S0-GQF-155

13051

The Library Reference Series

BASIC REFERENCE SOURCES

The Library Reference Series

Lee Ash

General Editor

BIOGRAPHY
BY
AMERICANS
1658 - 1936

A Subject Bibliography

By
EDWARD O'NEILL

GREGG PRESS
Boston   1972

This is a complete photographic reprint of a work
first published in Philadelphia
by the University of Pennsylvania Press in 1939.

First Gregg Press edition published 1972.

Copyright 1939 by University of Pennsylvania Press
Copyright renewed 1967 by Mrs. Edward H. O'Neill
Reprinted with permission.

Printed on permanent/durable acid-free paper in
The United States of America.

Library of Congress Cataloging in Publication Data

O'Neill, Edward Hayes, 1898-
    Biography by Americans, 1658-1936.

    1. Biography-Bibliography.   I. Title.
Z5301.O58 1972   016.92   72-7496
ISBN 0-8398-1455-0

BIOGRAPHY BY AMERICANS

BIOGRAPHY BY AMERICANS

1658 - 1936

A Subject Bibliography

By

EDWARD H. O'NEILL

Philadelphia

UNIVERSITY OF PENNSYLVANIA PRESS

LONDON: HUMPHREY MILFORD: OXFORD UNIVERSITY PRESS

1939

Copyright 1939

UNIVERSITY OF PENNSYLVANIA PRESS

Manufactured in the United States of America

by the Lancaster Press, Inc., Lancaster, Pa.

To

ARTHUR HOBSON QUINN

PREFACE

NEARLY ten years ago, I began the collection which has now grown
to the proportions of a book. The work was interrupted many times
and in many ways, but always I have had in mind the publication of
a bibliography of American biography which would make work a little
easier for other investigators in the field.

Though it is incomplete, I think this bibliography is the most
comprehensive accumulation of purely biographical material written
by Americans that has yet been made. It covers every possible field of
life. It has been my purpose to record only the important books in the
case of particularly famous men; otherwise, I have tried to note every
known biography.

Following the precedent established in my *History of American
Biography* (1935), I have excluded autobiographies, diaries, and journals. It may be that certain items of this kind have crept into the list,
for I was not able to examine every book recorded here. I have seen
about five thousand out of approximately seven thousand items.

Because of the necessity of keeping the volume within reasonable
size, I have reduced the information to a minimum and have used abbre-
viations wherever possible. I have tried to provide title, author, place
and date of publication, and pagination for each item. I have not
attempted to give the date of the first edition; the date given is that
of the edition available. Omissions will be noted: these occurred when
the particular volume was not obtainable in the various libraries where
I have worked during the last three years. Though this book is
intended to list only lives written by Americans, it is likely that an
occasional English biography has been included because individual
examination of some seven thousand items was impossible. Where
there was any doubt, I preferred inclusion to exclusion, error to omis-
sion. I shall greatly appreciate any additions or corrections which
the users of this volume may offer.

From the day of its first projection until that of its publication, this
book has had the fostering care and consideration of Professor Arthur
Hobson Quinn, of the University of Pennsylvania, to whom I could not
possibly make adequate acknowledgment.

PREFACE

Without the grants provided by the Board of Graduate Education and Research of the University of Pennsylvania my work could not have been completed in its present form.

I am particularly indebted to Mr. Clarence S. Brigham and Mr. R. W. G. Vail of the American Antiquarian Society, and Mr. K. D. Metcalf, Librarian at Harvard, and Mr. R. W. Henderson of the New York Public Library for the gracious manner in which they opened to me the resources of their libraries. Mr. C. Seymour Thompson of the Library of the University of Pennsylvania was most patient and helpful in answering the many questions put to him. I am also deeply obliged to the Huntington Library, the John Carter Brown Library, the William L. Clements Library, and the Burton Historical Collection of the Detroit Public Library for coöperation in checking this bibliography for the location of copies.

I wish also to thank my colleague, Dr. William A. Thomas, for his assistance in checking this bibliography with the catalogue of the Library of Congress.

E. H. O'N.

University of Pennsylvania
January, 1939

CONTENTS

ABBREVIATIONS USED IN TEXT

1. American Crisis Biographies: (A.C.B.)
2. American Men of Letters: (A.M.L.)
3. American Statesmen: (A.S.)
4. English Men of Letters: (E.M.L.)
5. Great Commanders: (G.C.)
6. Library of American Biography: (L.A.B.)

LIBRARY SYMBOLS USED

1. Library of Congress: *DLC*
2. New York Public Library: *NN*
3. American Antiquarian Society: *MWA*
4. Huntington Library: *CSmH*
5. University of Pennsylvania: *PU*
6. Burton Historical Collection: *MiD:B*
7. William L. Clements Library: *MiU:C*
8. John Carter Brown Library: *RP:JCB*

Note: Those titles in Part II that have been itemized are referred to in Part I thus: ABBOT, ABIEL. 2:681; ADAMS, HENRY. 2:84.

PART I

INDIVIDUAL BIOGRAPHIES

Listed by Subjects

AAKHNATAN. 2:665

AARON, SAMUEL. *Rev. Samuel Aaron. His Life, Sermons, Correspondence.* Samuel Aaron. Norristown, Pa., 1890. 252 p.
DLC, NN, CSmH, PU

ABBEY, EDWIN. 2:123–429

ABBOT, ABIEL. 2:681

ABBOTT, BENJAMIN. *The Experience and Gospel Labours of the Rev. Benjamin Abbott, With a Narrative of His Life and Death.* John Ffirth. Phila., 1825. 202 p. *DLC, NN, MWA, CSmH, MiD:B*

ABBOTT, EMMA. *Life and Professional Career of Emma Abbott.* Sadie E. Martin. Minneapolis, 1891. 192 p. *DLC, NN*

ABBOTT, HENRY. *In Memoriam, H. L. A.* Francis W. Palfrey. Boston, 1864. 31 p. *CSmH*

ABBOTT, JACOB. 2:6

ABBOTT, JOHN S. C. *A Memorial of John S. C. Abbott, D.D.* Horatio O. Ladd. Boston, 1878. 36 p. *DLC, NN, MWA, MiD:B*

ABBOTT, JOSIAH GARDNER. *Memoir of Josiah Gardner Abbott.* Charles Cowley. Boston, 1892. 92 p. *DLC, NN, MWA, MiD:B*

ABBOTT, MATHER ALMON. *Bott, the Story of a Schoolmaster.* William H. Husted. N. Y., 1936. 307 p. *DLC, NN*

ABEEL, DAVID. *Memoir of the Rev. David Abeel, D.D., Late Missionary to China.* G. R. Williamson. N. Y., 1848. 315 p. *DLC*

ABÉLARD, PETER. *Peter Abélard.* Joseph McCabe. N. Y., 1901. 402 p. *DLC, NN, PU*
2:371

ADAIR, JOHN. *Biographical Sketch of Gen. John Adair.* Washington, 1830. 23 p. *CSmH*

ADAMIC, LOUIS. *Louis Adamic & Shadow-America.* Carey McWilliams. Los Angeles, 1935. 100 p. *DLC, NN*

ADAMS. *The Adams Family.* James Truslow Adams. Boston, 1930. 364 p. Prologue; John Adams; John Quincy Adams; Charles Francis Adams; John Quincy, Charles Francis, Henry, and Brooks Adams. *DLC, NN, MWA, CSmH, PU*

1

ADAMS, ABIGAIL.
Letters of Abigail Adams, With a Memoir. Charles F. Adams. Boston, 1840. 447 p. *DLC, NN, MWA, CSmH, PU, MiU:C*
Abigail Adams, the Second First Lady. Dorothie Bobbé. N. Y., 1929. 336 p. *DLC, NN, MWA, CSmH, PU*
Abigail Adams and Her Times. Laura E. Richards. N. Y., 1917. 282 p. *DLC, NN, MWA, CSmH*
2:92–144–453

ADAMS, CHARLES FRANCIS. *Charles Francis Adams, the First.* Charles F. Adams, Jr. Boston, 1900. 426 p. (A.S.)
DLC, NN, MWA, CSmH, PU, MiD:B
2:128

ADAMS, CHARLES KENDALL.
Memoir of Charles K. Adams. James D. Butler. Worcester, Mass., 1905. 12 p. *DLC, MWA*
Charles Kendall Adams. A Life Sketch. Charles F. Smith. Madison, Wis., 1924. 150 p. *DLC, NN, CSmH, PU*

ADAMS, HENRY. *Henry Adams.* James Truslow Adams. N. Y., 1933. 246 p. *DLC, NN, MWA, PU*
2:84

ADAMS, HERBERT BAXTER.
Herbert B. Adams. John M. Vincent. (Annual Report of American Hist. Assoc., 1901. pp. 197–210)
DLC, NN, CSmH, PU
Herbert B. Adams, Tributes of Friends. Balt., 1902. (J. H. U. Studies in History, Ser. XX) *CSmH*

ADAMS, JAMES CAPEN.
The Adventures of James Capen Adams, Mountaineer and Grizzly Bear Hunter of California. Theodore H. Hittell, ed. San Francisco, 1860. N. Y., 1911. 373 p.
DLC, NN, MWA, CSmH, MiD:B
Life of J. C. Adams, Known as Old Adams . . . N. Y., 1860.
CSmH

ADAMS, JOHN.
The Works of John Adams, Second President of the United States. With a Life of the Author. John Q. Adams and Charles F. Adams. Boston, 1856. 10 vols.
DLC, NN, MWA, CSmH, PU, MiU:C
Honest John Adams. Gilbert Chinard. Boston, 1933. 359 p.
DLC, NN, CSmH, PU, MiD:B
Memoir of the Life . . . of John Adams. William Cranch.

Wash., 1827. 70 p. *CSmH*

This Man Adams; the Man Who Never Died. Samuel D. Mc-Coy. N. Y., 1928. 333 p. *DLC, NN, MWA, PU*

John Adams. John T. Morse, Jr. Boston, 1884, 1898. 337 p. (A.S.) *DLC, NN, MWA, CSmH, PU*

Famed in American History: Lives of John Adams and John Quincy Adams. Gideon T. Stewart. Norwalk, O., 1906. 55 p. *DLC*

John Adams and Thomas Jefferson. William O. Stoddard. N.Y., 1887. 358 p. *DLC, NN, MWA, PU*

John Adams. A Character Sketch. Samuel Willard. Milwaukee, 1898. 165 p. *DLC, NN, MWA, PU, MiD:B* 2:77–505–662

ADAMS, JOHN. *The Story of John Adams, a New England Schoolmaster.* Mary E. and H. G. Brown. N. Y., 1900. 275 p. *NN, MiD:B*

ADAMS, MR. AND MRS. JOHN QUINCY. *Mr. and Mrs. John Quincy Adams; An Adventure in Patriotism.* Dorothie Bobbé. N. Y., 1930. 310 p. *DLC, PU*

ADAMS, JOHN QUINCY.
John Quincy Adams, "Old Man Eloquent." Bennett Champ Clark. Boston, 1932. 437 p. *DLC, NN, MWA, CSmH, PU, MiD:B*

John Quincy Adams. Worthington C. Ford. N. Y., 1902. 52 p. *DLC, NN, MWA, CSmH*

History of the Life, Administration and Times of John Quincy Adams. John R. Irelan. Chicago, 1887. 682 p. *NN, MWA*

John Quincy Adams. John T. Morse, Jr. Boston, 1882. 315 p. (A.S.) *DLC, NN, MWA, CSmH, PU, MiD:B*

Memoir of the Life of John Quincy Adams. Josiah Quincy. Boston, 1858. 429 p. *DLC, NN, MWA, PU, MiD:B*

Life and Public Services of John Quincy Adams. William H. Seward. Auburn, 1849. 404 p. *DLC, NN, MWA, CSmH, MiD:B, MiU:C* 2:329–662

ADAMS, JONATHAN EDWARDS. *Jonathan Edwards Adams and Maine Congregationalism.* William C. Adams. Portland, Me., 1933. 164 p. *DLC, NN*

ADAMS, LOUISA. 2:453

ADAMS, MARY H. *Memoir of Mrs. Mary H. Adams.* John G. Adams. Boston, 1865. 144 p. *NN*

ADAMS, MAUDE.
  Maude Adams. Acton Davies. N. Y., 1901. 110 p.   *DLC*
  Maude Adams: A Biography. Ada Patterson. N. Y., 1907.
  109 p.   *DLC, NN*
ADAMS, SAMUEL.
  Samuel Adams: a Character Sketch. Samuel Fallows. Mil-
  waukee, 1903. 178 p.   *DLC, NN, MWA, PU, MiD:B*
  *Samuel Adams, Promoter of the American Revolution; a Study
  in Psychology and Politics.* Ralph V. Harlow. N. Y., 1923. 363 p.
                                  DLC, NN, CSmH, PU
  Samuel Adams. J. K. Hosmer. Boston, 1884, 1898. 442 p.
  (A.S.)   *DLC, NN, MWA, CSmH, PU, MiD:B*
  Sam Adams, Pioneer in Propaganda. John C. Miller. Boston,
  1936. 437 p.   *DLC, NN, MWA, CSmH*
  The Life and Public Services of Samuel Adams. William V.
  Wells. Boston, 1866. 3 vols.
                 DLC, NN, MWA, CSmH, MiD:B, MiU:C
    2:329
ADAMS, SEYMOUR W. *Memoir.* J. P. Bishop, ed. Cleveland, 1866.
  237 p.   *MiD:B*
ADDAMS, JANE.
  Jane Addams; a Biography. James W. Linn. N. Y., 1935.
  457 p.   *DLC, NN, PU*
  Jane Addams of Hull House. Winifred E. Wise. N. Y., 1935.
  255 p.   *DLC, NN, PU*
    2:9–301–395–506
ADDISON, JOSEPH. *Joseph Addison and His Time.* Charles J. Finger.
  Girard, Kan., 1922. 94 p.   *DLC*
ADDISON, WALTER DULANEY. *One Hundred Years Ago; or, the Life
  and Times of Rev. Walter Dulaney Addison.* Elizabeth H. Murray,
  comp. Phila., 1895. 215 p.   *DLC, NN, MWA, CSmH, MiD:B*
AELFRIC. *Aelfric: A New Study of His Life and Writings.* Caroline
  L. White. Boston, 1898. 218 p. (Yale Studies in English, No. 2.)
                                  DLC, NN, CSmH, PU
AGASSIZ, ELIZABETH CARY. *Elizabeth Cary Agassiz.* Lucy A. Paton.
  Boston, 1919. 423 p.   *DLC, NN, PU*
AGASSIZ, LOUIS.
  Louis Agassiz: His Life and Correspondence. Elizabeth C.
  Agassiz, ed. Boston, 1885. 2 vols.
                          DLC, NN, MWA, CSmH, PU, MiD:B

4

Louis Agassiz. Alice B. Gould. Boston, 1901. 154 p. (Beacon Biographies.) *DLC, NN*

Memoir of Louis Agassiz, 1807–1873. Arnold Guyot. Princeton, N. J., 1883. 49 p. (Pamphlet.) *DLC, NN, MWA, PU*

Louis Agassiz: His Life and Work. C. F. Holder. N. Y., 1893. 327 p. (Leaders in Science Series.) *DLC, CSmH*

Life, Letters, and Works of Louis Agassiz. Jules Marcou. N. Y., 1896. 2 vols. *DLC, NN*
2:79–340

AGNEW, DAVID HAYES. *History of the Life of D. Hayes Agnew.* J. Howe Adams. Phila., 1892. 376 p.
DLC, NN, MWA, PU, MiD:B

AGUINALDO, EMILIO. *Aguinaldo and His Captor; the Life Mysteries of Emilio Aguinaldo and Adventures and Achievements of General Funston.* Murat Halstead. Cincinnati, 1901. 437 p.
DLC, NN

AIKEN, ELIZABETH. *The Story of Aunt Lizzie Aiken.* Mary Eleanor Roberts Anderson. Chicago, 1880. 226 p. *DLC, NN*

AITCHISON, WILLIAM. *The Life and Observations of Rev. William Aitchison, Five Years in China.* C. B. Bush. Phila., 1865. 284 p.
DLC

AKE, JEFF. *They Die But Once; the Story of a Tejano.* James B. O'Neil. N. Y., 1935. 228 p. *DLC, NN, MWA*

ALBEE, HARRIET RYAN. *Harriet Ryan Albee. A Memorial Sketch.* James De Normandie. Boston, 1901. 68 p. *DLC, NN, PU*

ALCOTT, AMOS BRONSON.
Father of Little Women. Honoré W. Morrow. Boston, 1927. 283 p. *DLC, NN, PU*

A. Bronson Alcott; His Life and Philosophy. Franklin B. Sanborn and Wm. T. Harris. Boston, 1893. 2 vols.
DLC, NN, MWA, PU

ALCOTT, LOUISA MAY.
Louisa May Alcott, Her Life, Letters, and Journals. Ednah D. Cheney. Boston, 1889. 404 p. *DLC, NN, MWA*

Louisa May Alcott, Dreamer and Worker. Belle Moses. N. Y., 1909. 334 p. *DLC, NN, CSmH*
2:92

ALCOTT, MAY. *May Alcott; a Memoir.* Caroline Ticknor. Boston, 1928. 315 p. *DLC, NN, MWA*

ALCUIN, EALHWINE. *Alcuin and the Rise of the Christian Schools.* Andrew F. West. N. Y., 1892. 205 p. (Great Educators Series.)
DLC

ALDEN, JOHN. *Pilgrim Alden; the Story of the Life of the First John Alden in America.* Alexander H. Burr, ed. Boston, 1902. 214 p.
MWA, PU

ALDRICH, NELSON WILMARTH. *Nelson W. Aldrich; a Leader in American Politics.* Nathaniel W. Stephenson. N. Y., 1930. 496 p.
DLC, MWA, PU

ALDRICH, THOMAS BAILEY. *The Life of Thomas Bailey Aldrich.* Ferris Greenslet. Boston, 1908. 303 p.
DLC, NN, MWA, CSmH, PU, MiD:B

ALESSOR, MARY. 2:670

ALEXANDER THE GREAT.
History of Alexander the Great. Jacob Abbott. N. Y., 1859. 278 p.
DLC, NN
Alexander. Theodore A. Dodge. Boston, 1890. 2 vols. (Great Captains.)
DLC, NN, CSmH, PU

ALEXANDER, ANDREW JONATHAN. *The Life and Services of Brevet Brigadier-General Andrew Jonathan Alexander, U. S. Army.* James Harrison Wilson. N. Y., 1887. 135 p.
DLC, MiD:B

ALEXANDER, ARCHER. *The Story of Archer Alexander; from Slavery to Freedom, March 30, 1863.* William G. Eliot. Boston, 1885. 123 p.
NN

ALEXANDER, ARCHIBALD. *The Life of Archibald Alexander, D.D.* James W. Alexander. N. Y., 1854. 700 p.
DLC, NN, MWA, CSmH, PU

ALEXANDER, CHARLES. *" Charlie " Alexander: a Study in Personality.* Philip I. Roberts. N. Y., Chicago, 1920. 95 p.
DLC, NN

ALEXANDER, FRANCESCA. *Francesca Alexander.* Constance G. Alexander. Cambridge, 1927. 227 p.
DLC, NN

ALEXANDER, JOHN HENRY. *Memoir of John H. Alexander.* William Pinkney. Balt., 1867. 31 p.
CSmH

ALEXANDER, JOSEPH ADDISON. *Life of Joseph Addison Alexander.* Henry C. Alexander. N. Y., 1869. 2 vols.
DLC, NN, MWA

ALEXANDER, ROBERT. *Robert Alexander and the Early Methodist Church in Texas.* Anne Ayers Lide. Le Grange, Tex., 1935. 176 p.
DLC, NN, CSmH

ALEXANDER, WILLIAM. (EARL OF STIRLING.)
Life of William Alexander, Earl of Stirling. William A. Duer. N. Y., 1847. 272 p. (N. J. Historical Society Collections. vol. 2.)
DLC, NN, MWA, MiD:B
Major-General, the Earl of Stirling; Essays in Biography. Ludwig Schumacher. N. Y., 1897. 57 p.
DLC

ALEXANDER, WILLIAM PATTERSON.
Mission Life in Hawaii. Memoir of Rev. William P. Alexander.
James M. Alexander. Oakland, Cal., 1888. 196 p.

NN, MWA, CSmH

William Patterson Alexander in Kentucky, the Marquesas, Hawaii. Mary C. Alexander. Honolulu, 1934. 516 p. (Privately Printed.)

DLC

ALFRED THE GREAT. *History of Alfred the Great.* Jacob Abbott. Phila., 1900. 226 p.

DLC, NN

2: 336.

ALGER, HORATIO. *Alger; a Biography Without a Hero.* Herbert R. Mayes. N. Y., 1928. 241 p.

DLC, NN, MWA, PU

ALLAN, JOHN. *Memoir of Colonel John Allan.* George Hayward Allan. Albany, 1867. 32 p.

DLC, NN, MWA, CSmH, MiD:B

ALLEN, ALEXANDER VIETS GRISWOLD. *Alexander Viets Griswold Allen.* Charles Lewis Slattery. N. Y., 1911. 296 p.

DLC, NN

ALLEN, BENJAMIN. *Memoir of Rev. Benjamin Allen, Late Rector of St. Paul's Church, Philadelphia.* Thomas G. Allen. Phila., 1832. 548 p.

DLC, NN, PU, MiD:B

ALLEN, ETHAN.
Ethan Allen. Charles W. Brown. Chicago, 1902. 281 p.

DLC, NN

Ethan Allen and the Green Mountain Heroes of '76. H. W. De Puy. Buffalo, 1853. 428 p.

DLC, NN, MWA, CSmH, PU, MiU:C

Ethan Allen, the Robin Hood of Vermont. Henry Hall. N. Y., 1892. 207 p.

DLC, NN, MWA

Memoir of Colonel Ethan Allen. Hugh Moore. Plattsburgh, N. Y., 1834. 252 p. DLC, NN, MWA, CSmH, MiD:B, MiU:C

Ethan Allen. John Pell. Boston and N. Y., 1929. 331 p.

DLC, NN, MWA, CSmH, PU

Life of Ethan Allen. Jared Sparks. (L.A.B.)

DLC, NN, MWA, CSmH, PU, MiU:C

The Life and Times of Colonel Ethan Allen. Orville J. Victor. N. Y., 1876. 81 p.

DLC, NN

ALLEN, GEORGE. *Reminiscences of the Rev. George Allen, of Worcester.* Franklin P. Rice. Worcester, Mass., 1883. 127 p.

DLC, NN, MWA, MiD:B

ALLEN, HENRY WATKINS. *Recollections of Henry Watkins Allen, Brigadier-General Confederate States Army, Ex-Governor of Louisiana.* Sarah Anne Ellis Dorsey. N. Y., 1866. 420 p.

DLC, MWA, CSmH, PU

ALLEN, IRA.
> *Ira Allen, Founder of Vermont, 1751–1814.* James B. Wilbur. Boston, 1928. 2 vols.
> *DLC, NN, MWA, CSmH, PU, MiD:B, MiU:C, RP:JCB*
> *Life, Character and Times of Ira Allen.* Daniel P. Thompson. 1909. 194 p. *MiD:B*

ALLEN, JAMES LANE.
> *James Lane Allen and the Genteel Tradition.* Grant C. Knight. Chapel Hill, 1935. 313 p. *DLC, NN, CSmH, PU*
> *James Lane Allen, a Personal Note.* John W. Townsend. Louisville, Ky., 1928. 149 p. *DLC, NN, MWA, PU*

ALLEN, JOHN. *The Life of Rev. John Allen, Better Known as " Camp-Meeting John."* Stephen Allen. Boston, 1888. 140 p. *MWA*

ALLEN, JONATHAN. *Life and Sermons of Jonathan Allen, Ph.D., D.D., LL.D., President of Alfred University.* Abigail A. Allen. Oakland, Cal., 1894. 404 p. *NN*

ALLEN, MYRA W. *Memoir of Myra W. Allen.* Cyrus Mann. Boston, 1834. 256 p. *NN*

ALLEN, NATHANIEL TOPLIFF. *Nathaniel T. Allen. Teacher, Reformer, Philanthropist.* Mary A. Greene. Cambridge, 1906. 272 p. (Privately Printed.) *DLC, NN, MWA*

ALLEN, PICKERING DODGE. *Memorial of Pickering Dodge Allen.* John F. Allen. Boston, 1867. 174 p. *CSmH*

ALLEN, RICHARD. *Richard Allen, Apostle of Freedom.* Charles H. Wesley. Washington, D. C., 1935. 300 p. *DLC, NN, CSmH*

ALLEN, WILLIAM. *William Allen, a Study in Western Democracy.* Reginald C. McGrane. Columbus, Ohio, 1925. 279 p. (Ohio State Arch. and Hist. Soc.) *DLC, NN, MWA, MiD:B*
2: 128

ALLEN, YOUNG JOHN. *Young J. Allen, " The Man Who Seeded China."* Warren A. Candler. Nashville, 1931. 245 p.
DLC, NN

ALLEN, ZACHARIAH. *Memorial of Zachariah Allen, 1795–1882.* Amos Perry. Cambridge, 1883. 108 p. *DLC, NN, MWA, MiD:B*

ALLOUEZ, CLAUDE JEAN. *Claude Jean Allouez, the Apostle of the Ottawas.* Joseph S. La Boule. 1897. (Parkman Club Papers, No. 17.)
NN

ALLSTON, WASHINGTON.
> *The Life and Letters of Washington Allston.* J. B. Flagg. N. Y., 1892. 435 p. *DLC, NN, MWA, CSmH, PU*

The Life of Washington Allston. Moses F. Sweetser. Cambridge, 1879. 192 p. *DLC, NN*
2:394

ALLYN, JOHN. 2:681

ALSTON, THEODOSIA BURR. *Theodosia, the First Gentlewoman of Her Time.* Charles F. Pidgin. Boston, 1907. 484 p. *DLC, NN*

ALTGELD, JOHN PETER. *Altgeld of Illinois.* Waldo R. Browne. N. Y., 1924. 342 p. *DLC, NN*
2:150

ALVARADO, PEDRO DE. *Pedro de Alvarado, Conquistador.* John E. Kelly. Princeton, N. J., 1932. 279 p. *DLC, NN, MWA, PU*

ALVORD, CLARENCE WALWORTH. *Clarence W. Alvord, Historian.* Solon J. Buck. Cedar Rapids, 1928. *CSmH*

AMBROSE, SAINT. 2:554

AMERICAN HORSE. 2:204

AMES, FISHER. *Life and Works of Fisher Ames.* Seth Ames. Boston, 1854. 2 vols. *DLC, NN, MWA, CSmH, PU*

AMES, OAKES. *Oakes Ames: A Memoir.* Oakes Ames. Cambridge, 1883. 143 p. *DLC, NN, MWA, CSmH, MiD:B*

AMHERST, JEFFREY.
Lord Jeffrey Amherst, a Soldier of the King. John C. Long. N. Y., 1933. 373 p. *DLC, NN, MWA, CSmH, PU, MiU:C*
Jeffrey Amherst: a Biography. Lawrence S. Mayo. N. Y., 1916. 344 p. *DLC, NN, MWA, CSmH, PU*

AMORY, AUGUSTINE HEARD. *Memoirs of Augustine H. Amory.* Arthur W. Moulton. Salem, Mass., 1909. 205 p. *DLC, NN, MWA*

AMPÈRE, ANDRÉ MARIE. 2:25

AMUNDSEN, ROALD. *Amundsen, the Splendid Norseman.* Bellamy Partridge. N. Y., 1929. 276 p. *DLC, NN*

ANAGNOS, MICHAEL. *Michael Anagnos, 1837–1906.* F. B. Sanborn. Boston, 1907. 155 p. (Privately Printed.)
DLC, NN, MWA, PU

ANCENY, CHARLES L. 2:233

ANDERSON, ALEXANDER.
Life and Works of Alexander Anderson, The First American Wood Engraver. Frederic M. Burr. N. Y., 1893. 210 p. (Privately Printed.) *NN, MWA, CSmH, PU, MiU:C*
A Memorial of Alexander Anderson, M.D., the First Engraver on Wood in America. Benson J. Lossing. N. Y., 1872. 107 p.
CSmH

ANDERSON, JOHN TODD. *A Greatheart of the South, John T. Anderson, Medical Missionary*. Gordon Poteat. N. Y., 1921. 123 p.
DLC, NN

ANDERSON, MARTIN BREWER. *Martin B. Anderson, a Biography*. Asahel C. Kendrick and F. K. Cooper. Phila., 1895. 295 p.
DLC, PU

ANDERSON, MARY.
Life of Mary Anderson. J. M. Farrar. N. Y., 1885. 83 p.
DLC, NN

The Stage Life of Mary Anderson. William Winter. N. Y., 1886. 151 p. *DLC, NN*

ANDERSON, MAXWELL. *Maxwell Anderson, the Man and His Plays*. Barrett H. Clark. N. Y., 1933. 32 p. *DLC, NN, PU*

ANDERSON, RICHARD CLOUGH. *Soldier and Pioneer: a Biographical Sketch of Richard C. Anderson of the Continental Army*. E. L. Anderson. N. Y., 1879. 63 p. *DLC, NN, MiD:B*

ANDERSON, RICHARD HERON. *The Life of Lieutenant General Richard Heron Anderson, of the Confederate States Army*. Cornelius I. Walker. Charleston, S. C., 1917. 269 p.
DLC, NN, MWA, CSmH

ANDERSON, SHERWOOD. *Sherwood Anderson*. Cleveland B. Chase. N. Y., 1927. 84 p. (Modern American Writers.)
DLC, NN, MWA, PU
2:366

ANDERSON, THOMAS JEFFERSON. *Life and Letters of Judge T. J. Anderson and Wife*. J. H. Anderson, ed. Columbus, Ohio, 1904. 535 p. *DLC, NN*

ANDERSON, W. H. 2:546

ANDERSON, W. H. P. 2:675

ANDRÉ, JOHN. *The Life and Career of Major John André*. Winthrop Sargent. Boston, 1861. new ed., N. Y., 1902. 471 p.
DLC, NN, MWA, CSmH, MiD:B, MiU:C
See HALE, NATHAN.

ANDRÉ, LOUIS. *Sketch of Father Louis André, S.J., an Early Wisconsin Missionary*. Arthur E. Jones. N. Y., 1890. 15 p. *NN*

ANDREIS, FELIX.
Life of the Very Rev. Felix de Andreis. Joseph Rosati. St. Louis, 1900. 308 p. *DLC*

Sketches of the Life of the Very Rev. Felix de Andreis . . . J. B. Semeria. Balt., 1861. 276 p. *CSmH*

ANDREW, JAMES OSGOOD. *The Life and Letters of James Osgood Andrew, Bishop of the Methodist Episcopal Church South.* George G. Smith. Nashville, 1883. 562 p. *NN, MiD:B*

ANDREW, JOHN ALBION.
Sketch of the Life of Governor Andrew. Albert G. Brown. N. Y., 1868. 211 p. *DLC, NN, MWA, MiD:B*
Memoir of Governor Andrew. Peleg W. Chandler. Boston, 1880. 298 p. *DLC, NN, MWA, CSmH, PU*
The Life of John A. Andrew, Governor of Massachusetts, 1861–1865. Henry G. Pearson. Boston, 1904. 2 vols. *DLC, NN, CSmH, PU*
2:144

ANDREWS, CHARLES WESLEY. *Memoir of Rev. C. W. Andrews.* Cornelius Walker. N. Y., 1877. 224 p. *DLC, NN, MWA*

ANDREWS, CHRISTOPHER COLUMBUS. *Christopher C. Andrews, Pioneer in Forestry Conservation in the U. S.* C. C. Andrews. Cleveland, 1928. 327 p. *NN, CSmH, PU, MiD:B*

ANDREWS, EDWARD GAYER. *Edward Gayer Andrews, Bishop of the M. E. Church.* F. J. McConnell. N. Y., 1909. 291 p. *DLC*

ANDREWS, JOHN. *Biographical Notice of the Late Rev. John Andrews, D.D., Provost of the University of Pennsylvania.* Phila., 1813. 15 p. (The Portfolio, Ser. 3, v. 1, no. 5, May, 1813.) *NN, CSmH, PU*

ANDREWS, RICHARD SNOWDEN. *Richard Snowden Andrews, Lieut.-Col., C. S. A., A Memoir.* Tunstall Smith, ed. Baltimore, 1910. 151 p. *DLC*

ANDREWS, ROY CHAPMAN. *Roy Chapman Andrews, Dragon Hunter.* Fitzhugh Green. N. Y. and London, 1930. 173 p. *DLC, NN*

ANDREWS, WILLIAM WATSON. *William Watson Andrews.* S. J. Andrews. N. Y., 1900. 280 p. *DLC, NN*

ANDROS, EDMUND. *Memoir of Sir Edmund Andros.* W. H. Whitmore. Boston, 1868. 49 p. (Reprinted from the "Andros Tracts," Prince Society Publications.) *DLC, NN, MWA, CSmH, PU, MiD:B, MiU:C, RP:JCB*

ANGELICO, FRA. *Fra Angelico.* Moses F. Sweetser. Boston, 1879. 140 p. · *NN*
2:248

ANGELL, ISRAEL. *Israel Angell, Colonel of the 2nd Rhode Island Regiment.* Louise L. Lovell. N. Y., 1921. 360 p. *DLC, NN, MWA*

ANSELM, SAINT. *Saint Anselm; a Critical Biography.* Joseph Clayton. Milwaukee, 1933. 162 p. *DLC, NN*
2:371

ANTHONY, HENRY BOWEN. *Henry Bowen Anthony. A Memorial.* Providence, R. I., 1885. 198 p.

DLC, NN, MWA, MiD:B, RP:JCB

ANTHONY, SUSAN B.

Susan B. Anthony, the Woman Who Changed the Mind of a Nation. Rheta L. Dorr. N. Y., 1928. 367 p.

DLC, NN, CSmH, PU

Life and Works of Susan B. Anthony. Ida H. Harper. Indianapolis, 1898–1908. 3 vols. DLC, NN, PU
2:205–325

ANTHONY, SUSANNA. *Life . . . of Miss Susanna Anthony . . .* Worcester, 1796. RP:JCB

ANTIN, MARY. 2:506–672

ANTOINE, SIMON. 2:406

ANTONY, MARK. 2:330

APGAR, EDGAR KELSEY. *In Memoriam Edgar Kelsey Apgar: Obiit A.D. 1885.* Moses C. Tyler. Ithaca, 1886. 145 p. NN, MiD:B

APPLETON, NATHAN. *Memoir of Nathan Appleton.* R. C. Winthrop. Boston, 1861. 79 p. DLC, NN, MWA, MiD:B

APPLETON, WILLIAM. *Memoir of Hon. William Appleton.* Chandler Robbins. Boston, 1863. 64 p. CSmH

APPLETON, THOMAS GOLD. *Life and Letters of Thomas Gold Appleton.* Susan Hale. N. Y., 1885. 348 p. DLC, MWA, CSmH, PU

APULEIUS. *Apuleius and His Influence.* Elizabeth H. Haight. N. Y., 1927. 190 p. (Our Debt to Greece and Rome.)

DLC, NN, CSmH, PU

AQUINAS, SAINT THOMAS. 2:371

ARBLAY, MADAME D'. 2:93

ARBUTHNOT, JOHN. *John Arbuthnot, Mathematician and Satirist.* Lester M. Beattie. Cambridge, 1935. 432 p.

DLC, NN, CSmH, PU

ARC, JOAN OF.

Sword of God: Jeanne d'Arc. Guy Endore. N. Y., 1931. 492 p.

DLC, NN

Blessed Joan of Arc. E. A. Ford. N. Y., 1910. 314 p. DLC
My Jeanne d'Arc: Her Wonderful Story in the Light of Recent Researches. Michael Monahan. N. Y., 1928. 298 p.

DLC, NN, PU

Joan of Arc. John A. Mooney. N. Y., 1919. 144 p. DLC
Joan of Arc, Maid of France. Albert B. Paine. N. Y., 1925. 2 vols. DLC, NN

Joan of Arc. Laura E. Richards. N. Y. and London, 1919. 268 p.   *DLC, NN*

ARCHER, WILLIAM. *William. Archer, Life, Work and Friendships.* Charles Archer. New Haven, 1931. 451 p.   *DLC, NN, PU*

ARDEN, ELEANOR. *Eleanor Arden, Royalist.* M. C. Du Bois. N. Y., 1904. 283 p.   *DLC, NN*

ARETINO, PIETRO. 2:573

ARMINIUS, JACOBUS. 2:371

ARMOUR, PHILIP. 2:331

ARMOUR, PHILIP DANFORTH. 2:623

ARMSTRONG, SAMUEL CHAPMAN.

    Samuel Chapman Armstrong. Edith A. Talbot. N. Y., 1904. 301 p.   *DLC, NN, MWA, CSmH*

    Leader of Freemen, the Life Story of Samuel Chapman Armstrong, Brevet Brigadier-General, U. S. A. Everett T. Tomlinson and P. G. Tomlinson. Phila., 1917. 86 p.

         DLC, NN, MWA, CSmH, PU, MiD:B

    2:6–519

ARNOLD, BEN. See CONNOR, BENJAMIN.

ARNOLD, BENEDICT.

    Life of Benedict Arnold; His Patriotism and His Treason. Isaac N. Arnold. Chicago, 1880. 444 p.

         DLC, NN, MWA, CSmH, PU, MiU:C

    Benedict Arnold, Son of the Havens. Malcolm Becker. Tarrytown, N. Y., 1932. 534 p.   *DLC, NN, MWA, CSmH, MiU:C*

    Benedict Arnold, the Man. Charles S. Haight. n.p., n.d. 73 p.

         DLC, NN

    Benedict Arnold. A Biography. George C. Hill. Boston, 1858, 1892. 295 p.   *NN, CSmH, MiU:C*

    Benedict Arnold, the Proud Warrior. Charles C. Sellers. N. Y., 1930. 303 p.   *DLC, NN, PU, MiU:C*

    Benedict Arnold, Patriot and Traitor. Oscar Sherwin. N. Y., 1931. 395 p.   *DLC, NN, MWA, PU*

    Life and Treason of Benedict Arnold. Jared Sparks. (L.A.B.)

         DLC, NN, MWA, CSmH, PU

    Benedict Arnold, Military Racketeer. Edward D. Sullivan. N. Y., 1932. 306 p.   *DLC, NN, PU*

    The Real Benedict Arnold. Charles Burr Todd. N. Y., 1903. 235 p.   *DLC, NN, CSmH, PU*

    2:89

ARNOLD, MARGARET. *The Exquisite Exile, the Life and Fortunes of Mrs. Benedict Arnold.* Harry S. Tillotson. Boston, 1932. 205 p.
DLC, NN

2:97

ARNOLD, THOMAS. 2:336

ARRHENIUS, SVANTE. 2:286–348

ARROWSMITH, GEORGE. *Reminiscences and Letters of George Arrowsmith of New Jersey, Late Lt.-Col. of the 157th Regt., N. Y. State Volunteers.* John S. Applegate. Red Bank, N. J., 1893. 254 p.
DLC, NN, MWA, CSmH

ARTHUR, CHESTER ALAN. *Chester A. Arthur: A Quarter Century of Machine Politics.* George F. Howe. N. Y., 1934. 307 p.
DLC, NN, CSmH, PU

See GARFIELD, JAMES.

ASBURY, FRANCIS.
A Methodist Saint; the Life of Bishop Asbury. Herbert Asbury. N. Y., 1927. 355 p. *DLC, NN*

Francis Asbury; Biographical Study. Horace M. Du Bose. Nashville, 1909. 245 p. *DLC, NN*

Francis Asbury; Founder of American Methodism and Unofficial Minister of State. William L. Duren. N. Y., 1928. 276 p.
DLC, NN, CSmH, PU

Francis Asbury. George P. Mains. N. Y. and Cincinnati, 1909. 128 p. *DLC, NN*

Life and Labors of Francis Asbury, Bishop of the Methodist Episcopal Church in America. George G. Smith. Nashville, 1896. 311 p. *DLC, NN*

The Pioneer Bishop: or, The Life and Times of Francis Asbury. William P. Strickland. N. Y., 1858. 496 p.
NN, CSmH, MiD:B

Francis Asbury, the Prophet of the Long Road. Ezra S. Tipple. N. Y., 1916. 333 p. *DLC, NN*

Character and Career of Francis Asbury, Bishop of the M. E. Church. N. Y., 1872. 615 p. *MiD:B*

ASHBY, TURNER. *General Turner Ashby, the Centaur of the South.* Clarence Thomas. Winchester, Va., 1907. 211 p. *DLC, M*

ASHHURST, JOHN. *John Ashhurst, Junior . . . M.D. . . . A Memoir.* Richard H. Harte. Cambridge, 1902. 23 p. *PU*

ASHLEY, WILLIAM HENRY. 2:46

ASHMUN, JEHUDI. *Life of Jehudi Ashmun, Late Colonial Agent in Liberia.* Ralph R. Gurley. Wash., 1835. 396 p.
DLC, NN, MWA, CSmH, PU

ASTELL, MARY. *Mary Astell.* Florence M. Smith. N. Y., 1916. 193 p.
DLC, NN, CSmH, PU

ASTOR, JOHN JACOB.
The Life and Adventures of the Original John Jacob Astor.
Elizabeth L. Gebhard. N. Y., 1915. 321 p. DLC, NN, MWA
Life of John Jacob Astor. James Parton. N. Y., 1865. 121 p.
DLC, MWA, PU
John Jacob Astor, Business Man. Kenneth W. Porter. Cambridge, 1931. 2 vols. DLC, NN, CSmH, PU
John Jacob Astor. Arthur D. H. Smith. Phila., 1929. 296 p.
DLC, MWA, PU
2:331–451–511–623

ASTOR, LADY NANCY. 2:425

ATHANASIUS, SAINT. 2:371

ATKINSON, EDWARD. *Edward Atkinson. The Biography of an American Liberal, 1827–1905.* Harold F. Williamson. Boston, 1934.
304 p. DLC, NN, MWA, PU

ATKINSON, EDWARD LINCOLN. *Edward Lincoln Atkinson.* C. L. Slattery. N. Y., 1904. 195 p. DLC, NN, CSmH, PU

ATKINSON, THOMAS. 2:295

ATKINSON, WILMER. 2:497

ATLEE, SAMUEL JOHN. 2:521

ATWELL, GEORGE. *Memoirs of the Life and Character of the Late Rev. George Atwell.* Ezekiel Terry. Palmer, Mass., 1814. 144 p.
NN, MWA, CSmH

AUDUBON, JOHN JAMES.
Life of John James Audubon, the Naturalist. Lucy Audubon, ed. N. Y., 1869. 443 p. DLC, NN, MWA, MiD:B
John James Audubon. John Burroughs. Boston, 1902. 144 p. (Beacon Biographies.) DLC, CSmH, PU
Audubon, the Naturalist; a History of His Life and Times.
Francis H. Herrick. N. Y., 1917. 2 vols. DLC, NN, PU
Audacious Audubon. Edward A. Muschamp. N. Y., 1929.
312 p. DLC, NN, PU
Singing in the Wilderness; a Salute to John James Audubon.
Donald Culross Peattie. N. Y., 1935. 245 p. DLC, NN
Audubon. Constance Rourke. N. Y., 1936. 342 p.
DLC, NN, PU
Life of Audubon, Naturalist of the New World. Mrs. S. R. St.
John. N. Y., 1856. 311 p. NN, CSmH, PU
2:79

AUENBRUGGER, LEOPOLD. 2:678

AUGUSTINE, SAINT. *St. Augustine and His Age.* Joseph McCabe.
N. Y., 1903. 516 p. *DLC, NN*
2:371

AURELIUS, MARCUS.
Marcus Aurelius; a Biography. Henry D. Sedgwick. New
Haven, 1922. 309 p. *DLC, NN*
Marcus Aurelius Antoninus. Paul B. Watson. N. Y., 1884.
338 p. *DLC, NN, PU*
2:332

AUSTEN, JANE.
Story of Jane Austen's Life. Oscar F. Adams. Chicago, 1891.
277 p. *DLC, MWA, PU*
Jane Austen. Oscar W. Firkins. N. Y., 1920. 254 p.
DLC, NN, PU
2:93

AUSTIN, CHELLIS ASAHEL. *A Gallant Gentleman; the Life of Chellis
A. Austin.* Edna Page Austin. N. Y., 1932. 293 p. *DLC, NN*

AUSTIN, GEORGE. *George W. Austin, His Life and Work.* Rex F.
Harlow. Oklahoma City, Okla., 1927. 137 p. *DLC*

AUSTIN, STEPHEN FULLER. *Life of Stephen F. Austin.* Eugene C.
Barker. Nashville, 1925. 551 p. *DLC, NN, CSmH, PU, MiD:B*
2:46

AUSTIN, WILLIAM.
*Literary Papers of William Austin; With a Biographical Sketch
by His Son.* James W. Austin. Boston, 1890. 394 p.
DLC, NN, MWA
*William Austin, the Creator of Peter Rugg; Being a Biographical
Sketch of William Austin . . . by His Grandson.* Walter Austin.
Boston, 1925. 338 p. *DLC, NN, PU*

AVOGADRO, AMADEO. 2:348

AYCOCK, CHARLES BRANTLEY. 2:493

AYER, EDWARD EVERETT. *The Life of Edward E. Ayer.* Frank C.
Lockwood. Chicago, 1929. 300 p.
DLC, NN, MWA, CSmH, PU, MiU:C

AZARIAS, BROTHER. [MULLANY, PATRICK FRANCIS.] *Brother Azarias:
The Life Story of an American Monk.* John T. Smith. N. Y.,
1897. 280 p. *DLC, PU*

BABCOCK, MALTBIE DAVENPORT. *Maltbie Davenport Babcock, a Reminiscent Sketch and Memorial.* Charles E. Robinson. N. Y. and
Chicago, 1904. 161 p. *DLC, NN*

BACA, ELFEGO. *Law and Order Ltd.; the Rousing Life of Elfego Baca of New Mexico.* Kyle S. Crichton. Santa Fe, New Mexico, 1928. 219 p. *DLC, NN*

BACH, JOHANN SEBASTIAN.
Bach. Rutland Boughton. N. Y., 1907. 156 p. (Music of the Masters.) *DLC, NN*
Bach, the Master; a New Interpretation of His Genius. Rutland Boughton. N. Y., 1930. 291 p. *DLC, NN*
2:187

BACHE, EDWARD and WALTER. *Brother Musicians: Edward and Walter Bache.* Constance Bache. N. Y., 1901. 330 p. *DLC, NN*

BACHE, FRANKLIN. *Biographical Memoir of Franklin Bache, M.D.* George B. Wood. Phila., 1865. 66 p. *DLC, NN, PU*

BACHMAN, JOHN. *John Bachman . . . the Pastor of St. John's Lutheran Church, Charleston.* C. L. Bachman, ed. Charleston, S. C., 1888. 436 p. *DLC, NN, MWA*

BACKHOUSE, ANNA. *A Brief Sketch of the Life of Anna Backhouse.* Burlington, N. J., 1852. 201 p. *NN, MWA*

BACKUS, ISAAC. *A Memoir of the Life and Times of the Rev. Isaac Backus.* Alvah Hovey. Boston, 1858. 369 p.
NN, MWA, CSmH, MiD:B

BACON, DAVID. *Sketch of the Rev. David Bacon.* Leonard Bacon. Boston, 1876. 104 p. *NN*

BACON, DELIA. *Delia Bacon; a Biographical Sketch.* Theodore Bacon. Boston, 1888. 322 p. *DLC, NN, MWA, CSmH*

BACON, FRANCIS. *Sir Francis Bacon, the First Modern Mind.* Byron Steel. N. Y., 1930. 208 p. *DLC, NN*

BACON, LEONARD.
Leonard Bacon; Pastor of the First Church in New Haven. New Haven, 1882. 260 p. *DLC, NN, MWA, CSmH, MiD:B*
Leonard Bacon, a Statesman in the Church. Theodore D. Bacon. New Haven, 1931. 563 p. *DLC, NN*

BACON, LYDIA B. *Biography of Mrs. Lydia B. Bacon.* Boston, 1856. 348 p. *DLC, NN, MWA*

BACON, NATHANIEL. *Memoir of Nathaniel Bacon.* William Ware. (L.A.B.) *DLC, NN, MWA, CSmH*

BACON, ROGER. 2:393

BACON, SAMUEL. *Memoir of the Life and Character of the Rev. Samuel Bacon, A.M.* Jehudi Ashmun. Washington City, 1822. 288 p.
DLC, NN, MWA, CSmH

BACON, WILLIAM KIRKLAND. *Memorial of William Kirkland Bacon, Late Adjutant of the 26th Regiment of New York State Volunteers.* William J. Bacon. Utica, N. Y., 1863. 83 p.

DLC, NN, MWA, CSmH, MiD:B

BACOT, JOHN VACHER. *In Memoriam: John Vacher Bacot, 1857–1921.* Utica, 1922. 15 p.

BACOT, WILLIAM SINCLAIR. *In Memoriam: William Sinclair Bacot, 1860–1917.* Utica, 1918. 14 p. *DLC, NN*

BADGER, JOSEPH. *Memoir of Rev. Joseph Badger.* Elihu G. Holland. N. Y., 1854. 473 p. *NN, MiD:B*

BAGBY, GEORGE WILLIAM. *Dr. George William Bagby: A Study of Virginian Literature, 1850–1880.* Joseph L. King, Jr. N. Y., 1927. 193 p. (Col. Univ. Studies in English.) *DLC, NN, CSmH, PU*

BAGLEY, WORTH. *The First Fallen Hero; a Biographical Sketch of Worth Bagley, Ensign, U. S. N.* Josephus Daniels. Norfolk, Va., 1898. 88 p. *DLC, MWA*

BAILEY, HORACE WARD. *Horace Ward Bailey, Vermonter.* Frank L. Fish, ed. Rutland, Vt., 1914. 339 p. (Privately Printed.)

DLC, NN, MWA, CSmH, MiD:B

BAILEY, JACOB. *The Frontier Missionary; a Memoir of the Life of the Rev. Jacob Bailey.* William S. Bartlet. Boston, 1853. 365 p.

DLC, NN, MWA, CSmH

BAILEY, JOSEPH. *Joe Bailey, the Last Democrat.* Sam H. Acheson. N. Y., 1932. 420 p. *DLC, NN, MWA, PU*

BAILEY, NELLIE C. BENTHUSEN. *The Life of Nellie C. Bailey; or, a Romance of the West.* Mary E. Jackson. Topeka, Kan., 1885. 399 p. *DLC, NN*

BAILLIE, JOANNA. *The Life and Work of Joanna Baillie.* Margaret S. Carhart. New Haven, 1923. 215 p. (Yale Studies in English, No. 64.) *DLC, NN, CSmH, PU*

BAINBRIDGE, EDWIN. *Edwin Bainbridge; a Memoir.* Thomas Darlington. London, 1887. 125 p. *MWA*

BAINBRIDGE, LUCY SEAMAN. *Triumphant Christianity; the Life and Work of Lucy Seaman Bainbridge.* Alexander H. McKinney. N. Y., 1932. 206 p. *DLC*

BAINBRIDGE, WILLIAM.

Commodore Bainbridge. James Barnes. N. Y., 1897. 168 p.

MiD:B

The Life of William Bainbridge, Esq. of the U. S. Navy. Henry A. S. Dearborn. Princeton, 1931. 218 p. *DLC, NN, CSmH*

Life and Services of Commodore William Bainbridge. Thomas Harris. Phila., 1837. 254 p. *DLC, NN, CSmH*

BAIRD, ROBERT. *The Life of Rev. Robert Baird.* Henry M. Baird. N. Y., 1866. 347 p. *DLC, NN*

BAIRD, SPENCER FULLERTON. *Spencer Fullerton Baird; a Biography With Selections From His Correspondence.* William H. Dall. Phila., 1915. 462 p. *DLC, NN, MWA, PU, MiD:B*

BAKER, CHARLES MINTON. *Charles Minton Baker and the Pioneer Trail.* E. L. Baker, ed. Chicago, 1928. 403 p. *MiD:B*

BAKER, DANIEL. *Life and Labors of Rev. Daniel Baker.* William M. Baker. Phila., 1859. 569 p. *NN*

BAKER, EDWARD DICKINSON. *Sketch of the Life and Public Services of Edward D. Baker, U. S. Senator From Oregon.* Joseph Wallace. Springfield, Ill., 1870. 144 p. *DLC, NN, CSmH*

BAKER, GEORGE. *God In a Rolls Royce; the Rise of Father Divine.* John Hoshor. N. Y., 1936. 272 p. *DLC, NN*

BAKER, HOBART. 2:425

BAKER, JAMES. *The Life of Jim Baker, 1818–1898. Trapper, Scout, Guide and Indian Fighter.* Nolie Mumey. Denver, 1931. 234 p. *DLC, NN, MWA, CSmH*

BAKER, JEREMIAH. *Jeremiah Baker, M.D., Gorham and Falmouth, Maine, 1752–1835.* James A. Spalding. Portland, Me., 1909. 24 p. *NN*

BAKER, NELSON HENRY. *A Modern Apostle of Charity; Father Baker and His "Lady of Victory Charities."* Thomas A. Galvin. Buffalo, N. Y., 1925. 310 p. *DLC, NN*

BAKER, NORMAN. *The Throttle; a Fact Story of Norman Baker, of Injustices, Confiscation and Suppression.* Alvin Winston. Muscatine, Ia., 1934. 676 p. *DLC, NN*

BAKER, WILLIAM GEORGE. *The Christian Lawyer; Being a Portraiture of the Life and Character of William George Baker.* W. G. Baker. N. Y., 1859. *DLC*

BAKER, WILLIAM TAYLOR. *Life and Character of William Taylor Baker, President of the World's Columbian Exposition and of the Chicago Board of Trade.* Charles H. Baker. N. Y., 1908. 293 p. *DLC, NN*

BALBOA, VASCO NÚÑEZ DE. *Vasco Núñez de Balboa.* F. A. Ober. N. Y. and London, 1906. 285 p. (Heroes of Am. History) *DLC, NN*

BALCH, ELISE WILLING. *Elise Willing Balch. In Memoriam.* Edwin Swift Balch. Phila., 1917. 162 p. (Privately Printed) *DLC, NN, MWA, PU*

BALCHEN, BERNT. *Bernt Balchen, Viking of the Air.* John Lawrence. N. Y., 1931. 165 p. *DLC, NN*

BALDWIN, ABRAHAM. *Abraham Baldwin, One of the Founders of the Republic, and Father of the Univ. of Georgia, the First of American State Universities.* Henry Clay White. Athens, Ga., 1926. 196 p. *DLC, CSmH, MiD:B*

BALDWIN, ELIAS JACKSON. *Lucky Baldwin, the Story of an Unconventional Success.* C. B. Glasscock. Indianapolis, 1933. 308 p. *DLC, NN, MWA, CSmH*

BALDWIN, ELIHU WHITTLESEY. *Patient Continuance in Well-Doing; a Memoir of Elihu W. Baldwin, D.D.* Edwin F. Hatfield. N. Y., 1843. 404 p. *NN, MWA*

BALDWIN, FRANK DWIGHT. *Memoirs of the Late Frank D. Baldwin, Major General, U. S. A.* Alice B. Baldwin. Los Angeles, 1929. 204 p. *DLC, NN, CSmH*

BALDWIN, HENRY. 2:110

BALDWIN, JOHN. *Life of John Baldwin, Sr., of Berea, Ohio.* Amos R. Webber. Cincinnati, 1925. 279 p. *DLC, NN, MiD:B*

BALDWIN, JOHN B. *Memorial of Col. John B. Baldwin, of Staunton, Va.* Staunton, Va., 1874. *CSmH*

BALDWIN, MATTHIAS WILLIAM. *Memorial of Matthias W. Baldwin.* Wolcott Calkins. Phila., 1867. 237 p. *DLC, PU*

BALDWIN, SIMEON. *Life and Letters of Simeon Baldwin.* Simeon E. Baldwin. New Haven, 1919. 503 p. *DLC, MWA, PU*

BALDWIN, THOMAS. *Memoir of Rev. Thomas Baldwin.* Daniel Chessman. Boston, 1841. 107 p. *MiD:B*

BALDWIN, WILLIAM HENRY. *An American Citizen: Life of William Henry Baldwin, Jr.* J. G. Brooks. Boston, 1910. 341 p. *DLC, NN, MKA, CSmH, PU*

BALLIET, STEPHEN. *Colonel Stephen Balliet, Soldier, Patriot and Statesman of the Revolution.* James B. Laux. Allentown, Pa., 1918. 24 p. *DLC, NN*

BALLOU, ADIN AUGUSTUS. *Memoir of Adin Augustus Ballou.* Adin Ballou. Hopedale, Mass., 1853. 192 p. *NN, MWA, PU, MiD:B*

BALLOU, HOSEA.

Biography of Rev. Hosea Ballou. Maturin M. Ballou. Boston, 1852. 404 p. *NN, MWA, CSmH*

Hosea Ballou. A Marvelous Life-Story. Oscar F. Safford. Boston, 1889. 290 p. *NN*

Life of Rev. Hosea Ballou. Thomas Whittemore. Boston, 1854. 2 vols. *NN, MWA*

BALLOU, HOSEA, 2ND. *Hosea Ballou, 2d, D.D., First President of Tufts College.* Hosea Starr Ballou. Boston, 1896. 312 p.
DLC, NN, MWA, PU

BANCROFT, AARON. 2:681

BANCROFT, GEORGE.
Life and Writings of George Bancroft. Oliver Dyer. N. Y., 1891. 264 p. *DLC, NN*
Life and Letters of George Bancroft. M. A. de Wolfe Howe. N. Y., 1908. 2 vols. *DLC, NN, MWA, CSmH, PU*

BANCROFT, HUBERT HOWE. 2:531

BANGS, NATHAN.
Life and Times of Nathan Bangs, D.D. Abel Stevens. N. Y., 1863. 426 p. *DLC, NN, MiD:B*
Nathan Bangs. Alexander H. Tuttle. N. Y., 1909. 127 p.
DLC

BANTING, FREDERICK G. 2:175

BARAGA, FREDERICK.
The Apostle of the Chippewas, the Life Story of the Most Rev. Frederick Baraga, D.D., the First Bishop of Marquette. Joseph Gregorich. Chicago, 1932. 104 p. *DLC, NN, MiD:B*
Life and Labors of Frederick Baraga, First Bishop of Marquette, Mich.; With Sketches of Other Indian Missionaries of the Northwest. C. Verwyst. Milwaukee, 1900. 476 p. *DLC, NN, MiD:B*

BARBAULD, ANNA LAETITIA. *A Memoir of Mrs. Anna Laetitia Barbauld.* Grace E. Ellis. Boston, 1874. 350 p. *DLC, MWA*

BARBEE, JAMES D. *Life and Memories of Rev. J. D. Barbee . . .* Horace M. Du Bose. Nashville, 1906. 243 p. *DLC, NN*

BARBELIN, FELIX J. *Memoir of Father Felix J. Barbelin, S.J., Pastor of St. Joseph's Church, Phila.* Eleanor C. Donnelly. Phila., 1886. 468 p.

BARD, SAMUEL. *A Domestic Narrative of the Life of Samuel Bard, M.D. . . . Late President of the College of Physicians and Surgeons of the University of the State of New York.* John M'Vickar. N. Y., 1822. 244 p. *DLC, NN, MWA, PU*

BARGE, BENJAMIN FRANKLIN. *Benjamin F. Barge, 1832–1902; His Life, His Travels.* M. B. Hurlbut. Phila., 1905. 212 p.
DLC, NN, PU

BARKER, GEORGE PAYSON. *Life of George P. Barker, With Sketches of Some of His Celebrated Speeches.* George J. Bryan. Buffalo. 1849. 215 p. *DLC, NN, MWA, CSmH, MiD:B*

BARKER, JAMES NELSON. *James Nelson Barker, 1784–1858.* Paul H. Musser. Phila., 1929. 230 p. *DLC, NN, MWA, CSmH, PU*

BARLOW, JOEL.
  The Life and Letters of Joel Barlow, LL.D., Poet, Statesman, Philosopher. Charles B. Todd. N. Y., 1886. 306 p.
    DLC, NN, MWA, CSmH, PU, MiD:B
  The Early Days of Joel Barlow, a Connecticut Wit, Yale Graduate, Editor, Lawyer and Poet, Chaplain During the Revolutionary War. Theodore A. Zunder. New Haven, 1934. 320 p.
    DLC, NN, MWA, CSmH, PU
BARNARD, CHARLES FRANCIS. *Charles Francis Barnard; a Sketch of His Life and Work.* Francis Tiffany. Boston, 1895. 201 p.
    DLC, NN, MWA
BARNARD, FREDERICK AUGUSTUS P. *Memoirs of Frederick A. P. Barnard, Tenth President of Columbia College, in the City of New York.* John Fulton. N. Y., 1896. 485 p. (Columbia Univ. Press Series) *DLC, NN, PU*
BARNARD, GEORGE GREY. 2:430
BARNARD, HENRY. *Life of Henry Barnard, the First U. S. Commissioner of Education, 1867–1870.* Bernard C. Steiner. Washington, 1919. 131 p. *DLC, NN*
BARNERT, NATHAN. *Biography of Nathan Barnert . . .* Michael T. Baum. Paterson, N. J., 1914. 165 p. *DLC, NN*
BARNES, ALPHEUS GEORGE. *Al G. Barnes, Master Showman.* Dave Robeson. Caldwell, Idaho, 1935. 460 p. *DLC, NN*
BARNES, BARNABE. 2:604
BARNEY, EVERETT HOSMER. *Everett Hosmer Barney, His Family Connections, a Record of His Life Work.* William F. Adams, comp. Springfield, Mass., 1912. 133 p. *DLC, NN, PU*
BARNEY, JOSHUA.
  Commodore Joshua Barney. William F. Adams. Springfield, Mass., 1912. 228 p. *CSmH*
  A Biographical Memoir of the Late Commodore Joshua Barney. Mary Barney, ed. Boston, 1832. 328 p.
    DLC, NN, MWA, CSmH, PU, MiU:C
  Joshua Barney, a Forgotten Hero of Blue Water. Ralph D. Paine. N. Y., 1924. 410 p. *DLC, NN, MWA*
BARNUM, PHINEAS TAYLOR.
  Life of P. T. Barnum. Joel Benton. Phila., 1891. 621 p.
    DLC, NN, MWA, CSmH
  Life of Barnum, the Man Who Lured the Herd. C. J. Finger. Girard, Kansas, 1924. 96 p. *DLC*

Unknown Barnum. Harvey W. Root. N. Y., 1927. 376 p.
DLC, NN, MWA

Barnum. M. R. Werner. N. Y., 1923. 381 p.
DLC, NN, MWA, CSmH, PU
2:6–89–180–581

BARRETT, LAWRENCE. *Lawrence Barrett. A Professional Sketch.* Elwyn A. Barron. Chicago, 1889. 98 p. *DLC, NN*

BARRETT, SAMUEL. *Memoir of the Rev. Samuel Barrett, D.D., With a Selected Series of His Discourses.* Lewis G. Pray. Boston, 1867. 207 p. *DLC, NN, MWA*

BARRIOS, JUSTO RUFINO. *Justo Rufino Barrios; a Biography.* Paul Burgess. Phila., 1926. 286 p. *DLC, NN, PU*

BARROW, DAVID CRENSHAW. *David Crenshaw Barrow.* Thomas W. Reed. Athens, Ga., 1935. 295 p. *DLC, NN*

BARROWS, JOHN HENRY. *John Henry Barrows: A Memoir.* M. E. Barrows. N. Y., 1904. 450 p. *DLC, MiD:B*

BARROWS, SAMUEL JUNE. *Sunny Life: the Biography of Samuel June Barrows.* Isabel C. Barrows. Boston, 1913. 323 p. *DLC, NN*

BARRY, JOHN.
Commodore John Barry. Martin I. J. Griffin. (Annual Report of American Hist. Assoc., 1895. pp. 339–68)
DLC, NN, MWA, PU
The History of Commodore John Barry. Martin I. J. Griffin. Phila., 1897. 261 p. *DLC, NN, MWA*
Commodore John Barry, " the Father of the American Navy." Martin I. J. Griffin. Phila., 1903. 424 p. *DLC, NN, MWA*
Commodore John Barry, Father of the American Navy. Joseph Gurn. N. Y., 1933. 318 p. *DLC, NN, CSmH*
Commodore John Barry, the Father of the American Navy; a Survey of Extraordinary Episodes in His Naval Career. William B. Meany. N. Y., 1911. 74 p. *DLC, NN*
2:634

BARTLETT, EDWIN. *A Memoir of Edwin Bartlett.* William S. Ruschenberger. Phila., 1868. 126 p. *DLC, NN, MWA, PU*

BARTLETT, JOHN RUSSELL. *Life and Services of the Hon. John Russell Bartlett.* William Gammell. Providence, 1886. 20 p.
DLC, NN, MWA, CSmH, MiD:B

BARTLETT, NORMAN HOWARD. *Norman Howard Bartlett.* G. Waldo Browne. Manchester, N. H., 1904. 183 p. *NN, MWA*

BARTLETT, PAUL WAYLAND. 2:430

BARTLETT, WILLIAM FRANCIS. *Memoir of William F. Bartlett.* Francis W. Palfrey. Boston, 1878. 309 p.

DLC, NN, MWA, CSmH, PU, MiD:B

BARTON, CLARA.
Life of Clara Barton. William E. Barton. Boston and N. Y., 1922. 2 vols. *DLC, NN, MWA*
Life of Clara Barton. Percy H. Epler. N. Y., 1915. 438 p.

DLC, NN, MiD:B

2:9–325–506

BARTON, JOHN WAIT. *Falling in Harness: a Sketch of the Life of J. W. Barton.* Henry Clay Trumbull. Phila., 1867. 81 p.

BARTON, WILLIAM. *Biography of Revolutionary Heroes; Containing the Life of Brigadier-General William Barton, and Also, of Captain Stephen Olney.* Catherine R. Williams. Providence, N. Y., 1839. 312 p. *DLC, NN, MWA, CSmH, MiD:B MiU:C*

BARTRAM, JOHN, and MARSHALL, HUMPHREY. *Memorials of John Bartram and Humphrey Marshall, With Notices of Their Botanical Contemporaries.* William Darlington. Phila., 1849. 585 p.

DLC, NN, MWA, PU

2:225

BARTRAM, WILLIAM. *William Bartram, Interpreter of the American Landscape.* N. B. Fagin. Balt., 1933. 229 p.

DLC, NN, MWA, CSmH, PU, MiD:B

BASCOM, HENRY BIDLEMAN. *The Life of Henry Bidleman Bascom ...* Moses M. Henkle. Louisville, 1854. 408 p. *DLC, NN, MWA*

BASHFORD, JAMES WHITFORD. *James W. Bashford, Pastor, Educator, Bishop.* George R. Grose. N. Y., 1922. 252 p.

DLC, NN, MiD:B

BASS, EDWARD.
Life and Times of Edward Bass, First Bishop of Massachusetts, 1726–1803. Daniel D. Addison. Boston and N. Y., 1897. 350 p.

DLC, NN

Life of Bishop Bass of Massachusetts. John N. Norton. N. Y., 1854. 192 p.

BASS, SAMUEL. *Sam Bass.* Wayne Gard. Boston, 1936. 262 p.

DLC, NN, MWA

BASSETT, S. *Memoir of Rev. S. Bassett.* L. G. Pray. Boston, 1867. 207 p. *NN*

BATE, WILLIAM BRIMAGE. *Life of William B. Bate, Citizen, Soldier, and Statesman.* Park Marshall. Nashville, 1908. 363 p.

DLC, NN

BATES, FREDERICK. *The Life and Papers of Frederick Bates.* Thomas M. Marshall, ed. St. Louis, 1926. 2 vols.
DLC, NN, MWA, CSmH, PU, MiD:B

BATES, HERBERT ROSWELL. *The Life of H. Roswell Bates.* S. Ralph Harlow. N. Y., 1914. 159 p. *DLC, NN*

BATES, JOSEPH. *The Early Life and Later Experience and Labors of Elder Joseph Bates.* James White, ed. Battle Creek, Mich., 1877. 320 p. *DLC, NN, MWA, MiD:B*

BATTELL, ROBBINS. *Biography of Robbins Battell.* Charles S. Elliot. N. Y., 1895. 80 p. *DLC, NN*

BATZ, JEAN. *Marie Antoinette's Henchman; the Career of Jean, Baron de Batz, in the French Revolution.* Meade Minnigerode. N. Y., 1936. 317 p. *DLC, NN*

BAUDELAIRE, CHARLES PIERRE. *Baudelaire; Flesh and Spirit.* Lewis P. Shanks. Boston, 1930. 265 p. *DLC, NN, PU*

BAXTER, PERCY. 2:151

BAYARD, GEORGE DASHIELL. *The Life of George Dashiell Bayard.* Samuel J. Bayard. N. Y., 1874. 337 p.
DLC, NN, MWA, CSmH, MiD:B

BAYARD, JOHN. *Colonel John Bayard (1738–1807) and the Bayard Family of America . . .* James Grant Wilson. N. Y., 1885. 24 p.
DLC, NN, MWA, MiU:C, RP:JCB

BAYARD, LEWIS P. *Memorial of the Rev. Lewis P. Bayard, D.D.* John W. Brown, ed. N. Y., 1841. 272 p. *DLC, NN, MWA*

BAYARD, PIERRE D. T. *Life of Chevalier Bayard.* William G. Simms. N. Y., 1847. 401 p. *DLC, NN, CSmH, PU*

BAYARD, THOMAS FRANCIS. *Outline of the Public Life and Services of Thomas F. Bayard, Senator of the U. S. From Delaware, 1869–1880.* Edward Spencer. N. Y., 1880. 303 p.
DLC, NN, MWA, PU, MiD:B

BAYNES, ERNEST HAROLD. *Ernest H. Baynes, Naturalist and Crusader.* Raymond Gorges. Boston, 1928. 255 p. *DLC, NN*

BEADLE, WILLIAM. *A Narrative of the Life of William Beadle.* Hartford, 1783. *RP:JCB*

BEADLE, WILLIAM HENRY HARRISON. *A Complete Biographical Sketch of General W. H. H. Beadle.* Oscar W. Coursey. Mitchell, S. D., 1913. 99 p. *DLC, NN*

BEALE, CHARLES FREDERICK T. *Charles Frederick Tiffany Beale.* Marcus Benjamin. Wash., 1902. 13 p. (Memorial Papers of Soc. of Colonial Wars in D. C., no. 4) *DLC, NN, MWA, MiD:B*

BEALE, EDWARD FITZGERALD. *Edward Fitzgerald Beale, a Pioneer in the Path of Empire, 1822–1903.* Stephen Bonsal. N. Y., 1912. 312 p. *DLC, NN, CSmH, MiD:B*

BEAN, ROY. *Law West of the Pecos, the Story of Roy Bean.* Everett Lloyd. San Antonio, 1931. 168 p. *DLC, NN, MWA*

BEARD, W. H. 2:52

BEAUHARNAIS, HORTENSE. *History of Hortense, Daughter of Josephine.* J. S. C. Abbott. N. Y., 1870. 379 p. *DLC, NN*

BEAUMARCHAIS, [CARON, PIERRE A.]. *Beaumarchais and the War of American Independence.* Elizabeth S. Kite. Boston, 1918. 2 vols. *DLC, NN, PU*

BEAUMONT, FRANCIS. *Beaumont, the Dramatist.* Charles M. Gayley. N. Y., 1914. 445 p. *DLC, NN, CSmH, PU*

BEAUMONT, WILLIAM. *Life and Letters of Dr. William Beaumont; including Hitherto Unpublished Data Concerning the Case of Alexis St. Martin.* Jesse S. Myer. St. Louis, 1912. 317 p. *DLC, NN*

BEAUREGARD, PIERRE GUSTAVE TOUTANT. *Beauregard, the Great Creole.* Hamilton Basso. N. Y., 1933. 333 p. *DLC, NN, PU* 2:88–612

BEAVER, HUGH MCALLISTER. *A Memorial of a True Life; a Biography of Hugh McAllister Beaver.* Robert E. Speer. N. Y., 1898. 308 p. *DLC, NN, PU*

BEAVER, JAMES ADAMS. *Life and Achievements of James Adams Beaver.* Frank A. Burr. Phila., 1882. 224 p. *DLC, NN, MWA, CSmH, PU, MiD:B*

BECHER, JOHN JOACHIM. 2:348

BECKNELL, WILLIAM. 2:46

BEDE, VENERABLE. 2:7

BEDELL, GREGORY TOWNSEND. *Memoirs of Rev. G. T. Bedell.* Stephen H. Tyng. Phila. and Boston, 1836. 402 p. *DLC, NN, MWA, PU*

BEDINGER, GEORGE MICHAEL. *George Michael Bedinger: A Kentucky Pioneer.* Danske Dandridge. Charlottesville, Va., 1909. 232 p. *DLC, NN, MWA, PU*

BEECHER, CATHERINE ESTHER. *Catherine Esther Beecher, Pioneer Educator.* Mae Elizabeth Harveson. Phila., 1932, 295 p. *DLC, NN, PU*

BEECHER, HENRY WARD.
Henry Ward Beecher: A Sketch of His Career; With Analysis of His Power as a Preacher, Lecturer, etc. Lyman Abbott. N. Y., 1883. 604 p. *DLC, NN*

Henry Ward Beecher. Lyman Abbott. Boston, 1903. 457 p.
DLC, NN, PU

Henry Ward Beecher; A Sketch of His Career. Lyman Abbott and S. B. Halliday. Hartford, 1887. 670 p. *DLC, NN, MWA*

Henry Ward Beecher: The Shakespeare of the Pulpit. J. H. Barrows. N. Y., 1893. 541 p. (American Reformers Series)
DLC, NN, MiD:B

A Biography of Rev. Henry Ward Beecher. Wm. C. Beecher and Samuel Scoville, assisted by Mrs. Henry Ward Beecher. N. Y., 1888. 713 p. *DLC, NN, MWA, CSmH, MiD:B*

Beecher, Christian Philosopher, Pulpit Orator, Patriot and Philanthropist. Thomas W. Handford. Chicago, 1887. 317 p.
DLC

Henry Ward Beecher; An American Portrait. Paxton Hibben. N. Y., 1927. 390 p. *DLC, NN, MWA, PU*

Henry Ward Beecher. John R. Howard. Phila., 1887. 161 p.
DLC, NN, PU

Life of Henry Ward Beecher. Joseph Howard, Jr. Phila., 1887. 651 p. *DLC, NN, MWA, MiD:B*

The Life and Work of Henry Ward Beecher. Thomas W. Knox. Hartford, 1887. 544 p. *DLC, NN, MWA*

Beecher and His Accusers. Francis P. Williamson. Phila., 1874. 415 p. *DLC, PU*

2:6–12–40–98–330–511–581–624

BEECHER, LYMAN. *Lyman Beecher.* E. F. Hayward. Boston, 1904. 114 p. *DLC, NN*

2:40–581

BEER, GEORGE LOUIS. *George Louis Beer, a Tribute . . .* N. Y., 1924. 164 p. *CSmH*

BEER, THOMAS. 2:236

BEETHOVEN, LUDWIG VAN.

Beethoven, the Man Who Freed Music. Robert H. Schauffler. N. Y., 1929. 2 vols. *DLC, NN, PU*

Beethoven. Marion M. Scott. N. Y., 1934. 339 p.
DLC, NN

The Life of Ludwig Van Beethoven. Alexander W. Thayer. N. Y., 1925. 3 vols. *DLC, NN, PU*

2:5–187

BEHMEN, JACOB. 2:406

BEHRING, EMIL. 2:176

BELASCO, DAVID. *The Life of David Belasco.* William Winter. N. Y., 1918. 2 vols. *DLC, NN, CSmH, PU*

BELDEN, DAVID. *Life of David Belden . . .* David Belden. N. Y., 1891. 472 p. *NN, CSmH*

BELDING, WARREN ASA. *Biography of Dr. W. A. Belding, Including Sixty Years of Ministerial Pioneer Work.* Warren S. Belding. Cincinnati, 1897. 140 p. *NN*

BELKNAP, JEREMY. *Life of Jeremy Belknap With Selections From His Writings . . . Arranged by His Granddaughter.* Jane M. Belknap. N. Y., 1847. 253 p. *DLC, NN, MWA, CSmH, MiU:C*

BELL, ALEXANDER GRAHAM. *Alexander Graham Bell, The Man Who Contracted Space.* Catherine D. Mackenzie. Boston, 1928. 382 p. *DLC, NN, MWA*

2:388–675

BELL, CHARLES HENRY. *Memoir of Charles Henry Bell, LL.D.* Edmund F. Slafter. Boston, 1895. 24 p. (Privately Printed) *DLC, NN, MWA, MiD:B*

BELL, JOHN. *The Life, Speeches, and Public Services of John Bell, Together With a Sketch of the Life of Edward Everett.* N. Y., 1860. 118 p. *DLC, NN, CSmH, MiD:B*

BELL, LOUIS. *A Memoir of Gen. Louis Bell.* J. B. Bouton. N. Y., 1865. 53 p. *DLC, MWA, CSmH*

BELL, LUTHER VOSE. *Memoir of Luther V. Bell, M.D., LL.D.* George E. Ellis. Boston, 1863. 75 p. *CSmH*

BELLASIS, SERGEANT. *Memorials of Mr. Sergeant Bellasis, 1800–1875.* E. Bellasis. N. Y., 1893. 215 p. *DLC, NN*

BELLOMONT, EARL OF. *The Life and Administration of Richard, Earl of Bellomont.* Frederic De Peyster. N. Y., 1879. 17 p. *DLC, NN, CSmH, PU, MiU:C*

BELLOWS, ALBERT FITCH. 2:52

BELLOWS, BENJAMIN. *Sketch of Col. Benjamin Bellows.* H. W. Bellows. N. Y., 1855. 125 p. *MiD:B*

BELLOWS, GEORGE WESLEY. *George W. Bellows; His Lithographs; With an Essay by Thomas Beer.* N. Y., 1927. 254 p. *DLC, NN* 2:114

BELLOWS, HENRY WHITNEY. *Henry Whitney Bellows: a Biographical Sketch.* Russell N. Bellows. Keene, N. H., 1897. 283 p. *NN*

BELZONI, GIOVANNI BATTISTA. 2:598

BEMIS, JUDSON MOSS. *Judson Moss Bemis, Pioneer.* William C. Edgar. Minneapolis, 1926. 340 p. *DLC, NN*

BENEDICT, SAINT. 2:336–680

BENEDICT, LEWIS. *A Memorial of Brevet Brigadier General Lewis Benedict.* Henry M. Benedict. Albany, 1866. 155 p.

DLC, NN, MWA, CSmH

BENES, EDWARD. 2:30

BENEZET, ANTHONY. *Memoirs of Anthony Benezet.* Robert Vaux. Phila., 1817. 136 p. *MiD:B*

BENJAMIN, JUDAH PHILIP.

Judah P. Benjamin. Pierce Butler. Phila., 1907. 459 p. (A.C.B.) *DLC, NN, MWA, PU*

Judah P. Benjamin, Statesman of the Lost Cause. Rollin Osterweis. N. Y., 1933. 205 p. *DLC, NN, CSmH*
2:88

BENNETT, ALFRED. *Memoir of Rev. Alfred Bennett.* H. Harvey. N. Y., 1852. 231 p. *NN, MiD:B*

BENNETT, CEPHAS. *Sketch of the Lives and Missionary Work of Cephas Bennett and His Wife, S. K. Bennett.* Ruth W. Ranney. N. Y., 1892. 142 p. *DLC*

BENNETT, CHRISTINE IVERSON. 2:237

BENNETT, CONSTANCE. *The Life Story of Constance Bennett.* Mary M. McBride. N. Y., 1932. 61 p. *DLC*

BENNETT, FLOYD. *Floyd Bennett; With a Foreword by Rear Admiral Richard E. Byrd.* Cora L. Bennett. N. Y., 1932. 168 p.

DLC, NN

BENNETT, HENRY. *Henry Bennett, Earl of Arlington, Secretary of State to Charles II.* Violet Barbour. Washington, 1914. 303 p.

DLC, NN, CSmH

BENNETT, JAMES GORDON, AND BENNETT, JAMES GORDON, JR.

James Gordon Bennett and His Times. Isaac C. Pray. N. Y., 1855. 488 p. *DLC, NN, MWA, PU, MiD:B*

The James Gordon Bennetts. Don C. Seitz. Indianapolis, 1928. 405 p. *DLC, NN, PU*

When James Gordon Bennett Was Caliph of Bagdad. Albert S. Crockett. N. Y., 1926. 414 p. *DLC, NN, MWA, PU*
2:511

BENNETT, TIMOTHY. 2:406

BENSON, JOSEPH. *Life of Rev. Joseph Benson.* R. Treffry. N. Y., 1853. 292 p. *DLC*

BENTON, ANDREW. *Andrew Benton, 1620–1683.* J. H. Benton, Jr. Boston, 1900. 30 p. (Privately Printed) *DLC, MWA, MiD:B*

BENTON, THOMAS HART.

The Life of Thomas Hart Benton. W. M. Meigs. Phila., 1904. 535 p. *DLC, NN, MWA, CSmH, PU*

Thomas H. Benton. Joseph M. Rogers. Phila., 1905. 361 p. (A.C.B.) *DLC, NN, PU*

Thomas Hart Benton. Theodore Roosevelt. Boston, 1886. 372 p. (A.S.) *DLC, NN, MWA, CSmH, PU, MiD:B*

BERCOVICI, KONRAD. 2:366

BERGERAC, CYRANO. *Cyrano.* Cameron Rogers. N. Y., 1929. 308 p. *DLC, NN, PU*

BERING, VITUS. 2:387

BERKELEY, GEORGE.
> *Life of Bishop Berkeley.* J. N. Norton. N. Y., 1861. 299 p. *NN*
>
> *George Berkeley; a Study of His Life and Philosophy.* John Wild. Cambridge, 1936. 552 p. *DLC, NN, CSmH*

BERKOWITZ, HENRY. *The Beloved Rabbi; an Account of the Life and Works of Henry Berkowitz, D.D.* Max E. Berkowitz. N. Y., 1932. 285 p. *DLC, NN, MWA*

BERLIN, IRVING. *Story of Irving Berlin.* Alexander Woollcott. N. Y., 1925. 237 p. *DLC, NN*

BERLINER, EMILE. *Emile Berliner; Maker of the Microphone.* Frederic W. Wile. Indianapolis, 1926. 353 p. *DLC, NN, PU*

BERLIOZ, HECTOR. 2:187

BERNARD, SAINT. *Bernard of Clairvaux; the Times; the Man and His Work.* Richard S. Storrs. N. Y., 1892. 598 p. *DLC, NN, PU*

BERNARD, CLAUDE. 2:678

BERNAYS, AUGUSTUS CHARLES. *Augustus Charles Bernays; A Memoir.* Thekla Bernays. St. Louis, 1912. 309 p. *DLC, NN*

BERNHARDT, SARAH. 2–90

BERNON, ESTHER LEROY. *The Star of La Rochelle.* Elizabeth N. White. Providence, 1930. 130 p. *DLC, NN, MWA*

BERRY, HIRAM GREGORY. *Major-General Hiram G. Berry.* Edward K. Gould. Rockland, Me., 1899. 312 p. *DLC, NN*

BERRY, MARTHA. *Martha Berry, the Sunday Lady of Possum Trot.* Tracy Byers. N. Y., 1932. 268 p. *DLC, NN*

BERZELIUS, JOHN JACOB. 2:348

BETHUNE, GEORGE WASHINGTON. *Memoir of George W. Bethune.* Abraham R. Van Nest. N. Y., 1867. 446 p. *NN, MWA, MiD:B*

BETHUNE, JOANNA.
> *Memoirs of Mrs. Joanna Bethune.* George W. Bethune. N. Y., 1862. 250 p. *NN*
>
> *Memoirs of Mrs. Joanna Bethune.* George W. Bethune. N. Y., 1863. 125 p. *NN, MWA, MiD:B*

BETTS, SAMUEL ROSSITER. *Life and Career of Samuel Rossiter Betts.*
Georgina B. Wells. N. Y., 1934. 38 p. *DLC, NN*

BEVERIDGE, ALBERT JEREMIAH. *Beveridge and the Progressive Era.*
Claude G. Bowers. Boston, 1932. 610 p.
DLC, NN, MWA, CSmH, PU, MiD:B

BEZA, THEODORE. *Theodore Beza: The Counsellor of the French Reformation.* Henry M. Baird. N. Y., 1899. 376 p. (Heroes of the
Reformation) *DLC, NN, PU*

BICKEL, LUKE. *Captain Bickel of the Inland Sea.* Charles K. Harrington. N. Y., 1919. 301 p.

BICKERDYKE, MARY ANN.
Mother Bickerdyke. Florence S. Kellogg. Chicago, 1907.
176 p. *DLC, CSmH*
*The Woman Who Battled For the Boys in Blue. Mother Bick-
erdyke. Her Life and Labors.* Margaret A. Davis. San Francisco, 1886. 166 p. *DLC, NN, CSmH*

BIDDLE, CHAPMAN. *Memoir of Chapman Biddle . . .* Charles G.
Leland. Phila., 1882. 24 p. *NN, MWA, CSmH, PU*

BIDWELL, JOHN. *John Bidwell; Pioneer, Statesman, Philanthropist.*
C. C. Royce. Chico, California, 1906. 66 p. (Privately Printed)
DLC, NN, CSmH

BIENVILLE, LE MOYNE. 2:127

BIERCE, AMBROSE.
Portrait of Ambrose Bierce. Adolphe D. De Castro. N. Y.,
1929. 351 p. *DLC, NN, MWA, PU*
Bitter Bierce; A Mystery of American Letters. C. Hartley
Grattan. N. Y., 1929. 291 p. *DLC, PU*
Ambrose Bierce; A Biography. Carey McWilliams. N. Y.,
1929. 358 p. *DLC, NN, MWA, CSmH, PU*
Life of Ambrose Bierce. Walter Neale. N. Y., 1929. 489 p.
DLC, NN, MWA, PU
Ambrose Bierce; A Study. Vincent Starrett. Chicago, 1920.
50 p. (Privately Printed) *DLC, NN, MWA, CSmH*

BIGELOW, HENRY JACOB.
A Memoir of Henry Jacob Bigelow, M.D. William S. Bigelow.
Boston, 1900. 297 p. *NN, PU*
Memoir of H. J. Bigelow. Oliver Wendell Holmes. Boston,
1900.

BIGELOW, JACOB. *Memoir of Jacob Bigelow, M.D.* George E. Ellis.
Cambridge, 1880. 105 p. *NN, MWA, PU*

BIGGS. HERMAN M. *The Life of Herman M. Biggs, M.D., D.Sc., LL.D.* Charles E. A. Winslow. Phila., 1929. 432 p. *DLC, NN*

BILLINGS, EMILY SANFORD. *A Biographical Sketch of Emily Sanford Billings.* Edward C. Billings. New Orleans, 1887. 100 p.
DLC, NN

BILLINGS, JOHN SHAW.
John Shaw Billings: A Memoir. Fielding H. Garrison. N. Y., 1915. 432 p. *DLC, NN, MWA, PU, MiD:B*
John Shaw Billings, Creator of the National Medical Library and its Catalogue. Harry M. Lydenberg. Chicago, 1924. 94 p.
DLC, NN, CSmH

BILLINGS, JOSH. [HENRY W. SHAW]
Life and Adventures of Josh Billings. Francis S. Smith. N. Y., 1883. 92 p. *DLC, NN*
Josh Billings. A. P. Thompson. (New Eng. Mag. n.s. vol. 19)
NN

BINGHAM, GEORGE CALEB. *George Caleb Bingham, the Missouri Artist.* Fern H. Rusk. Jefferson City, Mo., 1917. 135 p.
DLC, NN, MWA

BINGHAM, HARRY. *Memorial of Hon. Harry Bingham, LL.D., Lawyer, Legislator, Author.* H. H. Metcalf. Concord, N. H., 1910. 505 p.
DLC, NN, MiD:B

BINNER, PAUL. *Paul Binner and His Noble Work Among the Deaf.* Hypatia Boyd. Milwaukee, 1901. 58 p. *DLC*

BINNEY, HORACE. *Life of Horace Binney.* Charles C. Binney. Phila., 1903. 460 p. *DLC, NN, PU, MiD:B*

BINNEY, HORACE, JR. *A Memoir of Horace Binney, Jr.* Charles J. Stillé. Phila., 1870. 24 p. *DLC, NN, PU, MiD:B*

BINNEY, JOSEPH GETCHELL. *Twenty-Six Years in Burma: Records of the Life and Work of Joseph G. Binney, D.D.* Juliette P. Binney. Phila., 1880. 384 p. *DLC, NN, MWA*

BIRD, FRANCIS WILLIAM. *Francis William Bird, A Biographical Sketch.* Boston, 1897. 168 p. *DLC, NN, MWA*

BIRD, ROBERT MONTGOMERY. *Life and Dramatic Works of Robert Montgomery Bird.* Clement E. Foust. N. Y., 1919. 725 p.
DLC, NN, PU, MWA, CSmH

BIRNEY, DAVID BELL. *Life of David Bell Birney . . .* Phila., 1867. 418 p. *CSmH, MiD:B*

BIRNEY, JAMES GILLESPIE.
James G. Birney and His Times. William Birney. N. Y., 1890. 443 p. *DLC, NN, CSmH, PU, MiD:B*

Sketches of the Life and Writings of James Gillespie Birney.
Beriah Green.   Utica, N. Y., 1844.   119 p.

DLC, NN, CSmH, MiD:B

BISE, MARY ANN.   *The Mountain Wild Flower; or, Memoirs of Mrs.
Mary Ann Bise.*   Charles Lester.   N. Y., 1838.   243 p.   *NN*

BISHOP, JOSEPH.   *The Life of Joseph Bishop.*   John W. Gray.   Nashville, 1858.   236 p.   *DLC, NN*

BISHOP, LEVI.   *Poetical Works of Levi Bishop, With a Sketch of the
Author.*   Albany, 1881.   590 p.   *DLC, NN*

BISMARCK, OTTO.   *Life of Prince Otto von Bismarck.*   F. P. Stearns.
Phila., 1899.   431 p.   *DLC, NN, PU*

BITTER, KARL.   *Karl Bitter; a Biography.*   Ferdinand Schevill.   Chicago, 1917.   68 p.   *DLC, NN*

BIXBY, MOSES HOMAN.   *Life and Work of Moses H. Bixby.*   Jennie
B. Johnson.   N. Y., 1904.   157 p.   *DLC*

BLACK HAWK.

Life and Adventures of Black Hawk.   Benjamin Drake.   Cincinnati, 1839.   288 p.   *DLC, NN, CSmH*

Black Hawk Wars, Including a Review of Black Hawk's Life.
Frank E. Stevens.   Chicago, 1903.   323 p.

DLC, NN, MWA, CSmH

BLACK, JEREMIAH SULLIVAN.

*Essays and Speeches of Jeremiah S. Black, With a Short Bio-
graphical Sketch.*   Chauncey F. Black.   N. Y., 1885.   621 p.

DLC, NN, CSmH, PU

Jeremiah Sullivan Black.   William N. Brigance.   Phila., 1934.
303 p.   *DLC, NN, CSmH, PU*
2:100

BLACKMAN, ANSON ALFONSO.   *Ali Baba; An Appreciation of the Life,
Labors and Public Services of a Good Man and True.*   Elbert Hubbard.   East Aurora, N. Y., 1926.   113 p.   *DLC, NN*

BLACKSTONE, TIMOTHY BEACH.   *Biography of Timothy B. Blackstone.*
Ida Hinman.   N. Y., 1917.   40 p.   *DLC, NN*

BLAINE, JAMES GILLESPIE.

*An American Career and Its Triumph; Life of James G. Blaine;
With the Career of J. A. Logan.*   W. R. Balch.   Phila., 1884.   546 p.

DLC, NN

*James G. Blaine; Sketch of His Life; With Record of the Life
of J. A. Logan.*   C. W. Balestier.   N. Y., 1884.   296 p.

DLC, NN, CSmH

Life and Public Services of Hon. James G. Blaine.   James P.
Boyd.   n.p., 1893.   704 p.   *DLC, MWA, MiD:B*

Life and Public Services of James G. Blaine; Also, Life of J. A. Logan. Russell H. Conwell. Augusta, Me., 1884. 504 p.

              DLC, NN, MiD:B

Biographies of James G. Blaine and J. A. Logan. T. V. Cooper. Chicago and N. Y., 1884. 503 p.   *DLC, MiD:B*

The Biography and Public Services of Hon. James G. Blaine. Hugh Craig. N. Y., 1884. 503 p.   *DLC, NN*

Life of Hon. James G. Blaine. Theron C. Crawford. Phila., 1893. 644 p.   *DLC, NN, MWA, MiD:B*

Pine to Potomac; Life of James G. Blaine; With Sketch of the Life of Gen. J. A. Logan. E. K. Cressey. Boston, 1884. 421 p.

              DLC, MWA

Biography of James G. Blaine. Mary A. Dodge. (Gail Hamilton) Norwich, Conn., 1895. 722 p.

        DLC, NN, MWA, PU, MiD:B

Early Life and Public Career of Hon. James G. Blaine . . . Including a Biography of Gen. J. A. Logan. Walter R. Houghton. Des Moines, Iowa, 1884. 576 p.   *DLC, NN*

American Statesman: the Work and Words of James G. Blaine. Willis F. Johnson. Phila., 1892. 535 p.   *DLC, NN*

The Lives of James G. Blaine and John A. Logan. Thomas W. Knox. Hartford, 1884. 502 p.   *DLC, MWA, CSmH*

Life and Great Speeches of the Hon. James G. Blaine. James B. McClure. Chicago, 1890. 287 p.   *DLC*

James G. Blaine; a Political Idol of Other Days. David S. Muzzey. N. Y., 1934. 514 p. *DLC, NN, CSmH, PU*

Life and Public Services of Hon. James G. Blaine. Henry D. Northrop. Phila., 1893. 604 p.   *DLC, NN, MiD:B*

Life of Hon. James G. Blaine. James W. Pierce. Balt., 1893. 565 p.   *DLC, PU*

Life and Public Services of Hon. James G. Blaine. H. J. Ramsdell. Phila., 1884. 678 p.   *DLC, NN, CSmH*

Life and Work of James G. Blaine. John C. Ridpath. Phila., 1893. 505 p.   *DLC, NN, PU, MiD:B*

Blaine of Maine; His Life and Times. Charles E. Russell. N. Y., 1931. 446 p.   *DLC, NN*

James Gillespie Blaine. Edward Stanwood. Boston, 1905. 377 p. (A.S. 2d Series) *DLC, NN, MWA, CSmH, PU, MiD:B*

Biographical Sketch of James G. Blaine; also, Life of J. A. Logan. Walter S. Vail, ed. 1884.   *DLC, NN, PU*

  2:84–107–590

BLAINE, MRS. JAMES GILLESPIE. 2:97

BLAIR. *The Blairs of Kentucky.* George Baber. (Register of the Kentucky Hist. Soc., XIV) *NN*

BLAIR, FRANCIS PRESTON. See SEYMOUR, HORATIO.

BLAIR, JAMES. *Life of Commissary James Blair, Founder of William and Mary College.* Dan E. Motley. Balt., 1901. 57 p. (J. H. U. Studies in Hist. and Pol. Science. Series 19, v. 10)
DLC, NN, MWA, CSmH, PU

BLAIR, JAMES LAWRENCE. *Life and Death of James L. Blair, Original General Counsel of Louisiana Purchase Exposition.* George E. Vogle. St. Louis, 1904. 128 p. *DLC*

BLAIR, MONTGOMERY. 2:218

BLAIR, R. DOWNEY. *Life of Rev. R. Downey Blair.* L. V. B. Hanshraugh. Washville, 1908. 248 p. *DLC*

BLAKE, WILLIAM. *William Blake, Artist and Poet.* Charles E. Norton. Boston, 1875.
2:161

BLAKE, WILLIAM R. 2:367

BLANCHARD, CHARLES ALBERT. *The Life of Charles Albert Blanchard.* Frances C. Blanchard. N. Y., 1932. 220 p. *DLC, NN*

BLANCHARD, THOMAS. 2:343

BLAND, RICHARD PARKS. *"An American Commoner"; The Life and Times of Richard Parks Bland.* William V. Byars, ed. Columbia, Mo., 1900. 404 p. *DLC, NN, PU*
2:314.

BLANKENBURG, RUDOLPH. *The Blankenburgs of Philadelphia.* Lucretia Blankenburg. Phila., 1929. 238 p. *DLC, NN, PU*

BLAUSTEIN, DAVID. *Memoirs of David Blaustein; Educator and Communal Worker.* Miriam Blaustein. N. Y., 1913. 308 p.
DLC, NN, PU

BLAVATSKY, HELENA P. *Madame Blavatsky.* G. B. Butt. Phila., 1927. 269 p. *DLC, NN*

BLEECKER, HARMANUS. *Harmanus Bleecker, an Albany Dutchman (1779–1849).* Harriet L. P. Rice. Albany, 1924. 253 p. (Ltd. Ed.) *DLC, NN, MWA, CSmH, MiD:B*

BLENNERHASSETT, HARMAN. *Life of Harman Blennerhassett, Comprising an Authentic Narrative of the Burr Expedition.* Wm. H. Safford. Cincinnati, 1850. 239 p.
DLC, NN, CSmH, PU, MiD:B, MiU:C

BLINN, HENRY CLAY. *In Memoriam; Elder Henry C. Blinn, 1824–1905.* Concord, N. H., 1905. 131 p. *DLC, NN*

BLISS, DANIEL. 2:6

BLISS, FRANKLIN S. *Sermons of Rev. Franklin S. Bliss . . . With a Sketch of His Life.* Moses Marston. Boston, 1878. 66 p.
MWA

BLISS, PHILIP PAUL. *Memoirs of Philip P. Bliss.* D. W. Whittle, ed. N. Y., 1877. 367 p. *MWA, MiD:B*

BLISS, TASKER HOWARD. *Bliss, Peacemaker; the Life and Letters of General Tasker Howard Bliss.* Frederick Palmer. N. Y., 1934. 477 p. *DLC, NN*

BLOCH, ERNEST. 2:336

BLOOD, THOMAS. *Colonel Thomas Blood, Crown-Stealer, 1618–1680.* Wilbur C. Abbott. New Haven, 1911. 98 p.
DLC, NN, MWA, CSmH, MiD:B
2:7

BLOOMER, AMELIA. *Life and Writings of Amelia Bloomer.* D. C. Bloomer. Boston, 1895. 387 p. *DLC, NN, CSmH*

BLOOMFIELD, ROBERT. 2:406

BLOUNT, JAMES. *Life, Treason and Death of James Blount of Breckenow.* Beulah M. Dix. N. Y., 1903. 345 p.

BLOUNT, WILLIAM. *Some Account of the Life . . . of William Blount.* Marcus J. Wright. Wash., 1884. 142 p. *CSmH*

BOARDMAN, GEORGE DANA. *Memoir of George Dana Boardman.* A. King. Boston, 1835. 320 p. *NN, MWA*

BOARDMAN, MARY ANNA. *Memoir of the Life and Character of Mrs. Mary Anna Boardman.* John F. Schroeder. New Haven, 1849. 478 p. *DLC, NN, MWA, MiD:B*

BOARDMAN, TIMOTHY. *Biographical Sketch of Timothy Boardman.* Samuel W. Boardman. Stanhope, N. J., n.d. 48 p.
DLC, NN, MWA, PU

BOARDMAN, WILLIAM EDWIN. *Life and Labors of Rev. W. E. Boardman.* Mrs. W. E. Boardman. N. Y., 1887. 260 p. *DLC, CSmH*

BOCCACCIO, GIOVANNI. *Life of Giovanni Boccaccio.* Thomas C. Chubb. N. Y., 1930. 286 p. *DLC, NN*

BOEHM, JOHN PHILIP. *Life and Letters of Rev. John Philip Boehm.* Wm. J. Hinke. Phila., 1916. 501 p. *DLC*

BOETHIUS, ANICIUS M. 2:554

BOKER, GEORGE HENRY. *George Henry Boker: Poet and Patriot.* Edward S. Bradley. Phila., 1927. 361 p. *DLC, NN, CSmH, PU*

BOLIVAR, SIMON.
Simon Bolivar, South American Liberator. Hildegarde Angell. N. Y., 1930. 296 p. *DLC, NN, PU*

Memoirs of Simon Bolivar . . . and of His Principal Generals.
H. L. V. Ducoudray Holstein. Boston, 1829. 383 p.

NN, MWA, CSmH, PU, MiD:B, MiU:C

Bolivar, Liberator of Venezuela, Colombia, Ecquador, Peru and Bolivia. Henry R. Lemly. Boston, 1923. 452 p. *DLC, NN, PU*

Simon Bolivar. Guillermo A. Sherwell. Wash., 1921. Balt., 1930. 232 p. *DLC, NN, MWA, PU, MiD:B*

Bolivar, the Passionate Warrior. Thomas R. Ybarra. N. Y., 1929. 365 p. *DLC, NN, MWA, PU*

BOLTON, CHARLES EDWARD. *Charles E. Bolton. A Memorial Sketch.* Sarah K. Bolton. Cambridge, 1907. 119 p. *DLC, NN, MWA*

BONAPARTE, CHARLES JOSEPH. *Charles Joseph Bonaparte; His Life and Public Services.* Joseph B. Bishop. N. Y., 1922. 304 p.

DLC, NN, MWA

BONAPARTE, ELIZABETH PATTERSON. *The Life and Letters of Madame Bonaparte.* Eugene L. Didier. N. Y., 1879. 276 p.

DLC, NN, MWA, CSmH, MiD:B

BONAPARTE, JOSEPH. *History of Joseph Bonaparte, King of Naples and of Italy.* J. S. C. Abbott. N. Y., 1869. 391 p.

DLC, NN, MWA, CSmH

BONAPARTE, JOSEPHINE.

History of the Empress Josephine. J. S. C. Abbott. N. Y., 1851. 285 p. *DLC, NN, MWA*

The Life of the Empress Josephine, First Wife of Napoleon. P. C. Headley. Auburn, 1851. 383 p. *DLC, NN, MWA*

Memoirs of the Empress Josephine. John S. Memes. N. Y., 1843. 396 p. *DLC, MWA*

Josephine, Empress of the French. F. A. Ober. N. Y., 1895. 458 p. *DLC*

2:1

BONAPARTE, MARIE LOUISE. 2:1

BONAPARTE, NAPOLEON.

History of Napoleon Bonaparte. J. S. C. Abbott. N. Y., 1855. 2 vols. *DLC, NN*

Napoleon, An Outline. Colin R. Ballard. N. Y., 1924. 325 p. *DLC, NN*

Napoleon: Self-Destroyer. Leon P. Clark. N. Y., 1929. 253 p. *DLC, NN, PU*

Napoleon the First; An Intimate Biography. Walter Geer. N. Y., 1921. 390 p. *DLC, NN*

Napoleon and Josephine; the Rise of the Empire. Walter Geer. N. Y., 1924. 395 p. *DLC, NN*

Napoleon and Marie-Louise; the Fall of the Empire. Walter Geer. N. Y., 1925. 337 p. *DLC, NN*

Napoleon and His Family; the Story of a Corsican Clan. Walter Geer. N. Y., 1927. 353 p. *DLC, NN*

Napoleon and the Marshals of the Empire. Rufus W. Griswold. Phila., 1848. 2 vols. *DLC*

Napoleon and His Marshals. J. T. Headley. N. Y., 1846. 2 vols. *DLC, NN, MWA, PU*

Life of Napoleon Bonaparte. William M. Sloane. N. Y., 1896–97. 4 vols. *DLC, NN, MWA, CSmH, PU*

Short Life of Napoleon Bonaparte. Ida M. Tarbell. N. Y., 1896. 248 p. *DLC, NN, MWA, PU*

Napoleon and the End of the French Revolution. Charles F. Warwick. Phila., 1910. 481 p. *DLC, NN, PU*

Napoleon: A Sketch of His Life, Character, Struggles and Achievements. Thomas E. Watson. N. Y., 1901. 719 p. *DLC, NN, PU*

BONAPARTE, NAPOLEON III.
History of Napoleon III. J. S. C. Abbott. Boston, 1868. 690 p. *DLC, NN, MWA*

Napoleon the Third. Walter Geer. N. Y., 1920. 348 p. 2:386

BONAPARTE, PAULINE. *Pauline, Favorite Sister of Napoleon.* William N. C. Carlton. N. Y., 1930. 372 p. *DLC, NN*

BOND, ELIZABETH POWELL. *Dean Bond of Swarthmore, a Quaker Humanist.* Emily C. Johnson. Phila., 1927. 239 p. *DLC, NN, MWA, PU*

BOND, SCOTT. *From Slavery to Wealth, the Life of Scott Bond.* Daniel A. Rudd and T. Bond. Madison, Ark., 1917. 383 p. *DLC, NN*

BOND, WILLIAM CRANCH. *Memorials of William Cranch Bond . . . and of His Son George Phillips Bond . . .* Edward S. Holden. San Francisco, 1897. 296 p. *DLC, NN, PU*

BONER, JOHN HENRY. *John Henry Boner.* Marcus Benjamin. Washington, 1903. 9 p. *DLC, NN*

BONFILS, FREDERICK. *Timber Line; a Story of Bonfils and Tammen.* Gene Fowler. N. Y., 1933. 480 p. *DLC, NN*

BONNEVILLE, BENJAMIN LOUIS. *Bonneville the Bold, the Story of His Adventures and Explorations in the Old Oregon Country.* Walter E. Meacham. Portland, Ore., 1934. 47 p. *DLC, NN*

BONNEY, CALVIN F. *Calvin Fairbanks Bonney.* S. G. Bonney. Concord, N. H., 1930. 320 p. *MiD:B*

BONNEY, WILLIAM H.

Saga of Billy the Kid. Walter N. Burns. N. Y., 1926. 322 p.
DLC, NN, MWA, CSmH, PU

Authentic Life of Billy the Kid. Pat F. Garrett. N. Y., 1927. 233 p. *DLC, MWA, PU*

The Real Billy the Kid. Miguel A. Otero. N. Y., 1936. 200 p.
DLC, NN, MWA

BONNY, ANNE. 2:576.

BOOMER, GEORGE BOARDMAN. *Memoir of George Boardman Boomer.* Amelia M. Stone. Boston, 1864. 284 p.
DLC, NN, MWA, CSmH

BOONE, ARTHUR UPSHAW. *Biography of Dr. A. U. Boone, Thirty-Two Years Pastor of the First Baptist Church, Memphis, Tennessee.* Leslie S. Howell. Shawnee, Okla., 1932. 232 p. *DLC, NN*

BOONE, DANIEL.

Daniel Boone; the Pioneer of Kentucky. John S. C. Abbott. N. Y., 1872. 331 p. *DLC, NN, MWA, MiD:B*

Daniel Boone and the Hunters of Kentucky. W. H. Bogart. Auburn, 1854. 390 p. *DLC, NN, CSmH, MiD:B*

Daniel Boone and the Wilderness Road. H. A. Bruce. N. Y., 1910. 349 p. *DLC, NN, PU*

Life and Times of Col. Daniel Boone. Edward S. Ellis. Phila., 1884. 269 p. *DLC, NN*

Life and Adventures of Col. Daniel Boone . . . John Filson. Brooklyn, 1823. *MiD:B*

Biographical Memoir of Daniel Boone, the First Settler of Kentucky. Timothy Flint. Cincinnati, 1833. 267 p.
DLC, NN, MWA, CSmH, MiD:B

The First White Man; or, the Life and Exploits of Col. Daniel Boone. Timothy Flint. Cincinnati, 1856. 252 p.
DLC, NN, MWA, PU, MiD:B

Daniel Boone, Backwoodsman. Charles H. Forbes-Lindsay. Phila., 1908. 319 p. *DLC, NN*

Daniel Boone. Lucile Gulliver. N. Y., 1916. 244 p.
DLC, NN

Life and Times of Col. Daniel Boone. Cecil B. Hartley. Phila., 1859. 351 p. *DLC, NN, CSmH, MiD:B*

The Adventures of Daniel Boone, the Kentucky Rifleman. Francis L. Hawks. N. Y., 1863. 174 p.
DLC, NN, CSmH, PU, MiD:B

Daniel Boone, the Pioneer of Kentucky. George C. Hill. N. Y., 1884. 262 p.   *DLC, NN, MiD:B*

Life of Daniel Boone. John M Peck. (L.A.B.)
DLC, NN, MWA, CSmH, MiD:B

Daniel Boone, Pioneer. Flora W. Seymour. N. Y. and London, 1931. 206 p.   *DLC, NN*

Daniel Boone. Reuben G. Thwaites. N. Y., 1902. 257 p.
DLC, NN, CSmH, PU, MiD:B

Daniel Boone, Wilderness Scout. Stewart E. White. N. Y., 1922. 308 p.   *DLC, NN, CSmH*
2:358

BOOTH, EDWIN.

Edwin Booth. C. T. Copeland. Boston, 1901. 159 p. (Beacon Biographies)   *DLC, MWA*

Edwin Booth. Laurence Hutton. N. Y., 1893. 59 p. (Black and White Series)   *DLC, NN, MWA, PU*

Darling of Misfortune; Edwin Booth, 1833–1893. Richard Lockridge. N. Y., 1932. 358 p.   *DLC, NN*

Life and Art of Edwin Booth. William Winter. N. Y., 1893. 308 p.   *DLC, NN, MWA, CSmH, PU*
2:6–85

BOOTH, EDWIN GILLIAM. *Life and Character of Edwin G. Booth.* Henry E. Dwight. Phila., 1886. 76 p.   *DLC, NN, PU*

BOOTH, HERBERT. *Herbert Booth; a Biography.* Ford C. Ottman. Garden City, N. Y., 1928. 477 p.   *DLC, NN*

BOOTH, JOHN WILKES.

The Life and Crime of John Wilkes Booth. George A. Townsend. N. Y., 1865. 79 p.   *DLC, NN, MWA, CSmH*

John Wilkes Booth; Fact and Fiction of Lincoln's Assassination. Francis Wilson. Boston and N. Y., 1929. 321 p.
DLC, NN, MWA, CSmH, PU

BOOTH, JUNIUS BRUTUS.

The Actor; or, A Peep Behind the Curtain. N. Y., 1846. 180 p.
DLC, MWA

Life of Junius B. Booth the Elder. Rosalie Booth. N. Y., 1866. 162 p.

The Elder and the Younger Booth. Asia B. Clarke. Boston, 1882. 194 p. (American Actor Series. V. 1)
DLC, NN, MWA, PU

BOOTH, WILLIAM. 2:6

BORAH, WILLIAM. *Borah of Idaho.* Claudius O. Johnson. N. Y., 1936. 511 p. *DLC, NN*

BORDET, JULES. 2:175

BORDLEY. *Biographical Sketches of the Bordley Family of Maryland.* Elizabeth B. Gibson. Phila., 1885. 158 p.

Thomas Bordley and Ariana, His Wife; Stephen Bordley; William Bordley; Elizabeth Bordley; John Bordley; Thomas Bordley; Matthias Bordley; John Beale Bordley. *DLC, NN, MWA*

BORGIA, CAESAR. 2:95

BORGLUM, GUTZON. 2:430

BORROW, GEORGE. *George Borrow.* Samuel M. Elam. N. Y., 1929. 139 p. *DLC, NN, PU*

BOSWELL, JAMES.

Young Boswell. Chauncey B. Tinker. Boston, 1922. 266 p. *DLC, NN, CSmH, PU*

A New Portrait of James Boswell. Chauncey B. Tinker and Frederic A. Pottle. Cambridge, 1927. 17 p. *DLC, NN*

BOUCICAULT, DION. *Career of Dion Boucicault.* Townsend Walsh. N. Y., 1915. 224 p. (Dunlap Soc. Publications) *DLC, NN, PU*

BOUCK, WILLIAM C. 2:349

BOUDINOT, ELIAS. *Life . . . of Elias Boudinot, President of the Continental Congress.* Jane J. Boudinot, ed. Boston, 1896. 2 vols. *DLC, NN, MiD:B*

BOUQUET, HENRY.

Col. Henry Bouquet and His Campaigns of 1763 and 1764. Cyrus Cort. Lancaster, Pa., 1883. 96 p. *DLC, PU, MiD:B, MiU:C*

History of Col. Henry Bouquet and the Western Frontiers of Pennsylvania. Mary C. Darlington. Cleveland, 1920. 232 p. *CSmH*

BOURGEOYS, MARGARET. *Life and Times of Margaret Bourgeoys (The Venerable).* Margaret Mary Drummond. Boston, 1907. 275 p. *DLC, NN*

BOWDITCH, HENRY INGERSOLL.

Life and Correspondence of H. I. Bowditch. Vincent Y. Bowditch. Boston, 1903. 2 vols. *DLC, NN, MWA, CSmH, PU*

Henry I. Bowditch; A Sketch. Frederick I. Knight. (Reprinted from the *Boston Medical and Surgical Journal* of August 25, 1892) *NN*

BOWDITCH, NATHANIEL.

Memoir of Nathaniel Bowditch. Nathaniel I. Bowditch. Boston, 1840. 172 p. (2d ed.) *DLC, NN, CSmH, PU*

Navigator; the Story of Nathaniel Bowditch. Alfred B. Stanford. N. Y., 1927. 308 p. [Biographical Fiction] *DLC, NN*
The Varieties of Human Greatness. A Discourse on the Life and Character of the Hon. Nathaniel Bowditch . . . Alexander Young. Boston, 1838. 119 p. *DLC, NN, MWA, PU*

BOWEN, NATHANIEL. *The Life of Bishop Bowen, of South Carolina.* John N. Norton. N. Y., 1859. 161 p. *NN*

BOWLES, CHARLES. *The Life, Labors and Travels of Elder Charles Bowles.* John W. Lewis. Watertown, 1852. 226 p.
DLC, NN, MWA, MiD:B

BOWLES, SAMUEL. *Life and Times of Samuel Bowles.* George S. Merriam. N. Y., 1885. 2 vols. *DLC, NN, MWA, CSmH, PU*
2:96

BOWNE, BORDEN PARKER. *Borden Parker Bowne, His Life and His Philosophy.* Francis J. McConnell. N. Y., 1929. 291 p.
DLC, NN

BOYCE, JAMES PETIGRU. *Memoir of James Petigru Boyce, Late President of the Southern Baptist Theological Seminary, Louisville, Ky.* John A. Broadus. Nashville, 1927. 428 p. *DLC, NN, PU*

BOYD, BELLE. 2:703

BOYD, THOMAS DUCKETT. *Thomas Duckett Boyd; the Story of a Southern Educator.* Marcus M. Wilkerson. Baton Rouge, La., 1935. 374 p. *DLC, NN, CSmH, PU, MiD:B*

BOYLE, ROBERT. 2:393

BRACE, CHARLES LORING. *The Life of Charles Loring Brace, Chiefly Told in His Own Letters.* Emma Brace, ed. N. Y., 1894. 503 p.
DLC, NN, CSmH, PU

BRACKENRIDGE, HUGH HENRY.
Memoir of H. H. Brackenridge in "Modern Chivalry." Henry M. Brackenridge. Phila., 1847. *DLC, NN, MWA*
Life and Writings of Hugh Henry Brackenridge. Claude M. Newlin. Princeton, 1932. 328 p. *DLC, NN, CSmH, PU*
2:110

BRADBURY, JOHN M. *Sketch of the Life of John M. Bradbury.* John W. Dean. Boston, 1877. *CSmH*

BRADFORD, VINCENT LOOCKERMAN. *The Life and Writings of the Hon. Vincent L. Bradford.* Henry E. Dwight, ed. Phila., 1885. 297 p. (Privately Printed) *MWA, PU*

BRADFORD, WILLIAM.
William Bradford of Plymouth. Albert H. Plumb. Boston, 1920. 112 p. *DLC, NN*

Governor William Bradford and His Son, Major William Brad-ford. J. Shepard. New Britain, Conn., 1900. 103 p.

DLC, NN, MWA, CSmH

2:141

BRADFORD, WILLIAM. *An Old Philadelphian, Colonel William Brad-ford, the Patriot Printer of 1776.* J. W. Wallace. Phila., 1884. 517 p. *DLC, PU*

BRADLEE, CALEB DAVIS. *Caleb D. Bradlee, D.D.* Alfred Manchester. Boston, 1897. 266 p. *NN, MWA*

BRADSTREET, ANNE.

Anne Bradstreet and Her Time. Helen S. Campbell. Boston, 1891. 373 p. *DLC, NN, MWA*

The Works of Anne Dudley Bradstreet. John H. Ellis, ed. Charlestown, Mass., 1867. [71 p. memoir]

DLC, NN, MWA, CSmH

2:464

BRADSTREET, JOHN. 2:542

BRADY, JAMES BUCHANAN. *Diamond Jim; the Life and Times of James Buchanan Brady.* Parker Morell. N. Y., 1934. 286 p.

DLC, NN, PU

BRADY, SAMUEL. 2:358

BRAGG, BRAXTON. *Braxton Bragg.* Don C. Seitz. Columbia, S. C., 1924. 544 p. *DLC, NN, MWA, CSmH, MiD:B*

2:612

BRAINERD, DAVID.

Memoirs of the Rev. David Brainerd, Missionary to the In-dians . . . Jonathan Edwards. Boston, 1749, New Haven, 1822. 507 p. *DLC, NN, MWA, CSmH, PU, MiD:B, MiU:C*

David Brainerd, the Apostle to the North American Indians. Jesse Page. N. Y., 1891. 160 p. (Missionary Biography Series)

DLC

Life of David Brainerd. W. B. O. Peabody. (L.A.B.)

DLC, NN, MWA, CSmH, PU

Life of David Brainerd. John Styles. Boston, 1821. 322 p.

MiD:B

BRAINERD, JOHN. *The Life of John Brainerd.* Thomas Brainerd. Phila., 1865. 492 p. *DLC, NN, PU*

BRAINERD, JOHN G. C. *The Literary Remains of John G. C. Brainerd, With a Sketch of His Life.* John Greenleaf Whittier. Hartford, 1832. 228 p. *NN, CSmH*

BRAINERD, THOMAS. *The Life of Rev. Thomas Brainerd.* M. Brain-erd. Phila., 1870. 455 p. *DLC, NN, MWA, PU*

BRANCH, JOHN. *John Branch, 1782–1863.* Marshall De Lancey Haywood. Raleigh, N. C., 1915. 55 p. *DLC, NN*

BRAND, SAMUEL. *A Melancholy Narrative of the Unhappy Samuel Brand, Who Was Executed for the Murder of His Brother . . .* Lancaster, 1774. *RP:JCB*

BRANDEIS, LOUIS.

Louis Brandeis; a Biographical Sketch. Jacob De Haas. N. Y., 1929. 296 p. *DLC, NN, MWA*

Brandeis; the Personal History of An American Ideal. Alfred Lief. N. Y., 1936. 508 p. *DLC, NN*

Brandeis: Lawyer and Judge in the Modern State. Alpheus T. Mason. Princeton, 1933. 203 p. *DLC, NN, PU*

BRANNAN, SAMUEL. *The First Forty-Niner and the Story of the Golden Teacaddy.* James A. B. Scherer. N. Y., 1925. 127 p.
DLC, NN, MWA, CSmH, PU

BRANT, JOSEPH.

Memoir of the Distinguished Mohawk Indian Chief, Sachem and Warrior, Capt. Joseph Brant. William E. Palmer. Brantford, Ont., 1872. 114 p. *DLC, NN, CSmH*

Brant and Red Jacket. E. E. Seelye and E. Eggleston. N. Y., 1879. 370 p. *DLC, NN, CSmH*

Life of Joseph Brant and History of the Border Wars of the American Revolution. William L. Stone. Cooperstown, N. Y., 1846. 2 vols. *DLC, NN, MWA, CSmH, PU, MiU:C*

BRATHWAITE, RICHARD. *Richard Brathwaite, An Account of His Life and Works.* Matthew W. Black. Phila., 1928. 176 p.
DLC, NN, CSmH, PU

BRATIANO, JOHN. 2:30

BRECK, JAMES LLOYD.

Life of James Lloyd Breck, D.D., Chiefly From Letters Written By Himself. C. Breck, comp. N. Y., 1883. 557 p.
DLC, NN, MWA

An Apostle of the Wilderness: James Lloyd Breck. Theodore I. Holcombe. N. Y., 1903. 195 p. *DLC*

BRECK, SAMUEL.

Memoir of Samuel Breck, Late President of the Pennsylvania Institution for the Instruction of the Blind. J. Francis Fisher. Phila., 1863. 45 p. *DLC, NN, MWA, PU, MiD:B*

Memoir of the Late Samuel Breck. Joseph R. Ingersoll. Phila., 1863. 56 p. *DLC, NN, MWA, PU*

BRECKENRIDGE, WILLIAM CLARK. *William Clark Breckenridge, Historical Research Writer and Bibliographer of Missouriana; His Life, Lineage and Writings.* James M. Breckenridge. St. Louis, 1932. 380 p. *DLC, NN, MWA, CSmH, MiD:B*

BRECKINRIDGE, JOHN CABELL. *Biographical Sketches of Hon. J. C. Breckinridge and General Joseph Lane.* Wash., 1860. 32 p.
DLC, PU, MiD:B

BRECKINRIDGE, JOSEPH CABELL. *Joseph Cabell Breckinridge, Junior, Ensign in the U. S. Navy.* Ethelbert D. Warfield. N. Y., 1898. 101 p. *DLC, NN, PU*

BRECKINRIDGE, MADELINE McDOWELL. *Madeline McDowell Breckinridge; A Leader in the New South.* Sophonisba P. Breckinridge. Chicago, 1921. 275 p. *DLC, NN*
2:493

BRECKINRIDGE, ROBERT JEFFERSON. 2:144

BREESE, SYDNEY. *Biographical Memoir of Sydney Breese in Breese's "Early History of Illinois"* . . . M. W. Fuller. n.p., 1884. 60 p.
DLC, NN, PU

BRENGLE, SAMUEL LOGAN. *Samuel Logan Brengle; Portrait of a Prophet.* Clarence W. Hall. N. Y., 1933. 387 p. *DLC, NN*

BREWER, EDWARD HAMILTON. *Life of E. H. Brewer.* Jeremiah Taylor. Boston, 1863. 140 p. *DLC, MWA, CSmH*

BREWSTER, BENJAMIN HARRIS. *Life of Benjamin Harris Brewster.* Eugene C. Savidge. Phila., 1891. 370 p.
DLC, NN, MWA, MiD:B

BREWSTER, WILLIAM. *Chief of the Pilgrims; or, the Life and Times of William Brewster.* Ashbel Steele. Phila., 1857. 416 p.
DLC, NN, MWA, CSmH, PU, MiU:C
2:141

BRIDGER, JAMES. *James Bridger, Trapper, Frontiersman, Scout and Guide.* J. Cecil Alter. Salt Lake City, 1925. 546 p.
DLC, NN, MWA, CSmH, PU

BRIDGMAN, ELIJAH. *The Pioneer of American Missions in China; Life and Labors of Elijah Bridgman.* Eliza J. C. Bridgman. N. Y., 1864. 296 p. *NN*

BRIDGMAN, LAURA.
Laura Bridgman, Dr. Howe's Famous Pupil. Maud Howe and F. M. Hall. Boston, 1903. 394 p. *DLC, NN, CSmH, PU*
Life and Education of Laura D. Bridgman, the Deaf, Dumb and Blind Girl. M. S. Lamson. Boston, 1879. 373 p.
DLC, NN, MWA, CSmH, PU

Laura Bridgman; the Story of an Opened Door. Laura E. Richards. N. Y., 1928. 154 p.   *DLC, NN, CSmH*

BRIGGS, GEORGE NIXON. *Great in Goodness; a Memoir of George N. Briggs, Governor of the Commonwealth of Massachusetts 1844–1851.* William C. Richards. Boston, 1866. 451 p.
    DLC, NN, MWA

BRIGGS, LeBARON RUSSELL. *Dean Briggs.* Rollo W. Brown. N. Y., 1926. 331 p.   *DLC, NN*

BRIGHAM, AMARIAH. *A Biographical Sketch of Amariah Brigham, M.D., Late Supt. of New York State Lunatic Asylum.* Ebenezer K. Hunt. Utica, N. Y., 1858. 123 p.   *NN*

BRIGHAM, J. C. *Life and Services of Rev. J. C. Brigham.* W. Adams. N. Y., 1863. 38 p.   *NN*

BRIGHT, JOHN. 2:334

BRILL, ABRAHAM ARDEN. 2:236

BRINCKLÉ, WILLIAM DRAPER. *A Biographical Memoir of Dr. W. D. Brincklé.* E. B. Gardette. Phila., 1863. 55 p.   *DLC, MWA*

BRISBANE, ALBERT. *Albert Brisbane, A Mental Biography.* Redelia Brisbane. Boston, 1893. 377 p.   *DLC, NN, CSmH*

BROAD, HARRIET CASWELL. *" Blue Sky ", The Life of Harriet Caswell Broad.* Joseph B. Clark. N. Y., 1911. 238 p.
    DLC, MWA

BROADUS, JOHN ALBERT. *Life and Letters of John Albert Broadus.* Archibald T. Robertson. Phila., 1901. 462 p.   *DLC, NN, PU*

BRODERICK, DAVID COLBRETH. *Senator of the Fifties: David C. Broderick of California.* Jeremiah Lynch. San Francisco, 1911. 246 p.
    DLC, NN

BROME, RICHARD. *Richard Brome: A Study of His Life and Works.* Clarence E. Andrews. N. Y., 1913. 140 p. (Yale Studies in English, No. 46)   *DLC, NN, PU*

BROMFIELD, JOHN.
    Memoir of John Bromfield. Josiah Quincy. Cambridge, 1850. 34 p.   *DLC, NN, MWA, MiD:B*
    Reminiscences of John Bromfield. A. B. Tracy. Salem, 1852. 210 p.   *DLC, NN, MWA*

BRONSON, HENRY. *Biographical Sketch of the Life and Writings of the Late Professor Henry Bronson, M.D.* Stephen G. Hubbard. New Haven, 1895. 117 p.   *DLC, NN, MWA*

BROOKE, RUPERT. 2:507

BROOKES, JAMES HALL. *James H. Brookes; A Memoir.* David R. Williams. St. Louis, 1897. 286 p.   *DLC*

BROOKS, CHARLES. *Charles Brooks and His Work for Normal Schools.* J. Albree. Medford, Mass., 1907. 31 p.   *DLC, NN, PU*

BROOKS, CHARLES TIMOTHY. *Memoir of Charles T. Brooks in Brooks' "Poems, Original and Translated."* Charles Wm. Wendte. Boston, 1885. 235 p.   *DLC, NN, PU*

BROOKS, ELBRIDGE GERRY. *Life-work of Elbridge Gerry Brooks, Minister in the Universalist Church.* Elbridge S. Brooks. Boston, 1881. 247 p.   *DLC, MWA*

BROOKS, PHILLIPS.

The Life and Letters of Phillips Brooks. Alexander V. G. Allen. N. Y., 1900. 3 vols.   *DLC, NN, MWA, CSmH, PU*

Phillips Brooks. Arthur Brooks. N. Y., 1893. 50 p.
    DLC, NN

Sketch of the Late Rt. Rev. Phillips Brooks, D.D. William H. Brooks. Boston, 1894. 54 p.   *DLC, NN, MWA, PU*

Phillips Brooks, Bishop of Massachusetts. Newell Dunbar. Boston, 1891. 93 p.   *DLC, NN, MWA*

Phillips Brooks; His Character and Teachings. H. R. Harris. N. Y., 1893. 32 p.   *DLC*

Phillips Brooks. M. A. de W. Howe. Boston, 1899. 120 p. (Beacon Biographies)   *DLC, NN, MWA, PU*

Life of Phillips Brooks. William Lawrence. N. Y., 1930. 151 p.   *DLC, NN, MWA, PU*

    2:6–12–98–109–325–519

BROPHY, JOSEPH FRANCIS. *A Heroic Priest: Memoir of Joseph Francis Brophy, Apostle of Coney Island.* Mrs. Paul Boynton, comp. n.p., 1910. 134 p.   *NN*

BROUGHAM, JOHN. *John Brougham.* William Winter. Boston, 1881. 461 p.   *NN, MWA, CSmH, PU*

    2:367

BROWN, ABEL. *Memoir of Rev. Abel Brown.* C. S. Brown. Worcester, Mass., 1849. 228 p.   *DLC, MWA*

BROWN, ABRAM BURWELL. *Sketch of the Life and Writings of A. B. Brown, Professor of English in Richmond College, Va.* William E. Hatcher and Mrs. W. E. Hatcher. Balt., 1886. 351 p.
    DLC, CSmH

BROWN, ALANSON DAVID. *A Man With a Purpose.* John T. M. Johnston. Chicago, 1906. 176 p.   *DLC, NN*

BROWN, CATHERINE. *Memoir of Catherine Brown, a Christian Indian of the Cherokee Nation.* Rufus Anderson. Boston, 1825. 180 p.
    DLC, NN, MWA, CSmH, PU

BROWN, CHARLES BROCKDEN.

Charles Brockden Brown; a Critical Biography. David Lee Clark. n.p., n.d. 49 p. *DLC, NN, PU*

Life of Charles Brockden Brown. William Dunlap. Phila., 1815. 2 vols. *DLC, NN, MWA, CSmH, MiU:C*

Life of Charles Brockden Brown. William H. Prescott. (L.A.B.) *DLC, NN, MWA, CSmH*

Charles Brockden Brown. A Study of Early American Fiction. Martin S. Vilas. Burlington, Vt., 1904. 66 p.

DLC, MWA, CSmH, PU

BROWN, GEORGE LORING. 2:52

BROWN, HENRY ARMITT. *Memoir of Henry Armitt Brown.* J. M. Hoppin. Phila., 1880. 395 p. *DLC, NN, PU* 2:521

BROWN, HERBERT. *Herbert Brown.* Oliver B. Whitaker. N. Y., 1905. 314 p. *DLC*

BROWN, JACOB. *Life of General Jacob Brown. With Memoirs of Generals Ripley and Pike.* N. Y., 1847. 256 p.

DLC, NN, MWA, MiD:B

BROWN, JAMES. *A Memoir of James Brown.* George S. Hillard. Boston, 1856. 138 p. (Privately Printed) *DLC, NN, MWA*

BROWN, JOHN. *Col. John Brown, His Services in the Revolutionary War, Battle of Stone Arabia.* Garret L. Roof. Utica, N. Y., 1884. 24 p. *DLC, NN, MWA, CSmH*

BROWN, JOHN.

The Life, Trial and Execution of Captain John Brown. N. Y., 1859. 108 p. *DLC, NN, MWA, CSmH*

John Brown. James E. Chamberlain. Boston, 1899. 138 p. (Beacon Biographies) *DLC, NN, CSmH, MiD:B*

John Brown. W. E. Connelly. Topeka, 1900. 426 p.

DLC, NN, CSmH

John Brown. William E. B. DuBois. Phila., 1909. 406 p.

DLC, NN, CSmH

John Brown and His Men. R. J. Hinton. N. Y., 1894. 752 p. (American Reformers) *DLC, NN*

John Brown. Hermann E. Von Holst. Boston, 1888. 232 p.

DLC, NN, CSmH, PU, MiD:B

John Brown: Terrible Saint. David Karsner. N. Y., 1934. 340 p. *DLC, NN, PU*

The Public Life of Captain John Brown, With an Autobiography of His Childhood and Youth. James Redpath. Boston, 1860. 407 p. *DLC, NN, MWA, CSmM, PU, MiD:B*

Captain John Brown, Life and Letters. F. B. Sanborn, ed. Boston, 1885. 645 p. *DLC, NN, CSmH, MiD:B*
John Brown, Liberator of Kansas and Martyr of Virginia, Life and Letters. F. B. Sanborn. Cedar Rapids, Ia., 1910. 645 p.
DLC, NN, MWA, CSmH, MiD:B
John Brown, 1800–1859; Biography Fifty Years After. Oswald G. Villard. Boston, 1910. 738 p. *DLC, NN, CSmH, PU, MiD:B*
John Brown; the Making of a Martyr. Robert P. Warren. N. Y., 1929. 474 p. *DLC, NN*
John Brown, Soldier of Fortune, a Critique. Hill P. Wilson. Lawrence, Kan., 1913. 450 p. *DLC, NN, CSmH, PU*
2:89

BROWN, JOSEPH EMERSON. *Life, Times and Speeches of Joseph E. Brown.* Herbert Fielder. Springfield, 1883. 785 p.
DLC, NN

BROWN, MARGARET. *Memoir of Margaret Brown.* Benjamin Hallowell. Phila., 1872. 174 p. *NN, PU*

BROWN, MOSES. *Moses Brown, Captain U. S. N.* Edgar S. Maclay. N. Y., 1904. 220 p. *DLC, NN, MWA, CSmH, MiD:B*

BROWN, NATHANIEL. *Captain Nathaniel Brown; an Old-Time Sailor of the Sea.* John R. Spears. N. Y., 1922. 252 p. *NN*

BROWN, SAMUEL ROLLINS. *A Maker of the New Orient; Samuel Rollins Brown.* W. E. Griffis. N. Y., 1902. 332 p. *DLC, NN*

BROWN, THURLOW WEED. 2:40

BROWNE, CHARLES FARRAR. (ARTEMUS WARD)
Artemus Ward: His Works Complete. With a Biographical Sketch. Melville D. Landon. N. Y., 1875. 347 p.
DLC, NN, CSmH, PU
Artemus Ward. Don C. Seitz. N. Y., 1919. 338 p.
DLC, NN, MWA, CSmH, PU

BROWNE, JOHN. *John Browne, Gentleman, of Plymouth.* G. T. Brown. Providence, 1919. *RP:JCB*

BROWNE, JOHN ROSS. *J. Ross Browne: A Biography.* Francis J. Rock. Wash., 1929. 80 p. *DLC, NN, CSmH, PU, MiU:C*

BROWNE, JOHN WHITE. *In Memoriam.* Albert G. Browne. Boston, 1860. 90 p. *DLC, NN, MWA, CSmH*

BROWNING, ELIZABETH BARRETT.
Elizabeth Barrett Browning. Louise S. Boas. N. Y., 1930. 216 p. *DLC, NN, PU*
Elizabeth Barrett Browning. Martha Foote Crow. N. Y., 1907. 232 p. *DLC, NN*

A Study of Elizabeth Barrett Browning. Lilian Whiting. Boston, 1899. 191 p. *DLC, NN, MWA*

BROWNING, ROBERT.

Browning, Poet and Man: a Survey. Elizabeth L. Cary. N. Y., 1899. 282 p. *DLC, NN, PU*

Early Literary Career of Robert Browning. Thomas R. Lounsbury. N. Y., 1911. 205 p. *DLC, NN, CSmH*

Robert Browning: How to Know Him. Wm. L. Phelps. Indianapolis, 1915. 381 p. *DLC, NN, PU*

BROWNINGS.

The Brownings; a Victorian Idyll. David G. Loth. N. Y., 1929. 289 p. *DLC, NN*

The Brownings; Their Life and Art. Lilian Whiting. Boston, 1911. 304 p. *DLC, NN*

BROWNSON, ORESTES AUGUSTUS. *Orestes A. Brownson's Life.* H. F. Brownson. Detroit, 1898–1900. 3 vols. *DLC, NN, MiD:B*

BRUCE, ELI. *The Masonic Martyr.* Robert Morris. Louisville, 1861. 313 p. *CSmH*

BRUCE, JAMES 2:598

BRUNOT, FELIX REVILLE. *Felix Reville Brunot 1820–1898.* Charles Lewis Slattery. N. Y., 1901. 304 p. *DLC, NN, CSmH, PU*

BRUSH, GEORGE DE FOREST. 2:123

BRUSQUET. 2:71

BRUTÉ, SIMON WILLIAM GABRIEL.

Memoirs of Rt. Rev. Simon Wm. G. Bruté, First Bishop of Vincennes (Ind.). J. R. Bayley. N. Y., 1860. 225 p. *DLC, NN, PU, RP:JCB*

Simon Bruté de Remur, First Bishop of Vincennes. Sister M. Silesia Godecker. St. Meinard, Indiana, 1931. 441 p. *DLC*

BRYAN, JAMES ALEXANDER. *Religion in Shoes; or, " Brother Bryan of Birmingham."* Hunter B. Blakely. Richmond, 1934. 186 p. *DLC, NN*

BRYAN, GEORGE. *George Bryan and the Constitution of Pennsylvania, 1731–1791.* Burton A. Konkle. Phila., 1922. 381 p. *DLC, NN, PU*

BRYAN, JONATHAN. *Life and Times of Jonathan Bryan, 1708–1788.* Isabella R. Redding. Savannah, 1901. 97 p. *DLC, NN, MiD:B, MiU:C*

BRYAN, WILLIAM JENNINGS.

Bryan, the Man; the Great Commoner at Close Range. A. L. Gale and G. W. Kline. St. Louis, 1908. 191 p. *DLC, NN*

The Life of William Jennings Bryan. Genevieve F. Herrick and John O. Herrick. Chicago, 1925. 424 p.   *DLC, NN, MWA*

Peerless Leader; William Jennings Bryan. Paxton Hibben. N. Y., 1929. 446 p.   *DLC, NN, CSmH, PU*

Bryan, the Great Commoner. John C. Long. N. Y., 1928. 421 p.   *DLC, NN, PU*

Life and Patriotic Services of Hon. William J. Bryan. Richard L. Metcalfe. n.p., 1896. 500 p.   *DLC, NN*

Victorious Democracy: Embracing Life of William J. Bryan; Life of Adlai I. Stevenson by J. A. Munson. R. L. Metcalfe. Chicago, 1900. 562 p.   *DLC, NN*

William Jennings Bryan, a Concise but Complete Story of His Life and Service. Harvey E. Newbranch. Lincoln, Neb., 1900. 178 p.   *DLC*

Life and Speeches of William J. Bryan. John S. Ogilvie. N. Y., 1896. 328 p.   *DLC, NN*

Bryan. Morris R. Werner. N. Y., 1929. 374 p.
DLC, NN, MWA, PU

William Jennings Bryan. Wayne C. Williams. N. Y., 1936. 516 p.   *DLC, NN*

2:395–590

BRYANT, WILLIAM CULLEN.

William Cullen Bryant. John Bigelow. Boston and N. Y., 1890. 355 p. (A.M.L.)   *DLC, NN, CSmH, PU*

William Cullen Bryant. W. A. Bradley. N. Y., 1905. 229 p. (E.M.L.)   *DLC, NN, CSmH, PU*

The Life, Character and Writings of William Cullen Bryant. George W. Curtis. N. Y., 1879. 64 p. . *DLC, NN, CSmH, MiD:B*

A Biography of William Cullen Bryant. Parke Godwin. N. Y., 1883. 2 vols.   *DLC, NN, CSmH, PU*

William Cullen Bryant. D. J. Hill. N. Y., 1879. 240 p. (American Authors)   *DLC, NN, MWA*

William Cullen Bryant. A. J. Symington. N. Y. and London, 1880. 256 p.   *DLC, NN, MWA, CSmH, PU*

2:40

BRYSKETT, LODOWICK. *The Life and Correspondence of Lodowick Bryskett.* Henry R. Plomer and Tom-Peete Cross. Chicago, 1927. 89 p.   *DLC, NN, CSmH, PU*

2:604

BUC, SIR GEORGE.   2:604

BUCER, MARTIN. *Martin Bucer.* Hastings Eells. New Haven, 1931.
539 p. *DLC, NN, CSmH*

BUCHANAN, CLAUDIUS. *Memoirs of Claudius Buchanan.* Hugh Pearson. N. Y., n.d. 475 p. *DLC, NN, MWA*

BUCHANAN, FRANKLIN. *Admiral Franklin Buchanan, Fearless Man of Action.* Charles L. Lewis. Balt., 1929. 285 p. *DLC, NN, PU*

BUCHANAN, JAMES.
Life of James Buchanan. George T. Curtis. N. Y., 1883.
2 vols. *DLC, NN, MWA, CSmH, PU, MiD:B*
Life of James Buchanan. R. G. Horton. N. Y., 1856. 428 p.
DLC, NN, MWA, PU, MiD:B, MiU:C

BUCKINGHAM. *The Dukes of Buckingham; Playboys of the Stuart World.* Robert P. T. Coffin. N. Y., 1931. 358 p.
DLC, NN, PU

BUCKINGHAM, WILLIAM ALFRED. *The Life of William A. Buckingham, the War Governor of Connecticut.* Samuel G. Buckingham. Springfield, Mass., 1894. 537 p. *DLC, NN, MWA, CSmH, MiD:B*
2: 624

BUCKLEY, JAMES MONROE. *James Monroe Buckley.* George P. Mains. N. Y., 1917. 305 p. *DLC, NN, MiD:B*

BUCKMINSTER, JOSEPH. *Memoirs of Rev. Joseph Buckminster, D.D., and of His Son, Rev. Joseph Stevens Buckminster.* Eliza B. Lee. Boston, 1849. 486 p. *DLC, NN, MWA, CSmH*

BUCKMINSTER, JOSEPH STEVENS. *Sermons of Joseph Stevens Buckminster, With a Memoir of His Life and Character.* Samuel C. Thacher. Boston, 1814; 2nd ed. 1815. 2 vols.
DLC, NN, CSmH, PU

BUEL, JESSE. 2:497

BULFINCH, CHARLES.
Life and Letters of Charles Bulfinch, Architect. E. S. Bulfinch, ed. Boston, 1896. 323 p. *DLC, NN, MWA*
Charles Bulfinch, Architect and Citizen. Charles A. Place. Boston, 1925. 294 p. *DLC, NN, MWA, PU*

BUNTING, JABEZ. *The Life of Rev. Jabez Bunting, With Notices of Contemporary Persons and Events.* Thomas P. Bunting. N. Y., 1859. 389 p. *NN, MWA*

BUNYAN, JOHN.
Life of John Bunyan. Helen C. Knight. Phila., 1855. 372 p.
NN
Life and Writings of John Bunyan. Harold E. B. Speight. N. Y., 1928. 224 p. *DLC, NN, CSmH, PU*

John Bunyan, Mechanick Preacher. William Y. Tindall. N. Y.,
1935. 309 p. *DLC, CSmH, PU*
 The Life of John Bunyan. Stephen B. Wickens. N. Y., 1844.
336 p. *DLC, NN, MWA*
BURBANK, LUTHER. *The Early Life and Letters of Luther Burbank.*
Emma B. Beeson. San Francisco, 1927. 155 p.
             DLC, NN, MWA
 2:388
BURDEN, HENRY. *Henry Burden; His Life and a History of His In-*
ventions. Margaret B. Proudfit, comp. Troy, N. Y., 1904. 112 p.
               DLC, NN
BURDETTE, ROBERT JONES. *Robert J. Burdette. His Message.* Clara
B. Burdette, ed. Phila., 1922. 460 p. *DLC, NN*
BURGESS, GEORGE. *Memoir of George Burgess, First Bishop of Maine.*
Alexander Burgess. Phila., 1869. 419 p. *NN, MWA, CSmH*
BURGESS, TRISTRAM. *Memoirs of Tristram Burgess.* Henry L. Bowen.
Phila., 1835. 404 p. *NN, MWA*
BURGHLEY, LORD DAVID. 2:425
BURK, JOHN DALY. *Memoir of John Daly Burk . . . With a Sketch of*
the Life and Character of His Only Child, John Junius Burk.
Charles Campbell. Albany, N. Y., 1868. 123 p.
        DLC, NN, CSmH, PU, MiD:B
BURKE, EDMUND. 2:330
BURKE, MARY ELLEN. [CALAMITY JANE] 2:576
BURKE, THOMAS. *Thomas Burke, 1849–1925.* Charles T. Conover.
Seattle, 1926. 173 p. *DLC, NN, PU*
BURLESON, RUFUS CLARENCE. *The Life and Writings of Rufus C.*
Burleson . . . George J. Burleson, comp. Waco, Tex., 1901. 887 p.
             DLC, NN, CSmH
BURLINGAME, ANSON. *Anson Burlingame and the First Chinese Mis-*
sion to Foreign Powers. Frederick W. Williams. N. Y., 1912.
370 p. *DLC, NN*
BURNES, JAMES NELSON. *James Nelson Burnes, Late Representative*
in Congress from Missouri. E. W. De Knight. Chicago, 1889.
480 p. *DLC, NN, MiD:B*
BURNETT, FRANCES HODGSON. *Romantick Lady; the Life Story of an*
Imagination. Vivian Burnett. N. Y., 1927. 423 p.
            DLC, NN, MWA, PU
BURNETTE, WILLIAM. *An Inside Story of Success; Life of William*
Burnette. Neil M. Clark. Garden City, N. Y., 1929. 320 p.
               DLC, NN

Burnham, Daniel Hudson. *Daniel H. Burnham, Architect; Planner of Cities.* Charles Moore. Boston, 1921. 2 vols.

DLC, NN, CSmH

Burnham, Major. 2:172

Burns, Marcia. 2:518

Burns, Otway. *Capt. Otway Burns: Patriot, Privateer and Legislator.* W. F. Burns, comp. N. Y., 1905. 166 p. *DLC, NN, CSmH*

Burns, Robert.

A Man for A' That; the Story of Robert Burns. Charles J. Finger. Boston, 1929. 259 p. *DLC, NN*

Life of Robert Burns. Franklyn B. Snyder. N. Y., 1932. 524 p. *DLC, NN, CSmH, PU*

Burns, William J. 2:395

Burnside, Ambrose Everett. *Life and Public Services of Ambrose E. Burnside.* Benjamin P. Poore. Providence, 1882. 448 p.

DLC, NN, MWA, CSmH, MiD:B

Burr, Aaron.

Memoirs of Aaron Burr, With Miscellaneous Selections From His Correspondence. Matthew L. Davis. N. Y., 1836–37. 2 vols.

DLC, NN, MWA, CSmH, PU, MiU:C

Aaron Burr; a Romantic Biography. Johnston D. Kerkhoff. N. Y., 1931. 279 p. *DLC, NN, MWA*

Life of Aaron Burr. Samuel L. Knapp. N. Y., 1935. 290 p.

DLC, NN, MWA, CSmH, MiD:B, MiU:C

An American Patrician: Aaron Burr. Alfred H. Lewis. N. Y., 1908. 335 p. *DLC, NN, MiD:B*

Aaron Burr. H. C. Merwin. Boston, 1899. 150 p.

DLC, NN

The Life and Times of Aaron Burr. James Parton. N. Y., 1858. Boston, 1872. 2 vols.

DLC, NN, MWA, CSmH, PU, MiD:B, MiU:C

Life of Col. Aaron Burr, Vice-President of the U. S. Charles Burr Todd. N. Y., 1879. 426 p.

DLC, NN, MWA, MiD:B, MiU:C

True Aaron Burr; A Biographical Sketch. Charles Burr Todd. N. Y., 1902. 77 p. *DLC, NN, MWA, CSmH, PU*

Aaron Burr: A Biography Written in Large Part From Original and Hitherto Unused Material. Samuel H. Wandell and Meade Minnigerode. N. Y., 1927. 2 vols.

DLC, NN, MWA, CSmH, PU

2:89–501–590

BURR, THEODOSIA. 2:97–452–511–518. See ALSTON, THEODOSIA BURR.

BURR, WILLIAM. *Life of William Burr.* J. M. Brewster. Dover, N. H., 1871. 208 p. *DLC, MWA*

BURRAGE, JOSEPH PERRIN. *Memorial of Lieut. J. P. Burrage.* D. R. Cady. Boston, 1864. 48 p. *DLC, MWA, CSmH*

BURRELL, DAVID JAMES. *David James Burrell; a Biography.* David De F. Burrell. N. Y. and Chicago, 1929. 221 p. *DLC, NN*

BURRITT, ELIHU. *Elihu Burritt. Sketch of His Life and Labors.* C. Northend, ed. N. Y., 1880. 479 p. *NN, MWA, CSmH*
2:40–225

BURROUGH, EDWARD. 2:55

BURROUGHS, JOHN.
Our Friend John Burroughs. Clara Barrus. Boston and N. Y., 1914. 286 p. *DLC, NN*
Life and Letters of John Burroughs. Clara Barrus. Boston, 1925. 2 vols. *DLC, NN, CSmH, PU*
2:388–507

BURROWS, JULIUS CAESAR. *Burrows of Michigan and the Republican Party; a Biography and a History.* William Dana Orcutt. N. Y., 1917. 2 vols. *DLC, NN*

BURTON, ERNEST DE WITT. *Ernest De Witt Burton; a Biographical Sketch.* Thomas W. Goodspeed. Chicago, 1926. 93 p.
DLC, NN, CSmH, PU

BURTON, RICHARD. *Burton, Arabian Nights Adventurer.* Fairfax D. Downey. N. Y., ·1931. 300 p. *DLC, NN*

BURTON, WILLIAM EVANS.
William E. Burton, Actor, Author and Manager. William L. Keese. N. Y., 1885. 230 p. *NN, MWA, CSmH, PU, MiD:B*
William Evans Burton. A Sketch of His Career Other Than That of Actor. William L. Keese. N. Y., 1891. 56 p. (Dunlap Soc. Pub. Ser. 1. v. 14) *DLC, NN, MWA, CSmH, PU, MiD:B*

BUSHNELL, HORACE.
Horace Bushnell. Warren S. Archibald. Hartford, 1930. 155 p.
DLC
Life and Letters of Horace Bushnell. Mary B. Cheney and others. Boston, 1880; with portraits and illustrations, 1903. 579 p.
DLC, NN, MWA, CSmH
Horace Bushnell, Preacher and Theologian. Theodore T. Munger. N. Y. and Boston, 1899. 425 p.
DLC, NN, MWA, CSmH
2:12–40–98–109

BUSHNELL, WILLIAM. *Memoirs and Select Remains of William Bushnell*. New Haven, 1833. 162 p.   *MWA*

BUTLER, BENJAMIN FRANKLIN.

    Life and Public Services of Major-General Butler, the Hero of New Orleans. Phila., 1864. 108 p.   *DLC, NN, CSmH*

    Life of Benjamin F. Butler. T. A. Bland. N. Y., 1879. 202 p.
                                                  DLC, NN, MWA, CSmH

    The Life and Public Services of Benjamin F. Butler. Marcus M. Pomeroy. N. Y., 1868. 63 p.   *DLC, NN, MWA, CSmH*
    2:89–590

BUTLER, MRS. BENJAMIN F.   2:97

BUTLER, SAMUEL. *Samuel Butler; a Mid-Victorian Modern*. Clara G. Stillman. N. Y., 1932. 319 p.   *DLC, NN, PU*

BUTLER, WILLIAM. *William Butler, the Founder of Two Missions of the M. E. Church*. Clementina Butler. N. Y., 1902. 239 p.
                                                  DLC

BUTTERFIELD, DANIEL. *Biographical Memorial of Gen. Daniel Butterfield*. Julia L. Butterfield, ed. N. Y., 1904. 379 p.
                                      DLC, NN, MWA, CSmH, PU

BYLES, MATHER. *The Famous Mather Byles*. Arthur W. H. Eaton. Boston, 1914. 258 p.   *DLC, NN, MWA, CSmH, RP:JCB*

BYRD, RICHARD EVELYN.

    Rear Admiral Byrd and the Polar Expeditions; With an Account of His Life and Achievements. Coram Foster. N. Y., 1930. 256 p.
                                                    DLC, NN

    Struggle; the Life and Exploits of Commander Richard E. Byrd. Charles J. V. Murphy. N. Y., 1928. 368 p.   *DLC, NN*

BYRD, WILLIAM. *William Byrd of Westover*. Richmond C. Beatty. Boston, 1932. 233 p.   *DLC, NN, MWA, CSmH, PU*

BYRON, GEORGE GORDON.

    Byron; Romantic Paradox. William J. Calvert. Chapel Hill, N. C., 1935. 235 p.   *DLC, NN, PU*

    Allegra; the Story of Byron and Miss Clairmont. Armistead C. Gordon. N. Y., 1926. 266 p.   *DLC, NN, CSmH, PU*
    2:95–701

CABELL, JAMES BRANCH. *James Branch Cabell*. Carl Van Doren. N. Y., 1932. 89 p.   *DLC, NN, MWA, PU*

CABLE, GEORGE WASHINGTON. *George W. Cable; His Life and Letters*. Lucy L. C. Bikle. N. Y., 1928. 306 p.
                                        DLC, NN, MWA, CSmH, PU

CABOT, FREDERICK PICKERING. *The Children's Judge, Frederick Pickering Cabot.* M. A. De Wolfe Howe. Boston, 1932. 162 p.
DLC, NN, MWA

CABOT, GEORGE. *Life and Letters of George Cabot.* Henry C. Lodge. Boston, 1877. 615 p. *DLC, NN, MWA, CSmH, PU, MiU:C*

CABOT, JOHN AND SEBASTIAN.
John and Sebastian Cabot. F. A. Ober. N. Y., 1908. 299 p. (Heroes of American History) *DLC, NN*

Sebastian Cabot—John Cabot. Henry Stevens, ed. Boston, 1870. 32 p. *DLC, NN, MWA, PU, MiU:C*

A Memoir of Sebastian Cabot. Richard Biddle. Phila., 1831. 327 p. *DLC, NN, MWA, CSmH, MiU:C*

Life of Sebastian Cabot. Charles Hayward, Jr. (L.A.B.)
DLC, NN, MWA, CSmH, MiU:C

CADAVERE, HENRY. *Henry Cadavere; Study of Life and Work.* H. W. Bellsmith. N. Y., 1897. 239 p. *DLC, NN*

CADILLAC, ANTOINE. *Cadillac, Knight Errant of the Wilderness.* Agnes C. Laut. Indianapolis, 1931. 298 p.
DLC, NN, CSmH, PU, MiD:B

CADMAN, SAMUEL PARKES. *S. Parkes Cadman, Pioneer Radio Minister.* Fred Hamlin. N. Y., 1930. 148 p. *DLC, NN*
2:487–546

CADWALADER, THOMAS. *Sketch of the Life of Dr. Thomas Cadwalader.* Charles W. Dulles. Phila., 1903. 17 p. *DLC, NN, MWA*

CADWALLADER, PRISCILLA. *Memoir of Priscilla Cadwallader.* Phila., 1862. 142 p. *NN, PU*

CAESAR, JULIUS.
History of Julius Caesar. Jacob Abbott. N. Y., 1849. 278 p.
DLC, NN, PU

Caesar. A History of the Art of War Among the Romans . . . With a Detailed Account of the Campaigns of . . . Caesar. Theodore A. Dodge. Boston, 1892. 2 vols. (Great Captains)
DLC, NN, PU

Hail, Caesar! Fletcher Pratt. N. Y., 1936. 349 p.
DLC, NN

Annals of Caesar. Ernest G. Sihler. N. Y., 1911. 330 p.
DLC, NN, PU

Julius Caesar and the Grandeur That Was Rome. Victor Thaddeus. N. Y., 1927. 321 p. *DLC, NN, PU*

CALDWELL, CHARLES. *Biographical Notice of Charles Caldwell.* Phila., 1855. 31 p. *DLC, NN*

CALDWELL, DAVID. *A Sketch of the Life and Character of the Rev. David Caldwell, D.D.* Eli W. Caruthers. Greensborough, N. C., 1842. 302 p. *DLC*

CALDWELL, ZENAS. *Life in Earnest; or, Memoirs and Remains of Rev. Zenas Caldwell, A.B.* Stephen M. Vail. Boston, 1855. 188 p.

CALHOUN, JOHN CALDWELL.

Private Life of John C. Calhoun. Mary Bates. Charleston, 1852. 31 p. *DLC, NN, MWA, CSmH*

John C. Calhoun. H. E. von Holst. Boston, 1884. 356 p. (A.S.)

John C. Calhoun. Gaillard Hunt. Phila., 1908. 335 p. (A.C.B.) *DLC, NN, PU*

Life of John C. Calhoun. R. M. T. Hunter. N. Y., 1843. 74 p. *DLC, NN, MWA*

Life of John Caldwell Calhoun. J. S. Jenkins. Auburn, N. Y., 1850. 454 p. *DLC, NN, MWA, CSmH, PU, MiD:B*

Life of John Caldwell Calhoun. William M. Meigs. N. Y., 1910. 2 vols. *DLC, NN, CSmH, PU*

Life of John C. Calhoun. G. M. Pinckney. Charleston, 1903. 251 p. *DLC, NN, CSmH, PU*

The Cast-Iron Man; John C. Calhoun and American Democracy. Arthur Styron. N. Y., 1935. 426 p. *DLC, NN, CSmH, PU*

2:85–107–431–511–590–654

CALLAGHAN, JAMES FREDERIC. *Memoirs . . . of the Very Rev. James F. Callaghan.* Emily A. Callaghan, comp. Cincinnati, 1903. 568 p. *DLC, NN*

CALVERT, GEORGE. (LORD BALTIMORE)

George Calvert and Cecilius, Barons Baltimore of Baltimore. W. H. Browne. N. Y., 1890. 181 p. (Makers of America Series) *DLC, NN, MWA, PU*

The Lords Baltimore and the Maryland Palatinate. Clayton C. Hall. Balt., 1902. 216 p. *DLC, NN, CSmH, PU*

The Lords Baltimore. John G. Morris. Balt., 1874. 61 p. (Md. Hist. Soc. Fund—Publication No. 8) *DLC, NN, CSmH, PU*

Sir George Calvert, Baron of Baltimore. Lewis W. Wilhelm. Balt., 1884. 172 p. (Md. Hist. Soc. Fund—Publication No. 20) *DLC, NN, MWA, PU*

CALVERT, LEONARD. *Life of Leonard Calvert.* George W. Burnap. (L.A.B.) *DLC, NN, MWA, CSmH, PU*

CALVIN, JOHN.
    John Calvin; A Study in French Humanism . . . Quirinus Breen. Grand Rapids, Mich., 1931. 174 p.
                                     DLC, NN, CSmH, PU
    John Calvin; the Man and His Ethics. Georgia E. Harkness. N. Y., 1931. 256 p.   *DLC, NN*
    John Calvin, the Organizer of Reformed Protestantism. William Walker. N. Y., 1906. 456 p. (Heroes of the Reformation)
                                       DLC, NN, CSmH, PU
    Memoirs of the Life and Writings of John Calvin. Elijah Waterman. Boston, 1813. 412 p.   *NN, MWA*
    2:371

CAMERON, DONALDINA. *Chinatown Quest; the Life Adventures of Donaldina Cameron.* Carol G. Wilson. Stanford, Calif., 1931. 263 p.   *DLC, NN*

CAMP, HENRY WARD. *The Knightly Soldier: A Biography of Major Henry Ward Camp.* Henry Clay Trumbull. Boston, 1865. 331 p.
                                     DLC, MWA, CSmH

CAMP, WALTER. *Walter Camp, the Father of American Football; an Authorized Biography.* Harford W. H. Pamel. Boston, 1926. 238 p.   *DLC, NN, PU*

CAMPBELL, JOHN ARCHIBALD. *John Archibald Campbell.* Henry G. Connor. Boston, 1920. 310 p.   *DLC, NN*

CAMPBELL, PRINCE LUCIEN. *Prince Lucien Campbell.* Joseph Schafer. Eugene, Ore., 1926. 216 p.   *DLC, NN*

CAMPBELL, REGINALD J. 2:487

CAMPBELL, THOMAS. *A Biographical Sketch of Thomas Campbell by a Gentleman of New York, Prefixed to the "Poetical Works of Thomas Campbell . . ."* Washington Irving. Phila., 1810. 27 p.
                                  DLC, NN, MWA, CSmH

CAMPBELL, WALTER. *The Life of Walter L. Campbell.* Mary R. Campbell. N. Y., 1917. 301 p.   *DLC, NN*

CAMPEGGIO, LORENZO. *Cardinal Lorenzo Campeggio, Legate to the Courts of Henry VIII and Charles V.* Edward V. Cardinal. Boston, 1935. 198 p.   *DLC, NN, CSmH*

CAMPION, EDMUND. *Blessed Edmund Campion.* Louise I. Guiney. London, 1914. 182 p. (St. Nicholas Series)   *DLC, NN*

CANDLER, WILLIAM ROBERT. *A Century and One; Life Story of William Robert Candler.* Henry E. Candler. N. Y., 1933. 319 p.
                                DLC, NN, CSmH, MiD:B

CANFIELD, RICHARD. *Canfield: the True Story of the Greatest Gambler.* Alexander Gardiner. N. Y., 1930. 350 p.

DLC, NN, MWA

CANNING, GEORGE. 2–662

CANNON, HARRIET STARR. *Harriet Starr Cannon, First Mother Superior of the Sisterhood of St. Mary: Brief Memoir.* Morgan Dix. N. Y., 1896. 149 p. *DLC, PU*

CAPEN, SAMUEL BILLINGS. *Samuel Billings Capen; His Life and Work.* Chauncey J. Hawkins. N. Y., 1914. 258 p. *DLC*

CAPERS, ELLISON. *The Soldier-Bishop, Ellison Capers.* Walter B. Capers. N. Y., 1912. 367 p. *DLC*

CAPERS, WILLIAM. *Life of Rev. William Capers.* William M. Wrightman. Nashville, 1858. 516 p. *DLC, NN, CSmH*

CAPLES, WILLIAM GOFF. *The Life of Rev. William Goff Caples.* E. M. Marvin. St. Louis, 1870. 440 p. *MWA*

CAPONE, ALPHONSE. *Al Capone; the Biography of a Self-Made Man.* Fred D. Pasley. N. Y., 1930. 355 p. *DLC, NN, MWA, PU*

CARDOZO, BENJAMIN. *Mr. Justice Cardozo; a Liberal Mind in Action.* Joseph P. Pollard. N. Y., 1935. 327 p. *DLC, NN*

CAREW, BAMPFYLDE-MOORE. 2:71

CAREY, MATHEW. *Mathew Carey. Editor, Author and Publisher.* Earl L. Bradsher. N. Y., 1912. 144 p. (Col. Univ. Studies in English) *DLC, NN, MWA, CSmH, PU*

CAREY, WILLIAM.

William Carey. A Biography. Joseph Belcher. Phila., 1853. 306 p. *MWA*

William Carey, Prophet to India. Russell Olt. Anderson, Ind., 1930. 128 p. *DLC, NN*

CARLIELL, LODOWICK. *Lodowick Carliell, His Life: a Discussion of His Plays and " The Deserving Favorite "; a Tragi-Comedy Reprinted From the Original Edition of 1629.* C. H. Gray. Chicago, 1905. 177 p. *DLC, NN, CSmH, PU*

CARLISLE, JOHN GRIFFIN. *John G. Carlisle, Financial Statesman.* James A. Barnes. N. Y., 1931. 552 p. *DLC, NN, CSmH, PU*

CARLYLE, JANE WELSH.

Jane Welsh and Jane Carlyle. Elizabeth A. Drew. N. Y., 1928. 282 p. *DLC, NN*

Life of Jane Welsh Carlyle. Annie E. N. Ireland. N. Y., 1891. 329 p. *DLC, NN, CSmH, PU*

CARLYLE, THOMAS.

Thomas Carlyle. Moncure D. Conway. N. Y., 1881. 253 p.

DLC, NN

Carlyle. Emery E. Neff. N. Y., 1932. 282 p.
DLC, NN, PU

CARNEGIE, ANDREW.
Andrew Carnegie, the Man and His Work. Bernard Alderson.
N. Y., 1902. 232 p. *DLC, NN, PU*
Life of Andrew Carnegie. Burton J. Hendrick. N. Y., 1932.
2 vols. *DLC, NN, PU*
The Incredible Carnegie. John C. Winkler. N. Y., 1931. 307 p.
DLC, NN, PU
2:331–340–388

CARON, PIERRE. See BEAUMARCHAIS.

CARPENTER, MATTHEW HALE. *Life of Matthew Hale Carpenter.*
Frank A. Flower. Madison, Wis., 1883. 584 p.
DLC, NN, MWA, PU

CARREL, ALEXIS. 2:388

CARROLL, ANNA ELLA. *Military Genius: Life of Anna Ella Carroll of
Maryland.* Sarah E. Blackwell. Washington, 1892. 2 vols.
DLC, NN, MWA, CSmH

CARROLL, CHARLES.
Charles Carroll of Carrollton, 1737–1832. Joseph Gurn. N. Y.,
1932. 312 p. *DLC, NN, CSmH, PU*
Life of Charles Carroll of Carrollton. Lewis A. Leonard. N. Y.,
1918. 313 p. *DLC, NN, MWA*
The Life of Charles Carroll of Carrollton. Kate M. Rowland.
N. Y., 1898. 2 vols. *DLC, NN, MWA, CSmH, PU, MiD:B*
2:218–634

CARROLL, JOHN.
*Biographical Sketch of . . . John Carroll, First Archbishop of
Baltimore.* Daniel Brent. Balt., 1843. 321 p.
DLC, NN, CSmH
Life and Times of John Carroll, Archbishop of Baltimore. Pe-
ter Guilday. N. Y., 1922. 2 vols. *DLC, NN, CSmH*
*Life and Times of the Most Rev. John Carroll, Bishop and First
Archbishop of Baltimore.* John D. G. Shea. N. Y., 1888. 695 p.
DLC, MWA, CSmH

CARSON, ALEXANDER. *Life of Alexander Carson.* George C. Moore.
N. Y., 1851. 156 p. *NN, MWA*

CARSON, CHRISTOPHER. [KIT CARSON]
Christopher Carson, Familiarly Known as Kit Carson. John S.
C. Abbott. N. Y., 1873. 348 p.
DLC, NN, MWA, CSmH, PU, MiD:B

Kit Carson. The Life and Adventures of Christopher Carson. the Celebrated Rocky Mountain Hunter, Trapper and Guide . . . Charles Burdett. Phila., 1860. 374 p.

DLC, NN, CSmH, MiD:B

The Life and Times of Christopher Carson, the Rocky Mountain Scout and Guide. Edward S. Ellis. N. Y., 1889. 260 p.

DLC, NN, CSmH

The Life of Kit Carson, Hunter, Trapper, Guide, Indian Agent, and Colonel U. S. A. Edward S. Ellis. N. Y., 1889. 260 p.

DLC, NN

The Daring Adventures of Kit Carson and Frémont. John C. Frémont. N. Y., 1887. 493 p. *NN*

The Life and Adventures of Kit Carson, the Nestor of the Rocky Mountains. Dewitt C. Peters. N. Y., 1858. 534 p.

DLC, NN, MWA, CSmH, PU

Kit Carson's Life and Adventures, From Facts Narrated by Himself . . . Dewitt C. Peters. Hartford, Conn., 1874. 604 p.

DLC, NN, MWA, MiD:B

Kit Carson Days. Edwin L. Sabin. Chicago, 1914. 669 p.

DLC, NN, CSmH, PU, MiD:B

Kit Carson; a Happy Warrior of the West; a Biography. Stanley Vestal. Boston, 1928. 297 p. *DLC, NN, MWA, PU*
2:41–358

CARTER, JOHN. *The Life of John Carter.* Frederick J. Mills. N. Y., 1868. 122 p. *DLC, NN, MWA, CSmH*

CARTER, ROBERT. *Robert Carter, His Life and Work, 1807–1889.* Annie Carter Cochran. 1891. 250 p. *DLC, NN*

CARTIER, JACQUES. *A Memoir of Jacques Cartier, Sieur De Limoilou.* James P. Baxter. N. Y., 1906. 464 p.

DLC, NN, MWA, CSmH, PU, MiU:C
2:127

CARTWRIGHT, PETER.

Peter Cartwright: Pioneer. Helen H. Grant. N. Y., 1931. 222 p. *DLC, NN, PU*

Peter Cartwright. Philip M. Watters. N. Y., 1910. 128 p.

DLC, NN

CARTY, JOHN JOSEPH. *John J. Carty, an Appreciation.* Frederick L. Rhodes. N. Y., 1932. 280 p. *DLC, NN, MWA, PU*

CARUSO, ENRICO.

Wings of Song; the Story of Caruso. Dorothy Caruso and Mrs. Torrance Goddard. N. Y., 1928. 218 p. *DLC, NN, PU*

Enrico Caruso; a Biography. Pierre V. R. Key and Bruno Zirato. Boston, 1922. 455 p. *DLC, NN*

CARVER, GEORGE WASHINGTON. *From Captivity to Fame; or, The Life of George Washington Carver.* Raleigh H. Merritt. Boston, 1929. 196 p. *DLC, NN, MWA*
2:675

CARVER, JOHN. 2:141

CARVER, JONATHAN. 2:262

CARY, ALICE AND PHOEBE. *A Memorial of Alice and Phoebe Cary.* Mary C. Ames. N. Y., 1873. 238 p. *NN, MWA, CSmH, PU*

CARY, LOTT. *Biography of Elder Lott Cary, Late Missionary to Africa.* James B. Taylor. Balt., 1837. 108 p. *NN*

CASALS, PABLO. *Pablo Casals.* Lillian Littlehales. N. Y., 1929. 216 p. *DLC, NN*

CASANOVA, JACQUES. *Casanova; His Known and Unknown Life.* S. Guy Endore. N. Y., 1929. 390 p. *DLC, NN*
2:95

CASAS, BARTOLOMÉ DE LAS. *The Life of Bartolomé de Las Casas, and the First Leaves of American Ecclesiastical History.* Louis A. Dutto. St. Louis, 1902. 592 p. *DLC, NN*

CASS, LEWIS.
Biography of General Lewis Cass. N. Y., 1843. 36 p. [Pamphlet] *DLC, NN, MWA. MiU:C*
Life and Public Services of General Lewis Cass. Boston, 1848. 25 p. [Pamphlet] *NN, MWA*
The Life of General Lewis Cass. Balt., 1848. 72 p. [Pamphlet] *MWA, PU*
Life of General Lewis Cass. George H. Hickman. Phila., 1848. 210 p. *DLC, NN, MWA, MiD:B*
Life of Lewis Cass. Andrew C. McLaughlin. Boston, 1891. 363 p. (A.S.) *DLC, NN, MWA, CSmH, PU, MiD:B*
Outlines of the Life and Character of Lewis Cass. Henry R. Schoolcraft. Albany, 1848. 64 p. *DLC. NN, MWA, MiD:B*
Fifty Years of Public Life. The Life and Times of Lewis Cass. William L. G. Smith. N. Y., 1856. 781 p.
DLC, NN, CSmH, MiD:B
Sketches of the Life and Public Services of Lewis Cass. William T. Young. Detroit, 1852. 420 p. *DLC, NN, MiD:B*
2:431–590

CASSARD, JACQUES. 2:488

CASSIDY, WILLIAM. *Memorial of William Cassidy.* Albany, 1874.
142 p. CSmH
CASTANG, REUBEN. *Wild Animal Man; Being the Story of the Life
of Reuben Castang.* Reginald W. Thompson. N. Y., 1934. 296 p.
DLC, NN
CASTIGLIONE, BALDASSARE. 2:573
CASTLE, VERNON. *My Husband.* Irene Castle. N. Y., 1919. 264 p.
DLC, NN
CATALÁ, MAGIN. *Holy Man of Santa Clara; or, Life, Virtues and
Miracles of Fr. Magin Catalá.* Zephyrin Engelhardt. San Fran-
cisco, 1909. 199 p. DLC, NN, CSmH
CATHER, WILLA. *Willa Cather.* Rene Rapin. N. Y., 1930. 115 p.
DLC, NN, MWA, PU
2:592
CATHERINE THE GREAT. *Catherine the Great.* Katharine S. Anthony.
N. Y., 1925. 331 p. DLC, NN, PU
CAVENDISH, HENRY. 2:348–393
CAVOUR, CAMILLO BENSO. *Life and Times of Cavour.* William R.
Thayer. Boston, 1911. 2 vols. DLC, NN, MWA, PU
CAWEIN, MADISON. *Madison Cawein. The Story of a Poet.* Otto A.
Rothert. Louisville, 1921. 545 p. (Filson Club Pub. No. 30)
DLC, NN, MWA, CSmH, PU, MiD:B
CELLINI, BENVENUTO. *Benvenuto Cellini and His Florentine Dagger.*
Victor Thaddeus. N. Y., 1933. 348 p. DLC, NN
CERVANTES, MIGUEL. *Cervantes.* Rudolph Schevill. N. Y., 1919.
388 p. (Master Spirits of Literature) DLC, NN, PU
CÉZANNE, PAUL. 2:161
CHACE, ELIZABETH BUFFUM. *Elizabeth Buffum Chace, 1806–1899.*
Lillie B. and Arthur C. Wyman. Boston, 1914. 2 vols.
NN, MWA
CHACE, GEORGE IDE. *George Ide Chace; a Memorial.* James O.
Murray. Cambridge, 1886. 271 p.
DLC, NN, MWA, MiD:B, RP:JCB
CHADWICK, JOHN. *Cap'n Chadwick, Marblehead Skipper and Shoe-
maker.* John W. Chadwick. Boston, 1906. 87 p. DLC, NN
CHAFFEE, ADNA ROMANZA. *Life of Lieut.-Gen. Chaffee.* William G.
H. Carter. Chicago, 1917. 296 p. DLC, NN, CSmH
CHAFFEY, GEORGE. *Life of George Chaffey; a Story of Irrigation Be-
ginnings in California and Australia.* J. A. Alexander. Melbourne,
1928; N. Y., 1929. 382 p. DLC, NN, CSmH

CHALLISS, JAMES. *Memoir of Rev. James Challiss.* John R. Murphy. Phila., 1870. 370 p. (Privately Printed) *NN, MWA*

CHALMERS, THOMAS.
Thomas Chalmers: A Biographical Study. J. Dodds. N. Y., 1870. 394 p. *NN*
Life of Thomas Chalmers. James C. Moffat. Cincinnati, 1853. 435 p. *NN, PU*

CHAMBERS, CHARLOTTE. See RISKE, CHARLOTTE.

CHAMBERS, JOHN. *John Chambers and His Ministry in Philadelphia.* W. E. Griffis. Ithaca, N. Y., 1903. 159 p. *DLC, MWA*

CHAMBERS, JOHN. *John Chambers.* J. C. Parish. Iowa City, Ia., 1909. 279 p. (Iowa Biographical Series)
DLC, NN, MWA, CSmH, MiD:B

CHAMPLAIN, SAMUEL DE.
Champlain, the Founder of New France. E. A. Dix. N. Y., 1903. 246 p. (Series of Historic Lives)
DLC, NN, MWA, CSmH, PU, MiU:C
Samuel de Champlain. H. D. Sedgwick, Jr. Boston, 1902. 126 p. (Riverside Biographies) *DLC, NN, CSmH*
Voyages of Samuel de Champlain . . . and a Memoir. Edmund F. Slafter, ed. Boston, 1880. (Prince Society Publications)
DLC, NN, MWA, CSmH, PU, MiU:C
2:127

CHANDLER, CHARLES. *Dr. Charles Chandler; His Place in the American Scene.* Josephine C. Chandler. Springfield, Ill., 1932. 184 p.
DLC, NN, MWA

CHANDLER, DANIEL MEEKER. *Memoir of the Rev. Daniel Meeker Chandler.* C. Prindle. Middlebury, Vt., 1842. 114 p.
NN, MWA

CHANDLER, ZACHARIAH. *Outline Sketch of Life of Zachariah Chandler.* C. K. Backus. N. Y., 1880. 436 p.

CHANNING, GEORGE. *Life of George Channing.* Walter A. Phillips. N. Y., 1905. 185 p.

CHANNING, WALTER. 2:144

CHANNING, WILLIAM ELLERY.
William Ellery Channing. A Centennial Memory. Charles T. Brooks. Boston, 1880. 259 p. *NN, MWA*
William Ellery Channing, Minister of Religion. J. W. Chadwick. Boston, 1903. 463 p. *DLC, NN, MWA, CSmH, PU*
Memoir of William Ellery Channing. William H. Channing (ed.). Boston, 1848. 3 vols. *DLC, NN, MWA, CSmH, PU*

The Life of William Ellery Channing, D.D. William H. Channing. Boston, 1880. 719 p. *DLC, NN*

William Ellery Channing. Paul R. Frothingham. Boston and N. Y., 1903. 52 p. *DLC*
2:12–144

CHANNING, WILLIAM HENRY. *Memoir of William H. Channing.* O. B. Frothingham. Boston and N. Y., 1886. 491 p. *DLC, NN*

CHAPIN, ALFRED CLARK. *Alfred Clark Chapin, March 8, 1848–Oct. 2, 1936.* L. E. Osborne. Portland, Me., 1937. *RP:JCB*

CHAPIN, EDWIN HUBBELL. *Life of Edwin H. Chapin, D.D.* Sumner Ellis. Boston, 1882. 332 p. *DLC, NN, MWA*
2:40

CHAPIN, JAMES HENRY. *James Henry Chapin; Sketch of His Life and Work.* G. S. Weaver. N. Y., 1894.

CHAPIN, SAMUEL. *Life of Deacon Samuel Chapin of Springfield.* Howard M. Chapin. Providence, 1908. 73 p. *DLC, NN, MWA*

CHAPLIN, CHARLES. *Charlie Chaplin; His Life and Art.* William D. Bowman. N. Y., 1931. 134 p. *DLC, NN, PU*
2:236

CHAPMAN, HENRY CADWALADER. *A Biographical Notice of Henry Cadwalader Chapman, M.D., Sc.D.* Edward J. Nolan. Phila., 1910. 115 p. *DLC, NN, PU*

CHAPMAN, HENRY G. *Henry G. Chapman, 1860–1913.* John J. Chapman. N. Y., 1914. 13 p. *DLC, NN*

CHAPMAN, JOHN. *Johnny Appleseed and His Time.* Henry A. Pershing. Strasburg, Va., 1930. 377 p. *DLC, NN, MWA, PU*

CHAPMAN, JOHN WILBUR. *J. Wilbur Chapman.* Ford C. Ottman. N. Y., 1920. 326 p. *DLC, NN*

CHAPPE, CLAUDE. 2:25

CHARLEMAGNE. *Charlemagne; the First of the Moderns.* Charles E. Russell. Boston, 1930. 305 p. *DLC, NN, PU*

CHARLES, FATHER. *Life of Father Charles of the Congregation of the Most Holy Cross.* Rev. Austin. N. Y., 1893.

CHARLES THE BOLD. *Charles the Bold, Last Duke of Normandy.* Ruth Putnam. N. Y. and London, 1908. 484 p. *DLC, NN*

CHARLES I. *History of King Charles the First of England.* Jacob Abbott. N. Y., 1848. 285 p. *DLC, NN, PU*

CHARLES II.

History of King Charles II of England. Jacob Abbott. N. Y., 1899. 245 p. *DLC, NN, PU*

Royal Charles, Ruler and Rake. David G. Loth. N. Y., 1930. 343 p. *DLC, NN, PU*

CHARLES V. *The Life of Charles the Fifth After His Abdication.* Wm.
H. Prescott. Boston, 1857. 185 p. *DLC, NN*

CHASE, KATE. *Kate Chase, Dominant Daughter; the Life Story of a
Brilliant Woman and Her Famous Father.* Mary M. Phelps. N. Y.,
1935. 316 p. *DLC, NN, CSmH, PU*
2:518

CHASE, GEORGE COLBY. *George C. Chase, a Biography.* George M.
Chase. Boston, 1924. 153 p. *DLC, NN, PU*

CHASE, IRA J. See HOVEY, ALVIN P.

CHASE, PHILANDER.
The Life of Bishop Chase. John N. Norton. N. Y., 1857.
99 p. *NN*
Life of Philander Chase. Laura C. Smith. N. Y., 1903. 341 p.
DLC, NN, PU

CHASE, SALMON PORTLAND.
Salmon Portland Chase. Albert B. Hart. Boston, 1899. 465 p.
(A.S.) *DLC, NN, MWA, CSmH, PU*
Life and Public Services of Salmon Portland Chase. Jacob W.
Schuckers. N. Y., 1874. 669 p. *DLC, NN, MWA, CSmH, PU*
*An Account of the Private Life and Public Services of Salmon P.
Chase.* Robert B. Warden. Cincinnati, 1874. 838 p.
DLC, NN, MWA, CSmH, PU
2:107–624

CHASE, SAMUEL. 2:218

CHASE, WILLIAM MERRITT. *Life and Art of William Merritt Chase.*
Katharine M. Roof. N. Y., 1917. 352 p. *DLC, NN*
2:52–429

CHATFIELD, JULIA. *Cross in the Wilderness; a Biography of Pioneer
Ohio.* Sr. Mary Monica. N. Y., 1930. 290 p. *DLC, NN*

CHATTERTON, THOMAS.
Thomas Chatterton, the Marvelous Boy. Esther P. Ellinger.
Phila., 1930. 75 p. *DLC, NN, CSmH, PU*
*Thomas Chatterton, the Marvelous Boy, The Story of a Strange
Life.* Charles E. Russell. N. Y., 1908. 289 p. *DLC, NN, PU*

CHAUCER, GEOFFREY.
Chaucer and His Poetry. George L. Kittredge. Cambridge,
1925. 230 p. *DLC, NN, CSmH, PU*
Studies in Chaucer: His Life and Writings. Thomas R. Louns-
bury. N. Y., 1892. 3 vols. *DLC, NN, CSmH, PU*
Dan Chaucer. Henry D. Sedgwick. Indianapolis, 1934. 391 p.
DLC, NN, PU

CHECKLEY, JOHN. *John Checkley; or, the Evolution of Religious Tolerance in Massachusetts Bay.* Edmund F. Slafter, ed. Boston, 1897. 2 vols. (Prince Soc. Pub.)

> *DLC, NN, MWA, CSmH, PU, MiU:C*

CHEEVER, EZEKIEL. *Ezekiel Cheever, Schoolmaster.* Elizabeth P. Gould. Boston, 1904. 94 p. *DLC, NN, MWA*

CHEEVER, NATHANIEL. *Memorials of the Life and Trials of a Youthful Christian . . . Nathaniel Cheever, M.D.* Henry T. Cheever. N. Y., 1851. 355 p. *DLC, MWA*

CHENEY, MARTIN. *The Life of . . . Martin Cheney.* George J. Day. Providence, 1853. 471 p. *NN*

CHESTER, PETER. *Peter Chester, Third Governor of the Province of British West Florida Under British Dominion, 1770–1781.* Eron O. M. Rowland. (In Miss. Hist. Soc. Publications. Centenary Series. Jackson, Miss., 1925. vol. V. p. (IX–XI) 1–183)

> *DLC, NN, CSmH*

CHEVERS, SARAH. 2:55

CHEW, BENJAMIN. *Benjamin Chew, 1722–1810.* Burton A. Konkle. Phila., 1932. 316 p. *DLC, NN, MWA, CSmH, PU*

CHILD, FRANCIS JAMES. 2:85

CHILD, HARRY W. 2:233

CHILD, LYDIA MARIA. *Letters of Lydia Maria Child With a Biographical Introduction.* John G. Whittier. Boston, 1883. 305 p.

> *DLC, NN, CSmH*

> 2:43

CHILD, ROBERT. *Dr. Robert Child.* George L. Kittredge. Cambridge, 1919. 146 p. (Pub. of Col. Soc. of Mass., XXI, 1–146)

> *DLC, NN, MWA, CSmH*

> 2:464

CHILDS, JOHN WESLEY. *Life of Rev. J. W. Childs.* John E. Edwards. Richmond, 1852. 295 p. *DLC, NN*

CHILTON, MARY. 2:337

CHIPMAN, NATHANIEL. *Life of Hon. Nathaniel Chipman With Selections From His Miscellaneous Papers.* Daniel Chipman. Boston, 1846. 402 p. *DLC, NN, MiD:B*

CHISHOLM, JAMES. *Memoir of Rev. James Chisholm . . . Late Rector of St. John's Church, Portsmouth, Va.* David H. Conrad. N. Y., 1856. 193 p. *DLC, NN, CSmH*

CHITTENDEN, THOMAS. *A Memoir of Thomas Chittenden, First Governor of Vermont.* Daniel Chipman. Middlebury, Vt., 1849. 222 p.

> *DLC, NN, MWA, MiD:B*

CHIVERS, THOMAS HOLLEY. *Thomas Holley Chivers, Friend of Poe
. . . a Strange Chapter in American Literary History.* S. Foster
Damon. N. Y., 1930. 305 p.   *DLC, NN, MWA, CSmH, PU*

CHOATE, JOSEPH HODGES.
   Life of Joseph Hodges Choate. Edward S. Martin. N. Y.,
1920. 2 vols.   *DLC, NN, MWA, PU*
   *Joseph H. Choate. New Englander, New Yorker, Ambassador,
Lawyer.* Theron G. Strong. N. Y., 1917. 390 p.
                                   DLC, NN, MWA, CSmH, PU

CHOATE, RUFUS.
   Memoir of Rufus Choate. Samuel G. Brown. Boston, 1862.
316 p.
   The Life of Rufus Choate. Samuel G. Brown. Boston, 1870.
468 p.   *DLC, NN, MWA, CSmH, MiD:B*
   Rufus Choate, the Wizard of the Law. Claude M. Fuess. N. Y.,
1928. 278 p.   *DLC, NN, CSmH, PU*
   Reminiscences of Rufus Choate, the Great American Advocate.
Edward G. Parker. N. Y., 1860. 522 p.
                              DLC, NN, MWA, CSmH, PU, MiD:B
   Some Recollections of Rufus Choate. Edwin P. Whipple. N. Y.,
1879. 100 p.   *DLC, NN*

CHOISEUL, MME DE. 2:93
CHOISY, FRANÇOIS TIMOLEAN DE. 2:71
CHOPIN, FREDERICK. *Chopin, the Man and His Music.* James G.
Huneker. N. Y., 1900. 415 p.   *DLC, NN*
      2:187
CHOPIN, KATE. *Kate Chopin and Her Creole Stories.* Daniel S.
Rankin. Phila., 1932. 313 p.   *DLC, NN, PU*
CHRISTEN, RODOLPHE. *Rodolphe Christen: Story of An Artist's Life.*
Mrs. Sydney M. T. Christen. N. Y., 1910. 264 p.   *DLC*
CHRISTIAN IV. *Christian IV, King of Denmark and Norway; a Pic-
ture of the Seventeenth Century.* John A. Gade. Boston, 1928.
319 p.   *DLC, NN, PU*
CHRISTINA, QUEEN. *Christina of Sweden, a Psychological Biography.*
Margaret L. Goldsmith. N. Y., 1933. 308 p.   *DLC, NN*
CHRISTMAS, LEON WINFIELD. *The Incredible Yanqui; the Career of
Lee Christmas.* Hermann B. Deutsch. N. Y., 1931. 242 p.
                                                  DLC, NN
CHRISTOPHE I. *Black Majesty.* John W. Vandercook. N. Y., 1928.
207 p.   *DLC, NN, PU*

CHURCHILL, CHARLES. *Charles Churchill: Vagabond Poet.* W. H. Miner. Cedar Rapids, Ia., 1907. 42 p.

CHURCHILL, SYLVESTER. *Sketch of the Life of Bvt.-Gen. Sylvester Churchill, Inspector General U. S. Army.* Franklin H. Churchill. N. Y., 1888. 201 p. *DLC, NN*

CHURCHILL, WINSTON S. 2:172

CHURCHMAN, JOHN. *An Account of the Gospel Labors and Christian Experiences of John Churchman; With a Short Memorial of the Life and Death of . . . Joseph White . . .* Phila., 1779. 256 p. *DLC, NN, MWA, PU, RP:JCB*

CICERO, MARCUS TULLIUS.
Cicero; a Study. George C. Richards. Boston, 1935. 298 p. *DLC, NN*
Cicero of Arpinun. Ernest G. Sihler. New Haven, 1914, 1933. 487 p. *DLC, NN, PU*
Cicero, a Sketch of His Life and Work. Hannis Taylor. Chicago, 1916. 615 p. *DLC, NN, PU*

CILLEY, JOSEPH. *Life of Gen. Joseph Cilley.* John Scales. Manchester, N. H., 1921. 59 p. *DLC, MWA, MiD:B*

CLAFLIN, HORACE BRIGHAM. 2:623

CLAGGETT, THOMAS JOHN.
Life of Bishop Claggett, of Maryland. J. N. Norton. N. Y., 1859. 135 p. *DLC, NN*
The Life and Times of Thomas John Claggett, First Bishop of Maryland. George B. Utley. Chicago, 1913. 184 p. *DLC, NN, MWA*

CLARK, ABRAHAM. *Abraham Clark; Signer of the Declaration of Independence.* Ann C. Hart, ed. San Francisco, 1923. 176 p. *DLC, NN, MiD:B*

CLARK, CHAMP. 2:314

CLARK, DAVIS WASGATT. *Life-Story of Rev. Davis Wasgatt Clark . . . Bishop of the Methodist Episcopal Church.* Daniel Curry. N. Y., 1874. 336 p. *NN*

CLARK, ELIJAH. 2:135

CLARK, GEORGE ROGERS.
George Rogers Clark; His Life and Public Services. Temple Bodley. Boston, 1926. 425 p. *DLC, NN, MWA, PU, MiD:B*
Life of Gen. George Rogers Clark; With Sketches of Men Who Served Under Clark. W. H. English. Indianapolis, 1896. 2 vols. *DLC, NN, CSmH*

Life of George Rogers Clark. James A. James. Chicago, 1928. 534 p.   *DLC, NN, CSmH, PU, MiD:B*

George Rogers Clark; Pioneer Hero of the Old Northwest. Ross F. Lockridge. N. Y. and Chicago, 1927. 210 p.   *DLC, NN*

Clark of the Ohio; the Life of George Rogers Clark. Frederick Palmer. N. Y., 1929. 482 p.   *DLC, NN, PU*

George Rogers Clark and His Illinois Campaign. Dan B. Starkey. Milwaukee, 1897. 62 p. (Parkman Club Papers, No. 12)   *DLC, NN, MWA*

Hero of Vincennes; the Story of George Rogers Clark. Lowell J. Thomas. Boston and N. Y., 1929. 195 p.   *DLC*

CLARK, JOHN. *The Life of Rev. John Clark.* B. M. Hall. N. Y., 1856. 276 p.   *NN, CSmH, MiD:B*

CLARK, JONAS GILMAN. *In Memoriam, Jonas Gilman Clark.* Susan W. Clark. N. Y., 1900. 55 p.   *DLC, NN, PU*

CLARK, SOLOMON. *Professor Clark, a Short Memoir.* Barrett H. Clark. Chautauqua, N. Y., 1928. 86 p.

CLARK, THOMAS MARCH. *Thomas March Clark, Fifth Bishop of Rhode Island.* Mary C. Sturtevant. Milwaukee, 1927. 235 p.   *DLC, NN, MWA*

CLARK, WILLIAM. 2:41–262–358 See LEWIS, MERIWETHER.

CLARKE, ADAM. 2:293

CLARKE, JAMES FREEMAN. 2:519

CLARKE, JOHN. *Story of Dr. John Clarke, of Rhode Island.* Thomas W. Bicknell. Providence, 1915. 212 p.   *DLC, NN, MWA, CSmH*

CLARKE, PITT AND MARY JONES. *Memorial of the Rev. Pitt Clarke and of Mary Jones Clarke, His Wife.* Cambridge, 1867. 94 p. (Privately Printed)   *DLC, NN, MWA*

CLARKE, WILLIAM NEWTON. *William Newton Clarke; a Biography, With Additional Sketches of His Friends and Colleagues.* Emily A. S. Clarke. N. Y., 1916. 262 p.   *DLC, NN*

CLARKSON, GERARDUS AND MATTHEW. *Memoirs of Matthew Clarkson of Philadelphia, 1735–1800; and His Brother, Gerardus Clarkson, 1737–1790.* John Hall and S. Clarkson. Phila., 1890. 259 p.   *DLC, NN, MWA*

CLAVER, PETER. *The Life of St. Peter Claver, S.J., the Apostle of the Negroes.* John R. Slattery. Phila., 1892. 264 p.   *DLC*

CLAY, HENRY.

Henry Clay. Howard W. Caldwell. Milwaukee, 1903. 180 p. (Great Americans of History)   *DLC, NN, CSmH*

Monument to the Memory of Henry Clay. A. H. Carrier Phila., 1858. 516 p. *PU*

The Life and Times of Henry Clay. Calvin Colton. N. Y.. 1845, 1856. 2 vols. *DLC, NN, MWA, CSmH, PU*

Henry Clay. Thomas H. Clay and Ellis P. Oberholtzer. Phila., 1910. 450 p. (A.C.B.) *DLC, NN, CSmH, PU*

The Clay Minstrel . . . to Which is Prefixed a Sketch of the Life, Public Services and Character of Henry Clay. John S. Littell. N. Y. and Phila., 1844. 288 p. *DLC, PU*

Life and Speeches of Henry Clay. D. Mallory, ed. Hartford, 1843. 2 vols. *NN, MWA, PU*

Biography of Henry Clay. G. D. Prentice. Hartford, 1831. 304 p. 2nd ed. rev. N. Y., 1831. 312 p. *DLC, NN, MWA, CSmH, PU, MiD:B*

The True Henry Clay. Jos. M. Rogers. Phila., 1904. 388 p. *DLC, NN, CSmH, PU*

The Life of Henry Clay. Nathan Sargent. Phila., 1844. 16 p. *DLC, NN, CSmH, MiD:B*

The Life and Public Services of Henry Clay. Epes Sargent and Horace Greeley. Phila., 1852. 423 p. *DLC, NN, MWA, CSmH, PU, MiD:B*

The Life and Times of Henry Clay. Samuel M. Schmucker. Phila., 1860. 432 p. *DLC*

Henry Clay. Carl Schurz. Boston, 1887. 2 vols. (A.S.) *DLC, NN, MWA, CSmH, PU, MiD:B*

Life and Speeches of Henry Clay Between 1810 and 1842. James B. Swain. 1842. 2 vols. *NN, CSmH*

Memoir of Henry Clay. R. C. Winthrop. Cambridge, 1880. 39 p. *DLC, NN, MWA*

2:35–77–85–107–329–431–501–511–590

CLAYTON, JOHN MIDDLETON. *Memoir of John M. Clayton.* Joseph P. Comegys. Wilmington, 1882. 307 p. (Papers, Hist. Soc. of Del., Vol. 4) *DLC, NN, CSmH, PU, MiD:B*

CLEMENCEAU, GEORGES. *The Tiger: Georges Clemenceau, 1841–1929.* George J. Adams. N. Y., 1930. 282 p. *DLC, NN, PU*

CLEMENS, SAMUEL. [MARK TWAIN]

Mark Twain, Son of Missouri. Minnie M. Brashear. Chapel Hill, N. C., 1934. 294 p. *DLC, NN, CSmH, PU*

Ordeal of Mark Twain. Van Wyck Brooks. N. Y., 1920. 267 p. *DLC, NN, PU*

My Father: Mark Twain. Clara Clemens. N. Y., 1931. 292 p.
DLC, NN, MWA, PU

Mark Twain: His Life and Works. A Biographical Sketch.
Will M. Clemens. San Francisco, 1892. 211 p.
DLC, NN, CSmH

Mark Twain's America. Bernard De Voto. Boston, 1932.
353 p. *DLC, NN, CSmH, PU*

Mark Twain. Archibald Henderson. N. Y., 1910. 230 p.
DLC, NN, CSmH, PU

My Mark Twain. William D. Howells. N. Y., 1910. 186 p.
DLC, NN, CSmH, PU, MiD:B

Mark Twain. A Biography. Albert B. Paine. N. Y., 1912.
3 vols. *DLC, NN, MWA, CSmH, PU*

A Short Life of Mark Twain. Albert B. Paine. N. Y., 1920.
343 p. *DLC, NN*

Mark Twain, the Man and His Work. Edward C. Wagenknecht. New Haven, 1935. 301 p. *DLC, NN, CSmH, PU*
2:41–84–180–314–388

CLEMENT, JOHN. *Memoir of Mr. John Clement, Surgeon.* John
Hooper. Boston, 1813. 200 p. *MWA*

CLEMMER, MARY. *A Memorial of Mary Clemmer.* Edmund Hudson.
Boston, 1886. 243 p. *DLC, NN, MWA, CSmH*

CLEOPATRA. *History of Cleopatra, Queen of Egypt.* Jacob Abbott.
N. Y., 1879. 318 p. *DLC, NN*

CLEVELAND, GROVER.

Grover Cleveland as Buffalo Knew Him. Charles H. Armitage.
Buffalo, 1926. 278 p. *DLC, NN, CSmH*

Life and Public Services of Grover Cleveland. W. Dorsheimer.
Phila., 1884. 578 p. *DLC, NN, MWA, MiD:B*

Grover Cleveland. R. W. Gilder. N. Y., 1910. 270 p.
DLC, NN, MWA, PU

The Life and Public Services of Grover Cleveland . . . Frederick E. Goodrich. Portland, Me., 1884. 504 p.
DLC, NN, MiD:B

*Life and Public Services of Grover Cleveland and John Thur-
man.* W. U. Hensel and G. F. Parker. Phila., 1888. 588 p.
DLC, NN

Grover Cleveland; a Study in Political Courage. Roland
Hugins. Washington, 1922. 94 p. (Admirable Americans)
DLC, NN

Life and Public Services of Grover Cleveland. Pendleton King. N. Y., 1884. 224 p. *DLC, NN, MWA, CSmH*

Grover Cleveland; a Man Four-Square. Denis T. Lynch. N. Y., 1932. 581 p. *DLC, NN, CSmH, PU*

The Life of Hon. Grover Cleveland . . . Also the Life of Hon. Thomas A. Hendricks. James B. McClure. Chicago, 1884. 218 p. *DLC, NN*

Grover Cleveland, the Man and the Statesman. Robert Mc-Elroy. N. Y., 1923. 2 vols.
DLC, NN, MWA, CSmH, PU, MiD:B

Grover Cleveland; a Study in Courage. Allan Nevins. N. Y., 1932. 832 p. *DLC, NN, CSmH, PU*

Life of Grover Cleveland; With Sketch of Adlai E. Stevenson. George F. Parker. N. Y., 1892. 333 p. *NN, MWA*

Recollections of Grover Cleveland. George F. Parker. N. Y., 1909. 427 p. *DLC, NN, CSmH, PU*

Grover Cleveland. William O. Stoddard. N. Y., 1888. 263 p.
DLC, NN, MiD:B

Grover Cleveland. J. L. Whittle. London, 1896. 240 p.
DLC, NN, MiD:B

2:14–84–107–525

CLEVENGER, SHOBAL VAIL. *The Don Quixote of Psychiatry. A Biography of Dr. Schobal Vail Clevenger.* Victor Robinson. N. Y., 1919. 339 p. *DLC, NN*

CLIFFORD, NATHAN. *Nathan Clifford, Democrat (1803–1881).* Philip G. Clifford. N. Y., 1922. 356 p. *DLC, NN, MWA, PU*

CLINTON, DE WITT.

De Witt Clinton. Dorothie Bobbé. N. Y., 1933. 308 p.
DLC, NN

Life and Writings of De Witt Clinton. W. W. Campbell. N. Y., 1849. 381 p. *NN, MWA, CSmH, MiD:B*

Memoir of De Witt Clinton: With An Appendix Containing Numerous Documents, etc. David Hosack. N. Y., 1829. 530 p.
DLC, NN, MWA, CSmH, MiD:B, MiU:C

Life of Dewitt Clinton. James Renwick. N. Y., 1840. 334 p.
DLC, NN, MWA, CSmH

Tribute to the Memory of De Witt Clinton, Late Governor of the State of New York. Cuyler Staats. Albany, 1828. 204 p.
DLC, NN, MWA, CSmH

2:349–501–660

CLINTON, GEORGE. 2:349

CLINTON, JAMES. 2:542

CLOPTON, ABNER W *A Memoir of Abner W. Clopton.* Jeremiah B. Jeter. Richmond, 1837. 283 p. *NN, CSmH*

CLOUGH, JOHN EVERETT.

John E. Clough, Missionary to the Telugres of South India. Emma R. Clough. Boston, 1902. 28 p. *DLC, NN*

Clough, Kingdom-Builder in South India. Herbert W. Hines. Phila., 1929. 168 p. *DLC, NN*

CLUM, JOHN PHILIP. *Apache Agent; the Story of John P. Clum.* Woodworth Clum. Boston, 1936. 297 p.

DLC, NN, MWA, CSmH

COAN, TITUS. *Titus Coan. A Memorial.* Lydia B. Coan. Chicago, 1884. 248 p. *NN*

COATES, ROBERT. *Life of Robert Coates, Known as " Romeo " and " Diamond " Coates, the Celebrated Amateur of Fashion.* J. R. Robinson and H. Hunter. N. Y., 1891. 255 p. *DLC, NN, CSmH*

COBB, ALICE CULLER. *The Portal of Wonderland; the Life Story of Alice Culler Cobb.* Mary G. White. N. Y., 1925. 240 p.

DLC, NN

COBB, ELIJAH. *Elijah Cobb, 1768–1848; a Cape Cod Skipper.* Elijah Cobb. New Haven, 1925. 111 p. *DLC, NN, MWA*

COBB, IRVIN SHREWSBURY. *Irvin S. Cobb; His Life and Achievements.* Fred Gus Neuman. Paducah, Ky., 1934. 275 p. *DLC, NN*

COBB, SYLVANUS, JR. *A Memoir of Sylvanus Cobb, Jr.* Ella W. Cobb. Boston, 1891. 323 p. (Privately Printed)

DLC, NN, MWA

COBBS, NICHOLAS HAMNER. *Saint of the Southern Church: Memoir of Nicholas Hamner Cobbs.* Greenough White. N. Y., 1897. 183 p.

DLC, CSmH

COBDEN, RICHARD. 2:334

COBURN, ABNER. *The Life of Abner Coburn . . . A Review of the . . . Career of the Late Ex-Governor of Maine . . .* Charles E. Williams. Bangor, Me., 1885. 220 p. *DLC, NN*

COCHRAN, JOSEPH PLUMB. *" The Hakim Sahib," the Foreign Doctor; a Biography of Joseph Plumb Cochran, M.D., of Persia.* Robert E. Speer. N. Y., 1911. 384 p. *DLC, NN*
2:237

COCKE, CHARLES LEWIS. *Charles Lewis Cocke: Founder of Hollins College.* William R. L. Smith. Boston, 1921. 161 p.

DLC, NN, PU

COCKENOE. *Cockenoe-de-Long-Island, John Eliot's First Indian Teacher and Interpreter: The Story of His Career.* W. W. Tooker. N. Y., 1896. 60 p. *DLC, NN*

CODDING, ICHABOD. 2:40

CODMAN, JOHN. *Memoir of John Codman, D.D.* William Allen. Boston, 1853. 408 p. *DLC, NN, MWA, PU, MiD:B*

CODY, WILLIAM FREDERICK.

" *Buffalo Bill* " *From Prairie to Palace.* John M. Burke. Chicago, 1893. 275 p. *DLC, NN, CSmH*

Memories of Buffalo Bill. Louise F. Cody and C. R. Cooper. N. Y., 1919. 325 p. *DLC, NN*

Buffalo Bill, the Scout. Clarence E. Ray. Chicago, n.d. 189 p. *DLC, NN*

Making of Buffalo Bill; a Study in Heroics. Richard J. Walsh and Milton Salsbury. Indianapolis, 1928. 391 p. *DLC, NN*

Last of the Great Scouts: Life Story of Col. William F. Cody. Helen C. Wetmore. Duluth, 1899. 267 p. *DLC, NN, MWA, CSmH*

Buffalo Bill: Full Account of His Adventurous Life. H. L. Williams. N. Y., 1887.

Thrilling Lives of Buffalo Bill, Colonel Wm. F. Cody, Last of the Great Scouts, and Pawnee Bill, Major Gordon W. Lillie, White Chief of the Pawnees. Frank Winch. N. Y., 1911. 224 p. *DLC, NN, CSmH*

2:358

COEUR, JACQUES. *Jacques Coeur, Merchant Prince of the Middle Ages.* Albert B. Kerr. N. Y., 1927. 327 p. *DLC, NN, PU*

COFFIN, CHARLES CARLETON. *Charles C. Coffin, War Correspondent, Traveler, Statesman.* W. E. Griffis. Boston, 1898. 357 p. *DLC, NN*

COFFIN, CHARLES F. *Charles F. Coffin, a Quaker Pioneer.* Mary Johnson. Richmond, 1923. 214 p. *MiD:B*

COFFIN, JAMES HENRY. *Life of James H. Coffin, LL.D.* John C. Clyde. Easton, 1881. 373 p. *DLC, NN*

COGSWELL, JOSEPH GREEN. *Life of Joseph Green Cogswell . . . in His Letters.* Anna E. Tichnor, comp. Cambridge, 1874. 377 p. (Privately Printed) *DLC, NN, MWA, CSmH, MiD:B*

COIT, DANIEL LATHROP. *A Memoir of Daniel Lathrop Coit of Norwich, Connecticut (1754–1833).* William C. Gilman. Norwich, 1907. 70 p. (Privately Printed) *NN, MWA, CSmH*

COIT, DANIEL WADSWORTH. *Memoir of Daniel W. Coit, of Norwich, Conn., 1787–1876.* W. C. Gilman. Cambridge, 1908. 178 p.

NN, MWA, CSmH, PU

COIT, HENRY AUGUSTUS.

Memories of a Great Schoolmaster, Dr. Henry A. Coit. James P. Conover. Boston, 1906. 270 p. DLC, NN, PU

Henry Augustus Coit. First Rector of Saint Pauls School, Concord, New Hampshire. James C. Knox. N. Y., 1915. 149 p.

DLC, NN, PU

COKE, EDWARD. *Edward Coke, Oracle of the Law* . . . Walter H. Lyon and Herman Block. Boston and N. Y., 1929. 383 p.

DLC, NN, PU

COKE, THOMAS.

Life of Thomas Coke. Warren A. Candler. Nashville, 1923. 408 p. DLC, NN

Thomas Coke. F. B. Upham. N. Y., 1910. 128 p. (Makers of Methodism) DLC

COLBURN, WARREN. *Memoir of Warren Colburn.* Theodore Edson. Boston, 1856. 27 p. DLC, NN, MiD:B

COLDEN, CADWALLADER. *Cadwallader Colden, a Representative 18th Century Official.* Alice M. Keys. N. Y., 1906. 375 p.

DLC, NN, MWA, CSmH, PU

COLE, FRED W. *Poems of Fred W. Cole, With a Sketch of His Life.* S. W. Fisher. Albany, 1845. 128 p. DLC, NN, MWA, CSmH

COLE, GEORGE E. *Citizen Cole of Chicago.* Hoyt King. Chicago, 1931. 158 p. DLC, NN

COLE, THOMAS. *Life and Works of Thomas Cole.* L. L. Noble. N. Y., 1853. 415 p. DLC, NN, MWA, PU

COLE, TIMOTHY. *Timothy Cole, Wood-Engraver.* Alpheus P. Cole and Margaret W. Cole. N. Y., 1936. 172 p. DLC, NN, CSmH

COLES, ABRAHAM. *Abraham Coles: Biographical Sketch.* Jonathan A. Coles. N. Y., 1892. 267 p. DLC, NN, MWA

COLES, EDWARD.

Governor Edward Coles. Clarence W. Alvord. Springfield, Ill., 1920. 435 p. (Ill. State Hist. Library Col. v. 15)

DLC, NN, MWA, CSmH, PU

Sketch of Edward Coles, Second Governor of Illinois. E. B. Washburne. Chicago, 1882. 253 p.

DLC, NN, MWA, CSmH, PU, MiD:B

COLFAX, SCHUYLER.

Life of Schuyler Colfax. O. J. Hollister. N. Y., 1886. 535 p.

DLC, NN, CSmH

Life and Public Services of Schuyler Colfax. James D. McCabe. Chicago, 1888. 512 p. *MiD:B*

Life and Public Services of Schuyler Colfax. E. W. Martin. N. Y., 1868. *DLC, MiD:B*

Life of Schuyler Colfax. Ambrose Y. Moore. Phila., 1868. 394 p. *DLC, NN, MWA, CSmH, MiD:B*

    2:264 See GRANT, ULYSSES.

COLLES, JAMES. *James Colles, 1788–1883. Life and Letters.* Emily J. De Forest. N. Y., 1926. 295 p. (Privately Printed) *DLC, NN, MWA, CSmH*

COLLINGWOOD, HERBERT W. 2:497

COLLINS, CASPAR. *Caspar Collins; the Life and Exploits of an Indian Fighter in the Sixties.* Agnes W. Spring. N. Y., 1927. 187 p. *DLC, NN, CSmH*

COLLINS, JOHN. *A Sketch of the Life of the Rev. John Collins.* John McLean. Cincinnati, 1849. 122 p. *CSmH*

COLLINS, PATRICK ANDREW. *Life of Patrick A. Collins, With Some of His Most Notable Public Addresses.* Michael P. Curran. Norwood, Mass., 1906. 276 p. *DLC, NN, MiD:B*

COLLYER, ROBERT. *Life and Letters of Robert Collyer, 1823–1912.* John H. Holmes. N. Y., 1917. 2 vols. *DLC, NN, CSmH*

COLMAN, BENJAMIN. *Life of Rev. Benjamin Colman.* Ebenezer Turrell. Boston, 1749. *RP:JCB*

COLMAN, GEORGE. *George Colman, the Elder; Essayist, Dramatist and Theatrical Manager.* Eugene R. Page. N. Y., 1935. 334 p. *DLC, NN, CSmH, PU*

COLMAN, NORMAN JAY. 2:497

COLMAN, SAMUEL. 2:52

COLT, SAMUEL. *Yankee Arms Maker; the Incredible Career of Samuel Colt.* Jack Rohan. N. Y., 1935. 301 p. *DLC, NN, CSmH, PU*

COLTER, JOHN. *John Colter, Discoverer of Yellowstone Park.* Stallo Vinton. N. Y., 1926. 114 p. *DLC, NN, CSmH*
    2:46

COLTON, WALTER. *Memoirs of Walter Colton in Colton's " The Sea and the Sailor."* H. T. Cheever. N. Y., 1851. 437 p. *DLC, NN, MWA, CSmH*

COLUMBUS, CHRISTOPHER.

Life of Christopher Columbus. John S. C. Abbott. N. Y., 1875. 345 p. *DLC, NN, MiU:C*

Christopher Columbus, His Life and Work. Charles K. Adams. N. Y., 1892. 261 p. (Makers of America) *DLC, NN, MWA, PU, MiU:C*

Christopher Columbus, (1440–1506) The First American Citizen (*By Adoption*). W. A. Alden. N. Y., 1881. 287 p. (Lives of American Worthies) *DLC, MWA, PU*

A History of the Character and Achievements of the So-Called Christopher Columbus. Aaron Goodrich. N. Y., 1874. 403 p. *DLC, NN, MWA, MiU:C*

The Life of Christopher Columbus. Edward E. Hale. Chicago, 1891. 320 p. *DLC, NN, MWA*

Life and Adventures of Christopher Columbus. Alexander Innes. N. Y., 1892.

A History of the Life and Voyages of Christopher Columbus. Washington Irving. N. Y., 1828. 3 vols. *DLC, NN, MWA, CSmH, PU, MiU:C*

The Life and Voyages of Christopher Columbus. Washington Irving. N. Y., 1829. 311 p. *DLC, NN, MWA, CSmH, PU, MiU:C*

Columbus, the Discoverer. F. A. Ober. N. Y., 1906. 299 p. (Heroes of American History) *DLC, NN, MiU:C*

Christopher Columbus, His Life, His Remains . . . J. B. Thacher. N. Y., 1903. 3 vols. *DLC, NN, PU, RP:JCB*

Christopher Columbus. Justin Winsor. Boston, 1891. 674 p. *DLC, NN, MWA, CSmH, PU, MiU:C*

2:78

COLVER, NATHANIEL, AND ROSENBERGER, SUSAN E. *Through Three Centuries; Colver and Rosenberger Lives and Times, 1620–1922.* Jesse L. Rosenberger. Chicago, 1922. 407 p. *DLC, NN, MWA, MiD:B*

COMBER, THOMAS J. *Thomas J. Comber, Missionary Pioneer to the Congo.* John B. Myers. N. Y., 1890. 160 p. *NN*

COMEGYS, CORNELIUS GEORGE. *Cornelius George Comegys, M.D. His Life and Career in the Development of Cincinnati for Nearly Half a Century.* Charles G. Comegys. Cincinnati, 1899. 128 p. (Privately Printed) *DLC, NN, PU*

COMENIUS, JOHN AMOS. *John A. Comenius, Bishop of the Moravians; His Life and Educational Works.* S. S. Laurie. N. Y., 1884. 272 p. *DLC, NN, PU*

COMISKEY, CHARLES ALBERT. *"Commy", the Life Story of Charles A. Comiskey, the "Grand Old Roman" of Baseball.* Gustaf W. Axelson. Chicago, 1919. 320 p. *DLC, NN*

COMSTOCK, ANTHONY.
Anthony Comstock, Roundsman of the Lord. Heywood C. Broun and Margaret Leech. N. Y., 1927. 285 p.
DLC, NN, MWA, PU
Anthony Comstock, Fighter. Charles G. Trumbull. N. Y., 1913. 240 p. *DLC, NN*
COMTE, AUGUSTE. 2:332
CONANT, AUGUSTUS H. *A Man in Earnest: Life of A. H. Conant.* Robert Collyer. Boston, 1868. 230 p. *NN, MWA, CSmH*
CONANT, MRS. JOHN H. *Biography of Mrs. J. H. Conant, the World's Medium of the 19th Century.* John W. Day. Boston, 1873. 322 p.
NN, PU
CONDON, THOMAS. *Thomas Condon, Pioneer Geologist of Oregon.* Ellen C. McCornack. Eugene, Ore., 1928. 355 p. *DLC, NN*
CONDORCET, MARIE JEAN.
Condorcet, the Torch Bearer of the French Revolution. Anne E. Burlingame. Boston, 1930. 249 p. *DLC, NN*
Condorcet and the Rise of Liberalism. Jacob S. Schapiro. N. Y., 1934. 311 p. *DLC, NN*
CONE, SPENCER HOUGHTON. *Life of Spencer H. Cone.* Edward W. and S. W. Cone. N. Y., 1856. 484 p. *DLC, NN, MWA, CSmH*
CONEY, JOHN. *John Coney, Silversmith, 1655–1722.* Hermann F. Clarke. Boston, 1932. 16 p. *DLC, NN, MWA*
CONFUCIUS. 2:336–665
CONKLING, ROSCOE.
Roscoe Conkling; the Distinguished American Statesman and Brilliant Advocate. James P. Boyd. Phila., 1888. 64 p.
DLC, NN
The Gentleman From New York; a Life of Roscoe Conkling. Donald B. Chidsey. New Haven, 1935. 438 p. *DLC, NN, PU*
Life and Letters of Roscoe Conkling, Orator, Statesman, Advocate. Alfred R. Conkling. N. Y., 1889. 709 p.
DLC, NN, MWA, CSmH, PU, MiD:B
CONNOLLY, JOHN. *John Connolly, a Tory of the Revolution.* C. M. Burton. Worcester, Mass., 1909. 38 p. *DLC, NN, MiD:B*
CONNOR, BENJAMIN. *Rekindling Camp Fires, the Exploits of Ben Arnold (Connor) (Wa-si-cu Tam-a-he-ca).* Lewis F. Crawford. Bismarck, N. D., 1926. 324 p. *DLC, NN, CSmH*
CONRIED, HEINRICH. *Life of Heinrich Conried.* Montrose J. Moses. N. Y., 1916. 367 p. *DLC, NN*

CONSTANT, BENJAMIN. *Benjamin Constant.* Elizabeth W. Schermerhorn. Boston, 1924. 424 p. *DLC, NN, PU*

CONWELL, RUSSELL HERMAN.

Modern Temple and Temples; a Sketch of the Life and Works of Russell H. Conwell. Robert J. Burdette. N. Y., 1894. 385 p. *DLC, NN, PU*

Russell H. Conwell, Founder of the Institutional Church in America, the Work and the Man ... Agnes R. Burr. Phila., 1905. 365 p. *DLC, NN*

Russell H. Conwell and His Works. One Man's Interpretation of Life. Agnes R. Burr. Phila., 1917. 438 p. *DLC, NN, MWA, PU*

Life of Russell H. Conwell, Preacher, Lecturer, Philanthropist. Albert H. Smith. N. Y., 1899. 335 p. *DLC, PU*

CONYNGHAM, GUSTAVUS. *Captain Gustavus Conyngham.* Charles H. Jones. Phila., 1903. 32 p. *DLC, NN, CSmH, PU*

COOK, DAVID. *Dave Cook of the Rockies.* Edwin V. Westrate and William R. Collier. N. Y., 1936. 224 p. *DLC, MWA*

COOK, GEORGE CRAM. *Road to the Temple; the Life of George Cram Cook.* Susan Glaspell. N. Y., 1927. 445 p. *DLC, NN, PU*

COOK, JAMES. *The Boy Who Loved the Sea; the Story of Capt. James Cook.* Mary H. Wade. N. Y., 1931. 247 p. *DLC*
2:387

COOKE, GEORGE FREDERICK. *Memoirs of George Frederick Cooke.* William Dunlap. London, 1813. 2 vols. *DLC, NN, CSmH, PU*

COOKE, JAY. *Jay Cooke, Financier of the Civil War.* Ellis P. Oberholtzer. Phila., 1907. 2 vols. *DLC, NN, MWA, PU*
2:451

COOKE, JOHN ESTEN. *John Esten Cooke, Virginian.* John O. Beaty. N. Y., 1922. 175 p. (Col. Univ. Studies in Eng.)
DLC, NN, MWA, CSmH, PU

COOKE, PHILIP PENDLETON. 2:503

COOKMAN, ALFRED. *Life of ... Alfred Cookman; With Some Account of His Father, George G. Cookman.* Henry B. Ridgaway. N. Y., 1873. 480 p. *DLC, NN, PU MiD:B*

COOLIDGE, ARCHIBALD CARY. *Archibald Cary Coolidge, Life and Letters.* Harold J. Coolidge. Boston, 1932. 368 p.
DLC, NN, MWA, CSmH

COOLIDGE, CALVIN.

The Boyhood Days of President Calvin Coolidge; or, From the Green Mountains to the White House. Ernest C. Carpenter. Rutland, Vt., 1925. 188 p. *DLC, NN, MWA*

The Rise of Saint Calvin; Merry Sidelights on the Career of Mr. Coolidge. Duff Gilfond. N. Y., 1932. 294 p.

DLC, NN, MWA

Life of Calvin Coolidge. Horace Green. N. Y., 1924. 263 p.

DLC, NN, PU

Calvin Coolidge, From a Green Mountain Farm to the White House. Michael E. Hennessy. N. Y., 1924. 197 p.

DLC, NN, MWA

Legend of Calvin Coolidge. Cameron Rogers. N. Y., 1928. 179 p. *DLC, NN, MWA, PU*

Cal Coolidge, President. Roland D. Sawyer. Boston, 1924. 128 p. *DLC, NN, MWA*

Calvin Coolidge. His First Biography. R. M. Washburn. Boston, 1923. 150 p. *DLC, NN, MWA, CSmH, PU*

Calvin Coolidge, the Man Who is President. William A. White. N. Y., 1925. 252 p. *DLC, NN, MWA, PU*

President Coolidge; a Contemporary Estimate. Edward E. Whiting. Boston, 1923. 208 p. *DLC, NN, CSmH, PU*

The Preparation of Calvin Coolidge. An Interpretation. Robert A. Woods. Boston, 1924. 288 p. *DLC NN, PU, MiD:B* 2:94

COOMBS, ISAAC. *A Sketch of the Life and Confessions of Isaac Coombs.* Middletown, 1787. *DLC*

COOPER, JAMES FENIMORE.

James Fenimore Cooper. Henry W. Boynton. N. Y., 1931. 408 p. *DLC, NN, MWA, CSmH, PU*

James Fenimore Cooper. W. B. S. Clymer. Boston, 1900. 149 p. (Beacon Biographies) *DLC, NN, PU*

James Fenimore Cooper. Thomas R. Lounsbury. Boston and N. Y., 1883. 306 p. (A.M.L.) *DLC, NN, MWA, CSmH, PU*

James Fenimore Cooper. Mary E. Phillips. N. Y., 1913. 368 p. *DLC, NN, MWA, PU*

Fenimore Cooper, Critic of His Times. Robert E. Spiller. N. Y., 1931. 337 p. *DLC, NN, MWA, PU*

COOPER, JOSEPH W. *A Pastoral Prince; the History of . . . J. W. Cooper.* Frank Sands. Santa Barbara, 1893. 190 p. *CSmH*

COOPER, MYLES. *Myles Cooper . . . Second President of King's College.* C. H. Vance. N. Y., 1930. 286 p. *CSmH*

COOPER, PETER.

Life and Character of Peter Cooper. Charles E. Lester. N. Y., 1883. 116 p. *DLC*

Peter Cooper. Rositer W. Raymond. Boston and N. Y., 1901.
109 p. (Riverside Biographies) *DLC, NN*
Sketch of the Life and Opinions of Peter Cooper. J. C. Zachos,
ed. N. Y., 1876. 96 p. *DLC, NN, MWA*
2:109–128–331–623–660. See HEWITT, ABRAM S.
COONER, SAMUEL. 2:612
COOPER, THOMAS. *Public Life of Thomas Cooper, 1783–1839.*
Dumas Malone. New Haven, 1926. 432 p. (Yale Hist. Pub.)
DLC, NN, CSmH, PU, MiD:B
COOPER, THOMAS ABTHORPE. *Life of Thomas A. Cooper.* Jas. N.
Ireland. N. Y., 1888. 162 p. (Dunlap Society of New York,
Ser. 1. v. 5) *DLC, NN, MWA, CSmH, PU*
COPE, EDWARD DRINKER.
Biographical Memoir of Edward Drinker Cope, 1840–1897.
Henry F. Osborn. Washington, 1930. 317 p. *DLC, PU*
*Cope: Master Naturalist; the Life and Letters of Edward
Drinker Cope.* Henry F. Osborn and Helen A. Warren. Prince-
ton, 1931. 740 p. *DLC, NN, PU*
COPELAND, CHARLES TOWNSEND. 2:592
COPERNICUS, NIKOLAUS. 2:79–335
COPLAND, PATRICK. *Memoir of Rev. Patrick Copland, Rector Elect
for the First Projected College in the U. S.* Edward D. Neill.
N. Y., 1871. 96 p. *DLC, NN, MWA, MiD:B, RP:JCB*
COPLEY, JOHN SINGLETON.
Domestic and Artistic Life of J. Singleton Copley, R.A. Martha
B. Amory. Boston, 1882. 478 p. *DLC, NN, MWA, CSmH*
Life and Works of John Singleton Copley. F. W. Bayley. Bos-
ton, 1915. 285 p. *CSmH*
*A Sketch of the Life and a List of Some of the Works of John
Singleton Copley.* Augustus T. Perkins. Boston, 1873. 144 p.
DLC, NN, MWA, MiD:B, MiU:C
2:429
COREY, ARTHUR DELORAINE. *Arthur Deloraine Corey, 1866–1891.* A
Memorial. Cambridge, 1892. 231 p. *DLC, NN, MWA*
CORNEILLE, PIERRE. *Corneille.* Leon H. Vincent. Boston, 1901.
198 p. *DLC, NN, PU*
CORNELIUS, ELIAS. *Memoir of Elias Cornelius.* B. B. Edwards.
Boston, 1833. 360 p. *DLC, NN, MWA, PU*
CORNELL, KATHERINE. 2:336
CORNELL, EZRA.
Biography of Ezra Cornell, Founder of Cornell University.
Alonzo B. Cornell. N. Y., 1884. 322 p. *DLC, NN, MWA, PU*

Ezra Cornell; a Character Study. Albert W. Smith. Ithaca, 1934. 238 p. *DLC, NN, CSmH, PU*

CORNPLANTER, CHIEF. *Historical Sketch of . . . the Cornplanter.* J. R. Snowden. Harrisburg, 1867. 115 p. *CSmH*

CORNWALL, BARRY. (BRYAN W. PROCTER) See PROCTER, BRYAN W.

CORNWALEYS, THOMAS. *Thomas Cornwaleys, Commissioner and Counsellor of Maryland.* George B. Stratemeier. Washington, 1922. 139 p. (Cath. Univ. of America Studies in Amer. Church History. vol. II) *DLC, NN, CSmH, PU*

CORNWELL, HENRY SYLVESTER. *Henry S. Cornwell, Poet of Fancy.* Ellen M. Frisbie. New London, Conn., 1906. 23 p. *DLC, NN*

CORRIGAN, DOMINIC. 2:678

CORTEZ, HERNANDO.
History of Hernando Cortez. J. S. C. Abbott. N. Y., 1855. 348 p. *DLC, NN, MWA*
Hernando Cortez, Conqueror of Mexico. F. A. Ober. N. Y., 1905. 291 p. (Heroes of Am. History) *DLC, NN, PU, MiU:C*
Mexico, and the Life of the Conqueror Fernando Cortez. William H. Prescott. N. Y., 1902. 2 vols. *DLC, NN, MWA, MiU:C*
Stout Cortez; a Biography of the Spanish Conquest. Henry M. Robinson. N. Y., 1931. 347 p. *DLC, NN, PU*
Cortes the Conqueror; the Exploits of the Earliest and Greatest of the Gentlemen Adventurers in the New World. Henry D. Sedgwick. Indianapolis, 1926. 390 p. *DLC, NN, PU*
2:293

CORWIN, THOMAS.
Life and Speeches of Thomas Corwin. Josiah Morrow. Cincinnati, 1896. 477 p. *DLC, NN, MWA, CSmH*
Thomas Corwin. A Sketch. A. P. Russell. Cincinnati, 1881. 128 p. *DLC, NN, MWA, CSmH*
2:431

COTTON, CHARLES. *Life and Poetry of Charles Cotton.* C. J. Sembower. Phila., 1911. 127 p. *CSmH*

COTTON, JOHN.
The Life of John Cotton. Alexander W. M'Clure. Boston, 1846. 300 p. *DLC, NN, MWA, CSmH*
The Life and Death of the Deservedly Famous Mr. John Cotton, Late Reverend Teacher of the Church of Christ in Boston. John Norton. Cambridge, 1658. 51 p. *MWA, RP:JCB*
Reprinted London, 1658 with the Title; *Abel Being Dead Yet Speaketh, or, the Life and Death of . . . John Cotton . . .*
CSmH, MiU:C

Reissued as *Memoirs of John Cotton,* with preface and notes by
Enoch Pond. Boston, 1834. 108 p.   *NN*
    John Cotton's Life and Letters. A. Young. Boston, 1846.
(Chronicles of the First Planters, etc.)
    2:246–405

COUGHLIN, CHARLES EDWARD.
    *Father Coughlin of the Shrine of the Little Flower; an Account
of the Life, Work and Message of Rev. Charles E. Coughlin.* Ruth
Migglebee. Boston, 1933. 321 p.   *DLC, NN*
    Father Charles E. Coughlin; an Authorized Biography. Louis
B. Ward. Detroit, 1933. 352 p.   *DLC, NN*

COVELL, ALANSON AND LEMUEL.
    *Memoir of the Late Rev. Lemuel Covell, Missionary to the Tus-
carora Indians and the Province of Upper Canada* . . . Deidamia C.
Brown. Brandon, Vt., 1839. 226 p.   *NN, MiD:B*
    *Memoir of the Late Rev. Lemuel Covell . . . also A Memoir of
Rev. Alanson L. Covell.* D. C. Brown. Brandon, Vt., 1839. 174 p.
226 p. 2 vols. in 1.   *DLC, NN, MWA*

COWELL, EDWARD BYLES. *Life and Letters of Edward Byles Cowell.*
G. Cowell. N. Y., 1904. 480 p.   *DLC*

COWLEY, JOSEPH. *Sketch of the Life and Character of the Late Mr.
Joseph Cowley.* John Holland. N. Y., 1847. 104 p.   *NN*

COWPER, WILLIAM. *William Cowper.* Mary V. H. Terhune. N. Y.,
1899. 237 p.   *DLC, NN, CSmH*

COX, JACOB D. *Gen. Jacob Dolson Cox; Early Life and Military
Services.* W. C. Cochran. Oberlin, 1901.   *CSmH*

COX, JAMES M. *Cox—The Man.* Roger W. Babson. N. Y., 1920.
128 p.   *DLC, MWA*

COX, MELVILLE BEVERIDGE. *Remains of Melville B. Cox, Late Missionary to Liberia. With a Memoir.* Gershom F. Cox. Boston,
1835. 240 p.   *DLC, NN, MiD:B*

COX, SAMUEL SULLIVAN. *Life of Samuel S. Cox.* W. V. Z. Cox and
M. H. Northrup. Syracuse, N. Y., 1899. 280 p.   *DLC, NN*

COX, THOMAS. *Thomas Cox.* Harvey Reid. Iowa City, 1909. 257 p.
    (Iowa Biographical Series)   *DLC, NN, MWA, MiD:B*

CRABBE, GEORGE. 2:293

CRABTREE, LOTTA. *Troupers of the Gold Coast; or, the Rise of Lotta
Crabtree.* Constance M. Rourke. N. Y., 1928. 262 p.
        DLC, NN, MWA, CSmH, PU

CRAIG, AUSTIN. *Life and Letters of Austin Craig.* W. S. Harwood.
N. Y., 1908. 394 p.   *DLC, NN*

CRAIG, ISAAC. *Sketch of the Life and Services of Isaac Craig.* Neville B. Craig. Pittsburgh, 1854. 70 p.

DLC, NN, MWA, CSmH, MiU:C

CRAIG, LEWIS. *Lewis Craig, the Pioneer Baptist Preacher; His Life, Labors, and Character.* Lewis N. Thompson. Louisville, 1910. 90 p. *DLC*

CRAMP, CHARLES HENRY. *Memoirs of Charles H. Cramp.* A. C. Buell. Phila., 1906. 269 p. *DLC, NN*

CRANCH, CHRISTOPHER PEARSE. *The Life and Letters of Christopher Pearse Cranch.* Leonora C. Scott. Boston, 1917. 395 p.

DLC, NN, MWA, CSmH, PU

CRANE, AARON. *Aaron Crane.* Henry Tate. N. Y., 1901. 248 p.

DLC, NN

CRANE, JAMES CAMPBELL. *A Christian Merchant. A Memoir of James C. Crane.* J. L. Burrows. Charleston, 1858. 90 p.

DLC, NN, CSmH

CRANE, STEPHEN. *Stephen Crane: A Study in American Letters.* Thomas Beer. N. Y., 1923. 248 p. *DLC, NN, CSmH, PU*

CRANE, WINTHROP MURRAY. *W. Murray Crane, a Man and Brother.* Solomon B. Griffin. Boston, 1926. 202 p. *DLC, NN, MWA, PU*

CRANE, ZENAS. *Pioneer Paper Making in Berkshire. Life, Life-Work and Influence of Zenas Crane.* Joseph E. A. Smith. Holyoke, Mass., n.d. 55 p. *DLC, NN, CSmH*

CRANMER, THOMAS.

The Life and Times of Thomas Cranmer. Hannah F. S. Lee. Boston, 1841. 277 p. *DLC, NN, MWA*

The Life of Archbishop Cranmer. J. N. Norton. N. Y., 1863.

The Three Pelicans: Archbishop Cranmer and the Tudor Juggernaut. Arthur Styron. N. Y., 1932. 414 p. *DLC, NN*

CRAPO, HENRY HOWLAND. *The Story of Henry Howland Crapo, 1804–1869.* Henry H. Crapo. Boston, 1933. 272 p.

DLC, NN, MWA, CSmH, MiD:B, MiU:C

CRAPSEY, ADELAIDE. *Adelaide Crapsey.* Mary E. Osborn. Boston, 1933. 119 p. *DLC, NN, PU*

CRATTY, MABEL. *Mabel Cratty, Leader in the Art of Leadership.* Margaret E. Burton. N. Y., 1929. 248 p. *DLC, NN*

CRAVEN. *Reverend Craven of Virginia, The Bold Frontier Preacher.* J. B. Wakeley. Cincinnati, 1869. *DLC*

CRAVEN, AUGUSTUS. *Memoir of Mrs. Augustus Craven.* M. C. Bishop. N. Y., 1895. 2 vols. *DLC, NN*

CRAVEN, BRATON. *The Life of Braton Craven.* Jerome Dowd. Raleigh, N. C., 1896. 246 p. *DLC, NN*

CRAWFORD, FRANCIS MARION. *My Cousin, F. Marion Crawford.* Maud H. Elliott. N. Y., 1934. 318 p. *DLC, NN, PU*

CRAWFORD, THOMAS. 2:394

CRAWFORD, WILLIAM HARRIS. *Giant Days; or, The Life and Times of William H. Crawford.* J. E. D. Shipp. Americus, Ga., 1909. 266 p. *DLC, NN, PU, MiU:C*

2:590

CRAZY HORSE. 2:204

CREE, THOMAS KIRBY. *Thomas Kirby Cree; a Memorial.* John K. Cree and H. S. Ninde. N. Y., 1914. 200 p. *DLC, NN*

CREED, WIGGINTONE. 2:233

CREIGHTON, THOMAS. *Thomas Creighton.* John C. Mendenhall. n.p., n.d. 12 p. (Papers of Hist. Soc. of Frankford, Phila., Pa.)

CRESAP, MICHAEL. *Biographical Sketch of the Late Capt. Michael Cresap.* J. J. Jacob. Cumberland, 1826. 123 p. *DLC, NN, MWA, CSmH, MiD:B*

CRÈVECŒUR, ST. JEAN DE. *St. Jean de Crèvecœur.* Julia P. Mitchell. N. Y., 1916. 362 p. (Col. Univ. Studies in Eng.) *DLC, NN, MWA, CSmH, PU*

CRISPIN, SAINT. 2:406

CRITTENDEN, ALONZO. *Sketch of the Life, Character and Work of Alonzo Crittenden, A.M., Ph.D.* Margaret E. Winslow, ed. N. Y., 1885. 241 p. *DLC, NN*

CRITTENDEN, JOHN JORDAN. *Life of John J. Crittenden. With Selections From His Correspondence and Speeches.* C. Coleman, ed. Phila., 1871. 2 vols. *DLC, NN, CSmH, PU*

CRITTENDEN, THOMAS THEODORE. *The Crittenden Memoirs.* Henry H. Crittenden, comp. N. Y., 1936. 542 p. *DLC, NN, CSmH*

CROCKER, ALVAH. *Life and Times of Alvah Crocker.* William B. Wheelwright. Boston, 1923. 114 p. (Privately Printed) *DLC, NN, MWA, PU*

CROCKER, NATHAN BOURNE. *A Memorial of Nathan B. Crocker, Late Rector of St. John's Church, Providence, R. I.* Richard B. Duane. Providence, 1866. 103 p. *DLC, NN, MWA, MiD:B*

CROCKER, WILLIAM G. *Memoir of William G. Crocker, Missionary in West Africa.* Rebecca B. Medbery. Boston, 1848. 300 p.

CROCKETT, DAVID.
Life and Adventures of David Crockett. Cincinnati, 1833. 204 p. *CSmH*

David Crockett. J. S. C. Abbott. N. Y., 1874. 350 p.
DLC, NN, CSmH
David Crockett. Charles F. Allen. Phila., 1911. 308 p.
DLC

Life of Col. David Crockett: Added Sketches of Gen. Sam Houston, Santa Anna, and Others. Edward S. Ellis. Phila., 1884. 271 p. *DLC, NN, CSmH*

Davy Crockett. Constance M. Rourke. N. Y., 1934. 276 p.
DLC, NN, MWA, CSmH, PU

2:358

CROCKETT, JOSEPH. *Biographical Sketch of Colonel Joseph Crockett.* Samuel W. Price. Louisville, 1909. 85 p. (Filson Club Pub. No. 24) *DLC, NN, MWA, MiU:C*

CROES, JOHN. *Life of Bishop Croes of New Jersey.* John N. Norton. N. Y., 1859. 208 p. *DLC, NN, MWA*

CROGHAN, GEORGE. *George Croghan and the Westward Movement, 1741–1782.* Albert T. Volwiler. Cleveland, 1926. 370 p.
DLC, NN, MWA, CSmH, PU

CROKER, RICHARD.

Richard Croker. Alfred H. Lewis. N. Y., 1901. 372 p.
DLC, NN, MWA, CSmH

Master of Manhattan; the Life of Richard Croker. Theodore L. Stoddard. N. Y., 1931. 279 p. *DLC, NN, MWA, PU, MiD:B*

CROMWELL, OLIVER.

Life of Oliver Cromwell. Charles Adams. N. Y., 1867. 268 p.
DLC

Life of Oliver Cromwell. J. T. Headley. N. Y., 1848. 446 p.
DLC, NN, CSmH, PU

Oliver Cromwell. Theodore Roosevelt. N. Y., 1900. 260 p.
DLC, NN, MWA, CSmH

2:7–246–293–334–386

CROSBY, ENOCH. *The Spy Unmasked; or, Memoirs of Enoch Crosby.* H. L. Barnum. N. Y., 1829. 2 vols. *DLC, NN, MWA, CSmH*

CROSWELL, WILLIAM. *A Memoir of the Late Rev. William Croswell.* Harry Croswell. N. Y., 1853. 528 p. *DLC, NN, MWA, PU*

CROTHERS, SAMUEL. *Life and Writings of Rev. Samuel Crothers.* A. Ritchie. Cincinnati, 1857. *MiD:B*

CROTHERS, SAMUEL McCHORD. 2:487

CROZER, JOHN PRICE. *Life of John P. Crozer.* J. W. Smith. Phila., 1868. 264 p. *DLC, MWA, CSmH, PU*

CROZET, CLAUDIUS. *Claudius Crozet, Soldier.* William Couper. Charlottesville, 1936. 221 p.   *CSmH*

CRUMMER, LEROY. *A Doctor's Odyssey; a Sentimental Record of LeRoy Crummer.* Alexander G. Beaman. Balt., 1935. 340 p.   *DLC, NN, CSmH*

CUDWORTH, WARREN HANDEL. *Memorial of Warren H. Cudworth.* Angeline M. Cudworth. Boston, 1884. 380 p.   *DLC, NN, MWA*

CULBERSON, CHARLES ALLEN. *Charles Allen Culberson. His Life, Character and Public Service.* James W. Madden. Austin, Tex., 1929. 351 p.   *DLC, NN*

CUMBERLAND, RICHARD. *Richard Cumberland, His Life and Dramatic Works.* Stanley T. Williams. New Haven, 1917. 365 p.   *DLC, NN, CSmH, PU*

CUMINGS, HENRY H. *In Memoriam Henry H. Cumings.* J. N. Fradenburgh. Oil City, Pa., 1913. 236 p.   *CSmH*

CUMMINS, GEORGE DAVID. *Memoir of G. D. Cummins, First Bishop of Reformed Episcopal Church.* Mrs. G. D. Cummins. Phila., 1878. 544 p.   *MWA, PU*

CURIE, MME MARIE. 2:286–301–348–506

CURLEY, MICHAEL JOSEPH. *Life of Archbishop Curley, Champion of Catholic Education.* Vincent de Paul Fitzpatrick. Balt., 1929. 124 p.   *DLC, NN*

CURRIER, WARREN. *A Christian Lawyer. A Sketch of the Life and Work of Hon. Warren Currier.* George C. Adams. St. Louis, 1893. 124 p.   *NN*

CURRY, JABEZ LAMAR MONROE. *J. L. M. Curry, a Biography.* E. A. Alderman and A. C. Gordon. N. Y., 1911. 468 p.   *DLC, NN, PU*

CURTIN, ANDREW GREGG.

    Andrew Gregg Curtin: His Life and Services. W. H. Egle. Phila., 1895. 521 p.   *DLC, NN, CSmH, PU*

    Life and Services of Andrew Curtin. A. K. McClure. Harrisburg, Pa., 1895. 35 p.   *DLC, NN, CSmH, PU*

CURTIS, ALFRED ALLEN. *Life and Characteristics of Right Rev. Alfred A. Curtis, D.D., Second Bishop of Wilmington.* Sisters of the Visitation, comp. N. Y., 1913. 446 p.   *DLC, NN*

CURTIS, BENJAMIN ROBBINS. *Memoir of Benjamin R. Curtis.* George T. Curtis. Boston, 1879. 2 vols.   *DLC, NN, MWA, PU*

CURTIS, CHARLES. *From Kaw Tepee to Capitol; the Life Story of Charles Curtis, Indian.* Don C. Seitz. N. Y., 1928. 223 p.   *DLC, NN, MWA, PU*

2:190

CURTIS, CYRUS HERMANN KOTZSCHMAR. *A Man From Maine; Cyrus H. K. Curtis.* Edward Bok. N. Y., 1923. 278 p.
DLC, NN, PU

CURTIS, GEORGE WILLIAM. *George William Curtis.* Edward Cary. Boston, 1894. 343 p. (A.M.L.) *DLC, NN, MWA, CSmH, PU*

CURTIS, JOSEPH. *Memoir of Joseph Curtis, a Model Man.* Catharine M. Sedgwick. N. Y., 1858. 200 p. *DLC, NN*

CUSHING, CALEB.
A Memorial of Caleb Cushing, From the City of Newburyport ... Newburyport City Council, 1879. 178 p. *DLC, NN, MWA*
Life of Caleb Cushing. Claude M. Fuess. N. Y., 1923. 2 vols. *DLC, NN, MWA, CSmH, PU*

CUSHING, WILLIAM. 2:230

CUSHMAN, CHARLOTTE.
Charlotte Cushman. Clara E. Clement. Boston, 1882. 193 p. (American Actor Series) *DLC, NN, MWA*
A Life of Charlotte Cushman. William T. Price. N. Y. and Paris, 1894. 180 p. *DLC, NN*
Charlotte Cushman. Her Letters and Memories of Her Life. Emma Stebbins. Boston, 1878. 308 p.
DLC, NN, MWA, CSmH, PU, MiD:B
Charlotte Cushman. Clara E. C. Waters. Boston, 1882. 193 p. *DLC, NN, PU*
2:87

CUSHMAN, PAULINE. *Life and Adventures of Pauline Cushman.* F. L. Sarmiento. Phila., 1865. 374 p. *DLC, NN, MWA, CSmH*

CUSHMAN, ROBERT. 2:141

CUSTER, GEORGE ARMSTRONG.
Custer, the Last of the Cavaliers. Frazier Hunt. N. Y., 1928. 209 p. *DLC, NN, MWA*
Glory Hunter. A Life of General Custer. Frederick F. Van de Water. Indianapolis, 1934. 394 p. *DLC, NN, MiD:B*
A Complete Life of Gen. George A. Custer. Frederick Whittaker. N. Y., 1876. 648 p. *DLC, NN, MWA, CSmH, MiD:B*

CUTBUSH, EDWARD. *Edward Cutbush, M.D. The Nestor of the Medical Corps of the Navy.* F. L. Pleadwell. N. Y., 1923. (Reprinted from Annals of Medical History, vol. 5, No. 4, pp. 337–386) *DLC, NN, MWA*

CUTBUSH, JAMES. *James Cutbush, an American Chemist, 1788–1823.* Edgar F. Smith. Phila., 1919. 94 p. *DLC, NN, PU*

CUTLER, BENJAMIN CLARKE.
   Memoir of Benjamin C. Cutler. Horatio Gary. N. Y., 1865.
   439 p.   *DLC, NN, MWA, MiD:B*
   Sketch of the Life and Ministry of B. C. Cutler. S. Tyng.
   N. Y., 1863. 162 p.   *DLC, NN, MiD:B*
CUTLER, EBENEZER. *A Memorial of Rev. Ebenezer Cutler.* Ezra H.
   Byington, ed. Boston, n.d. 64 p.   *MWA*
CUTLER, EPHRAIM. *Life and Times of Ephraim Cutler; Prepared from
   His Journals and Correspondence . . . ; With Biographical Sketches
   of Jervis Cutler and W. P. Cutler.* Julia P. Cutler. Cincinnati,
   1890. 353 p.   *DLC, NN, MWA, CSmH, MiD:B*
CUTLER, MANASSEH. *Life, Journals and Correspondence of Manasseh
   Cutler.* Julia and W. P. Cutler. Cincinnati, 1888. 2 vols.
                            DLC, NN, MWA, CSmH, PU
CUTTER, CHARLES AMMI. *Charles Ammi Cutter.* William P. Cutter.
   Chicago, 1931. 72 p.   *DLC, NN, PU*
CUTTER, LEONARD R. *Leonard R. Cutter. In Memoriam.* Boston,
   1898. 301 p. (Privately Printed)   *DLC, MWA*
CUTTS, ADELE. 2:518
CUVIER, GEORGES. *Memoirs of Baron Cuvier.* Sarah W. Lee. N. Y.,
   1833. 197 p.   *DLC, NN, MWA, CSmH*
   2:79–293.
CYRUS. *History of Cyrus the Great.* Jacob Abbott. N. Y., 1878.
   289 p.   *DLC, NN, PU*
DABNEY, ROBERT LEWIS. *Life and Letters of Robert L. Dabney.* T.
   C. Johnson. Richmond, 1903. 585 p.   *DLC, NN, CSmH*
DABNEY, THOMAS SMITH GREGORY. *Memorials of a Southern Planter.*
   Susan D. Smedes. Balt., 1888. 341 p.   *DLC, NN, MWA*
DAHLGREN, JOHN ADOLPHUS. *Memoir of John A. Dahlgren, Rear-
   Admiral, U. S. N.* Mrs. M. V. Dahlgren. Boston, 1882. 660 p.
                            DLC, NN, MWA, CSmH
DAHLGREN, ULRIC.
   In Memoriam. Colonel Ulric Dahlgren. Boston, 1865. 108 p.
                            DLC, MWA, CSmH
   Memoir of Ulric Dahlgren. John A. Dahlgren. Phila., 1872.
   308 p.   *DLC, NN, MWA, CSmH*
DAHLMAN, JAMES. *Mayor Jim.* Fred Carey. Omaha, 1930. 175 p.
                            DLC, NN
DALE, SAMUEL. *Life and Times of . . . Samuel Dale, the Mississippi
   Partisan.* J. F. H. Claiborne. N. Y., 1860. 233 p.
                    DLC, NN, MWA, PU, MiD:B, MiU:C

DALLAS, ALEXANDER JAMES. *Life and Writings of Alexander James Dallas.* George M. Dallas. Phila., 1871. 487 p.   *DLC, NN*
2:110

DALLAS, GEORGE MIFFLIN.
Brief Memoir of George Mifflin Dallas. Phila., 1853. 18 p.
DLC, MWA
Eulogy Upon the Hon. George Mifflin Dallas. Charles J. Biddle.
n.p., n.d. 51 p. (Delivered Before the Bar of Philadelphia, Feb.
11, 1865)   *DLC, NN, MWA, PU, MiD:B*

DALTON, CHARLES HENRY. *Memoir of Charles Henry Dalton.* Roger
B. Merriman. Cambridge, 1909. 28 p.   *DLC, NN, MWA*

DALTON, EDWARD BARRY. *Memorial of Edward B. Dalton, M.D.*
N. Y., 1872. 49 p.   *DLC, NN, MWA*

DALTON, JOHN. 2:348

DALTON, JOHN CALL. *A Memorial of John C. Dalton.* John O.
Green. Cambridge, 1864. 18 p.   *DLC, NN, MWA, MiD:B*

DALY, ARNOLD. *Arnold Daly.* Berthold H. Goldsmith. N. Y., 1927.
57 p.   *DLC, NN*

DALY, AUGUSTIN. *Life of Augustin Daly.* Joseph F. Daly. N. Y.,
1917. 672 p.   *DLC, NN, CSmH, PU*

DAMEN, ARNOLD. *Arnold Damen; a Chapter in the Making of Chicago.* Joseph P. Conroy. N. Y., 1930. 329 p.   *DLC, NN*

DAMIEN, FATHER. [JOSEPH DAMIEN DE VEUSTER] *The Samaritans
of Molokai: the Lives of Father Damien and Brother Dutton Among
the Lepers.* Charles J. Dutton. N. Y., 1932. 286 p.
DLC, NN

DAMPIER, WILLIAM. *Captain William Dampier, Buccaneer-Author.*
Willard H. Bonner. Stanford Univ., Calif., 1934. 234 p.
DLC, NN, CSmH, PU

DANA, CHARLES ANDERSON.
When Dana Was the Sun; a Story of Personal Journalism.
Charles J. Rosebault. N. Y., 1931. 294 p.
DLC, NN, MWA, CSmH, PU
Life of Charles A. Dana. James H. Wilson. N. Y., 1907. 544 p.
DLC, NN, MWA, CSmH, PU, MiD:B

DANA, FRANCIS. *Francis Dana, a Puritan Diplomat at the Court of
Catherine the Great.* William P. Cresson. N. Y., 1930. 397 p.
DLC, NN, MWA, CSmH

DANA, HENSHAW. *Five Songs of Henshaw Dana. With a Memoir.*
Charles A. Chase. Boston, 1884. 57 p.   *NN, MWA*

DANA, JAMES DWIGHT. *Life of James Dwight Dana, Scientific Explorer, Mineralogist, Geologist, Professor in Yale University.* Daniel C. Gilman. N. Y., 1899. 409 p. *DLC, NN, CSmH, PU, MiD:B*

DANA, JOHN COTTON. *John Cotton Dana, 1856–1929.* Newark, N. J., 1930. 125 p. *DLC, NN, MWA, CSmH*

DANA, RICHARD HENRY.
Richard Henry Dana. A Biography. Charles F. Adams, Jr. Boston, 1890. Rev. Ed., Boston, 1891. 2 vols.
DLC, NN, MWA, CSmH, PU
Richard Henry Dana, 1851–1931. Bliss Perry. Boston, 1933. 265 p. *DLC, NN*

DANICAN, FRANÇOIS ANDRÉ. *The Life of Philidor, Musician and Chess-Player.* George Allen. Phila., 1863. 156 p.
DLC, MWA, CSmH, PU

DANIELS, JOHN MONCURE.
John M. Daniels' Latch-Key: A Memoir of the Late Editor of the " Richmond Examiner." G. W. Bagby. Lynchburg, 1868. 40 p. *DLC*
The Richmond Examiner During the War; or, The Writings of John M. Daniels, With a Memoir of His Life. F. S. Daniel. N. Y., 1868. 232 p. *DLC, CSmH*

DANIELSON, GEORGE WHITMAN. *Memorial of George Whitman Danielson.* Providence, 1872. 78 p. *DLC, MWA*

DANTE.
Dante and His Influence. Thomas N. Page. N. Y., 1922. 306 p. *DLC, NN, PU*
Life of Dante Alighieri. Charles A. Dinsmore. Boston, 1919. 239 p. *DLC, NN, PU*
Dante. An Elementary Book For Those Who Seek in The Great Poet The Teacher of Spiritual Life. Henry D. Sedgwick. New Haven, 1918. 187 p. *DLC, NN, PU*
A Biography of Dante Alighieri, Set Forth as His Life Journey. Denton J. Snider. St. Louis, 1922. 478 p. *DLC, NN, PU*
2:82

DANTON, GEORGES-JACQUES. *Danton and the French Revolution.* Charles F. Warwick. Phila., 1908. 467 p. *DLC, NN, PU*

DARIUS. *History of Darius the Great.* Jacob Abbott. Phila., 1900. 231 p. *DLC, NN*

DARLINGTON, WILLIAM. *The Life and Exploits of " Bristol Bill " the Notorious Burglar.* Boston, 1850. *MWA*

DARROW, CLARENCE. *Clarence Darrow.* Charles Y. Harrison. N. Y., 1931. 380 p.   *DLC, NN*
   2:366

DARWIN, CHARLES.
   Darwin. Gamaliel Bradford. Boston, 1926. 314 p.
                       DLC, NN, PU
   Evolution of Charles Darwin. George A. Dorsey. N. Y., 1927. 300 p.   *DLC, NN*
   Charles Darwin; the Man and His Warfare. Charles H. Ward. Indianapolis, 1927. 472 p.   *DLC, NN*
   2:5–79–335

DAVENANT, WILLIAM. *Sir William Davenant, Poet Venturer, 1606–1668.* Alfred Harbage. Phila., 1935. 317 p.
                      DLC, NN, CSmH, PU

DAVENPORT. *The Davenport Brothers, Spirit Mediums: Their Biographies and Adventures.* Orrin Abbott. N. Y., 1864. Boston, 1869. 48 p.   *NN*

DAVENPORT, EDWARD LOOMIS. *Edward Loomis Davenport.* Edward F. Edgett. N. Y., 1901. 145 p. (Dunlap Soc. Pub. Ser. 2. v. 14)   *DLC, NN, MWA, CSmH*

DAVENPORT, JOHN. 2:428

DAVENPORT, RUSSELL WHEELER. *Russell W. Davenport, Father of Rowing at Yale, Maker of Guns and Armor Plate Used by the U. S. Government.* C. A. Brinley, ed. N. Y., 1905. 79 p.
                      DLC, NN, PU

DAVENPORT, THOMAS. *Biography of Thomas Davenport, the "Brandon Blacksmith" Inventor of the Electric Motor.* Walter R. Davenport. Montpelier, Vt., 1929. 165 p.   *DLC, NN, MWA*

DAVIDSON, GEORGE. 2:531

DAVIDSON, LUCRETIA MARIA.
   Biographical Sketch in "Remains of Lucretia Maria Davidson." Samuel F. B. Morse. N. Y., 1829. 26 p.   *NN*
   Biography of Lucretia Maria Davidson in "Poetical Remains of . . . Lucretia Maria Davidson." Catherine M. Sedgwick. Phila., 1841. 312 p.   *DLC, NN, MWA, CSmH, PU*

DAVIDSON, MARGARET MILLER. *Biography and Poetical Remains of the Late Margaret Miller Davidson.* Washington Irving. Phila., 1842. 359 p.   *DLC, NN, CSmH, PU*

DAVIE, WILLIAM RICHARDSON.
   Memoir of William Richardson Davie. J. G. de R. Hamilton. Chapel Hill, 1907. 75 p. (Univ. of N. C., James Sprunt Historical Monograph)   *DLC, NN, CSmH, PU*

Life of Wiliam R. Davie. Fordyce M. Hubbard. (L.A.B.)
DLC, NN, MWA, CSmH

DAVIS, CHARLES HENRY. *Life of Charles Henry Davis, Rear-Admiral, 1807–1877.* Charles H. Davis. Boston, 1899. 349 p.
DLC, NN, CSmH

DAVIS, GUSTAVUS FELLOWES. *Memoir of Rev. Gustavus F. Davis, D.D.* Abigail L. Davis. Hartford, 1837. 167 p. *MWA, CSmH*

DAVIS, HENRY GASSAWAY. *The Life and Times of Henry Gassaway Davis, 1823–1916.* Charles M. Pepper. N. Y., 1920. 318 p.
DLC, NN, PU

DAVIS, HENRY WINTER. *Life of Henry Winter Davis.* Bernard C. Steiner. Balt., 1916. 416 p. *DLC, NN, CSmH*
2:218

DAVIS, JAMES A. *" Our Jim."* *A Biography.* Joe M. Chapple. Boston, 1928. 299 p. *DLC, NN, MWA*

DAVIS, JEFF.
Jeff Davis, Governor and U. S. Senator. L. S. Dunaway. Little Rock, 1913. 255 p. *DLC, NN*
The Life Story of Jeff Davis, the Stormy Petrel of Arkansas Politics. Charles Jacobson. Little Rock, 1925. 241 p.
DLC, NN

DAVIS, JEFFERSON.
Life and Imprisonment of Jefferson Davis, Together With the Life and Military Career of Stonewall Jackson . . . Markinfield Addey. N. Y., 1866. 300 p. *NN, CSmH*
Life of Jefferson Davis. F. H. Alfriend. Cincinnati, 1868. 645 p. *DLC, NN, MWA, CSmH, PU*
Life and Death of Jefferson Davis. A. C. Bancroft. N. Y., 1889. 256 p. *DLC*
Prison Life of Jefferson Davis. John J. Craven. N. Y., 1866. 319 p. *DLC, NN, MWA, CSmH*
Jefferson Davis, Political Soldier. Elisabeth D. Cutting. N. Y., 1930. 361 p. *DLC, NN, PU*
Jefferson Davis, Ex-President of the Confederate States of America. Varina H. Davis. N. Y., 1890. 2 vols.
DLC, NN, MWA, CSmH, PU
Jefferson Davis. William E. Dodd. Phila., 1907. 396 p. (A.C.B.) *DLC, NN, MWA, CSmH, PU*
Jefferson Davis, President of the South. H. J. Eckenrode. N. Y., 1923. 371 p. *DLC, NN, CSmH, PU*

Jefferson Davis. Armistead C. Gordon. N. Y., 1918. 329 p.
DLC, NN, CSmH

Real Jefferson Davis. Landon Knight. Battle Creek, Mich.,
1904. 203 p. *DLC, NN, CSmH, PU*

*Life of Jefferson Davis, With a Secret History of the Southern
Confederacy, Gathered " Behind the Scenes in Richmond "* . . . Ed-
ward A. Pollard. Phila., 1869. 536 p.
DLC, NN, MWA, CSmH, PU, MiD:B

Jefferson Davis; His Life and Personality. Morris Schaff.
Boston, 1922. 277 p. *DLC, NN, CSmH*

Jefferson Davis; His Rise and Fall; a Biographical Narrative.
Allen Tate. N. Y., 1929. 311 p. *DLC, NN, MWA, CSmH, PU*

High Stakes and Hair Trigger: The Life of Jefferson Davis.
Robert W. Winston. N. Y., 1930. 306 p. *DLC, NN, PU*
2:654

DAVIS, JOHN. *Life of John Davis.* Wm. W. H. Davis. Doylestown,
Pa., 1886. 195 p. (Privately Printed) *DLC, NN, MWA*

DAVIS, JOHN. *Life and Works of John Davis, 1774–1853.* Thelma L.
Kellogg. Orono, Me., 1924. 139 p. (Univ. of Maine Studies
Ser. 2, vol. 1) *DLC, NN, MWA, CSmH, PU*

DAVIS, JOHN WILLIAM. *Life of John W. Davis.* Theodore A. Hunt-
ley. N. Y., 1924. 295 p. *DLC, NN*

DAVIS, NATHAN SMITH. *Life of Nathan Smith Davis . . . 1817–1904.*
I. N. Danforth. Chicago, 1907. 193 p. *DLC*

DAVIS, OZORA STEARNS. *Ozora Stearns Davis, His Life and Poems.*
Grace E. T. Davis. Boston, 1932. 124 p. *DLC, NN*

DAVIS, RICHARD HARDING.

Adventures and Letters of Richard Harding Davis. Charles B.
Davis. N. Y., 1917. 417 p. *DLC, NN, MWA, CSmH, PU*

Richard Harding Davis; His Day. Fairfax Downey. N. Y.,
1933. 322 p. *DLC, NN, PU*

DAVIS, VARINA HOWELL. *Varina Howell Davis, Wife of Jefferson
Davis.* Eron Rowland. 1927–1931. 2 vols.
DLC, NN, MWA, CSmH, PU
2:97

DAVISON, HENRY POMEROY. *Henry P. Davison; the Record of a Useful Life.* Thomas W. Lamont. N. Y., 1933. 373 p. *DLC, NN*

DAVY, SIR HUMPHREY. 2:79–293

DAWES, CHARLES.

Dawes, the Doer. Carl W. Ackerman. N. Y., 1924. 87 p.
DLC, NN, PU

That Man Dawes. Paul R. Leach. Chicago, 1930. 349 p.

DLC, NN, PU

DAY, GEORGE TIFFANY. *Memoir of George T. Day, D.D., Minister and Editor, 1846–1875.* William H. Bowen. Dover, N. H., 1876. 431 p. *DLC, NN, MWA*

DAY, GERSHOM. *Pioneer Days; the Life-Story of Gershom and Elizabeth Day.* Mary E. D. Trowbridge. Phila., 1895. 160 p.

DLC, NN, MWA, MiD:B

DAY, THOMAS. *The Author of Sandford and Merton; a Life of Thomas Day, Esq.* George W. Gignilliat. N. Y., 1932. 361 p.

DLC, NN, CSmH, PU

DAY, TIMOTHY CRANE. *The Man On A Hill Top.* Sarah J. Day. Phila., 1931. 319 p. *DLC, NN*

DEANE, G. W. *Memoir of G. W. Deane in Deane's " Lectures on the Evidence of Revealed Religion."* W. C. Doane. N. Y., 1890. 661 p. *DLC, NN*

DEANE, SILAS. *Silas Deane: a Connecticut Leader in the American Revolution.* George L. Clark. N. Y., 1913. 287 p. *NN, CSmH*

DEARBORN, HENRY. 2:149

DEBS, EUGENE VICTOR.

Eugene V. Debs; a Man Unafraid. McAlister Coleman. N. Y., 1930. 345 p. *DLC, NN, PU*

Debs: His Authorized Life and Letters. From Woodstock Prison to Atlanta. David Karsner. N. Y., 1919. 244 p.

DLC, NN

That Man Debs and His Life Work. Floy R. Painter. Bloomington, Ind., 1929. 209 p. *DLC, NN, PU*

Debs, His Life, Writings and Speeches. Stephen M. Reynolds. Girard, Kansas, 1908. 76 p. *DLC, NN*

The Story of Eugene Debs. Henry T. Schnittkind. Boston, 1929. 204 p. *DLC, NN*

2:150

DECATUR, STEPHEN.

Decatur. Irvin Anthony. N. Y., 1931. 319 p.

DLC, NN, PU

Stephen Decatur. Cyrus T. Brady. Boston, 1900. 142 p. (Beacon Biographies) *DLC, NN, CSmH*

Life of Stephen Decatur. Alexander S. Mackenzie. Boston, 1846. 443 p. (L.A.B.) *DLC, NN, MWA, CSmH*

Life and Character of Stephen Decatur. S. P. Waldo. Hartford, 1821. 312 p. *NN, MWA, CSmH, PU, MiD:B*

2:396

DEERING, NATHANIEL. *The Life and Works of Nathaniel Deering (1791–1881) With the Text . . . of Carabasset and the Clairvoyants.* Leola B. Chaplin. Orono, Me., 1934. 224 p. (Univ. of Maine Studies, Second Series, No. 32) *DLC, NN, CSmH, PU*

DEFFAND, MME DU. 2:93

DEFOE, DANIEL. *Daniel Defoe, How to Know Him.* William P. Trent. Indianapolis, 1916. 329 p. *DLC, NN, CSmH, PU*

DEFOREST, JOHN HYDE. *The Evolution of a Missionary. A Biography of John Hyde DeForest . . . Missionary . . . in Japan.* Charlotte B. DeForest. N. Y., 1914. 309 p. *DLC, NN, MWA*

DEFOREST, LEE. *Conqueror of Space; an Authorized Biography of the Life and Work of Lee DeForest.* Georgette Carneal. N. Y., 1930. 296 p. *DLC, NN*

DEHON, THEODORE.
  An Essay on the Life of the Right Reverend Theodore Dehon, D.D. Christopher E. Gadsden. Charleston, 1833. 341 p.
  DLC, NN
  Life of Theodore Dehon. John N. Norton. N. Y., 1857. 144 p.
  PU

DEKKER, THOMAS. *Thomas Dekker.* Mary L. Hunt. N. Y., 1911. 213 p. (Col. Univ. Studies in Eng.) *DLC, NN, CSmH, PU*

DELACROIX, FERDINAND V. 2:161

DELANY, MARTIN ROBINSON. *Life and Public Services of Martin R. Delany.* Frank A. Rollin. Boston, 1868. 367 p.
  DLC, NN, MWA, CSmH

DELCASSÉ, THÉOPHILE. *The Career of Théophile Delcassé.* Charles W. Porter. Phila., 1936. 356 p. *DLC, NN*

DE LISLE, LECONTE. *Leconte De Lisle: A Study of the Man and His Poetry.* Irving Brown. N. Y., 1924. 274 p. (Col. Univ. Studies in Romance) *DLC, NN*

DE LONG, GEORGE WASHINGTON. 2:262

DE MILT, ALONZO PIERRE. *The Life, Travels and Adventures of an American Wanderer: a Truthful Narrative of Events in the Life of Alonzo P. De Milt.* Franklin Y. Fitch. N. Y., 1883. 228 p.
  DLC, NN, CSmH

DE MORNY, DUC. *Imperial Brother; the Life of the Duc De Morny.* Maristan Chapman. 1931. 418 p. *DLC, NN*

DEMOSTHENES. *Demosthenes and His Influence.* Charles D. Adams. N. Y., 1927. 184 p. (Our Debt to Greece and Rome)
  DLC, NN, CSmH, PU

DENCK, JOHANNES. *The Life, Teachings and Works of Johannes Denck, 1495–1527.* Frederick L. Weis. Strasbourg, 1924. 93 p.
DLC, MWA

DENNIE, JOSEPH.
Joseph Dennie: Editor of the Port Folio and Author of "The Lay Preacher." William W. Clapp. Cambridge, 1880. 41 p.
DLC, NN, MWA
Joseph Dennie and His Circle, A Study in American Literature from 1792 to 1812. Harold M. Ellis. Austin, 1915. 285 p. (Univ. of Texas Bulletin No. 40—Studies in English, No. 3)
DLC, NN, MWA, CSmH, PU

DENNING, WILLIAM. *The Life and History of William Denning.* J. W. Strohm. Newville, Pa., 1890. 37 p.
DLC

DENNIS, JOHN. *John Dennis: His Life and Criticism.* Harry G. Paul. N. Y., 1911. 299 p. (Col. Univ. Studies in English)
DLC, NN, CSmH, PU

DENNISON, ELIPHALET WHORF. *E. W. Dennison. A Memorial.* Mrs. E. W. Dennison. Boston, 1909. 103 p.
DLC, NN, MWA, CSmH, PU

DENTON, JOHN B. *Captain John B. Denton . . .* William Allen. Chicago, 1905. 171 p.
CSmH

DENTON, WILLIAM. *William Denton, the Geologist and Radical. A Biographical Sketch.* James H. Powell. Boston, 1870. 36 p.
DLC, MWA

DEPEW, CHAUNCEY MITCHELL. 2:623

DE QUINCEY, THOMAS. *Thomas De Quincey.* Horace A. Eaton. N. Y., 1936. 542 p.
DLC, NN, CSmH, PU

DERBY, RICHARD. *The Life and Times of Richard Derby, Merchant of Salem, 1712 to 1783.* James D. Phillips. Cambridge, 1929. 116 p.
DLC, NN, MWA

DESMOND, PHILIP. *Philip Desmond.* Cora S. Day. N. Y., 1900. 68 p.

DE SERVIER, JEAN GROLIER. *Jean Grolier De Servier, Viscount d'-Aguisy. Some Account of His Life and of His Famous Library.* William L. Andrews. N. Y., 1892. 68 p.
DLC, NN, CSmH

DE VALERA, EAMON. 2:190

DE VAUX, JAMES. 2:394

DE VEAUX, JAMES. *A Memoir of James De Veaux of Charleston, S. C.* Robert W. Gibbes. Columbia, S. C., 1846. 258 p. (Privately Printed)
DLC, NN, MWA, PU

DE VINNE, THEODORE LOW. *Theodore Low De Vinne, Printer.* N. Y.,
1915. 111 p. *DLC, NN, MWA*

DEWEES, SAMUEL. *History of the Life and Services of Captain Samuel
Dewees.* J. S. Hannah. Balt., 1844. 360 p.
DLC, NN, CSmH, MiU:C

DEWEY, GEORGE.

*Dewey and Other Great Naval Commanders. Series of Biog-
raphies.* W. H. D. Adams. N. Y., 1899. 487 p. *NN*

Admiral George Dewey: Sketch of the Man. John Barrett.
N. Y., 1899. 279 p. *DLC, NN, MWA, CSmH, PU, MiD:B*

Life of Admiral George Dewey. Will M. Clemens. N. Y.,
1899. 196 p. *DLC, NN, CSmH*

Life of Admiral George Dewey . . . Adelbert M. Dewey, ed.
Westfield, Mass., 1898. 1117 p. *DLC, NN, CSmH*

The Life and Letters of Admiral Dewey . . . Adelbert M.
Dewey, ed. N. Y., 1899. 452 p. *DLC, NN, MWA, CSmM, PU*

Dewey, the Defender; a Life Sketch of America's Great Admiral.
Margherita A. Hamm. N. Y., 1899. 187 p. *DLC, NN*

Life and Achievements of Admiral Dewey. Murat Halstead.
Chicago, 1899. 452 p. *DLC, NN, MWA, CSmH, MiD:B*

*Admiral Dewey, the Hero of Manila: Record of His Life and
Achievements; With Brief Sketches of Our Early Naval Heroes.*
T. W. Handford. Chicago, 1899. 349 p. *DLC, NN*

The Hero of Manila; Dewey on the Mississippi and the Pacific.
Rossiter Johnson. N. Y., 1899. 152 p. *DLC, NN, CSmH*

Life and Glorious Deeds of Admiral Dewey. Joseph L. Stickney. Chicago, 1898. 434 p. *DLC, NN, MWA, CSmH*

*Life and Heroic Deeds of Admiral Dewey, Including Battles in
the Philippines . . .* Louis S. Young and H. D. Northrop. Phila.,
1899. 546 p. *DLC, NN, MiD:B*
2:180–396

DEWEY, JOHN. 2:236

DEWEY, MELVIL. *Melvil Dewey, Seer: Inspirer: Doer, 1851–1931.*
George G. Dawe. Lake Placid, N. Y., 1932. 391 p.
DLC, NN, CSmH, PU

DE WITT, JOHN. *Sketch of the Life and Times of John De Witt.*
Robert G. Barnwell. N. Y., 1856. 108 p. *NN, PU*

DEXTER, SAMUEL. *Samuel Dexter, 1726–1810.* Carlton A. Staples.
Dedham, Mass., 1892. 18 p. *DLC, MWA*

DEXTER, TIMOTHY.

Life of Lord Timothy Dexter. S. L. Knapp. Boston, 1848.
107 p. *DLC, NN, MWA, PU, MiD:B, MiU:C*

Lord Timothy Dexter of Newburyport, Massachusetts. John P. Marquand. N. Y., 1925. 378 p.

DLC, NN, MWA, CSmH, PU

DIAZ, PORFIRIO.

Porfirio Diaz, Dictator of Mexico. Carleton Beals. Phila. and London, 1932. 463 p. *DLC, NN, PU*

Diaz, Master of Mexico. James Creelman. N. Y., 1911. 441 p.

DLC, NN, MWA, PU

DICKENS, CHARLES.

Boz; an Intimate Biography of Charles Dickens. Joseph C. Boarman and James L. Harte. Boston, 1936. 234 p. *DLC, NN*

Charles Dickens. Richard E. Burton. Indianapolis, 1919. 308 p. *DLC, NN, PU*

Life and Writings of Charles Dickens. Phoebe A. Hanaford. Boston, 1882. 401 p. *DLC, MWA*

Short Life of Charles Dickens. C. H. Jones. N. Y., 1880. 260 p. *DLC, NN, CSmH, PU*

Dickens, the Immortal. Edward B. Lupton. Kansas City, 1923. 117 p. *DLC, NN, CSmH, PU*

Life of Charles Dickens. R. Shelton Mackenzie. Phila., 1870. 479 p. *DLC, NN, MWA, CSmH*

Charles Dickens; A Sketch of His Life and Works. Frederic B. Perkins. N. Y., 1870. 264 p. *DLC, NN*

The Man Charles Dickens; a Victorian Portrait. Edward C. Wagenknecht. Boston and N. Y., 1929. 364 p. *DLC, NN, PU*

Charles Dickens; an Appreciation. Charles D. Warner. Newark, N. J., 1913. 17 p. *DLC, NN, CSmH*

Charles Dickens; the Man and His Works. Edwin P. Whipple. Boston, 1912. 2 vols. *DLC, NN, CSmH*

DICKERMAN, ELIZABETH H., ABBIE A., and SARAH F. *A Memoir of Elizabeth H., Abbie A., and Sarah F. Dickerman.* Israel P. Warren. Boston, 1859. 282 p. *NN*

DICKINSON, EMILY.

The Life and Letters of Emily Dickinson. Martha D. Bianchi. Boston, 1924. 386 p. *DLC, NN, CSmH, PU*

Emily Dickinson; Friend and Neighbor. MacGregor Jenkins. Boston, 1930. 150 p. *DLC, NN, PU*

Emily Dickinson: The Human Background of Her Poetry. Josephine Pollitt. N. Y., 1930. 350 p. *DLC, NN, PU*

The Life and Mind of Emily Dickinson. Genevieve Taggard. N. Y., 1930. 378 p. *DLC, NN, PU*

2:92–114

DICKINSON, JOHN. *Life and Times of John Dickinson.* Charles J. Stillé. Phila., 1891. 437 p.
DLC, NN, MWA, CSmH, PU, MiD:B, MiU:C
2:594

DICKSON, ROBERT. *Robert Dickson, British Fur Trader on the Upper Mississippi: A Story of Trade, War and Diplomacy.* Louis A. Tohill. Ann Arbor, Mich., 1927. 124 p. *DLC, NN, PU*

DICKSTEIN, SAMUEL. *American Defender.* Dorothy Waring. N. Y., 1935. 267 p. *DLC, NN*

DILLARD, JAMES HARDY. *Doctor Dillard of the Jeanes Fund.* Benjamin Brawley. N. Y., 1930. 151 p. *DLC, NN*

DILLINGHAM, JOHN HOAG. *John H. Dillingham, 1839–1910, Teacher, Minister in the Society of Friends, Editor.* Jarvis H. Bartlett. N. Y., 1911. 190 p. *DLC, NN, PU*

DILLON, ANNA PRICE. *Anna Price Dillon; Memoir and Memorials.* J. F. Dillon. N. Y., 1900. 489 p. (Privately Printed)
DLC, NN, MWA, CSmH

DILLON, JOHN BROWN. *Life and Services of John B. Dillon.* John Coburn. Indianapolis, 1886. 30 p. (Ind. Hist. Soc. Pamph. No. 2) *DLC, NN, MWA, CSmH, MiD:B*

DIMAN, JEREMIAH LEWIS. *Memoirs of the Rev. Jeremiah Lewis Diman, D.D.* Caroline Hazard. Boston, 1887. 363 p.
DLC, NN, MWA, MiD:B

DIMITROV, GEORG. *. . . Dimitrov; a Biography.* Stella D. Blagoyeva. N. Y., 1934. 124 p. *DLC, NN*

DIMOCK, SUSAN. *Memoir of Susan Dimock, Resident Physician of the New England Hospital for Women and Children.* Boston, 1875. 103 p. *MWA*
2:144

DINGLEY, NELSON. *Life and Times of Nelson Dingley, Jr.* E. N. Dingley. Kalamazoo, Mich., 1902. 22 p.
DLC, NN, MWA, MiD:B

DISRAELI, BENJAMIN. *Young Mr. Disraeli.* Helen R. Beebe. N. Y., 1936. 337 p. *DLC, NN, CSmH*
2:7

DIX, DOROTHEA LYNDE. *Life of Dorothea Lynde Dix.* Francis Tiffany. Boston, 1890. 392 p. *DLC, NN, MWA, CSmH, PU*
2:43

DIX, HENRY A. *An American Business Adventure; the Story of Henry A. Dix.* Mark H. Dix. N. Y., 1928. 181 p. *DLC, NN, PU*

DIX, JOHN ADAMS. *Memoirs of John Adams Dix.* Morgan Dix, comp. N. Y., 1883. 2 vols.

DLC, NN, MWA, CSmH, PU, MiD:B

DOANE. *The Doane Family: Deacon John Doane of Plymouth; John Doane of Maryland.* Alfred A. Doane. Boston, 1902. 533 p.

DLC, NN, MWA

DOANE, GEORGE WASHINGTON. *A Memoir of the Life of George Washington Doane, Bishop of New Jersey.* William C. Doane. N. Y., 1860. 577 p.

DLC, NN, PU

DOBIE, GILMOUR C. 2:425

DOCK, CHRISTOPHER. 2:521

DODD, WALTER JAMES. *Walter James Dodd.* N. Y., 1918. 63 p.

MWA

DODDRIDGE, JOSEPH. *Memoir of Joseph Doddridge in Doddridge's "Notes on the Settlement and Indian Wars of the Western Parts of Virginia and Pennsylvania, 1763–1783."* Narcissa Doddridge. Albany, N. Y., 1876. 320 p. *DLC, NN, MWA, CSmH*

DODDRIDGE, PHILIP.

Memoir of the Life, Character and Writings of Philip Doddridge, D.D. With a Selection From His Correspondence. James R. Boyd. N. Y., 1860. 480 p. *DLC, NN, CSmH, PU*

Life of Philip Doddridge. D. A. Harsha. Albany, 1864. 241 p.

NN, MWA, CSmH, MiD:B

Philip Doddridge, His Life and Labors, A Centenary Memorial. John Stoughton. Boston, 1853. 222 p. *NN, MWA, CSmH*

See WATTS, ISAAC.

DODGE, ALLEN WASHINGTON. *Divine Guidance; Memorial of Allen W. Dodge.* Mary A. Dodge. N. Y., 1881. 328 p. *DLC, PU*

DODGE, AUGUSTUS CAESAR. *Augustus Caesar Dodge.* Louis Pelzer. Iowa City, 1908. 369 p. (Iowa Biographical Series)

DLC, NN, MWA, CSmH, PU

DODGE, GRACE HOADLEY. *Grace H. Dodge; Merchant of Dreams.* Abbie Graham. N. Y., 1926. 329 p. *DLC, NN, MWA*

DODGE, GRENVILLE MELLEN. *Trails, Rails and War; the Life of General G. M. Dodge.* Jacob R. Perkins. Indianapolis, 1929. 371 p.

DLC, NN, CSmH, PU

DODGE, HENRY.

Henry Dodge. Louis Pelzer. Iowa City, 1911. 266 p. (Iowa Biographical Series) *DLC, NN, CSmH, PU, MiD:B*

The Life of Henry Dodge, From 1782 to 1833. William Salter. Burlington, Ia., 1890. 76 p. *DLC, NN, CSmH*

DODGE, WILLIAM EARL.
    Memorials of William E. Dodge. D. S. Dodge, ed. N. Y., 1887. 407 p.   *DLC, NN, MWA, CSmH, PU*
    William E. Dodge: the Christian Merchant. Carlos Martyn. N. Y., 1890. 349 p.   *DLC, NN, CSmH*

DOHENY, EDWARD LAURENCE. 2:233

DOLLAR, ROBERT. 2:233

DONAHEY, VICTOR. 2:151

DONGAN, THOMAS.
    Thomas Dongan, Colonial Governor of New York, 1683–1688. Thomas P. Phelan. N. Y., 1933. 154 p.   *DLC, NN, CSmH*
    Thomas Dongan, Governor of New York. John H. Kennedy. Wash., 1930. 131 p.   *CSmH*

DONNE, JOHN. 2:91

DONNELLY, CHARLES. *Charles Donnelly. A Memoir.* Mabel W. Cameron and Katherine E. Conway. N. Y., 1909. 265 p. (Privately Printed)   *DLC, NN, MWA, PU*

DONNELLY, IGNATIUS. *Biography of Ignatius Donnelly.* Everett W. Fish. Chicago, 1892. 144 p.   *DLC, NN*

DORR, THOMAS WILSON. *The Life and Times of Thomas Wilson Dorr.* Dan King. Boston, 1859. 368 p.
    DLC, NN, MWA, CSmH, MiD:B

D'ORSAY, ALFRED GUILLAUME. *D'Orsay; or, The Complete Dandy.* William T. Shore. N. Y., 1911. 324 p.   *DLC, NN*

DOSTIE, ANTHONY PAUL. *Life of A. P. Dostie.* Emily H. Reed. N. Y., 1868. 374 p.   *DLC, NN, MWA, CSmH*

DOSTOEVSKÝ, FEODOR. *Dostoevsky.* Avraham Yarmolinsky. N. Y., 1934. 447 p.   *DLC, NN*

DOUGHERTY, CARDINAL. 2:679

DOUGLAS, PAUL. *Paul Douglas, Journalist.* C. M. Sheldon. Chicago, 1909. 305 p.   *DLC*

DOUGLAS, STEPHEN ARNOLD.
    Life of Stephen A. Douglas, U. S. Senator From Illinois. A Member of the Western Bar. N. Y., 1860. 270 p.
    DLC, NN, MWA, CSmH, PU
    Stephen Arnold Douglas. Wm. G. Brown. Boston, 1902. 141 p.
    DLC, NN, MWA, PU
    Stephen A. Douglas. Clark E. Carr. Chicago, 1909. 293 p.
    DLC, NN, MWA, CSmH, PU
    Life of Stephen A. Douglas. Henry M. Flint. N. Y., 1860. 278 p.   *DLC, NN, MWA, CSmH, MiD:B*

Life of Stephen A. Douglas. W. Gardner. Boston, 1905. 239 p.
DLC, NN

Stephen A. Douglas. Louis Howland. N. Y., 1920. 375 p.
(Figures from American History) *DLC, NN*

Stephen A. Douglas: A Study in American Politics. Allen Johnson. N. Y., 1908. 503 p. *DLC, NN, CSmH, PU*

The Eve of Conflict: Stephen A. Douglas and the Needless War. George F. Milton. Boston, 1934. 608 p. *DLC, NN, CSmH, PU*

Life of Stephen A. Douglas. James W. Sheahan. N. Y., 1860. 528 p. *DLC, NN, MWA, CSmH*

Life of Stephen A. Douglas. Frank E. Stevens. Springfield, Ill., 1924. 426 p. (Journal Ill. State His. Soc. XVI)
NN, MiD:B

A Voter's Version of the Life and Character of Stephen A. Douglas. Robert B. Warden. Columbus, 1860. 131 p.
DLC, MiD:B

Stephen A. Douglas. Henry P. Willis. Phila., 1910. 371 p.
(A.C.B.) *DLC, NN, PU*
2:501–590–624

DOUGLASS, FREDERICK.

Frederick Douglass. C. W. Chesnutt. Boston, 1899. 141 p.
DLC, NN, MWA

Frederick Douglass, the Orator. James M. Gregory. Springfield, Mass., 1893. 215 p. *DLC, NN*

Frederick Douglass: The Colored Orator. F. M. Holland. N. Y., 1891. Rev. Ed., 1895. 423 p. *DLC, NN, CSmH*

Frederick Douglass. Booker T. Washington. Phila., 1906–1907. (A.C.B.) *DLC, NN, PU*
2:40–128

DOUGLASS, WILLIAM. *Life and Writings of William Douglass.* G. H. Weaver. (In the Collection of the Soc. of Medical History of Chicago. Vol. IV. 1921)

DOW, LORENZO.

Lorenzo Dow, the Bearer of the Word. Charles C. Sellers. N. Y., 1928. 275 p. *DLC, NN, MWA, PU, MiD:B*

The Eccentric Preacher, or, A Sketch of the Life of . . . Lorenzo Dow. Lowell, 1841. 204 p. *CSmH*

DOWIE, JOHN ALEXANDER.

John Alexander Dowie and the Christian Catholic Apostolic Church in Zion. Rolvix Harlan. Evansville, Wis., 1906. 204 p.
DLC, NN, PU, MiD:B

Dowie, Anointed of the Lord. Arthur Newcomb. N. Y., 1930. 403 p. *DLC, NN, MWA, PU*

DOWNING, ANDREW JACKSON. *Memoir of A. J. Downing, in Downing's " Rural Essays."* George W. Curtis. n.p., 1853. 47 p. *DLC, NN, PU*

DOWNS, SARAH J. C. *Life of Mrs. Sarah J. C. Downs.* Jacob B. Graw, ed. Camden, N. J., 1892. 84 p. *DLC, NN, MWA*

DOWSE, EDMUND. *Fifty Years a Pastor. A Biographical Sketch of Dr. Edmund Dowse, With a History of His Church.* Charles F. Adams. Sherborn, 1888. 128 p. *NN, MWA*

DOWSE, WILLIAM BRADFORD HOMER. *William Bradford Homer Dowse, A Memoir.* William V. Kellen. Boston, 1929. 44 p. (Privately Printed) *DLC, NN, MWA, CSmH*

DRAKE, DANIEL.
Biographical Sketch of Daniel Drake, 1870, in Daniel Drake's " Pioneer Life in Kentucky." Charles D. Drake. Cincinnati, 1870. 37 p. *DLC, NN, PU*
Daniel Drake and His Followers. Otto Juettner. Cincinnati, 1909. 496 p. *DLC, NN, CSmH*
Memoirs of the Life and Services of Daniel Drake, M.D. Edward D. Mansfield. Cincinnati, 1855. 408 p. *DLC, NN, CSmH, PU, MiD:B*

DRAKE, JOSEPH RODMAN. *The Life and Works of Joseph Rodman Drake (1795–1820).* Frank L. Pleadwell. Boston, 1935. 424 p. (Privately Printed) *DLC, NN*

DRAKE, SAMUEL GARDNER. *A Memoir of S. G. Drake.* John H. Sheppard. Albany, 1863. 36 p. (Privately Printed) *DLC, NN, MWA, CSmH*

DRAPER, ANDREW SLOAN. *The Life and Work of Andrew Sloan Draper.* Harlan H. Horner. Urbana, Ill., 1934. 291 p. *DLC, NN*

DRAPER, LYMAN COPELAND. *Lyman Copeland Draper. A Memoir.* Reuben G. Thwaites. 22 p. (Wis. Hist. Soc. Coll. XII, 1892) *DLC, NN, MWA, CSmH*

DREISER, THEODORE.
Forgotten Frontiers; Dreiser and the Land of the Free. Dorothy Dudley. N. Y., 1932. 485 p. *DLC, NN, PU*
Theodore Dreiser. Burton Rascoe. N. Y., 1925. 91 p. (Modern American Writers) *DLC, NN, MWA, CSmH, PU*
2:236–366

DREW, DANIEL. *Book of Daniel Drew: A Glimpse of the Fisk-Gould-Tweed Régime From the Inside.* Bouck White. N. Y., 1910. 423 p. (Fictionized Biography) *DLC, NN, PU* 2:451

DREW, JOHN.
John Drew. E. A. Dithmar. N. Y., 1900. 137 p. *DLC, NN, MWA, PU*
A Splendid Gypsy: John Drew. Peggy Wood. N. Y., 1928. 64 p. *DLC, NN, PU*

DRUM, WALTER. *The Life and Letters of Walter Drum, S.J.* Joseph P. Gorayeb. N. Y., 1928. 313 p. *DLC, NN*

DRUMMOND, HENRY. 2:519

DRUMMOND, WILLIAM. *William Drummond, First Governor of North Carolina.* S. B. Weeks. N. Y., 1892. *CSmH*

DU BARRY, JEANNE. *The Story of Du Barry.* James L. Ford. N. Y., 1902. 288 p. *DLC, NN*

DUCAT, ARTHUR C. *Memoir of Gen. A. C. Ducat.* Chicago, 1897. *CSmH*

DUCHAILLU, PAUL B. 2:262

DUCHESNE, PHILIPPINE. *Mother Philippine Duchesne.* Marjory Erskine. N. Y., 1926. 400 p. *DLC, NN, MiD:B*

DUDEVANT, AMANTINE, BARONESS. See SAND, GEORGE.

DUDLEY, CHARLES BENJAMIN. *Memorial Volume Commemorative of the Life and Life-Work of Charles Benjamin Dudley, Ph.D.* American Society For Testing Materials. Phila., 1911. 269 p. *DLC, NN, PU*

DUDLEY, JOSEPH. *The Public Life of Joseph Dudley.* Everett Kimball. N. Y., 1911. 239 p. (Harvard Hist. Studies, XV) *DLC, NN, CSmH, PU, MiD:B*

DUDLEY, THOMAS.
Life and Work of Thomas Dudley, Second Governor of Massachusetts. Augustine Jones. Boston and N. Y., 1899. 484 p. *DLC, NN, MWA, PU, MiD:B*
Thomas Dudley, 1576–1653, Governor of Massachusetts Bay Colony. George E. Koues. Boston, 1914. 103 p. *DLC, NN*

DUFF, MARY ANN. *Mrs. Duff.* Joseph N. Ireland. Boston, 1882. 188 p. (American Actor Series) *DLC, NN, MWA, CSmH, PU*

DUFFY, FRANCIS PATRICK. *Chaplain Duffy of the Sixty-Ninth Regiment, New York.* Ella M. Flick. Phila., 1935. 203 p. *DLC, NN*

DUKE, JAMES BUCHANAN. *James B. Duke, Master Builder.* John W. Jenkins. N. Y., 1927. 302 p. *DLC, NN, CSmH, PU*

DULL KNIFE. 2:204

DUMAS, ALEXANDER. *Dumas, The Incredible Marquis.* Herbert Gorman. N. Y., 1929. 466 p. *DLC, NN, PU*
2:91

DUMMER, JEREMIAH. *Jeremiah Dummer, Colonial Craftsman and Merchant, 1645–1718.* Hermann F. Clarke and Henry W. Foote. Boston, 1935. 209 p. *DLC, NN, MWA, CSmH*

DUNBAR, DUNCAN. *Duncan Dunbar: Sketch of the Late Pastor of the McDougal St. Baptist Church.* Jeremiah Chaplin. N. Y., 1865. 312 p. *MWA, CSmH*

DUNBAR, JAMES ROBERT. *James Robert Dunbar. A Memorial.* Boston, 1916. 45 p. (Privately Printed) *DLC, MWA*

DUNBAR, PAUL LAURENCE.
Biography of Paul Laurence Dunbar in His " Life and Works." Lida K. Wiggins. Naperville, Indiana, 1895–1907. 111 p.
DLC, NN, PU
Paul Laurence Dunbar; Poet of His People. Benjamin Brawley. Chapel Hill, 1936. 159 p. *DLC, NN, CSmH, PU*

DUNBAR, WILLIAM. *Life, Letters and Papers of William Dunbar of Elgin, Morayshire, Scotland, and Natchez, Mississippi.* William Dunbar. Jackson, Miss., 1930. 410 p.
DLC, NN, CSmH, PU, MiD:B

DUNCAN, JAMES HENRY. *In Memoriam; James Henry Duncan.* Cambridge, n.d. 80 p. *DLC, NN, MWA, MiD:B*

DUNCAN, JOSEPH. *Biographical Sketch of Joseph Duncan, Fifth Governor of Illinois.* Julia D. Kirby. Chicago, 1888. 97 p.
DLC, NN, CSmH, MiD:B

DUNCAN, WILLIAM. *The Apostle of Alaska; the Story of William Duncan, of Metlaktla.* John W. Arctander. N. Y., Chicago, 1909. 395 p. *DLC, NN*

DUNLAP, WILLIAM.
William Dunlap: A Study of His Life and Works and of His Place in Contemporary Culture. Oral S. Coad. N. Y., 1917. 313 p. (Dunlap Soc. Pub. Ser. 3. vol. 2) *DLC, NN, MWA, CSmH*
William Dunlap and His Writings. Oscar Wegelin. n.p., n.d. 8 p. (Privately Reprinted from the *Literary Collection,* Jan. 1904)
DLC, NN, MWA, CSmH

DUNN, ROBINSON POTTER. *In Memoriam. Robinson Potter Dunn.* Samuel L. Caldwell. Cambridge, 1867. 237 p.
DLC, NN, MWA, MiD:B

DUNN, WILLIAM MCKEE. *William McKee Dunn, Brigadier-General U. S. A. A Memoir. With Extracts From His Speeches, Decisions and Correspondence.* William W. Woollen. N. Y., 1892. 115 p.
DLC, NN

DUNNING, ALBERT ELIJAH. *Albert Elijah Dunning. A Book of Remembrance.* Harriet W. Dunning. n.p., 1927. 217 p. (Privately Printed)
DLC, MWA

DUNSTER, HENRY. *Life of Henry Dunster, First President of Harvard College.* Jeremiah Chaplin. Boston, 1872. 315 p.
DLC, NN, MWA, CSmH, PU
2:464

DUPONT, SAMUEL FRANCIS. *Rear-Admiral Samuel Francis DuPont, U. S. N. A Biography.* H. A. DuPont. N. Y., 1926. 320 p.
DLC, NN, PU

DUPUIS, AUGUSTE. *The White Monk of Timbuctoo.* William B. Seabrook. N. Y., 1934. 279 p.
DLC, NN

DUQUESNE, FRITZ JOUBERT. *The Man Who Killed Kitchener; the Life of Fritz Joubert Duquesne, 1879–.* Clement Wood. N. Y., 1932. 429 p.
DLC, NN

DURAND, ASHER BROWN.
The Life and Times of A. B. Durand. John Durand. N. Y., 1894. 232 p.
NN, MWA
Asher B. Durand. Daniel Huntington. N. Y., 1887. 48 p. (Privately Printed)
DLC, NN, PU

DURANT, HENRY FOWLE. *Life of Henry Fowle Durant, Founder of Wellesley College.* Florence M. Kingsley. N. Y., 1924. 354 p.
DLC, NN, PU

DURANT, WILL. 2:366

DURBIN, JOHN PRICE. *Life of John Price Durbin.* John A. Roche. N. Y., 1889. 369 p.
DLC, NN

DÜRER, ALBRECHT. *Dürer.* Moses F. Sweetser. Boston, 1877. 158 p.
DLC, NN

DU SIMITIERE, PIERRE EUGENE. *Du Simitiere: Artist, Antiquary, and Naturalist, Projector of the First American Museum.* William J. Potts. Phila., 1889. 37 p. (Reprinted from Pa. Mag. of Hist. and Biog.)
NN, MWA, PU

DUTTON, BROTHER. See DAMIEN, FATHER.

DUTTON, SAMUEL TRAIN. *Samuel Train Dutton; a Biography.* Charles H. Levermore. N. Y., 1922. 280 p.
DLC, NN, MWA, PU

DUY, ALBERT WILLIAM. *Memoir of Rev. Albert W. Duy, With Biography.* Samuel Adams Clark. Phila., 1847. 196 p.
DLC, NN, PU

DUYCKINCK, EVERT AUGUSTUS.
Memorial Sketch of the Life and Literary Labors of Evert A. Duyckinck. W. A. Butler. N. Y., 1879. 14 p.
DLC, NN, MWA, CSmH, PU, MiD:B
Evert A. Duyckinck, His Life, Writings and Influence. Samuel Osgood. Boston, 1879.
CSmH

DWIGHT, ELIZABETH B. *Memoir of Mrs. Elizabeth B. Dwight.* H. G. O. Dwight. N. Y., 1840. 323 p.   *DLC, NN, MWA, MiD:B*

DWIGHT, JOHN SULLIVAN. *John Sullivan Dwight, Brook-Farmer, Editor and Critic of Music.* George W. Cooke. Boston, 1898. 297 p.
DLC, NN

DWIGHT, SERENO EDWARDS. *Select Discourses of S. E. Dwight With a Memoir of His Life.* W. T. Dwight. Boston, 1851. 382 p.
DLC, MWA

DWIGHT, TIMOTHY.
Life of Timothy Dwight. William Sprague. (L.A.B.)
DLC, NN, MWA, CSmH
A Memoir of the Late Timothy Dwight, With the Sermon Delivered on the Occasion of His Death. Joseph P. Thompson. New Haven, 1844. 148 p.   *DLC, NN, MiU:C*
2:12–326

DWIGHT, WILDER. *Life and Letters of Wilder Dwight, Lieut.-Col. Second Mass. Inf. Vols.* Boston, 1868. 351 p.
DLC, NN, MWA, CSmH

DWINELL, ISRAEL EDSON. *Israel Edson Dwinell: A Memoir.* Henry E. Jewett. Oakland, Calif., 1892. 320 p.
DLC, NN, MWA, CSmH

DYCKMAN, HANNAH. *A Sketch of the Life and Death of Miss Hannah Dyckman, Kings Ferry.* Andrew Fowler. Danbury, 1795. 36 p.

DYER, EDWARD. *At the Court of Queen Elizabeth; the Life and Lyrics of Sir Edward Dyer.* Ralph M. Sargent. N. Y., 1935. 229 p.
DLC, NN, CSmH, PU

DYER, MARY. *Mary Dyer of Rhode Island, the Quaker Martyr That Was Hanged on Boston Common June 1, 1660.* Horatio Rogers. Providence, 1896. 115 p.   *DLC, NN, MWA, MiD:B*
2:55

DYKES, J. B. *Life and Letters of J. B. Dykes.* J. B. Fowler, ed. N. Y., 1898. 344 p.   *DLC*

DYSON, JULIA A. PARKER. *Life and Thought; or, Cherished Memorials of the Late Julia A. Parker Dyson.* Elizabeth W. Latimer. Boston, 1856. 314 p. *DLC, MWA*

EADS, JAMES BUCHANAN. *James Buchanan Eads.* L. How. Boston, 1900. 120 p. (Riverside Biographies) *DLC, NN*

EAGELS, JEANNE. *The Rain Girl, the Tragic Story of Jeanne Eagels.* Edward J. Doherty. Phila., 1930. 313 p. *DLC, NN*

EARLE, PLINY. *Memoirs of Pliny Earle, M.D.* Franklin B. Sanborn, ed. Boston, 1898. 409 p. *DLC, NN, MWA, PU*

EARP, WYATT. *Wyatt Earp, Frontier Marshal.* Stuart N. Lake. Boston, 1931. 392 p. *DLC, NN, MWA*

EASTBURN, JOSEPH. *Memoirs of the Rev. Joseph Eastburn, Stated Preacher in the Mariners Church, Philadelphia.* Ashbel Green. Phila., 1828. 208 p. *DLC, NN, MWA, PU, MiD:B*

EASTMAN, GEORGE. *George Eastman.* Carl W. Ackerman. Boston, 1930. 522 p. *DLC, NN, MWA, PU*

EATON, HORACE. *A Memorial of Rev. Horace Eaton, D.D.* Anna R. Eaton. Boston, 1885. 306 p. *DLC, NN*

EATON, PEGGY. *Peggy Eaton, Democracy's Mistress.* Queena Pollack. N. Y., 1931. 295 p. *DLC, NN, PU*
2:453–518

EATON, WILLIAM.

Life of William Eaton. Cornelius Felton. (L.A.B.)
DLC, NN, MWA, CSmH, PU, MIU:C

Life of William Eaton, Principally Collected From His Correspondence and Other Manuscripts. Charles Prentiss, ed. Brookfield, 1813. 448 p. *DLC, NN, MWA, CSmH, PU*
2:452

ECKERT, STEPHEN. *A Herald of the Great King, Stephen Eckert, O.M. Cap.* Berchmans Bittle. Milwaukee, 1933. 179 p. *DLC, NN*

EDDY, MARY BAKER.

Mary Baker Eddy; the Truth and the Tradition. Ernest S. Bates and J. V. Dittemore. N. Y., 1933. 476 p.
DLC, NN, MWA, PU

Mary Baker G. Eddy. Arthur Brisbane. Boston, 1908. 62 p.
DLC, NN, MWA

Mrs. Eddy: the Biography of a Virginal Mind. Edwin F. Dakin. N. Y., 1929. 553 p. *DLC, NN, MWA, PU*

Memoirs of Mary Baker Eddy. Adam Dickey. London, 1927. 141 p. *DLC, NN*

The Life of Mary Baker G. Eddy and the History of Christian Science. Georgine Milmine. N. Y., 1909. 495 p.
DLC, NN, MWA, PU

The Life of Mary Baker Eddy. Sybil W. O'Brien. N. Y., 1908. 384 p. *DLC, NN, PU*

Mary Baker Eddy; a Life Size Portrait. Lyman P. Powell. N. Y., 1930. 364 p. *DLC, NN, MWA, PU*

According to the Flesh: A Biography of Mary Baker Eddy. Fleta C. Springer. N. Y., 1930. 497 p. *DLC, NN, PU*
2:336

EDDY, THOMAS. *Life of Thomas Eddy.* S. L. Knapp. N. Y., 1834. 394 p. *DLC, NN, PU*

EDDY, THOMAS MEARS. *Life of Thomas M. Eddy, D.D.* Charles N. Sims. N. Y., 1879. 392 p. *NN, MiD:B*

EDEN, ROBERT. *Life and Administration of Sir Robert Eden.* Bernard C. Steiner. Balt., 1898. 135 p. (Johns Hopkins Univ. Studies, 16th Series, Nos. 7–9. v. 16. pp. 341–476)
DLC, NN, MWA, CSmH, PU

EDES, PETER. *Peter Edes, Pioneer Printer in Maine, A Biography.* Samuel L. Boardman, ed. Bangor, 1901. 159 p.
DLC, MWA, CSmH

EDGEWORTH, MARIA. *A Study of Maria Edgeworth.* Grace A. Oliver. Boston, 1882. 567 p. *DLC, NN, PU*

EDISON, THOMAS ALVA.

Edison, the Man and His Work. George S. Bryan. N. Y., 1926. 350 p. *DLC, NN, PU*

Thomas A. Edison. Frederic T. Cooper. N. Y., 1914. 236 p.
DLC, NN

Thomas A. Edison and Samuel F. B. Morse. V. B. Denslow and Jane M. Parker. 1887. (World's Workers Series) *NN*

Life and Invention of Thomas Edison. W. K. L. and A. Dickinson. N. Y., 1894. 362 p. *DLC, NN*

Thomas A. Edison. His Life and Inventions. Frank L. Dyer and Thomas C. Martin. N. Y., 1910, 1929. 2 vols. *DLC, NN*

Thomas Alva Edison: Sixty Years of an Inventor's Life. Francis A. Jones. N. Y., 1907. 375 p. *DLC*

Thomas Alva Edison, an Intimate Record. Francis A. Jones. N. Y., 1924. 399 p. *DLC*

The Life Story of Thomas Alva Edison. Francis A. Jones. N. Y., 1931. 405 p. *DLC, NN*

Thomas Alva Edison: The Telegraph Boy Who Became a Great Inventor. Edith C. Kenyon. N. Y., 1896. 128 p.   *DLC, NN*
Recollections of Edison. David T. Marshall. Boston, 1931. 117 p.   *DLC, NN*
Thomas A. Edison, Benefactor of Mankind. Francis T. Miller. Phila., 1931. 320 p.   *DLC, NN, MWA*
Thomas A. Edison, a Modern Olympian. Mary C. Nerney. N. Y., 1934. 334 p.   *DLC, NN, CSmH*
Thomas Alva Edison. Francis W. Rolt-Wheeler. N. Y., 1915. 201 p. (True Stories of Great Americans)   *DLC*
Edison; His Life, His Work, His Genius. William A. Simonds. N. Y., 1934. 364 p.   *DLC, NN*
2:94–301–388

EDWARD III. *Life of Edward the Black Prince, 1330–1376.* Henry D. Sedgwick. Indianapolis, 1932. 315 p.   *DLC, NN*

EDWARDS, BELA BATES. *Writings of Prof. B. B. Edwards, With a Memoir.* Edwards A Park. Boston, 1853. 2 vols.
DLC, NN, MWA

EDWARDS, DAN. *This Side of Hell; Dan Edwards, Adventurer.* Lowell J. Thomas. Garden City, N. Y., 1932. 316 p.   *DLC, NN*

EDWARDS, DAVID. *Life of Rev. David Edwards, Late Bishop of the United Brethren in Christ.* Lewis Davis. Dayton, Ohio, 1883. 322 p.   *DLC*

EDWARDS, JAMES GARDINER. *The Life and Works of James Gardiner Edwards.* Philip D. Jordan. Springfield, Ill., 1931. 46 p. (Pamphlet) (Reprinted from Journal of Ill. State Hist. Soc. Vol. 23, No. 3, Oct., 1930)   *NN, MWA, CSmH*

EDWARDS, JOHN NEWMAN. *John N. Edwards; Biography, Memoirs, Reminiscences and Recollections.* Mary V. P. Edwards, comp. Kansas City., Mo., 1889. 428 p.   *DLC, NN, CSmH*

EDWARDS, JONATHAN.
Life of President Edwards. Phila., 1832. 143 p.   *DLC, PU*
Jonathan Edwards. A. V. G. Allen. Boston, 1889. 401 p. (American Religious Leaders)   *DLC, NN, MWA, CSmH, PU*
Jonathan Edwards. I. Crook. N. Y., 1903. 95 p. (Modern Messages)   *DLC, NN*
Jonathan Edwards: A Psychological Study. J. H. Crooker. Boston, 1890. (N. E. Mag. Vol. 2, (N.S.) no. 2 pp. 159–172)
NN
The Life of President Jonathan Edwards. Sereno E. Dwight. N. Y., 1830. 766 p.   *DLC, NN, MWA, CSmH*

Jonathan Edwards, a Retrospect. Harry N. Gardiner. Boston, 1901. 168 p. *CSmH*

The Life and Character of the Late Mr. Jonathan Edwards, President of the College of New Jersey . . . Samuel Hopkins. Boston, 1765. 373 p. *DLC, MWA, CSmH, RP:JCB*

Jonathan Edwards. Arthur C. McGiffert. N. Y. and London, 1932. 225 p. *DLC, NN, CSmH, PU*

Life of Jonathan Edwards. Samuel Miller. (L.A.B.)
DLC, NN, MWA, CSmH, PU, MiU:C

Jonathan Edwards; the Fiery Puritan. Henry B. Parkes. N. Y., 1930. 271 p. *DLC, NN, MWA, CSmH, PU*
2:707

EDWARDS, JUSTIN. *A Sketch of the Life and Labors of the Rev. Justin Edwards, D.D.* William A. Hallock. N. Y., 1855. 556 p.
DLC, NN, MWA, CSmH

EDWARDS, RICHARD. *The Life and Poems of Richard Edwards.* Leicester Bradner. New Haven, 1927. 144 p. (Yale Studies in English No. 74) *DLC, NN, CSmH, PU*

EDWARDS, SARAH. *Mrs. Sarah Edwards, Wife of . . . President Edwards.* S. E. Dwight. *CSmH*

EGAN, MICHAEL. *History of Michael Egan, First Bishop of Philadelphia.* Martin I. J. Griffin. Phila., 1893. 128 p. *DLC, NN*

EGGLESTON, EDWARD. *The First of the Hoosiers.* George C. Eggleston. Phila., 1903. 382 p. *DLC, NN, MWA, PU*

EHRLICH, PAUL. 2:176

EINSTEIN, ALBERT. *Albert Einstein, a Biographical Portrait.* Anton Reiser. N. Y., 1930. 255 p. *DLC, NN, PU*
2:301

ELAGABALUS, EMPEROR. 2:71

ELDER, BEN. *The Drummer Boy of the Ozarks; or, Sketches in the Life of Ben Elder.* W. S. Kirby. West Plains, Mo., 1893. 112 p.
NN

ELDER, SAMUEL JAMES. *Life of Samuel J. Elder; With Chapters by Edwin A. Whitman and William C. Wait.* Margaret M. Elder. New Haven, 1925. 370 p. *DLC, NN*

ELIOT, CHARLES. *Charles Eliot, Landscape Architect.* Charles W. Eliot, ed. Boston, 1902. 770 p. *DLC, NN, MWA, PU*

ELIOT, CHARLES WILLIAM.

The Life of Charles W. Eliot. E. H. Cotton. Boston, 1926. 424 p. *DLC, NN, PU*

Charles W. Eliot, President of Harvard University, 1869–1909.
Henry James. Boston, 1930. 2 vols.   *DLC, NN, CSmH, PU*
Charles·W. Eliot, Puritan Liberal. Henry H. Saunderson. N. Y.,
1928. 253 p.   *DLC, NN, PU*
2:114–246–326–519

ELIOT, GEORGE. [MARY ANN EVANS]
George Eliot: Critical Study. G. W. Cooks. Boston, 1883.
438 p.   *DLC, NN, CSmH*
George Eliot; a Biography. Blanche C. Williams. N. Y.,
1936. 341 p.   *DLC, NN, CSmH, PU*
2:337

ELIOT, JOHN.
Life of Rev. John Eliot. Nehemiah Adams. Boston, 1847.
324 p.   *DLC, NN, MWA, CSmH*
John Eliot, the Puritan Missionary to the Indians. Ezra H.
Byington. 34 p. (Amer. Soc. Church Hist. Vol. VIII., 1897)
DLC, NN
Life and Labors of John Eliot, the Apostle Among the Indians.
Robert B. Caverly. Lowell, Mass., 1881. 98 p.
DLC, NN, MWA
A Sketch of the Life of the Apostle Eliot. Henry A. S. Dear-
born. Roxbury, Mass., 1850. 32 p.
DLC, NN, MWA, CSmH, MiU:C
Life of John Eliot, Apostle to the Indians. Convers Francis.
N. Y., 1849. 357 p. (L.A.B.)   *DLC, NN, MWA, CSmH, PU*
*Memoirs of the Life and Character of Rev. John Eliot, Apostle
of the N. A. Indians.* Martin Moore. Boston, 1822. 174 p.
DLC, NN, MWA, CSmH, MiD:B
2:405–464

ELIOT, WILLIAM GREENLEAF. *William Greenleaf Eliot, Minister, Educator, Philanthropist.* C. C. Eliot. Boston, 1904. 376 p.
DLC, NN, CSmH, PU

ELIZABETH, QUEEN.
History of Queen Elizabeth. Jacob Abbott. N. Y., 1849. 281 p.
DLC, NN, PU
Queen Elizabeth. Katharine S. Anthony. N. Y., 1929. 263 p.
DLC, NN, PU
Tudor Wench. Elswyth Thane. N. Y., 1932. 390 p.
DLC, NN

ELLER, FRANKLIN PLATO and JOHN CARLTON. *Lives of Franklin
Plato Eller and John Carlton Eller.* Jay B. Hubbell. Durham,
N. C., 1910. 245 p.   *DLC, NN*

ELLERY, WILLIAM. *Life of William Ellery.* Edward T. Channing. (L.A.B.)   *DLC, NN, MWA, CSmH, PU*

ELLICOTT, ANDREW. *Andrew Ellicott: His Life and Letters.* Catherine V. C. Matthews. N. Y., 1908. 256 p.
                                           DLC, NN, MWA, PU

ELLINWOOD, FRANK FIELD. *Frank Field Ellinwood. His Life and Work.* Mary G. Ellinwood. N. Y., 1911. 246 p.   *DLC*

ELLIOTT, JESSE DUNCAN. *A Biographical Notice of Com. Jesse D. Elliott . . .* Russell Jarvis. Phila., 1835. 480 p.
                                           DLC, NN, CSmH, PU

ELLIOTT, JOHN. *John Elliott; the Story of an Artist.* Maud H. Elliott. Boston, 1920. 265 p. (Ltd. Ed.)   *DLC, NN, MWA*

ELLIOTT, STEPHEN. *Memoir of Stephen Elliott, D.D.* Thomas M. Hanckel. N. Y., 1867. 594 p.

ELLIS, HAVELOCK.

Havelock Ellis; a Biographical and Critical Survey, With a Supplementary Chapter on Mrs. Edith Ellis. Isaac Goldberg. N. Y., 1926. 359 p.   *DLC, NN, PU*

Havelock Ellis; Philosopher of Love. Houston Peterson. Boston, 1928. 432 p.   *DLC, NN, PU*

ELLIS, MARY MERCER. *Memoir of Mrs. Mary Mercer Ellis, Wife of Rev. William Ellis . . . Including . . . the Details of Missionary Life . . .* William Ellis. Boston, 1836. 286 p.
                                           DLC, NN, CSmH

ELLIS, RUFUS. *Memoir of Rufus Ellis.* Arthur B. Ellis. Boston, 1891. 324 p.   *MWA*

ELLIS, WILLIAM. *Memoir of William Ellis.* Ethel E. Ellis. N. Y., 1888. 201 p.

ELLSWORTH, OLIVER. *The Life of Oliver Ellsworth.* William G. Brown. N. Y., 1905. 369 p.   *DLC, NN, CSmH, PU, MiD:B* 2:230–666

EMERSON, GEORGE BARRELL. *Memoir of George Barrell Emerson . . .* Robert C. Waterston. Cambridge, 1884. 124 p.
                                           NN, MWA, MiD:B

EMERSON, JOHN EDWARDS. *Memoir of Rev. John Edwards Emerson.* Rufus W. Clark, N. Y., 1852. 406 p.
                                           DLC, NN, MWA, CSmH, MiD:B

EMERSON, JOSEPH. *Life of the Rev. Joseph Emerson, Pastor of the Third Congregational Church in Beverly, Mass.* Ralph Emerson. Boston, 1834. 454 p.   *DLC, NN, MWA, PU, MiD:B*

EMERSON, RALPH WALDO.

Ralph Waldo Emerson . . . An Estimate of His Character and Genius, etc. Bronson Alcott. Boston, 1882. 81 p.　*DLC, NN*
Ralph Waldo Emerson. Sarah K. Bolton. N. Y., 1904. 27 p.
　　　　　　　　　　　　　　　　　　　　　DLC, NN
Life of Emerson. Van Wyck Brooks. N. Y., 1932. 315 p.
　　　　　　　　　DLC, NN, MWA, CSmH, PU
A Memoir of Ralph Waldo Emerson. James E. Cabot. Boston and N. Y., 1887. 2 vols.
　　　　　　DLC, NN, MWA, CSmH, PU, MiD:B
Emerson, Poet and Thinker. Elisabeth L. Cary. N. Y., 1904. 284 p.　　　　　　　　　　　　　　*DLC, PU*
Ralph Waldo Emerson: His Life, Writings and Philosophy. George W. Cooke. Boston, 1881. 422 p. *DLC, NN, CSmH, PU*
Ralph Waldo Emerson. Samuel M. Crothers. Indianapolis, 1921. 234 p.　　　　　　*DLC, NN, CSmH, PU*
Emerson in Concord. A Memoir. Edward W. Emerson. Boston, 1888. 266 p.　　　*DLC, NN, MWA, CSmH, PU*
Ralph Waldo Emerson. Oscar W. Firkins. Boston, 1915. 379 p.　　　　　　*DLC, NN, CSmH, PU*
Emerson: a Study of the Poet as Seer. Robert M. Gay. N. Y., 1928. 250 p. (Murray Hill Biographies) *DLC, NN, CSmH, PU*
Ralph Waldo Emerson, Philosopher and Poet. Alfred H. Guernsey. N. Y., 1881. 327 p.　　　*DLC, NN, MWA*
Ralph Waldo Emerson. William Hague. N. Y., 1884. 31 p.
　　　　　　　　　　　　　　　　　　　　　DLC, NN
Youth's Captain, the Story of Ralph Waldo Emerson. Hildegarde Hawthorne. N. Y., 1935. 205 p.　　　*DLC, NN*
Ralph Waldo Emerson. Oliver W. Holmes. Boston and N. Y., 1885, 1912. 441 p. (A.M.L.)
　　　　　DLC, NN, MWA, CSmH, PU, MiD:B
Emerson Today. Bliss Perry. Princeton, N. J., 1931. 140 p.
　　　　　　　　　　　DLC, NN, CSmH, PU
Emerson, the Wisest American. Phillips Russell. N. Y., 1929. 320 p.　　　　　　*DLC, NN, CSmH, PU*
Ralph Waldo Emerson. F. B. Sanborn. Boston, 1901. 140 p. (Beacon Biographies)　　　　　　*DLC, CSmH, PU*
A Biography of Ralph Waldo Emerson, Set Forth as His Life Essay. Denton J. Snider. St. Louis, 1921. 384 p.　*DLC, NN*

Ralph Waldo Emerson. George E. Woodberry. Boston, 1907.
205 p. *DLC, NN, MWA, CSmH, PU*
2:5–47

EMERY, MATTHEW G. *Biography of Matthew G. Emery.* Wm. V.
Cox. Wash., 1904. *RP:JCB*

EMERY, NOAH. *Noah Emery of. Exeter, Member of the Provincial
Congress and Clerk of the Assembly in New Hampshire in the Revo-
lution.* Charles E. Stevens. n.p., 1886. 39 p. (Privately
Printed) *DLC, MWA, MiD:B*

EMERY, SAMUEL HOPKINS. *The Life of Samuel Hopkins Emery.*
Ralph Davol. Taunton, Mass., 1902. 206 p. *NN, MWA, MiD:B*

EMMET, JOHN PATTEN. *Memoir of John Patten Emmet, Formerly
Professor of Chemistry and Materia Medica in the University of
Virginia.* Thomas A. Emmet. N. Y., 1898. 66 p.
DLC, NN, MWA, CSmH

EMMET, ROBERT.
Robert Emmet, A Survey of His Rebellion and of His Romance.
Louise I. Guiney. London, 1904. 102 p. *DLC, NN, CSmH*
Dear Robert Emmet, a Biography. Raymond W. Postgate.
N. Y., 1932. 278 p. *DLC, NN*

EMMET, THOMAS ADDIS. *Memoir of Thomas Addis Emmet and Robert
Emmet.* Thomas A. Emmet. N. Y., 1915. 2 vols.
DLC, NN, MWA

EMMET, THOMAS ADDIS. *Memoir of Thomas Addis Emmet With a
Biographical Notice of C. G. Haines.* C. G. Haines. N. Y., 1829.
132 p. *DLC, NN, PU*

EMMONS, NATHANIEL. *Memoir of Nathaniel Emmons.* Edwards A.
Park. Boston, 1861. 468 p. *DLC, NN, MWA*

EMORY, JOHN. *The Life of John Emory, D.D.* Robert Emory. N. Y.,
1841. 380 p. *DLC, NN*

EMORY, WILLIAM HEMSLEY. *The Life of an American Sailor: Rear
Admiral William Hemsley Emory, U. S. N., From His Letters and
Memoirs.* Albert Gleaves. N. Y., 1923. 359 p. *DLC, NN*

EMRICH, FREDERICK ERNEST. *Frederick Ernest Emrich, Lover of Humanity.* Winfred Rhoades. Boston, 1933. 152 p. *DLC, NN*

ENDECOTT, JOHN.
Memoir of John Endecott . . . Charles M. Endecott. Salem,
1847. 116 p. *CSmH*
John Endecott, a Biography. Lawrence F. S. Mayo. Cambridge, 1936. 301 p. *DLC, NN, MWA, CSmH*

ENDICOTT, HENRY B. *Henry B. Endicott. A Brief Memoir of His Life and His Services to the Nation.* Boston, 1921. (Privately Printed) *MWA*

ENGLAND, JOHN.
Life and Times of John England, First Bishop of Charleston (1786–1842). Peter K. Guilday. N. Y., 1927. 2 vols.
DLC, NN, CSmH, MiD:B
John England, Bishop of Charleston, the Apostle to Democracy. Joseph L. O'Brien. N. Y., 1934. 222 p. *DLC, NN, CSmH*

ENNEKING, JOHN JOSEPH. 2:52

ERASMUS, DESIDERIUS.
Desiderius Erasmus of Rotterdam. Ephraim Emerton. N. Y., 1899. 469 p. *DLC, NN, PU*
The Youth of Erasmus. Albert Hyma. Ann Arbor, Mich., 1930. 350 p. *DLC, NN, MWA, CSmH, PU*
Life, Character and Influence of Desiderius Erasmus of Rotterdam; Derived From a Study of His Works and Correspondence. John J. Mangan. N. Y., 1927. 2 vols. *DLC, NN, CSmH, PU*
Erasmus: a Study of His Life, Ideals and Place in History. Preserved Smith. N. Y., 1923. 479 p. *DLC, NN, CSmH, PU*
2:5–336–371

ERICSSON, JOHN.
Life of John Ericsson. W. C. Church. N. Y., 1890. 2 vols.
DLC, NN, MWA, CSmH, PU
The Miner Boy and His Monitor; the Career and Achievements of John Ericsson, Engineer. Phineas C. Headley. Boston, 1864. 297 p. *DLC, NN*
2:340–343

ERRETT, ISAAC. *Memoirs of Isaac Errett.* James S. Lamar. Cincinnati, 1893. 2 vols. *DLC*

ERSKINE, ROBERT. *The Forgotten General. Robert Erskine, F.R.S. (1735–1780), Geographer and Surveyor-General to the Army of the U. S. of America.* Albert H. Heusser. Paterson, N. J., 1928. 216 p. *DLC, NN, MWA, CSmH*

ESSEX, 2D EARL OF. *The Career of the Earl of Essex From the Islands' Voyage in 1597 to His Execution in 1601.* Laura H. Cadwallader. Phila., 1923. 128 p. *DLC, NN, CSmH, PU*

EURIPIDES. *Euripides; a Student of Human Nature.* William N. Bates. Phila., 1930. 315 p. *DLC, NN, PU*

EVANS, ALICE C. 2:175

EVANS, HUGH DAVEY. *Hugh Davey Evans. A Memoir.* Hall Harrison. Hartford, 1870. 182 p. *DLC, NN*

EVANS, JAMES. *Apostle of the North, Rev. James Evans.* Egerton R. Young. N. Y., 1899. 262 p. *DLC, NN*

EVANS, JOHN. *Life of Governor Evans, Second Territorial Governor of Colorado.* Edgar G. MacMechen. Denver, 1924. 224 p.
DLC, NN

EVANS, KATHERINE. 2:55

EVANS, OLIVER. *Oliver Evans; a Chronicle of Early American Engineering.* Grenville Bathe and Dorothy Bathe. Phila., 1935. 362 p.
DLC, NN, CSmH, PU

EVANS, ROBERT. *Fighting Bob Evans.* Edwin A. Falk. Annapolis, 1931. 495 p. *DLC, NN, PU*

EVARTS, JEREMIAH. *Memoir of the Life of Jeremiah Evarts, Esq., Late Corresponding Secretary of the American Board of Commissioners for Foreign Missions.* E. C. Tracy. Boston, 1845. 448 p.
NN, MWA

EVERETT, ANNE GORHAM. *Memoir of Anne Gorham Everett.* Philippa C. Bush. Boston, 1857 320 p. (Privately Printed)
DLC, NN, MWA, CSmH

EVERETT, CHARLES C. 2:519

EVERETT, EDWARD.
An Address Upon the Life and Services of Edward Everett.
Richard H. Dana, Jr. Cambridge, 1865. 70 p.
DLC, NN, MWA, MiD:B
Edward Everett; Orator and Statesman. Paul R. Frothingham.
Boston, 1925. 495 p. *DLC, NN, MWA*
See BELL, JOHN.

EVERETT, SERAPHINA H. *The Missionary Sisters: A Memorial of Mrs. Seraphina H. Everett and Mrs. Harriet M. Hamlin, Late Missionaries . . . at Constantinople.* M. G. Benjamin. Boston, 1860. 335 p. *DLC, NN, MWA*

EVERETT, WILLIAM. 2:246

EVERHART, JAMES BOWEN. *A Memorial of the Life and Character of James Bowen Everhart.* Thomas L. Ogier, ed. N. Y., 1889. 156 p. *DLC, NN*

EVERTS, WILLIAM WALLACE. *The Life of Rev. W. W. Everts, D.D.* William W. Everts, Jr. Phila., 1891. 136 p. *DLC, NN, MiD:B*

EWELL, RICHARD STODDERT. 2:612

EWING, ELLEN. *Ellen Ewing, Wife of General Sherman.* Anna S. McAllister. N. Y., 1936. 379 p. *DLC, NN, CSmH*

EWING, GEORGE. *George Ewing, Gentleman, a Soldier of Valley Forge.* Thomas Ewing. Yonkers, 1928.   CSmH

EWING, THOMAS. *Memorial of Thomas Ewing, of Ohio.* Ellen E. Sherman. N. Y., 1873. 289 p.   DLC, NN

FABRE, HENRY. *The Boy Who Found Out; the Story of Henry Fabre.* Mary H. Wade. N. Y., 1928. 215 p.   DLC
   2:79

FAIRBANKS, CHARLES WARREN. *Life and Speeches of Hon. Charles W. Fairbanks.* W. H. Smith. Indianapolis, 1904. 252 p. *DLC, NN*

FAIRBANKS, JOSEPH PADDOCK. *A Memorial of Joseph P. Fairbanks.* Samuel H. Taylor. Riverside, 1865. 169 p.   DLC, MWA

FAIRCHILD, JAMES HARRIS. *James Harris Fairchild; or, Sixty-Eight Years With a Christian College.* Albert T. Swing. N. Y., 1907. 396 p.   DLC, NN, CSmH, PU

FAIRFAX. *The Fairfaxes of England and America in the 17th and 18th Centuries.* E. D. Neill. N. Y., 1868. 234 p.
        DLC, NN, MWA, CSmH

FAIRFAX, SALLY C. *Sally Cary; a Long Hidden Romance of Washington's Life.* Wilson M. Cary. N. Y., 1916. 104 p.
        DLC, NN, CSmH

FAIRFIELD, SUMNER LINCOLN. *The Life of Sumner Lincoln Fairfield* . . . Jane Fairfield. N. Y., 1847. 132 p.
        DLC, NN, MWA, PU, MiD:B

FALCKNER, JUSTICE. *Justice Falckner, Mystic and Scholar.* J. F. Sachse. Phila., 1903. 141 p. (Privately Printed)
        DLC, NN, MWA, CSmH, PU

FALLON, WILLIAM JOSEPH. *Great Mouthpiece; a Life Story of William J. Fallon.* Gene Fowler. N. Y., 1931. 403 p. DLC, NN

FALLOWS, SAMUEL. *Everybody's Bishop; Life and Times of Samuel Fallows.* Alice K. Fallows. N. Y., 1927. 461 p.
        DLC, NN, MWA, MiD:B

FANCHER, MARY J. *Mollie Fanchèr, the Brooklyn Enigma* . . . *Life of Mary J. Fancher.* Abram H. Dailey. Brooklyn, N. Y., 1894. 262 p.   DLC, NN, PU

FANNING, CHARLOTTE. *Life Work of Mrs. Charlotte Fanning.* Emma Page, ed. Nashville, 1907. 201 p.   DLC

FARADAY, MICHAEL. *Michael Faraday (1791–1867).* Wilfred L. Randell. Boston, 1924. 186 p.   DLC, NN
   2:79

FARLEY, CARDINAL. 2:679

FARMER, JOHN. *A Memorial of John Farmer, A.M.* John Le Bosquet. Boston, 1884. 138 p. *DLC, NN, MWA, MiD:B*

FARRAGUT, DAVID GLASGOW.
David G. Farragut. James Barnes. Boston, 1899. 132 p. (Beacon Biographies) *DLC, NN, CSmH, MiD:B*
Life of David G. Farragut, First Admiral, U. S. N., Embodying His Journals and Letters. Loyall Farragut. N. Y., 1879. 586 p. *DLC, NN, MWA, CSmH*
Life and Naval Career of Admiral David G. Farragut. P. C. Headley. N. Y., 1865. 342 p. *MiD:B*
Admiral Farragut. Alfred T. Mahan. N. Y., 1892. 333 p. (G.C.) *DLC, NN, MWA, CSmH, PU, MiD:B*
David G. Farragut. John R. Spears. Phila., 1905. 407 p. (A.C.B.) *DLC, NN, PU*
2:104–396–624

FARRAR, GERALDINE. *Geraldine Farrar, an Authorized Record of Her Career.* Edward C. Wagenknecht. Seattle, 1929. 91 p. *DLC, NN*

FARWELL, JOHN VILLIERS. *Reminiscences of John V. Farwell.* Abby Farwell. Chicago, 1928. 2 vols. *DLC*

FECHTER, CHARLES ALBERT. *Charles Albert Fechter.* Kate Field. Boston, 1882. 205 p. (American Actor Series) *DLC, MWA, PU*

FEKE, ROBERT. *Robert Feke, Colonial Portrait Painter.* Henry W. Foote. Cambridge, 1920. 223 p. *DLC, NN, MWA*

FELL, MARGARET. 2:55

FELS, JOSEPH. *Joseph Fels: His Life Work.* Mary Fels. N. Y., 1916. 271 p. *DLC, NN, PU*

FÉNELON, FRANÇOIS. *Memoir of Fénelon.* J. R. G. Hassard. N. Y., 1865. *NN*
2:95

FENWICK, EDWARD DOMINIE. *The Right Rev. Edward Dominie Fenwick, O.P.* Victor F. O'Daniel. Washington, 1920. 473 p. *DLC, NN, MiD:B*

FENWICK, JOHN. *Sketch of the Life and Character of John Fenwick.* John Clement. Phila., 1875. 95 p. *DLC, PU, MiD:B*

FERDINAND of AUSTRIA. 2:1

FERDINAND of ROUMANIA. 2:30

FESSENDEN, THOMAS GREEN. *The Life and Works of Thomas Green Fessenden, 1771–1837.* Porter G. Perrin. Orono, Me., 1925. 206 p. (Univ. of Maine Studies, Sec. Ser., No. 4)
DLC, NN, MWA, CSmH, PU

FESSENDEN, WILLIAM PITT. *Life and Public Services of William Pitt Fessenden.* Francis Fessenden. Boston, 1907. 2 vols.
DLC, NN, MWA, CSmH, PU

FIEGLER, MARY AQUINATA. *Memoirs of Mother Mary Aquinata Fiegler, O.P.* Sister Mary P. Kildee. Grand Rapids, Mich., 1928. 128 p. *DLC, NN*

FIELD, CYRUS WEST. *Cyrus W. Field. His Life and Work, 1819–1892.* Isabella F. Judson, ed. N. Y., 1896. 322 p.
DLC, NN, PU

2:623

FIELD, DAVID DUDLEY. *The Life of David Dudley Field.* Henry M. Field. N. Y., 1898. 361 p. *DLC, NN, MWA, CSmH*

FIELD, EUGENE.
Eugene Field in His Home. Ida C. Below. N. Y., 1898. 111 p.
DLC, NN, MWA
Eugene Field's Creative Years. Charles H. Dennis. N. Y., 1924. 339 p. *DLC, NN, MWA, CSmH*
Works of Eugene Field With a Memoir. R. M. Field. N. Y., 1896. 10 vols. (Sabine Ed.) *DLC*
Eugene Field; a Study in Heredity and Contradictions. Slason Thompson. N. Y., 1901. 2 vols. *DLC, NN, MWA, CSmH, PU*
Life of Eugene Field; the Poet of Childhood. Slason Thompson. N. Y. and London, 1927. 407 p. *DLC, NN, MWA, PU*
The Eugene Field I Knew. Francis Wilson. N. Y., 1898. 128 p. *DLC, NN, MWA, CSmH*

FIELD, FATHER. *Cross of Iron; With a Sketch of the Life and Work of Father Field.* Wilton Tournier. Phila., 1891. 92 p.

FIELD, KATE. *Kate Field; a Record.* Lilian Whiting. Boston, 1899. 610 p. *DLC, NN, MWA, CSmH*

FIELD, MARSHALL. 2:623

FIELD, NATHANIEL. *Nathaniel Field, the Actor-Playwright.* Roberta F. Brinkley. New Haven, 1928. 159 p. (Yale Studies in Eng.)
DLC, NN, CSmH, PU

FIELD, STEPHEN JOHNSON. *Stephen J. Field, Craftsman of the Law.* Carl B. Swisher. Washington, 1930. 473 p.
DLC, NN, CSmH, PU

FIELDE, ADELE MARION. *Memorial Biography of Adele M. Fielde, Humanitarian.* Helen N. Stevens. N. Y., 1918. 377 p.
DLC, NN

FIELDING, HENRY. *History of Henry Fielding.* Wilbur L. Cross. New Haven, 1918. 3 vols. *DLC, CSmH, PU*

FIGUEROA, CRISTÓBAL SUAREZ. *Life and Works of Cristóbal Suarez de Figueroa* . . . James P. W. Crawford. Phila., 1907. 159 p. (Pub. of the Univ. of Penn., Series in Romance Languages and Literatures, v. 1)   *DLC, NN, PU*

FILLMORE, MILLARD.
 Biography of Millard Fillmore. Ivory Chamberlain. Buffalo, 1856. 215 p.   *DLC, NN, MWA*
 Life and Public Services of Millard Fillmore. W. L. Barre. Buffalo, 1856. 408 p.   *DLC*
 Millard Fillmore, Constructive Statesman, Defender of the Constitution, President of the United States. William E. Griffis. Ithaca, N. Y., 1915. 159 p.   *DLC, NN, MWA, CSmH, PU*

FILSON, JOHN. *John Filson, the First Historian of Kentucky: Account of His Life and Writings.* Reuben T. Durrett. Louisville, 1884. 132 p.   *DLC, MWA, CSmH, MiD:B, MiU:C*

FINCH, JOHN BIRD. *John B. Finch. His Life and Work* . . . Francis E. Finch and Frank J. Sibley. N. Y., 1888. 569 p.
               DLC, NN, MiD:B

FINDLAY, JONATHAN SMITH. *Life and Letters of Jonathan Smith Findlay.* ·Ellen Duvall. n.p., n.d. 51 p.   *DLC, MWA*

FINK, MIKE. *Mike Fink, King of Mississippi Keelboatmen.* Walter Blair and Franklin J. Meine. N. Y., 1933. 283 p.
           DLC, NN, MWA, CSmH, PU

FINLEY, ROBERT. *Memoirs of the Rev. Robert Finley, D. D. . . . With Brief Sketches of Some of His Contemporaries.* Isaac V. Brown. New Brunswick, N. J., 1819. 296 p.
        DLC, NN, MWA, CSmH, PU, MiD:B

FINNEY, CHARLES GRANDISON.
 Life of Charles G. Finney. A. M. Hills. Cincinnati, 1902. 240 p.   *DLC, NN*
 Charles G. Finney. George F. Wright. Boston and N. Y., 1891. 329 p. (American Religious Leaders) *DLC, NN, MWA* 2:40

FINSEN, NIELS R. 2:175

FIRKINS, OSCAR W. *Memoirs and Letters of Oscar W. Firkins.* Ina Ten Eyck Firkins. Minneapolis, 1934. 312 p.   *DLC, NN*

FIRTH, FRANK RUSSELL. *The Young Engineer; a Memoir of Frank Russell Firth.* Boston, 1874. 122 p.   *DLC, NN, MWA*

FISCHER, EMIL. 2:286

FISH, HAMILTON.
 Hamilton Fish. Amos E. Corning. N. Y., 1918. 108 p.
                DLC, NN

Hamilton Fish, the Inner History of Grant's Administration. Allan Nevins. N. Y., 1936. 932 p.   *DLC, NN, CSmH, PU*

FISHER, EBENEZER. *Memoir of Rev. Ebenezer Fisher.* G. H. Emerson. Boston, 1880. 263 p.   *NN*

FISHER, ELIJAH JOHN. *The Master's Slave, Elijah John Fisher; a Biography.* Miles M. Fisher. Phila., 1922. 194 p.   *DLC, NN*

FISHER, MARY. 2:55

FISHER, SAMUEL S. *In Memoriam. Samuel S. Fisher.* Cincinnati, 1874. 92 p.   *DLC, NN, MWA, CSmH*

FISHER, THOMAS JEFFERSON. *The Life of Thomas Jefferson Fisher, the Pulpit Orator and Evangelist.* J. H. Spencer. Louisville, 1866. 208 p.

FISK, CLINTON BOWEN. *The Life of Clinton B. Fisk, With a Brief Sketch of John A. Brooks.* Alphonso A. Hopkins. N. Y., 1888. 295 p.   *DLC, NN, MiD:B*

FISK, JAMES, JR.

    James Fisk, Jr. The Life of a Green Mountain Boy. Phila., 1872. 128 p.   *NN, MWA*

    A Life of James Fisk, Jr., Being a Full and Accurate Narrative of All the Enterprises in Which He Has Been Engaged. N. Y., 1871. 300 p.   *DLC, NN*

    Jubilee Jim: The Life of Colonel James Fisk, Jr. Robert H. Fuller. N. Y., 1928. 566 p. (Biographical Fiction)
DLC, NN, MWA, PU

    James Fisk, Jr. The Life of a Green Mountain Boy. The Story of His Struggle From Poverty and Weakness up to Health and Power. Willoughby Jones. Phila., 1872. 512 p.
DLC, NN, CSmH

    The Life and Times of Col. James Fisk, Jr., Being the Full and Impartial Account of the Remarkable Career of a Most Remarkable Man. R. W. McAlpine. N. Y., 1872. 504 p.   *DLC, NN*

    A Life of James Fisk, Jr., Being a Full and Accurate Narrative of All the Enterprises in Which He Has Been Engaged. Marshall P. Stafford. N. Y., 1872. 325 p.   *DLC, MiD:B*
    2:451

FISK, PLINY. *Memoirs of Pliny Fisk.* Alvan Bond. Boston, 1828. 437 p.   *DLC, NN, MWA, PU*

FISK, WILBUR.

    Wilbur Fisk. George Prentice. Boston, 1890. 289 p. (American Religious Leaders)   *DLC, NN, MWA*

    Life of Wilbur Fisk, D.D., First President of the Wesleyan University. Joseph Holdich. N. Y., 1842. 455 p. *NN, PU, MiD:B*

FISKE, JOHN.
 Life and Letters of John Fiske. John S. Clark. Boston, 1917.
 2 vols. *DLC, NN, MWA, CSmH, PU*
 Life of John Fiske. Thomas S. Perry. Boston, 1906. 105 p.
 (Beacon Biographies) *DLC, NN, MWA, CSmH*
 2:6–246–335
FISKE, MINNIE MADDERN. *Mrs. Fiske.* Frank C. Griffith. N. Y.,
 1912. 146 p. *NN*
FISKE, NATHAN. *Memoir of Rev. Nathan Fiske, Professor of Intel-
 lectual and Moral Philosophy in Amherst College.* H. Humphrey.
 Amherst, Mass., 1850. 392 p. *DLC, NN, MWA*
FISKE, WILLARD. *Willard Fiske: Life and Correspondence.* Horatio
 S. White. N. Y., 1925. 485 p. *DLC, NN, CSmH, PU*
FITCH, CLYDE. *Clyde Fitch and His Letters.* Montrose J. Moses and
 Virginia Gerson. Boston, 1924. 406 p. *DLC, NN*
FITCH, EBENEZER. *Sketch of the Late Rev. Ebenezer Fitch, D.D.,
 First President of Williams College.* Calvin Durfee. Boston, 1865.
 163 p. *DLC, NN, MWA*
FITCH, JOHN.
 Poor John Fitch; Inventor of the Steamboat. Thomas A. Boyd.
 N. Y., 1935. 315 p. *DLC, NN, MWA, CSmH, PU, MiD:B*
 Life of John Fitch, the Inventor of the Steamboat. Thompson
 Westcott. Phila., 1857. 415 p. *DLC, NN, MiD:B*
 Life of John Fitch. Charles Whittlesey. (L.A.B.)
 DLC, NN, MWA, CSmH
FITZGERALD, EDWARD. 2:86
FITZGERALD, OSCAR PENN. 2:531
FITZSIMMONS, ROBERT. *"Ruby Robert" alias Bob Fitzsimmons.*
 Robert H. Davis. N. Y., 1926. 134 p. *DLC, NN, PU*
FITZSIMONS, THOMAS. *Thomas Fitzsimons, Pennsylvania's Catholic
 Signer of the Constitution of the United States.* Martin I. J.
 Griffin. Phila., 1887. 26 p. *DLC, NN, MWA, CSmH, PU*
FLAGET, BENEDICT JOSEPH. *Sketches of the Life, Times and Char-
 acter of . . . Benedict Joseph Flaget, First Bishop of Louisville.*
 Martin J. Spalding. Louisville, 1852. 406 p.
 NN, CSmH, MiD:B
FLAMEL, NICHOLAS. 2:393
FLAUBERT, GUSTAVE. *Flaubert's Youth, 1821–1845.* Lewis P. Shanks.
 Balt., 1927. 250 p. *DLC, NN, PU*
 2:86

FLECHERE, JOHN WILLIAM. *The Life of the Rev. John W. de la Flechere* ... Joseph Benson. N. Y., 1833. 361 p.

DLC, NN, MWA

FLEISHHACKER, HERBERT. 2:233

FLETCHER, ALICE C. 2:506

FLETCHER, MARY. *Life of Mrs. Mary Fletcher.* Henry Moore. Phila., 1819. 2 vols. *DLC, NN, MWA, CSmH*

FLETCHER, PHILIP CONE. *The Radiant Philip Cone Fletcher.* Silas W. Rogers. Cedar Rapids, Ia., 1923. 313 p. *DLC, NN*

FLETCHER, WILLIAM S. *At Sea and In Port; or, Life and Experience of William S. Fletcher.* Harvey K. Hines, comp. Portland, Ore., 1898. 251 p. *DLC, NN, CSmH*

FLINT, TIMOTHY. *Timothy Flint, Pioneer, Missionary, Author, Editor, 1780–1840.* John E. Kirkpatrick. Cleveland, 1911. 331 p.

DLC, NN, MWA, CSmH, PU

FLOWER, GEORGE EDWARD. *Life and Writings of George Edward Flower.* Isaac Errett, ed. Cincinnati, 1885. 338 p. *DLC, NN*

FLOYD, JOHN. *Life and Diary of John Floyd, Governor of Virginia and Father of Oregon Country.* Charles H. Ambler. Richmond, 1918. 248 p. *DLC, NN, CSmH, PU, MiD:B*

FOCH, FERDINAND.
General Foch; the Man of the Hour. R. M. Johnston. N. Y., 1918. 53 p. *DLC, NN, MWA, PU*
Foch the Man; a Life of the Supreme Commander of the Allied Armies. Clara E. Laughlin. N. Y., 1918. 155 p. *DLC, NN*

FOLGER, HENRY CLAY. *Henry C. Folger, 1857–1930.* Henry C. Folger. New Haven, 1931. 114 p. *DLC, NN, MWA*

FOLLEN, CHARLES. *Life of Charles Follen.* Eliza Lee Follen. Boston, 1844. 386 p. *DLC, NN, MWA*

FOLLEN, KARL. *The Life of Karl Follen; a Study in German American Cultural Relations.* George W. Spindler. Chicago, 1917. 234 p.

NN, PU

FOLTZ, JONATHAN MESSERSMITH. *Surgeon of the Seas; the Adventurous Life of Surgeon General Jonathan M. Foltz in the Days of Wooden Ships.* Charles S. Foltz. Indianapolis, 1931. 351 p.

DLC, NN, PU

FONZI, GIUSEPPANGELO. *The Life and Works of Giuseppangelo Fonzi.* Vincenzo Guerini. Phila., 1925. 136 p. *DLC, NN*

FOOTE, ANDREW HULL. *Life of Andrew Hull Foote, Rear-Admiral U. S. N.* James M. Hoppin. N. Y., 1874. 411 p.

DLC, NN, MWA, CSmH

FOOTE, SAMUEL. *The Dramatic Works of Samuel Foote.* Mary M. Belden. New Haven, 1929. 224 p. (Yale Studies in English. No. 80)   *DLC, NN, CSmH, PU*

FOOTE, SAMUEL EDMOND. *Memoirs of the Life of Samuel E. Foote.* John P. Foote. Cincinnati, 1860. 307 p.   *DLC, MiD:B*

FOOTE, ZIBA. *Life of Ziba Foote.* S. Morrison. Indianapolis, 1893. (Ind. Hist. Soc. Pub. Vol. 2, No. 9)   *DLC, NN, CSmH*

FORBES, JOHN MURRAY. *Life and Recollections of John M. Forbes.* Sarah F. Hughes. Boston, 1899. 2 vols.

DLC, NN, MWA, CSmH

FORBES, JOHN MURRAY. *American Railroad Builder: John Murray Forbes.* Henry G. Pearson. Boston, 1911. 196 p.

DLC, NN, MiD:B

FORBES, VIRGINIA ISABEL. *Virginia Isabel Forbes.* Francis W. Halsey. N. Y., 1900. 180 p.   *DLC, NN*

FORCE, PETER. *The Life and Labors of Peter Force.* Ainsworth R. Spofford. Washington, 1898. 13 p. (Records of the Dist. of Columbia Hist. Soc. vol. 2, p. 1)   *DLC, NN, MiD:B*

FORD, HENRY.
  New Henry Ford; an Authentic Biography. Allan L. Benson. N. Y., 1923. 360 p.   *DLC, NN*
  Truth About Henry Ford. Sarah T. Bushnell. Chicago, 1922. 222 p.   *DLC, NN, MWA*
  Henry Ford, the Man, the Worker, the Citizen. Joseph G. de R. Hamilton. N. Y., 1927. 322 p.   *DLC, NN, PU*
  Henry Ford's Own Story. Rose W. Lane. Forest Hills, N. Y., 1917. 184 p.   *DLC, NN*
  The Tragedy of Henry Ford. Jonathan N. Leonard. N. Y., 1932. 245 p.   *DLC, NN, MWA*
  Henry Ford; an Interpretation. Samuel S. Marquis. Boston, 1923. 206 p.   *DLC, NN, PU, MiD:B*
  And Then Came Ford. Charles Merz. N. Y., 1929. 321 p.
                                             DLC, NN, PU

  The Amazing Story of Henry Ford, the Ideal American and the World's Most Famous Private Citizen. James M. Miller. Chicago, 1922. 400 p.   *DLC, NN*
  Henry Ford, Motor Genius. William A. Simonds. N. Y., 1929. 205 p.   *DLC, NN, MiD:B*
  Henry Ford, the Man and His Motives. William L. Stidger. N. Y., 1923. 207 p.   *DLC, NN, PU*
    2:94–301

FORDNEY, JOSEPH WARREN. *Joseph Warren Fordney; an American Legislator.* John A. Russell. Boston, 1928. 246 p.

DLC, NN, MWA

FORREST, EDWIN.

Life of Edwin Forrest: The American Tragedian. William R. Alger. Phila., 1877. 2 vols. *DLC, NN, CSmH, PU*

Edwin Forrest. Lawrence Barrett. Boston, 1881. 171 p. (American Actor Series) *DLC, NN, MWA, CSmH, PU*

Edwin Forrest; the Actor and the Man. Gabriel Harrison. Brooklyn, N. Y., 1889. 210 p. *DLC, NN, MWA, CSmH, PU*

The Fabulous Forrest; the Record of an American Actor. Montrose J. Moses. Boston, 1929. 369 p. *DLC, NN, PU*

The Life of Edwin Forrest. With Reminiscences and Personal Recollections. James Rees. Phila., 1874. 524 p.

DLC, NN, CSmH, PU

FORREST, NATHAN BEDFORD.

Life of Nathan B. Forrest. Hamilton J. Eckenrode. Richmond, 1918. 187 p. *DLC, NN*

Bedford Forrest and His Critter Company. Andrew N. Lytle. N. Y., 1931. 402 p. *DLC, NN, CSmH, PU*

General Forrest. James H. Mathes. N. Y., 1902. 395 p. (G.C.) *DLC, NN, CSmH, PU*

Bedford Forrest: the Confederacy's Greatest Cavalryman. Eric W. Sheppard. N. Y., 1920. 320 p. *DLC, NN, PU*

Life of Nathan B. Forrest. John A. Wyeth. N. Y., 1899. 667 p. *DLC, NN, CSmH*

FOSTER, JOHN. *John Foster, the Earliest American Engraver and the First American Printer.* Samuel A. Green. Boston, 1909. 149 p.

NN, MWA, CSmH, PU, MiD:B

FOSTER, JOHN WELCH. *A Memorial of John W. Foster.* Andrew P. Peabody, ed. Portsmouth, 1852. 400 p. *DLC, NN, MWA*

FOSTER, JUDITH ELLEN. 2:9

FOSTER, LAFAYETTE SABINE. *Memorial Sketch of Lafayette S. Foster, U. S. Senator From Connecticut.* W. H. W. Campbell. Boston, 1881. 129 p. (Privately Printed) *DLC, NN, MWA*

FOSTER, NAT. *Life and Adventures of Nat. Foster, Trapper and Hunter of the Adirondacks.* Arthur L. B. Curtiss. Utica, N. Y., 1897. 286 p. *DLC, NN*

See STONER, NICHOLAS.

FOSTER, STEPHEN COLLINS.

My Brother Stephen. Morrison Foster. Indianapolis, 1932. 55 p. (Privately Printed) *DLC, NN, MWA*

Stephen Foster, America's Troubadour. John T. Howard. N. Y.,
1934. 445 p.   *DLC, NN, MWA, CSmH*
    *Stephen Collins Foster; a Biography of America's Folk-Song
Composer.* Harold V. Milligan. N. Y. and Boston, 1920. 116 p.
                                                     DLC, NN
    Stephen Foster. Raymond Walters. Princeton, 1936. 160 p.
FOTHERGILL, SAMUEL. *Memoirs of the Life and Gospel Labours of
Samuel Fothergill, With Selections From His Correspondence.*
George Crosfield. N. Y., 1844. 544 p.   *NN, MWA, MiD:B*
FOX, GEORGE.
    Story of George Fox. Rufus M. Jones. N. Y., 1919. 169 p.
                                                 DLC, NN, CSmH
    George Fox, Seeker and Friend. Rufus M. Jones. N. Y., 1930.
224 p.   *DLC, NN, CSmH, PU*
        2:55–406

FOX, MARGARET AND CATHERINE.   2:703
FOX, WILLIAM. *Upton Sinclair Presents William Fox.* Upton Sin-
clair. Los Angeles, 1933. 377 p.   *DLC, NN, MWA*
FRANCE, ANATOLE. *Anatole France.* Lewis P. Shanks. Chicago,
1919. 241 p.   *DLC, NN, PU*
FRANCIS I. *Francis I.* Francis Hackett. N. Y., 1935. 448 p.
                                                 DLC, NN, PU

FRANCIS JOSEPH.
    Francis Joseph, Emperor of Austria—King of Hungary. Eugene
Bagger. N. Y., 1927. 572 p.   *DLC, NN, PU*
    Emperor Francis Joseph of Austria. Josef Redlich. N. Y.,
1929. 547 p.   *DLC, NN, PU*
FRANCIS, SAINT. *Everybody's St. Francis.* Maurice F. Egan. N. Y.,
1912. 191 p.   *DLC, NN*
        2:5–95–205–670

FRANCIS DE SALES, SAINT.   2:91
FRANCIS XAVIER, SAINT.   2:680
FRANCIS, JOHN WAKEFIELD. *Memoir of John W. Francis in Francis'
"Old New York."* Henry T. Tuckerman. N. Y., 1855. 143 p.
                                            DLC, NN, MWA, CSmH, PU
FRANCISCO, PETER. *The Romantic Record of Peter Francisco " a Revo-
lutionary Soldier."* Nannie F. Porter. Staunton, Va., 1929. 103 p.
                                                     DLC, NN
FRANCKE, AUGUSTUS HERMANN.. .See SPENCER, PHILIP JACOB.
FRANK, WALDO. *Waldo Frank. A Study.* Gorham B. Munson. N. Y.,
1923. 95 p.   *DLC, NN*

FRANKLIN, BENJAMIN.

Benjamin Franklin, a Picture of the Struggles of Our Infant Nation, One Hundred Years Ago. John S. C. Abbott. N. Y., 1876. 373 p. (American Pioneers and Patriots) *DLC, NN, PU*

Life of Benjamin Franklin. John Bigelow. Phila., 1874. 3 vols. *DLC, NN*

The True Story of Benjamin Franklin. E. S. Brooks. Boston, 1898. 250 p. *DLC*

Benjamin Franklin, Self-Revealed. William C. Bruce. N. Y., 1917. 2 vols. *DLC, NN, PU*

The Life of Benjamin Franklin. Jeremiah Chaplin. Boston and Dover, N. H., 1876. 398 p. *DLC, NN*

Benjamin Franklin. E. L. Dudley. N. Y., 1915. 232 p. *PU*

The True Benjamin Franklin. Sydney G. Fisher. Phila., 1899. 369 p. *DLC, NN, MWA, PU, MiD:B, MiU:C*

The Many-Sided Franklin. Paul L. Ford. N. Y., 1899. 516 p. *DLC, NN, MWA, CSmH, PU, MiD:B*

Life and Times of Benjamin Franklin. Joseph Franklin and J. A. Headington. St. Louis, 1879. 508 p. *DLC, NN*

Memoirs of the Life and Writings of Benjamin Franklin . . . William Temple Franklin. London, 1818. 2 vols. *DLC, NN, MWA, CSmH*

Benjamin Franklin. A Biography. G. C. Hill. Phila., 1865. 333 p. *DLC, NN, PU*

Life of Benjamin Franklin. Orville L. Holley. Phila., 1848. 468 p. *DLC, NN, PU, MiD:B*

Benjamin Franklin. Samuel Hutchins. Cambridge, 1852. 36 p. *DLC*

Benjamin Franklin, as a Man of Letters. John B. McMaster. Boston, 1887. 293 p. (A.M.L.) *DLC, NN, MWA, CSmH, PU*

Benjamin Franklin. Paul E. More. Boston, 1900. 140 p. *DLC, NN*

Benjamin Franklin. John T. Morse, Jr. Boston, 1889. 428 p. (A.S.) *DLC, NN, MWA, CSmH, PU*

Life of Dr. Franklin. J. N. Norton. Clairmont, N. H., 1861. 258 p. *DLC*

Benjamin Franklin, Printer. John C. Oswald. N. Y., 1917. 244 p. *DLC, NN, MWA, CSmH, PU, MiU:C*

Life and Times of Benjamin Franklin. James Parton. N. Y., 1864. 2 vols. *DLC, NN, MWA, CSmH, PU, MiD:B, MiU:C*

Benjamin Franklin, Printer, Statesman, Philosopher, and Practical Citizen. Edward Robins. N. Y., 1898. 354 p. (American Men of Energy) DLC, NN, PU

Benjamin Franklin, the First Civilized American. Phillips. Russell. N. Y., 1926. 323 p. DLC, NN, CSmH, PU

The Writings of Benjamin Franklin . . . With a Life. Albert H. Smyth. N. Y., 1905–07. 10 vols. DLC, NN, CSmH, PU

The Amazing Benjamin Franklin. John H. Smythe, Jr., ed. N. Y., 1929. 296 p. DLC, NN, PU

The Works of Benjamin Franklin; With Notes and a Life of the Author. Jared Sparks, ed. Boston, 1836–40. 10 vols.
DLC, NN, MWA, CSmH, PU, MiU:C

Benjamin Franklin. Frank Strong. Milwaukee, 1903. 174 p. (Great Americans of History) DLC, NN

Benjamin Franklin. Lindsay Swift. Boston, 1910. 154 p. (Beacon Biographies) DLC

From Boyhood to Manhood; the Life of Benjamin Franklin. William M. Thayer. Boston, 1890. 497 p. DLC, MWA

Benjamin Franklin. E. M. Tomkinson. N. Y., 1885. 128 p. (World's Workers Series) DLC

Benjamin Franklin; a Biography in Wood Cuts. Charles Turzak. N. Y., 1935. 92 p. DLC, NN, PU

The Life of Benjamin Franklin; With Many Choice Anecdotes and Admirable Sayings of the Great Man . . . Mason L. Weems. Phila., 1817. 264 p. DLC, NN, MWA, CSmH, PU, MiU:C
2:77–109–264–329–505–562–662–675–707

FRANKLIN, SIR JOHN. 2:78

FRANKS, REBECCA. *Rebecca Franks, An American Jewish Belle of the Last Century.* Max J. Kohler. N. Y., 1894. 27 p. (Privately Printed) NN

FRASER, JAMES EARLE. 2:430

FREDERICK THE GREAT.
Frederick the Great. Charles B. Brackenburg. N. Y., 1890. 266 p. DLC, NN

Frederick the Great. Margaret Goldsmith. N. Y., 1929. 206 p. DLC, NN, PU

Frederick the Great, the Philosopher King. Victor Thaddeus. N. Y., 1930. 330 p. DLC, NN

FREEMAN, GEORGE WASHINGTON. *Life of Bishop Freeman of Arkansas.* John N. Norton. N. Y., 1867. 203 p. DLC, MiD:B

FREEMAN, JAMES. 2:144–681

FREEMAN, SAMUEL. *Samuel Freeman; His Life and Services.* William Freeman. Portland, Me., 1893. 32 p.
DLC, NN, MWA, PU

FREEMAN, THOMAS B. *Thomas B. Freeman, Missionary Pioneer to Ashanti, Dahomey and Egba.* J. Milum. N. Y., 1893. 160 p. (Missionary Biography Series)

FRELINGHUYSEN, THEODORE. *Memoir of the Life and Character of Hon. Theo. Frelinghuysen.* T. W. Chambers. N. Y., 1863. 289 p.
DLC, NN, MWA

FRÉMONT, JESSIE BENTON. *Jessie Benton Frémont; a Woman Who Made History.* Catherine Phillips. San Francisco, 1936. 361 p.
DLC, NN, CSmH
2:518

FRÉMONT, JOHN CHARLES.
Man Unafraid; the Story of John C. Frémont. Herbert Bashford and Harr Wagner. San Francisco, 1927. 406 p.
DLC, NN, PU
Memoir of the Life and Public Services of John Charles Frémont. John Bigelow. N. Y., 1856. 480 p.
DLC, NN, MWA, CSmH, PU, MiD:B
Frémont and '49. Frederick S. Dellenbaugh. N. Y., 1914. 547 p. *DLC, NN, CSmH*
John Charles Frémont; an Explanation of His Career. Cardinal L. Goodwin. Stanford U., Calif., 1930. 285 p.
DLC, NN, CSmH
Frémont; the West's Greatest Adventurer . . . Allan Nevins. N. Y., 1928. 2 vols. *DLC, NN, CSmH, PU*
Life, Explorations and Adventures of Col. J. C. Frémont. Samuel M. Schmucker. N. Y., 1856. 493 p. *MWA, PU*
Life, Explorations and Public Services of John Charles Frémont. Charles W. Upham. Boston, 1856. 356 p.
DLC, NN, MWA, CSmH, MiD:B
Life of J. C. Frémont. F. C. Woodworth. N. Y., 1856. 282 p.
DLC, CSmH
2:41–262–590

FRENCH, DANIEL CHESTER. 2:430

FRENCH, EDWIN DAVIS. *Edwin D. French. A Memorial. His Life —His Art.* N. Y., 1908. 95 p. (Privately Printed)
DLC, NN, MWA

FRENEAU, PHILIP.
Philip Freneau, The Poet of the Revolution. Mary Austin. N. Y., 1901. 285 p. *DLC, NN, CSmH*

Philip Freneau, the Huguenot Patriot-Poet of the Revolution and His Poetry. E. F. De Lancey. (Proc. of the Huguenot Soc. of America Vol. II, no. 2, 1891) *NN, CSmH*

The Political Activities of Philip Freneau. S. E. Forman. Balt., 1902. 105 p. (Johns Hopkins Studies in Hist. and Political Science, Series XX, nos. 9–10) *DLC, NN, CSmH, MiD:B*

Life of Philip Freneau. In " The Poems of Philip Freneau, Poet of the American Revolution." Fred L. Pattee. Princeton, 1902. 3 vols. *DLC, NN, CSmH, PU*

FRICK, HENRY CLAY. *Henry Clay Frick, the Man.* George B. Harvey. N. Y., 1928. 382 p. *DLC, NN, PU*

FRIES, FRANCIS HENRY. *The Life Story of a Trust Man; Being That of Francis Henry Fries, President of the Wachovia Bank and Trust Company.* Gilbert T. Stephenson. N. Y., 1930. 267 p.
DLC, NN

FRITCHIE, BARBARA.
Barbara Fritchie. A Study. Caroline H. Dall. Boston, 1892. 99 p. *DLC, NN, CSmH*

Life of Whittier's Heroine, Barbara Fritchie. H. M. Nixdorff. Frederick, Md., 1887. 77 p. *DLC, NN, MWA*

FROEBEL, FREDERICK. *Life of Frederick Froebel.* D. J. Snider. Chicago, 1900. 470 p. *DLC, NN, PU*
2:336

FROHMAN, CHARLES. *Charles Frohman: Manager and Man. With an Appreciation by James M. Barrie.* Daniel Frohman and Isaac Marcosson. N. Y., 1916. 439 p. *DLC, NN, CSmH, PU*

FRONTENAC, LOUIS. 2:127

FROST, ROBERT.
Robert Frost, Original " Ordinary Man." Sidney Cox. N. Y., 1929. 43 p. *DLC, NN, PU*

Robert Frost; a Study in Sensibility and Good Sense. Gorham B. Munson. N. Y., 1927. 135 p. (Murray Hill Biographies)
DLC, NN, PU

2:592

FROTHINGHAM, NATHANIEL LANGDON. *Boston Unitarianism, 1820–1850; A Study of the Life and Work of Nathaniel L. Frothingham.* Octavius B. Frothingham. N. Y., 1890. 272 p.
DLC, NN, MWA, CSmH, PU

FROTHINGHAM, OCTAVIUS BROOKS. *Octavius B. Frothingham and the New Faith.* E. C. Stedman. N. Y., 1876. 50 p.
DLC, NN, CSmH, PU

FROTHINGHAM, PAUL REVERE. *The Life of Paul Revere Frothingham.*
Howard C. Robbins. Boston, 1935. 171 p. *DLC, NN*

FRY, ELIZABETH.
 Elizabeth Fry; or, the Christian Philanthropist. Phila., 1851.
450 p. *CSmH*
 Elizabeth Fry. Emma R. Pitman. Boston, 1886. 269 p.
DLC, NN, PU
 Elizabeth Fry; the Angel of the Prisons. Laura E. Richards.
N. Y., 1916. 205 p. *DLC, NN*
 *Elizabeth Fry. Life and Labors of the Eminent Philanthropist,
Preacher, and Prison Reformer.* Edward Ryder. N. Y., 1884.
389 p. *DLC*
 Elizabeth Fry; Quaker Heroine. Janet Whitney. Boston,
1936. 337 p. *DLC, NN, MWA, CSmH*
 2:9–670

FRY, JOSEPH. *Life of Captain Joseph Fry, the Cuban Martyr.* Jeanie
M. Walker. Hartford, 1875. 589 p. *DLC, NN, MWA, CSmH*

FRY, JOSHUA. *Memoir of Col. Joshua Fry, Professor in William and
Mary College, Va., and Washington's Senior in Command of Va
Forces, 1754.* Philip Slaughter. Richmond, 1880. 112 p.
NN, MWA, CSmH

FULLER, ANDREW. *Life of Andrew Fuller.* John Ryland. Charleston, 1818. 362 p. *DLC, NN, MWA*

FULLER, ARTHUR BUCKMINSTER. *Chaplain Fuller: Being a Life
Sketch of a New England Clergyman and Army Chaplain.* Richard
F. Fuller. Boston, 1863. 342 p. *DLC, NN, MWA, MiD:B*

FULLER, GEORGE. 2:123

FULLER, HOMER TAYLOR. *In Memoriam. Homer Taylor Fuller.*
Zelotes W. Coombs. n.p., n.d. 69 p. *MWA*

FULLER, MARGARET.
 Margaret Fuller: a Psychological Biography. Katharine An-
thony. N. Y., 1920. 223 p. *DLC, NN, CSmH, PU*
 Margaret Fuller. Margaret Bell. N. Y., 1930. 320 p.
DLC, NN, MWA, PU
 Memoirs of Margaret Fuller Ossoli. R. W. Emerson and J. F.
Clarke and W. H. Channing. Boston, 1852. 2 vols.
DLC, NN, CSmH
 Margaret Fuller Ossoli. Thomas W. Higginson. Boston, 1884.
323 p. (A.M.L.) *DLC, NN, MWA, CSmH, PU*
 Margaret Fuller. Julia W. Howe. Boston, 1883. 298 p.
(Famous Women) *DLC, NN, CSmH, PU*
 2:43–92

FULLER, RICHARD. *Life of R. Fuller.* J. H. Cuthbert. N. Y., 1879.
325 p.   NN
FULLER, THOMAS. *The Great Tom Fuller.* Dean B. Lyman. Berkeley, Cal., 1935. 198 p.   DLC, NN, CSmH
FULTON, ROBERT.

   The Life of Robert Fulton. Cadwallader D. Colden. N. Y.,
   1817. 371 p.   DLC, NN, MWA, PU, RP:JCB
   Robert Fulton, Engineer and Artist. H. W. Dickinson. N. Y.,
   1913. 333 p.   DLC, NN, MWA, CSmH, PU
   Life of Robert Fulton and a History of Steam Navigation.
   Thomas W. Knox. N. Y., 1896. 507 p.   DLC, NN
   The Story of Robert Fulton. Peyton F. Miller. N. Y., 1908.
   113 p.   DLC, NN, MWA
   Life of Robert Fulton. J. Franklin Reigart. Phila., 1856.
   297 p.   DLC, NN, MWA, CSmH, PU
   Life of Robert Fulton. James Renwick. (L.A.B.)
                                             DLC, NN, MWA, CSmH, PU
   Robert Fulton and the " Clermont." Alice C. Sutcliffe. N. Y.,
   1909. 367 p.   DLC, NN, MWA, CSmH, PU, MiD:B
   Robert Fulton: His Life and its Results. Robert H. Thurston.
   N. Y., 1891. 194 p. (Makers of America)   DLC, NN, PU
   2:343–660–707

FUNSTON, FREDERICK. See AGUINALDO, EMILIO.
FURMAN, JAMES CLEMENT. *The Life Work of James Clement Furman.*
Harvey T. Cook. Greenville, S. C., 1926. 363 p.   DLC, NN
GABLE, CLARK. *The Life Story of Clark Gable; the Child, the
Trouper, the Screen Sensation.* Mary M. McBride. N. Y., 1932.
61 p.   DLC
GABRIEL, SAINT. *Saint Gabriel, Passionist.* Father Camillus, C.P.
N. Y., 1923. 278 p.   NN
GADSDEN, CHRISTOPHER EDWARDS. *Life of Bishop Gadsden of South
Carolina.* John N. Norton. N. Y., 1858.   DLC
GAGE, FRANCES COUSENS. *The Road Ahead, Experiences in the Life
of Frances C. Gage.* Elizabeth Wilson. N. Y., 1918. 114 p.
                                                                                     DLC, NN
GALILEO. 2:79–335
GALL, FRANÇOIS JOSEPH. *Some Accounts of the Life and Labors of
Dr. François Joseph Gall, Founder of Phrenology, and His Disciple, Dr. John Gaspar Spurzheim.* Charlotte F. Wells. N. Y.,
1896. 154 p.   DLC, NN

GALLATIN, ALBERT.
 Life of Albert Gallatin. Henry Adams. Phila., 1879. 697 p.
DLC, NN, MWA, CSmH, PU, MiU:C
 Albert Gallatin. John A. Stevens. Boston and N. Y., 1883,
1899. 423 p. (A.S.) DLC, NN, MWA, CSmH, PU, MiD:B
GALLAUDET, THOMAS HOPKINS.
 *Tribute to Gallaudet. A Discourse in Commemoration of the
Life, Character and Services of the Rev. Thomas H. Gallaudet.*
Henry Barnard. Hartford, 1852. 264 p.
DLC, NN, MWA, MiD:B
 *Life of Thomas H. Gallaudet, Founder of Deaf-Mute Instruction
in America.* E. M. Gallaudet. N. Y., 1888. 339 p. DLC, PU
GALLITZIN, PRINCE DEMETRIUS AUGUSTINE. *Memoir on the Life and
Character of Rev. Prince Demetrius A. Gallitzin.* Thomas Heyden.
Balt., 1869. 200 p.
GALLOWAY, CHARLES BETTS. *Charles Betts Galloway, Orator,
Preacher, and " Prince of Christian Chivalry."* William L. Duren.
Emory U., Ga., 1932. 331 p. DLC, NN
GALLOWAY, JOSEPH. *Joseph Galloway, the Loyalist Politician: A Bi-
ography.* Ernest H. Baldwin. Phila., 1902. 113 p.
DLC, MWA, CSmH
GALVANI, LUIGI. 2–678
GAMMELL, WILLIAM. *William Gammell, LL.D. A Biographical
Sketch With Selections From His Writings.* James O. Murray.
Cambridge, 1890. 95 p. DLC, NN, MWA, PU, RP:JCB
GANDHI, MAHATMA. *That Strange Little Brown Man, Gandhi.* Fred-
erick B. Fisher. N. Y., 1932. 239 p. DLC, NN
 2:276–301
GANNETT, EZRA STILES. *Ezra Stiles Gannett, Unitarian Minister in
Boston, 1824–1871.* William C. Gannett. Boston, 1875. 572 p.
DLC, NN, MWA, CSmH
 2:144
GANSEVOORT, HENRY SANFORD. *Memorial of Henry Sanford Ganse-
voort.* J. C. Hoadley, ed. Boston, 1875. 335 p.
DLC, NN, CSmH, MiD:B
GANSFORT, WESSEL. *Wessel Gansfort: Life and Writings.* Edward
W. Miller and Jared W. Scudder. N. Y., 1917. 2 vols.
DLC, NN, PU
GANTT, HENRY LAWRENCE. *Henry Lawrence Gantt, Leader in Indus-
try.* Leon P. Alford. N. Y., 1935. 315 p. DLC, NN

GARBO, GRETA.

The Life Story of Greta Garbo. Mary M. McBride. N. Y., 1932. 61 p. *DLC*

The Private Life of Greta Garbo. Rilla P. Palmborg. Garden City, N. Y., 1931. 282 p. *DLC, NN*

GARCIA, MANUEL. *Manuel Garcia: A Biography.* Malcolm S. Mackinlay. N. Y., 1908. 335 p. *DLC, NN*

GARDINER, LION. *The Papers and Biography of Lion Gardiner, 1599–1663.* Curtiss C. Gardiner, ed. St. Louis, 1883. 106 p. (Privately Printed) *NN, MWA*

GARDNER, ISABELLA STEWART. *Isabella Stewart Gardner and Fenway Court.* Morris Carter. Boston, 1925. 254 p. *DLC, NN, CSmH*

GARESCHÉ, JULIUS PETER. *Biography of Lieut. Col. Julius P. Garesché.* Louis Garesché. Phila., 1887. 505 p. *CSmH*

GARFIELD, JAMES ABRAM.

From Canal Boy to President; or, The Boyhood and Manhood of James A. Garfield. Horatio Alger. Boston, 1881. 334 p. *DLC, NN*

Life of James Abram Garfield, Late President of the U. S. . . . William R. Balch. Phila., 1881. 860 p. *DLC, NN, MWA, CSmH, PU*

The Early Life and Public Career of James A. Garfield . . . Including Also a Sketch of the Life of Chester A. Arthur . . . James S. Brisbin. Hartford, 1880. 585 p. *DLC, NN, PU*

Life of James A. Garfield. Emma E. Brown. Boston, 1881. 519 p. *DLC, NN, CSmH*

The Life of Gen. James A. Garfield. J. M. Bundy. N. Y., 1880. 239 p. *DLC, NN, CSmH, PU, MiD:B*

Nation's Hero—In Memoriam; Life of James A. Garfield, 20th President of the United States. Jonas M. Bundy. N. Y., 1881. 274 p. *DLC, NN, MWA*

James A. Garfield, Party Chieftain. Robert G. Caldwell. N. Y., 1931. 383 p. *DLC, NN, CSmH, PU*

The Life of James A. Garfield. Charles C. Coffin. Boston, 1880. 379 p. *DLC, NN*

The Life, Speeches and Public Services of Gen. James A. Garfield of Ohio. Russell H. Conwell. Boston, 1880. 354 p. *DLC, NN, MWA, CSmH, MiD:B*

The Life, Speeches and Public Services of Gen. James A. Garfield . . . Including an Account of His Assassination, Lingering Pain, Death and Burial. Russell H. Conwell. Boston, 1881. 384 p. *DLC, NN*

Lives of James A. Garfield and Chester A. Arthur. With a Brief Sketch of the Assassin . . . Burton T. Doyle and Homer H. Swaney. Washington, 1881. 224 p. *DLC, NN*

Life of James A. Garfield. J. R. Gilmore. N. Y., 1880. 64 p. *DLC, NN, MiD:B*

Biography of James A. Garfield. B. J. Lossing. N. Y., 1882. 840 p. *DLC, MiD:B*

Gen. Garfield From the Log Cabin to the White House. James B. McClure. Chicago, 1881. 228 p. *DLC, NN, MiD:B*

Biographical Sketches of Gen'l James A. Garfield and Gen'l Chester A. Arthur. David J. Nevin. Phila., 1880. 120 p. *DLC, NN*

Life and Death of Jas. A. Garfield . . . With an Account of His Assassination; History C. J. Guiteau. J. S. Ogilvie. Cincinnati, 1881. 428 p. *DLC, NN*

The Life, Character and Public Services of Jas. A. Garfield. Albert G. Riddle. Phila. and N. Y., 1880. 427 p. *DLC, NN, CSmH, MiD:B*

The Life and Work of James A. Garfield. John C. Ridpath. Cincinnati, 1881. 672 p. *DLC, NN, PU, MiD:B*

Life and Letters of James Abram Garfield. Theodore C. Smith. New Haven, 1925. 2 vols. *DLC, NN, CSmH, PU*

From Log Cabin to the White House: Life of James A. Garfield. William M. Thayer. Boston, 1881. 478 p. *DLC, NN, MWA, CSmH, MiD:B*

2:107–190–521–525

GARGAN, THOMAS J. *Thomas J. Gargan. A Memorial.* Joseph Smith. Boston, 1910. 166 p. *DLC, MWA*

GARIBALDI, GIUSEPPE.

Life of Giuseppe Garibaldi. J. T. Bent. N. Y., 1881. 60 p. *DLC*

2:334

The Life of Joseph Garibaldi, the Liberator of Italy . . . O. J. Victor. N. Y., 1860. 103 p. (Beadle's Dime Biographical Library) *DLC, NN, PU*

GARNER, JOHN N. *The Speaker of the House; the Romantic Story of John N. Garner.* George R. Brown. N. Y., 1932. 162 p. *DLC, NN, MWA*

GARRETTSON, FREEBORN.

Life of Rev. F. Garrettson. N. Bangs, comp. N. Y., 1829, 1838. 294 p. *MWA, CSmH, MiD:B*

Freeborn Garrettson. Ezra S. Tipple. N. Y., 1910. 128 p.
DLC, MiD:B

GARRISON, WILLIAM LLOYD.
William Lloyd Garrison. John J. Chapman. N. Y., 1913.
278 p. *DLC, NN, PU*
William Lloyd Garrison, 1805–79. Wendell P. Garrison and
Francis J. Garrison. N. Y., 1885–89. 4 vols.
DLC, NN, MWA, CSmH, PU, MiD:B
William Lloyd Garrison, the Abolitionist. A. H. Grimké. N. Y.,
1891. 405 p. (American Reformer Series) *DLC, NN, MWA*
William Lloyd Garrison and His Times. Oliver Johnson. Bos-
ton, 1879, Rev. Ed., 1882. 490 p.
DLC, NN, MWA, CSmH, PU, MiD:B
William Lloyd Garrison. Nina Moore. N. Y., 1888. 33 p.
DLC, NN
William Lloyd Garrison. Lindsay Swift. Phila., 1911. 412 p.
(A.C.B.) *DLC, NN, PU, MiD:B*
2:40–205–624

GARY, ELBERT HENRY. *Life of Elbert H. Gary; the Story of Steel.*
Ida M. Tarbell. N. Y., 1925. 361 p. *DLC, NN, PU*

GASCOIGNE, GEORGE. *Life and Writings of George Gascoigne.* Felix
E. Schelling. Boston, 1893. 131 p. *DLC, NN, CSmH, PU*

GASS, PATRICK. *The Life and Times of Patrick Gass.* J. G. Jacob.
Wellsburg, 1859. 280 p. *CSmH*

GATCH, PHILIP. *Sketch of Rev. Philip Gatch.* John McLean. Cincinnati, 1854. 190 p. *NN*

GATES, JOHN WARNE. *Bet-a-Million Gates; the Story of a Plunger.*
Robert I. Warshow. N. Y., 1932. 187 p. *DLC, NN, MWA*

GATES, THEOPHILUS. *Theophilus, the Battle-Axe. A History of the
Lives and Adventures of Theophilus Ransom Gates and the Battle-
Axes.* Charles C. Sellers. Phila., 1930. 61 p. *DLC, NN, MWA*

GATES, WILLIAM. *The True Life Story of Swiftwater Bill Gates.* Iola
Beebe. Seattle, 1908. 139 p. (Privately Printed) *DLC, CSmH*

GATTINGER, AUGUSTIN. *A Brief Sketch of the Life and Works of
Augustin Gattinger.* Henry N. Oakes. Nashville, 1932. 152 p.
DLC, NN

GAUTAMA. [BUDDHA] 2:665

GAUTIER, THEOPHILE. *Gautier and the Romantics.* John G. Palache.
N. Y., 1926. 186 p. *DLC, NN*

GAVIN, MICHAEL FREEBERN. *Michael Freebern Gavin. A Biography.*
Cambridge, 1915. 158 p. *DLC, NN, MWA*

GAY, JOHN. *Mr. Gay; Being a Picture of the Life and Times of the Author of the Beggar's Opera.* Oscar Sherwin. N. Y., 1929. 184 p.
DLC, NN

GAYLORD, REUBEN. *Life and Labors of Rev. Reuben Gaylord.* Mary W. Gaylord. Omaha, 1889. 437 p. *DLC, NN, MWA*

GAYNOR, WILLIAM JAY. *Gaynor, the Tammany Mayor Who Swallowed the Tiger.* Louis H. Pink. N. Y., 1931. 256 p.
DLC, NN, MWA

GENÊT, EDMOND CHARLES. *Jefferson, Friend of France, 1793; the Career of Edmond Charles Genêt, Minister Plenipotentiary From the French Republic to the U. S.* Meade Minnigerode. N. Y., 1928. 447 p. *DLC, NN*
2:452

GENGHIS KHAN.
History of Genghis Khan. Jacob Abbott. N. Y., 1860. 335 p.
DLC, NN
Genghis Khan. Ralph W. Fox. N. Y., 1936. 285 p.
DLC, NN
Genghis Kahn; the Emperor of All Men. Harold Lamb. N. Y., 1927. 270 p. *DLC, PU*

GENTH, FREDERICK AUGUSTUS. *Memoir of Frederick Augustus Genth, 1820–1893.* George F. Barker. Washington, 1902. 231 p.
DLC, NN, PU, MiD:B

GENTZ, FRIEDRICH. *Friedrich Gentz.* Paul M. Reif. Urbana, Ill., 1912. 159 p. *CSmH*

GEORGE, HENRY.
The Life of Henry George. Henry George, Jr. (Vol. 10 of Memorial Edition N. Y., 1898–1900) Published Separately N. Y., 1900. 634 p. *DLC, NN, PU*
The Prophet of San Francisco; Personal Memories and Interpretations of Henry George. Louis F. Post. N. Y., 1930. 335 p.
DLC, NN, PU
2:150–334

GERHARD, CALVIN S. *Life of Rev. Calvin S. Gerhard.* T. W. Dickert, ed. Phila., 1904. 256 p. *DLC*

GERONIMO. *The Truth About Geronimo.* Britton Davis. New Haven, 1929. 253 p. *DLC, NN, CSmH, PU*

GERRY, ELBRIDGE. *The Life of Elbridge Gerry, With Contemporary Letters, to the Close of the American Revolution.* James T. Austin. Boston, 1828–29. 2 vols.
DLC, NN, MWA, CSmH, PU, MiD:B, MiU:C

GERSHWIN, GEORGE. *George Gershwin, a Study in American Music.* Isaac Goldberg. N. Y., 1931. 305 p. *DLC, NN*

GIANAVELLO, JOSHUA. *Joshua Gianavello, Captain of the Vineyards of Lucerna.* Russell H. Conwell. Phila., 1884. 319 p.

GIANNINI, AMADEO P. 2:233

GIBB, WILLIAM. *Glimpses of the Life of William Gibb, Late Pastor, Advent Christian Church, Bristol, Conn.* Millie A. Gibb. Springfield, Mass., 1898. 144 p. *DLC, NN*

GIBBONS, FLOYD. *Floyd Gibbons.* Douglas Gilbert. N. Y., 1930. 96 p. *DLC, NN, MWA, PU*

GIBBONS, JAMES CARDINAL.
 Cardinal Gibbons, Churchman and Citizen. Albert E. Smith. Balt., 1921. 301 p. *DLC, NN*
 Life of James, Cardinal Gibbons. Allen S. Will. N. Y., 1911. 414 p. *DLC, NN*
 Life of Cardinal Gibbons, Archbishop of Baltimore. Allen S. Will. N. Y., 1922. 2 vols. *DLC, NN, PU*
 2:679

GIBBONS, JOSEPH K. *Poet-Soldier: A Memoir of Joseph K. Gibbons.* P. L. Buell. N. Y., 1868. 48 p. *NN, CSmH*

GIBBONS, WILLIAM. *A Memoir of William Gibbons.* T. Tebbets. N. Y., 1856. 129 p. (Privately Printed) *DLC, NN, MWA*

GIBSON, CHARLES DANA. *Portrait of an Era as Drawn by C. D. Gibson. A Biography.* Fairfax Downey. N. Y., 1936. 391 p.
 DLC, NN, CSmH

GIBSON, JOHN BANNISTER.
 An Essay on the Life, Character and Writings of John B. Gibson, Lately Chief Justice of the Supreme Court of Pennsylvania. William A. Porter. Phila., 1855. 140 p. *DLC, PU*
 Memoirs of John Bannister Gibson, Late Chief Justice of Pennsylvania. Thomas P. Roberts. Pittsburgh, 1890. 247 p.
 DLC, CSmH, PU
 2:110

GIBSON, WILLIAM HAMILTON. *William Hamilton Gibson, Artist-Naturalist-Author.* John C. Adams. N. Y., 1901. 275 p.
 NN, MWA

GIBSON, WILLIAM HARVEY. *Ohio's Silver-Tongued Orator; Life and Speeches of General William H. Gibson . . .* David D. Bigger. Dayton, O., 1901. 558 p. *DLC, NN*

GIDDINGS, JOSHUA REED.
 Joshua R. Giddings. Walter Buell. Cleveland, 1882. 213 p.
 DLC, NN, MWA, MiD:B

Life of Joshua R. Giddings. George W. Julian. Chicago, 189?.
473 p.   *DLC, CSmH, PU, MiD:B*
    2:40

GIFFORD, ROBERT SWAIN. 2:52

GIFFORD, SANFORD ROBINSON. 2:52

GIFFORD, WILLIAM. *William Gifford, Tory Satirist, Critic, and Editor.*
Roy B. Clark. N. Y., 1930. 294 p. (Col. Univ. Studies in Eng.)
                                                DLC, CSmH, PU

    2:406

GILBERT, HUMPHREY.
    Sir Humphrey Gilbert. Donald B. Chidsey. N. Y., 1932.
204 p.   *DLC, NN*
    *Sir Humphrey Gylberte and His Enterprise of Colonization in
America.* Carlos Slafter, ed. Boston, 1903. 335 p. (Prince Soc.
Pub.)   *DLC, NN, MWA, PU, MiU:C*

GILBERT, JOHN. *A Sketch of the Life of John Gilbert.* William
Winter. N. Y., 1890. 55 p. (Dunlap Soc. Pub. Ser. I. v. 11)
                                             DLC, NN, CSmH, PU

    2:128

GILBERT, JOHN WESLEY. *The Spirit of John Wesley Gilbert.* Joseph
C. Colclough. Nashville, 1925. 108 p.   *DLC, NN*

GILBERT, MAHLON NORRIS. *Mahlon Norris Gilbert, Bishop Coadjutor
of Minnesota, 1886–1900.* Francis L. Palmer. Milwaukee, 1912.
303 p.   *DLC, CSmH*

GILDER, RICHARD WATSON. *Richard Watson Gilder, Edward Markham, Edward Rowland Sill.* D. G. Downey. N. Y., 1906. 183 p.
                                                       DLC

GILES, CHAUNCEY. *The Life of Chauncey Giles; as Told in His Diary
and Correspondence.* Chauncey Giles. Boston, 1920. 478 p.
                                                DLC, NN, MiD:B

GILES, WILLIAM BRANCH. *William Branch Giles: A Study of Politics
in Virginia and the Nation From 1790 to 1830.* Dice R. Anderson.
Menasha, Wis., 1914. 271 p.
                            DLC, NN, MWA, CSmH, PU, MiD:B

GILL, CHARLES. *Charles Gill: The First Actuary in America.* Emory
McClintock. N. Y., 1913–14. (Reprint: Actuarial Soc. of Amer.
Transac.)   *NN*

GILLETTE, A. D. *Reminiscences . . . of A. D. Gillette.* N. Y., 1883.
174 p.   *CSmH*

GILLETTE, DANIEL HOLBROOK. *Memoir of Rev. Daniel Holbrook Gillette, of Mobile, Alabama.* Walter D. and Abram D. Gillette.
Phila., 1846. 234 p.   *DLC, NN, CSmH*

GILLEY, JOHN. *John Gilley.* Charles W. Eliot. Boston, 1904. 73 p.
DLC, NN, MWA

GILMAN, DANIEL COIT. *Life of Daniel Coit Gilman.* Fabian Franklin. N. Y., 1910. 446 p. *DLC, NN*

GILPIN, HENRY DILWORTH. *A Memorial of Henry D. Gilpin.* Eliza Gilpin, comp. Phila., 1860. 211 p. *DLC, NN, PU, MiD:B*

GILPIN, WILLIAM. *History of the Life of William Gilpin.* Hubert H. Bancroft. San Francisco, 1889. 62 p. *DLC, NN*

GIOTTO. 2:161

GIRARD, STEPHEN.

Stephen Girard, Founder. C. A. Herrick. Phila., 1923. 203 p. (Privately Printed) *DLC, NN, CSmH, PU*

Life and Character of Stephen Girard. H. Atlee Ingram. Phila., 1884. 185 p. *DLC, NN, PU*

Life and Times of Stephen Girard, Mariner and Merchant. John B. McMaster. Phila., 1918. 2 vols.
DLC, NN, MWA, PU

Biography of Stephen Girard. Together With a Detailed History of His Banking and Financial Operations. Stephen Simpson. Phila., 1832. 281 p. *DLC, NN, MWA, CSmH, PU*
2:331–348–451–511

GIRTY, SIMON. *Simon Girty, the White Savage.* Thomas A. Boyd. N. Y., 1928. 252 p. *DLC, NN, MiD:B*

GISH, LILLIAN.

Life and Lillian Gish. Albert B. Paine. N. Y., 1932. 303 p.
DLC, NN

Lillian Gish; an Interpretation. Edward C. Wagenknecht. Seattle, 1927. 26 p. *DLC, NN, MWA*

GLADDEN, WASHINGTON. 2:109

GLADSTONE, WILLIAM EWART.

William Ewart Gladstone. Jabez L. M. Curry. Richmond, 1891. 239 p. *DLC, NN, CSmH, PU*

William Ewart Gladstone; Life and Public Services. T. W. Handford. Chicago, 1898. 424 p. *DLC*

Short Life of W. E. Gladstone. C. E. Jones. N. Y., 1880. 254 p. *DLC, NN*

Life and Times of William E. Gladstone. John C. Ridpath. N. Y., 1898. 624 p. *NN, MWA*

GLANVILL, JOSEPH. *Joseph Glanvill: A Study in English Thought and Letters of the Seventeenth Century.* Ferris Greenslet. N. Y., 1900. 235 p. *DLC, NN, CSmH*

GLAZIER, WILLARD. *Sword and Pen; or, Ventures and Adventures of Willard Glazier, the Soldier-Author.* John A. Owens. Phila., 1881. 436 p. *DLC, NN, MWA, CSmH, PU*

GLINKA, MIKHAIL I. 2:187

GLOVER, JOHN. *A Memoir of Gen. John Glover, of Marblehead.* Wm. P. Upham. Salem, 1863. 61 p. *NN*

GLOVER, T. REAVELEY. 2:487

GLUCK, CHRISTOPH W. 2:187

GODFREY, THOMAS. *Biography of Thomas Godfrey in " Prince of Parthia."* Archibald Henderson. Boston, 1917. 75 p.
DLC, NN, PU

GODKIN, EDWIN LAWRENCE. *Life and Letters of Edwin Lawrence Godkin.* Rollo Ogden, ed. N. Y., 1907. 2 vols.
DLC, NN, MWA, CSmH, PU

GODWIN, MARY. *Life of Mary Wollstonecraft.* Elizabeth R. Pennell. Boston, 1884. 360 p. *DLC, NN, PU*

GODWIN, SAMUEL P. *Life of Samuel P. Godwin, First President of the Godwin Association of the Franklin Reformatory Homes for In-ebriates, of Philadelphia.* Phila., 1889. 283 p. *NN*

GOERING, JACOB. 2:294

GOETHALS, GEORGE WASHINGTON. *Goethals, Genius of the Panama Canal, A Biography.* Joseph B. and Farnham Bishop. N. Y., 1930. 493 p. *DLC, NN, PU*
2:388–507–675

GOETHE, JOHANN WOLFGANG.
Goethe and Schiller. Their Lives and Works. Hjalmar H. Boyesen. N. Y., 1879. 424 p. *DLC, NN, PU*
Goethe. His Life and Works. An Essay. George H. Calvert. Boston, 1872. 276 p. *DLC, NN, MWA, CSmH*
Goethe, the Man and His Character. Joseph McCabe. Phila., 1912. 378 p. *DLC, NN, PU*
Goethe's Life-Poem as Set Forth in His Life and Works. Denton J. Snider. St. Louis, 1915. 601 p. *DLC, NN, PU*
Goethe. Calvin Thomas. N. Y., 1917. 368 p. *DLC, PU*
2:82

GOFF, CHARLES BRADFORD. *Charles Bradford Goff (1834–1898).* W. A. Mowry. Boston, 1900. 72 p. (Privately Printed) *DLC, NN*

GOLDMAN, EMMA. 2:395

GOLDONI, CARLO.
Goldoni: A Biography. Hobart C. Chatfield-Taylor. N. Y., 1913. 695 p. *DLC, NN, PU*

Goldoni and the Venice of His Time. Joseph S. Kennard. N. Y., 1920. 551 p. *DLC, NN, PU*

GOLDSMITH, OLIVER. *Oliver Goldsmith: A Biography.* Washington Irving. N. Y., 1849. 448 p.

DLC, NN, MWA, CSmH, PU, MiD:B

GOMPERS, SAMUEL. *Samuel Gompers; Champion of the Toiling Masses.* Rowland H. Harvey. Stanford, 1935. 376 p.

DLC, NN, CSmH, PU

2:150–325

GONZAGA, MARY. *Life of Sister Mary Gonzaga Grace, of the Daughters of Charity of St. Vincent de Paul, 1812–1897.* Eleanor C. Donnelly. Phila., 1900. 334 p. *DLC*

GOOD, ADOLPHUS CLEMENS. *A Life For Africa; Rev. Adolphus Clemens Good . . . American Missionary in Equatorial West Africa.* Ellen C. Parsons. N. Y., 1897. 316 p. *DLC, NN*

GOODE, GEORGE BROWN. *Memoir of George Brown Goode, 1851–1896.* Samuel P. Langley. Washington, 1897. 30 p.

DLC, NN, MWA, CSmH, PU, MiD:B

GOODELL, CONSTANS LIBERTY. *Life of Constans L. Goodell, D.D.* A. H. Currier. N. Y., 1887. 486 p. *DLC, NN, MWA*

GOODELL, HENRY HILL. *Henry Hill Goodell. The Story of His Life, With Letters and a Few of His Addresses.* Calvin Stebbins. Cambridge, 1911. 340 p. *DLC, NN, MWA*

GOODELL, WILLIAM. *Forty Years in the Turkish Empire; or, Memoirs of Rev. William Goodell.* E. D. G. Prime. N. Y., 1876. 489 p.

DLC, NN, MWA

GOODNIGHT, CHARLES. *Charles Goodnight, Cowman and Plainsman.* J. Evetts Haley. Boston, 1936. 485 p.

DLC, NN, MWA, CSmH

2:46

GOODNOW, EDWARD A. *A Souvenir Sketch of Edward A. Goodnow.* N. Y., Worcester, Mass., 1904. 2d ed. *MWA, MiD:B*

GOODPASTURE, JEFFERSON DILLARD. *Life of Jefferson Dillard Goodpasture.* A. V. and W. H. Goodpasture. Nashville, 1897. 308 p.

DLC, NN, MWA

GOODRICH, CHAUNCEY ALLEN. *Discourse Commemorative of the Life and Services of Rev. Chauncey A. Goodrich, D.D.* T. D. Wooley. New Haven, 1860. 32 p. *DLC, NN, PU*

GOODWIN, WILLIAM RANSDALL. 2:497

GOODYEAR, CHARLES. *Trials of an Inventor: Life and Discoveries of Charles Goodyear.* Bradford K. Peirce. N. Y., 1866. 224 p.
DLC, NN, MWA, CSmH
2:343–511

GORDON, ADONIRAM JUDSON. *Adoniram J. Gordan: Biography With Letters.* E. B. Gordon. N. Y., 1898. 386 p. *DLC, NN*

GORDON, GEORGE ANGIER. 2:487

GORDON, HENRY S. *Life and Labors of Rev. Henry S. Gordon, Founder of the Free Baptist Church in Southern Illinois, With Pictures and Sketches of Other Free Baptists.* George A. Gordon. Campbell Hill, Ill., 1901. 93 p. *DLC*

GORDON, WILLIAM FITZHUGH. *William F. Gordon . . . His Life, Times and Contemporaries (1787–1858).* Armistead C. Gordon. N. Y., 1909. 412 p. *DLC, NN, PU, MiD:B*

GORGAS, WILLIAM CRAWFORD. *William Crawford Gorgas, His Life and Work.* Marie D. Gorgas and Burton J. Hendrick. N. Y., 1924. 359 p. *DLC, NN, PU*
2:388

GORGES, FERDINAND. *Sir Ferdinand Gorges and His Province of Maine.* James P. Baxter, ed. Boston, 1890. 3 vols. (Prince Soc. Pub.)
DLC, NN, MWA, PU, MiU:C

GORKY, MAXIM. *Maxim Gorky, His Life and Writings.* E. J. Dillon. London, 1902. 389 p. *DLC*

GORMAN, ARTHUR PUE. 2:218

GORTON, SAMUEL.
Life and Times of Samuel Gorton. Adelos Gorton, comp. Phila., 1907. 154 p. *DLC, NN, MWA, CSmH*
Samuel Gorton . . . First Settler of Warwick, R. I. Lewis G. Janes. Providence, 1906. 141 p. *DLC, NN, MWA, MiD:B*
Life of Samuel Gorton. John M. Mackie. (L.A.B.)
DLC, NN, CSmH

GOSDEN, THOMAS. *An English XIX Century Sportsman Bibliopole and Binder of Angling Books.* William L. Andrews. N. Y., 1906. 60 p. *DLC, CSmH*

GOTTSCHALK, LOUIS MOREAU. *Life and Letters of Louis Moreau Gottschalk.* Octavia Hensel. Boston, 1870. 213 p. *NN*

GOUGH, JOHN BARTHOLOMEW.
John B. Gough, the Apostle of Cold Water. Carlos Martyn. N. Y., 1893. 336 p. *DLC, NN, MWA*

Tiger! Tiger! The Life Story of John B. Gough. Honoré
W. Morrow. N. Y., 1930. 296 p. [Biographical Fiction]
DLC, NN, PU

2:6–40

GOULD, EMILY BLISS. *A Life Worth Living. Memorials of Emily
Bliss Gould of Rome.* Leonard W. Bacon. N. Y., 1879. 284 p.
DLC, NN, MWA, CSmH, MiD:B

GOULD, JAY.

Life of Jay Gould, How He Made His Millions. Murat Halstead and J. Frank Beale, Jr. Phila., 1892. 490 p. *DLC, PU*

*The Life and Achievements of Jay Gould, the Wizard of Wall
Street.* Henry D. Northrop. Phila., 1892. 512 p. *DLC, NN*

Life and Death of Jay Gould and How He Made His Millions.
John S. Ogilvie. N. Y., 1892. 208 p. *DLC, NN, CSmH*

Jay Gould; the Story of a Fortune. Robert I. Warshow. N. Y.,
1928. 200 p. *DLC, NN, PU*

*The Wizard of Wall Street and His Wealth, or, The Life and
Deeds of Jay Gould.* Trumbull White. Chicago, 1892. 312 p.
DLC, NN

2:451

GOYA, FRANCISCO. 2:161

GRADY, HENRY WOODFIN.

Life and Labors of Henry W. Grady, His Speeches, Writings, etc.
Atlanta, 1890. 488 p. *DLC, NN*

Life of Henry W. Grady. Gentry Dugat. Edinburg, Texas,
1927. 150 p. *DLC*

The New South, With a Character Sketch of Henry W. Grady.
Oliver Dyer. N. Y., 1890. 273 p. *DLC*

Joel Chandler Harris' Life of Henry W. Grady. Joel Chandler
Harris, ed. N. Y., 1890. 628 p.
DLC, NN, MWA, CSmH, MiD:B

Henry W. Grady. The Editor, the Orator, the Man. James
W. Kee. N. Y., 1896. 106 p. *NN*

GRAFTON, JOSEPH. *Life of the Rev. Joseph Grafton, Late Pastor of the
First Baptist Church, Newton, Mass.* S. F. Smith. Boston, 1849.
213 p. *DLC, NN, MWA, MiD:B*

GRAHAM, EDWARD KIDDER. 2:493

GRAHAM, WILLIAM S. *Remains of William S. Graham, With a Memoir.*
George Allen, ed. Phila., 1849. 264 p. *DLC, MWA, MiD:B*

GRANGER, LAUNCELOT. *Launcelot Granger of Newbury, Mass., and
Suffield, Conn.; a Biographical History.* James M. Granger.
Hartford, 1893. 587 p. *DLC, MWA*

GRANT, JUDITH S.   *A Memoir of Mrs. Judith S. Grant, Late Missionary to Persia.*   William W. Campbell.   N. Y., 1844.   200 p.

GRANT, ULYSSES SIMPSON.

Illustrated Life, Campaigns and Public Services of Lieut. General Grant.   Phila., 1865.   271 p.   NN, CSmH, PU

Life of General U. S. Grant.   J. S. C. Abbott.   Boston, 1868.   309 p.   DLC, NN, MWA, CSmH, MiD:B

Grant as a Soldier.   A. W. Alexander.   St. Louis, 1887.   249 p.
                DLC, NN, MWA

Ulysses S. Grant.   Walter Allen.   Boston, 1901.   153 p.   (Riverside Biographies, no. 7)   DLC, NN, CSmH

Life and Public Services of Gen. Grant.   Wm. R. Balch.   Phila., 1885.   613 p.   CSmH

Campaign Lives of U. S. Grant and Schuyler Colfax.   James S. Brisbin.   Cincinnati, 1868.   411 p.   DLC, CSmH, PU

Grant and Colfax; Their Lives and Services.   L. P. Brockett.   N. Y., 1868.   136 p.   DLC, NN, MWA

Original and Authentic Record of the Life and Deeds of General Ulysses S. Grant.   Frank A. Burr.   Phila., 1885.   1032 p.
                DLC, CSmH, PU

Ulysses S. Grant.   W. C. Church.   N. Y., 1897.   473 p.   (Heroes of the Nation)   DLC, NN, CSmH

Rise of U. S. Grant.   Arthur L. Conger.   N. Y., 1931.   390 p.
                DLC, NN, MWA, PU

Ulysses S. Grant.   Louis A. Coolidge.   Boston, 1917.   596 p.   (A.S. Ser. 2.   v. 1)   DLC, NN, MWA, CSmH, PU

U. S. Grant.   Francis L. Coombs.   N. Y., 1916.   244 p.
                CSmH

Grant and His Campaigns: A Military Biography.   Henry Coppée.   N. Y., 1866.   521 p.
                DLC, NN, MWA, CSmH, PU, MiD:B

Life and Services of U. S. Grant.   Henry Coppée.   N. Y., 1868.   465 p.   DLC, NN, MWA, CSmH, MiD:B

Life of U. S. Grant.   W. A. Crafts.   Boston, 1868.   172 p.
                DLC, NN, MWA, CSmH, MiD:B

The Modern Ulysses S. Grant; His Political Record.   Nelson Cross.   N. Y., 1872.   182 p.   DLC, NN, MWA, CSmH, MiD:B

Life of Ulysses S. Grant.   Charles A. Dana and James G. Wilson.   Springfield, Mass., 1868.   424 p.
                DLC, NN, MWA, CSmH, PU

Life of U. S. Grant. H. C. Deming. Hartford, 1868. 533 p.
DLC, NN, MWA, CSmH, MiD:B

Life and Public Services of Gen. U. S. Grant. J. S. Dye.
Phila., 1868. 48 p. *DLC, CSmH*

Ulysses S. Grant. Franklin S. Edmonds. Phila., 1915. 376 p.
(A.C.B.) *DLC, NN, CSmH*

The Generalship of Ulysses S. Grant. John F. C. Fuller. N. Y.,
1929. 452 p. *DLC, NN, CSmH, PU*

Ulysses S. Grant; His Life and Character. Hamlin Garland.
N. Y., 1898. 524 p. *DLC, NN, MWA, CSmH, PU*

General Grant's Last Stand. Horace Green. N. Y., 1936. 334 p.
DLC, NN, PU

The Life of Ulysses S. Grant. J. T. Headley. N. Y., 1868.
458 p. *DLC, NN, MWA, CSmH, MiD:B*

The Life and Travels of General Grant. J. T. Headley. Phila.,
1879. 599 p. *DLC, NN, MWA*

The Hero Boy; or, the Life and Deeds of Lieut-Gen. Grant.
Phineas C. Headley. N. Y., 1864. 340 p.
DLC, NN, CSmH, MiD:B

The Life and Campaigns of General U. S. Grant. Phineas C.
Headley. N. Y., 1868. 752 p. *DLC, NN, MWA, CSmH, MiD:B*

The Life and Deeds of Gen. U. S. Grant. Phineas C. Headley
and G. L. Austin. Boston, 1885. 425 p. *DLC, NN*

Ulysses S. Grant, Politician. William B. Hesseltine. N. Y.,
1935. 480 p. *DLC, NN, CSmH, PU*

Grant as a Soldier and a Statesman. Edward Howland. Hartford, 1868. 631 p. *DLC, NN, MWA, CSmH*

True Ulysses S. Grant. Charles King. Phila., 1914. 400 p
(True Biographies) *DLC, NN, MWA, CSmH, PU*

General Grant and His Campaigns. Julian K. Larke. N. Y.,
1864. 473 p. *NN, MWA, CSmH, MiD:B*

*Gen. U. S. Grant; His Early Life and Military Career; Brief
Account of His Presidential Administration and Tour Around the
World.* J. K. Larke. N. Y., 1879. 512 p. *CSmH, MiD:B*

Life, Campaigns and Battles of Gen. Ulysses S. Grant. Benson J. Lossing, ed. N. Y., 1868. 502 p. *CSmH, PU*

Ulysses S. Grant, the Great Soldier of America. Robert R.
McCormick. N. Y., 1934. 343 p. *DLC, NN, MWA*

The Life . . . and Death of Gen. U. S. Grant. John Bach Mc-
Master. Phila., 1885. 112 p. *CSmH*

A Popular and Authentic Life of U. S. Grant. Edward D. Mansfield. Cincinnati, 1868. 377 p.   *DLC, CSmH, MiD:B*

    Lives and Campaigns of Grant and Lee: Comparison of the Two Great Opponents in the Civil War. S. W. Odell. Chicago, 1895. 602 p.   *DLC, CSmH*

    The Life of Gen. U. S. Grant. Loomis T. Palmer. N. Y., 1888. 772 p.   *DLC, NN, CSmH, MiD:B*

    Life and Public Services of Gen. U. S. Grant, and Biographical Sketch of Colfax. Charles A. Phelps. Boston, 1868. 344 p.   *DLC, NN, MWA, CSmH, MiD:B*

    Life of U. S. Grant. Benjamin P. Poore and O. H. Tiffany. Phila., 1885. 594 p.   *DLC, CSmH*

    The Life of Gen. U. S. Grant. His Early Life, Military Achievements, etc. L. T. Remlap, ed. Chicago, 1885. 772 p.   *NN, CSmH*

    A Personal History of Ulysses S. Grant. Albert D. Richardson. Hartford, 1868. 560 p.   *DLC, NN, MWA, CSmH, PU, MiD:B*

    Grant, the Man of Mystery. Nicholas Smith. Milwaukee, 1909. 381 p.   *CSmH*

    Ulysses S. Grant. W. O. Stoddard. N. Y., 1886. 362 p. (Lives of the Presidents)   *DLC, NN, MWA, CSmH*

    From Tannery to the White House; the Life of Ulysses S. Grant. William M. Thayer. N. Y., 1880. 480 p.   *DLC, MWA, CSmH*

    Gen. U. S. Grant. A Story of His Life and Military Services. William H. Van Orden. N. Y., 1885. 34 p.   *DLC, NN, CSmH*

    Life and Military Services of Gen. U. S. Grant. William H. Van Orden. N. Y., 1896. 236 p.   *DLC, NN, CSmH*

    Life and Public Services of Ulysses S. Grant. James G. Wilson. N. Y., 1885. 168 p.   *DLC, NN, MWA, CSmH, MiD:B*

    General Grant. James G. Wilson. N. Y., 1897. 390 p.   *DLC, NN, CSmH, MiD:B*

    Ulysses S. Grant. Owen Wister. Boston, 1900. 145 p.   *DLC, NN, MWA, CSmH*

    Meet General Grant. William E. Woodward. N. Y., 1928. 512 p.   *DLC, NN, PU*

    2:104–562–624

GRASSI, BATISTA. 2:176

GRATZ, REBECCA. *Rebecca Gratz; a Study in Charm.* Rollin G. Osterweis. N. Y., 1935. 244 p.   *DLC, NN, CSmH, PU*

GRAVES, ROBERT. 2:678

GRAY, ASA. 2:85

GRAY, BRYANT. *Bryant Gray; the Student, the Christian, the Soldier.* Joseph P. Thompson. N. Y., 1864. 148 p.   *DLC, NN, CSmH*

GRAY, DAVID. *Story of David Gray: A Memoir.* Robert W. Buchanan. Portland, Me., 1900. 85 p.   *DLC, NN, CSmH*

GRAY, JOHN CHIPMAN. *John Chipman Gray.* Boston, 1917. 142 p. (Privately Printed)   *DLC, NN, PU*

GRAY, ROBERT. 2:262–387

GRAY, THOMAS. 2:86

GRAY, WILLIAM. *William Gray of Salem, Merchant; a Biographical Sketch.* Edward Gray. Boston, 1914. 134 p.

   DLC, NN, MWA, CSmH

GREBLE, JOHN TROUT. *Memoir of Lieut.-Col. John T. Greble.* Benson J. Lossing. Phila., 1870. 99 p.   *DLC, NN, CSmH, PU*

GRECO, EL. 2:161

GREELEY, HORACE.

   Life and Public Career of Hon. Horace Greeley. William M. Cornell. Boston, 1872. 317 p.   *DLC, NN, MWA*

   Journalist, Reformer, and Philanthropist. Life of Horace Greeley. L. D. Ingersoll. Phila., 1874. 574 p.   *DLC, NN*

   The Life of Horace Greeley, Founder of the New York Tribune, With Extended Notices of Many of His Contemporary Statesmen and Journalists. L. D. Ingersoll. Chicago, 1873. 688 p.

   DLC, NN, MWA

   Horace Greeley, Founder and Editor of the New York Tribune. W. A. Linn. N. Y., 1903. 267 p. (Historic Lives Series)

   DLC, NN, MWA, PU

   The Life of Horace Greeley, Editor of the New York Tribune. James Parton. Boston, 1855, 1868, 1872. 548 p.

   DLC, NN, MWA, CSmH, PU, MiD:B

   Horace Greeley in 1872. J. S. Pike. N. Y., 1873. 15 p.

   DLC, NN

   A Representative Life of Horace Greeley, With an Introduction by Cassius M. Clay. L. U. Reavis. N. Y., 1872. 579 p.

   DLC, NN, MWA, MiD:B

   Horace Greeley, Founder of the New York Tribune. Don C. Seitz. Indianapolis, 1926. 433 p.   *DLC, NN, CSmH, PU*

   Horace Greeley and Other Pioneers of American Socialism. Charles Sotheran. N. Y., 1892. 349 p. *DLC, NN, MWA, CSmH*

   Horace Greeley, the Editor. Franklin N. Zabriskie. N. Y., 1890. 398 p.   *DLC, NN, MWA, MiD:B*

   2:40–85–581–590–624

GREELY, ADOLPHUS WASHINGTON. *General Greely; the Story of a Great American.* William Mitchell. N. Y., 1936. 242 p.

DLC, NN

2:78

GREEN, ANDREW HASWELL. *The Life and Public Services of Andrew Haswell Green.* John Foord. N. Y., 1913. 322 p.

DLC, NN, MWA, PU, MiD:B

GREEN, ALEXANDER LITTLE P. *Life and Papers of A. L. P. Green, D.D.* William M. Green. Nashville, 1877. 592 p. DLC, NN

GREEN, HETTY. *Hetty Green, a Woman Who Loved Money.* Boyden Sparks and Samuel T. Moore. N. Y., 1930. 338 p.

DLC, NN, PU

GREEN, JOHNSON. *The Life and Confession of Johnson Green, Who Is to Be Executed This Day, August 17th, 1786, For the Atrocious Crime of Burglary* . . . Worcester, 1787.

GREEN, LEWIS WARNER. *Memoir of the Life and Character of Rev. Lewis Warner Green, D.D. With a Selection From His Sermons.* LeRoy L. Halsey. N. Y., 1871. 491 p. DLC, MWA

GREEN, PAUL. *Paul Green.* Barrett H. Clark. N. Y., 1928. 36 p.

DLC, NN, MWA, PU

GREEN, RALPH ROBINSON. *All Around Boy: Life and Letters of Ralph Robinson Green.* Rufus S. Green. N. Y., 1893. 255 p.

DLC, NN, PU

GREEN, SAMUEL. *Memoir of the Rev. Samuel Green.* Richard S. Storrs. Boston, 1836. 412 p. DLC, NN, MWA

GREEN, SAMUEL FISK. *Life and Letters of Samuel Fisk Green, M.D. of Green Hill.* Ebenezer Cutler, comp. n.p., 1891. 456 p. (Privately Printed) NN, MWA

GREEN, SAMUEL SWETT. *Samuel Swett Green.* R. K. Shaw. Chicago, 1926. 92 p. (American Library Pioneers)

DLC, NN, MWA, CSmH, PU

GREEN, WILLIAM. *Brief Sketch of the Life of William Green, LL.D.* Philip Slaughter. Richmond, 1883. 131 p.

DLC, NN, MWA, CSmH, MiD:B

2:258

GREENE, CORDELIA AGNES. *Biography of Cordelia Agnes Greene, M.D. in Her "Art of Keeping Well."* Elizabeth P. Gordon. N. Y., 1906. 418 p. DLC, NN

GREENE, DANIEL CROSBY. *New-Englander in Japan; Daniel Crosby Greene.* Evarts B. Greene. Boston, 1927. 374 p.

DLC, NN, MWA, CSmH, PU

GREENE, NATHANAEL.
*Memoirs of the Life and Campaigns of the Hon. Nathaniel
Greene, Major General in the Army of the United States* . . .
Charles Caldwell. Phila., 1819. 452 p.
DLC, NN, MWA, CSmH, PU, MiD:B
General Greene. Francis V. Greene. N. Y., 1893. 332 p.
(G.C.) DLC, NN, CSmH, PU
Life of Nathanael Greene. George W. Greene. Boston, 1846.
403 p. (L.A.B.) DLC, NN, MWA, CSmH, MiU:C
*Life of Nathanael Greene, Major General in the Army of the
Revolution.* George W. Greene. N. Y., 1867–71. 3 vols.
DLC, NN, PU, MiD:B, MiU:C
Sketches of the Life and Correspondence of Nathanael Greene.
William Johnson. Charleston, 1822. 2 vols.
DLC, NN, MWA, CSmH, PU, MiU:C, RP:JCB
Life of Nathanael Greene. William G. Simms. N. Y., 1849.
393 p. DLC, NN, MWA, CSmH, PU, MiD:B, MiU:C
GREENE, ROBERT. *Robert Greene.* John C. Jordan. N. Y., 1915.
231 p. (Col. Univ. Studies in English) DLC, NN, CSmH, PU
GREENE, STEPHEN. *Stephen Greene; Memories of His Life.* Ben-
jamin A. Greene. n.p., 1903. (Privately Printed) DLC, MWA
GREENE, WILLIAM PARKINSON. *The Life and Character of the Hon.
William Parkinson Greene.* Elbridge Smith. Cambridge, 1865.
137 p. DLC, NN, MWA, CSmH, MiD:B
GREENHALGE, FREDERICK THOMAS. *Life and Work of Frederick T.
Greenhalge, Governor of Massachusetts.* James E. Nesmith.
Boston, 1897. 456 p. DLC, NN, MWA, MiD:B
GREENLEAF, MOSES. *Moses Greenleaf; Maine's First Map-Maker.*
Edgar C. Smith. Bangor, Me., 1902. 165 p. (De Burians Pubs.
no. 2) DLC, NN, MWA, CSmH, MiD:B, RP:JCB
GREENOUGH, HORATIO. *Memorial of Horatio Greenough.* Henry T.
Tuckerman. N. Y., 1853. 245 p. DLC, NN, MWA, CSmH, PU
GREENWOOD, CALEB. *Old Greenwood; the Story of Caleb Greenwood,
Trapper, Pathfinder* . . . Charles Kelly. Salt Lake City, 1936.
128 p. DLC, NN, CSmH
GREENWOOD, JAMES M. 2:314
GREER, DAVID HUMMELL. *David Hummell Greer, Eighth Bishop of
N. Y.* Charles L. Slattery. N. Y., 1921. 328 p. DLC, NN
GREGG, ALEXANDER. *Alexander Gregg, First Bishop of Texas.* Wilson
Gregg. Sewanee, Tenn., 1912. 138 p. DLC, NN

GREGG, WILLIAM. *William Gregg; Factory Master of the Old South.* Broadus Mitchell. Chapel Hill, N. C., 1928. 331 p.
DLC, NN, CSmH, PU

GREGORY, JOHN MILTON. *John M. Gregory; A Biography.* Allene Gregory. Chicago, 1923. 372 p. *DLC, NN*

GRELLET, STEPHEN.
A Short Life of Stephen Grellet (1773–1855). Alfred C. Garrett. Phila., n.d. 128 p. *NN*
Stephen Grellet. William Guest. Phila., 1881. 264 p.
DLC, NN, MWA, PU

GRENELL, ZELOTES. *Life and Labors of Elder Zelotes Grenell: For Sixty-Four Years . . . Baptist Minister.* L. O. Grenelle. n.p., 1885. 248 p.

GRENFELL, WILFRED THOMASON.
Forty Years on the Labrador; Life Story of Sir Wilfred Grenfell, K.C.M.G. Ernest H. Hayes. N. Y., 1930. 128 p.
DLC, NN
Grenfell: Knight-Errant of the North. Fullerton L. Waldo. Phila., 1924. 315 p. *DLC, NN*
2:507

GRESHAM, WALTER QUINTIN. *Life of Walter Quintin Gresham, 1832–1895.* Matilda Gresham. Chicago, 1918. 2 vols.
DLC, NN, MWA, PU

GRIBBLE, JAMES. *Undaunted Hope; Life of James Gribble.* Florence N. Gribble. Ashland, O., 1932. 438 p. *DLC, NN*

GRIER, ROBERT COOPER. 2:110

GRIFFIN, EDMUND DORR.
E. D. Griffin. Remains With Memoir. Francis Griffin, comp. 1831. 2 vols. *DLC, NN*
A Biographical Memoir of the Rev. Edmund D. Griffin. John McVickar. N. Y., 1832. 117 p. *DLC, NN, MWA*

GRIFFIN, EDWARD DORR.
Memoir of Edward Dorr Griffin, D.D., President of Williams College. Ansel Nash. N. Y., 1842. 72 p. *MWA*
Memoir of Rev. Edward D. Griffin. Wm. B. Sprague. N. Y., 1839. 270 p. *DLC, NN, MWA*

GRIFFIN, GASTON. *Gaston Griffin, a Country Banker.* Gaston W. Ames. Port Jervis, N. Y., 1900. 194 p. *NN*

GRIFFITH, BENJAMIN. *Benjamin Griffith, Biographical Sketches Contributed by Friends.* Charles H. Banes, ed. Phila., 1894. 296 p.
MWA

GRIFFITTS, SAMUEL POWEL. *Biographical Memoir of Dr. Samuel P. Griffitts.* G. Emerson. Phila., 1827. 22 p. *MWA, PU*

GRIMALD, NICHOLAS. *The Life and Poems of Nicholas Grimald.* L. R. Merrill. New Haven, 1925. 458 p. (Yale Studies in English. No. 69) *DLC, NN, CSmH*

GRIMES, JAMES WILSON. *The Life of James W. Grimes, Governor of Iowa, 1854–58.* William Salter. N. Y., 1876. 398 p. *DLC, NN, MWA, PU, MiD:B*

GRIMKÉ, SARAH and ANGELINA. *Sarah and Angelina Grimké.* Catherine H. Birney. Boston and N. Y., 1885. 319 p. *DLC, NN, MWA*

GRISCOM, JOHN. *Memoir of John Griscom, With an Account of the N. Y. High School; Society for the Prevention of Pauperism . . . and Other Institutions.* John H. Griscom. N. Y., 1859. 427 p. *DLC, NN*

GRISWOLD, ALEXANDER VIETS.
   The Life of Bishop Griswold. John N. Norton. N. Y., 1858. 86 p. *NN, PU*
   Memoir of the Life of the Rt. Rev. Alexander Viets Griswold, D.D. John S. Stone. Phila., 1844. 620 p. *NN, MWA, CSmH, MiD:B*
   Memoir of Bishop A. V. Griswold. J. S. Stone. N. Y., 1857. 263 p. (Abridged) *DLC*

GROSS, SAMUEL DAVID. *Biographical Sketch of Samuel D. Gross.* J. M. Da Costa. Phila., 1884. 16 p. *DLC, NN, PU*

GROTIUS, HUGO. *Hugo Grotius; the Father of the Modern Science of International Law.* Hamilton Vreeland. N. Y., 1917. 246 p. *DLC, NN, PU*

GROW, GALUSHA AARON. *Galusha A. Grow, Father of the Homestead Law.* James T. Dubois and Gertrude S. Mathews. Boston and N. Y., 1917. 305 p. *DLC, NN, CSmH, PU*

GRUBB, SARAH. *Some Account of the Life . . . of Sarah Grubb.* Trenton, 1795. 418 p. *CSmH*

GRUBER, JACOB. *The Life of Jacob Gruber.* William P. Strickland. N. Y., 1860. 384 p. *DLC, NN, CSmH, PU*

GRÜNEWALD, MATTHIAS. *Matthias Grünewald, Personality and Accomplishment.* Arthur Burkhard. Cambridge, 1935. 123 p. *NN*

GUÉRIN, EUGÉNIE. 2:93

GUESCLIN, BERTRAND. *The Life and Times of Bertrand Du Guesclin: a History of the Fourteenth Century.* D. F. Jamison. Charleston, S. C., 1864. 2 vols. *DLC, MWA, PU*

GUGGENHEIM, WILLIAM. *William Guggenheim.* Gatenby Williams and C. M. Heath. N. Y., 1934. 252 p. *DLC, NN*

GUINEY, LOUISE IMOGEN. *Louise Imogen Guiney.* Alice Brown. N. Y., 1921. 111 p. *DLC, NN, MWA, CSmH, PU*

GUITEAU, CHARLES J. *The Life and Trial of Guiteau, the Assassin.* John C. Ridpath. Cincinnati, 1882. 131 p.

GULICK, ALICE GORDON. *Alice Gordon Gulick; Her Life and Work in Spain.* Elizabeth P. Gordon. N. Y., 1917. 283 p. *DLC*

GULICK, JOHN THOMAS. *Evolutionist and Missionary, John Thomas Gulick, Portrayed Through Documents and Discussions.* Addison Gulick. Chicago, 1932. 555 p. *DLC, NN*

GULICK, LUTHER HALSEY.
  Luther Halsey Gulick, 1865–1918. Ethel J. Dorgan. N. Y., 1934. 180 p. *NN, PU*
  Luther H. Gulick, Missionary in Hawaii. F. G. Jewett. Boston, 1895. 314 p. *NN*

GUNN, MOSES. *Memorial Sketches of Dr. Moses Gunn.* Jane A. Gunn. Chicago, 1889. 380 p. *DLC, NN, MWA*

GUNN, WALTER. *Memoir of Rev. Walter Gunn.* G. A. Lintner. Albany, 1852. 156 p. *DLC*

GUNSAULUS, FRANK. 2:487

GURLEY, WILLIAM. *Memoir of Rev. William Gurley, Late of Milan, Ohio . . . Including a Sketch of the Irish Insurrection and Martyrs of 1798.* L. B. Gurley. Cincinnati, 1852. 268 p. *NN*

GURNEY, ELIZA P. *Memoir and Correspondence of Eliza P. Gurney.* Richard F. Mott. Phila., 1884. 377 p. *NN, MWA, MiD:B*

GUTHRIE, THOMAS. 2:98

GUTHRIE, WILLIAM. *Life of William Guthrie.* William Dunlap. Exeter, N. H., 1796.

GUYON, JEANNE MARIE. *Life and Religious Opinions of Madame De La Mothe Guyon: Together With Some Account of . . . Fénelon, Archbishop of Cambray.* Thomas C. Upham. N. Y., 1847. 2 vols. *NN, MWA*
  2:90–138

GWINETT, AMBROSE. *The Life and Adventures of Ambrose Gwinett . . . To Which is Added An Account of John Matthieson . . .* Phila., 1784. 32 p. *NN*

GWINNETT, BUTTON.
  Button Gwinnett, . . . a Brief Biographical Review. William M. Clemens. Pompton Lakes, N. J., 1921. 13 p. *DLC, NN, MWA, PU*

Button Gwinnett, Signer of the Declaration of Independence. Charles F. Jenkins. N. Y., 1926. 291 p.

DLC, NN, MWA, CSmH, PU, MiD:B, MiU:C

HACKETT, HORATIO BALCH. *Memorials of Horatio Balch Hackett.* George H. Whittemore. Rochester, 1876. 303 p.

DLC, NN, MWA, MiD:B

HACKETT, WILLIAM HENRY YOUNG. *Memoir of William H. Y. Hackett, With Selections From His Writings.* Frank W. Hackett. Portsmouth, 1879. 156 p. DLC, NN, MWA, MiD:B

HADDOCK, GEORGE CHANNING. *Life of Rev. George C. Haddock.* Frank C. Haddock. N. Y., 1887. 541 p.

DLC, NN, MWA, PU, MiD:B

HADDON, ELIZABETH. 2:55

HADLEY, SAMUEL HOPKINS. *Samuel H. Hadley of Water Street.* J. W. Chapman. N. Y., 1906. 289 p. DLC, NN

HADLOCK, SAMUEL. *God's Pocket. The Story of Captain Samuel Hadlock.* Rachel Field. N. Y., 1934. 163 p. DLC, NN

HAECKEL, ERNEST. 2:335

HAGERT, HENRY SCHELL. *Henry S. Hagert. Memorial.* Phila., 1886. 123 p. (Privately Printed) DLC, NN, CSmH, PU

HAHNEMAN, SAMUEL.

Life and Letters of Dr. Samuel Hahneman. T. L. Bradford. Phila., 1895. 513 p. DLC, NN

Life of Samuel Hahneman, M.D. A. G. Hull. N. Y., 1841. 18 p. DLC, NN

HAIG, AXEL HERMANN. *Axel Hermann Haig and His Work.* E. A. Armstrong. N. Y., 1905. 176 p. DLC, NN, CSmH

HAKLUYT, RICHARD. *Richard Hakluyt and the English Voyages.* George B. Parks. N. Y., 1928. 289 p.

DLC, NN, MWA, CSmH, PU

HALE, DAVID. *Memoirs of David Hale; Late Editor of the Journal of Commerce.* Joseph P. Thompson. N. Y., 1850. 520 p.

DLC, NN, MWA, PU

HALE, EDWARD EVERETT. *The Life and Letters of Edward Everett Hale.* Edward E. Hale, Jr. Boston, 1917. 2 vols.

DLC, NN, MWA, CSmH, PU

2:6–109–246–431–519

HALE, NATHAN.

Memoir of Captain Nathan Hale. New Haven, 1844. 16 p.

DLC, NN, MWA, MiU:C

Nathan Hale, the Martyr Spy. Charles W. Brown. N. Y.,
1899. 149 p.   *DLC, CSmH*

Nathan Hale, the Martyr Spy. Charlotte M. Holloway. N. Y.,
1900. 246 p.   *DLC, MWA*

Nathan Hale, 1776; Biographical and Memorial. Henry P.
Johnston. New Haven, 1914. 208 p.

          DLC, NN, MWA, CSmH, PU, MiU:C

Two Spies: Nathan Hale and John André. Benson J. Lossing.
N. Y., 1886. 169 p.   *DLC, NN, MWA, CSmH*

Nathan Hale, the Ideal Patriot. W. O. Partridge. N. Y., 1902.
134 p.   *DLC, NN*

The Two Spies: Nathan Hale and Robert Townsend. Morton
Pennypacker. Boston, 1930. 118 p.   *DLC, NN, MWA, PU*

Nathan Hale. Jean C. Root. N. Y., 1915. 160 p.

          DLC, NN, MWA

*Captain Nathan Hale; Major John Palsgrave Wyllys . . . A
Digressive History.* George D. Seymour. New Haven, 1933. 296 p.

          DLC, NN, MWA, CSmH

*Life of Captain Nathan Hale, the Martyr-Spy of the American
Revolution.* Isaac W. Stuart. Hartford and N. Y., 1856. 271 p.

          DLC, NN, MWA, CSmH, PU, MiU:C

HALE, SAMUEL WHITNEY. *Memorial of Samuel Whitney Hale.* William De L. Love. Hartford, 1895. 27 p.   *DLC, MWA*

HALE, SARAH JOSEPHA. *Lady of Godey's: Sarah Josepha Hale.* Ruth
Finley. Phila., 1931. 318 p.   *DLC, NN, MWA, CSmH, PU*
2:703

HALIBURTON, THOMAS CHANDLER. *Thomas Chandler Haliburton
(Sam Slick); a Study in Provincial Toryism.* Victor L. O. Chit-
tick. N. Y., 1924. 695 p. (Col. Univ. Studies in English)

          DLC, NN, MWA, CSmH, PU

HALL, ANGELINE. *An Astronomer's Wife; the Biography of Angeline
Hall.* Angelo Hall. Balt., 1908. 129 p.

          DLC, NN, MWA, PU, MiD:B

HALL, ARTHUR CRAWSHAY ALLISTON. *Arthur C. A. Hall, Third
Bishop of Vermont.* George L. Richardson. Boston and N. Y.,
1932. 249 p.   *DLC, NN*

HALL, CHARLES FRANCIS. 2:78, 262

HALL, EDWARD KIMBALL. 2:425

HALL, EVELYN SARAH. *The Life Story of Evelyn S. Hall, Principal of
Northfield Seminary From 1883 to 1911.* Mary E. Silverthorne.
N. Y., 1914. 309 p.   *DLC, NN*

HALL, GEORGE ALONZO. *George Alonzo Hall; Tribute to Consecrated Personality.* G. A. Warburton. N. Y., 1905. 169 p. *DLC, NN*

HALL, GORDON. *Memoir of Rev. Gordon Hall, A.M.; One of the First Missionaries . . . at Bombay.* Horatio Bardwell. Andover, 1834. 260 p. *NN, MWA*

HALL, GRANVILLE STANLEY.
    G. Stanley Hall; a Biography of a Mind. Lorine Pruette. N. Y., 1926. 266 p. *DLC, NN, PU*
    G. Stanley Hall: A Sketch. Louis N. Wilson. N. Y., 1914. 144 p. *DLC, NN, PU*

HALL, JAMES. *James Hall of Albany, Geologist and Paleontologist, 1811–1898.* John M. Clarke. Albany, 1923. 565 p.
DLC, NN, PU

HALL, JAMES. *Judge James Hall; Literary Pioneer of the Middle West.* Davis L. James. Columbus, 1909. 15 p. (Reprinted from *Ohio Archeological and Historical Publications*) *DLC, NN, PU*

HALL, JOHN. *John Hall, Pastor and Preacher.* Thomas C. Hall. N. Y., 1901. 341 p. *DLC, NN, MWA*

HALL, JOHN. *John Hall of Wallingford, Conn.* James Shepard. New Britain, Conn., 1902. 60 p. *DLC, NN*

HALL, JOHN NEWTON. *Memoirs of Elder J. N. Hall, the Peerless Defender of the Baptist Faith.* W. M. Barker and Lillian J. S. Hall. Fulton, Ky., 1907. 349 p. *DLC*

HALL, LOUISE. *In Memoriam. Sister Louise, the Story of Her Life Work.* Maunsell Van Rensselaer. N. Y., 1883. 107 p.
DLC, NN

HALL, WILLARD. *Memoir of Willard Hall.* Daniel M. Bates. Wilmington, Del., 1879. 60 p. (Papers of the Hist. Soc. of Delaware, Vol. 1) *DLC, NN, MWA, CSmH, MiD:B*

HALLECK, FITZ-GREENE.
    Fitz-Greene Halleck; an Early Knickerbocker Wit and Poet. Nelson F. Adkins. New Haven, 1930. 461 p.
DLC, NN, MWA, CSmH, PU
    Some Notices on the Life and Writings of Fitz-Greene Halleck. William C. Bryant. N. Y., 1869. 43 p.
DLC, NN, MWA, CSmH
    Fitz-Greene Halleck. A Memorial. F. S. Cozzens. N. Y., 1868. 32 p. *NN, MWA, CSmH*
    The Life and Letters of Fitz-Greene Halleck. James G. Wilson. N. Y., 1869. 607 p. *DLC, NN, MWA, CSmH, PU*

HALLOCK, GERARD. *Life of Gerard Hallock, Thirty-Three Years Editor of the New York Journal of Commerce.* W. H. Hallock. N. Y., 1869. 287 p.   *DLC, NN, MWA*

HALLOCK, JEREMIAH and MOSES.

Life of Rev. Jeremiah Hallock, Late Pastor of the Congregational Church in Canton, Conn. Cyrus Yale. N. Y., 1828. 316 p.   *NN, MWA*

Life of Rev. Jeremiah Hallock of Canton, Conn., To Which is Added . . . the Life of the Rev. Moses Hallock, of Plainfield, Mass. Cyrus Yale. N. Y., 1854. 404 p.   *DLC, NN, MWA*

HALSTED, WILLIAM STEWART. *William Stewart Halsted, Surgeon.* William G. MacCallum. Balt., 1930. 241 p.   *DLC, NN*

HAMILTON, ALEXANDER.

An American Colossus; the Singular Career of Alexander Hamilton. Ralph E. Bailey. Boston, 1933. 318 p.   *DLC, NN*

Alexander Hamilton, the Constructive Statesman. Lewis H. Boutell. Chicago, 1890. 66 p.   *DLC, NN, MWA, CSmH*

Alexander Hamilton. C. A. Conant. Boston and N. Y., 1901. 145 p. (Riverside Biography Series)   *DLC, NN*

Alexander Hamilton: An Essay. William S. Culbertson. New Haven, 1911. 153 p.   *DLC, NN*

Alexander Hamilton. E. S. Ellis. Milwaukee, 1903. 173 p. (Great Americans of History)   *DLC, NN, PU*

Alexander Hamilton. Henry J. Ford. N. Y., 1920. 381 p. (Figures from American History)   *DLC, NN, PU*

Study in Alexander Hamilton. Fontaine T. Fox. N. Y., 1911. 171 p.   *DLC, NN, CSmH, PU*

Alexander Hamilton, Nevis-Weehawken. J. E. Graybill. N. Y., 1897. 80 p.   *DLC, NN, CSmH, MiD:B*

The Intimate Life of Alexander Hamilton. Allan McLane Hamilton. N. Y., 1910. 483 p.   *DLC, NN, MWA, CSmH, PU, MiD:B*

The Life of Alexander Hamilton. John C. Hamilton. N. Y., 1834. 422 p.   *DLC, NN, CSmH, MiU:C*

Life of Alexander Hamilton. John C. Hamilton. Boston, 1879. 7 vols.   *DLC, NN, CSmH, MiU:C*

Alexander Hamilton. Henry C. Lodge. Boston, 1882. 317 p. (A.S.)   *DLC, NN, MWA, CSmH, PU, MiD:B*

The Life of Alexander Hamilton. J. T. Morse, Jr. Boston, 1876. 2 vols.   *DLC, NN, MWA, CSmH, PU, MiD:B, MiU:C*

Alexander Hamilton; An Essay on American Union.   Frederick
S. Oliver.   N. Y., 1921.   502 p.   *DLC, NN, MWA, CSmH, PU*
  Alexander Hamilton: a Study of the Revolution and the Union.
John C. Ridpath.   Cincinnati, 1881.   43 p.   *DLC, MiU:C*
  The Life and Times of Alexander Hamilton.   Samuel M.
Schmucker.   Phila., 1857.   408 p.   *DLC, NN, MWA, CSmH*
  Alexander Hamilton.   James Schouler.   N. Y., 1901.   140 p.
(Beacon Biographies)   *DLC*
  Life and Epoch of Alexander Hamilton.   A Historical Study.
George Shea.   Boston, 1879.   470 p.
DLC, NN, MWA, CSmH, MiD:B, MiU:C
  Alexander Hamilton.   Johan J. Smertenko.   N. Y., 1932.   307 p.
DLC, NN, PU
  Alexander Hamilton.   William G. Sumner.   N. Y., 1890.   281 p.
DLC, NN, MWA, MiD:B
  Greatest American: Alexander Hamilton.   Arthur H. Vanden-
berg.   N. Y., 1921.   353 p.
DLC, NN, CSmH, PU, MiD:B, MiU:C
  Hamilton.   The Trail of a Tradition.   Arthur H. Vandenberg.
N. Y. and London, 1926.   405 p.   *DLC, NN*
  Alexander Hamilton, First American Business Man.   Robert I.
Warshow.   N. Y., 1931.   241 p.   *DLC, NN, MWA PU*
  2:35–77–264–329–660
HAMILTON, ALICE.   2:592
HAMILTON, WILLIAM STEPHEN.   *Alexander Hamilton's Pioneer Son:
The Life and Times of Colonel William Stephen Hamilton; 1797–
1850.*   Sylvan J. Muldoon.   Harrisburg, Pa., 1930.   246 p.
DLC, NN, MWA, CSmH, PU, MiD:B
HAMLIN, CYRUS.   *In Memoriam; Rev. Cyrus Hamlin* . . . Alfred
D. G. Hamlin, comp.   Boston, 1903.   118 p.   *DLC, NN, MWA*
HAMLIN, HANNIBAL.   *Life and Times of Hannibal Hamlin.*   C. E.
Hamlin.   Cambridge, 1899.   627 p.   *DLC, NN, MWA, CSmH*
  2:128   See LINCOLN, ABRAHAM.
HAMLIN, HARRIET M.   See EVERETT, SERAPHINA H.
HAMLINE, LEONIDAS LENT.
  *Biography of Rev. Leonidas L. Hamline, Late Bishop of the
M. E. Church.*   F. G. Hibbard.   Cincinnati, 1880.   447 p.
NN, MiD:B
  Life and Letters of Rev. L. L. Hamline.   Walter C. Palmer.
N. Y., 1866.   544 p.   *DLC, NN*

HAMM, ARTHUR ELLIS. *In White Armor; the Life of Captain Arthur Ellis Hamm, 326th Infantry, U. S. Army.* Elizabeth G. Hamm. N. Y., 1919. 185 p. *DLC, NN*

HAMMOND, JAMES HENRY. *James Henry Hammond.* Elizabeth Merritt. Balt., 1923. 151 p. *CSmH*

HAMMOND, MAXIMILIAN MONTAGU. *Memoir of Capt. M. M. Hammond.* Egerton D. Hammond. N. Y., 1858. 372 p.
DLC, NN, MWA

HAMPTON, WADE. 2:612

HANCOCK, GEORGE A. *A Pioneer Heritage.* Sam T. Clover. Los Angeles, 1932. 291 p. *CSmH*

HANCOCK, JOHN.
John Hancock, His Book. A. E. Brown. Boston, 1898. 286 p.
DLC, NN, MWA, PU
John Hancock. J. R. Musick. Milwaukee, 1903. 178 p.
(Great Americans of History) *DLC, NN, PU, MiD:B*
John Hancock, the Picturesque Patriot. Lorenzo Sears. Boston, 1912. 351 p. *DLC, NN, MWA, PU, MiD:B*
Biographical Sketch of the Life and Character of His Late Excellency Governor Hancock. James Sullivan. Boston, 1793. 16 p.
MWA

2:329

HANCOCK, JOHN. *John Hancock, Ph.D. A Memoir, With Selections From His Writings.* William E. Venable. Cincinnati, 1892. 195 p.
DLC, MWA

HANCOCK, WINFIELD SCOTT.
Life of Winfield Scott Hancock. J. R. Cole. Cincinnati, 1880. 424 p. *DLC*
Winfield; the Lawyer's Son, and How He Became a Major-General. Charles W. Denison. Phila., 1865. 323 p.
DLC, NN, CSmH
Hancock " The Superb." The Early Life and Public Career of Winfield S. Hancock . . . Including Also a Sketch of the Life of Hon. William H. English . . . Charles W. Denison and G. B. Herbert. Cincinnati, 1880. 431 p. *DLC, NN, CSmH*
Life and Military Career of Winfield Scott Hancock, Also a Biographical Sketch of Hon. Wm. H. English . . . John W. Forney. Phila., 1880. 502 p. *DLC, NN, CSmH*
Life and Public Services of Winfield Scott Hancock. A. T. Freed. Chicago, 1880. 94 p. *DLC, NN*

Life of Gen. Winfield S. Hancock. F. E. Goodrich. Boston, 1886. 352 p. *DLC, NN, MWA, CSmH, PU*

Reminiscences of Winfield Scott Hancock. Almira R. Hancock. N. Y., 1887. 340 p. *DLC, NN, MWA, CSmH, PU*

Life of Winfield Scott Hancock, Personal, Military, and Political. D. X. Junkin and F. H. Norton. N. Y., 1880. 398 p.
NN, CSmH, MiD:B

Life of Gen. Hancock. James B. McClure, ed. Chicago, 1880. 124 p. *NN, CSmH*

Life of Gen. Winfield S. Hancock. Alvan S. Southworth. N. Y., 1880. 256 p. *DLC, NN*

General Hancock. Francis A. Walker. N. Y., 1894. 332 p. (G.C.) *DLC, NN, MWA, CSmH, PU*
2:590

HAND, FATHER. *Father Hand, Founder of All Hallow's Catholic College For Foreign Missions.* J. Macdevitt. 1885.

HANDEL, GEORG FRIEDRICH. 2:187

HANFORD, LEVI. *A Narrative of the Life and Adventures of Levi Hanford.* Charles I. Bushnell. N. Y., 1863. 80 p. (Privately Printed) *DLC, NN, MWA, MiU:C*

HANKS, NANCY. *Nancy Hanks: Story of Abraham Lincoln's Mother.* C. H. Hitchcock. N. Y., 1899. 105 p. *DLC, NN, MWA, CSmH*

HANLAN, EDWARD. *Edward Hanlan, America's Champion Oarsman . . . , Also, History of E. A. Trickett.* W. E. Harding. N. Y., 1881. 48 p. *NN*

HANLY, JOSEPH J. *Memoir of the Late Rev. Joseph J. Hanly, M.D., of the New Jersey Conference.* Joanna P. R. Hanly. Phila., 1861. 368 p. *DLC, MWA*

HANNA, MARCUS ALONZO.
Hanna. Thomas Beer. N. Y., 1929. 325 p.
DLC, NN, MWA

Marcus Alonzo Hanna: His Life and Work. Herbert D. Croly. N. Y., 1912. 495 p. *DLC, NN, CSmH, PU*

HANNIBAL.
History of Hannibal, the Carthaginian. Jacob Abbott. N. Y., 1849. 295 p. *DLC, NN*

Hannibal. Theodore A. Dodge. Boston and N. Y., 1891. 2 vols. (Great Captains) *DLC, NN, PU*

HANSON, JOHN. *John Hanson, Our First President.* Seymour W. Smith. N. Y., 1932. 140 p. *DLC, NN, MWA, CSmH*
2:218

HARBOUGH, HENRY. *Life of Rev. Henry Harbough.* Linn Harbough. Phila., 1900. 302 p. *DLC*

HARDEE, WILLIAM JOSEPH. 2:612

HARDEN-HICKEY, JAMES. 2:172

HARDEY, MARY ALOYSIA. *Mary Aloysia Hardey, Religious of the Sacred Heart, 1809–1886.* Mother Mary Garvey. N. Y., 1910. 405 p. *DLC, NN*

HARDIE, JAMES KEIR. 2:205

HARDIE, JOHN. *John Hardie of Thornhill; His Life and Letters and Times.* Benjamin P. Lewis. N. Y., 1928. 167 p. *DLC, NN*

HARDIN, BENJAMIN. *Ben Hardin: His Times and Contemporaries, With Selections From His Speeches.* Lucius P. Little. Louisville, 1887. 640 p. *DLC, NN*

HARDIN, JOHN WESLEY. *They Died With Their Boots On. Biography of One of the Most Notorious of the Texas " Bad Men," John Wesley Hardin.* Thomas Ripley. N. Y., 1935. 285 p. *DLC, NN, MWA*

HARDING, BENJAMIN FOSDICK. *Benjamin Fosdick Harding, 1857–1923.* Mrs. Benjamin F. Harding and Wm. L. W. Field. Cambridge, 1925. 30 p. (Privately Printed) *MWA*

HARDING, SETH. *Seth Harding, Mariner. A Naval Picture of the Revolution.* James L. Howard. New Haven, 1930. 301 p. *DLC, NN, MWA, CSmH*

HARDING, WARREN GAMALIEL.

Warren G. Harding, The Man. Joe M. Chapple. Boston, 1920. 128 p. *DLC, NN, MWA*

Life and Times of Warren G. Harding, Our After-War President. Joe M. Chapple. Boston, 1924. 386 p. *DLC, NN, MWA, PU*

From Printer to President. Sherman A. Cuneo. Phila., 1922. 153 p. *DLC, NN*

The Life of Warren G. Harding. Willis F. Johnson. Phila., 1923. 288 p. *DLC, NN*

The Illustrious Life and Work of Warren G. Harding, Twenty-Ninth President of the U. S. . . . Thomas H. Russell. Chicago, 1923. 320 p. *DLC, NN*

HARDY, THOMAS. *Thomas Hardy, Poet and Novelist.* Samuel C. Chew. N. Y., 1928. 196 p. *DLC, NN, CSmH, PU*
2:406

HARE, ROBERT. *Life of Robert Hare, the American Chemist.* Edgar Fahs Smith. Phila., 1917. 508 p. *DLC, NN, PU*

HARE, WILLIAM HOBART. *Life and Labors of Bishop Hare, Apostle to the Sioux*. M. A. De Wolfe Howe. N. Y., 1911. 417 p.

DLC, NN, MiD:B

HARI, MATA. See ZELLE, MARGARETHA G.

HARLAN, JAMES. *James Harlan*. Johnson Brigham. Iowa City, 1913. 398 p. (Iowa Hist. Soc.) *DLC, NN, CSmH, PU*

HARNETT, CORNELIUS. *Cornelius Harnett: Essay in N. Carolina History*. Robert D. W. Connor. Raleigh, 1909. 209 p.

DLC, NN, MiU:C

HARNEY, WILLIAM SELBY. *Life and Military Services of Gen. William S. Harney*. L. U. Reavis. St. Louis, 1878. 477 p.

DLC, CSmH, PU

2:358

HARPER, JESSE. *Life of Col. Jesse Harper of Danville, Ill., Farm-Boy, Lawyer, Editor, Author, Orator, Scholar and Reformer. Brief Biography With Selections From His Speeches and Writings*. A. C. Barton and W. B. Gallaher. Chicago, 1904. 371 p. *DLC, NN*

HARPER, ROBERT D. *In Memoriam of the Rev. Robert D. Harper, D.D.* Wellington E. Loucks, ed. n.p., n.d. 131 p.

DLC, MWA, PU

HARPER, ROBERT GOODLOE. *Robert Goodloe Harper*. C. W. Sommerville. Washington, 1899. 43 p. *DLC, NN, PU*

HARPER, WILLIAM RAINEY. *William R. Harper, First President of the University of Chicago*. Thomas W. Goodspeed. Chicago, 1928. 241 p. *DLC, NN, CSmH, PU*

HARRIMAN, EDWARD HENRY.

E. H. Harriman, the Little Giant of Wall Street. H. J. Eckenrode and Pocahontas W. Edmunds. N. Y., 1933. 242 p.

DLC, NN, MWA

E. H. Harriman: A Biography. George E. Kennan. Boston, 1922. 2 vols. *DLC, NN, CSmH, PU*

Edward H. Harriman. John Muir. N. Y., 1911. 38 p.

DLC, NN, CSmH

HARRIMAN, WALTER. *Life of Walter Harriman, Governor of New Hampshire*. Amos Hadley. Boston, 1888. 385 p. *DLC*

HARRINGTON, JOSEPH. *A Memoir of Rev. Joseph Harrington in His " Sermons."* William Whiting. Boston, 1854. 67 p.

NN, MWA

HARRIOT, THOMAS. *Thomas Harriot. The Mathematician, the Philosopher and the Scholar*. Henry Stevens. London, 1900. 213 p. (Privately Printed) *DLC, NN, MWA, CSmH, MiU:C*

HARRIS, FRANK. *Frank Harris; a Study in Black and White.* A. I. Tobin and Elmer Gertz. Chicago, 1931. 393 p. *DLC, NN, MWA, PU*

HARRIS, GEORGE N. AND BUSHROD W. *The Confederate Soldier. A Memorial Sketch of G. N. and B. W. Harris.* J. E. Edwards. N. Y., 1868. 139 p. *DLC, NN, MWA, CSmH*

HARRIS, JOEL CHANDLER.
Life and Letters of Joel Chandler Harris. Julia F. Harris. Boston, 1918. 620 p. *DLC, NN, MWA, CSmH, PU, MiD:B*
The Life of Joel Chandler Harris. R. L. Wiggins. Nashville, 1918. 447 p. *DLC, NN, MWA, CSmH, PU*
2:493

HARRIS, THADDEUS WILLIAM. *Memoir of Thaddeus W. Harris.* Thomas W. Higginson. Boston, 1869. (Occasional Papers of the Boston Society of Natural History) *NN, MWA, PU*
2:681

HARRIS, TOWNSEND. *Townsend Harris, First American Envoy in Japan.* W. E. Griffis. Boston, 1895. 351 p. *DLC, NN, PU*

HARRISON, BENJAMIN.
The Life and Public Services of Benjamin Harrison. James P. Boyd. Phila., 1901. 246 p. *DLC*
Lives of Benjamin Harrison and Levi P. Morton. Gilbert L. Harney. Providence, R. I., 1888. 479 p. *DLC, NN*
Life of Gen. Benjamin Harrison. Waldo Messaros. Phila., 1892. 511 p. *CSmH*
The Life and Public Services of Gen. Benj. Harrison. Henry D. Northrop. Phila., 1888. 624 p. *NN, CSmH*
Life of Gen. Benjamin Harrison. Lew Wallace. Hartford, 1888. 348 p. *NN, MWA, CSmH, PU, MiD:B*

HARRISON, CARTER HENRY.
Carter Henry Harrison; a Memoir. Willis J. Abbott. N. Y., 1895. ·254 p. *DLC, NN, MWA, CSmH, MiD:B*
Carter Henry Harrison I., Political Leader. Claudius O. Johnson. Chicago, 1928. 306 p. *DLC, NN*

HARRISON, WILLIAM HENRY.
The Life and Times of William Henry Harrison. Samuel J. Burr. N. Y., 1840. 300 p. *DLC, NN, MWA, MiD:B*
Outlines of the Life and Public Services, Civil and Military, of William Henry Harrison. Caleb Cushing. Boston, 1840. 21 p. *DLC, NN, MWA, CSmH, MiD:B*
A Historical Narrative of the Civil and Military Services of Major-General William Henry Harrison. Moses Dawson. Cincinnati, 1824. 464 p. *DLC, NN, MWA, CSmH, MiD:B*

William Henry Harrison. Dorothy B. Goebel. Indianapolis, 1926. 456 p. (Indiana Hist. Coll. Vol. 14)

DLC, NN, CSmH, PU

A Memoir of the Public Services of William Henry Harrison, of Ohio. James Hall. Phila., 1838. 323 p.

DLC, NN, MWA, MiD:B

The People's Presidential Candidate, or Life of William H. Harrison. Richard Hildreth. Boston, 1839. 211 p.

DLC, NN, MiD:B

Life of W. H. Harrison; the Peoples Candidate for the Presidency. Isaac R. Jackson. Phila., 1840. 60 p. *NN*

The Life of William Henry Harrison (of Ohio), the Peoples' Candidate for the Presidency. Isaac S. Jackson. Phila., 1840. 212 p. *DLC, NN, MWA, CSmH, MiD:B*

Life of William Henry Harrison. Henry Montgomery. Cleveland, 1853. 465 p. *DLC, NN, CSmH, MiD:B*

Sketches of the Civil and Military Services of William Henry Harrison. Charles S. Todd and Benjamin Drake. Cincinnati, 1840. 165 p. *DLC, NN, MWA, MiD:B*

William Henry Harrison, John Tyler, and James Knox Polk. William O. Stoddard. N. Y., 1888. 280 p. *DLC*

HARRISSE, HENRY *Henry Harrisse. Biographical and Bibliographical Sketch.* Adolph Growoll. N. Y., 1899. 13 p. (Dibden Club Leaflets, No. 3) *DLC, NN, CSmH*

HART, WILLIAM H. *A Biographical and Historical Sketch of William H. Hart, 1834–1919.* Lillian H. Tryon. Hartford, 1929. Unpaged. (Privately Printed) *MWA*

HARTE, BRET.

Bret Harte. Henry W. Boynton. N. Y., 1903. 117 p. (Contemporary Men of Letters Series) *DLC, NN, CSmH, PU*

The Life of Bret Harte. H. C. Merwin. Boston and N. Y., 1911. 362 p. *DLC, NN, MWA, CSmH, PU*

Bret Harte; Argonaut and Exile. George R. Stewart. Boston, 1931. 384 p. *DLC, NN, CSmH, PU*
2:41

HARTLEY, ROBERT MILHAM. *Memorial of Robert Milham Hartley.* Isaac S. Hartley. Utica, 1882. 549 p. *DLC, NN, PU*

HARVARD, JOHN. *John Harvard and His Times.* Henry C. Shelley. Boston, 1907. 331 p. *DLC, NN, MWA, CSmH, PU*

HARVEY, ELIAS. 2:343

HARVEY, GEORGE. *George Harvey, a Passionate Patriot.* Willis F. Johnson. Boston, 1929. 436 p.   *DLC, NN, MWA, PU*

HARVEY, HAYWARD AUGUSTUS. *Memoir of Hayward Augustus Harvey.* N. Y., 1900. 82 p.   *DLC, NN, MWA, PU*

HARVEY, WILLIAM. *William Harvey.* Archibald E. Malloch. N. Y., 1929. 103 p.   *DLC, NN, CSmH*

HARWARD, WILLIAM EUGENE. *Life of W. Eugene Harward.* F. E. Clark. Portland, Me., 1879. 176 p.   *NN, MWA*

HASKELL, ALEXANDER CHEVES. *Alexander Cheves Haskell; the Portrait of a Man.* Louise H. Daly. Norwood, Mass., 1934. 224 p. (Privately Printed)   *DLC, NN, MWA, CSmH*

HASKINS, CHARLES WALDO. *Charles Waldo Haskins. An American Pioneer in Accountancy.* William G. Jordan. N. Y., 1923. 128 p.   *DLC, NN, PU*

HASKINS, GEORGE FOXCROFT. *Life of Father Haskins.* William D. Kelly. Boston, 1899. 152 p.   *DLC, NN*

HASSELQUIST, TUFVE NILSSON. *T. N. Hasselquist. The Career and Influence of a Swedish-American Clergyman, Journalist and Educator.* Oscar F. Ander. Rock Island, Ill., 1931. 260 p.   *DLC, NN, MWA, CSmH, PU*

HASSLER, FERDINAND RUDOLPH. *The Chequered Career of Ferdinand Rudolph Hassler, First Superintendent of the U. S. Coast Survey; a Chapter in the History of Science in America.* Florian Cajori. Boston, 1929. 245 p.   *DLC, NN, CSmH*

HASWELL, ANTHONY. *Anthony Haswell; Printer-Patriot-Ballader.* John Spargo. Rutland, Vt., 1925. 293 p.   *DLC, NN, MWA, CSmH*

HATCHER, WILLIAM ELDRIDGE. *William E. Hatcher, D. D. . . . A Biography.* Eldridge B. Hatcher. Richmond, 1915. 696 p.   *DLC, NN, CSmH, PU*

HATTON, ROBERT. *Life of General Robert Hatton, Including His Most Important Public Speeches; Together With Much of His Washington and Army Correspondence.* James V. Drake. Nashville, 1867. 458 p.   *DLC, NN, CSmH*

HAVEMEYER, JOHN CRAIG. *Life, Letters and Addresses of John Craig Havemeyer . . .* John C. Havemeyer. N. Y., 1914. 372 p.   *DLC, NN*

HAVEN, ALICE BRADLEY. *Cousin Alice: A Memoir of Alice B. Haven.* Cornelia H. B. Richards. N. Y., 1865. 392 p. *DLC, NN, CSmH*

HAVEN, GILBERT.
    Memorials of Gilbert Haven, Bishop of the Methodist Episcopal Church. W. H. Daniels, ed. Boston, 1880. 359 p.   *MWA*

Life of Gilbert Haven, Bishop of the M. E. Church. George Prentice. N. Y., 1884. 526 p. *PU*

HAVEN, HENRY PHILEMON. *A Model Superintendent . . . Henry P. Haven of the International Lesson Committee.* Henry C. Trumbull. N. Y., 1880. 188 p. *DLC, NN, MWA, PU*

HAVEN, NATHANIEL APPLETON. *The Remains of Nathaniel Appleton Haven, With a Memoir of His Life.* George Ticknor, ed. n.p., 1827. 368 p. *DLC, NN, MWA*

HAVERGAL, FRANCES RIDLEY.

Frances Ridley Havergal. Edward Davies. Reading, Mass., 1884. 192 p. *DLC, MWA*

Memorials of Frances Ridley Havergal. Maria V. G. Havergal. N. Y., n.d. 391 p. *DLC, NN, MWA, PU, MiD:B*

HAWKINS, BENJAMIN. 2:135

HAWKINS, JOHN HENRY WILLIS. *Life of John H. W. Hawkins.* Wm. George Hawkins. Boston, 1859. 423 p.

DLC, NN, MWA, MiD:B

HAWKINS, MICAH. *Micah Hawkins and the Saw-Mill. A Sketch of the First Successful American Opera and Its Author.* Oscar Wegelin. N. Y., 1917. Unpaged. (Privately Printed)

DLC, NN, MWA, CSmH, PU

HAWKS, FRANCIS LISTER. *A Memorial of Francis L. Hawks, D.D., LL.D.* Evert A. Duyckinck. N. Y., 1871. 166 p.

DLC, NN, MWA, MiD:B

HAWLEY, JOSEPH.

Historical Sketch of Major Joseph Hawley of Northampton, Mass., 1723–1788 Elias Hawley. Buffalo, N. Y., 1890. 48 p.

DLC, NN, MWA, CSmH, MiD:B

Joseph Hawley, Colonial Radical. E. Francis Brown. N. Y., 1931. 213 p. *DLC, NN, MWA, CSmH, PU*

HAWTHORNE, NATHANIEL.

Hawthorne. Newton Arvin. Boston, 1929. 303 p.

DLC, NN, MWA, CSmH, PU

Personal Recollections of Nathaniel Hawthorne. Horatio Bridge. N. Y., 1893. 200 p. *DLC, PU*

Life of Nathaniel Hawthorne. Moncure D. Conway. N. Y. and London, 1890. 224 p. *DLC, NN, MWA, CSmH, PU*

Nathaniel Hawthorne. Annie Fields. Boston, 1899. 136 p.

DLC, NN, MWA, CSmH, MiD:B

Hawthorne. James T. Fields. Boston, 1871. 128 p.

DLC, NN, PU

Hawthorne; a Study in Solitude. Herbert S. Gorman. N. Y., 1927. 179 p. (Murray Hill Biographies)

          DLC, NN, CSmH, PU

Romantic Rebel. The Story of Nathaniel Hawthorne. Hildegarde Hawthorne. N. Y., 1932. 231 p.   *DLC, NN, MWA, PU*

Nathaniel Hawthorne and His Wife. Julian Hawthorne. Boston, 1884. 2 vols.   *DLC, NN, MWA, CSmH, PU*

Nathaniel Hawthorne. Henry James, Jr. N. Y., 1879. 177 p. (E.M.L.)   *DLC, NN, MWA, CSmH, PU*

A Study of Hawthorne. George P. Lathrop. Boston, 1876. 350 p.   *DLC, NN, MWA, CSmH, PU*

Memories of Hawthorne. Rose Hawthorne Lathrop. Boston, 1897. 494 p.   *DLC, NN, MWA, PU*

The Rebellious Puritan; Portrait of Mr. Hawthorne. Lloyd R. Morris. N. Y., 1927. 369 p.   *DLC, NN, MWA, CSmH, PU*

Hawthorne and His Friends; Reminiscence and Tribute. Franklin B. Sanborn. Cedar Rapids, Ia., 1908. 84 p.

       DLC, NN, MWA, CSmH, PU, MiD:B

Life and Genius of Nathaniel Hawthorne. F. P. Stearns. Phila., 1906. 463 p.   *DLC, NN, MWA, PU*

Nathaniel Hawthorne; a Memoir. Richard H. Stoddard. N. Y., 1879. 16 p.   *DLC, CSmH*

Nathaniel Hawthorne. George E. Woodberry. Boston, 1902. 302 p. (A.M.L.)   *DLC, NN, MWA, CSmH, PU*
  2:47

HAY, JOHN.

John Hay, Scholar and Statesman. Joseph B. Bishop. Providence, 1906. 29 p.   *DLC, NN, MWA, CSmH, PU*

John Hay, From Poetry to Politics. Tyler Dennett. N. Y., 1933. 476 p.   *DLC, NN, CSmH, PU*

John Hay, Author and Statesman. Lorenzo Sears. N. Y., 1914. 150 p.   *DLC, NN, CSmH, PU*

The Life and Letters of John Hay. William R. Thayer. Boston, 1908. 2 vols. Boston, 1929. 1 vol.

      DLC, NN, MWA, CSmH, PU, MiD:B
  2:77

HAYDN, FRANZ JOSEPH. 2:187

HAYES, PATRICK CARDINAL. 2:190–679

HAYES, ISAAC ISRAEL. 2:262

HAYES, RUTHERFORD BIRCHARD.

Gov. Rutherford B. Hayes. Life and Public Services. R. H. Conwell. Boston, 1876. 328 p.   *DLC, NN, CSmH*

Rutherford B. Hayes, Statesman of Reunion. Hamilton J. Eckenrode and Pocahontas W. Wight. N. Y., 1930. 363 p. (American Political Leaders)   *DLC, NN, CSmH, PU*

The Life, Public Services and Select Speeches of Rutherford B. Hayes. J. Q. Howard. Cincinnati, 1876. 260 p.
DLC, NN, MWA, CSmH, PU, MiD:B

Sketch of the Life and Character of Rutherford B. Hayes. William D. Howells. N. Y., 1876. 195 p.
DLC, NN, MWA, CSmH, PU, MiD:B

Rutherford Birchard Hayes, James Abram Garfield, and Chester Alan Arthur. William O. Stoddard. N. Y., 1889. 275 p.
DLC, NN

Life of Rutherford B. Hayes, Nineteenth President of the United States. Charles R. Williams. Boston, 1914. 2 vols.
DLC, NN, CSmH, PU, MiD:B
2:6–190

HAYGARTH, JOHN. *John Haygarth, Clinician, Investigator, Apostle of Sanitation, 1740–1827.* George H. Weaver. Chicago, 1930. 45 p.
DLC

HAYNE, PAUL H. 2:503

HAYNE, ROBERT YOUNG.
Robert Y. Hayne and His Times. T. D. Jervey. N. Y., 1909. 555 p.   *DLC, NN, CSmH, PU*

Lives of Robert Young Hayne and Hugh Swinton Legaré. Paul H. Hayne. Charleston, 1878. 158 p.   *NN, MWA, CSmH*

HAYNES, LEMUEL. *Sketches of the Life and Character of the Rev. Lemuel Haynes . . . of . . . Rutland, Vt.* Timothy M. Cooley. N. Y., 1839. 348 p.   *DLC, NN, MWA, CSmH, MiD:B*

HAYS, ALEXANDER. *Life and Letters of Alexander Hays, Brevet Colonel U. S. Army, Brigadier General and Brevet-Major General U. S. Volunteers.* George T. Fleming. Pittsburgh, 1919. 708 p.
DLC, NN

HAYS, JACOB. 2:662

HAYS, WILL H. 2:546

HAYWOOD, ELIZA. *Life and Romances of Mrs. Eliza Haywood.* George F. Whicher. N. Y., 1915. 211 p. (Col. Univ. Studies in Eng.)   *DLC, NN, CSmH, PU*

HAZARD, THOMAS. *Thomas Hazard Son of Robert, Call'd College Tom. A Study of Life in Narragansett in the 18th Century.* Caroline Hazard. Boston, 1893. 324 p.   *DLC, NN, MWA, PU, MiD:B*

HAZELTINE, NELLIE. 2:518

HEARD, AUGUSTINE. *Augustine Heard and His Friends.* Thomas F.
Waters. Salem, Mass., 1916. 108 p. *DLC, NN, MWA, CSmH*
HEARN, LAFCADIO.
　　Life and Letters of Lafcadio Hearn. Elizabeth Bisland. N. Y.,
1906. 2 vols. *DLC, NN, MWA, CSmH, PU*
　　Concerning Lafcadio Hearn. George M. Gould. Phila., 1908.
416 p. *CSmH*
　　Lafcadio Hearn. Nina H. Kennard. N. Y., 1912. 356 p.
　　　　　　　　　　　　　　　　　　DLC, NN, CSmH, PU
　　Blue Ghost; a Study of Lafcadio Hearn. Jean Temple. N. Y.,
1931. 328 p. *DLC, NN, PU*
　　Lafcadio Hearn's American Days. Edward L. Tinker. N. Y.,
1924. 374 p. *DLC, NN, CSmH, PU*
HEARST, PHOEBE APPERSON. *The Life . . . of Phoebe A. Hearst.*
Winifred Black. San Francisco, 1928. 155 p. *CSmH*
HEARST, WILLIAM RANDOLPH.
　　Hearst, Lord of San Simeon. Oliver Carlson and Ernest S.
Bates. N. Y., 1936. 332 p. *DLC, NN, PU*
　　Imperial Hearst; a Social Biography. Ferdinand Lundberg.
N. Y., 1936. 406 p. *DLC, NN, PU*
　　William Randolph Hearst, American. Cora M. Older. N. Y.,
1936. 581 p. *DLC, NN, PU*
　　W. R. Hearst; an American Phenomenon. John K. Winkler.
N. Y., 1928. 354 p. *DLC, NN, PU*
HEATH, ISAAC. *Lives of Isaac Heath, and John Bowles . . . and . . .
John Eliot, Jr.* J. W. Thornton. n.p., 1850. 216 p. (Privately
Printed) *DLC, NN, MWA, CSmH*
HEATHCOTE, CALEB. *Caleb Heathcote, Gentleman Colonist; the Story
of a Career in the Province of New York, 1692–1721.* Dixon R.
Fox. N. Y., 1926. 301 p. *DLC, NN, MWA, CSmH, PU, MiU:C*
HEAVISIDE, OLIVER. 2:25
HEBER, REGINALD. *The Life of Bishop Heber.* J. N. Norton. N. Y.,
1858. 144 p. *DLC, NN*
HECHT, BEN. 2:366
HECKER, ISAAC.
　　Life of Father Hecker. Walter Elliott. N. Y., 1891. 428 p.
　　　　　　　　　　　　　　　　　　　　NN
　　Father Hecker. H. D. Sedgwick, Jr. N. Y., 1900. 157 p.
　　(Beacon Biographies) *DLC, NN, MWA*
HECKEWELDER, JOHN. *Life of John Heckewelder.* Edward Rond-
thaler. Phila., 1847. 149 p.
　　　　　　DLC, NN, MWA, CSmH, PU, MiD:B, MiU:C

HEDDING, ELIJAH. *Life and Times of Rev. Elijah Hedding.* D. W. Clark. N. Y., 1855. 686 p. NN, CSmH

HEDLEY, FRANK. 2:546

HEILPRIN, MICHAEL. *Michael Heilprin and His Sons.* Gustav Pollak. N. Y., 1912. 540 p. DLC, NN

HEINE, HEINRICH.
That Man Heine; a Biography. Lewis Browne and Elsa Weihl. N. Y., 1927. 420 p. DLC, NN, PU
Heinrich Heine; Romance and Tragedy of the Poet's Life. Michael Monahan. N. Y., 1924. 199 p. DLC, NN, PU

HEINZ, HENRY JOHN. *Henry J. Heinz. A Biography.* E. D. Mc-Cafferty. N. Y., 1923. 233 p. DLC, NN, CSmH, PU

HELEN OF TROY. *A Daughter of the Gods; the Story of Helen of Troy.* Lea Donald. N. Y., 1906. 135 p. DLC, NN

HELMONT, JAN BAPTISTA. 2:71

HENCK, F. W. *Memoir of F. W. Henck, With Notes and Comments.* John S. Keen. Highway, Ky., 1899. 247 p. DLC, NN

HENDERSON, ARCHIBALD. *Archibald Henderson: Artist and Scientist.* George H. McCoy. Chapel Hill, 1930. DLC, MWA

HENDRICKS, THOMAS ANDREWS. *Life and Public Services of Thomas A. Hendricks.* John W. Holcombe and Hubert M. Skinner. Indianápolis, 1886. 637 p. DLC, PU, MiD:B
See CLEVELAND, GROVER.

HENLE, JACOB. *Life of Jacob Henle.* Victor Robinson. N. Y., 1921. 117 p. DLC, PU

HENRY IV.
History of Henry the Fourth, King of France and Navarre. J. S. C. Abbott. N. Y., 1856. 335 p. DLC, NN
Henry of Navarre. Henry D. Sedgwick. Indianapolis, 1930. 324 p. DLC, NN

HENRY VIII. *Henry VIII.* Francis Hackett. N. Y., 1929. 452 p. DLC, NN, PU

HENRY, JOSEPH.
A Memoir of Joseph Henry. William B. Taylor. Washington, 1879. 142 p. DLC, NN, PU, MiD:B
Notes on the Life and Character of Joseph Henry. James C. Welling. Phila., 1878. (Extract from Bull. of Philos. Soc. of Washington v. 2. 1878. p. 203–29) DLC, NN, MWA, PU

HENRY, O. [See PORTER, WILLIAM SYDNEY]

HENRY, PATRICK.
The Life of Patrick Henry of Virginia. S. G. Arnold. Auburn, 1854. 271 p. DLC, MWA, CSmH, PU

Life of Patrick Henry. Alexander H. Everett. (L.A.B.)
DLC, MWA, CSmH, MiU:C
Patrick Henry: Life, Correspondence and Speeches. Wm. W.
Henry. N. Y., 1891. 3 vols.
DLC, NN, MWA, CSmH, PU, MiU:C
The True Patrick Henry. George Morgan. Phila., 1907. 492 p.
DLC, NN, CSmH, PU
Patrick Henry. Moses C. Tyler. Boston, 1887. 454 p.
(A.S.) DLC, NN, MWA, CSmH, PU, MiD:B, MiU:C
Sketches of the Life and Character of Patrick Henry. William
Wirt. Phila., 1817. 468 p.
DLC, NN, MWA, CSmH, PU, MiD:B, MiU:C, RP:JCB
2:330–662

HENRY, WILLIAM. *Life of William Henry of Lancaster, Pa., 1729–
1786, Patriot, Military Officer, Inventor of the Steamboat.* Francis
Jordan, Jr. Lancaster, Pa., 1910. 185 p.
DLC, NN, PU, MiD:B

HENSHAW, JOHN PRENTISS. *Life of Bishop Henshaw, of Rhode Island.*
J. N. Norton. N. Y., 1859. 164 p. NN

HEPBURN, ALONZO BARTON. *A. Barton Hepburn; His Life and Service to His Time.* Joseph B. Bishop. N. Y., 1923. 421 p.
DLC, NN, CSmH

HEPBURN, JAMES CURTIS. *Hepburn of Japan and His Wife and Help-
mate.* Wm. E. Griffis. Phila., 1913. 238 p. DLC, NN, PU
2:237

HEPBURN, WILLIAM PETERS. *William Peters Hepburn.* John E.
Briggs. Iowa City, 1919. 469 p. (Iowa State Hist. Soc.)
DLC, NN, CSmH

HEPWORTH, GEORGE. *George Hepworth; Preacher, Journalist, Friend
of the People.* Susan H. Ward. N. Y., 1903. 294 p.
DLC, NN, MWA

HERBERT, GEORGE. *The Life of George Herbert.* G. L. Duyckinck.
N. Y., 1858. 197 p. DLC, NN

HERBERT, HENRY WILLIAM.
Frank Forester (Henry William Herbert); A Tragedy in Exile.
William S. Hunt. Newark, N. J., 1933. 128 p.
DLC, NN, MWA, CSmH
Life and Writings of Frank Forester. [H. W. Herbert.] David
W. Judd, ed. N. Y., 1882. 2 vols. DLC, NN, MWA

HERFORD, BROOKE. *Brooke Herford. A Memoir.* John Cuckson.
Boston, 1904. 84 p. DLC, MWA

HERKOMER, HUBERT VON. *Hubert Von Herkomer.* Alfred L. Baldry. N. Y., 1901. 135 p. *DLC, PU*

HEROD THE GREAT. *Herod; a Biography.* Jacob S. Minkin. N. Y., 1936. 277 p. *DLC, NN*

HERODOTUS. *Father of History: Account of Herodotus.* Denton J. Snider. St. Louis, 1907. 451 p. *DLC, NN, PU*
2:5

HERRICK, MYRON TIMOTHY. *Myron T. Herrick, Friend of France. An Autobiographical Biography.* T. Bentley Mott. N. Y., 1929. 399 p. *DLC, NN, MWA, PU*

HERRICK, ROBERT. *Youth Immortal: A Life of Robert Herrick.* Emily Easton. Boston, 1934. 220 p. *DLC, NN, PU*

HERRON, FRANCIS. *Two Discourses Upon the Life and Character of the Rev. Francis Herron, D.D.* William M. Paxton. Pittsburgh, 1861. 141 p. *DLC, NN, MiD:B*

HERSCHEL, SIR WILLIAM. 2:79–335

HERSHEY, MILTON SNAVELY. *Milton S. Hershey, Builder.* Joseph R. Snavely. Hershey, Pa., 1935. 237 p. *DLC, NN, PU*

HERTZ, HEINRICH. 2:25

HERZL, THEODOR. *Theodor Herzl; a Biography.* Jacob De Haas. N. Y., 1927. 2 vols. *DLC, NN*

HETZER, LUDWIG. *The Life and Teachings of Ludwig Hetzer, 1500–1529.* Frederick L. Weis. Dorchester, Mass., 1930. 239 p.
DLC, NN, MWA

HEWES, GEORGE ROBERT TWELVES.
A Retrospect of the Boston Tea Party, With a Memoir of George R. T. Hewes, a Survivor of the . . . Patriots Who Drowned the Tea in Boston Harbor in 1773. James Hawkes. N. Y., 1834. 210 p. *DLC, NN, MWA, CSmH, MiU:C*
Traits of the Tea Party; Being a Memoir of George R. T. Hewes, One of the Last of Its Survivors. B. B. Thatcher. Boston, 1835. 265 p. *DLC, NN, MWA, CSmH, MiU:C*

HEWITT, ABRAM STEVENS. *Abram S. Hewitt; With Some Account of Peter Cooper.* Allan Nevins. N. Y., 1935. 623 p.
DLC, NN, CSmH, PU

HEYWOOD, JOHN. *Life and Work of John Heywood.* Robert G. W. Bolwell. N. Y., 1921. 188 p. (Col. Univ. Studies in English)
DLC, NN, CSmH, PU

HIBBS, RUSSELL AUBRA. *Russell A. Higgs, Pioneer in Orthopedic Surgery, 1869–1932.* George M. Goodwin. N. Y., 1935. 136 p.
DLC, NN

HICK, SAMUEL. *The Village Blacksmith; or, Piety and Usefulness Exemplified in a Memoir of the Life of Samuel Hick . . .* James Everett. N. Y., 1844. 352 p. *DLC, NN, MWA*

HICKOK, JAMES BUTLER.

Life and Marvelous Adventures of Wild Bill, the Scout . . . James W. Buel. Chicago, 1880. 92 p. *DLC, NN*

Wild Bill and His Era. The Life and Adventures of James Butler Hickok. William E. Connelley. N. Y., 1933. 229 p. *DLC, NN, CSmH*

" Wild Bill." Oscar W. Coursey. Mitchell, S. D., 1924. 80 p. *DLC, NN*

The Real Wild Bill Hickok; Famous Scout and Knight Chivalric of the Plains. Wilbert E. Eisele. Denver, 1931. 364 p. *DLC, NN, MWA*

Wild Bill Hickok; the Prince of Pistoleers. Frank J. Wilstach. N. Y., 1926. 304 p. *DLC, NN, MWA*
2:358

HICKS, THOMAS HOLLIDAY. *Gov. Thomas H. Hicks of Maryland.* George L. P. Radcliffe. Balt., 1901. 141 p. *CSmH*

HIDALGO, MIGUEL. *The Life and Times of Miguel Hidalgo y Costilla.* Arthur H. Noll and A. P. McMahon. Chicago, 1910. 200 p. *DLC, NN, CSmH*

HIDDEN, SAMUEL. *Memoir of the Rev. Samuel Hidden.* E. C. Cogswell. Boston, 1842. 332 p. *DLC, NN, MWA*

HIGGINSON, FRANCIS. *Life of Francis Higginson.* Thomas W. Higginson. N. Y., 1891. 158 p. *DLC, NN, MWA, MiD:B*

HIGGINSON, HENRY LEE. *Life and Letters of Henry Lee Higginson.* Bliss Perry. Boston, 1921. 557 p. *DLC, NN, MWA, CSmH*

HIGGINSON, NATHANIEL. *Nathaniel Higginson, Royal Governor of Madras, 1692–1698.* B. C. Steiner. Durham, N. C., 1902. 13 p. *DLC, NN, PU, MiD:B*

HIGGINSON, STEPHEN. *Life and Times of Stephen Higginson.* Thomas W. Higginson. Boston, 1907. 305 p. *DLC, NN, MWA, CSmH, PU, MiD:B*

HIGGINSON, THOMAS WENTWORTH. *Thomas Wentworth Higginson: The Story of His Life.* Mary P. T. Higginson. Boston, 1914. 435 p. *DLC, NN, MWA, CSmH, PU*

HILDRETH, AZRO BENJAMIN FRANKLIN. *The Life and Times of Azro B. F. Hildreth.* Charles Aldrich, ed. Des Moines, Ia., 1891. 556 p. *DLC, NN, MWA, MiD:B*

HILDRETH, EDWARD. *Edward Hildreth; in Memoriam.* Philo C. Hildreth. n.p., 1908. 56 p. *DLC, NN, MWA*

HILL, AMBROSE POWELL. 2:612 p.

HILL, AARON. *Aaron Hill, Poet, Dramatist, Projector.* Dorothy Brewster. N. Y., 1913. 301 p. (Col. Univ. Studies in English) *DLC, NN, CSmH, PU*

HILL, BENJAMIN HARVEY.

Senator Benjamin H. Hill, of Georgia. His Life, Speeches and Writings. Benj. H. Hill, Jr. Atlanta, 1891. 823 p. *DLC, NN, CSmH*

Benjamin H. Hill, Secession and Reconstruction. Haywood J. Pearce. Chicago, 1928. 330 p. *DLC, NN, CSmH, PU*

HILL, DAVID. 2:14

HILL, DAVID OCTAVIUS. *David Octavius Hill: Master of Photography.* Heinrich Schwarz. N. Y., 1931. 67 p. *DLC, NN*

HILL, EVERETT WENTWORTH. *A Biography of Everett W. Hill.* Rex. F. Harlow. Oklahoma City, Okla., 1930. 115 p. *DLC, NN, MWA, PU*

HILL, GEORGE HANDEL. *Life and Recollections of " Yankee " Hill.* W. K. Northall, ed. N. Y., 1850. 203 p. *DLC, NN, MWA, CSmH, PU, MiD:B*

HILL, ISAAC.

Biography of Isaac Hill. Cyrus P. Bradley. Concord, N. H., 1835. 245 p. *DLC, NN, MWA*

The Work of Isaac Hill in the Presidential Election of 1828. Charles E. Perry. (Concord, N. H., *Monitor and Patriot*, Feb. 2–15, 1932) *DLC, NN*

HILL, JAMES JEROME. *Life of James J. Hill.* Joseph G. Pyle. N. Y., 1917. 2 vols. *DLC, NN, PU*

2:180–331–340

HILL, JOSEPH BANCROFT. *Joseph Bancroft Hill.* Brief Memoir. Edwin R. Hodgman. Boston, 1868. *MWA*

HILL, THOMAS. *Thomas Hill, Twentieth President of Harvard.* William G. Land. Cambridge, 1933. 267 p. *DLC, NN, CSmH, PU*

HILLGAS, MICHAEL. *Memoir of the First Treasurer of the United States.* Michael R. Minnich. Phila., 1905. 87 p. *DLC, NN, PU*

HILLHOUSE, AUGUSTUS and JAMES. *Sketch of the Life and Public Services of Hon. James Hillhouse of New Haven; With a Notice of His Son, Augustus Lucas Hillhouse.* Leonard Bacon. New Haven, 1860. 572 p. *DLC, NN, MWA, MiD:B, MiU:C*

HILTY, CARL. 2:519

HINDENBURG, PAUL. *Hindenburg, the Man With Three Lives.* Thomas R. Ybarra. N. Y., 1932. 316 p. *DLC, NN*

HINKEY, FRANK. 2:425

HINKLEY, HOLMES. *Holmes Hinkley, an Industrial Pioneer, 1793–1866.* Walter S. Hinchman, ed. Cambridge, 1913. 43 p.
DLC, NN, MWA

HOAR, EBENEZER ROCKWOOD. *Ebenezer Rockwood Hoar.* Moorfield Storey and E. W. Emerson. Boston and N. Y., 1911. 355 p.
DLC, NN, MWA, PU

HOAR, GEORGE FRISBIE. *George Frisbie Hoar.* Frederick H. Gillett. Boston, 1934. 311 p. *DLC, NN, MWA, CSmH, PU*

HOAR, SAMUEL. *Memoir of Samuel Hoar, Sept. 27, 1845–April. 11, 1904.* Woodward Hudson. Cambridge, 1904. 52 p. (Privately Printed) *DLC, NN*

HOARD, WILLIAM DEMPSTER. *William Dempster Hoard.* George W. Rankin. Fort Atkinson, Wis., 1925. 261 p. *DLC, NN, MiD:B*
2:497

HOBART, GARRET AUGUSTUS. *Life of Garret A. Hobart, Twenty-Fourth Vice-President of the United States.* David Magie. N. Y., 1910. 300 p. *DLC, NN*
See MCKINLEY, WILLIAM.

HOBART, JOHN HENRY.
Memoir of J. H. Hobart in Hobart's "Posthumous Works." William Berrian. N. Y., 1833. 423 p. *DLC, NN*
The Early Life and Professional Years of J. H. Hobart. John McVicar. N. Y., 1834. 2 vols. London, 1838. 728 p.
NN, MWA, CSmH
Life of the Rt. Rev. John Henry Hobart. John N. Norton. N. Y., 1857. 96 p. *NN, PU*

HOBART, SAMUEL. *Sam Hobart, the Locomotive Engineer.* Justin D. Fulton. N. Y., 1883. 252 p. *DLC, MWA, PU*

HODGE, CHARLES. *The Life of Charles Hodge, Professor in the Theological Seminary, Princeton, N. J.* Archibald A. Hodge. N. Y., 1880. 620 p. *DLC, NN, MWA, PU*

HODGE, WILLIAM. *A Memoir of the Late William Hodge.* William Hodge. Buffalo, 1855. 160 p. *CSmH*

HODGES, GEORGE. *George Hodges; a Biography.* Julia S. Hodges. N. Y., 1926. 242 p. *DLC, NN, MWA*
2:246

HODGES, JACOB. *Life of Jacob Hodges, an African.* A. D. Eddy. Phila., 1842. 94 p. *DLC, NN, MWA*

HOFF, GRACE WHITNEY. *Grace Whitney Hoff, the Story of an Abundant Life.* Carolyn Patch. Cambridge, 1933. 223 p.
DLC, NN, CSmH, PU, MiD:B

HOFF, JACOBUS HENDRICUS. 2:286

HOFFMAN, CADWALLADER COLDEN. *A Memoir of Rev. C. C. Hoffman.* George T. Fox. N. Y., 1868. 365 p. *DLC, MWA*

HOFFMAN, CHARLES FENNO. *Charles Fenno Hoffman.* Homer F. Barnes. N. Y., 1930. 361 p. (Col. Univ. Studies in English)
DLC, NN, PU

HOFFMAN, EUGENE AUGUSTUS. *A Memorial Biography of the Very Rev. Eugene A. Hoffman, Late Dean of the General Theological Seminary.* Theodore M. Riley. N. Y., 1904. 2 vols. (Privately Printed) *DLC, NN, PU*

HOFFMAN, VIRGINIA HALE. *Life of Mrs. Virginia Hale Hoffman.* George D. Cummins. Phila., 1859. 256 p. *DLC, NN*

HOGARTH, WILLIAM. 2:161

HOGE, MOSES DRURY. *Moses Drury Hoge; Life and Letters.* Payton H. Hoge. Richmond, 1899. 518 p. *DLC, NN*

HOLCOMBE, STEVE P. *Steve P. Holcombe, the Converted Gambler: His Life and Work.* Gross Alexander. Louisville, 1891. 218 p. *NN*

HOLCROFT, THOMAS. 2:406

HOLE-IN-THE-DAY. 2:204

HOLLAND, GEORGE. *Sketch of the Life of George Holland, the Veteran Comedian.* T. H. Morell. N. Y., 1871. 124 p. *DLC, NN*
2:367

HOLLAND, JOSIAH GILBERT. *The Life of Josiah G. Holland.* Harriette Plunkett. N. Y., 1894. 208 p. *DLC, MWA, MiD:B*

HOLLAND, LADY. 2:93

HOLLEY, ALEXANDER LYMAN. *Memorial of Alexander Lyman Holley ... July 20, 1832–Jan. 29, 1882.* N. Y., 1884. 224 p.
DLC, NN, MWA, PU

HOLLEY, HORACE. *Discourse on the Genius and Character of the Rev. Horace Holley, LL.D., Late President of Transylvania University.* Charles Caldwell. Boston, 1828. 294 p. *NN, MWA, CSmH, PU*

HOLLEY, MYRON. *Myon Holley; and What He Did for Liberty and True Religion.* Elizur Wright. Boston, 1882. 328 p. (Privately Printed) *DLC, NN, MWA, PU, MiD:B*

HOLLINGSWORTH, DAVID ADAMS. *Biographical Sketch of Hon. David A. Hollingsworth.* Lavina Ada J. Burtoft. Cleveland, 1920. 339 p.
DLC, NN, MWA

HOLLIS, GEORGE CHARLES. *George Charles Hollis; a Memoir.* Henry
Barnard. N. Y., 1901. 39 p. *DLC, NN*

HOLMES, ABIEL. *Memoir of Rev. Abiel Holmes.* William Jenks.
(Mass. Hist. Soc. Coll. Ser. III. Vol. 7) *DLC, NN, MWA, CSmH*

HOLMES, MEAD. ...*Memoir of Mead Holmes.* Boston, 1864. 240 p.
CSmH

HOLMES, OLIVER WENDELL.
Life of Oliver Wendell Holmes. Emma E. Brown. Boston,
1884. 304 p. *DLC, CSmH*
Oliver Wendell Holmes, Poet, Littérateur, Scientist. William S.
Kennedy. Boston, 1883. 356 p. *DLC, NN, MWA, CSmH, PU*
Life and Letters of Oliver Wendell Holmes. John T. Morse,
Jr. Boston, 1896. 2 vols. *DLC, NN, MWA, CSmH, PU*
Oliver Wendell Holmes. Centenary Biography. Lewis W.
Townsend. London, 1909. 180 p. *DLC*
2:592

HOLMES, OLIVER WENDELL, JR. *Justice Oliver Wendell Holmes.* Silas
Bent. N. Y., 1932. 386 p. *DLC, NN, MWA*

HOMER. 2:82

HOMER, WILLIAM BRADFORD. *Writings of Rev. William Bradford
Homer, ... With ... a Memoir.* Edwards A. Park. Boston, 1842.
395 p. *DLC, NN, MWA*

HOMER, WINSLOW. *Life and Work of Winslow Homer.* William H.
Downes. Boston, 1911. 306 p. *DLC, NN, PU*
2:123–429

HOOD, JOHN. 2:612

HOOD, ROBIN. *Historical Sketch of Robin Hood and Captain Kidd.*
W. W. Campbell. N. Y., 1853. 263 p. *DLC, NN*

HOOK, THEODORE. *Theodore Hook and His Novels.* Myron F. Bright-
field. Cambridge, 1928. 381 p. *DLC, NN, CSmH, PU*

HOOKER, JOSEPH. 2:96

HOOKER, PHILIP. *Philip Hooker; a Contribution to the Study of the
Renaissance of America.* Edward W. Root. N. Y., 1929. 242 p.
DLC, NN, PU

HOOKER, THOMAS.
The Life of Thomas Hooker. Edward W. Hooker. Boston,
1849. 324 p. *DLC, NN, MWA*
Thomas Hooker, Preacher, Founder, Democrat. G. L. Walker.
N. Y., 1891. 203 p. (Makers of America)
DLC, NN, MWA, CSmH, PU

HOOKER, ZIBEON. *An Account of the Life and Military Services of Zibeon Hooker, a Lieutenant in the Army of Washington.* Clarence A Wiswall, comp. n.p., 1918. 35 p.

DLC, MWA, CSmH, MiU:C

HOOVER, HERBERT.

The Truth About Hoover. Herbert Corey. Boston, 1932. 318 p. *DLC, NN, MWA*

Herbert Hoover and American Individualism, a Modern Interpretation of a National Ideal. Walter E. Dexter. N. Y., 1932. 256 p. *DLC, NN*

Hoover and His Times; Looking Back Through the Years. Edwin Emerson. N. Y., 1932. 632 p. *DLC, NN, MWA*

The Strange Career of Mr. Hoover Under Two Flags. John Hamill. N. Y., 1931. 381 p. *DLC, NN, MWA*

Who's Hoover? William Hard. N. Y., 1928. 274 p. *DLC, PU*

Herbert Hoover; a Reminiscent Biography. Will Irwin. N. Y., 1928. 315 p. *DLC, NN, MWA, PU*

Herbert Hoover; the Man and His Work. Vernon L. Kellogg. N. Y., 1920. 375 p. *DLC, NN*

The Great Mistake. [Herbert Hoover.] John Knox. Washington, 1930. 176 p. *DLC, NN, MWA*

Making of Herbert Hoover. Rose W. Lane. N. Y., 1920. 356 p. *DLC, NN*

The Rise of Herbert Hoover. Walter W. Liggett. N. Y., 1932. 382 p. *DLC, NN, MWA*

Herbert Clark Hoover: An American Tragedy. Clement Wood. N. Y., 1932. 330 p. *DLC, NN*

2:190–507–546–703

HOPKINS, ALBERT. *Life of Professor Albert Hopkins.* Albert C. Sewall. N. Y., 1879. 340 p. *DLC, NN*

HOPKINS, ESEK. *Esek Hopkins, Commander-in-Chief of the Continental Navy During the American Revolution, 1775 to 1778.* Edward Field. Providence, 1898. 280 p.

DLC, NN, MWA, CSmH, PU, MiD:B

HOPKINS, JOHN HENRY. *The Life of the Late Rt. Rev. John Henry Hopkins, First Bishop of Vermont.* John H. Hopkins, Jr. N. Y., 1873. 481 p. *NN, MWA, PU*

HOPKINS, JOHNS. *Johns Hopkins; a Silhouette.* Helen H. Thom. Balt., 1929. 125 p. *DLC, NN, CSmH, PU*

HOPKINS, MARK.
> *Mark Hopkins.* Franklin Carter. Boston and N. Y., 1892.
> 375 p. (American Religious Leaders)   *NN, MWA, MiD:B*
> *Mark Hopkins; a Biography.* John H. Denison. N. Y., 1935.
> 327 p.   *DLC, NN*
> 2:326

HOPKINS, SAMUEL.
> *Memoir of the Life and Character of the Rev. Samuel Hopkins.*
> John Ferguson. Boston, 1830. 196 p.
>   *DLC, NN, MWA, MiD:B*
> *The Works of Samuel Hopkins . . . With Memoirs of His Life
> and Character.* Edwards A. Park. Boston, 1852. 3 vols.   *NN*
> *Memoir of the Life and Character of Samuel Hopkins.* Edwards
> A. Park. Boston, 1854. 264 p.
> *Reminiscences of the Late Rev. Samuel Hopkins, D.D.* William Patten. Providence, 1843. 157 p.   *MWA, MiD:B*

HOPKINS, STEPHEN. *Stephen Hopkins. A Rhode Island Statesman.*
William E. Foster. Providence, 1884. 2 vols. (R. I. Hist. Tracts.
First Series, No. 19, Parts I and II)
>   *DLC, NN, MWA, CSmH, MiD:B, MiU:C*

HOPKINSON, FRANCIS. *Life and Works of Francis Hopkinson.* George
E. Hastings. Chicago, 1926. 516 p.
>   *DLC, NN, MWA, CSmH, PU, MiD:B*

HOPKINSON, JOSEPH. *Joseph Hopkinson, 1770–1842, Jurist: Scholar:
Inspirer of the Arts: Author of Hail Columbia.* Burton A. Konkle.
Phila., 1931. 361 p.   *DLC, NN, CSmH, PU, MiD:B*

HOPPER, ISAAC TATEM. *Isaac T. Hopper: A True Life.* Lydia Maria
Child. Boston, 1853, 493 p.
>   *DLC, NN, MWA, CSmH, PU, MiD:B*

HOPSON, WINTHROP HARTLY. *Memoirs of Dr. Winthrop Hartly Hopson.* Ella L. Hopson. Cincinnati, 1887. 239 p.   *DLC, NN*

HORNBLOWER, JOSIAH. *Josiah Hornblower and the First Steam-Engine
in America.* W. Nelson. Newark, N. J., 1883. 80 p.
>   *NN, MWA, MiD:B*

HORR, GEORGE EDWIN. *George Edwin Horr; a Biographical Memoir.*
Howard B. Grose. N. Y., 1928. 128 p. (Privately Printed)
>   *DLC MWA, MiD:B*

HORTHY, ADMIRAL. 2:30
HOSMER, HARRIET. 2:430
HOTT, JAMES WILLIAM. *The Life and Career of James William Hott,
D.D., LL.D., Late Bishop of the United Brethren in Christ.* Marion
R. Drury. Dayton, O., 1902. 214 p.   *NN*

HOUDIN, JEAN ROBERT. See ROBERT-HOUDIN, JEAN.

HOUDINI, HARRY. *Houdini; His Life Story.* Harold Kellock. N. Y., 1928. 384 p. *DLC, NN, PU*

HOUDON, JEAN ANTOINE. *Memoirs of the Life and Works of Jean Antoine Houdon, Sculptor of Voltaire and Washington.* Charles H. Hart and Edward Biddle. Phila., 1911. 341 p. (Privately Printed) *DLC, NN, MWA, CSmH*

HOUGHTON, DOUGLASS. *Memoir of Douglass Houghton, First State Geologist of Michigan.* Alvah Bradish. Detroit, 1889. 302 p. *DLC, NN, MiD:B*

HOUGHTON, HENRY OSCAR. *Henry O. Houghton. A Biographical Outline.* Horace E. Scudder. Cambridge, 1897. 160 p. *DLC, NN, MWA, CSmH, PU*

HOUSE, EDWARD. *Real Colonel House.* Arthur D. H. Smith. N. Y., 1918. 306 p. *DLC, NN, MiD:B*

HOUSTON, SAMUEL.

    Life of General Houston, 1793–1863. Henry Bruce. N. Y., 1891. 232 p. (Makers of America Series) *DLC, NN, MWA, CSmH*

    Sam Houston. George S. Bryan. N. Y., 1917. 183 p. *DLC, CSmH*

    Life . . . of Samuel Houston of Texas. William C. Crane, ed. Phila., 1884. 672 p. *DLC, NN, CSmH*

    Sam Houston, Colossus in Buckskin. George Creel. N. Y., 1928. 340 p. *DLC, NN, MWA, PU*

    Sam Houston. Sarah B. Elliott. Boston, 1900. 149 p. (Beacon Biographies) *DLC, NN, CSmH*

    The Raven; a Biography of Sam Houston. Marquis James. Indianapolis, 1929. 489 p. *DLC, NN, CSmH*

    Sam Houston and His Republic. Charles E. Lester. N. Y., 1846. 208 p. *DLC, NN, CSmH, PU, MiD:B*

    The Life of Sam Houston. Charles E. Lester. N. Y., 1855. 402 p. *DLC, NN, CSmH*

    Life and Achievements of Sam Houston, Hero and Statesman. Charles E. Lester. N. Y., 1883. 242 p. *DLC, CSmH*

    A Texan Titan; the Story of Sam Houston. John M. Oskison. Garden City, N. Y., 1929. 311 p. *DLC, NN, MWA, PU*

    Sam Houston and the War of Independence in Texas. Alfred M. Williams. Boston, 1893. 405 p. *DLC, NN, CSmH, PU, MiD:B*

Following General Sam Houston, From 1795 to 1863.   Amelia
Williams.   Austin, 1935.   252 p.   *DLC, NN*
2:358
HOVEY, ALVIN PETERSON.   *Hovey and Chase. Life of Gen. Alvin P.
Hovey Together With a Sketch of Ira J. Chase.*   Charles M.
Walker.   Indianapolis, 1888.   200 p.   *DLC, NN, CSmH*
HOW, DAVID D.   *The Life and Confessions of David D. How, Who Was
Executed at Angelica, Allegany County, N. Y., on Friday, March
19, 1824, for the Murder of Othello Church.*   Joseph Badger.
N. Y., 1824.   24 p.   *DLC*
HOWARD, BRONSON.   *Bronson Howard; In Memoriam.*   Issued by the
American Dramatists Club.   N. Y., 1910.   130 p.
DLC, PU, MiD:B
HOWARD, CLARENCE HENRY.   *Fellowship; the Biography of a Man and
a Business.*   Albert F. Gilmore.   Boston, 1929.   287 p.
DLC, NN, MWA
HOWARD, JOHN.
A View of the Life of . . . John Howard.   Phila., 1794.   196 p.
CSmH
Memoir of John Howard, the Philanthropist.   J. B. Brown.
Boston, 1831.   352 p.   *NN, MWA, CSmH*
John Howard.   E. S. C. Gibson.   Boston, 1902.   211 p.   (Lit-
tle Biographies)   *PU*
Memoirs of John Howard, the Prisoner's Friend.   Charles K.
True.   Cincinnati, 1878.   225 p.
HOWARD, OLIVER OTIS.   2:624
HOWARD, WILLIAM JAMES.   *The Last of the California Rangers.*   Jill
L. Cossley-Bott.   N. Y., 1928.   294 p.   *DLC, NN, MWA*
HOWE, GEORGE ROWLAND.   *George Rowland Howe, 1847–1917; a
Son's Tribute . . .*   Herbert B. Howe.   Mount Kisco, N. Y., 1920.
160 p.   *DLC, NN, MWA*
HOWE, JOHN MOFFAT.   *Filial Tribute to the Memory of Rev. John
Moffat Howe, M.D.*   John M. Reid.   N. Y., 1889.   254 p.
DLC, NN, MWA, MiD:B
HOWE, JULIA WARD.
Julia Ward Howe.   Laura E. Richards and Maud H. Elliott.
Boston, 1915.   2 vols.   *DLC, NN, CSmH, PU*
Julia Ward Howe, 1819–1910.   Laura E. Richards and Maud
H. Elliott.   Boston, 1925.   457 p.   *DLC, NN, MWA*
2:9–506

Howe, Mary. *Memoir of Mrs. Mary Howe . . . Containing Selections From Her Letters and Diary.* John M. Howe. N. Y., 1843. 282 p. NN

Howe, Samuel Gridley.
Memoir of Dr. Samuel Gridley Howe. Julia Ward Howe. Boston, 1876. 127 p. DLC, NN, MWA, CSmH, MiD:B
Samuel Gridley Howe. Laura E. Richards. N. Y., 1935. 283 p. DLC, NN, MWA, CSmH, PU
Dr. S. G. Howe, the Philanthropist. Franklin B. Sanborn. N. Y., 1891. 370 p. DLC, NN, CSmH
2:144

Howe, William. *Sir Billy Howe.* Bellamy Partridge. N. Y., 1932. 301 p. DLC, NN, MiU:C

Howell, Varina. See Davis, Varina Howell.

Howells, William Dean.
William Dean Howells: A Critical Study. Delmar C. Cooke. N. Y., 1922. 279 p. DLC, NN, CSmH, PU
William Dean Howells; A Study. Oscar W. Firkins. Cambridge, 1924. 356 p. DLC, NN, CSmH, PU

Howland, John. *Life and Recollections of John Howland.* Edwin M. Stone. Providence, 1857. 348 p.
DLC, NN, MWA, MiD:B, RP:JCB

Hoxie, Solomon. *Solomon Hoxie; a Biography by His Daughter.* Jane L. Hoxie. N. Y., 1923. 224 p. DLC, NN

Hubbard, Elbert.
The Elbert Hubbard I Knew; An Intimate Biography From the Heart and Pen of His Sister. Mary H. Heath. East Aurora, N. Y., 1929. 221 p. DLC, NN, PU
Elbert Hubbard and His Work. Albert Lane. Worcester, Mass., 1901. 153 p. NN, MWA
Elbert Hubbard of East Aurora. Felix Shay. N. Y., 1926. 553 p. DLC, NN, MWA, PU

Hubbard, Richard Dudley. *Richard Dudley Hubbard; a Memorial. Born Sept. 6, 1818, Died February 28, 1884.* Hartford, 1884. 172 p. DLC, NN

Hubbard, Thomas Hamlin. *Thomas Hamlin Hubbard, Bvt. Brigadier General U. S. Vols.* Henry B. Burrage. Portland, Me., 1923. 66 p. DLC, NN, MWA, CSmH

Hubbs, Rebecca. *Memoir of Rebecca Hubbs, a Minister of the Gospel in the Society of Friends.* Phila., n.d. 114 p. MWA, PU

HUBMAIER, BALTHASAR. *Balthasar Hubmaier, the Leader of the Ana-baptists.* Henry C. Vedder. N. Y., 1905. 333 p. *DLC, NN*

HUDSON, HENRY.

Henry Hudson: His Times and His Voyages. Edgar M. Bacon. N. Y., 1907. 277 p. (American Men of Energy Series)

DLC, NN, CSmH

Life of Henry Hudson. Henry R. Cleveland. (L.A.B.)

DLC, NN, MWA, CSmH, PU

Adventures of Henry Hudson. Francis L. Hawks. N. Y., 1842. 161 p. *DLC, NN*

Henry Hudson. A Brief Statement of His Aims and His Achievements. Thomas A. Janvier. N. Y., 1908. 147 p.

DLC, NN, MWA, CSmH, PU, MiU:C

HUDSON, SIR JEFFREY. 2:71

HUGHES, HUGH PRICE. *Life of Hugh Price Hughes.* Dorothea P. Hughes. N. Y., 1904. 679 p. *DLC, MWA*

HUGHES, JOHN.

The Life of Archbishop Hughes, First Archbishop of New York. With a Full Account of His Life, Death and Burial. Phila., 1864. 70 p. *NN, MWA*

Most Reverend John Hughes, First Archbishop of New York. H. A. Brann. N. Y., 1892. 182 p. (Makers of America)

DLC, NN

Life of the Most Rev. John Hughes. J. R. G. Hassard. N. Y., 1866. 519 p. *DLC, NN, MWA, MiD:B*

HUGHES, JOHN. *John Hughes, Champion Pedestrian.* William E. Harding. N. Y., 1881. *DLC*

HUGHES, LEWIS. *Lewis Hughes, the Militant Minister of the Ber-mudas.* G. W. Cole. Worcester, Mass., 1928. 67 p. (American Antiquarian Soc.) *DLC, NN, MWA, CSmH, PU, MiU:C*

HUIDEKOPER, HARM JAN. *Harm Jan Huidekoper.* Nina M. and Francis Tiffany. Cambridge, 1904. 386 p.

DLC, NN, MWA, PU

2:225

HULBURD, LITTLE JUSTIN. *Life of Little Justin Hulburd, Medium, Actor and Poet.* Ebenezer W. Hulburd, comp. Descanso, Calif., 1909. 3 vols. *DLC, NN*

HULL, ISAAC. 2:396

HULL, JOHN. 2:464

HULL, WILLIAM.
> *Revolutionary Services and Civil Life of Maj.-Gen. William Hull.*
Maria Campbell, ed. N. Y. and Phila., 1848. 482 p.
> *DLC, NN, MWA, CSmH, PU, MiD:B, MiU:C*
> *William Hull and the Surrender of Detroit, a Biography.* James
F. Clarke. Boston, 1912. 32 p. *NN, MWA, PU, MiD:B*
2:144.

HULSE, ISAAC. *Dr. Isaac Hulse, Surgeon, U. S. Navy, 1797–1856.*
His Life and Letters. Charles J. Werner. N. Y., 1922. 47 p.
> *DLC, NN, MWA*

HUMBLE, JOSHUA. *Joshua Humble.* Edgar R. Beach. St. Louis,
1899. 328 p. *DLC*

HUMBOLDT, ALEXANDER VON. *The Life, Travels and Books of Alexander Von Humboldt.* Richard H. Stoddard. N. Y., 1859. 482 p.
> *DLC, NN, MWA, MiD:B*
> 2:79–335

HUMPHREYS, ANDREW ATKINSON.
> *Andrew Atkinson Humphreys, of Pennsylvania, Brigadier Gen-
eral and Brevet Major General, U. S. A.* John W. DePeyster.
Lancaster, 1886. 21 p. *NN, CSmH, PU*
> *Andrew Atkinson Humphreys, a Biography.* H. H. Humphreys.
Phila., 1924. 335 p. *DLC, NN, CSmH, PU*

HUMPHREYS, DAVID. *Life and Times of David Humphreys, 1752–
1818.* Francis L. Humphreys. N. Y., 1917. 2 vols.
> *DLC, NN, CSmH*

HUMPHREYS, JOSHUA. 2:225

HUNNEWELL, HORATIO HOLLIS. *Life, Letters and Diary of Horatio
H. Hunnewell, 1810–1902.* Hollis H. Hunnewell, ed. Boston and
·N. Y., 1906. 3 vols. (Privately Printed) *DLC*

HUNT, JOHN. *A Missionary Among Cannibals; or, the Life of John
Hunt.* George S. Rowe. N. Y., 1859. 286 p. *MWA*

HUNT, WALTER. *Walter Hunt, American Inventor.* Joseph N. Kane.
N. Y., 1935. 76 p. *NN, MWA, PU*

HUNT, WILLIAM. *Memoir of William Hunt.* T. G. Morton. Phila.,
1897. 14 p. *DLC, PU, MiD:B*

HUNT, WILLIAM HENRY. *The Life of William H. Hunt.* Thomas
Hunt. Brattleboro, Vt., 1922. 360 p. *DLC, NN, CSmH*

HUNT, WILLIAM MORRIS. 2:87

HUNTER, JOHN. *John Hunter and His Pupils.* Samuel D. Gross.
Phila., 1881. 106 p. *DLC, PU*

HUNTER, ROBERT MERCER TALIAFERRO.
>*Memoir of Robert M. T. Hunter.* Martha T. Hunter. Washington, 1903. 166 p.   *DLC, NN, CSmH*
>*Life of Robert M. T. Hunter; a Study in Sectionalism and Secession.* Henry H. Sims. Richmond, 1935. 234 p.
>   *DLC, NN, CSmH, PU*

HUNTINGTON, FREDERICK DAN. *Memoir and Letters of Frederick D. Huntington, First Bishop of Central New York.* Arria S. Huntington. Boston and N. Y., 1906. 435 p.   *DLC, MWA, CSmH, PU*

HUNTINGTON, WILLIAM REED. *Life and Letters of William Reed Huntington, a Champion of Unity.* John W. Suter. N. Y., 1925. 549 p.   *DLC, NN, MWA, PU*

HURD, AARON HAYNES. *The Wesleyan Student; or, Memoirs of Aaron Haynes Hurd* ... Joseph Holdich. Middletown, 1839. 281 p.
>   *NN*

HURD, HENRY MILLS. *Henry Mills Hurd, the First Superintendent of the Johns Hopkins Hospital.* Thomas S. Cullen. Balt., 1920. 147 p.   *DLC, NN, PU*

HURLEY, PATRICK. *" Pat " Hurley; the Story of an American.* Parker E. Moore. N. Y., 1932. 140 p.   *DLC, NN, MWA*

HURST, JOHN FLETCHER. *John Fletcher Hurst; a Biography.* Albert Osborn. N. Y., 1905. 509 p.   *DLC, NN, PU*

HUSS, JOHN.
>*Life and Times of John Huss.* Ezra H. Gillett. Boston, 1863–64. 2 vols.   *DLC, NN, PU*
>*John Huss; The Witness.* Oscar Ruhns. Cincinnati, 1907. 174 p.
>*John Huss: His Life, Teachings and Death, After Five Hundred Years.* David S. Schaff. N. Y., 1915. 349 p. *DLC, NN, PU*
>*John Hus, the Martyr of Bohemia; a Study of the Dawn of Protestantism.* William N. Schwarze. N. Y., 1915. 152 p.
>   *DLC, NN*

HUSSEY, OBED. *Obed Hussey, Who, of All Inventors, Made Bread Cheap.* Follett L. Greene, ed. Rochester, N. Y., 1912. 228 p.
>   *DLC, NN, MWA, PU*

HUTCHINSON, ANNE.
>*An American Jezebel; the Life of Anne Hutchinson.* Helen Augur. N. Y., 1930. 320 p.   *DLC, NN, CSmH, PU*
>*A Woman Misunderstood. Anne, Wife of William Hutchinson.* Reginald P. Bolton. N. Y., 1931. 137 p.   *DLC, NN, MWA*

Anne Hutchinson; a Biography. Edith Curtis. Cambridge, 1930. 122 p. *DLC, NN, CSmH*

Life of Anne Hutchinson. George E. Ellis. (L.A.B.)
DLC, NN, MWA, CSmH

Unafraid; a Life of Anne Hutchinson. Winifred K. Rugg. Boston, 1930. 263 p. *DLC, NN, MWA, CSmH, PU*
2:334

HUTCHINSON, THOMAS. *Life of Thomas Hutchinson, Royal Governor of the Province of Massachusetts Bay.* James K. Hosmer. Boston, 1896. 453 p. *DLC, NN, MWA, CSmH, PU, MiD:B*

HUTTON, JOHN A. 2:487

HUXLEY, THOMAS.
Huxley. Clarence E. Ayres. N. Y., 1932. 254 p. *DLC, NN*
Huxley, Prophet of Science. Houston Peterson. N. Y., 1932. 338 p. *DLC, NN*
2:79–335

HUYCK, EDMUND NILES. *Edmund Niles Huyck; the Story of a Liberal.* Francis Brown. N. Y., 1935. 255 p. *DLC, NN, PU*

HYATT, ANNA V. 2:430

HYDE, ALBERT ALEXANDER. *Master of Money; A. A. Hyde of Wichita.* George Irving. N. Y., 1936. 157 p. *NN*

HYDE, ALVAN. *Memoir of Rev. Alvan Hyde . . . of Lee, Mass.* Boston, 1835. 408 p. *DLC, NN, MWA*

HYDE, AMMI BRADFORD. *The Story of Ammi Bradford Hyde.* Arthur H. Harrop. Cincinnati, 1912. 195 p. *NN*

HYDE, CAROLINE. *Memoir of Caroline Hyde.* Charles Hyde. N. Y., 1836. 72 p. *NN, MWA, PU*

HYDE, EDWARD. [EARL OF CLARENDON] 2:91

HYDE, HENRY BALDWIN. *Henry Baldwin Hyde. A Biographical Sketch.* N. Y., 1901. 244 p. (Privately Printed)
DLC, NN, MWA, CSmH, PU

HYDE, WILLIAM DE WITT. *Hyde of Bowdoin, a Biography of William De Witt Hyde.* Charles T. Burnett. Boston, 1931. 364 p.
DLC, NN, PU

HYPATIA. 2:336

IBERVILLE, LEMOYNE. 2:127

IBRAHIM PASHA. *Ibrahim Pasha, Grand Vizir of Suleiman the Magnificent.* Hester D. Jenkins. N. Y., 1911. 123 p. (Col. Univ. Studies in History, vol. 46, no. 2) *DLC, NN*

IBSEN, HENRIK.
Henrik Ibsen; the Man and His Plays. Montrose J. Moses. N. Y., 1908. 522 p. *DLC, NN*

Ibsen, the Master Builder. Adolph E. Zucker. N. Y., 1929. 312 p.   *DLC, NN, PU*

ILIFF, THOMAS CORWIN. *Thomas Corwin Iliff, Apostle of Home Missions in the Rocky Mountains.* James D. Gillilan. N. Y., 1919. 193 p.   *DLC, NN*

INGALLS, HENRY AUGUSTUS. *Memoir of Henry Augustus Ingalls . . . With Selections From His Writings.* George W. Burnap. N. Y., 1845. 224 p.   *DLC, NN, MWA, MiD:B*

INGALLS, JOHN.

Ingalls of Kansas. W. E. Connelley. Topeka, 1909. 234 p.
DLC, NN, CSmH

John J. Ingalls . . . A Biographical Sketch. Granville H. Meixell. Atchison, Kansas, 1896. 45 p. (Pamphlet)
DLC, NN, CSmH, PU

INGE, DEAN. 2:487

INGERSOLL, CHARLES JARED. *Life of Charles Jared Ingersoll.* W. M. Meigs. Phila., 1897. 351 p.   *DLC, NN, MWA, PU*

INGERSOLL, JARED. *Jared Ingersoll: A Study of American Loyalism in Relation to British Colonial Government.* Lawrence H. Gipson. New Haven, 1920. 432 p. (Yale Hist. Pub.)
DLC, NN, MWA, CSmH, PU, MiD:B
2:110

INGERSOLL, ROBERT GREEN.

An Intimate View of Robert G. Ingersoll. Isaac N. Baker. N. Y., 1920. 207 p.   *DLC, NN*

Ingersoll. Herman E. Kittredge. N. Y., 1911. 581 p.
DLC, NN

Colonel Bob Ingersoll; a Biographical Narrative of the Great American Orator and Agnostic. Cameron Rogers. N. Y., 1927. 293 p.   *DLC, NN*

Life and Reminiscences of Robt. G. Ingersoll. Edward G. Smith. N. Y., 1904. 225 p.   *DLC, NN*
2:330

INGLE, JAMES. *James A. Ingle.* (*Yin-Teh-Sen.*) W. H. Jefferys. N. Y., 1913. 286 p.   *DLC, NN, PU*

INMAN, HENRY. 2:394

INNESS, GEORGE. *Life, Art, and Letters of George Inness.* George Inness, Jr. N. Y., 1917. 290 p.   *DLC, NN*
2:123–429

INSKIP, JOHN SWANEL. *Life of John S. Inskip.* W. McDonald and J. E. Searle. Boston, 1885. 378 p.

IREDELL, JAMES. *Life and Correspondence of James Iredell.* Griffith J. McRee. N. Y., 1857. 2 vols. *DLC, MWA*

IRISH, JAMES. *A Sketch of the Life of General James Irish of Gorham, Maine, 1776–1863.* Lyndon Oak. Boston, 1898. 70 p.
DLC, NN, MWA, MiD:B

IRVING, HENRY. *Henry Irving.* William Winter. N. Y., 1885. 123 p.
DLC, NN, MWA, CSmH

IRVING, WASHINGTON.
Memoir of Washington Irving. Charles Adams. N. Y., 1870. 299 p. *DLC, NN*
Washington Irving. H. W. Boynton. Boston, 1901. 116 p. (Riverside Biographical Series) *DLC, NN, PU*
A Discourse on the Life, Character and Genius of Washington Irving. William C. Bryant. N. Y., 1860. 46 p.
DLC, NN, MWA, CSmH
Washington Irving: a Sketch. George W. Curtis. N. Y., 1891. 115 p. *DLC, NN, CSmH, PU*
Washington Irving, Esquire, Ambassador at Large From the New World to the Old. George S. Hellman. N. Y., 1925. 355 p.
DLC, NN, CSmH, PU
Washington Irving. D. J. Hill. N. Y., 1879. 234 p. *DLC*
Life and Letters of Washington Irving. Pierre M. Irving, ed. N. Y., 1862–64. 4 vols. *DLC, NN, MWA, CSmH, PU, MiD:B*
Washington Irving. Charles D. Warner. Boston, 1882. 304 p. (A.M.L.) *DLC, NN, MWA, CSmH, PU*
Life of Washington Irving. Stanley T. Williams. New Haven, 1935. 2 vols. *DLC, NN, CSmH, PU*
2:660–662

IRWIN, AGNES. *Agnes Irwin, a Biography.* Agnes Repplier. N. Y., 1934. 125 p. *DLC, NN, MWA, PU*

ISABELLA of CASTILE.
Isabella of Castile. O. O. Howard. N. Y., 1894. 349 p.
DLC, NN, MWA
Isabella of Spain; the Last Crusader. William T. Walsh. N. Y., 1930. 515 p. *DLC, NN*
Isabella the Crusader. William T. Walsh. N. Y., 1935. 308 p.
DLC, NN

ISABELLA II. 2:1
ISAIAH. 2:665
ITO, PRINCE. 2:276

IVES, LEVI SILLIMAN. *Levi Silliman Ives, Pioneer Leader in Catholic Charities.* John O'Grady. N. Y., 1933. 98 p.   *DLC, NN*

IVEY, THOMAS NEAL. *Thomas Neal Ivey.* Marion T. Plyler. Nashville, 1925. 166 p.   *DLC*

JACKSON, ALICE. *A Memorial of Alice Jackson.* Robert· E. Speer. N. Y., 1908. 128 p.   *DLC, NN*

JACKSON, ANDREW.

Lives of Andrew Jackson and General Marion. Boston, 1881. 208 p.   *MWA*

Memoirs of Andrew Jackson . . . Compiled by a Citizen of Massachusetts. [J. H. Eaton.]   Boston, 1828.   334 p.
      NN, MWA, CSmH

Memoirs of General Andrew Jackson . . . Compiled by a Citizen of Western New York.   Auburn, N. Y., 1845.   270 p.   *NN, MWA*

Some Account of General Jackson, Drawn Up From the Hon. Mr. Eaton's Very Circumstantial Narrative.   Balt., 1828.   272 p.
      NN

Civil and Military History of Andrew Jackson . . . by an American Officer.   N. Y., 1825.   359 p.   *NN, PU*

The Life of Andrew Jackson.   John S. Bassett.   N. Y., 1911. 2 vols.   N. Y., 1925.   1 vol.   *DLC, NN, MWA, CSmH, PU*

True Andrew Jackson.   Cyrus T. Brady.   Phila., 1906.   504 p.
      DLC, NN, PU

Andrew Jackson.   W. G. Brown.   Boston, 1900.   156 p.
      DLC, NN, PU

History of Andrew Jackson, Pioneer, Patriot, Soldier, Politician, President.   A. C. Buell.   N. Y., 1904.   2 vols.
      DLC, NN, MWA, MiD:B

Life and Times of Andrew Jackson.   Arthur St. C. Colyar. Nashville, 1904.   2 vols.   *DLC, NN*

General Andrew Jackson; Hero of New Orleans and 7th President of the United States.   Oliver Dyer.   N. Y., 1891.   378 p.
      DLC, NN, CSmH

Life of Andrew Jackson.   John H. Eaton.   Phila., 1824.   468 p.
      DLC, NN, MWA, CSmH, MiD:B

Pictorial Life of Andrew Jackson.   John Frost.   Phila., 1845. 183 p.   *DLC, NN, MWA, MiD:B, MiU:C*

Biography of Andrew Jackson.   Philo A. Goodwin.   Hartford, 1832.·   456 p.   *DLC, NN, MWA, CSmH, MiD:B*

Andrew Jackson: Border Captain.   Marquis James.   Indianapolis, 1933.   461 p.   *DLC, NN, CSmH, PU*

Life and Public Services of General Andrew Jackson. John S. Jenkins. Buffalo, 1850. 397 p.

DLC, NN, MWA, CSmH, PU, MiD:B

Jackson and the Generals of the War of 1812. John S. Jenkins. Phila., 1856. 407 p. *NN, MWA*

Jacob Brown, Edmund Pendleton Gaines, William Henry Harrison, Alexander Macomb, Zebulon Montgomery Pike, and Winfield Scott.

Andrew Jackson: An Epic in Homespun. Gerald W. Johnson. N. Y., 1927. 303 p. *DLC, NN, MWA, CSmH, PU, MiD:B*

Andrew Jackson, the Gentle Savage. David Karsner. N. Y., 1929. 399 p. *DLC, NN*

Life of Andrew Jackson. Amos Kendall. N. Y., 1843. 288 p. *DLC, NN*

When Men Grow Tall; or, the Story of Andrew Jackson. Alfred H. Lewis. N. Y., 1907. 330 p. *DLC, NN, PU, MiD:B*

Life of Andrew Jackson. James Parton. N. Y., 1860. 3 vols. *DLC, NN, MWA, CSmH, PU, MiD:B, MiU:C*

Memoirs of Andrew Jackson, Late Major General and Commander-in-Chief of the Southern Division of the Army of the U. S. Jerome van C. Smith. Boston, 1828. 334 p. *NN*

A Short and Impartial History of the Life and Actions of Andrew Jackson. Wm. J. Snelling. (A Free Man.) Boston, 1831. 210 p. *DLC, NN, MWA, CSmH, MiD:B*

Andrew Jackson and Martin Van Buren. William O. Stoddard. N. Y., 1887. 317 p. (The Lives of the Presidents Series)

DLC, NN

Andrew Jackson as a Public Man. William G. Sumner. Boston, 1882. 503 p. (A.S.) *DLC, NN, MWA, CSmH, MiD:B*

Memoirs of Andrew Jackson . . . Commander in Chief of the Division of the South. S. Putnam Waldo. Hartford, 1818. 316 p.

DLC, NN, MWA

Memoirs of Andrew Jackson, Major-General in the Army of the U. S. Samuel P. Waldo. Hartford, 1819. 336 p.

DLC, NN, CSmH, MiD:B

The Life of Andrew Jackson . . . [and] An Authentic Narrative . . . of the American Army at New Orleans. Alexander Walker. Phila., 1860. 414 p. *DLC, NN, MWA*

Life and Times of Andrew Jackson. Thomas E. Watson. Thompson, Ga., 1912. 408 p. *DLC, PU*

2:35–77–190–662

JACKSON, JAMES. *Life of Maj.-Gen. James Jackson.* T. U. P. Charlton. Augusta, Ga., 1809. 215 p. (Reprinted, 1895)

DLC, NN, CSmH, MiU:C

2:135

JACKSON, JAMES.

A Memoir of James Jackson, Jr., M.D. James Jackson. Boston, 1835. 444 p. *DLC, NN, MWA, CSmH, PU, MiD:B*

Memoir of Dr. James Jackson: Sketches of His Father, Hon. Jonathan Jackson, and His Brothers. James J. Putnam. N. Y. and Boston, 1905. 456 p. *DLC, NN, MWA, PU, MiD:B*

JACKSON, RACHEL. 2:453

JACKSON, SHELDON. *Sheldon Jackson: Pathfinder and Prospector of the Missionary Vanguard in the Rocky Mountains and Alaska.* Robert L. Stewart. Chicago, 1903. 488 p. *DLC, NN*

2:225

JACKSON, THOMAS JONATHAN.

" Stonewall Jackson"; The Life and Military Career of Thomas Jonathan Jackson. Markinfield Addey. N. Y., 1863. 240 p.

DLC, NN, MWA, CSmH, MiD:B

Early Life and Letters of General Thomas J. Jackson, Stonewall Jackson. Thomas J. Arnold. N. Y., 1916. 379 p.

DLC, NN, CSmH, PU

Story of Stonewall Jackson: the Career of Thomas Jonathan Jackson. W. C. Chase. Atlanta, 1901. 568 p. *DLC, CSmH*

The Life of Stonewall Jackson, from Official Papers, Contemporary Narratives and Personal Acquaintance. By a Virginian. John E. Cooke. Richmond, 1864. 305 p. (Pirated ed. N. Y., 1863) *DLC, NN, MWA, CSmH, PU*

Stonewall Jackson: A Military Biography. John E. Cooke. N. Y., 1866. 470 p. *DLC, NN, MWA, CSmH*

The Life and Campaigns of Lieut.-Gen. Thomas J. (Stonewall) Jackson. R. L. Dabney. N. Y., 1866. 742 p.

DLC, NN, MWA, CSmH

The Life of Stonewall Jackson. John W. Daniel. Richmond, 1863. 305 p. *MWA, MiD:B*

Stonewall Jackson. Carl Hovey. Boston, 1900. 131 p.

NN, CSmH

Life and Letters of General Thomas J. Jackson (Stonewall Jackson). Mary A. M. Jackson. N. Y., 1892. 479 p.

DLC, NN, CSmH

Memoirs of Stonewall Jackson. Mary A. Jackson. Louisville, 1895. 647 p. *DLC, NN*

The Life of Gen. Thomas J. Jackson. Sarah N. Randolph. Phila., 1876. 363 p. *DLC, NN, MWA, CSmH*

Stonewall Jackson, the Good Soldier. Allen Tate. N. Y., 1928. 322 p. *DLC, NN, CSmH, PU*

Stonewall Jackson. Henry A. White. Phila., 1909. 378 p. (A.C.B.) *DLC, NN, CSmH, PU*

2:190–612

JACOBI, MARY PUTNAM. *Life and Letters of Mary Putnam Jacobi.* Ruth Putnam, ed. N. Y., 1925. 354 p. *DLC, NN*

JAGGARD, WILLIAM. *A Printer of Shakespeare; the Books and Times of William Jaggard.* Edwin E. Willoughby. N. Y., 1935. 304 p. *DLC, NN, CSmH, PU*

JAMES. *Three Jameses; a Family of Minds.* C. Hartley Grattan. N. Y., 1932. 376 p. *DLC, NN, PU*

JAMES, HENRY, SR. *The Elder Henry James.* Austin Warren. N. Y., 1934. 269 p. *DLC, NN*

JAMES, HENRY, JR.

Pilgrimage of Henry James. Van Wyck Brooks. N. Y., 1925. 170 p. *DLC, NN, CSmH*

Henry James, Man and Author. Pelham Edgar. Boston, 1927. 351 p. *DLC, NN, CSmH, PU*

2:84

JAMES, JESSE.

Jesse James; a Romance of Terror, Vividly Portraying the Daring Deed of the Most Fearless and Fearsome Bandit . . . Balt., 1910. 189 p. *NN*

Rise and Fall of Jesse James. Robertus Love. N. Y., 1926. 446 p. *DLC, NN*

Train and Bank Robbers of the West . . . The Adventures and Exploits of Frank and Jesse James. Chicago, 1882. 287 p. *NN*

The Border Outlaws, Frank and Jesse James; Historical and Complete Life and Death of the Notorious Bandits From the Cradle to the Grave. Clarence E. Ray. Chicago, 1921. 185 p. *NN*

2:84

JAMES, JOSHUA. *Joshua James, Life-Saver.* Sumner I. Kimball. Boston, 1909. 102 p. *DLC, MWA*

JAMES, WILLIAM. *The Thought and Character of William James.* Ralph B. Perry. Boston, 1935. 2 vols.

DLC, NN, CSmH, PU

JAMESON, JOHN ALEXANDER. *In Memoriam, John Alexander Jameson.* F. N. Thorpe. Phila., 1890. 26 p. *DLC, NN, MWA, PU*

JANES, LEWIS GEORGE. *Lewis G. Janes, Philosopher, Patriot, Lover of Man.* L. G. Janes. Boston, 1902. 215 p. *DLC, NN, MWA*

JANEWAY, JACOB JONES. *Memoir of . . . Jacob J. Janeway.* Thomas L. Janeway. Phila., 1861. 304 p. *DLC, NN*

JARVES, JAMES JACKSON. *Pepero, the Boy Artist: Memoir of James J. Jarves, Jr.* James J. Jarves. Boston, 1891. 69 p.

JARVIS, WILLIAM. *The Life and Times of Hon. William Jarvis, of Weathersfield.* Mary P. S. Cutts. N. Y., 1869. 446 p.
DLC, NN, MWA, MiD:B

JASPER, JOHN.
John Jasper, the Unmatched Negro Philosopher and Preacher. William E. Hatcher. N. Y., 1908. 183 p. *DLC, NN, MWA*
The Life of John Jasper From His Birth to the Present Time, With His Theory on the Rotation of the Sun. E. A. Randolph. Richmond, 1884. 167 p. *DLC, NN, CSmH*

JAY, JOHN.
Life of John Jay. William Jay. N. Y., 1833. 2 vols.
DLC, NN, MWA, CSmH, PU, MiD:B
John Jay. Frank Monaghan. N. Y., 1935. 497 p.
DLC, NN, MiD:B, MiU:C
John Jay. George Pellew. Boston, 1890. 374 p. (A.S.)
DLC, NN, MWA, CSmH, PU
Lives of John Jay and Alexander Hamilton. J. Renwick. N. Y., 1841. 341 p. *NN, MWA, PU*
Life and Times of John Jay. William Whitelock. N. Y., 1887. 370 p. *DLC, NN, CSmH, PU*
2:230–329–349–666

JAY, PETER AUGUSTUS. *Memorials of Peter A. Jay.* John Jay. N. Y., 1905. 308 p. (Privately Printed)
DLC, NN, MWA, CSmH, PU, MiD:B

JAY, WILLIAM. *William Jay and the Constitutional Movement For the Abolition of Slavery.* Bayard Tuckerman. N. Y., 1893. 185 p.
DLC, NN, CSmH, PU, MiD:B

JEFFERS, ROBINSON.
Robinson Jeffers, the Man and His Work. Lawrence C. Powell. Los Angeles, 1934. 215 p. *DLC, NN, PU*
Robinson Jeffers, the Man and the Artist. George Sterling. N. Y., 1926. 40 p. *DLC, NN, MWA, CSmH*

JEFFERSON, CHARLES EDWARD. 2:487

JEFFERSONS. *The Jeffersons.* William Winter. Boston, 1881. 252 p.

DLC, NN, CSmH, PU

JEFFERSON, JOSEPH.

Joseph Jefferson at Home. Nathan Haskell Dole. Boston, 1898. 110 p. *DLC, NN, MWA, PU*

Joseph Jefferson. Francis Wilson. N. Y., 1906. 354 p.

DLC, NN, CSmH, PU

Life and Art of Joseph Jefferson. William Winter. N. Y., 1894. 319 p. *DLC, NN, MWA, CSmH, PU*
2:84–128

JEFFERSON, THOMAS.

The Living Jefferson. James Truslow Adams. N. Y. and London, 1936. 403 p. *DLC, NN, PU*

Memoirs of Thomas Jefferson: Containing a Concise History of the U. S. From 1783. Stephen C. Carpenter. N. Y., 1809. 2 vols.

DLC, NN, CSmH

Thomas Jefferson, the Apostle of Americanism. Gilbert Chinard. Boston, 1929. 548 p. *DLC, NN, CSmH, PU*

The True Thomas Jefferson. William E. Curtis. Phila., 1901. 395 p. *DLC, NN, MWA, PU, MiD:B*

Sketch of the Life, Character and Public Services of Thomas Jefferson. Thomas J. Davis. Phila., 1876. 179 p. *DLC, NN*

The Character of Thomas Jefferson as Exhibited in His Own Writings. Theodore Dwight. Boston, 1839. 371 p.

DLC, NN, MWA

Thomas Jefferson. Edward S. Ellis. Milwaukee, 1903. 180 p. (Great Americans of History) *DLC, NN, PU, MiD:B*

Thomas Jefferson. Paul L. Ford. Boston, 1904. 37 p. (Monographs of American Revolution)

DLC, MWA, CSmH, MiD:B, MiU:C

The Life and Writings of Thomas Jefferson. Samuel E. Forman. Indianapolis, 1900. 476 p. *CSmH*

A Biographical Sketch of Thomas Jefferson. Henry D. Gilpin. Phila., 1828. 372 p. *DLC, NN*

Jefferson and His Colleagues; a Chronicle of the Virginian Dynasty. Allen Johnson. New Haven, 1921. 343 p.

DLC, NN, CSmH, PU

The Life of Thomas Jefferson . . . Third President of the United States. William Linn. Ithaca, N. Y., 1834. 267 p.

DLC, NN, MWA, MiD:B

Thomas Jefferson. Henry C. Merwin. Boston, 1901. 164 p.
(Riverside Biographies) *DLC, NN, PU*
Thomas Jefferson. John T. Morse, Jr. Boston, 1883. 351 p.
(A.S.) *DLC, NN, MWA, CSmH, PU, MiD:B*
Thomas Jefferson. David S. Muzzey. N. Y., 1918. 319 p.
DLC, NN, CSmH
Jefferson. Albert J. Nock. N. Y., 1926. 340 p.
DLC, NN, CSmH, PU, MiD:B
The Life of Thomas Jefferson. James Parton. Boston, 1874.
764 p. *DLC, NN, MWA, PU*
Life of Thomas Jefferson. Henry S. Randall. N. Y., 1858.
3 vols. *DLC, NN, MWA, CSmH, PU, MiD:B, MiU:C*
The Domestic Life of Thomas Jefferson . . . Sarah N. Ran-
dolph. N. Y., 1871. 432 p.
DLC, NN, MWA, CSmH, PU, MiD:B
Life of Thomas Jefferson, With Letters. B. L. Rayner. Bos-
ton, 1834. 431 p. *DLC, NN, MWA, CSmH*
Life and Times of Thomas Jefferson . . . Samuel M. Schmucker.
Phila., 1854. 400 p. *DLC, NN, MWA*
Thomas Jefferson. James Schouler. N. Y., 1893. 252 p.
(Makers of America) *DLC, NN, CSmH, PU, MiD:B*
*Life of Thomas Jefferson and Part of His Unpublished Corre-
spondence.* George Tucker. Phila., 1847. 2 vols.
DLC, NN, MWA, CSmH, MiU:C
The Boy Who Loved Freedom; the Story of Thomas Jefferson.
Mary H. Wade. N. Y., 1930. 234 p. *DLC*
Thomas Jefferson. Thomas E. Watson. Boston, 1900. 150 p.
(Beacon Biographies) *DLC, NN*
The Life and Times of Thomas Jefferson. Thomas E. Watson.
N. Y., 1903. 534 p. *DLC, NN, CSmH*
Thomas Jefferson. John S. Wiliams. N. Y., 1913. 330 p.
DLC, NN, PU
Jefferson and Monticello. Paul Wilstach. Garden City, N. Y.,
1925. 258 p. *DLC, NN, CSmH, PU*
2–5–35–77–150–264–329–505–562–654–662–678
JEFFREY, FRANCIS. *A Famous Reviewer, Francis Jeffrey.* Adrian H.
Joline. N. Y., 1910. 109 p. *DLC, NN, CSmH*
JEMISON, MARY. *Narrative of the Life of Mary Jemison (De-he-was-
mis, Otherwise Called the White Woman).* Jas. E. Seaver. N. Y.,
1824. 312 p. *DLC, NN, MWA*

JENNISON, ISAAC. *The Christian Student. Memoirs of Isaac Jennison, Jr.* Edward Otheman. N. Y., 1843. 271 p.   *DLC, NN*

JENSEN, JAMES. *A Biographical Sketch of James Jensen.* J. M. Tanner. Salt Lake City, 1911. 190 p.   *NN, MWA, CSmH*

JEROME, SAINT. 2:554

JEROME, JENNIE. 2:518

JESSUP, MORRIS KETCHUM. *Morris Ketchum Jessup: a Character Sketch.* William A. Brown. N. Y., 1910. 247 p.
DLC, NN, MiD:B

JETER, JEREMIAH BELL. *Life of J. B. Jeter.* W. E. Hatcher. Balt., 1887. 508 p.   *CSmH*

JEWETT, CHARLES. *Charles Jewett, Life and Recollections.* William M. Thayer. Boston, 1880. 464 p.
DLC, NN, MWA, CSmH, MiD:B

JEWETT, SARAH ORNE. *Sarah Orne Jewett.* Francis O. Matthiessen. Boston, 1929. 159 p.   *DLC, NN, MWA, CSmH, PU*

JILLSON, WILLARD ROUSE. *Willard Rouse Jillson, Kentuckian, Geologist, Author, Public Servant; a Biographical Sketch.* George L. Willis. Louisville, 1930. 211 p.   *DLC, NN*

JOGUES, ISAAC.
The Saint of the Wilderness; St. Isaac Jogues, S.J. John J. Birch. N. Y., 1936. 236 p.   *DLC, NN*
Life of Father Isaac Jogues. Felix Martin. N. Y., 1885. 263 p.
DLC, NN, MiD:B
Isaac Jogues, S.J., Discoverer of Lake George. Thomas J. Campbell. N. Y., 1911. 55 p.   *DLC, NN*
Isaac Jogues, Missioner and Martyr. Martin J. Scott, S.J. N. Y., 1927. 233 p.   *DLC, NN*
Saint Among Savages; the Life of Isaac Jogues. Francis X. Talbot. N. Y., 1935. 466 p.   *DLC, NN, CSmH*
2:680

JOHNSEN, BIRGER. *The Far Horizon; Twenty Years of Adventure, Development, and Invention on the New Air Frontier, the Life Story of Birger Johnsen.* Henry W. Lanier. N. Y., 1933. 284 p.
DLC, NN

JOHNSON, ANDREW.
Andrew Johnson . . . His Life and Speeches. Lillian Foster. N. Y., 1866. 316 p.   *DLC, MWA, CSmH*
Andrew Johnson, Military Governor of Tennessee. Clifton R. Hall. Princeton, N. J., 1916. 234 p.   *DLC, NN, PU*

Life of Andrew Johnson, Seventeenth President of the U. S.
James S. Jones. Greenville, Tenn., 1901. 400 p.   *DLC*
Age of Hate: Andrew Johnson and the Radicals. George F.
Milton. N. Y., 1930. 787 p.   *DLC, NN, CSmH, PU*
Life and Public Services of Andrew Johnson. John Savage.
N. Y., 1866. 565 p.   *DLC, NN, MWA, CSmH*
Andrew Johnson: A Study in Courage. Lloyd P. Stryker. N.
Y., 1929. 881 p.   *DLC, CSmH, PU*
Andrew Johnson, Plebian and Patriot. Robert W. Winston.
N. Y., 1928. 549 p.   *DLC, NN, CSmH, PU*
2:190

JOHNSON, HERSCHEL VESPASIAN. *Herschel V. Johnson of Georgia,*
State Rights Unionist. Percy S. Flippin. Richmond, 1931. 336 p.
          DLC, NN, CSmH, PU

JOHNSON, JACOB. *Rev. Jacob Johnson, M.A., Pioneer Preacher of*
Wyoming Valley (Wilkes-Barre, Pa.) 1772–1790. Frederick C.
Johnson. Wilkes-Barre, 1911. 100 p.   *DLC, NN, MiD:B*

JOHNSON, COLONEL JOHN. See PATTERSON, ROBERT.

JOHNSON, JOHN. *Life and Misfortunes and the Military Career of*
Brig.-Gen. Sir John Johnson. J. W. DePeyster. N. Y., 1882. 111 p.
          DLC, NN, CSmH

JOHNSON, JOHN ALBERT. *Life of John A. Johnson, Three Times Gov-*
ernor of Minnesota. F. A. Day and T. M. Kappen. Chicago,
1910. 429 p.   *DLC, CSmH*

JOHNSON, JOHN TRIMBLE. *Biography of Elder J. T. Johnson.* John
Rogers. Cincinnati, 1861. 408 p.   *DLC*

JOHNSON, LIZZIE LOUVIRA. *The Story of Lizzie L. Johnson, Twenty*
Years a Shut-In. Francis W. Warne. N. Y., 1927. 122 p.
          DLC, NN

JOHNSON, REVERDY. *Life of Reverdy Johnson.* Bernard C. Steiner.
Balt., 1914. 284 p.   *DLC, NN, CSmH, PU*
2:218

JOHNSON, RICHARD MENTOR.
          Authentic Biography of Colonel Richard M. Johnson of Ken-
tucky. William Emmons. N. Y., 1833. 107 p.
          DLC, NN, MWA, CSmH, MiD:B
          Life and Times of Richard M. Johnson. L. R. Meyer. N. Y.,
1932. 508 p.   *CSmH*

JOHNSON, SAMUEL.
          Doctor Johnson; His Life, Works and Table Talk. James
Macauley. N. Y., 1893. 156 p.   *NN*

Dr. Johnson and Mr. Boswell. Harry Saltpeter. N. Y., 1929. 265 p. *DLC, NN, PU*

Rasselas in the New World. Chauncey B. Tinker. New Haven, 1925. 31 p. *DLC, NN*

JOHNSON, SAMUEL.

Life and Correspondence of Samuel Johnson. E. E. Beardsley. N. Y., 1874. 380 p. *DLC, NN, MWA, PU*

Life of Samuel Johnson. Thomas B. Chandler. N. Y., 1805. 208 p. *DLC, NN, MWA, CSmH, PU*

JOHNSON, THOMAS. *Life of Thomas Johnson.* Edward S. Delaplaine. N. Y., 1927. 517 p. *DLC, NN, CSmH*

JOHNSON, THOMAS LOFTIN. *Tom L. Johnson, Mayor of Cleveland.* Carl Lorenz. N. Y., 1911. 203 p. *DLC, NN*

JOHNSON, WILLIAM.

Sir William Johnson. A. C. Buell. N. Y., 1903. 281 p. *DLC, NN, MWA, PU, MiD:B*

Sir William Johnson and the Six Nations. W. E. Griffis. N. Y., 1891. 227 p. (Makers of America Series) *DLC, NN, MWA, CSmH, PU, MiD:B*

Johnson of the Mohawks; a Biography of Sir William Johnson, Irish Immigrant, Mohawk War Chief, American Soldier, Empire Builder. Arthur Pound and Richard E. Day. N. Y., 1930. 568 p. *DLC, NN, CSmH, PU*

The Life and Times of Sir William Johnson. William L. Stone. Albany, N. Y., 1865. 2 vols. *DLC, NN, MWA, CSmH, PU, MiU:C, RP:JCB*

JOHNSON, WILLIAM AUGUSTINE B. *A Memoir of William Augustine B. Johnson.* S. H. Tyng. N. Y., 1853. 385 p. *CSmH*

JOHNSON, WILLIAM E. *" Pussyfoot " Johnson, Crusader—Reformer— a Man Among Men.* Frederick A. McKenzie. N. Y., 1920. 193 p. *DLC, NN, PU*

JOHNSON, WILLIAM SAMUEL. *Life and Times of William Samuel Johnson, LL.D., First Senator . . . From Connecticut, and President of Columbia College.* E. E. Beardsley. Boston, 1876. 225 p. *DLC, NN, MWA, MiD:B*

JOHNSTON, ADELIA A. FIELD. *The Life of Adelia A. Field Johnston, of Oberlin College.* Harriet L. Keeler. Cleveland, 1912. 254 p. *DLC, NN, PU*

JOHNSTON, ALBERT SIDNEY. *The Life of Gen. Albert Sidney Johnston.* William P. Johnston. N. Y., 1878. 755 p. *DLC, NN, CSmH, MiD:B*

2:612

JOHNSTON, JAMES J. *Wise Guy: James J. Johnston: A Rhapsody in Fistics.* Marcus Griffin. N. Y., 1933. 315 p.   *DLC, NN*

JOHNSTON, JOHN. *John Johnston of New York, Merchant.* Emily J. de Forest. N. Y., 1909. 196 p. (Privately Printed)
   DLC, NN, MWA

JOHNSTON, JOHN. *John Johnston: A Memoir.* W. W. Wight. Madison, 1905. 133 p.   *DLC, NN*

JOHNSTON, JOSEPH EGGLESTON.
   General Johnston. Robert M. Hughes. N. Y., 1893. 353 p. (G.C.)   *DLC, NN, PU*
   A Memoir of the Life and Public Services of Joseph E. Johnston . . . a General in the Army of the Confederate States of America. Bradley T. Johnson. Balt., 1891. 362 p.
   DLC, NN, MWA, CSmH
   Joseph E. Johnston. Leigh Robinson. Washington, 1891. 61 p.
   DLC, MWA, CSmH
   2:88–612

JOHNSTON, WILLIAM PRESTON. *William Preston Johnston, a Character Sketch.* Jacob Cooper. n.p., n.d. 32 p.   *DLC, PU*

JOINCARE, LOUIS T. *The Story of Joincare, His Life and Times on the Niagara.* F. H. Severance. Buffalo, 1906. 138 p. (Privately Printed)   *DLC, NN*

JOLIET, LOUIS. 2:262

JONES, ABNER. *Memoir of Elder Abner Jones.* A. D. Jones. Boston, 1842. 207 p.   *NN, MWA, MiD:B*

JONES, CHARLES COLCOCK. *In Memoriam. Col. Charles C. Jones, Jr., LL.D. Historian, Biographer, and Archeologist.* Charles E. Jones. Augusta, Ga., 1893. 13 p.   *DLC, NN, MWA, CSmH*

JONES, CHARLES FREMONT. *Biographical Sketch of Charles F. Jones and His People, With a Brief History of the Spanish Treaty Claims Commission and the Court of Claims.* Nellie E. G. Fealy. Washington, 1931. 271 p.   *DLC, NN*

JONES, CHARLES JESSE. *The Last of the Plainsmen.* Zane Grey. N. Y., 1908. 314 p.   *CSmH*

JONES, CHRISTOPHER. *Master of the Mayflower.* Henry Justin Smith. Chicago, 1936. 241 p.   *DLC, NN*

JONES, DAVID SAMUEL. *Memorial of the Late Hon. David S. Jones. With Notices of the Jones Family, of Queen's County.* William A. Jones. N. Y., 1849. 99 p. *DLC, NN, MWA, CSmH, MiD:B*

JONES, ELI. *Eli and Sybil Jones, Their Life and Work.* Rufus M. Jones. Phila., 1899. 316 p.   *DLC, NN, MWA, PU*

JONES, GEORGE WALLACE. *George Wallace Jones.* John C. Parish. Iowa City, 1912. 354 p. (Iowa Biographical Series)
DLC, MWA, CSmH, PU, MiD:B

JONES, JACOB. *Life, Character and Public Services of Commodore Jacob Jones.* Mark M. Cleaver. Wilmington, 1906. 32 p. (Papers of the Hist. Soc. of Delaware)
DLC, NN, MWA, CSmH, PU, MiD:B

JONES, JAMES KIMBROUGH. *James K. Jones, the Plumed Knight of Arkansas.* Farrar Newberry. Arkadelphia, Ark., 1913. 338 p.
DLC, NN, MiD:B

JONES, JEHU GLANCY. *Life and Public Services of J. Glancy Jones.* Charles H. Jones. Phila., 1910. 2 vols. *DLC, MWA, RP:JCB*

JONES, JOHN. *The Surgical Works of the Late John Jones, M.D.* . . . [and] *A Short Account of the Life of the Author.* James Mease, ed. Phila., 1795. 186 p. *DLC, MWA, PU*

JONES, JOHN BEAUCHAMP. 2–87

JONES, JOHN PAUL.

Life and Correspondence of John Paul Jones. N. Y., 1830. 555 p. *DLC, MWA, CSmH, PU, MiD:B*

Memoirs of Rear-Admiral John Paul Jones. Phila., 1830. 399 p.
DLC, MWA, CSmH, MiD:B, MiU:C

. . . The Life and Adventures of Rear-Admiral John Paul Jones, Commonly Called Paul Jones. J. S. C. Abbott. N. Y., 1874. 359 p.
DLC, NN, CSmH, MiD:B

Commodore Paul Jones. Cyrus T. Brady. N. Y., 1900. 480 p. (G.C.) *DLC, NN, CSmH*

John Paul Jones of Naval Fame. C. W. Brown. Chicago, 1902. 271 p. (American Patriot Series) *DLC, CSmH*

Paul Jones, Founder of the American Navy. A. C. Buell. N. Y., 1900. 2 vols. *DLC, NN, MWA, CSmH, PU, MiD:B, MiU:C*

Life and Letters of John Paul Jones. Anna F. DeKoven. N. Y., 1913. 2 vols. *DLC, NN, MWA, CSmH, PU*

Paul Jones. Hutchins Hapgood. Boston, 1901. 126 p. (Riverside Biographies) *DLC, NN, CSmH*

Admiral Paul Jones. Abraham V. D. Honeyman. Plainfield, N. J., 1905. 100 p. *DLC, NN*

Life of John Paul Jones. J. O. Kaler. N. Y., 1900. 407 p.
DLC, NN, CSmH

Story of Paul Jones. Alfred H. Lewis. N. Y., 1906. 308 p.
DLC, NN

The Life of Paul Jones. Alexander S. Mackenzie. Boston, 1841. 2 vols.   *DLC, NN, MWA, CSmH, MiD:B, MiU:C*
John Paul Jones, Man of Action. Phillips Russell. N. Y., 1927. 314 p.   *DLC, NN, CSmH, PU*
The Life and Correspondence of John Paul Jones. Robert C. Sands. N. Y., 1830.   *DLC, NN, CSmH, MiU:C*
Paul Jones. Molly E. Seawell. N. Y., 1893. 166 p.
    DLC, NN, MWA
Life and Character of the Chevalier John Paul Jones. John H. Sherburne. Washington, 1825. 364 p.
    DLC, NN, MWA, CSmH, MiD:B, MiU:C
Life of Paul Jones. William G. Simms. N. Y., 1845.   *DLC*
John Paul Jones. Lewis F. Tooker. N. Y., 1916. 210 p.
    DLC, NN
The Life and Exploits of John Paul Jones. Orville J. Victor. N. Y., 1864. 95 p. (Beadle's Dime Biographical Library)
    DLC, NN, MWA
    2:396

JONES, KILSBY. *Rev. Kilsby Jones.* Vyrnwy Morgan. Scranton, Pa., 1898. 374 p.   *PU*

JONES, ROBERT EDMOND. 2:592

JONES, ROGER. *Captain Roger Jones, of London and Virginia.* Lewis H. Jones. Albany, 1891. 295 p.   *DLC, NN*

JONES, SAMUEL MINOT. *Samuel Minot Jones; the Story of an Amherst Boy.* Charles S. Walker. Amherst, Mass., 1922. 90 p.
    DLC, NN, MWA, MiD:B

JONES, WILLIAM. *William Jones; Indian, Cowboy, American Scholar, and Anthropologist in the Field.* Henry M. Rideout. N. Y., 1912. 212 p.   *DLC, NN*

JONSON, BEN. *O Rare Ben Jonson.* Byron Steel. N. Y., 1927. 158 p.
    DLC, NN, PU

JORDAN, DAVID STARR. 2:109

JOSEPH, CHIEF. 2:204

JOSEPH, FRIAR. *His Grey Eminence; the True "Friar Joseph" of Bulwer Lytton's "Richelieu." A Historical Study of the Capuchin Père Joseph François Le Clerc du Tremblay.* Robert F. O'Connor. Phila., 1912. 112 p.   *DLC, NN*

JOURNEYCAKE. *The Indian Chief, Journeycake.* S. H. Mitchell. Phila., 1895. 108 p.   *DLC, NN*

JOYCE, ISAAC WILSON. *Life of Isaac Wilson Joyce.* Wilbur F. Sheridan. N. Y., 1907. 281 p.   *DLC, NN*

JOYCE, JAMES. *James Joyce; His First Forty Years.* Herbert Gorman. N. Y., 1924. 238 p. *DLC, NN*

JUDD, ORANGE. 2:497

JUDD, SYLVESTER. *Life and Character of the Rev. Sylvester Judd.* Arethusa Hall. Boston, 1854. 531 p. *DLC, NN, MWA, PU*

JUDGE, WILLIAM H. *An American Missionary: Record of the Work of Rev. William H. Judge, S.J.* Charles J. Judge. Balt., 1904. 293 p. *NN*

JUDSON, ADRONIRAM.

The Earnest Man. A Sketch of the Character and Labors of Adoniram Judson, First Missionary to Burmah.* Hannah O. C. Conant. Boston, 1856. 498 p. *NN, MiD:B*

A Sketch of the Labors, Sufferings and Death of . . . Adoniram Judson. Abram D. Gillette. Phila., 1851. 160 p. *NN*

The Life and Character of Adoniram Judson . . . a Commemorative Discourse. William Hague. Boston, 1851. 38 p. *NN, MWA*

The Life of Adoniram Judson, Missionary to Burmah. Julia H. Johnston. Chicago, 1887. 80 p. *NN*

The Life of Adoniram Judson. Edward Judson. N. Y., 1883. 601 p. *DLC, NN, MWA, MiD:B*

Adoniram Judson; a Biography. Edward Judson. Phila., 1894. 188 p. *NN*

Burmah's Great Missionary. Records of the Life . . . of Adoniram Judson. Robert T. Middleditch. N. Y., 1854. 456 p. *NN, MWA*

The Apostle of Burma . . . Adoniram Judson. William C. Richards. Boston, 1889. 146 p. *NN, MWA, PU*

Memoir of the Life and Labors of Rev. Adoniram Judson. Francis Wayland. Boston, 1853. 2 vols. *DLC, NN, MWA, CSmH, MiD:B*

JUDSON, ANN.

Ann of Ava. Ethel D. Hubbard. N. Y., 1913. 245 p. *DLC, MWA*

Memoir of Ann Judson. J. D. Knowles. Boston, 1829. 324 p. *DLC, MWA*

2:147

JUDSON, EDWARD. *Edward Judson, Interpreter of God.* Charles H. Sears. Phila., 1917. 150 p. *DLC*

JUDSON, EDWARD ZANE CARROLL. *Life and Adventures of "Ned Buntline."* Fred E. Pond. N. Y., 1919. 139 p. *DLC, NN, MWA, CSmH*

JUDSON, EMILY CHUBBUCK.
   The Life and Letters of Mrs. Emily C. Judson. A. C. Kendrick.
N. Y. and Boston, 1860. 426 p.   *DLC, NN, MWA*
   The Three Mrs. Judsons, and Other Daughters of the Cross.
Daniel C. Eddy. Boston, 1859. 270 p.   *MWA*
   Lives of the Three Mrs. Judsons. Arabella M. Wilson. Boston,
1869. 371 p.   *NN, MWA*
JUDSON, SARAH HALL BOARDMAN.
   Memoir of Sarah B. Judson. " Fanny Forester." N. Y., 1848.
250 p.   *DLC*
   Memoir of Mrs. Sarah B. Judson. Emily C. Judson. N. Y.,
1848. 250 p.   *NN, MWA*
JULIA, SISTER. *Sister Julia (Susan McGroarty) Sister of Notre Dame
de Namur.* Mary Francis Nugent. N. Y., 1928. 375 p.
          DLC, NN
JULIAN, GEORGE WASHINGTON. *George W. Julian.* Grace J. Clarke.
Indianapolis, 1923. 456 p. (Indiana Hist. Coll. XI)
          DLC, NN, MWA, CSmH, PU
JUMEL, ELIZA. *The Amazing Madame Jumel.* William C. Duncan.
N. Y., 1935. 321 p.   *DLC, NN, MWA*
JUMEL, STEPHEN. 2:452
JUNKIN, GEORGE. *The Rev. George Junkin, a Historical Biography* . . .
David X. Junkin. Phila., 1871. 609 p.   *DLC, NN*
KAGAWA, TOYOHIKO. 2:190
KAHN, OTTO. 2:236
KALB, JOHANN. *The Life of Johann Kalb, Major-General in the Revo-
lutionary Army.* Frederick Kapp. N. Y., 1870. 319 p.
          DLC, NN, MWA, CSmH, MiD:B, MiU:C
KAMEHAMEHA, KING. *Napoleon of the Pacific (Kamehameha of Ha-
waii).* Herbert H. Gowen. N. Y., 1919. 326 p.   *DLC, NN*
KANE, ELISHA KENT.
   Biography of Elisha Kent Kane. William Elder. Phila., 1857.
416 p.   *DLC, NN, MWA, CSmH, PU, MiD:B*
   *Life of Dr. Elisha Kent Kane and of Other Distinguished Amer-
ican Explorers.* Samuel M. Schmucker. Phila., 1858. 406 p.
          DLC, NN, PU

   2:78–262
KANT, IMMANUEL. 2:232
KAROLYI, MICHAEL. 2:30
KAVANAUGH, HUBBARD HINDE. *Life and Times of Hubbard H. Kav-
anaugh.* A. H. Redford. Nashville, 1884. 552 p.   *CSmH*

KEAN, EDMUND. *Edmund Kean.* Harold N. Hillebrand. N. Y., 1933. 387 p. *DLC, NN, CSmH, PU*

KEARNY, PHILIP.

Personal and Military History of Philip Kearny, Major Gen. U. S. Volunteers. John W. de Peyster. N. Y., 1870. 512 p. *DLC, NN, MWA, CSmH, PU, MiD:B*

Sketch of the Life of General Kearny. Valentine M. Porter. Los Angeles, 1911. 35 p. (Pub. of the Hist. Soc. of So. Cal. Vol. VII) *NN, CSmH*

KEATS, GEORGE. 2:144

KEATS, JOHN.

John Keats; a Literary Biography. Albert E. Hancock. Boston, 1908. 234 p. *DLC, NN, CSmH*

John Keats. Amy Lowell. Boston, 1925. 2 vols. Boston, 1929. 1 vol. *DLC, NN, CSmH, PU* 2:86–701

KEENE, LAURA. *The Life of Laura Keene. Actress, Artist, Manager and Scholar.* John Creahan. Phila., 1897. 254 p. *DLC, NN, CSmH, PU*

KEESE, JOHN. *John Keese, Wit, and Littérateur; Biographical Memoir.* W. L. Keese. N. Y., 1883. 96 p. *DLC, NN, MWA*

KEITH, CAROLINE P. *Memoir of Mrs. Caroline P. Keith.* William C. Tenney. N. Y., 1864. 392 p. *DLC, NN, MWA*

KELLER, EZRA. *Biography of Ezra Keller, D.D.; With an Introduction by S. Sprecher, D.D.* M. Diehl. Springfield, O., 1859. 382 p. *NN*

KELLEY, HALL JACKSON. *Hall Jackson Kelley, Prophet of Oregon.* Fred W. Powell. Portland, Ore., 1917. 185 p. *NN*

KELLOGG, ELIJAH. *Elijah Kellogg . . .* W. B. Mitchell. Boston, 1903. 424 p. *DLC, NN*

KELLY, ALFRED. *Alfred Kelly of Ohio; His Life and Work.* J. L. Bates. Columbus, O., 1888. 210 p. (Privately Printed) *NN*

KELLY, JOHN. *Life and Times of John Kelly, Tribune of the People.* James F. McLoughlin. N. Y., 1885. 309 p. *NN*

KELLY, ROBERT H. *Memoir of Robert Hendre Kelly, Librarian of N. Y. Historical Society.* Alexander J. Wall. N. Y., 1928. 16 p. *NN*

KELLY, WILLIAM. *William Kelly: A True History of the So-Called Bessemer Process.* J. N. Boucher. Greensburg, Pa., 1924. 258 p.

KELVIN, LORD. 2:79

KEMAL, MUSTAPHA. 2:276

KEMBLE, FANNY.
    Fanny Kemble. Dorothie Bobbé. N. Y., 1931. 351 p.
                                         DLC, NN, CSmH, PU
    Fanny Kemble. Leota S. Driver. Chapel Hill, N. C., 1933.
271 p.   *DLC, NN*
KEMPER, JACKSON. *Memoir of Rt. Rev. Jackson Kemper.* Greenough
White. N. Y., 1900. 231 p.   *DLC*
KEMPIS, THOMAS Á. 2:95
KENDRICK, ASAHEL CLARK. *An American Scholar; a Tribute to Asahel
Clark Kendrick, 1809–1895.* Florence K. Cooper. N. Y., 1913.
138 p.   *DLC, NN*
KENDRICK, NATHANIEL. *Memoirs of Rev. Nathaniel Kendrick, D.D.,
and Silas N. Kendrick.* Seymour W. Adams. Phila., 1860. 370 p.
                                  DLC, NN, MiD:B
KENDRICK, WILLIAM. *Memoir of William Kendrick, 1810–1880.*
Louisville, 1881. 126 p.   *DLC, NN*
KENNARD, JOSEPH H. *Joseph H. Kennard, D.D., a Memorial.* Joseph
S. Kennard. Phila., 1867. 288 p.   *DLC, NN*
KENNEDY, JOHN PENDLETON.
    John Pendleton Kennedy. Edward M. Gwathmey. N. Y.,
1931. 193 p.   *DLC, NN, CSmH, PU*
    The Life of John Pendleton Kennedy. Henry T. Tuckerman.
N. Y., 1871. 490 p.   *DLC, NN, MWA, CSmH, PU*
KENOLY, JACOB. *The Life and Work of Jacob Kenoly.* C. C. Smith.
Cincinnati, 1912. 160 p.   *DLC, NN*
KENRICK, FRANCIS PATRICK and PETER RICHARD. *The Two Ken-
ricks: Most Rev. E. P., Archbishop of Baltimore; Most Rev. P. R.,
Archbishop of St. Louis.* J. J. O'Shea. Phila., 1904. 495 p.
                                     DLC, NN
KENT, JAMES. *Memoirs and Letters of James Kent, LL.D. Late
Chancellor.* William Kent. Boston, 1898. 341 p.
                                 DLC, NN, CSmH
KENTON, SIMON. *Simon Kenton, His Life and Period, 1755–1836.*
Edna Kenton. N. Y., 1930. 352 p.
                      DLC, NN, MWA, CSmH, PU
    2:358–424
KEPHART, EZEKIEL BORING. *Life of Ezekiel B. Kephart, Statesman,
Educator, Preacher, Bishop of the Church of the United Brethren
in Christ.* Lewis F. John. Dayton, O., 1907. 417 p. *DLC, NN*
KEPHART, ISAIAH L. *Life of Rev. Isaiah L. Kephart . . .* Cyrus J.
Kephart and W. R. Funk. Dayton, O., 1909. 249 p. *DLC, NN*

KERFOOT, JOHN BARRETT. *Life of the Rev. John Barrett Kerfoot, D.D. . . . First Bishop of Pittsburgh.* Hall Harrison. N. Y., 1886. 2 vols. *DLC, NN, MWA*

KERR, WALTER CRAIG. *A Biography of Walter Craig Kerr.* Albert W. Smith. N. Y., 1927. 191 p. *DLC, PU*

KEY, FRANCIS SCOTT.
 Francis Scott Key, Author of the Star Spangled Banner; What Else He Was and Who. Francis Scott Key-Smith. Washington, 1911. 104 p. *DLC, NN, MWA*
 Spangled Banner; the Story of Francis Scott Key. Victor Weybright. N. Y., 1935. 307 p. *DLC, NN*
  2:503

KIDD, WILLIAM. *. . . Captain William Kidd, and Others of the Pirates or Buccaneers Who Ravaged the Seas, Islands and Continents of America Two Hundred Years Ago.* John S. C. Abbott. N. Y., 1874. 373 p. *DLC, NN, MWA, MiD:B*
 See HOOD, ROBIN.

KIDDER, DANIEL PARRISH. *Biography of the Rev. Daniel Parrish Kidder . . .* G. E. Strobridge. N. Y., 1804. 357 p. *NN, PU*

KILLIGREW, THOMAS. *Thomas Killigrew; Cavalier Dramatist, 1612–83.* Alfred B. Harbage. Phila., 1930. 247 p.
        DLC, NN, CSmH, PU

KILPATRICK, HUGH. *Kilpatrick and Our Cavalry . . . Sketch of the Life of General Kilpatrick.* James Moore. N. Y., 1865. 245 p.
        DLC, NN, MWA, CSmH

KIMBALL, CHARLES DEAN. *Pioneer of Old Superior: Charles Dean Kimball.* Lillian K. Stewart. Boston, 1930. 322 p.
        DLC, NN, MiD:B

KIMBALL, DAVID P. *Life of David P. Kimball and Other Sketches.* Solomon F. Kimball. Salt Lake City, 1918. 128 p. *NN*

KIMBALL, HEBER C. *Life of Heber C. Kimball.* Orson F. Whitney. Salt Lake City, 1888. 520 p. *NN*

KIMBALL, JONATHAN GOLDEN. *J. Golden Kimball; the Story of a Unique Personality.* Claude Richards. Salt Lake City, 1934. 398 p. *DLC, NN*

KIMBALL, JAMES PELEG. *A Soldier-Doctor of Our Army, James P. Kimball.* Maria B. Kimball. Boston, 1917. 192 p.
        DLC, NN, PU, MiD:B

KINCAID, EUGENIO. *A History of the Labors of Rev. E. Kincaid.* Alfred S. Patton. N. Y., 1858. 312 p. *MWA, PU*

KING, CLARENCE.
  Clarence King Memoirs. The Helmet of Mambrino. N. Y., 1904. 427 p. *MWA, CSmH*
  Biographical Memoir of Clarence King, 1842–1901. S. F. Emmons. Washington, 1907. 55 p. *NN, PU*
KING, RUFUS.
  Rufus King and His Times. Edward H. Brush. N. Y., 1926. 159 p. *DLC, NN, CSmH*
  The Life and Correspondence of Rufus King. Charles R. King, ed. N. Y., 1894–1900. 6 vols.
  DLC, NN, MWA, CSmH, PU, MiD:B, MiU:C
KING, THOMAS STARR.
  Life, Writings and Character of Thos. Starr King. C. C. Bradlee. Boston, 1870. 27 p. (Privately Printed)
  DLC, MWA, MiD:B
  Biographical Sketch of Rev. T. S. King in " King's Patriotism and Other Papers." Richard Frothingham. Boston, 1864. 359 p.
  DLC, NN, MWA
  A Tribute to Thomas Starr King. Richard Frothingham. Boston, 1865. 247 p. *DLC, NN, MWA, MiD:B*
  Thomas Starr King, Patriot and Preacher. Charles Wendte. Boston, 1921. 226 p. *DLC, NN, CSmH*
  2:41–330
KINGMAN, ABNER. *Memoir of Abner Kingman.* Henry Kingman. Boston, 1888. 135 p. *MWA*
KINGSBURY, KENNETH RALEIGH. 2:233
KINGSLEY, WILLIAM CHARLES. *William C. Kingsley, 1833–1885. His Career and Character, With the Expressions of Tribute and Sorrow Evoked by His Death.* St. Clair McKelway, ed. Brooklyn, 1885. 102 p. *NN*
KINO, EUSEBIO FRANCISCO.
  Rim of Christendom; a Biography of Eusebio Francisco Kino, Pacific Coast Pioneer. Herbert E. Bolton. N. Y., 1936. 644 p.
  DLC, NN, MWA, CSmH
  Pioneer Padre, the Life and Times of Eusebio Francisco Kino. Rufus Kay Wyllys. Dallas, 1935. 230 p. *DLC, NN, CSmH*
KINSEY, JOHN. *John Kinsey, Speaker of the Penna. Assembly and Justice of the Supreme Court of the Province.* Jas. S. Walton. Phila., 1900. 69 p. *DLC, NN, MWA*
  2:594

KINSOLVING, GEORGE HERBERT. *Texas George: The Life of George Herbert Kinsolving, Bishop of Texas, 1892–1928.* Arthur B. Kinsolving. Milwaukee, 1932. 137 p.   *DLC, NN, MWA*

KIPLING, RUDYARD. *A Ken of Kipling; Being a Biographical Sketch of Rudyard Kipling, With an Appreciation and Some Anecdotes.* Wm. M. Clemens. N. Y., 1899. 141 p.   *DLC, NN, CSmH* 2:301.

KIRBY, GUSTAVUS TOWN. 2:425

KIRBY, WILLIAM. *William Kirby; the Portrait of a Tory Loyalist.* Lorne Pierce. N. Y., 1930. Toronto, 1929. 477 p.
   DLC, NN, CSmH, MiD:B

KIRK, EDWARD NORRIS. *Life of Edward Norris Kirk.* David O. Mears. Boston, 1877. 432 p.   *DLC, NN, MWA*

KIRKLAND, JOHN THORNTON. 2:681

KIRKLAND, SAMUEL. *Life of Samuel Kirkland.* Samuel K. Lothrop. (L.A.B.)   *DLC, NN, MWA, CSmH*

KIRKPATRICK, ANDREW. *Memorials of Andrew Kirkpatrick, and His Wife, Jane Bayard.* James G. Wilson. N. Y., 1870. 75 p.
   DLC, NN, MWA, PU, MiD:B

KIRKPATRICK, JACOB. *The Kirkpatrick Memorial; or, Biographical Sketches of Father and Son, and a Selection From the Sermons of the Rev. Jacob Kirkpatrick, Jr., the Sketches by the Rev. George Hale, D.D.* Wm. M. Blackburn. Phila., 1867. 312 p.
   DLC, NN, MWA

KIRKWOOD, SAMUEL JORDAN. *Samuel Jordan Kirkwood.* Dan E. Clark. Iowa City, 1917. 464 p. (Iowa State Hist. Soc.)
   DLC, NN, MWA, CSmH, PU

KITE, THOMAS. *Memoirs and Letters of Thomas Kite . . . Prepared by His Family.* Phila., 1883. 479 p.   *MWA*

KITTO, JOHN. *From Poor-House to Pulpit; or, the Triumph of the Late Dr. John Kitto, From Boyhood to Manhood.* Wm. M. Thayer. Boston, 1859. 349 p.   *DLC, MWA*

KITTREDGE, ALFRED BEARD. *Biography of Senator Alfred Beard Kittredge; His Complete Life Work.* Oscar W. Coursey. Mitchell, S. D., 1915. 224 p.   *DLC, NN*

KLOPSCH, LOUIS. *Life Work of Louis Klopsch . . .* Charles M. Pepper. N. Y., 1910. 395 p.   *DLC, NN, PU*

KNAPP, SEAMAN ASAHEL. 2:493

KNIGHT, FREDERICK. *Thorn Cottage, or The Poet's House. A Memorial of Frederick Knight, Esq., of Rowley, Mass.* Frederick Knight. Boston, 1855. 108 p.   *DLC, NN, MWA*

KNIGHT, JOHN W. *"Saved by Fire." The Life of John W. Knight, Methodist Preacher.* George G. Smith. Macon, Ga., 1888. 135 p.

KNIGHT, WILLIAM HENRY. *William Henry Knight, California Pioneer.* Bertha K. Power, comp. N. Y., 1932. 252 p.
DLC, NN, CSmH

KNOWLTON, THOMAS. 2:149

KNOX, CHARLES. *The Story of Two Famous Hatters.* Robert R. Updegraff. N. Y., 1926. 76 p. (Privately Printed)
DLC, NN, PU

KNOX, FRANK. *Frank Knox, American; a Short Biography.* Norman Beasley. Garden City, N. Y., 1936. 184 p. *DLC, NN*

KNOX, HENRY.
Henry Knox: Soldier of the Revolution. Noah Brooks. N. Y., 1900. 286 p. (American Men of Energy)
DLC, NN, CSmH, MiD:B
Life and Correspondence of Henry Knox. Francis S. Drake. Boston, 1873. 160 p. *DLC, NN, MWA, CSmH, MiD:B, MiU:C*

KNOX, JOHN.
John Knox. A. Taylor Innes. N. Y., 1896. 158 p. *DLC*
The Life and Times of John Knox, the Soul of the Scottish Reformation. Charles K. True. Cincinnati, 1878. 357 p. *DLC*
2:334

KOCH, ROBERT. 2:176

KONSCAK, FERDINAND. *Life and Works of the Rev. Ferdinand Konscak, S.J., 1703–1759, an Early Missionary in California.* M. D. Krmpotic. Boston, 1923. 167 p. *DLC, NN, CSmH*

KOSCIUSZKO, THADDEUS. *Memoir of Thaddeus Kosciuszko, Poland's Hero and Patriot.* A. W. W. Evans. N. Y., 1888. 58 p. (Privately Printed) *DLC, NN, MWA, CSmH*

KOSSUTH, LOUIS. *The Life of Louis Kossuth.* P. C. Headley. Auburn, 1852. 461 p. *DLC, NN, MWA*

KRAUTH, CHARLES PORTERFIELD. *Charles Porterfield Krauth.* Adolph Spaeth. N. Y., 1898. 2 vols. *NN, PU*

KREUGER, IVAR. *The Life and Death of Ivar Kreuger.* William H. Stoneman. Indianapolis, 1932. 289 p. *DLC, NN, PU*

KROPOTKIN, PETR. ALEKSYEEVICH. *Comrade Kropotkin.* Victor Robinson. N. Y., 1908. 127 p. *DLC, NN*

KURTZ, BENJAMIN. 2:294

KUSSMAUL, ADOLF. *The Life and Time of Adolf Kussmaul.* Theodore H. Bast. N. Y., 1926. 131 p. *DLC, NN*

LABAGH, PETER. *Memoir of the Rev. Peter Labagh, D.D. With Notices of the History of the Reformed Protestant Dutch Church in North America.* John A. Todd. N. Y., 1860. 339 p.   *NN*

LA BARGE, JOSEPH. *Life and Adventures of Joseph La Barge, Pioneer Navigator and Indian Traveler.* H. M. Chittenden. N. Y., 1903. 2 vols.   *DLC, NN, CSmH, PU*

LACEY, JOHN. *Sketch of the Life and Character of John Lacey, a Brigadier-General in the Revolutionary Army.* Wm. W. H. Davis. n.p., 1868. 118 p.   *DLC, NN, MiD:B*

LACKINGTON, JAMES. 2:406

LACOMBE, ALBERT. *Father Lacombe, the Black-Robe Voyageur.* Katherine Hughes. N. Y., 1911. 467 p.   *DLC, NN*

LADD, WILLIAM. *The Apostle of Peace. Memoir of William Ladd.* John Hemmenway. Boston, 1872. 272 p.   *DLC, NN, MWA*

LAËNNEC, RENÉ THÉOPHILE HYACINTHE. *René Théophile Hyacinthe Laënnec; a Memoir.* Gerald B. Webb. N. Y., 1928. 146 p.
DLC, NN, PU
2:678

LA FARGE, JOHN. *John La Farge: A Memoir and a Study.* Royal Cortissoz. Boston, 1911. 268 p.   *DLC, NN, PU*
2:123–429

LAFAYETTE, MARIE JOSEPH PAUL, MARQUIS DE.
A Complete History of the Marquis De Lafeyette, Major-General in the Army of the U. S. A. in the War of the Revolution. Hartford, 1846. 503 p.   *NN, MWA, MiD:B*
Outlines of the Life of General Lafayette. Tappan, N. Y., 1830. 250 p.
Life of General Lafayette. John Q. Adams. N. Y., 1847. 255 p.
DLC
La Fayette. John Bigelow. Boston, 1882. 11 p.   *DLC*
Memoirs of the Marquis de Lafayette, Major-General in the Revolutionary Army of the United States of America, Together With His Tour Through the U. S. Frederick Butler. Wethersfield, Conn., 1825. 418 p.   *DLC, NN, CSmH*
Life of Lafayette. E. Cecil. Boston, 1860. 218 p.
DLC, NN, MWA
Lafayette. Martha F. Crow. N. Y., 1916. 201 p.
DLC, NN
The Life of General Lafayette. William Cutter. Boston, 1854. 408 p.   *DLC, NN, MiD:B*

Young Lafayette. Jeannette Eaton. Boston and N. Y., 1932. 253 p. *DLC, NN*

The Life of Lafayette. The Knight of Liberty in Two World and Two Centuries. Lydia H. Farmer. N. Y., 1888. 472 p.
DLC, NN, MWA

Lafayette Comes to America. Louis R. Gottschalk. Chicago, 1935. 184 p. *DLC, NN, CSmH, PU*

The Spirit of Lafayette. James M. Hallowell. Garden City, N. Y., 1918. 101 p. *DLC, NN, PU*

Life of General Lafayette. P. C. Headley. Auburn, 1851. 377 p. *DLC, NN*

Memoirs of General La Fayette; With an Account of His Visit to America, and Reception, Aug. 15–Oct. 19, 1824. Samuel L. Knapp. Boston, 1824. *DLC, NN*

The Life of Gilbert Motier de Lafayette. Ebenezer Mack. Ithaca, N. Y., 1841. 371 p. *DLC, NN, MWA, MiU:C*

True La Fayette. George Morgan. Phila., 1919. 488 p.
DLC, NN, PU

Lafayette in America. J. B. Nolan. Balt., 1934. 324 p.
CSmH

Lafayette and Three Revolutions. John S. Penman. Boston, 1929. 362 p. *DLC, NN, CSmH*

La Fayette. Henry D. Sedgwick. Indianapolis, 1928. 433 p.
DLC, NN, PU

Life of Gen. Lafayette. Bayard Tuckerman. N. Y., 1889. 2 vols. *DLC, NN, MWA, CSmH, PU, MiD:B, MiU:C*

Life of Marquis De La Fayette; Major-General . . . in the War of the Revolution. Robert Waln, Jr. Phila., 1825. 450 p.
DLC, NN, CSmH, MiU:C

La Fayette. Brand Whitlock. N. Y., 1929. 2 vols.
DLC, NN, PU. MiD:B

2:662

LAFAYETTE, ADRIENNE.

Madame de Lafayette and Her Family. M. Crawford. N. Y., 1907. 358 p. *DLC, NN*

Ardent Adrienne. The Life of Madame de La Fayette. Lida R. McCabe. N. Y., 1930. 325 p. *DLC, NN*

LAFITTE, JEAN.

Lafitte of Louisiana. M. Devereaux. Boston, 1902. 427 p.

Lafitte, the Pirate. Lyle Saxon. N. Y., 1930. 307 p.
DLC, NN, MWA, CSmH

LA FLECHERE, JOHN W. See FLECHERE, JOHN W.

LAMAR, JOSEPH RUCKER. *Life of Joseph Rucker Lamar, 1857–1916.*
Clarinda P. Lamar. N. Y., 1926. 284 p.   *DLC, NN, PU*

LAMAR, LUCIUS QUINTUS CINCINNATUS.
    Lucius Q. C. Lamar, Secession and Reunion. Wirt A. Cate.
Chapel Hill, N. C., 1935. 594 p.   *DLC, NN, CSmH, PU, MiU:C*
    Lucius Q. C. Lamar, His Life, Times and Speeches, 1825–1893.
Edward Mayes. Nashville, 1896. 820 p.
                            DLC, NN, MWA, CSmH, PU

LAMAR, MIRABEAU BONAPARTE.
    Mirabeau Bonaparte Lamar. Asa K. Christian. Austin, 1922.
208 p.   *DLC, NN, CSmH, PU*
    Mirabeau Bonaparte Lamar, Troubador and Crusader. Herbert
P. Gambrell. Dallas, 1934. 317 p.   *DLC, NN, CSmH, PU*

LAMAR, THOMAS JEFFERSON. *Thomas Jefferson Lamar; a Memorial
Sketch.* Samuel T. Wilson. Maryville, Tenn., 1920. 96 p.
                                  DLC, NN

LAMB, CHARLES. 2:86

LAMB, JOHN. *Memoir of the Life and Times of General John Lamb.*
Isaac Q. Leake. Albany, 1850. 431 p.
          DLC, NN, MWA, CSmH, PU, MiD:B, MiU:C

LAMB, MARY. 2:337

LAMBUTH, WALTER RUSSELL. *Walter Russell Lambuth, Prophet and
Pioneer.* William W. Pinson. Nashville, 1924. 261 p.
                                    DLC, NN

LANDELS, WILLIAM. *Memoir of William Landels.* T. D. Landels.
N. Y., 1900. 344 p.   *DLC*

LANDIS, KENESAW M. 2:546

LANDON, ALFRED.
    *This Man Landon; the Record and Career of Governor Alfred
M. Landon of Kansas.* Frederick Palmer. N. Y., 1936. 245 p.
                           DLC, NN, PU, MiD:B
    The Life of Alfred M. Landon. Willis Thornton. N. Y., 1936.
174 p.   *DLC, NN*
    Is It True What They Say About Landon? Cal Tinney. N. Y.,
1936. 204 p.   *DLC, NN*

LANDRUM, JOHN GILL. *The Life and Times of Rev. John G. Landrum.*
H. P. Griffith. Phila., 1885. 298 p.   *DLC*

LANE, HARRIET. 2:518

LANE, JAMES HENRY.
    James Henry Lane. Wm. E. Connelley. Topeka, 1899. 129 p.
                                    CSmH

The Grim chieftain of Kansas. R. M. Fish. Cherryvale, Kansas, 1885. 145 p. *CSmH*

Life of General James H. Lane. John Speer. Garden City, Kansas, 1896. 336 p. *DLC, NN, CSmH*

The Political Career of General James H. Lane. Wendell Holmes Stephenson. Topeka, 1930. 196 p. *CSmH*

LANE, JOEL. *Joel Lane, Pioneer and Patriot.* M. de L. Haywood. Raleigh, 1900. 23 p. *DLC, NN, MWA*

LANE, JOSEPH. See BRECKINRIDGE, JOHN C.

LANE, LUNSFORD. *Lunsford Lane; or, Another Helper From North Carolina.* William G. Hawkins. Boston, 1863. 305 p. *DLC, NN, MWA*

LANE, RALPH. *Life of Sir Ralph Lane.* Edward E. Hale. Worcester, Mass., 1860. 27 p. (Amer. Ant. Soc. Archaelogia Americana. V. 4) *DLC, NN, MWA, CSmH, PU, MiU:C*

LANGDON, SAMUEL. *President Langdon, a Biographical Tribute.* Franklin B. Sanborn. Boston, 41 p. *DLC, NN, MWA, PU*

LANGLADE, CHARLES. *Charles Langlade, First Settler in Wisconsin.* M. E. McIntosh. Wilwaukee, 1896. 223 p. (Parkman Club Papers, No. 8) *DLC, NN, MWA*

LANGLEY, SAMUEL PIERPONT. 2:507

LANGMUIR, IRVING. 2:348

LANIER, SIDNEY.

The Life of Sidney Lanier. Lincoln Lorenz. N. Y., 1935. 340 p. *DLC, NN, PU*

Sidney Lanier. Edwin Mims. Boston, 1905. 386 p. (A.M.L.) *DLC, NN, MWA, CSmH, PU*

Sidney Lanier. Henry N. Snyder. N. Y., 1906. 132 p. (Modern Poets and Christian Teaching) *DLC, NN*

Sidney Lanier; a Biographical and Critical Study. Aubrey H. Starke. Chapel Hill, 1933. 525 p. *DLC, NN, CSmH, PU*

Sidney Lanier—His Life and Writings. George S. Wills. 211 p. (Pub. of the Southern Hist. Asso., 3, July, 1898) *DLC, NN, CSmH* 2:84–503

LAO-TZE. 2:665

LARCOM, LUCY. *Lucy Larcom; Life, Letters and Diary.* Daniel D. Addison. Boston, 1894. 295 p. *DLC, NN, MWA*

LARNED, SYLVESTER. *Life of Rev. Sylvester Larned.* Ralph R. Gurley. N. Y., 1844. 412 p. *DLC, NN, MWA, MiD:B*

LARSEN, LAUR. *Laur Larsen, Pioneer College President.* Karen Larsen. Northfield, Minn., 1936. 358 p. *DLC, CSmH*

LASALLE, PHILIPPE. *Philippe de Lasalle; His Contribution to the Textile Industry of Lyons.* Belle M. Borland. Chicago, 1936. 49 p. *DLC, NN*

LA SALLE, ROBERT.
The Fatal River, the Life and Death of La Salle. Frances O. Gaithier. N. Y., 1931. 303 p. *DLC, NN*
La Salle. Louise S. Hasbrouck. N. Y., 1916. 212 p. *DLC, NN, CSmH*
La Salle. Leo V. Jacks. N. Y., 1931. 282 p. *DLC, NN*
La Salle. Ross F. Lockridge. Yonkers-on-Hudson, N. Y., 1931. 312 p. *DLC, NN*
Life of Robert Cavalier De La Salle. Jared Sparks. (L.A.B.) *DLC, NN, MWA, CSmH, MiU:C*
2:127

LA SALLE, ST. JOHN BAPTIST. *The Story of St. John Baptist de la Salle, Founder of the Institute of the Brothers of the Christian Schools.* Brother Leo. N. Y., 1921. 135 p. *DLC, NN*

LAS CASAS, BARTHOLOMÉ. *Bartholomew de Las Casas: His Life, His Apostolate and His Writings.* Francis A. MacNutt. N. Y., 1909. 472 p. *DLC, MWA, CSmH, PU, MiU:C*

LATHROP, JULIA. *My Friend, Julia Lathrop.* Jane Addams. N. Y., 1935. 228 p. *DLC, NN, PU*

LATHROP, ROSE HAWTHORNE. *Mother Alphonsa, Rose Hawthorne Lathrop.* James J. Walsh. N. Y., 1930. 275 p. *DLC, NN, PU*

LATIMER, HUGH. *The Life of Hugh Latimer.* George L. Duyckinck. N. Y., 1861. 204 p. *NN*

LATROBE, JOHN HAZELHURST BONEVAL. *John H. B. Latrobe and His Times.* John E. Semmes. Balt., 1917. 601 p. *DLC, NN, MWA*

LAUD, WILLIAM.
Laud, Storm Center of England. Robert P. T. Coffin. N. Y., 1930. 331 p. *DLC, NN, PU*
Life of Archbishop Laud. John N. Norton. Boston, 1864. 269 p. *DLC, NN, MWA*

LAURENS, HENRY AND JOHN. *The Life of Henry Laurens, With Sketch of the Life of Lieutenant-Colonel John Laurens.* David D. Wallace. N. Y., 1915. 539 p. *DLC, NN, MWA, CSmH*

LAVOISIER, ANTOINE. *Antoine Lavoisier; the Father of Modern Chemistry.* Douglas McKie. Phila., 1936. 303 p. *DLC, NN*
2:348:393

LAW, JOHN. *Judge John Law.* Charles Denby. Indianapolis, 1897.
213 p. *CSmH*

LAWRANCE, MARION. *Marion Lawrance; a Memorial Biography.*
Harold G. Lawrance. N. Y., 1925. 479 p. *DLC*

LAWRENCE, ABBOTT.
Memoir of Abbott Lawrence. Hamilton A. Hill. Boston, 1883.
243 p. *DLC, NN, MWA, CSmH, PU, MiD:B*
Memoir of the Hon. Abbott Lawrence. William H. Prescott.
n.p., 1856. 51 p. *DLC, NN, MWA*

LAWRENCE, AMOS ADAMS. *Life of Amos A. Lawrence.* William Lawrence. Boston and N. Y., 1888. 289 p.
DLC, NN, MWA, CSmH, MiD:B

LAWRENCE, EDWARD ALEXANDER. *Reminiscences of the Life and Work
of Edward A. Lawrence, Jr.* Margaret W. Lawrence. N. Y., 1900.
519 p. *DLC, NN, MWA*

LAWRENCE, JAMES. *James Lawrence, U. S. N., Commander of the
Chesapeake.* Albert Gleaves. N. Y., 1904. 337 p. (American
Men of Energy) *DLC, NN, CSmH, PU*

LAWSON, VICTOR. *Victor Lawson; His Time and His Work.* Charles
H. Dennis. Chicago, 1935. 470 p.
DLC, NN, MWA, CSmH, PU

LAY, W. P. *Soldiers of Progress and Industry.* John R. Hornady.
N. Y., 1930. 243 p. *DLC, NN*

LEA, HENRY CHARLES.
Henry Charles Lea. Edward S. Bradley. Phila., 1931. 391 p.
DLC, NN, CSmH, PU
Henry Charles Lea. Edward P. Cheyney. (Am. Philos. Soc.
Proc. L. Appendix 3–41) *DLC, CSmH*
Henry Charles Lea. Arthur H. Lea. Phila., 1910. 24 p.

LEACOCK, HAMBLE JAMES. *The Martyr of the Pongas; Being a Memoir of the Rev. Hamble James Leacock.* Henry Caswall. N. Y.,
1857. 281 p. *DLC, NN*

LEARY, ELIZA FERRY. *Through Historic Years With Eliza Ferry Leary.*
Laura V. Wagner. Seattle, 1934. 93 p. *DLC, NN*

LEAVELL, LANDRUM PINSON. *An Unashamed Workman, the Biography
of Landrum Pinson Leavell.* Roland Q. Leavell. Richmond, 1932.
146 p. *DLC, NN*

LE CONTE, JOHN. *Biography of John Le Conte.* Joseph Le Conte.
Wash., 1895. 393 p. *CSmH*

LECONTE, JOSEPH. 2:531

LECOUVREUR, ADRIENNE. 2:576

LEDYARD, JOHN.
 Memoirs of the Life and Travels of John Ledyard. Jared
Sparks. Cambridge, 1828. 428 p. (Reprinted in L.A.B. as *Life
of John Ledyard*)   *DLC, NN, MWA*
 Life of John Ledyard, the American Traveler. Jared Sparks.
Boston, 1847. 419 p.   *DLC, NN, MWA, CSmH, PU*
LEE, ALFRED. *Alfred Lee, First Bishop of Delaware.* Phila., 1888.
243 p. (Privately Printed)   *DLC, NN*
LEE, ANN. *The Life and Gospel Experience of Mother Ann Lee . . .*
Henry C. Blinn. East Canterbury, N. H., 1901. 264 p.
                                                       DLC, NN
LEES OF VIRGINIA.
 The Lees of Virginia; Biography of a Family. Burton J. Hen-
drick. Boston, 1935. 455 p.   *DLC, NN, CSmH*
 *Lee of Virginia. 1642–1892. Biographical and Genealogical
Sketches of the Descendants of Colonel Richard Lee.* Edmund J.
Lee. Phila., 1895. 586 p.   *DLC, NN, CSmH*
LEE, ARTHUR. *Life of Arthur Lee, LL.D.* Richard H. Lee. Boston,
1829. 2 vols.   *DLC, NN, MWA, CSmH, MiU:C, RP:JCB*
LEE, CHARLES.
 *Memoirs of the Life of the Late Charles Lee, Esq., . . . Second
in Command in the Services of the U. S. A. During the Revolution
. . .* Edward Langworthy. N. Y., 1792. London, 1792. N. Y.,
1813. 50 p.
        DLC, NN, MWA, CSmH, PU, MiD:B, MiU:C, RP:JCB
 Life of Charles Lee. Jared Sparks. (L.A.B.)
                        DLC, NN, MWA, CSmH, PU, MiU:C
LEE, HENRY.
 Light-Horse Harry Lee. Thomas A. Boyd. N. Y., 1931. 359 p.
                                                DLC, NN, CSmH, PU
 *Life of Maj.-Gen. Henry Lee, Commander of Lee's Legion in the
Revolutionary War, and Subsequently Governor of Va., Also the
Life of Gen. Thomas Sumter of South Carolina.* Cecil B. Hartley.
Phila., 1859. 352 p.   *DLC, NN, MiD:B*
 *Biography of Henry Lee in " Memoirs of the War in the South-
ern Department of the United States."* R. E. Lee. N. Y., 1869.
70 p.   *DLC, CSmH*
LEE, HENRY. *Memoir of Col. Henry Lee.* John T. Morse, Jr. Bos-
ton, 1905. 441 p.   *NN, MWA*
LEE, IVY L. 2:546

LEE, JASON. *Jason Lee, Prophet of the New Oregon.* Cornelius J. Brosnan. N. Y., 1932. 348 p.   *DLC, MWA, CSmH, MiD:B*

LEE, JESSE.
The Life and Times of the Rev. Jesse Lee. Leroy M. Lee. Louisville, 1848. 517 p.   *DLC, NN, CSmH, MiD:B*
Jesse Lee: a Methodist Apostle. William H. Meredith. N. Y., 1909. 128 p.   *DLC, NN*
Memoir of the Rev. Jesse Lee. Minton Thrift. N. Y., 1823. 360 p.   *DLC, NN, MWA, CSmH*

LEE, JOHN. *A Short Account of the Life and Death of the Rev. John Lee, a Methodist Minister in the United States of America.* Jesse Lee. Balt., 1805. 179 p.   *DLC, MWA, CSmH*

LEE, NATHANIEL. See THOMAS OTWAY.

LEE, RICHARD HENRY. *Memoir of the Life of Richard Henry Lee.* R. H. Lee. Phila., 1825. 2 vols.
DLC, NN, MWA, CSmH, MiU:C

LEE, ROBERT EDWARD.
Life of Gen. Robert E. Lee. Graeme M. Adams. N. Y., 1905. 321 p.   *CSmH*
Lee, the American. Gamaliel Bradford. Boston, 1912. 324 p.
DLC, NN, CSmH, PU
Gen. Robert Edward Lee. Robert A. Brock, ed. Richmond, 1897. 586 p.   *DLC*
Lee of Virginia; a Biography. William E. Brooks. Indianapolis, 1932. 361 p.   *DLC, NN, CSmH*
Robert E. Lee. Philip A. Bruce. Phila., 1907. 380 p. (A.C.B.)   *DLC, NN, MWA, CSmH*
The Life and Campaigns of General Lee. Edward L. Childs. Paris, 1874, London, 1875. 336 p.   *DLC, NN, MWA, CSmH*
A Life of Gen. Robert E. Lee. John E. Cooke. N. Y., 1871. As *Robert E. Lee.* N. Y., 1893. 577 p.
DLC, NN, MWA, CSmH, PU, MiD:B
R. E. Lee. A Biography. Douglas S. Freeman. N. Y., 1934–1935. 4 vols.   *DLC, NN, MWA, CSmH, PU*
Robert E. Lee. Bradley Gilman. N. Y., 1915. 205 p.
DLC, NN, CSmH
Robert E. Lee, the Christian. William J. Johnstone. N. Y., Cincinnati, 1933. 301 p.   *DLC, NN, CSmH*
Life and Letters of Robert Edward Lee. Soldier and Man. William J. Jones. N. Y., 1906. 486 p.   *NN, MWA, CSmH*

General Lee. Fitzhugh Lee. N. Y., 1894. 433 p. (G.C.)
DLC, NN, CSmH, PU, MiD:B

Memoirs of Robert E. Lee. A. L. Long and M. J. Wright, eds.
N. Y., 1887. 707 p. *DLC, NN, MWA, CSmH, PU*

Life and Campaigns of Gen. Robert E. Lee. James D. McCabe,
Jr. Atlanta, 1866. 717 p. *DLC, NN, CSmH, PU, MiD:B*

Soul of Lee. Randolph H. McKim. N. Y., 1918. 258 p.
DLC, NN, CSmH, PU

Popular Life of Gen. Robert Edward Lee. Emily V. Mason.
Balt., 1872. 432 p. *DLC, NN, MWA, CSmH, MiD:B*

Robert E. Lee, the Southerner. Thomas N. Page. N. Y., 1908.
312 p. *DLC, NN, MWA, CSmH*

Robert E. Lee: Man and Soldier. Thomas N. Page. N. Y.,
1911. 734 p. *DLC, NN, CSmH, PU*

*Lee and His Lieutenants; Comprising the Early Life, Public
Services and Campaigns of General Robert E. Lee and His Companions in Arms.* Edward A. Pollard. N. Y., 1867, 1871. 851 p.
DLC, NN, CSmH, PU

Gen. Robert E. Lee After Appomattox. F. L. Riley. N. Y.,
1922. 250 p. *CSmH, PU*

Life of Robert E. Lee. H. E. Shepherd. N. Y., 1906. 280 p.
DLC, CSmH

Robert E. Lee. W. P. Trent. Boston, 1899. 135 p. (Beacon
Biographies) *DLC, NN, CSmH, MiD:B*

Robert E. Lee and the Southern Confederacy. Henry A. White.
N. Y., 1897. 467 p. (Heroes of the Nations Series)
DLC, NN, CSmH

Robert E. Lee; a Biography. Robert W. Winston. N. Y.,
1934. 428 p. *DLC, NN, CSmH, PU*

Gen. Robert E. Lee. John A. Wyeth. N. Y., 1906. 22 p.
DLC, NN, CSmH

Marse Robert, Knight of the Confederacy. James C. Young.
N. Y., 1929. 362 p. *DLC, NN, MWA, PU*
2:264–612

LEETH, JOHN. *Short Biography of John Leeth; With an Account of
His Life Among the Indians; Reprinted From Original Edition of
1831.* Ewel Jeffries. Cleveland, 1904. 70 p. (Narratives of
Captivities) *DLC, NN, MWA, CSmH, PU*

LEEUWENHOEK, ANTON. 2:176

LEFFINGWELL, CLARA. *Clara Leffingwell, a Missionary.* W. A. Sellew. Chicago, 1907. 320 p. *DLC*

LEGARÉ, HUGH SWINTON. *Hugh Swinton Legaré, a Charleston Intellectual*. Linda Rhea. Chapel Hill, 1934. 279 p.

DLC, NN, CSmH, PU

LEHR, HARRY SYMES. *" King Lehr " and the Gilded Age*. Elizabeth D. Lehr. Phila., 1935. 332 p. *DLC, NN, MWA, PU*

LEIBNITZ, GODFREY WILLIAM. *Life of Godfrey William Von Leibnitz*. John M. Mackie. Boston, 1845. 288 p. *DLC, PU*

LEIBOWITZ, SAMUEL SHOWMAN. *Not Guilty! The Story of Samuel S. Leibowitz*. Fred D. Pasley. N. Y., 1933. 281 p. *DLC, NN*

LEISLER, JACOB. *Administration of Jacob Leisler*. Charles F. Hoffman. (L.A.B.) *DLC, NN, MWA, CSmH*

LEITER, MARY VICTORIA. 2:518

LELAND, CHARLES GODFREY. *Charles Godfrey Leland, a Biography*. Elizabeth R. Pennell. Boston, 1906. 2 vols.

DLC, NN, MWA, CSmH, PU

LEMAÎTRE, JULES. 2:91

LE MOYNE, CHARLES. 2:127

LE MOYNE, JEAN BAPTISTE. *Jean Baptiste Le Moyne, Sieur De Bienville*. Grace King. N. Y., 1892. 327 p. (Makers of America)

DLC, NN, MWA

LE MOYNE, PETER. 2:262

LENCLOS, NINON. 2:90

LENIN, NIKOLAI.

The Man Lenin. Isaac D. Levine. N. Y., 1924. 209 p.

DLC, NN, PU

Lenin. William C. White. N. Y., 1936. 172 p.

DLC, NN, PU

2:94

LEO XIII.

The Life and Life-Work of Pope Leo XIII. James J. McGovern. Chicago, 1903. 463 p. *DLC*

Life of Leo XIII: From an Authentic Furnished Memoir by His Order. Bernard O'Reilly. N. Y., 1887. 603 p. *DLC, NN, PU*

LEON, PONCE DE. *Juan Ponce de Leon*. F. A. Ober. N. Y. and London, 1908. 287 p. (Heroes of American History) *DLC, NN*

LEONARD, DANIEL. 0–43

LEONARD, JAMES FRANCIS. *Life of James Francis Leonard, the First Practical Sound Reader of the Morse Alphabet*. John W. Townsend. Louisville, 1909. 85 p. (Limited Ed.) (Filson Club Pub.)

DLC, NN, MWA, CSmH, PU, MiD:B, MiU:C

LEOPARDI, GIACOMO. 2:91

LEOPOLD I. 2:1

LESPINASSE, MLLE DE. 2:90

LETCHWORTH, WILLIAM PRYOR. *Life and Work of William P. Letch-worth.* Joseph N. Larned. Boston, 1912. 472 p. *DLC, NN, PU*

LE TOURNEUR, PIERRE. *Pierre Le Tourneur.* Mary G. Cushing. N. Y., 1908. 317 p. (Col. Univ. Studies in Romance) *DLC, NN, PU*

LEVETT, CHRISTOPHER. *Christopher Levett, of York, the Pioneer Colonist of Casco Bay.* James P. Baxter. Portland, Me., 1893. 166 p. (Gorges Soc., Pub., v. 5) *DLC, NN, MWA, CSmH, PU, MiD:B*

LEVILLE, JEAN BAPTISTE. 2:488

LEVY, SAMPSON. 2:110

LEWES, GEORGE. *George Lewes and George Eliot; a Review of Records.* Anna T. Kitchel. N. Y., 1933. 321 p. *DLC, NN, CSmH*

LEWGER, JOHN. *The First Catholic Secretary, John Lewger.* Sebastian Streeter. Balt., 1876. (Md. Hist. Soc. Fund—Publication No. 9. pp. 218–276) *NN, CSmH*

LEWIS, DIO. *Biography of Dio Lewis, M.D.* M. F. Eastman. N. Y., 1891. 398 p. *DLC, PU*

LEWIS, ELLIS. *Life of Chief Justice Ellis Lewis, 1798–1871.* Burton A. Konkle. Phila., 1907. 285 p. *DLC, NN, PU*
2:110

LEWIS, FRANCIS and MORGAN. *Biographies of Francis and Morgan Lewis.* Julia Delafield. N. Y., 1877. 2 vols.
DLC, NN, CSmH, MiD:B

LEWIS, MERIWETHER.
Lewis and Clark. William R. Lighton. Boston, 1901. 159 p. (Riverside Biographies) *DLC, NN*
Meriwether Lewis, of Lewis and Clark. Charles M. Wilson. N. Y., 1934. 305 p. *DLC, NN, CSmH, PU*
2:41–262–358
2:349

LEWIS, ROSA. *The Queen of Cooks and Some Kings.* Mary Lawton. N. Y., 1925. 208 p. *DLC, NN*

LEWIS, SAMUEL. *Biography of Samuel Lewis.* Wm. G. Lewis. Cincinnati, 1857. 429 p. *DLC, NN, MWA*

LEWIS, SINCLAIR. *Sinclair Lewis; a Biographical Sketch. With a Bibliography by Harvey Taylor.* Carl Van Doren. N. Y., 1933. 205 p. *DLC, NN, MWA, PU*
2:236–366

LEWIS, WILLIAM. 2:110

LEWISOHN, LUDWIG. . . . *Ludwig Lewisohn; the Artist and His Message*. Adolph Gillis. N. Y., 1933. 110 p.   *DLC, NN*

LEYPOLDT, FREDERICK. *Frederick Leypoldt. Biographical and Bibliographical Sketch*. Adolph Growoll. N. Y., 1898. 15 p. (Dibden Club Leaflets No. 2)   *NN*

LIBBEY, DAVID. *David Libbey, Penobscot Woodsman and River-Driver*. Fannie H. Eckstorm. Boston, 1907. 109 p. (True American Types)   *DLC*

LIEBER, FRANCIS.

Francis Lieber: His Life and Political Philosophy. L. R. Harley. N. Y., 1899. 213 p. (Columbia Univ. Press Series)
DLC, NN, CSmH

Life and Letters of Francis Lieber. Thomas S. Perry, ed. Boston, 1882. 439 p.   *DLC, NN, MWA, CSmH, PU, MiD:B*

LIGGETT, LOUIS KROH. *Rise and Fight Again; the Story of a Life-Long Friend*. Samuel Merwin. N. Y., 1935. 257 p.   *DLC, NN*

LILLIE, GORDON WILLIAM. *Pawnee Bill, His Experience and Adventures on the Western Plains; or, From the Saddle of a "Cowboy and Ranger" to the Chair of a "Bank President."* J. H. De Wolff. n.p., 1902. 108 p.   *DLC, NN*

LINCOLN, ABRAHAM.

Life of Abraham Lincoln. A. A. Abott. N. Y., 1864. 100 p.
DLC, NN, CSmH

Life of Abraham Lincoln . . . a Biographical Sketch of President Lincoln Taken From Abbott's "Lives of the Presidents" . . . John S. C. Abbott and R. H. Conwell. Chicago, n.d. 159 p.
DLC, NN, CSmH

The History of Abraham Lincoln and the Overthrow of Slavery. I. N. Arnold. Chicago, 1866. 736 p.
DLC, NN, MWA, CSmH, PU

Sketch of the Life of Abraham Lincoln. I. N. Arnold. N. Y., 1869. 75 p.   *DLC, NN, MWA, CSmH, MiD:B*

Life of Abraham Lincoln. Isaac N. Arnold. Chicago, 1885. 462 p.   *DLC, NN, CSmH*

Life of Abraham Lincoln, etc. Joseph H. Barrett. Cincinnati, 1865. 518 p.   *DLC, NN, CSmH*

Life of Abraham Lincoln. Joseph H. Barrett. Cincinnati, 1865. 842 p.   *DLC, NN, MWA, CSmH*

Life of Abraham Lincoln. Jos. H. Barrett and C. W. Brown. Chicago, 1902. 842 p. (Biographies of Famous Men)
DLC, NN, CSmH, RP:JCB

Abraham Lincoln and His Presidency. Jos. H. Barrett. Cincinnati, 1904. 2 vols.   *DLC, NN, CSmH*

The Life and Public Services of Abraham Lincoln . . . and A Biographical Sketch of Hon. Hannibal Hamlin. D. W. Bartlett. N. Y., 1860. 354 p.   *DLC, NN, MWA, CSmH, PU*

Life of Abraham Lincoln. William E. Barton. Indianapolis, 1925. 2 vols.   *DLC, NN, MWA, CSmH, PU*

President Lincoln. William E. Barton. Indianapolis, 1933. 2 vols.   *DLC, NN, CSmH, PU*

Abraham Lincoln . . . A Brief Biography. J. F. Beale. Phila., 1909. 48 p.   *DLC, NN, CSmH*

Abraham Lincoln, 1809–1858. Albert J. Beveridge. Boston, 1928. 2 vols.   *DLC, NN, MWA, CSmH, PU, MiD:B*

Life of Abraham Lincoln. H. B. Binns. N. Y., 1927. 379 p.   *DLC, NN, CSmH*

Abraham Lincoln, a Universal Man. Clark P. Bissett. San Francisco, 1923. 230 p.   *DLC, NN, CSmH*

Abraham Lincoln, the Type of American Genius. Rufus Blanchard. Wheaton, Ill., 1882. 141 p. (In Verse)   *NN, MWA, CSmH*

Abraham Lincoln. W. H. Branigan. Peterboro, N. H., 1909. 11 p.   *CSmH*

Life and Times of A. Lincoln. L. P. Brockett. Phila., 1865. 750 p.   *DLC, NN, MWA, CSmH*

Abraham Lincoln and the Downfall of American Slavery. Noah Brooks. N. Y., 1894. 471 p. (Heroes of the Nations Series)   *DLC, NN, CSmH*

Abraham Lincoln, His Youth and Early Manhood. With a Brief Account of His Later Life. Noah Brooks. N. Y., 1901. 204 p.   *DLC, NN, CSmH*

Every-Day Life of Abraham Lincoln. Francis F. Browne. Chicago, 1913. 622 p.   *DLC, NN, CSmH*

Abraham Lincoln and the Men of His Time. R. H. Browne. Cincinnati, 1901. 2 vols.   *DLC, NN, CSmH*

Lincoln. A. M. Bullock. Appleton, Wis., 1913. 156 p.   *DLC, CSmH*

Abraham Lincoln. J. E. Burton. Lake Geneva, Wis., 1903. 23 p.   *NN, CSmH*

Lincoln the Unknown. Dale Carnegie. N. Y., 1932. 305 p.   *DLC, NN, PU*

The Inner Life of Abraham Lincoln. Six Months At the White House. Francis B. Carpenter. N. Y., 1868. 359 p.

DLC, NN, MWA, CSmH, PU, MiD:B

Truth is Stranger Than Fiction; the True Genesis of a Wonderful Man. J. H. Cathey. Atlanta, 1899. 185 p. As: *The Genesis of Lincoln.* Atlanta, 1904. 307 p.   NN, CSmH, MiD:B

Lincoln, the Man of Sorrows. Eugene W. Chafin. Chicago, 1908. 97 p.   DLC, CSmH

Lincoln. A Psycho-Biography. L. Pierce Clark. N. Y., 1933. 570 p.   DLC, NN, CSmH, PU

Abraham Lincoln. C. C. Coffin. N. Y., 1893. 542 p.

DLC, NN, CSmH

Abraham Lincoln, a North Carolinian. James C. Coggins. Gastonia, N. C., 1927. 194 p.   DLC, NN

President Lincoln as War Statesman. Arthur L. Conger. Madison, 1916. 140 p.   DLC, NN

Abraham Lincoln: An Appreciation. B. R. Cowen. Cincinnati, 1909. 63 p.   NN, CSmH

Life of Abraham Lincoln. Frank Crosby. Phila., 1865. 476 p.

DLC, NN, MWA, CSmH, PU

The True Abraham Lincoln. William E. Curtis. Phila., 1903. 409 p.   DLC, NN, MWA, CSmH, PU

Abraham Lincoln. Ernest Foster. 1885. 128 p. (World's Workers Series)   DLC, CSmH

Abraham Lincoln, the Liberator. C. W. French. N. Y., 1891. 398 p. (American Reformers)   DLC, NN, CSmH

Abraham Lincoln. W. F. Gordy. N. Y., 1917. 266 p.

DLC, CSmH

Lincoln, the Man and the Statesman. Dwight Goss. Chicago, 1914. 61 p.   DLC, CSmH

The Story of Abraham Lincoln. Eleanor Gridley. Chicago, 1902. 355 p.   DLC, NN, CSmH

Abraham Lincoln; His Life and Public Services. Phoebe A. C. Hanaford. Boston, 1865. 216 p.   DLC, NN, MWA, CSmH

Abraham Lincoln: The Man of the People. Norman Hapgood. N. Y., 1899. 433 p.   DLC, NN, CSmH, MiD:B

Abraham Lincoln, the Great Commoner, the Sublime Emancipator. Franklin W. Hart. Pasadena, Calif., 1927. 274 p.

DLC, NN, CSmH

Herndon's Lincoln; The True Story of a Great Life . . . The History and Personal Recollections of Abraham Lincoln. William H. Herndon and Jesse W. Weik. Chicago, 1889. 3 v. [Various Incomplete Editions 1893–1930]   *DLC, CSmH, MiD:B*

Herndon's Life of Lincoln . . . Ed. by Paul M. Angle. N. Y., 1930. [Reprint of Original Ed.]   *DLC, NN, PU*

Abraham Lincoln; a New Portrait. Emanuel Hertz. N. Y., 1931. 2 vols.   *DLC, NN, MWA, CSmH, PU*

Lincoln, Emancipator of the Nation; a Narrative History of Lincoln's Boyhood and Manhood Based on His Own Writings. Frederick T. Hill. N. Y. and London, 1928. 284 p.
DLC, NN, CSmH, PU

Lincoln, the Lawyer. Frederick T. Hill. N. Y., 1906. 332 p.
DLC, NN, CSmH, PU

Abraham Lincoln, Man of God. John W. Hill. N. Y., 1920. 416 p.   *DLC, NN, CSmH*

Footprints of Abraham Lincoln. Jonathan T. Hobson. Dayton, 1909. 114 p.   *DLC, NN, CSmH*

Abraham Lincoln, the Politician and the Man. Raymond P. Holden. N. Y., 1929. 309 p.   *DLC, NN, MWA, CSmH*

The Life of Abraham Lincoln. J. G. Holland. Springfield, Mass., 1866. 544 p.   *DLC, NN, MWA, CSmH, PU, MiD:B*

The Life of Abraham Lincoln: With Extracts From His Speeches. J. Q. Howard. Columbus, 1860. 102 p.   *DLC, CSmH*

Lives and Speeches of Abraham Lincoln and Hannibal Hamlin. William D. Howells. Columbus, 1860. 406 p.   *DLC, NN, PU*

Abraham Lincoln. Robert G. Ingersoll. N. Y., 1907. 100 p.
DLC, NN, CSmH

The History of the Life, Administration and Times of Abraham Lincoln. J. R. Irelan. Chicago, 1888. 2 vols.
DLC, NN, MWA, CSmH

Abraham Lincoln. William Jayne. Chicago, 1908. 58 p.
NN, CSmH

Life of Abraham Lincoln. Henry Ketcham. N. Y., 1901. 435 p.
DLC, NN, CSmH, MiD:B

Life of Abraham Lincoln: From His Birth to His Inauguration as President. Ward H. Lamon. Boston, 1872. 547 p.
DLC, NN, MWA, CSmH

Recollections of Abraham Lincoln, 1847–1865. Ward H. Lamon. Chicago, 1895. 276 p. Wash., 1911. 337 p.
DLC, NN, CSmH, PU

Abraham Lincoln and the Abolition of Slavery in the United States. Charles G. Leland. N. Y., 1879. 246 p. (New Plutarch Series) DLC, NN, MWA, CSmH

Lincoln the Politician. T. A. Levy. Boston, 1918. 236 p. DLC, NN, CSmH

Set My People Free; a Negro's Life of Lincoln. William E. Lilly. N. Y., 1932. 269 p. DLC, NN

The Life Story of Abraham Lincoln. John D. Long. N. Y., 1930. 320 p. DLC, NN, MWA

Lincoln and His Generals. Clarence E. N. Macartney. N. Y., 1925. 226 p. DLC, NN, CSmH

Lincoln and His Cabinet. Clarence E. N. Macartney. N. Y., 1931. 366 p. DLC, NN, CSmH, PU

Lincoln as a Politician. Alexander K. McClure. Putnam, Conn., 1916. 21 p. (Privately Printed) DLC, CSmH

Lincoln, the Man of the People. W. H. Mace. Chicago, 1912. 191 p. DLC, CSmH

The Life and Public Services of Abraham Lincoln. Charles Maltby. Stockton, Cal., 1884. 326 p. DLC, NN, CSmH, MiD:B

Lincoln, the Man. Edgar L. Masters. N. Y., 1931. 520 p. DLC, NN, PU

The Life of Abraham Lincoln, In Verse. Stella T. Mathews. Seattle, 1923. 97 p. DLC

The Real Lincoln. C. L. C. Minor. Richmond, 1901, 1904. 66 p., 230 p. DLC, NN, MWA, CSmH, PU

Abraham Lincoln, the Man and the Crisis. Wilmot B. Mitchell. Portland, Me., 1910. 31 p. DLC, NN, CSmH

Abraham Lincoln, the Boy and the Man. James Morgan. N.Y., 1908. 435 p. DLC, NN, CSmH

Abraham Lincoln. John T. Morse, Jr. Boston and N. Y., 1893. 2 vols. (A.S.) DLC, NN, MWA, CSmH, PU, MiD:B

Abraham Lincoln. John G. Nicolay. Boston, 1882. 21 p. DLC, CSmH, MiD:B

Abraham Lincoln, a History. John G. Nicolay and John Hay. N. Y., 1890. 10 vols. DLC, NN, MWA, CSmH, PU, MiD:B

A Short Life of Abraham Lincoln; Condensed From Nicolay and Hay's Abraham Lincoln: A History. John G. Nicolay. N. Y., 1906. 578 p. DLC, NN, CSmH, PU

Abraham Lincoln. E. P. Oberholtzer. Phila., 1904. 389 p. (A.C.B.) DLC, NN, CSmH

Abraham Lincoln; A Short Study. Isaac N. Phillips. Bloomington, 1901. 62 p. *DLC, NN, CSmH*

Lincoln. I. N. Phillips. N. Y., 1910. 117 p.
DLC, NN, CSmH

Abraham Lincoln. His Life, Public Services, Death and Great Funeral Cortège. John C. Power. Springfield, Ill., 1882. 416 p.
DLC, MWA, CSmH

Abraham Lincoln . . . George H. Putnam. N. Y., 1909. 292 p.
DLC, NN, CSmH, PU

Life and Public Services of Abraham Lincoln. Henry J. Raymond. N. Y., 1865. 808 p.
DLC, NN, MWA, CSmH, PU, MiD:B

Abraham Lincoln. Whitelaw Reid. London, 1910. 50 p.
DLC, NN, CSmH, PU

Abraham Lincoln: The Lawyer-Statesman. John T. Richards. Boston, 1916. 260 p. *DLC, NN, CSmH*

Abraham Lincoln as a Man of Letters. Luther E. Robinson. N. Y., 1923. 344 p. *DLC, NN, CSmH, PU*

Lincoln, Master of Men. A Study in Character. Alonzo Rothschild. Boston, 1906. 531 p. *DLC, NN, CSmH, PU*

Abraham Lincoln: The Prairie Years. Carl Sandburg. N. Y., 1926. 2 vols. N. Y., 1926. 1 vol. Abridged Ed.
DLC, NN, MWA, CSmH, PU

Abraham Lincoln. A Biographical Essay . . . Carl Schurz. Boston, 1892. 134 p. *DLC, NN, MWA, CSmH, PU, MiD:B*

Life of Abraham Lincoln. John L. Scripps. Chicago, 1860. Detroit, 1900. 85 p. *DLC, NN, CSmH, MiD:B*

Lincoln, the Politician. Don C. Seitz. N. Y., 1931. 487 p.
DLC, NN, MWA, CSmH, PU

Abraham Lincoln; Profusely Illustrated With Contemporary Cartoons, Portraits and Scenes. Albert Shaw. N. Y., 1929. 2 vols. *DLC, NN, MWA, CSmH, PU*

The Lincoln Memorial; a Record of the Life, Assassination, and Obsequies of the Martyred President. John D. G. Shea, ed. N. Y., 1865. 288 p. *DLC, NN, MWA, CSmH, MiD:B*

The Life of Abraham Lincoln. R. D. Sheppard. Chicago, 1913. 179 p. *DLC, NN, CSmH*

Lincoln and the Doctors; a Medical Narrative of the Life of Abraham Lincoln. Milton H. Shutes. N. Y., 1933. 152 p.
DLC, NN, PU

Abraham Lincoln. Samuel G. Smith. N. Y., 1902. 31 p.
DLC, CSmH

Abraham Lincoln. An Interpretation in Biography. Denton J. Snider. St. Louis, 1908. 574 p.
DDLC, NN, CSmH, PU, MiD:B

Lincoln; an Account of His Personal Life, Especially of Its Springs of Action as Revealed and Deepened by the Ordeal of War. Nathaniel W. Stephenson. Indianapolis, 1922. 474 p. N. Y., 1924. 528 p.
DLC, NN, MWA, CSmH, PU

Abraham Lincoln: True Story of a Great Life. William O. Stoddard. N. Y., 1884. 508 p.
DLC, NN, CSmH

Abraham Lincoln and Andrew Johnson. William O. Stoddard. N. Y., 1888. 284 p.
DLC, NN, CSmH

Abraham Lincoln. Rose Strunsky. N. Y., 1914. 331 p.
DLC, NN, CSmH

Life of Abraham Lincoln. Ida Tarbell. N. Y., 1900, 1917, 1928. 2 vols.
DLC, NN, MWA, CSmH, PU, MiD:B

In the Footsteps of the Lincolns. Ida M. Tarbell. N. Y., 1924. 418 p.
DLC, NN

Early Life of Abraham Lincoln. Ida M. Tarbell and J. McC. Davis. N. Y., 1896. 240 p.
DLC, MWA, CSmH, MiD:B

From Pioneer Home to the White House. Life of Abraham Lincoln. William M. Thayer. Norwich, Conn., 1882. 469 p.
DLC, CSmH

Abraham Lincoln, the Pioneer Boy, and How He Became President; the Story of His Life. William M. Thayer. London, 1902. 395 p.
DLC, NN, CSmH

Abraham Lincoln, the First American. David D. Thompson. N. Y., 1894. 236 p.
DLC, NN, CSmH

Real Life of A. Lincoln. George A. Townsend. N. Y., 1867. 15 p.
DLC, NN, MWA, CSmH

Abraham Lincoln, Defendant. William H. Townsend. Boston, 1923. 40 p.
DLC, NN, CSmH

Lincoln, the Litigant. William H. Townsend. Boston, 1925. 116 p.
DLC, NN, MWA, CSmH

Lincoln, the Hoosier. Charles G. Vannest. St. Louis, 1928. 258 p.
DLC, NN, CSmH

The Private and Public Life of Abraham Lincoln. O. J. Victor. N. Y., 1864. 96 p.
DLC, NN, CSmH

The Prairie President; Living Through the Years With Lincoln, 1809–1861. Raymond Warren. Chicago, 1930. 427 p.
DLC, NN, CSmH

231

Real Lincoln; a Portrait. Jesse W. Weik. Boston, 1922. 323 p.
DLC, NN, CSmH
Abraham Lincoln. Daniel E. Wheeler. N. Y., 1916. 224 p.
DLC, NN, CSmH
Abraham Lincoln. Brand Whitlock. N. Y., 1909. 205 p.
(Beacon Biographies) *DLC, NN, CSmH*
Life of Lincoln. Henry C. Whitney. N. Y., 1908. 2 vols.
DLC, NN, CSmH, PU
Life on the Circuit With Lincoln. Henry C. Whitney. Boston,
1892. 601 p. *DLC, NN, CSmH*
2:2–6–77–107–109–114–264–329–386–435–624
LINCOLN, BENJAMIN. *Life of Benjamin Lincoln.* Francis Bowen.
(L.A.B.) *DLC, NN, MWA, CSmH*
LINCOLN, MARY TODD.
*Mrs. Abraham Lincoln; a Study of Her Personality and Her
Influence on Lincoln.* William A. Evans. N. Y., 1932. 364 p.
DLC, NN, CSmH, PU
Mary, Wife of Lincoln. Katherine Helm. N. Y., 1928. 309 p.
DLC, NN, MWA, CSmH, PU
*Mary Todd Lincoln; an Appreciation of the Wife of Abraham
Lincoln.* Honoré W. Morrow. N. Y., 1928. 248 p.
DLC, NN, PU
Mary Lincoln, Wife and Widow. Carl Sandburg and Paul M.
Angle. N. Y., 1932. 357 p. *DLC, NN, CSmH, PU*
LIND, JENNY.
Jenny Lind. Edward C. Wagenknecht. Boston, 1931. 230 p.
DLC, NN, PU
Memoranda of the Life of Jenny Lind. N. P. Willis. Phila.,
1851. 238 p. *DLC, NN*
LIND, JOHN. *John Lind of Minnesota.* George M. Stephenson. Min-
neapolis, 1935. 398 p. *DLC, NN, PU*
LINDBERGH, CHARLES AUGUSTUS.
*The Story of Lindbergh, the Lone Eagle, Including the Develop-
ment of Aviation, etc.* Richard J. Beamish. Phila., 1927. 288 p.
DLC, NN
Lindbergh, the Lone Eagle. George B. Fife. N. Y., 1933.
316 p. *DLC, NN*
The Lindberghs. Lynn Haines and D. B. Haines. N. Y., 1931.
307 p. *DLC, NN*
Charles Lindbergh, His Life. Dale Van Every and M. D. Tracy.
N. Y., 1927. 235 p. *DLC, NN*

The Lone Scout of the Sky; the Story of Charles A. Lindbergh.
James E. West. Phila., 1928. 275 p.   *DLC, NN*
     2:670–675

LINDSAY, VACHEL. *Vachel Lindsay, a Poet in America.* Edgar L.
Masters. N. Y., 1935. 392 p.   *DLC, NN, PU*

LINN, JOHN BLAIR. *Sketch of the Life and Character of John B. Linn.*
J. B. Linn. Phila., 1805. 24 p.   *PU*

LINN, LEWIS FIELDS. *Life and Public Services of Lewis F. Linn.*
Elizabeth A. Linn and Nathan Sargent. N. Y., 1857. 441 p.
     DLC, NN, MWA, CSmH

LINNÆUS, CARL. 2:79–335

LINNARD, ANNA JANE. *Memoir of Anna Jane Linnard.* Robert Baird.
Phila., 1835. 231 p.   *DLC, MiD:B*

LINTNER, JOSEPH ALBERT. *Memorial of Life and Entomologic Works
of Joseph Albert Lintner, Ph.D., State Entomologist, 1874–98.*
Ephraim P. Felt. Albany, 1899. 310 p.   *NN, PU*

LIPTON, SIR THOMAS. 2:425

LISZT, FRANZ. *Franz Liszt.* James G. Huneker. N. Y., 1911. 458 p.
     DLC, NN, CSmH, PU
     2:187

LITTLE, CHARLES JOSEPH. *In Memoriam. Charles Joseph Little.*
Charles M. Stuart. Chicago, 1912. 305 p.   *DLC, NN, MWA*

LITTLE CROW. 2:204

LITTLE, FERAMORZ. *Biographical Sketch of Feramorz Little.* James
A. Little. Salt Lake City, 1890. 191 p.   *NN*

LITTLE WOLF. 2:204

LIVERIGHT, HORACE. 2:236

LIVERMORE, GEORGE. *Memoir of George Livermore.* Charles Deane.
Cambridge, 1869. 60 p.
     NN, MWA, CSmH, MiD:B, MiU:C, RP:JCB

LIVINGSTON, CORA. 2:518

LIVINGSTON, EDWARD. *Life of Edward Livingston.* Charles H. Hunt.
N. Y., 1864. 448 p.   *DLC, NN, MWA, CSmH, PU, MiU:C*

LIVINGSTON, MRS. EDWARD. *Life of Mrs. Edward Livingston.* Louise
L. Hunt. N. Y., 1886. 182 p.   *DLC, NN, MWA*

LIVINGSTON, JOHN HENRY. *Memoirs of Rev. John H. Livingston.*
Alexander Gunn. N. Y., 1829. 540 p.
     DLC, NN, MWA, MiD:B

LIVINGSTON, WILLIAM. *Life and Letters of William Livingston.* Theodore Sedgwick. N. Y., 1833. 449 p.
     DLC, NN, MWA, CSmH, MiU:C

LIVINGSTONE, DAVID.

The Life and Labors of David Livingstone, LL.D., D.C.L. J.
E. Chambliss. Phila., 1875. 805 p. *DLC, NN, MWA*
*Lives and Travels of Livingstone and Stanley, Covering Their
Entire Career in Africa.* J. E. Chambliss, comp. Phila., 1881.
761 p. *DLC, NN*
David Livingstone, Explorer and Prophet. Charles J. Finger.
N. Y., 1927. 300 p. *DLC, NN, PU*
The Life and Explorations of David Livingstone, LL.D. John
S. Roberts. Boston, 1875. 384 p. *DLC, NN, MWA*
2:78

LLEWELLYN, MORRIS. *Morris Llewellyn of Haverford, 1647–1730.*
Morris L. Cooke. Phila., 1935. 19 p. (Privately Printed)
DLC, NN, MWA, CSmH

LLOYD, DAVID. 2:594

LLOYD, HENRY DEMAREST. *Henry Demarest Lloyd, 1847–1903: a
Biography.* Caroline A. Lloyd. N. Y., 1912. 2 vols.
DLC, NN, PU

LLOYD, THOMAS. 2:594

LOBDELL, HENRY. *Memoir of Henry Lobdell, M.D., Late Missionary
. . . at Mosul.* W. S. Tyler. Boston, 1859. 414 p. *MWA*

LOBO, FATHER JEROME. 2:680

LOCHMAN, GEORGE. 2:294

LOCKE, DAVID. [PETROLEUM V. NASBY] See NASBY, PETROLEUM V.

LOCKHART, JOHN WASHINGTON. *Sixty Years on the Brazos; the Life
and Letters of Dr. John Washington Lockhart, 1824–1900.* Mrs.
Jonnie L. Wallis and Laurance L. Hill. Los Angeles, 1930. 336 p.
DLC, NN

LOCKWOOD, J. D. *Memoirs of J. D. Lockwood.* Peter Lockwood.
N. Y., 1852. 231 p.

LOCKWOOD, JAMES BOOTH. *Farthest North; or, the Life and Explorations of Lt. James B. Lockwood, of the Greely Arctic Expedition.*
Charles Lanman. N. Y., 1885. 333 p. *DLC, NN, MWA, MiD:B*

LOCKWOOD, PETER. *Memorials of Rev. Peter Lockwood of Binghamp-
ton.* Peter Lockwood. N. Y., 1885. 101 p. *DLC, NN*

LODGE, GEORGE CABOT. *The Life of George Cabot Lodge.* Henry
Adams. Boston, 1911. 206 p. *DLC, NN, MWA, PU*

LODGE, HENRY CABOT.

Henry Cabot Lodge, the Statesman. Charles S. Grover. Boston, 1925. 152 p. *DLC, NN, MWA, PU*

Henry Cabot Lodge; a Biographical Sketch. William Lawrence. Boston, 1925. 203 p. *DLC, NN, MWA, CSmH*

LODGE, THOMAS.

Thomas Lodge; the History of an Elizabethan. Nathaniel B. Paradise. New Haven, 1931. 254 p. *DLC, NN, CSmH, PU*

Thomas Lodge. Edward A. Tenney. Ithaca, N. Y., 1935. 202 p. (Cornell Studies in English) *DLC, NN, CSmH, PU* 2:604

LOFLAND, JOHN. *The Life of John Lofland, " The Milford Bard," the Earliest and Most Distinguished Poet of Delaware.* William S. Smithers. Phila., 1894. 311 p. *DLC, MWA, PU*

LOGAN, CAPTAIN. *Captain Logan, Blair County's Indian Chief, a Biography.* H. W. Shoemaker. Altoona, Pa., 1915. 40 p. *DLC, PU*

LOGAN, GEORGE. *Memoir of Dr. George Logan of Stenton.* Deborah N. Logan. Phila., 1899. 207 p. *DLC, NN, MWA, PU, MiD:B*

LOGAN, JAMES. *Life and Public Services of James Logan.* Irma J. Cooper. N. Y., 1921. 77 p. (Col. Univ. Studies) *DLC, NN, MWA, CSmH, PU* 2:594

LOGAN, JOHN. *Logan the Mingo.* Franklin B. Sawvel. Boston, 1921. 110 p. *DLC*

LOGAN, JOHN ALEXANDER.

Life of Gen. John A. Logan. G. F. Dawson. Chicago, 1884. 580 p. *DLC, NN, MWA, CSmH, MiD:B*

Biographical Memoir of J. A. Logan in " Volunteer Soldier of America." C. A. Logan. Chicago, 1887. 706 p. *DLC, MWA*

See BLAINE, JAMES G.

LOINES, RUSSELL HILLARD. *Russell Hillard Loines, 1874–1922.* N. Y., 1927. 268 p. (Privately Printed) *MWA*

LONDON, JACK. *Book of Jack London.* Charmian K. London. N. Y., 1921. 2 vols. *DLC, NN, CSmH, PU*

LONDON, MEYER. *East Side Epic; the Life and Work of Meyer London.* Harry Ragoff. N. Y., 1930. 311 p. *DLC, NN*

LONG, CRAWFORD WILLIAMSON. *Crawford W. Long and the Discovery of Ether Anesthesia.* Frances L. Taylor. N. Y., 1928. 237 p. *DLC, NN, PU*

LONG, ENOCH. *Sketch of Enoch Long: an Illinois Pioneer.* Harvey Reid. Chicago, 1884. 134 p. *DLC, NN, MWA, CSmH*

LONG, HUEY PIERCE.

The Story of Huey P. Long. Carleton Beals. Phila., 1935. 414 p. *DLC, NN, PU*

Huey Long; a Candid Biography; With a Digest of the Share-Our-Wealth Principles Prepared by Senator Huey P. Long. Forrest Davis. N. Y., 1935. 312 p. *DLC, NN, PU*

The Kingfish, a Biography of Huey P. Long. Webster Smith. N. Y., 1933. 286 p. *DLC, NN*

LONG, MARY ELITCH. *The Lady of the Gardens, Mary Elitch Long.* Caroline L. Dier. Hollywood, 1932. 305 p. *DLC, NN*

LONGFELLOW, HENRY WADSWORTH.

Henry Wadsworth Longfellow: His Life, His Works, His Friendships. G. L. Austin. Boston, 1883. 419 p. *DLC, MWA, CSmH*

Longfellow, 1807–1882. H. S. Burrage, comp. Portland, Me., 1882. 171 p. *DLC, NN*

Henry Wadsworth Longfellow. George R. Carpenter. Boston, 1901. 150 p. (Beacon Biographies) *DLC, NN, PU*

H. W. Longfellow. Thomas Davidson. Boston, 1882. 17 p. *DLC*

Life and Works of Henry W. Longfellow. D. G. Dexter. Cambridge, 1882. 80 p. *DLC, MWA*

A Victorian American, Henry Wadsworth Longfellow. Herbert S. Gorman. N. Y., 1926. 363 p. *DLC, NN, MWA, CSmH, PU*

New Light on Longfellow, With Special Reference to His Relations to Germany. James T. Hatfield. Boston, 1933. 186 p. *DLC, NN, CSmH, PU*

Henry Wadsworth Longfellow. Thomas W. Higginson. Boston, 1902. 336 p. (A.M.L.) *DLC, NN, MWA, CSmH, PU*

Henry W. Longfellow: Biography, Anecdote, Letters, Criticism. W. S. Kennedy. Cambridge, 1882. 368 p. *DLC, MW,, CSmH, PU*

Life of Henry Wadsworth Longfellow, With Extracts From His Journals and Correspondence. Samuel Longfellow. Boston, 1886. 2 vols. Boston, 1891. 3 vols. *DLC, NN, MWA, CSmH, PU*

Henry Wadsworth Longfellow; a Sketch of His Life. Charles E. Norton. Boston, 1907. 121 p. *DLC, NN, MWA, CSmH, PU*

Memoir of Henry Wadsworth Longfellow. Horace E. Scudder. (Mass. Hist. Soc. Proc. vol. 8, 1892. pp. 152–167) *DLC, NN, MWA, CSmH*

Henry Wadsworth Longfellow. A Medley in Prose and Verse. Richard H. Stoddard. N. Y., 1882. 251 p. *DLC, CSmH*

Longfellow and Other Essays. William P. Trent. N. Y., 1910. 244 p. *DLC, NN, CSmH, PU*

The Life of Henry Wadsworth Longfellow; With Critical and Descriptive Sketches of His Writings. F. H. Underwood. Boston, 1882. 355 p.   DLC, NN, MWA, PU
  2:87

LONGFELLOW, SAMUEL. *Memoirs and Letters of Samuel Longfellow.* J. May, ed. Boston, 1894. 306 p.   DLC, NN, CSmH

LONGSTREET, AUGUSTUS BALDWIN. *Augustus Baldwin Longstreet; a Study of The Development of Culture in the South.* J. D. Wade. N. Y., 1924. 392 p.   DLC, NN, CSmH, PU
  2:493

LONGSTREET, JAMES. *James Longstreet, Lee's War Horse.* H. J. Eckenrode and Bryan Conrad. Chapel Hill, 1936. 399 p.
          DLC, NN, CSmH, PU
  2:88–612

LONGUEUIL, LE MOYNE. 2:127

LONGWORTH, NICHOLAS. *The Making of Nicholas Longworth. Annals of an American Family.* Clara L. De Chambrun. N. Y., 1933. 322 p.   DLC, NN, MWA

LOOMIS, HENRY. *Henry Loomis, Friend of the East.* Clara D. Loomis. N. Y., 1923. 150 p.   DLC, NN

LORD, JOHN. *Life of John Lord.* Alexander S. Twombly. N. Y., 1896. 326 p.   DLC

LORD, PAULINE. 2:592

LORRAINE, CLAUDE. *Claude Lorraine.* Moses F. Sweetser. Boston, 1878. 154 p.   DLC, NN, CSmH

LOTHROP, SAMUEL KIRKLAND. *Some Reminiscences of the Life of Samuel K. Lothrop.* Thornton K. Lothrop, ed. Cambridge, 1888. 266 p.   DLC, NN, MiD:B

LOUGHLIN, JOHN. *Golden Jubilee Celebration of the Rt. Rev. John Loughlin . . . First Bishop of Brooklyn, Oct. 18th, 1890 . . .* James H. Mitchell. Brooklyn, 1891. 238 p.   NN

LOUIS XIV. *History of Louis XIV.* J. S. C. Abbott. N. Y., 1870. 410 p.   DLC, NN

LOUIS XVII. *The Son of Marie Antoinette.* Meade Minnigerode. N. Y., 1934. 400 p.   DLC, NN

LOUIS PHILIPPE. *The Rise and Fall of Louis Philippe Ex-King of the French.* Ben Perley Poore. Boston, 1848. 316 p. DLC, MWA
  2:1

LOUIS, JOE. *Joe Louis, Man and Super-Fighter.* Edward Van Every. N. Y., 1936. 183 p.   DLC, NN

LOVEJOY, ELIJAH PARISH.
Memoir of the Rev. Elijah P. Lovejoy . . . Joseph C. Lovejoy.
N. Y., 1838. 382 p. *DLC, NN, MWA, CSmH, PU, MiD:B*
*The Martyrdom of Lovejoy. An Account of the Life, Trials and
Perils of Rev. Elijah P. Lovejoy.* Henry Tanner. Chicago, 1881.
233 p. *DLC, NN, MWA, CSmH*
LOW, SETH. *Seth Low.* Benjamin R. C. Low. N. Y., 1925. 92 p.
DLC, NN
LOWE, CHARLES. *Memoir of Charles Lowe.* Martha P. Lowe. Bos-
ton, 1884. 596 p. *DLC, NN, MWA, CSmH*
LOWELL, AMY.
*Amy Lowell, a Chronicle, With Extracts From Her Correspond-
ence.* S. Foster Damon. Boston, 1935. 773 p.
DLC, NN, CSmH, PU
Amy Lowell. Clement Wood. N. Y., 1926. 185 p.
DLC, NN, PU
2:592
LOWELL, CHARLES RUSSELL. *Life and Letters of Charles Russell
Lowell.* Edward W. Emerson. Boston and N. Y., 1907. 499 p.
DLC, NN, MWA, CSmH, PU
LOWELL, JAMES RUSSELL.
Life of James Russell Lowell. Emma E. Brown. Boston, 1887.
321 p. *DLC, NN*
James Russell Lowell. His Life and Work. Ferris Greenslet.
Boston, 1905. 309 p. (A.M.L.) *DLC, NN, CSmH, PU*
James Russell Lowell. Edward Everett Hale. Boston, 1899.
128 p. (Beacon Biographies) *DLC, NN, PU*
James Russell Lowell and His Friends. Edward E. Hale. Bos-
ton, 1899. 303 p. *DLC, NN, MWA, CSmH, PU, MiD:B*
Memoir of James Russell Lowell. Abbott L. Lowell. Cam-
bridge, 1896. 27 p. (Proc. Mass. Hist. Soc., 2nd Series, v. XI.
Cambridge, 1896) *NN, MWA, CSmH, PU*
James Russell Lowell: A Biography. Horace E. Scudder. Bos-
ton, 1901. 2 vols. *DLC, NN, MWA, CSmH, PU*
James Russell Lowell; a Biographical Sketch. F. H. Under-
wood. Boston, 1882. 167 p. *DLC, NN, PU*
*The Poet and the Man; Recollections and Appreciations of
James Russell Lowell.* F. H. Underwood. Boston, 1893. 138 p.
DLC, NN, PU
2:40

LOWELL, PERCIVAL. *Biography of Percival Lowell.* A. Lawrence Lowell. N. Y., 1935. 212 p.   *DLC, NN, PU*

LOWNDES, WILLIAM. *Life and Times of William Lowndes of South Carolina.* Harriott H. R. Ravenel. Boston, 1901. 257 p.
  DLC, NN, MWA, CSmH, PU

LOWRIE, LOUISA A. *Memoir of Mrs. Louisa A. Lowrie, of the Northern India Mission.* Ashbel G. Fairchild. Phila., 1837. 221 p.
  DLC, NN

LOWRIE, WALTER. *Memoirs of the Hon. Walter Lowrie.* John C. Lowrie. N. Y., 1896. 192 p.   *NN, MiD:B*

LOYOLA, IGNATIUS.
  Ignatius Loyola: a General in the Church Militant . . . Robert Harvey. Milwaukee, 1936. 273 p.   *DLC, NN*
  Ignatius Loyola; an Attempt at an Impartial Biography. Henry D. Sedgwick. N. Y., 1923. 399 p.   *DLC, NN*
  Ignatius Loyola; the Founder of the Jesuits. Paul Van Dyke. N. Y., 1926. 381 p.   *DLC, NN, PU*
  2:680

LUBIN, DAVID. *David Lubin: a Study in Practical Idealism.* Olivia R. Agresti. Boston, 1922. 372 p.   *DLC, NN, CSmH*

LUCAS, ROBERT.
  Robert Lucas. John C. Parish. Iowa City, 1907. 356 p. (Iowa Biographical Series)   *DLC, NN, MWA, CSmH*
  Biography of Gen. Robert Lucas. Caleb Stark. Columbus, 1908. 12 p. (In Ohio Archaeological and Hist. Quarterly v. 17. pp. 160–172)   *NN, MWA, CSmH*

LUCE, STEPHEN BLEECKER. *Life and Letters of Stephen B. Luce, Rear-Admiral, U. S. N.* Albert Gleaves. Annapolis, 1925. 381 p.
  DLC, NN, MWA, PU

LUCIAN. *Lucian, Satirist and Artist.* Francis G. Allinson. N. Y., 1926. 204 p. (Our Debt to Greece and Rome)
  DLC, NN, CSmH

LUCKNER, FELIX. *Count Luckner, the Sea Devil.* Lowell J. Thomas. N. Y., 1927. 308 p.   *DLC, NN, MWA, PU*

LUDINGTON, HENRY. *Colonel Henry Ludington.* A Memoir. Willis F. Johnson. N. Y., 1907. 235 p.   *DLC, NN*

LUDLOW, ISRAEL. *Sketch of the Life and Times of Col. Israel Ludlow, One of the Original Proprietors of Cincinnati . . .* Henry B. Teetor. Cincinnati, 1885. 52 p.   *NN, MWA, MiD:B*

LUDLOW, ROGER. *Roger Ludlow, the Colonial Lawmaker.* John M. Taylor. N. Y., 1900. 166 p.   *DLC, NN, MWA, CSmH*

LUDWICK, CHRISTOPHER. *An Account of the Life and Character of Christopher Ludwick . . . Baker-General of the Army of the United States During the Revolutionary War.* Benjamin Rush. Phila., 1801. Rev. Ed. 1831. 61 p.

> DLC, NN, MWA, PU, MiD:B, MiU:C

2:225

LUKE, FRANK. *Balloon Buster; Frank Luke of Arizona.* Norman S. Hall. N. Y., 1928. 191 p.   *DLC, NN*

LUNA Y ARELLANO, TRISTAN DE. *Tristan de Luna, Conquistador of the Old South; a Study of Spanish Imperial Strategy.* Herbert I. Priestley. Glendale, Calif., 1936. 215 p.

> DLC, NN, MWA, CSmH

LUNDY, BENJAMIN. *Life, Travels and Opinions of Benjamin Lundy.* Phila., 1847. 316 p.   *NN, MWA, CSmH, PU, MiD:B*

LUNGREN, FERNAND H. *Fernand Lungren.* John Berger. Santa Barbara, 1936. 347 p.   *CSmH*

LURTING, THOMAS. 2:55

LUTHER, KATHERINE. *Katherine Luther of the Wittenberg Parsonage.* Clara L. Dentler. Phila., 1924. 150 p.   *DLC, NN*

LUTHER, MARTIN.

Martin Luther, Oak of Saxony. Edwin P. Booth. N. Y., 1933. 271 p.   *DLC, NN, PU*

Young Luther; the Intellectual and Religious Development of Martin Luther to 1518. Robert H. Fife. N. Y., 1928. 232 p.

> DLC, NN

Martin Luther; the Formative Years, Being the Story of the First Thirty-Four Years of His Life. Barend K. Kuiper. Grand Rapids, Mich., 1933. 298 p.   *DLC, NN*

The Life and Times of Martin Luther. Hannah F. S. Lee. Boston, 1839. 324 p.   *NN, MWA*

Martin Luther, Germany's Angry Man. Abram Lipsky. N. Y., 1933. 305 p.   *DLC, NN, PU*

Martin Luther: The Man and His Work. Arthur C. McGiffert. N. Y., 1911. 397 p.   *DLC, NN, PU*

The Facts About Luther. Patrick F. O'Hare. N. Y., 1916. 367 p.   *DLC, NN*

The Life of Luther. Barnas Sears. Phila., 1850. 486 p.

> NN, MWA, PU

Martin Luther. Elsie Singmaster. Boston, 1917. 138 p.

> DLC, NN

Life and Letters of Martin Luther. Preserved Smith. Boston, 1911. 490 p.   *DLC, NN, PU*

The Conservative Character of Martin Luther. George M. Stephenson. Phila., 1921. 143 p.   *DLC, NN*
  2:205–330–371

LUZZATTO, MOSES CHAIM. *A Modern Hebrew Poet: Life and Writings of Moses Chaim Luzzatto.* A. S. Isaacs. N. Y., 1878. 73 p.
  NN

LYELL, SIR CHARLES. 2:79

LYLY, JOHN. 2:604

LYMAN, THEODORE. *Theodore Lyman, (1833–1897) and Robert C. Winthrop, Jr. (1834–1905). Two Memoirs.* Charles F. Adams, Jr. Cambridge, 1906. 200 p.   *DLC, MiD:B*
  2:295

LYNNE, MARY. 2:337

LYON, MARY.
  Life of Mary Lyon. Beth B. Gilchrist. Boston, 1910. 462 p.
  DLC, NN, PU

  The Power of Christian Benevolence, Illustrated in the Life and Labors of Mary Lyon. Edward Hitchcock. Northampton, Mass., 1851. 486 p.   *DLC, NN, MWA, PU, MiD:B*
  2:9–92–326–506

LYON, MATTHEW. *Matthew Lyon, the Hampden of Congress.* James F. McLaughlin. N. Y., 1900. 531 p.
  DLC, NN, MWA, CSmH, MiD:B

LYON, NATHANIEL.
  The Last Political Writings of Gen. Nathaniel Lyon, U. S. A., With a Sketch of His Life and Military Service. N. Y., 1861. 275 p.   *NN, MWA, CSmH, MiD:B*

  Gen. Nathaniel Lyon ... James Peckham. N. Y., 1866. 447 p.
  CSmH

  Life of General Nathaniel Lyon. Ashbel Woodward. Hartford, 1862. 360 p.   *NN, MWA, CSmH, MiD:B*

MABIE, CATHERINE L. 2:237

MABIE, HAMILTON WRIGHT. *Life and Letters of Hamilton Wright Mabie.* Edwin W. Morse. N. Y., 1920. 344 p.
  DLC, NN, CSmH, PU

McADOO, WILLIAM GIBBS. *McAdoo, the Man and His Times; a Panorama in Democracy.* Mary Synon. Indinapolis, 1924. 355 p.
  DLC, NN, CSmH, PU

McALL, ROBERT WHITAKER. *Robert Whitaker McAll, Founder of the McAll Mission, Paris.* Mrs. R. W. McAll. London, 1896. 252 p. NN, MWA, PU

McARTHUR, DUNCAN. 2:424

MACAULAY, THOMAS. *Lord Macaulay. His Life—His Writings.* Charles H. Jones. N. Y., 1880. 247 p. DLC, NN

McBURNEY, ROBERT ROSS. *Life of Robert R. McBurney.* Lawrence L. Doggett. Cleveland, 1902. 280 p.
DLC, NN, CSmH, PU, MiD:B

McCABE, CHARLES CARDWELL. *Life of Chaplain McCabe.* Frank M. Bristol. N. Y., 1908. 416 p. DLC, NN

McCABE, WILLIAM GORDON. *Memories and Memorials of William Gordon McCabe.* Armistead C. Gordon. Richmond, 1925. 2 vols. DLC, NN, MiD:B
2:558

McCALL, SAMUEL WALKER. *Samuel W. McCall, Governor of Massachusetts.* Lawrence B. Evans. Boston, 1916. 241 p.
DLC, NN, MWA, PU, MiD:B

McCARTEE, DIVIE BETHUNE. *A Missionary Pioneer in the Far East; a Memorial of Divie Bethune McCartee . . .* Robert E. Speer, ed. N. Y., 1922. 224 p. DLC, NN, PU

McCLELLAN, GEORGE. *Memoir of George McClellan, M.D.* William Darrach. Phila., 1847. 40 p. DLC, MiD:B

McCLELLAN, GEORGE BRINTON.
George Brinton McClellan, From Cadet to Major-General. Markinfield Addey. N. Y., 1864. 352 p. DLC, NN, MWA
McClellan, a Vindication of the Military Career of Gen. George B. McClellan. James H. Campbell. N. Y., 1916. 458 p.
DLC, NN, CSmH, PU
Life of George B. McClellan. Alexander Delmar. N. Y., 1864. 109 p. DLC
Life and Campaigns of George B. McClellan. G. S. Hillard. Phila., 1864. 396 p. DLC, NN, MWA, CSmH, PU, MiD:B
The Life of Maj.-Gen. George B. McClellan, General-in-Chief, U. S. A. Louis Legrand [Orville J. Victor]. N. Y., 1862. 98 p.
DLC, MWA
General McClellan. Peter S. Michie. N. Y., 1901. 489 p.
(G.C.) DLC, NN, CSmH
A Study in Personality, General George Brinton McClellan.

William S. Myers. N. Y., 1934. 520 p. *DLC, NN, CSmH, PU*
The Life of Major-Gen. George B. McClellan. Orville J. Victor.
N. Y., 1861. 98 p. (Beadle's Dime Biographical Library)
DLC, NN, CSmH
2:96–590

McCLELLAN, JAMES E. *The Christian Patriot: a Biography of James E. McClellan.* Gilbert Robbins. Worcester, 1865. 127 p.
NN, MWA

McCLOSKEY, JOHN. *The Life of John, Cardinal McCloskey, First Prince of the Church in America.* John, Cardinal Farley. N. Y., 1918. 401 p. *DLC, NN*
2:679

McCOMBS, WILLIAM FRANK. *William F. McCombs, the President Maker.* Maurice F. Lyons. Cincinnati, 1922. 147 p.
DLC, NN

McCORKLE, SAMUEL EUSEBIUS. *The Prophet of Zion-Parnassus, Samuel Eusebius McCorkle.* James F. Hurley and Julia G. Eagan. Richmond, 1934. 121 p. *DLC, NN, CSmH*

McCORMICK, ADRIAN IGNATIUS. *"Once Upon a Time," Being the Life of Adrian Ignatius McCormick, of the Society of Jesus.* David P. McAstocker. Boston, 1924. 238 p. *DLC, NN*

McCORMICK, CYRUS HALL.
In Memoriam. Cyrus Hall McCormick, 1809–1884. Cambridge, 1884. 143 p.
Cyrus Hall McCormick, His Life and Work. Herbert N. Casson. Chicago, 1909. 264 p. *DLC, NN, MWA, PU, MiD:B*
Cyrus Hall McCormick: Seed-Time, 1809–1856. William T. Hutchinson. N. Y., 1930. 493 p. Vol. 1.
DLC, NN, MWA, CSmH, PU, MiD:B
Cyrus Hall McCormick; Harvest, 1856–1884. William T. Hutchinson. N. Y., 1935. 793 p. Vol. 2.
DLC, NN, MWA, CSmH, PU, MiD:B
Cyrus Hall McCormick and the Reaper. Reuben G. Thwaites. Madison, 1909. 259 p. *CSmH*
2:343

McCOSH, JAMES. *The Life of James McCosh. A Record Chiefly Autobiographical.* William M. Sloane, ed. N. Y., 1896. 287 p.
DLC, NN, CSmH
2:326

McCOY, GEORGE WALTER. 2:175.

McCOY, ISAAC. *Isaac McCoy.* Walter N. Wyeth. Phila., 1895. 236 p. *CSmH*

McCoy, William. *The Real McCoy.* Frederic F. Van de Water. Garden City, N. Y., 1931. 305 p. *DLC, NN*

MacCracken, Henry Mitchell. *Henry Mitchell MacCracken; in Memoriam.* N. Y., 1923. 81 p. *DLC, NN, PU*

McCrea, Jane. *The Life of Jane McCrea.* David Wilson. N. Y., 1853. 155 p. *DLC, NN, MWA, MiD:B*

McCullagh, John. *"The Sunday School Man of the South."* A Sketch of the Life and Labors of the Rev. John McCullagh. Joseph H. McCullagh. Phila., 1889. 189 p. *NN, PU*

McCulloch, Ben. *The Life and Services of Gen. Ben McCulloch.* Victor M. Rose. Phila., 1888. 260 p. *DLC, NN*

McCulloch, Sam. 2:358

McCullough, John. *John McCullough as Man, Actor and Spirit.* Susie C. Clark. N. Y., 1914. 368 p. *NN*

McDaniel, George White. *George White McDaniel.* Martha D. S. McDaniel. Nashville, 1928. 256 p. *NN*

MacDonald, Flora. *Flora MacDonald; a History and a Message.* James A. MacDonald. Wash., 1916. 32 p. *DLC, NN, MWA*

McDonald, William. *Capt. Bill McDonald, Texas Ranger.* Albert B. Paine. N. Y., 1909. 448 p. *DLC, NN, CSmH*

McDonald, William Madison. *Life of William Madison McDonald, Ph.D.* William O. Bundy. Fort Worth, Tex., 1925. 333 p. *DLC, NN*

Macdonell, Alexander. *Life and Times of . . . Alexander Macdonell.* H. J. Somers. Wash., 1931. 232 p. *CSmH*

McDonogh, John. *Life and Work of John McDonogh.* William Allan. Balt., 1886. 105 p. *DLC, NN, MWA, PU, MiD:B*

MacDonough, Thomas. *Life of Commodore Thomas MacDonough, U. S. N.* Rodney MacDonough. Boston, 1909. 313 p. *DLC, NN, CSmH, MiD:B*
2:396

MacDowell, Edward.
Edward MacDowell. Laurence Gilman. N. Y., 1906. 80 p. (Living Masters of Music) *NN, PU*
Edward MacDowell: a Study. Laurence Gilman. N. Y., 1909. 190 p. *DLC, NN, PU*
Edward MacDowell, His Work and His Ideals. Elizabeth F. Page. N. Y., 1910. 85 p. *DLC, NN*
2:114

McDowell, Ephraim. *Biography of Ephraim McDowell, M.D.* Mary Y. Ridenbough. N. Y., 1890. 558 p. *DLC, NN, PU*

McDOWELL, JOHN and WILLIAM ANDERSON. *Memoirs of the Rev. John McDowell, D.D., and the Rev. William A. McDowell, D.D.* William B. Sprague. N. Y., 1864. 305 p.   *DLC, NN, MWA*

McDOWELL, MARY. *Mary McDowell, Neighbor.* Howard E. Wilson. Chicago, 1928. 235 p.   *DLC, NN*

McDUFFIE, GEORGE. *George McDuffie . . .* Edwin L. Green. Columbia, S. C., 1936. 262 p.   *DLC, NN, CSmH*
    2:431

McELLIONNEY, JOHN. *Recollections of the Rev. John McEllionney, D.D.* Rose W. Fry. Richmond, 1893. 291 p.   *NN*

MacENERY, JOHN. 2:680

MACFADDEN, BERNARR.
    True Story of Bernarr Macfadden. Fulton Oursler. N. Y., 1929. 281 p.   *DLC, NN, MWA*
    Bernarr Macfadden; a Study in Success. Clement Wood. N. Y., 1929. 316 p.   *DLC, NN, MWA*
    2:546

McFERRIN, JOHN BERRY. *John B. McFerrin. A Biography.* O. P. Fitzgerald. Nashville, 1888. 448 p.   *DLC, NN, MWA*

McGARVEY, WILLIAM. *William McGarvey and the Open Pulpit.* Edward Hawks. Phila., 1935. 258 p.   *DLC, NN*

McGEE, THOMAS D'ARCY. *Poems by T. D'A. McGee. With an Introduction and Biography.* Mrs. J. Sadlier. N. Y., 1869. 612 p.   *DLC, NN*

McGEE, WILLIAM JOHN. *Life of W. J. McGee, Distinguished Geologist, Ethnologist, Anthropologist, Hydrologist, etc., in Service of U. S. Government, With Extracts From Addresses and Writings.* Emma R. McGee. Farley, Ia., 1915. 240 p.   (Privately Printed)   *DLC, NN*

McGIFFIN, PHILO NORTON. 2:172

McGILLIVRAY, ALEXANDER. 2:135

McGLYNN, EDWARD. *Dr. Edward McGlynn.* Sylvester L. Malone, ed. N. Y., 1918. 135 p.   *DLC, NN*

McGUFFEY, WILLIAM HOLMES. *William Holmes McGuffey . . .* H. C. Minnich. N. Y., 1936. 203 p.   *DLC, NN, CSmH*

MACHEBEUF, JOSEPH PROJECTUS. *Life of the Rev. Joseph P. Machebeuf, D.D., Pioneer Priest of Ohio, of New Mexico, of Colorado; etc.* William J. Howlett. Pueblo, Colo., 1908. 419 p.   *DLC, NN, CSmH*

McHENRY, JAMES. *Sketch of the Life of Dr. James McHenry.* F. J. Brown. Balt., 1877. 44 p.   (Md. Hist. Soc. Fund-Pub. v. 10)   *DLC, NN, CSmH, PU*

McHENRY, JAMES. *Life and Correspondence of James McHenry, Secretary of War Under Washington and Adams.* Bernard C. Steiner. Cleveland, 1907. 640 p. *DLC, NN, MWA, CSmH, PU, MiD:B* 2:218

MACHIAVELLI, NICCOLÒ. 2:573

McINTIRE, SAMUEL. *Wood-Carver of Salem: Samuel McIntire; His Life and Work.* Frank Cousins and P. M. Riley. Boston, 1916. 168 p. *DLC, NN, MWA*

MACIVER, HENRY RONALD. *Soldier of Fortune. Life and Adventures of Gen. Henry R. Maciver.* J. W. McDonald. N. Y., 1888. 331 p. *NN, CSmH* 2:172

MACKAYE, STEELE. *Epoch; the Life of Steele Mackaye, Genius of the Theatre, in Relation to His Times and Contemporaries; a Memoir by His Son.* Percy Mackaye. N. Y., 1927. 2 vols. *DLC, NN, PU*

McKEAN, THOMAS. *Life of Hon. Thomas McKean . . .* Roberdeau Buchanan. Lancaster, Pa., 1890. 136 p. *DLC, NN, MWA, PU, MiD:B* 2:110

McKENNA, CHARLES HYACINTH. *Very Rev. Charles Hyacinth McKenna, O.P., P.G., Missionary and Apostle of the Holy Name Society.* Victor F. O'Daniel. N. Y., 1917. 409 p. *DLC, NN*

McKENZIE, ALEXANDER. *Life and Times of Alexander McKenzie.* Raymond Calkins. Cambridge, 1935. 455 p. *DLC, NN, CSmH, PU*

MacKENZIE, JOHN KENNETH. 2:237

McKIM, CHARLES FOLLEN.
Charles F. McKim; a Study of His Life and Work. Alfred H. Granger. Boston and N. Y., 1913. 145 p. *DLC, NN, PU*
Life and Times of Charles Follen McKim. Charles Moore. Boston, 1929. 356 p. *DLC, NN, PU*

McKINLEY, CARLYLE. *In Loving Memory of Carlyle McKinley.* William A. Courtenay. Walhalla, S. C., 1904. 23 p. *DLC, NN, CSmH, MiD:B*

McKINLEY, WILLIAM.
One of the People: Life and Speeches of William McKinley; With a Brief Sketch of Garrett A. Hobart. Byron Andrews. Chicago, 1896. 365 p. *DLC, NN, MWA, MiD:B*
William McKinley. Amos E. Corning. N. Y., 1907. 182 p. *DLC, NN*

Life of William McKinley. E. S. Ellis. N. Y., 1901. 243 p.
DLC

Life of William McKinley; With Short Biography of Lincoln and Garfield, and Life of President Roosevelt. S. Fallows, ed. Chicago, 1901. 453 p. DLC, NN, MiD:B

Life and Distinguished Services of William McKinley . . . With a Sketch of the Life of Garrett A. Hobart . . . Murat Halstead. Chicago, 1896. 540 p. DLC, NN, PU

The Illustrious Life of William McKinley. Murat Halstead. Chicago, 1901. 464 p. DLC, NN, PU, MiD:B

William McKinley. John Hay. N. Y., 1902. 27 p.
DLC, MWA, CSmH, PU, MiD:B

The Authentic Life of William McKinley . . . Together With a Life Sketch of Theodore Roosevelt. Alexander K. McClure and C. Morris. Phila., 1901. 503 p. DLC, NN, CSmH, PU

. . . Complete Life of William McKinley and Story of His Assassination. Henry Neil. Chicago, 1901. 448 p. NN, MiD:B

Life and Speeches of William McKinley. John S. Ogilvie. N. Y., 1896. 337 p. DLC

Life of William McKinley. Charles S. Olcott. Boston, 1916. 2 vols. DLC, NN, CSmH, PU

Biography of William McKinley. Elizabeth Owen. Toledo, 1902. 37 p. DLC, NN

McKinley and Men of Our Times. E. Pell, J. Buell, and J. Boyd. n.p., 1901. 544 p. DLC, NN, PU

Life of Wm. McKinley: Soldier, Lawyer, Statesman. Robert P. Porter. Cleveland, 1896. 538 p. DLC, NN, MWA, MiD:B

Life and Work of William McKinley. Edward T. Roe. Chicago, 1901. 193 p. DLC

Lives of William McKinley and Garrett A. Hobart. Henry B. Russell. Hartford, 1896. 346 p.
DLC, NN, MWA, CSmH, MiD:B

Life of William McKinley. Jane E. Snow. Cleveland, 1908. 98 p. DLC, NN

Life of William McKinley. J. W. Tyler. Chicago, 1901. 512 p.
DLC, MWA

2:525

MacLEAN, JOHN. *A Memoir of John MacLean, M.D., the First Professor of Chemistry in the College of New Jersey.* John MacLean. Princeton, 1876. 64 p. (Privately Printed) DLC, NN

McLELLAN, FRANCES E. H. *Memoir of Frances E. H. McLellan.* R. M. Haskell. N. Y., 1856. *MiD:B*

McLEOD, ALEXANDER. *Memoir of Alexander McLeod, D.D., New York.* Samuel B. Wylie. N. Y., 1855. 535 p.

DLC, NN, MiD:B

McLOUGHLIN, JOHN.

McLoughlin and Old Oregon. Eva E. Dye. Chicago, 1900. 381 p. *CSmH, PU*

Dr. John McLoughlin, the Father of Oregon. F. V. Holman. Cleveland, 1907. 301 p. *DLC, NN, CSmH*

John McLoughlin: Patriarch of the Northwest. Robert C. Johnson. Portland, Oregon, 1935. 302 p. *DLC, NN*

The White-Headed Eagle, John McLoughlin, Builder of an Empire. Richard G. Montgomery. N. Y., 1935. 358 p.

DLC, NN, CSmH

2:41–127

McLOUGHLIN, THOMAS PATRICK. *Father Tom: Life and Lectures of Rev. Thomas P. McLoughlin.* Peter P. McLoughlin. N. Y., 1919. 400 p. *DLC, NN*

McMAHON, JOHN VAN LEAR. *Life of John Van Lear McMahon.* John T. Mason and John T. Mason, Jr. Balt., 1879. 140 p.

DLC, NN, MiD:B

McMASTER, JOHN BACH. *John Bach McMaster, Historian of the American People.* William T. Hutchinson. n.p., 1929. 26 p. (Reprinted from Miss. Hist. Review, Vol. XVI, No. 1, June 1929)

NN, PU

MACMILLAN, ALEXANDER. *Life and Letters of Alexander Macmillan.* C. L. Graves. N. Y., 1910. 417 p. *DLC, NN, PU*

McMILLAN, JOHN. *Life and Work of Rev. John McMillan, D.D., Pioneer, Preacher, Educator, Patriot of Western Pennsylvania.* Daniel M. Bennett. Bridgeville, Pa., 1935. 525 p.

DLC, NN, CSmH

MACMONNIES, FREDERICK. 2:430

McMULLEN, JOHN. *Life of Rt. Rev. John McMullen, D.D.* Jos. J. McGovern. Chicago, 1888.

MACNEIL, HERMON ATKINS. 2:430

McNEMAR, RICHARD. *A Sketch of the Life and Labors of Richard McNemar.* John P. MacLean. Franklin, O., 1905. 67 p.

DLC, NN

McNIEL, JOHN WILLIAM THOMAS. *Rev. J. W. T. McNiel; a Brief Biography.* Mary C. Merritt, comp. Los Angeles, 1909. 130 p.

DLC

MACOMB, ALEXANDER. *Memoir of Alexander Macomb, the Major General Commanding the Army of the United States.* George H. Richards. N. Y., 1833. 130 p. *DLC, NN, MWA, PU, MiD:B*

MACON, NATHANIEL.
Life of . . . Nathaniel Macon, of North Carolina . . . His Public . . . and Private Life . . . Edward R. Cotton. Balt., 1840. 272 p.
DLC, NN

Life of Nathaniel Macon. William E. Dodd. Raleigh, 1903. 443 p. *DLC, NN, MWA, CSmH, PU*

McPHEETERS, SAMUEL BROWN. *Memoir of Rev. Samuel B. McPheeters, D.D.* John S. Grasty. St. Louis, 1871. 384 p.
DLC, NN, MWA

McPHERSON, AIMEE. *Sister Aimee McPherson.* Nancy B. Mavity. Garden City, N. Y., 1931. 360 p. *DLC, NN, PU*

McQUAID, BERNARD JOHN. *The Life and Letters of Bishop McQuaid, Prefaced With the History of Catholic Rochester Before His Episcopate.* Frederick J. Zwierlein. Rochester, N. Y., 1925–27. 3 vols. *DLC, NN*

McRAE, THOMAS CHIPMAN. *The Life of Thomas C. McRae, Arkansas' Educational Governor, 1921–1925.* James R. Grant. Russellville, Ark., 1932. 123 p. *DLC, NN*

McSHANE, DANIEL. *Father McShane of Maryknoll, Missioner in South China.* James E. Walsh. N. Y., 1932. 227 p. *DLC, NN*

MACURDY, ELISHA. *The Life of the Rev. Elisha Macurdy.* David Elliott. Allegheny, Pa., 1848. 323 p. *DLC, NN, MiD:B*

McVICKAR, JOHN. *Life of Rev. John McVickar . . . of Columbia College.* William A. McVickar. N. Y., 1872. 416 p.
DLC, NN, PU

MACY, ANNE SULLIVAN. *Anne Sullivan Macy, the Story Behind Helen Keller.* Nella Braddy. Garden City, N. Y., 1933. 365 p.
DLC, NN

MADDEN, MARTIN BARNABY. *Martin B. Madden, Public Servant; a Sketch.* Edgar W. Brent. Chicago, 1901. 316 p. *DLC, NN*

MADISON, DOLLY.
Life and Letters of Dolly Madison. Allen C. Clark. Washington, 1914. 517 p. *DLC, NN, CSmH, PU*
Dolly Madison, the Nation's Hostess. Elizabeth L. Dean. Boston, 1928. 250 p. *DLC, NN*
Dolly Madison. Maud W. Goodwin. N. Y., 1896. 287 p. (Women of Colonial and Revolutionary Times, No. 2)
DLC, NN, MWA, CSmH, MiD:B

2:97–453

MADISON, JAMES.

The Lives of James Madison and James Monroe, Fourth and Fifth Presidents of the United States. John Q. Adams. Boston, 1850, Buffalo, 1851. 432 p.

DLC, NN, MWA, CSmH, MiD:B, MiU:C

James Madison. Sydney H. Gay. Boston, 1884. 342 p. (A.S.) *DLC, NN, MWA, CSmH, PU, MiD:B*

The Life of James Madison. Gaillard Hunt. N. Y., 1902. 402 p. *DLC, NN, MWA, CSmH, PU, MiD:B*

History of the Life and Times of James Madison. William C. Rives. Boston, 1859–68. 3 vols.

DLC, NN, MWA, CSmH, PU, MiD:B, MiU:C

James Madison, James Monroe, and John Quincy Adams. William O. Stoddard. N. Y., 1887. 331 p. *DLC, MWA, MiD:B*

2:77–662

MAESER, KARL GOTTFRIED. *Karl G. Maeser, a Biography.* Reinhard Maeser. Provo, Utah, 1928. 184 p. *DLC, NN*

MAETERLINCK, MAURICE. 2:246

MAFFITT, JOHN NEWLAND. *Life and Services of John N. Maffitt.* Emma R. Maffitt. N. Y., 1906. 436 p. *DLC, NN, MiD:B*

MAGELLAN, FERDINAND.

Magellan; His Life and Adventures by Land and by Sea. Arthur S. Hildebrand. N. Y., 1924. 261 p. *DLC, NN, PU*

Ferdinand Magellan. F. A. Ober. N. Y., 1907. 300 p. (Heroes of Am. History) *DLC, NN*

2:78

MAGENDIE, FRANÇOIS. *Biography of François Magendie.* Percy M. Dawson. Brooklyn, 1908. 66 p. *DLC*

MAHAN, ALFRED THAYER. *The Life of Admiral Mahan, Naval Philosopher, Rear-Admiral U. S. N. . . .* Charles C. Taylor. N. Y., 1920. 359 p. *DLC, NN, CSmH, PU*

2:396

MAHOMET.

Mohammed. Roy F. Dibble. N. Y., 1926. 257 p.

DLC, NN

Mahomet and His Successors. Washington Irving. N. Y., 1849–1850. 2 vols. *DLC, NN, MWA, CSmH*

2:665

MAHONE, WILLIAM. *William Mahone of Virginia, Soldier and Political Insurgent.* Nelson M. Blake. Richmond, 1935. 323 p.

DLC, NN, CSmH, PU

MAHONEY, JAMES. *James Mahoney, 1862–1915.* Nellie M. Mahoney. Concord, N. H., 1920. 343 p. (Privately Printed) *DLC, MWA*

MAIMONIDES, MOSES.
The Boy of Cordova; an Incident in the Youth of Moses Maimonides. Abraham Burstein. N. Y., 1935. 124 p. *DLC*
Maimonides. Solomon Zeitlin. N. Y., 1935. 234 p.
DLC, NN

MAINTENON, MME. 2:90

MAISONNEUVE, PAUL DE C. 2:127

MAJOR, NOAH J. . . . *The Pioneers of Morgan County; Memoirs of Noah J. Major.* Logan Esarey, ed. Indianapolis, 1915. 516 p.
DLC, NN, CSmH

MAJORS, ALEXANDER. 2:46

MALCOM, LYDIA M. *A Brief Memoir of Mrs. Lydia M. Malcom, Late of Boston, Mass., Wife of Rev. Howard Malcom, D.D.* Boston, 1835. 122 p. 4th ed. *DLC, NN*

MALL, FRANKLIN PAINE. *Franklin Paine Mall; the Story of a Mind.* Florence R. Sabin. Balt., 1934. 342 p. *DLC, NN, MWA*

MALLERY, MRS. JERUSHA D. *Memoir of Mrs. Jerusha D. Mallery, Wife of Rev. S. S. Mallery, Pastor of the Baptist Church, Willington, Ct.* S. S. Mallery. Hartford, 1834. 113 p. *NN*

MALONE, DANA. *Dana Malone of Greenfield.* Howard C. Robbins. N. Y., 1928. 81 p. *DLC, NN, MWA*

MALORY, THOMAS. *Sir Thomas Malory, His Turbulent Career; a Biography.* Edward Hicks. Cambridge, 1928. 118 p.
DLC, NN, CSmH, PU

MANLEY, JOHN.
Captain John Manley; Second in Rank in the U. S. N., 1776–1783. Isaac J. Greenwood. Boston, 1915. 174 p.
DLC, NN, MWA
Naval Career of Captain John Manley of Marblehead. Rob. E. Peabody. Salem, Mass., 1909. 27 p. (Essex Institute) (Privately Printed) *DLC, NN, MWA*

MANLY, BASIL. *Dr. Basil Manly, the Founder of the Alabama Historical Society.* T. M. Owen. Montgomery, Ala., 1904. 15 p. (Ala. Hist. Soc. Reprint) *DLC, NN*

MANN, HORACE.
Horace Mann. B. A. Hinsdale. N. Y., 1898. 326 p. (Great Educators) *DLC, NN, CSmH*
Horace Mann, Educator, Patriot, Reformer: Study in Leadership. G. A. Hubbell. Phila., 1910. 285 p.
DLC, NN, MWA, CSmH, PU

The Life of Horace Mann. Mary T. Mann. Boston, 1865.
602 p. *DLC, NN, PU*

MANNING, JAMES. *Life, Times and Correspondence of James Manning.*
R. A. Guild. Boston, 1864. 523 p. *DLC, NN, MWA, MiD:B*

MANSFIELD, RICHARD.
Richard Mansfield, the Man and the Actor. Paul Wilstach.
N. Y., 1908. 500 p. *DLC, NN, MWA, PU*
Life and Art of Richard Mansfield. William Winter. N. Y.,
1910. 2 vols. *DLC, NN, MWA, CSmH, PU*

MAPES, CLARINDA. *Early Piety, Exemplified in the Life of Miss Clarinda Mapes.* J. Batey. N. Y., 1849. 99 p. *DLC, NN*

MARAT, JEAN PAUL. *Jean Paul Marat; a Study in Radicalism.* Louis
R. Gottschalk. N. Y., 1927. 221 p. *DLC, NN, PU*
2:330

MARBLE, DANFORTH. *Biographical Sketch of Dan Marble.* Jonathan
F. Kelly. N. Y., 1851. 235 p. *DLC, NN*

MARBURY, FRANCIS. *Rev. Francis Marbury.* Frederick L. Gay.
(Mass. Hist. Soc. Coll. Vol. 48, 1915) *NN*

MARCION. 2:371

MARCONI, GUGLIELMO. 2:301

MARCY, OLIVER. *In Memoriam, Oliver Marcy, LL.D.* . . . Chicago,
1899. 179 p. *NN, MWA, MiD:B*

MARCY, WILLIAM LEARNED. 2:349

MARDEN, ORISON SWETT. *Life Story of Orison Swett Marden, a Man
Who Benefited Men.* Margaret Connolly. N. Y., 1925. 216 p.
DLC, NN

MARGOT, ANTOINETTE. *The Story of Antoinette Margot, a Descendant
of the Huguenots.* Thomas D. Williams. Balt., 1931. 216 p.

MARGUERITE OF NAVARRE. *Marguerite of Navarre.* Samuel Putnam.
N. Y., 1935. 391 p. *DLC, NN, PU*

MARIANNE, MOTHER. *Mother Marianne of Molokai.* Leo V. Jacks.
N. Y., 1935. 203 p. *DLC, NN*

MARIE OF ROUMANIA. 2:30

MARIE ANTOINETTE.
History of Maria Antoinette. J. S. C. Abbott. N. Y., 1849.
322 p. *DLC, NN*
Marie Antoinette. Katharine S. Anthony. N. Y., 1933. 302 p.
DLC, NN, PU
Marie Antoinette, the Player Queen. John G. Palache. N. Y.,
1929. 322 p. *DLC, NN*

MARIE, MÈRE. *Mère Marie of the Ursulines; a Study in Adventure.*
Agnes Repplier. N. Y., 1931. 314 p.   *DLC, NN, PU*

MARIN, JOHN. *John Marin; the Man and His Work.* Emanuel M.
Benson. N. Y., 1936. 111 p.   *DLC, NN*

MARION, FRANCIS.
    The Life of Gen. Francis Marion. Cecil B. Hartley. Phila.,
1866. 320 p.   *DLC, MiD:B*
    The Life and Times of Gen. Francis Marion. H. N. Moore.
Phila., 1845. 210 p.   *DLC, NN, MWA, CSmH*
    Life of Francis Marion. William G. Simms. N. Y., 1844. 357 p.
        DLC, NN, MWA, CSmH, PU, MiD:B, MiU:C
    Life of General Francis Marion. Mason L. Weems and P.
Horry. Balt., 1809. 2nd ed. Balt., 1814. 270 p.
        DLC, NN, MWA, CSmH, PU, MiD:B, MiU:C
    2:290

MARK, JOHN. *John Mark.* James D. Hunter. N. Y., 1903. 113 p.
        DLC

MARKHAM, EDWIN. *Edwin Markham.* William L. Stidger. N. Y.,
1933. 287 p.   *DLC, NN, PU*

MARKSMAN, PETER. *Life of Rev. Peter Marksman, an Ojibwa Missionary; Illustrating the Triumphs of the Gospel Among the Ojibwa
Indians.* John H. Pitezel. Cincinnati, 1901. 286 p.   *NN*

MARLBOROUGH, JOHN, DUKE OF. *Marlborough: The Portrait of a
Conqueror.* Donald B. Chidsey. N. Y., 1929. 308 p. *DLC, NN*

MARLOWE, JULIA.
    Julia Marlowe. John D. Barry. Boston, 1899. 87 p.
        DLC, NN, MWA
    Julia Marlowe. John D. Barry. Bost., 1907. 117 p.   *NN*
    Julia Marlowe, Her Life and Art. Charles E. Russell. N. Y.,
1926. 582 p.   *DLC, NN, PU*

MARQUETTE, JACQUES.
    Father Marquette, the Discoverer of the Mississippi. S. Hedges.
N. Y., 1903. 164 p.   *DLC, CSmH*
    Père Marquette. Agnes Repplier. N. Y., 1929. 298 p.
        DLC, NN, MWA, PU
    *Life of Father Marquette in " Discovery and Exploration of the
Mississippi Valley."* John D. G. Shea. N. Y., 1852. 267 p.
        DLC, NN, MWA, CSmH, PU, MiU:C
    Life of Father Marquette. Jared Sparks. (L.A.B.)
        DLC, NN, MWA, CSmH, PU

Father Marquette. Reuben G. Thwaites. N. Y., 1902. 244 p.
DLC, NN, CSmH, PU, MiU:C
2:680

MARSH, GEORGE PERKINS. *Life and Letters of George Perkins Marsh.*
Caroline C. Marsh. N. Y., 1888. 479 p. DLC, MWA

MARSH, JAMES. *The Remains of the Rev. James Marsh, D.D. . . .
With a Memoir.* J. Torrey, ed. Boston, 1843. 642 p.
DLC, MWA, CSmH

MARSH, JOHN. *John Marsh, Pioneer, Life Story of a Trail Blazer on
Six Frontiers.* George D. Lyman. N. Y., 1930. 394 p.
DLC, NN, CSmH, PU, MiD:B

MARSHALL, CHARLES HENRY. *Memorial of Charles H. Marshall.*
William A. Butler. N. Y., 1867. 96 p. DLC, NN, MWA, CSmH

MARSHALL, EMILY. 2:518

MARSHALL, EMMA. *Emma Marshall. A Biographical Sketch.* Beatrice Marshall. N. Y., 1901. 342 p. DLC, NN

MARSHALL, HUMPHREY. See BARTRAM, JOHN.

MARSHALL, JAMES WILSON. *The Life of James W. Marshall.* G. F.
Parsons. San Francisco, 1935. 144 p. CSmH

MARSHALL, JOHN.
Life of John Marshall. Albert J. Beveridge. Boston, 1916–19.
4 vols. 4 vols. in 2, 1929. DLC, NN, CSmH, PU, MiD:B
John Marshall and His Times. Neal Brown. Wausaic, Wis.,
1902. 259 p. DLC, NN
Life of John Marshall. H. Flanders. Phila., 1905. 278 p.
DLC, CSmH, PU
John Marshall. Allan B. Magruder. Boston, 1885. 290 p.
(A.S.) DLC, NN, MWA, CSmH, PU, MiD:B
*A Discourse Upon the Life, Character and Services of the Hon-
orable John Marshall, Chief Justice of the United States of America.*
Joseph Story. Boston, 1835. 74 p.
DLC, NN, MWA, CSmH, PU, MiD:B
John Marshall. James B. Thayer. Boston, 1901. 157 p.
(Riverside Biography Series) DLC, NN, MWA, PU
2:5–77–230–666–707

MARSHALL, JOSEPH GLASS. *Joseph G. Marshall.* John L. Campbell.
Indianapolis, 1897. 200 p. DLC, CSmH

MARSHALL, LOUIS. *Louis Marshall, A Biographical Sketch.* Cyrus
Adler. N. Y., 1931. 121 p. DLC, NN, PU

MARTIN, SAINT. *The Greatest Saint of France.* Louis Foley. Milwaukee, 1931. 321 p. DLC, NN

MARTIN, HOMER. *Homer Martin: Poet in Landscape.* Frank J. Mather, Jr. N. Y., 1912. 76 p. *DLC, NN*
2:123

MARTIN, LUTHER. *Luther Martin; the Federal Bulldog.* Henry P. Goddard. Balt., 1887. 60 p. (Md. Hist. Soc. Fund—Pub. No. 24, pp. 1–42) *DLC, NN, MWA, CSmH, PU*

MARTINEAU, JAMES. *James Martineau. A Biography and a Study.* Abraham W. Jackson. Boston, 1900. 459 p. *DLC, NN, PU*

MARX, KARL. *Karl Marx: His Life and Work.* John Spargo. N. Y., 1910. 359 p. *DLC, NN, PU*

MARY THE VIRGIN. 2:337

MASARYK, THOMAS.
Masaryk: Nation Builder; the Man Who Changed the Map of Europe. Donald A. Lowrie. N. Y., 1930. 232 p. *DLC, NN*
Thomas Masaryk. C. J. C. Street. N. Y., 1930. 281 p.
DLC, NN, PU
2:30

MASON, EBENEZER PORTER. *Life and Writings of Ebenezer Porter Mason.* Denison Olmsted. N. Y., 1842. 252 p.
DLC, NN, MWA, CSmH, PU

MASON, GEORGE.
George Mason of Virginia. L. H. Machen. Washington, 1901. 35 p. *DLC*
Life of George Mason. Kate M. Rowland. N. Y., 1892. 2 vols. *DLC, NN, MWA, CSmH, PU, MiD:B, MiU:C*

MASON, JAMES MURRAY. *Public Life . . . of James M. Mason, With Some Personal History.* Virginia Mason, ed. and comp. Roanoke, Va., 1903. 603 p. *DLC, CSmH, PU*

MASON, JEREMIAH. *Memoir and Correspondence of Jeremiah Mason.* George S. Hillard. Cambridge, 1873. 467 p.
DLC, NN, MWA, CSmH

MASON, JOHN. *The Life and Times of Major John Mason of Connecticut: 1600–1672.* Louis B. Mason. N. Y., 1935. 350 p.
DLC, NN, CSmH

MASON, JOHN.
Capt. John Mason, the Founder of New Hampshire. John W. Dean, ed. Boston, 1887. 492 p. (Prince Soc. Pub., 1887)
DLC, NN, CSmH, MiD:B, MiU:C
Life of John Mason. George E. Ellis. (L.A.B.)
DLC, NN, MWA, CSmH

MASON, JOHN MITCHELL. *Memoirs of John M. Mason, D.D.* Jacob Van Vechten. N. Y., 1856. 559 p.   *DLC, NN, MWA, PU*

MASON, WILLIAM. *William Mason: A Study in Eighteenth Century Culture.* John W. Draper. N. Y., 1924. 397 p.
DLC, NN, CSmH, PU

MASSEY, GERALD. *Gerald Massey: Poet, Prophet and Mystic.* B. O. Flower. Boston, 1895. 113 p.   *NN, MWA*

MASSIE, NATHANIEL. *Nathaniel Massie: Pioneer of Ohio; Sketch of His Life.* David M. Massie. Cincinnati, 1896. 285 p.
DLC, MWA, PU
2:424

MASTERS, EDGAR LEE. 2:366

MASTERS, ELIZA BAILEY. *An American Schoolmistress; the Life of Eliza B. Masters, 1847–1921.* Marion B. Shelton. N. Y., 1927. 204 p.   *DLC, NN*

MATHERS, THE. *The Mathers (Cotton and Increase) Weighed in the Balance . . . and Found Not Wanting.* Delano A. Goddard. Boston, 1870. 32 p.   *DLC, NN, MWA, CSmH*

MATHER, COTTON.

Cotton Mather: Keeper of the Puritan Conscience. Ralph and Louise Boas. N. Y., 1928. 271 p.
DLC, NN, MWA, CSmH, PU
Memoir of Cotton Mather, With a Genealogy of the Family of Mather. S. G. Drake. Boston, 1851. 16 p.   *DLC, NN, MWA*
Life of Cotton Mather. S. G. Drake. 13 p. (In the 1853 ed. of the Magnalia)   *DLC, NN, CSmH, PU*
Life and Times of Cotton Mather; or, a Boston Minister of Two Centuries Ago, 1663–1728. Abijah P. Marvin. Boston, 1892. 582 p.   *DLC, NN, CSmH*
The Life of the Very Reverend and Learned Cotton Mather, D.D. and F.R.S. Late Pastor of the North Church of Boston, Who Died, February 13, 1727. Samuel Mather. Boston, 1729. 186 p.
DLC, NN, CSmH, PU, MiU:C, RP:JCB
Cotton Mather: Puritan Priest. Barrett Wendell. N. Y., 1891. 321 p. (Makers of America)   *DLC, NN, MWA, CSmH*

MATHER, INCREASE.

Increase Mather, the Foremost American Puritan. Kenneth B. Murdock. Cambridge, 1925. 442 p.
DLC, NN, MWA, CSmH, PU, MiU:C
Memoirs of the Rev. Increase Mather. W. H. Whitmore. (N. E. Hist. and Gen. Reg. II)   *NN, MWA, CSmH*
2:405

MATHER, RICHARD. *The Life and Death of That Reverend Man of God, Mr. Richard Mather, Teacher of the Church of Dorchester in New England.* Increase Mather. Cambridge, 1670. Another edtion, with title, *Life and Death of Mr. Richard Mather.* Boston, 1850. 58 p. *DLC, NN, CSmH, RP:JCB*

MATHER, SAMUEL. *Samuel Mather of Witney.* Thomas J. Holmes. Cambridge, 1928. 322 p. *CSmH*

MATTESON, H. *The Life and Character of the Rev. H. Matteson.* N. Vansant. N. Y., 1870. 252 p.

MATTHEWS, ROBERT. *Life of Matthias (the Impostor); or, the Progress of Fanaticism Illustrated in the Extraordinary Case of Robert Matthews.* William L. Stone. N. Y., 1835. 347 p.
DLC, MWA, CSmH, PU

MAULE, THOMAS. *Thomas Maule the Salem Quaker.* Matt B. Jones. Salem, 1936. *RP:JCB*

MAUPASSANT, GUY DE.
Guy de Maupassant; a Biographical Study. Ernest A. Boyd. N. Y., 1926. 258 p. *DLC, NN, PU*
The Private Life of Guy de Maupassant. Ronald de L. Kirkbride. N. Y., 1932. 252 p. *DLC, NN*

MAURETANIA, QUEEN OF. *Cleopatra's Daughter: the Queen of Mauretania.* Beatrice Chanler. N. Y., 1935. 365 p. *DLC, NN*

MAURY, MATTHEW FONTAINE.
Life and Letters of Matthew Fontaine Maury. Jacqueline A. Caskie. Richmond, 1928. 191 p. *DLC, PU*
Life of Matthew Fontaine Maury. Diana F. M. Corbin, comp. N. Y., 1888. 326 p. *DLC, NN, CSmH, PU*
Matthew Fontaine Maury, the Pathfinder of the Seas. Charles L. Lewis. Annapolis, 1927. 264 p. *DLC, NN, CSmH, PU*
The Pathfinder of the Seas; the Life of Matthew Fontaine Maury. John W. Wayland. Richmond, 1930. 191 p.
DLC, NN

MAXIM, HIRAM STEVENS. *A Genius in the Family. Sir Hiram Stevens Maxim Through a Small Son's Eyes.* Hiram P. Maxim. N. Y., 1936. 193 p. *DLC, NN*

MAXWELL, HUGH. *The Christian Patriot: Some Recollections of the Late Col. Hugh Maxwell, of Massachusetts.* N. Y., 1833. 139 p.
MWA

MAXWELL, JAMES CLARK. 2:25

MAXWELL, WILLIAM HENRY. *Dr. William H. Maxwell, the First Superintendent of Schools of the City of New York.* Samuel P. Abelow. Brooklyn, N. Y., 1934. 177 p. *DLC, NN, PU*

MAY, JAMES. *Life and Letters of Rev. James May.* Alexander
Shiras. Phila., 1865. 185 p. *DLC, NN, PU*
MAY, SAMUEL JOSEPH. *Memoir of S. J. May.* G. B. Emerson, S. May
and T. J. Mumford, eds. and comps. Boston, 1873. 297 p.
DLC, NN, MWA, MiD:B
    2:144
MAY, THOMAS. *Thomas May: Man of Letters, 1595–1650.* Allan G.
Chester. Phila., 1932. 204 p. (Privately Printed) *DLC, PU*
MAYER, LEVY. *Levy Mayer and the New Industrial Era.* Edgar L.
Masters. New Haven, 1927. 305 p. *DLC*
MAYER, PHILIP FREDERICK. *Memorial of Rev. Philip F. Mayer.* M.
L. Stower. Phila., 1858. 70 p. *DLC, NN, CSmH, PU*
MAYHEW, JONATHAN. *Memoir of the Life and Writings of Rev. Jona-
than Mayhew, D.D., Pastor of the West Church and Society in Bos-
ton, From June, 1747 to July, 1766.* Alden Bradford. Boston,
1838. 484 p. *NN, MWA, MiD:B*
MAYHEW, THOMAS. *Thomas Mayhew, Patriarch to the Indians 1593–
1682.* Lloyd C. M. Hare. N. Y., 1932. 231 p.
DLC, NN, CSmH
MAYNARD, DAVID SWINSON. *David S. Maynard and Catherine T.
Maynard: Biographies of Two of the Oregon Immigrants of 1850.*
T. W. Prosch. Seattle, 1907. 83 p. *DLC, NN, CSmH, MiD:B*
MAYO, SARAH C. EDGARTON. *Selections From the Writings of Mrs.
Sarah C. Edgarton Mayo: With a Memoir.* A. D. Mayo, ed. Bos-
ton, 1849. 432 p. *DLC, NN, MWA, CSmH*
MAZZINI, GIUSEPPE. *Mazzini; Portrait of an Exile.* Frank S. Barr.
N. Y., 1935. 308 p. *DLC, NN, PU*
MEADE, GEORGE GORDON.
    *Life of Gen. George Gordon Meade, Commander of the Army of
the Potomac.* R. M. Bache. Phila., 1897. 596 p.
DLC, NN, CSmH, PU
    Life and Letters of George Gordon Meade. G. Gordon Meade,
ed. N. Y., 1913. 2 vols. *DLC, NN, CSmH, PU*
    General Meade. I. R. Pennypacker. N. Y., 1901. 402 p.
(G.C.) *DLC, NN, CSmH, PU*
    2:96
MEADE, WILLIAM.
    A Memoir of the Life of Rt. Rev. William Meade. J. Johns.
Balt., 1867. 537 p. *DLC, NN*
    Memoir of the Life of Rt. Rev. William Meade, D.D. Philip
Slaughter. Cambridge, 1885. 51 p. *DLC, NN, MWA, CSmH*

MEAGHER, THOMAS FRANCIS.
 Memoirs of Gen. Thomas Francis Meagher. Michael Cavanagh.
Worcester, Mass., 1892. 38 p. *DLC, NN, MWA, CSmH, PU*
 *Brigadier-General Thomas Francis Meagher: His Political and
Military Career.* W. F. Lyons. N. Y., 1870. 357 p.
            DLC, NN, MWA, CSmH
MEDICI, CATHERINE. *Catherine de Medici.* Paul Van Dyke. N. Y.,
1922. 2 vols.   *DLC, NN*
MEDICI, LORENZO. *Lorenzo, the Magnificent.* David G. Loth. N.
Y., 1929. 329 p.   *DLC, NN*
MEEK, JOSEPH. *The River of the West . . . Contains a Life of the
Noted Trapper, Joe Meek.* Frances F. Victor. San Francisco,
1870. 602 p.   *DLC, NN, MWA, CSmH*
MEEKER, EZRA. 2:41
MEEKER, JOTHAM. *Jotham Meeker, Pioneer Printer of Kansas.* Doug-
las McMurtrie and Albert H. Allen. Chicago, 1930. 169 p.
            DLC, NN, MWA, CSmH
MEIER-SMITH, MATSON. *Matson Meier-Smith. Memories of His Life
and Work.* N. Y., 1891. 367 p. (Privately Printed)
             DLC, NN, MWA
MEIGS, JAMES ATKINS. *Biographical Sketch of James Atkins Meigs.*
George Hamilton. Phila., 1880. 22 p.   *DLC, PU*
MEIGS, JOHN. *Master of the Hill; a Biography of John Meigs.* Wal-
ter R. Bowie. N. Y., 1917. 372 p.   *DLC, NN, PU*
MEIGS, JOSIAH. *Life of Josiah Meigs.* W. M. Meigs. Phila., 1887.
132 p.   *DLC, NN, MWA, PU, MiD:B*
MELANCHTHON, PHILIP. *Life of Philip Melanchthon.* Joseph Stump.
Reading, Pa., 1897. 272 p.   *NN*
MELL, PATRICK HUES. *Life of Patrick Hues Mell.* P. H. Mell, Jr.
Louisville, 1895. 258 p.   *NN*
MELLON, ANDREW.
 Andrew W. Mellon—The Man and His Work. Philip Love.
Balt., 1929. 319 p.   *DLC, NN*
 *Mellon's Millions, the Biography of a Fortune; the Life and
Times of Andrew W. Mellon.* Harvey O'Connor. N. Y., 1933.
443 p.   *DLC, NN, PU*
MELVILLE, HERMAN.
 Herman Melville. Lewis Mumford. N. Y., 1928. 377 p.
         DLC, NN, MWA, CSmH, PU
 Biographical Sketch of Herman Melville. J. E. A. Smith.
Pittsfield, Mass., 1891. 32 p. (Pamphlet) *NN, MWA*

Herman Melville: Mariner and Mystic. Raymond M. Weaver. N. Y., 1921. 399 p.   *DLC, NN, MWA, CSmH, PU*

MEMBRE, ZENOBE. . . . *The Franciscan Père Marquette: a Critical Biography of Father Zenobe Membre, O.F.M., La Salle's Chaplain and Missionary Companion, 1645–1689.* Marion A. Habig. N. Y., 1934. 301 p.   *DLC, NN, CSmH*

MEMINGER, WILBUR FISK. *" The Little Man From Chicago"; the Life Story of Wilbur F. Meminger.* Laura S. Meminger. N. Y., 1910. 200 p.   *DLC*

MEMMINGER, CHRISTOPHER GUSTAVUS. *Life and Times of C. G. Memminger.* Henry D. Capers. Richmond, 1893. 604 p.
                     DLC, NN, CSmH, PU

MENCKEN, HENRY LOUIS.
   H. L. Mencken. Ernest A. Boyd. N. Y., 1925. 89 p. (Modern American Writers)   *DLC, NN, MWA, CSmH, PU*
   The Man Mencken; a Biographical and Critical Survey. Isaac Goldberg. N. Y., 1925. 388 p.   *DLC, NN, CSmH, PU*
   2:592

MENDELEEFF, DMITRI. 2:286–348

MENDELSSOHN, JAKOB J. F. 2:187

MENDOZA, ANTONIO. *Antonio de Mendoza, First Viceroy of New Spain.* Arthur S. Aiton. Durham, N. C., 1927. 240 p.
                     DLC, NN, CSmH, PU

MENELLY, ANDREW. *Memoir of Andrew Menelly . . . of West Troy, N. Y.* Oscar H. Gregory. N. Y., n.d. 159 p.   *MWA*

MENEFEE, RICHARD HICKMAN. *Richard Hickman Menefee.* John W. Townsend. N. Y., 1907. 111 p.   *DLC, NN, MiD:B*

MENENDEZ, PETER. 2:127

MERCER, CHARLES FENTON. *Biographical Sketch of Hon. Charles Fenton Mercer, 1778–1858, M.C. 1817–1840, of Aldie, Loudon County, Virginia . . .* James M. Garnett. Richmond, 1911. 95 p.
                     DLC, NN, CSmH

MERCER, HUGH. *Life of General Hugh Mercer.* J. T. Goolrick. N. Y., 1906. 140 p.   *DLC, NN, MWA, CSmH, PU, MiD:B*

MERCER, JESSE. *Memoirs of Elder Jesse Mercer.* C. D. Mallory. N. Y., 1844. 456 p.   *DLC, NN, MWA, CSmH*

MERCER, MARGARET. *Memoir of Miss Margaret Mercer.* Caspar Morris. Phila., 1848. 213 p.   *DLC, NN, MWA, CSmH, PU*

MERCIER, DÉSIRÉ CARDINAL.
   The Life of Cardinal Mercier. John A. Gade. N. Y., 1934. 312 p.   *DLC, NN*

Mercier, the Fighting Cardinal of Belgium. Charlotte Kellogg. N. Y., 1920. 248 p.   *DLC, NN, PU*

MEREDITH, GEORGE. *George Meredith; a Study and an Appreciation.* William Chislett, Jr. Boston, 1925. 225 p.   *DLC, NN, CSmH*

MEREDITH, WILLIAM MORRIS. *William M. Meredith.* R. Lewis Ashurst. n.p., 1901. 52 p.   *NN*

MERGENTHALER, OTTMAR. 2:343

MERICI, ANGELA.

Sant'Angela of the Ursulines; the Story of Angela Merici, Foundress of the Ursulines. Mother Frances D'Assisi. Milwaukee, 1935. 174 p.   *DLC*

Angela Merici and Her Teaching Idea (1474–1540). Sister Mary Monica. N. Y., 1927. 429 p.   *DLC, NN, PU*

MERRILL, DAVID. *Sketch of the Life of the Late Rev. David Merrill.* Thomas S. Pearson. Windsor, Vt., 1855. 24 p.   *MWA*

MERRIMAN, EDWARD. *A Memorial of the Reverend William Edward Merriman, D.D., 1825–1892.* Cambridge, 1893. 100 p. (Privately Printed)

MERRIMON, AUGUSTUS SUMMERFIELD. *A Memoir. Augustus Summerfield Merrimon.* Maud L. Merrimon. Raleigh, 1894. 100 p.   *DLC, NN*

MERRITT FAMILY. *Seven Iron Men (The Merritts).* Paul H. De-Kruif. N. Y., 1929. 241 p.   *DLC, NN, PU*

MESMER, FRANZ ANTON. *Franz Anton Mesmer; a History of Mesmerism.* Margaret L. Goldsmith. N. Y., 1934. 308 p.   *DLC, NN*

MESSER, LORING WILBUR.

L. Wilbur Messer; an Appreciation. C. S. Bishop. N. Y., 1931. 218 p.   *DLC, MWA*

Loring Wilbur Messer, Metropolitan General Secretary (Y. M. C. A.). Charles T. Goodspeed. Chicago, 1934. 183 p.   *DLC, NN, MWA*

METCHNIKOFF, ELIE. 2:176

MEYER, FREDERICK BROTHERTON. *F. B. Meyer, Preacher, Teacher, Man of God.* Philip I. Roberts. N. Y., 1929. 221 p.   *DLC*

MEYER, GEORGE VON LENGERKE. *George von Lengerke Meyer: His Life and Public Services.* Mark A. De W. Howe. N. Y., 1919. 556 p.   *DLC, NN, MWA*

MEYER, VICTOR. 2:286

MEYERBEER, GIACOMO. 2:187

MICHAEL, HELEN ABBOTT. *Helen Abbott Michael; Biographical Sketch.* Nathan H. Dole. Boston, 1907. 107 p. (In Michael, Mrs. T. and C. D. S. Abbott, " Studies in Plant and Organic Chemistry. . . .")   *DLC, PU*

MICHELANGELO.

Michelangelo, the Man. Donald L. Finlayson. N. Y., 1935. 356 p.   *DLC, NN*

Michelangelo. Moses F. Sweetser. Boston, 1878. 157 p.   *DLC*

2:161–248

MICHELSON, ALBERT ABRAHAM. 2:388

MIELZINER, MOSES. *Moses Mielziner, 1828–1903.* Ella M. F. Mielziner. N. Y., 1931. 254 p.   *DLC, NN, PU*

MIFFLIN, WARNER. *Life and Ancestry of Warner Mifflin, Friend— Philanthropist—Patriot.* Hilda Justice, comp. Phila., 1905. 240 p.   *DLC, NN, MWA, PU, MiD:B*

MILBURN, DEVEREUX. 2:425

MILES, RICHARD PIUS. *The Father of the Church in Tennessee; or, The life, Times, and Character of the Rt. Rev. Richard Pius Miles, O.P., the First Bishop of Nashville.* Victor F. O'Daniel. Washington, 1926. 607 p.   *DLC, NN*

MILLER, CHARLES. *Broncho Charlie; a Saga of the Saddle.* Gladys S. Erskine. N. Y., 1934. 316 p.   *DLC, NN*

MILLER, CHARLES RANSOM. *Mr. Miller of " The Times." The Story of an Editor.* F. Fraser Bond. N. Y., 1931. 264 p.   *DLC, NN, MWA, PU*

MILLER, CHRISTIAN. *Memoirs of an Old Disciple and His Descendants: Christian Miller, Sarah H. Miller, Isaac L. K. Miller, Rev. John E. Miller . . .* Francis M. Kip. N. Y., 1848. 309 p.   *DLC, NN, CSmH, MiD:B*

MILLER, DEWITT. *Dewitt Miller; a Biographical Sketch.* Leon H. Vincent. Cambridge, 1912. 148 p.   *DLC, NN*

MILLER, EDWARD. *Biographical Sketch of Edward Miller in His " Medical Works."* Samuel Miller. N. Y., 1814. 111 p.   *DLC, NN, PU*

MILLER, HENRY. *The Cattle King. A Dramatized Biography.* Edward F. Treadwell. N. Y., 1931. 367 p.   *DLC, NN, MWA, CSmH, PU*

MILLER, HUGH. *Memoir of Hugh Miller in " Miller's Footprints of the Creator."* Louis Agassiz. Boston, 1850.   *DLC, NN, MWA, PU*

MILLER, JOAQUIN. *Joaquin Miller and His Other Self.* Harr Wagner. San Francisco, 1929. 312 p.   *DLC, NN, MWA, CSmH, PU*
    2:41

MILLER, JAMES RUSSELL. *Life of Dr. J. R. Miller.* John T. Faris. Phila., 1912. 246 p.   *NN*

MILLER, JOHN B.   2:233

MILLER, LEWIS. *Lewis Miller; a Biographical Essay.* Ellwood Hendrick. N. Y., 1925. 208 p.   *DLC, NN*

MILLER, SAMUEL. *The Life of Rev. Samuel Miller.* Samuel Miller. Phila., 1869. 2 vols.   *DLC, NN, MWA*

MILLER, SAMUEL FREEMAN. *Samuel Freeman Miller.* Charles N. Gregory. Iowa City, 1907. 217 p. (Iowa Biographical Series)
                         DLC, NN, MWA, CSmH, PU

MILLER, WILLIAM. *Sketches of the Christian Life and Public Labors of William Miller.* James White. Battle Creek, Mich., 1875. 416 p.   *MWA*

MILLET, FRANÇOIS.   2:5

MILLIKAN, ROBERT ANDREWS.   2:388

MILLS, ROBERT. *Robert Mills; Architect of the Washington Monument, 1781–1855.* Helen M. Gallagher. N. Y., 1935. 233 p.
                              DLC, NN, PU

MILLS, SAMUEL JOHN.
    Samuel J. Mills, Missionary Pathfinder, Pioneer and Promoter. Thomas C. Richards. N. Y., 1906. 275 p.   *DLC, NN, MWA*
    Memoir of Samuel John Mills. Gardiner Spring. Boston, 1829. 259 p.   *DLC, NN, MWA, CSmH*

MILNER, MOSES EMBREE. *California Joe, Noted Scout and Indian Fighter.* Joe E. Milner and Earle R. Forrest. Caldwell, Idaho, 1935. 396 p.   *DLC, NN, MWA*

MILNOR, JAMES. *A Memoir of the Life of James Milnor.* John S. Stone. N. Y., 1848. 646 p.
               DLC, NN, MWA, CSmH, PU, MiD:B

MILTON, JOHN.
    Oliver's Secretary; John Milton in an Era of Revolt. Dora N. Raymond. N. Y., 1932. 341 p.   *DLC, NN, MWA, CSmH, PU*
    John Milton; a Short Study of His Life and Works. William P. Trent. N. Y., 1899. 285 p.   *DLC, NN*
    2:82

MINER, ALONZO AMES. *Life of Alonzo Ames Miner.* G. H. Emerson. Boston, 1896. 555 p.   *DLC, NN, MWA, MiD:B*

MINER, ASHER. *Asher Miner, Citizen and Soldier.* Margaret M. Miner. Cambridge, 1929. 129 p.   *DLC, NN*

MINER, CHARLES. *Charles Miner, a Pennsylvania Pioneer.* Charles F. Richardson and Eliz. M. Richardson. Wilkes-Barre, Pa., 1916. 195 p.   *DLC, NN, MWA, MiD:B*

MINER, MYRTILLA. *Myrtilla Miner. A Memoir.* Ellen M. O'Connor. Boston, 1885. 129 p.   *DLC, NN, MWA*

MINOT, CHARLES SEDGWICK. 2:175

MINTURN, ROBERT BOWNE. *Memoir of Robert Bowne Minturn.* N.Y., 1871. 353 p. (Privately Printed)   *DLC, NN, MiD:B*

MINUIT, PETER. 2:660

MIRABEAU, HONORÉ GABRIEL.
    Mirabeau and the French Revolution. Fred M. Fling. N. Y., 1908. 3 vols.   *DLC, NN, PU*
    Mirabeau and the French Revolution. Charles F. Warwick. Phila., 1905. 483 p.   *DLC, NN, PU*

MIRANDA, FRANCISCO. *Life of Miranda.* William S. Robertson. Chapel Hill, 1929. 2 vols.   *DLC, NN, MWA, CSmH*

MITCHEL, ORMSBY MACKNIGHT.
    The Patriot Boy: or, The Life and Career of Major-General Ormsby M. Mitchel. Phineas C. Headley. N. Y., 1865. 278 p.   *DLC, NN, MWA, CSmH*
    Ormsby Macknight Mitchel, Astronomer and General. F. A. Mitchel. Boston, 1887. 392 p.   *DLC, NN, MWA, CSmH*

MITCHELL, DONALD GRANT. *Life of Donald G. Mitchell.* [Ik Marvel.] Waldo H. Dunn. N. Y., 1922. 421 p.   *DLC, NN, CSmH, PU*

MITCHELL, JOHN. *John Mitchell, Miner, Labor's Bargain With the Gilded Age.* Elsie Gluck. N. Y., 1929. 270 p.   *DLC, NN*
    2:150

MITCHELL, MARIA. *Maria Mitchell; Life, Letters and Journals.* Phebe M. Kendall, comp. Boston, 1896. 293 p.
    DLC, NN, MWA, PU, MiD:B

MITCHELL, SILAS WEIR.
    Weir Mitchell: His Life and Letters. Anna R. Burr. N. Y., 1929. 424 p.   *DLC, NN, MWA, CSmH, PU*
    S. Weir Mitchell, a Brief Sketch of His Life. Beverley R. Tucker. Boston, 1914. 68 p.   *DLC, NN, PU*
    2:109

MITCHILL, SAMUEL LATHAM. *A Scientist in the Early Republic; Samuel Latham Mitchell, 1764–1831.* Courtney R. Hall. N. Y., 1934. 162 p.   *DLC, NN, CSmH, PU*

MIZNER FAMILY. *The Many Mizners.* Addison Mizner. N. Y., 1932. 305 p. *DLC, NN*

MIZNER, WILSON. *The Fabulous Wilson Mizner.* Edward D. Sullivan. N. Y., 1935. 324 p. *DLC, NN*

MOFFAT, ROBERT and MARY. *Lives of Robert and Mary Moffat.* John S. Moffat. N. Y., 1886. 484 p. *MWA*

MOHUN, CHARLES. *A Noble Rake: The Life of Charles, Fourth Lord Mohun. Being a Study in the Historical Background of Thackeray's " Henry Esmond."* Robert S. Forsythe. Cambridge, 1928. 310 p. *DLC, NN, CSmH*

MOISSAN, HENRY. 2:286

MOLIÈRE, JEAN.
Molière, a Biography. H. C. Chatfield-Taylor. N. Y., 1906. 434 p. *DLC, NN, PU*
Molière; His Life and Works. Brander Matthews. N. Y., 1910. 385 p. *DLC, NN*
Molière. Leon H. Vincent. Boston, 1902. 233 p. *DLC, NN, CSmH*

MOLINOS, MICHEL. *Molinos the Quietist.* John Bigelow. N. Y., 1882. 127 p. *DLC, NN, CSmH, PU*

MONAGHAN, JOHN ROBERT. *Life of John Robert Monaghan, the Hero of Samoa.* Henry L. McCulloch. Spokane, 1906. 415 p. (Privately Printed) *DLC, NN*

MONAHAN, JOHN JOSEPH. *The Padre of the Press; Recollections of Rev. John J. Monahan, S.J.* Thomas J. Feeney. N. Y., 1931. 161 p. *DLC, NN*

MONCRIEFFE, MARGARET. *Margaret Moncrieffe, the First Love of Aaron Burr.* C. Burditt. N. Y., 1860. 437 p. *DLC, CSmH*

MONHOLLAND, MARY. *Life of Mary Monholland, One of the Pioneer Sisters of the Order of Mercy in the West.* Chicago, 1894. 183 p.

MONK, MARIA. 2:703

MONROE, ELIZABETH. 2:453

MONROE, JAMES.
The Lives of James Madison and James Monroe. John Q. Adams. Buffalo, 1851. 432 p. *DLC, NN, CSmH, MiU:C*
James Monroe. Daniel C. Gilman. Boston, 1883, 1899. 312 p. (A.S.) *DLC, NN, MWA, CSmH, PU, MiD:B*
Life of James Monroe. George Morgan. Boston, 1921. 484 p. *DLC, NN, PU*
James Madison, James Monroe, and John Quincy Adams. W. O. Stoddard. N. Y., 1887. 331 p. *DLC, MWA*
2:262

MONSON, SIR WILLIAM. 2:7
MONTAGU, EDWARD WORTLEY. 2:71
MONTAGU, LADY MARY WORTLEY. 2:93
MONTALEMBERT, CHARLES FORBES. *Montalembert: a Biographical Sketch.* Joseph W. Wilstach. N. Y., 1885. 118 p.   *NN*
MONTBRUN, JEAN GIRARD. *Life of Jean Girard de Montbrun.* Henry A. Ingram. Phila., 1888. 121 p.   *DLC, NN*
MONTEFIORE, MOSES. *Moses Montefiore.* Paul Goodman. Phila., 1925. 255 p.   *DLC, NN, MWA*
MONTEZ, LOLA. 2:576
MONTGOMERY, JAMES. *Life of James Montgomery.* Helen C. Knight. Boston, 1857. 416 p.   *DLC, NN, PU, MiD:B*
MONTGOMERY, RICHARD. *Life of Richard Montgomery.* John Armstrong. (L.A.B.)   *DLC, NN, MWA, CSmH, PU*
MOODY. *Biography of the Moody Family.* C. C. P. Moody. Boston, 1847. 168 p.   *DLC, NN, MWA, RP:JCB*
MOODY, DWIGHT LYMAN.

    D. L. Moody: Worker in Souls. Gamaliel Bradford. 1927. 320 p.   *DLC, NN, PU*

    The Life and Work of Dwight L. Moody . . . John W. Chapman. Phila., 1900. 555 p.   *DLC, NN*

    D. L. Moody and His Work. W. H. Daniels. Hartford, 1876. 472 p.   *NN, MWA, MiD:B*

    Bush Aglow; The Life Story of Dwight Lyman Moody, Commoner of Northfield. Richard E. Day. Phila., 1936. 333 p.   *DLC, NN, CSmH*

    D. L. Moody, His Message For Today. Charles R. Erdman. N. Y., 1928. 156 p.   *DLC, NN*

    The American Evangelists, D. L. Moody and Ira D. Sankey, in Great Britain and Ireland. John Hall and G. H. Stuart. N. Y., 1875. 455 p.   *DLC, NN*

    The Life of Dwight Lyman Moody. W. R. Moody. N. Y., 1900. 590 p.   *DLC, NN, MWA, CSmH, PU, MiD:B*

    D. L. Moody. William R. Moody. N. Y., 1930. 556 p.   *DLC, NN*

    Lives of the Eminent American Evangelists, D. L. Moody, I. D. Sankey, With Account of Their Labors in Great Britain and America; Also Sketches of the Lives of P. P. Bliss and E. Tourgee. Elias Nason. Boston, 1877. 360 p.   *MWA*

    Life and Labors of Dwight L. Moody. Henry D. Northrop. Phila., 1899. 512 p.   *DLC*

Life and Sermons of Dwight L. Moody. John S. Ogilvie. N. Y., 1900. 402 p. *DLC*

Life and Work of Dwight L. Moody. Augustus W. Williams. Phila., 1900. 416 p. *DLC*
2:6

MOODY, WILLIAM VAUGHN.

William Vaughn Moody; a Study. David D. Henry. Boston, 1934. 276 p. *DLC, NN, PU*

William Vaughn Moody. E. H. Lewis. Chicago, 1914. 44 p. *DLC, NN, CSmH*

Selected Poems of William Vaughn Moody. Robert M. Lovett. Boston, 1931. *DLC, NN*

MOORE, EDWARD. *The Life and Works of Edward Moore.* John H. Caskey. New Haven, 1927. 202 p. (Yale Studies in English, No. 75) *DLC, NN, CSmH, PU*

MOORE, JOHN. *Memoir of Rev. John Moore.* John G. Adams. Boston, 1856. 360 p. *NN, MWA*

MOORE, PLINY. *Obituary of Judge Pliny Moore (1739–1822).* Hugh McLellan, ed. Champlain, N. Y., 1929. 27 p.
DLC, NN, MWA, CSmH

MOORE, RICHARD CHANNING.

Memoir of the Life of the Rt. Rev. Richard Channing Moore, Bishop of the Protestant Episcopal Church in the Diocese of Virginia. J. P. K. Henshaw. Phila., 1843. 503 p. *DLC, NN, PU*

The Life of . . . Richard Channing Moore . . . Bishop of Virginia . . . John N. Norton. N. Y., 1857. 95 p. *NN*

MOORE, THOMAS. *Biographical Sketch of Thomas Moore in Moore's " Complete Poetical Works."* Nathan H. Dole. N. Y., 1895.
DLC

MOORE, WILLIAM. 2:521

MORAY, ROBERT. *The Life of Sir Robert Moray, Soldier, Statesman and Man of Science.* Alexander Robertson. N. Y. and London, 1922. 223 p. *DLC, NN, CSmH, PU*

MORE, HANNAH.

A New Memoir of Hannah More. Helen C. Knight. N. Y., 1851. 311 p. *DLC, NN, PU*

Hannah More. Mary V. H. Terhune. N. Y., 1900. 238 p.
DLC, NN, PU

MORE, PAUL ELMER. *Paul Elmer More and American Criticism.* Robert Shafer. New Haven, 1935. 325 p. *DLC, NN, CSmH*

MORE, THOMAS.
> *The Century of Sir Thomas More.* Benjamin O. Flower. Boston, 1896. 293 p.   *NN, CSmH*
>> *Thomas More.* Daniel Sargent. N. Y., 1933. 299 p.
>>   *DLC, NN, CSmH, PU*

MOREHEAD, JOHN MOTLEY. *John Motley Morehead and the Development of North Carolina, 1796–1866.* Burton A. Konkle. Phila., 1922. 437 p.   *DLC, MiD:B*

MOREHOUSE, HENRY LYMAN. *Henry Lyman Morehouse.* Lathan A. Crandall. Phila., 1919. 240 p.   *DLC*

MORGAGNI, JOHN BAPTIST. 2:678

MORGAN, ARTHUR E. *Finding His World; the Story of Arthur E. Morgan.* Lucy G. Morgan. Yellow Springs, O., 1927. 108 p.
      DLC, NN

MORGAN, DANIEL.
> *The Life of General Daniel Morgan.* James Graham. N. Y., 1856. 475 p.   *DLC, NN, MWA, CSmH, PU, MiD:B, MiU:C*
>> *The Hero of Cowpens. A Centennial Sketch . . .* Rebecca M'Conkey. N. Y., 1881. 295 p.   *DLC, NN*

MORGAN, EDWIN DENISON. 2:623

MORGAN, GEORGE. *George Morgan, Colony Builder.* Max Savelle. N. Y., 1932. 266 p.   *DLC, NN, CSmH, PU*

MORGAN, GEORGE CAMPBELL. *G. Campbell Morgan, the Man and His Ministry.* John Harries. N. Y., 1930. 252 p.   *DLC, NN, PU*

MORGAN, HENRY.
> *Sir Henry Morgan, Buccaneer.* Merritt P. Allen. N. Y., 1931. 244 p.   *DLC, NN*
> *Sir Henry Morgan, Buccaneer.* Cyrus T. Brady. N. Y., 1903. 446 p.   *DLC*
> *Sir Henry Morgan, Buccaneer and Governor.* Walter A. Roberts. N. Y., 1933. 320 p.   *DLC, NN, PU*

MORGAN. *House of Morgan; a Social Biography of the Masters of Money.* Lewis Corey. N. Y., 1930. 479 p.   *DLC, NN, PU*

MORGAN, JOHN PIERPONT. *Life Story of J. Pierpont Morgan.* Carl Hovey. N. Y., 1911. 352 p.   *DLC, NN, PU, MiD:B*
> *Morgan, the Magnificent; the Life of J. Pierpont Morgan, (1837–1913).* John K. Winkler. N. Y., 1930. 313 p.
>   *DLC, NN, MWA, PU*

MORGAN, JOHN HUNT. *The Rebel Raider. The Life of John Hunt Morgan.* Howard Swiggett. Indianapolis, 1934. 341 p.
      DLC, NN, CSmH, PU

2:612

MORGAN, LEWIS HENRY.
    Memoir of Lewis H. Morgan of Rochester, N. Y. Charles H.
Hart. Phila., 1883. 12 p.   *DLC, NN, MWA*
    Lewis Henry Morgan, Social Evolutionist. Bernhard J. Stern.
Chicago, 1931. 221 p.   *DLC, NN, CSmH, PU*
MORGAN, WILLIAM. *The Strange Disappearance of William Morgan.*
Thomas A. Knight. Brecksville, O., 1932. 302 p.
        DLC, NN, MWA
MORISON, JOHN HOPKINS. *John Hopkins Morison, a Memoir.* George
S. Morison. Boston, 1897. 298 p.   *DLC, NN*
MORLEY, CHRISTOPHER. 2:366
MORRILL, JUSTIN SMITH. *Life and Public Services of Justin Smith
Morrill.* William B. Parker. Boston, 1924. 378 p.
        DLC, NN, MWA, PU, MiD:B
MORRIS, GEORGE SYLVESTER. *Life and Work of George Sylvester Mor-
ris.* Robert M. Wenley. N. Y., 1917. 332 p.
        DLC, NN, MWA, CSmH, PU
MORRIS, GOUVERNEUR.
    Gouverneur Morris. Theodore Roosevelt. Boston, 1888. 370 p.
(A.S.)   *DLC, NN, MWA, CSmH, PU, MiD:B*
    *Life of Gouverneur Morris, With Selections From His Corre-
spondence and Miscellaneous Papers.* Jared Sparks. Boston, 1832.
3 vols.   *DLC, NN, MWA, CSmH, PU, MiD:B, MiU:C*
MORRIS, ROBERT.
    Life of Robert Morris. David Gould. Boston, 1834. 126 p.
        DLC, MWA, MiU:C
    *Robert Morris, the Financier of the American Revolution; a
Sketch.* Charles H. Hart. Phila., 1877. 11 p.
        DLC, NN, MWA, CSmH, PU, MiD:B
    Robert Morris, Patriot and Financier. E. P. Oberholtzer. N. Y.,
1903. 372 p.   *DLC, NN, MWA, CSmH, PU, MiU:C, RP:JCB*
    Robert Morris. William G. Sumner. N. Y., 1892. 172 p.
(Makers of America)   *DLC, NN, MWA, PU, MiD:B*
MORRIS, SAMUEL. *Glimpses of the Life of Samuel Morris.* Hannah
P. Morris. Phila., 1907. 206 p.   *DLC, NN, MWA, PU*
MORRIS, THOMAS. *The Life of Thomas Morris . . . U. S. Senator
(from Ohio) from 1833 to 1839.* B. F. Morris. Cincinnati, 1856.
408 p.   *DLC, NN, MWA, CSmH, MiD:B*
MORRIS, THOMAS ASBURY. *The Life of Rev. Thomas A. Morris, D.D.,
Late Senior Bishop of the M. E. Church.* John F. Marlay. Cin-
cinnati, N. Y., 1875. 407 p.   *DLC, NN*

MORRIS, WILLIAM. *William Morris, Poet, Craftsman, Socialist.* Elizabeth L. Cary. N. Y., 1902. 296 p. *DLC, NN, PU*

MORRISON, HENRY CLAY. *A Biographical Sketch of Henry Clay Morrison, D.D., Editor of " The Pentecostal Herald": the Man and His Ministry.* Charles F. Wimberly. N. Y., 1922. 214 p.
DLC, NN

MORRISON, WILLIAM McCUTCHAN. *William McCutchan Morrison, Twenty Years in Central Africa.* T. C. Vinson. Richmond, Texarkana, Ark., 1921. 201 p. *DLC, NN*

MORROW, DWIGHT WHITNEY.
Dwight Whitney Morrow. Hewitt H. Howland. N. Y., 1930.
91 p. *DLC, NN, MWA, PU*
Story of Dwight W. Morrow. Mary M. McBride. N. Y.,
1930. 183 p. *DLC, NN, PU*

MORSE, JEDIDIAH. *The Life of Jedidiah Morse.* William B. Sprague.
N. Y., 1874. 333 p. *DLC, NN, MiD:B*

MORSE, SAMUEL FINLEY BREESE.
Samuel F. B. Morse: His Letters and Journals. Edward L.
Morse. Boston, 1914. 2 vols. *DLC, NN, MWA, CSmH, PU*
The Life of Samuel F. B. Morse. Samuel I. Prime. N. Y.,
1875. 776 p. *DLC, NN, MWA, CSmH, PU*
Samuel F. B. Morse. J. Trowbridge. N. Y., 1901. 134 p.
(Beacon Biographies) *DLC, MiD:B*
2:343–660

MORTIMER, MARY. *A True Teacher; Mary Mortimer . . . a Memoir.*
Minerva B. Norton. N. Y., 1894. 341 p. *DLC, CSmH*

MORTON, HENRY. *Biographical Notice of Pres't Henry Morton, of the Stevens Institute of Technology . . .* Coleman Sellers and Albert R. Leeds. N. Y., 1892. 138 p. *DLC, NN, PU*

MORTON, LEVI PARSONS.
Levi Parsons Morton. Robert M. McElroy. N. Y., 1930. 340 p.
DLC, NN, MWA, CSmH, PU
Benjamin Harrison and Levi P. Morton. Gilbert L. Harney.
Providence, 1888. 479 p. *DLC, NN*
2:623

MORTON, OLIVER PERRY.
Life of Oliver P. Morton. William D. Foulke. Indianapolis,
1899. 2 vols. *DLC, NN, MWA, PU, MiD:B*
*Sketch of the Life, Character and Public Services of Oliver P.
Morton.* C. M. Walker. Indianapolis, 1878. 191 p.
DLC, NN, MWA

MORTON, SARAH WENTWORTH. *Philenia, the Life and Works of Sarah Wentworth Morton.* Milton Ellis and Emily Pendleton. Orono, Me., 1931. 122 p. (University of Maine Studies, Second Series, No. 20) *DLC, NN, MWA, CSmH, PU*

MORTON, THOMAS. 2:598

MOSBY, JOHN SINGLETON. *Mosby and His Men: a Record of the Adventures of That Renowned Partisan Ranger.* J. Marshall Crawford. N. Y., 1867. 375 p. *DLC, NN, MWA, CSmH*

MOSELEY, HENRY G. J. 2:348

MOSES. 2:336–665

MOSLEY, EDWARD AUGUSTUS. *Life Work of Edward A. Mosley in the Service of Humanity.* James Morgan. N. Y., 1913. 378 p.
DLC

MOTLEY, JOHN LOTHROP. *Memoir of John Lothrop Motley.* Oliver Wendell Holmes. Boston, 1879. 278 p.
DLC, NN, MWA, CSmH, PU, MiD:B

MOTT, JAMES.
James Mott: a Biographical Sketch. Mary Grew. N. Y., 1868. 40 p. *NN, MWA*
James and Lucretia Mott: Life and Letters. Anna D. Hallowell, ed. Boston, 1884. 566 p. *DLC, NN, MWA, CSmH*

MOTT, JOHN RALEIGH. *John R. Mott, World Citizen.* Basil J. Mathews. N. Y., 1934. 469 p. *DLC, NN*

MOTT, VALENTINE.
Memoir of the Life and Character of Prof. Valentine Mott. S. W. Francis. N. Y., 1865. 32 p. *DLC, NN, CSmH, PU*
Memoir of Valentine Mott. Samuel D. Gross. N. Y., 1868. 96 p. *DLC, NN, PU*

MOTTEY, JOSEPH. 2:681

MOULTON, LOUISE CHANDLER. *Louise Chandler Moulton, Poet and Friend.* Lillian Whiting. Boston, 1910. 294 p.
DLC, NN, MWA, CSmH

MOULTRIE, WILLIAM. 2:290

MOUNTAIN, JOSEPH. *Sketches of the Life of Joseph Mountain, a Negro . . . Executed . . . for Rape . . .* David Daggett. New Haven, 1790. 20 p.

MOUNTFORT, WILLIAM. *The Life and Death of William Mountfort.* Albert S. Borgman. Cambridge, 1935. 221 p. (Harvard Studies in English. Vol. XV) *DLC, NN, CSmH, PU*

MOWRY, SALOME LINCOLN. *The Female Preacher; or, Memoir of Salome Lincoln. Afterwards the Wife of Elder Junia S. Mowry.* Almond H. Davis. Providence, 1843. 162 p. *DLC, NN*

MOYLAN, STEPHEN. *General Stephen Moylan, Muster-Master General, Secretary and Aide-de-Camp to General Washington* . . . Martin I. J. Griffin. Phila., 1909. 142 p. *DLC, NN, MWA, PU*

MOZART, WOLFGANG A. *Mozart.* Marcia Davenport. N. Y., 1932. 400 p. *DLC, NN, PU*
2:187

MOZLEY, JAMES BOWLING. 2:98

MUDD, SAMUEL ALEXANDER. *Life of Dr. Samuel A. Mudd . . . Imprisoned Four Years for Alleged Complicity in the Assassination of Abraham Lincoln.* Nettie Mudd. N. Y., 1906. 326 p.
DLC, NN, PU, MiD:B

MUHLENBERG, HENRY MELCHIOR.
Henry M. Muhlenberg. W. K. Frick. Phila., 1902. 200 p.
DLC, NN
Life and Times of Henry M. Muhlenberg. William J. Mann. Phila., 1887. 547 p. *DLC, NN, PU*
An Eagle of the Wilderness; the Story of Henry Melchior Muhlenberg. Margaret R. Seebach. Phila., 1924. 139 p. *DLC, NN*
Memoir of the Life and Times of Henry Melchior Muhlenberg, D.D., Patriarch of the Evangelical Lutheran Church in America. Martin L. Stoever. Phila., 1856. *DLC, NN, PU*

MUHLENBERG, PETER. *Life of Maj.-Gen. Peter Muhlenberg.* Henry A. Muhlenberg. Phila., 1849. 456 p.
DLC, NN, MWA, CSmH, PU

MUHLENBERG, WILLIAM AUGUSTUS.
Life and Work of William A. Muhlenberg. Anne Ayres. N. Y., 1880. 524 p. *DLC, NN, MWA, PU*
Dr. William A. Muhlenberg. William W. Newton. Boston, 1890. 272 p. (American Religious Leaders) *DLC, NN, MWA*

MUIR, JOHN. *Life and Letters of John Muir.* William F. Bade. Boston, 1924. 2 vols. *DLC, NN, CSmH, PU*
2:41–507–672

MUIR, JOHN. *John Muir of Wall Street.* O. M. Fuller. N. Y., 1927. 325 p. *DLC, NN*

MULDOON, WILLIAM. *Muldoon, the Solid Man of Sport.* Edward Van Every. N. Y., 1929. 364 p. *DLC, NN, PU*

MULLANY, PATRICK FRANCIS. See AZARIAS, BROTHER.

MULLER, GEORGE. 2:675

MÜLLER, JOHANN. 2:678

MULLIGAN, JAMES. *" In Kentucky " and Its Author, " Jim " Mulligan.* John W. Townsend. Lexington, Ky., 1909. 31 p. *DLC, NN*

MUNDELEIN, GEORGE CARDINAL. 2:679

MUNGER, THEODORE THORNTON. *Theodore Thornton Munger, New England Minister.* Benjamin W. Bacon. New Haven, 1913. 409 p.
DLC, NN

MUNSEY, FRANK ANDREW. *Forty Years—Forty Millions; the Career of Frank A. Munsey.* George Britt. N. Y., 1935. 309 p.
DLC, NN, MWA

MURDOCK, JOHN RIGGS. *A Biographical Sketch of John Riggs Murdock.* Joseph M. Tanner. Salt Lake City, 1909. 206 p. *NN*

MURILLO, BARTOLOME. *Murillo.* Moses F. Sweetser. Boston, 1877. 136 p. *DLC, NN*
2:248

MURPHY, JOHN FRANCIS. *J. Francis Murphy.* Eliot C. Clark. N. Y., 1926. 63 p. *DLC, NN*

MURRAY, HANNAH LINDLEY. *Memoirs of the Late Hannah L. Murray.* Gardiner Spring. N. Y., 1849. 312 p. *DLC, NN*

MURRAY, JUDITH SARGENT. *Constantia: a Study of the Life and Works of Judith Sargent Murray, 1751–1820.* Vena B. Field. Orono, Me., 1931. 118 p. (Univ. of Maine Studies, Second Series, No. 17) *DLC, NN, CSmH, PU*

MURRAY, LINDLEY. 2:293

MURRAY, NICHOLAS. *Memoirs of the Rev. Nicholas Murray.* Samuel I. Prime. N. Y., 1862. 438 p. *DLC, NN, MWA, CSmH, PU*

MURRAY, WILLIAM. *Alfalfa Bill, an Intimate Biography.* Gordon Hines. Oklahoma City, Okla., 1932. 308 p. *DLC, NN*

MURRAY, WILLIAM H. *Adirondack Murray.* Harry V. Radford. N. Y., 1905. 84 p. *DLC, NN, MWA, CSmH*

MURRIETA, JOAQUIN.
Joaquin Murieta, the Brigand Chief. San Francisco, 1932. 116 p. *CSmH*

The Robin Hood of El Dorado. The Saga of Joaquin Murrieta, Famous Outlaw of California's Age of Gold. Walter N. Burns. N. Y., 1932. 304 p. *DLC, NN, MWA*

The Life and Adventures of Joaquin Murrietta, the Brigand Chief of California. J. R. Ridge. San Francisco, 1871. 98 p.
DLC, CSmH

MUSSER, JOHN HERR. *Memoir of John Herr Musser, M.D.* George A. Piersol. 9 p. (Reprinted from the Transactions of the College of Physicians of Philadelphia, 1912) *NN, PU*

MUSSET, ALFRED DE. *Alfred de Musset, 1810–1857; a Biography.* Henry D. Sedgwick. Indianapolis, 1931. 343 p. *DLC, NN, PU*

MUSSOLINI, BENITO.
  Mussolini, the Wild Man of Europe. John Bond. Washington, 1929. 206 p.   *DLC, NN*
  Mussolini and the New Italy; Head of the Italian Government, Duce of the Fascisti. Alexander Robertson. N. Y., 1928. 156 p.
                                                          DLC, NN
  Sawdust Caesar; the Untold History of Mussolini and Fascism. George Seldes. N. Y., 1935. 459 p.   *DLC, NN, PU*
  2:94–301

MYLES, JOHN. *Rev. John Myles and the Founding of the First Baptist Church in Massachusetts.* Henry M. King. Providence, 1905. 112 p.   *DLC, NN, MWA*

NAJERA, MANUEL GUTIÉRREZ. *Life and Works of Manuel Gutiérrez Najera.* Nell Walker. Columbia, Mo., 1927. 83 p.   *DLC, NN*

NASBY, PETROLEUM V. (DAVID C. LOCKE.) *Petroleum Vesuvius Nasby.* Cyril Clemens. Webster Groves, Mo., 1936. 162 p.
                                                          DLC, NN

NAST, THOMAS. *Th. Nast, His Period and His Pictures.* Albert B. Paine. N. Y., 1904. 583 p.   *DLC, NN, CSmH, PU*

NATION, CARRY.
  Carry Nation. Herbert Asbury. N. Y., 1929. 307 p.
                                                          DLC, NN
  Use and Need of a Life of Carry A. Nation. Carry A. M. Nation. Topeka, 1904. 184 p.   *DLC, NN*

NEAL, DAVID DALHOFF. 2:52

NEALE, JOHN MASON. *John Mason Neale; a Memoir.* Eleanor A. Towle. N. Y., 1906. 238 p.   *DLC, NN*

NEESIMA, JOSEPH HARDY.
  Sketch of the Life of Joseph Hardy Neesima. J. D. Davis. N. Y., 1894. 156 p.   *DLC, NN, MWA*
  Life and Letters of Joseph Hardy Neesima. Arthur S. Hardy. Boston, 1891. 350 p.   *DLC, NN, MWA, CSmH*
  A Sketch of the Early Life of Joseph Hardy Neesima. Phebe F. McKeen. Boston, 1890. 52 p.   *DLC, NN*

NEIHARDT, JOHN G. *John G. Neihardt, Man and Poet.* Julius T. House. Wayne, Neb., 1920. 143 p.   *DLC, NN*

NELSON, HORATIO.
  Life of Nelson. Joseph Allen. N. Y., 1886. 160 p.
  The Life of Nelson, the Embodiment of the Sea Power of Great Britain. Alfred T. Mahan. Boston, 1897. 2 vols.
                                                   DLC, NN, CSmH, PU

NELSON, KNUTE. *The Life of Knute Nelson.* Martin W. Odland. Minneapolis, 1926. 335 p. *DLC, NN, PU*

NELSON, WILLIAM ROCKHILL. *William Rockhill Nelson; the Story of a Man, a Newspaper and a City.* Cambridge, 1915. 274 p. (Privately Printed) *DLC, NN, MWA, PU, MiD:B*

NERINCKX, CHARLES.

Life of Rev. Charles Nerinckx, Pioneer Missionary of Kentucky and Founder of the Sisters of Loretto at the Foot of the Cross. William J. Howlett. Techny, Ill., 1915. 447 p. *DLC, NN*

Life of Rev. C. Nerinckx; With a Chapter on the Early Catholic Missions of Kentucky . . . Camillus P. Maes. Cincinnati, 1880. 635 p. *NN*

NETTLETON, ASAHEL. *Memoir of the Life and Character of Rev. Asahel Nettleton, D.D.* Bennett Tyler. Hartford, 1844. 372 p. *DLC, NN, CSmH, MiD:B*

NEUMAN, JOHN NEPOMUCENE. *Short Life of the Venerable Servant of God, John N. Neuman, Bishop of Philadelphia.* J. Magnier. St. Louis, 1897. 99 p.

NEVIN, ETHELBERT.

Ethelbert Nevin. John Tasker Howard. N. Y., 1935. 423 p. *DLC, NN*

Life of Ethelbert Nevin, From His Letters and His Wife's Memories. Vance Thompson. Boston, 1913. 247 p. *DLC, NN*

NEVIN, JOHN WILLIAMSON. *Life and Work of John W. Nevin.* Theodore Appel. Phila., 1889. 776 p. *DLC*

NEVINS, WILLIAM. *Select Remains of the Rev. William Nevins, D.D. With a Memoir.* N. Y., 1836. 398 p. *DLC, NN, MWA*

NEVIUS, JOHN LIVINGSTON. *Life of John L. Nevius, For Thirty Years a Missionary in China.* Helen S. Nevins. N. Y., 1895. 476 p. *DLC, NN, MWA*

NEWCASTLE, THOMAS PELHAM-HOLLES, DUKE OF. *Thomas Pelham-Holles, Duke of Newcastle; His Early Political Career, 1693–1724.* Stebelton H. Nulle. Phila., 1931. 204 p. *DLC, NN, CSmH, PU*

NEWCOMB, EDGAR MARSHALL. *A Memorial Sketch of Lieut. Edgar M. Newcomb, of the Nineteenth Mass. Vols.* A. B. Weymouth. Malden, 1883. 134 p. *DLC, NN, MWA, CSmH*

NEWKIRK, MATTHEW. *A Memorial of Matthew Newkirk.* Matthew Newkirk, Jr. Phila., 1869. 123 p. (Privately Printed) *DLC, NN, PU*

NEWMAN, JOHN HENRY.

Life of Cardinal Newman. Gaius G. Atkins. N. Y., 1931. 338 p. *DLC, NN, PU*

John Henry Newman, the Romantic, the Friend, the Leader.
Sister Mary A. Kiener. Boston, 1933. 510 p. *DLC, NN*
Newman as a Man of Letters. Joseph J. Reilly. N. Y., 1925.
329 p. *DLC, NN, PU*
*John Henry Newman; Anglican Minister, Catholic Priest, Roman
Cardinal.* J. Elliot Ross. N. Y., 1933. 258 p. *DLC, NN, PU*
2:98

NEWPORT, ELIZABETH. *Memoir of Elizabeth Newport.* Ann A. Townsend, comp. Phila., 1874. 310 p. *NN, PU*

NEWSAM, ALBERT. *Memoir of Albert Newsam, Deaf Mute Artist.*
Joseph O. Pyatt. Phila., 1868. 160 p. *DLC, NN, MWA, PU*

NEWTON, ADELAIDE LEAPER. *A Memoir of Adelaide Leaper Newton.*
John Baillie. N. Y., 1858. 364 p. *DLC, NN, MWA*

NEWTON, ISAAC. *Isaac Newton; a Biography.* Louis T. More. N. Y.,
1934. 675 p. *DLC, NN*
2:79–335

NEWTON, ROBERT. *The Life of Rev. Robert Newton, D.D.* Thomas
Jackson. N. Y., 1855. 427 p. *DLC, NN, MWA*

NEY, MICHEL. *Marshal Ney Before and After Execution; With Numerous Illustrations.* James E. Smoot. Charlotte, N. C., 1929.
460 p. *DLC, NN*

NEZ PERCÉ JOSEPH. *Nez Percé Joseph, an Account of His Ancestors,
His Lands, His Confederates, His Enemies, His Murders, His. War,
His Pursuit and Capture.* Oliver O. Howard. Boston, 1881. 274 p.
NN

NICHOLAS I. *The Life and Reign of Nicholas I., Emperor of Russia.*
Samuel M. Schmucker. Phila., 1856. 407 p. *DLC, NN*
2:1

NICHOLSON, TIMOTHY. *Timothy Nicholson, Master-Quaker; a Biography.* Walter C. Woodward. Richmond, Ind., 1927. 252 p.
DLC, NN

NICOLL, DELANCEY. *DeLancey Nicoll, an Appreciation.* Joseph S.
Auerbach. N. Y., 1931. 125 p. *DLC, NN*

NIETZSCHE, FRIEDRICH. *Son of the Morning: a Portrait of Friedrich
Nietzsche.* Edward J. O'Brien. N. Y., 1932. 294 p. *DLC, NN*

NIGHTINGALE, FLORENCE.

A Lost Commander: Florence Nightingale. Mary R. S. An-
drews. Garden City, N. Y., 1929. 299 p. *DLC, NN*
Florence Nightingale, the Wounded Soldier's Friend. Eliza F.
Pollard. N. Y., 1891. 160 p. (World's Benefactors Series)
DLC, NN

Florence Nightingale; the Angel of the Crimea. Laura E. Richards. N. Y., 1909. 167 p.   *DLC, MWA*
2:9

NINDE, WILLIAM XAVIER. *William Xavier Ninde.* Mary L. Ninde. N. Y., 1902. 290 p.   *DLC, NN, MWA, MiD:B*

NISBET, CHARLES.
Memoir of the Rev. Charles Nisbet, Late President of Dickinson College, Carlisle. Samuel Miller. N. Y., 1840. 357 p.
    DLC, NN

Charles Nisbet, First President of Dickinson College; His Book, 1736–1804. Sarah W. Parkinson. n.p., 1908. 14 p.
    DLC, MWA

NIXON, JOHN. *Memoir of the Life and Services of Col. John Nixon.* Charles H. Hart. Phila., 1877. 19 p.
    DLC, NN, MWA, PU, MiD:B, MiU:C

NOAH, MORDECAI MANUEL. *Mordecai Manuel Noah.* Simon Wolf. Phila., 1897. 49 p.   *DLC, NN, MWA, CSmH*

NOGUCHI, HIDEYO. *Noguchi.* Gustav Eckstein. N. Y., 1931. 419 p.
    DLC, NN, PU

NOLAN, THOMAS. *The Barrister; Being Anecdotes of the Late Tom Nolan of the New York Bar.* Charles F. Stansbury. N. Y., 1902. 264 p.   *DLC, NN*

NORRIS, FRANK. *Frank Norris; a Biography.* Franklin Walker. N. Y., 1932. 317 p.   *DLC, NN, PU*

NORRIS, ISAAC. 2:594

NORSWORTHY, NAOMI. *Life of Naomi Norsworthy.* Frances C. Higgins. Boston, 1918. 243 p.   *DLC, NN*

NORTH, EDWARD. *Old Greek . . . a Memoir of Edward North.* S. N. D. North. N. Y., 1905. 417 p.   *DLC, NN, MWA*

NORTH, SIMEON. *Simeon North: First Official Pistol Maker of the United States. A Memoir.* S. N. D. North and Ralph H. North. Concord, N. H., 1913. 207 p.   *DLC, NN, MWA, PU*

NORTHROP, CYRUS. *Cyrus Northrop. A Memoir.* Oscar W. Firkins. Minneapolis, 1925. 634 p.   *DLC, NN, PU*

NORTON, CHARLES ELIOT. *Charles Eliot Norton.* E. W. Emerson. Boston, 1912. 53 p.   *DLC, NN, CSmH, PU*
2:114

NORTON, JOHN. 2:405–428

NORTON, JOHN PITKIN. *Memorials of John Pitkin Norton, Late Professor of Analytical and Agricultural Chemistry, in Yale College, New Haven, Conn.* John P. Norton. Albany, 1853. 85 p.
    DLC, NN, MWA

NOTT, ABNER KINGMAN. *Memoir of Abner Kingman Nott, Late Pastor of the First Baptist Church of New York.* Richard M. Nott. N. Y., 1860. 395 p.   *NN, MWA*

NOTT, ELIPHALET. *Memoirs of Eliphalet Nott.* Cornelius Van Santvoord and Lewis Taylor. N. Y., 1876. 390 p.
    DLC, NN, CSmH, PU

NOYES, JOHN HUMPHREY.
    John Humphrey Noyes, the Putney Community. George W. Noyes, ed. Oneida, N. Y., 1931. 393 p.
    DLC, NN, MWA, CSmH
    A Yankee Saint; John Humphrey Noyes and the Oneida Community. Robert A. Parker. N. Y., 1935. 322 p.
    DLC, NN, CSmH, PU, MiD:B

NUGENT, THOMAS LEWIS. *Life Work of Thomas L. Nugent.* Catherine Nugent, ed. Stephenville, Tex., 1896. 398 p.
    DLC, NN, CSmH

NUNN, LUCIEN LUCIUS. *L. L. Nunn, a Memoir.* Stephen A. Bailey. Ithaca, N. Y., 1933. 180 p.   *DLC, NN*

NURSE, REBECCA. *Rebecca Nurse; Saint but Witch Victim.* Charles S. Tapley. Boston, 1930. 105 p.   *DLC, NN, MWA, PU*

NYE, WILLIAM. *Bill Nye, His Own Life Story.* Frank W. Nye, comp. N. Y., 1926. 412 p.   *DLC, NN, MWA*

OAKLEY, ANNIE. *Annie Oakley, Woman at Arms.* Courtney R. Cooper. N. Y., 1927. 270 p.   *DLC, NN, PU*

OBERLIN, JOHN. *Oberlin, a Protestant Saint.* Marshall Dawson. Chicago, 1934. 166 p.   *DLC, NN*

OBREGÓN, ALVARO. *President Obregón—a World Reformer.* Emile J. Dillon. Boston, 1923. 350 p.   *DLC, NN, PU*

O'BRIEN, FITZ-JAMES. *Biographical Sketch of Fitz-James O'Brien in " The Poems and Stories of Fitz-James O'Brien."* William Winter. Boston, 1881. 485 p.   *DLC, NN, MWA*

O'BRIEN, JEREMIAH. *Life of Captain Jeremiah O'Brien of Machias, Maine.* A. M. Sherman. Morristown, N. J., 1902. 247 p.
    DLC, NN, CSmH, PU

O'CALLAGHAN, EDMUND BAILEY. *Edmund Bailey O'Callaghan; a Study in American Historiography (1797–1880).* Francis S. Guy. Washington, 1934. 93 p.   *DLC, NN, PU*

OCCOM, SAMSON.
    Samson Occom. Harold Blodgett. Hanover, N. H., 1935. 230 p.   *DLC, NN*
    Samson Occom and the Christian Indians of New England. W. De Loss Love. Boston, 1899. 379 p.   *DLC*

O'Connell, William Cardinal.   2:679
O'Connor, Michael Patrick.   *Life and Letters of M. P. O'Connor.*
Mary D. O'Connor.   N. Y., 1893.   561 p.   *DLC, CSmH*
Odoric, Friar.   2:680
O'Dwyer, Joseph.   2:678
Oersted, Hans Christian.   2:25
Officer, Morris.   *Life of Rev. Morris Officer.*   Alex. J. Imhoff.   Dayton, O., 1876.   464 p.   *DLC, NN*
Oglethorpe, James.
   Life of General Oglethorpe.   H. Bruce.   N. Y., 1890.   297 p.
   (Makers of America Series)   *NN, MWA, MiD:B*
   James Oglethorpe.   The Founder of Georgia.   H. C. Cooper.
   N. Y., 1904.   317 p.   *DLC, NN, MWA, CSmH*
   James Edward Oglethorpe, Imperial Idealist.   Amos A. Ettinger.   Oxford, 1936.   348 p.   *DLC, NN, CSmH, PU*
   *Biographical Memorials of James Oglethorpe, Founder of the
   Colony of Georgia* ...   Thaddeus M. Harris.   Boston, 1841.   424 p.
   (Privately Printed)   *DLC, NN, MWA, CSmH, PU, MiD:B*
   Life of General Oglethorpe.   William B. O. Peabody.   (L.A.B.)
           DLC, NN, MWA, CSmH
O'Hara, Theodore.   *" The Bivouac of the Dead " and its Author.
Contains a Memoir of Theodore O'Hara.*   George W. Ranck.   N. Y.,
1899.   50 p.   *DLC, NN, MWA, PU, MiD:B*
   2:503
Ohm, G. S.   2:25
O'Keeffe, Georgia.   2:236
Older, Fremont.   *Fremont Older.*   Evelyn Wells.   N. Y., 1936.
407 p.   *DLC*
Oliver, Fitch Edward.   *Memoir of Fitch Edward Oliver, M.D.*   Edmund F. Slafter.   Boston, 1894.   16 p.   (Privately Printed)
           DLC, NN, MWA
Oliver, James.   2:331
Olmsted, Arthur George.   *Arthur George Olmsted, Son of a Pennsylvania Pioneer* ... *Citizen, Jurist, Statesman.*   Rufus B. Stone.
Phila., 1919.   268 p.   *DLC, NN, CSmH, MiD:B*
Olmsted, Frederick Law.
   Frederick Law Olmsted: a Critic of the Old South.   Broadus
   Mitchell.   Balt., 1924.   158 p.   (Johns Hopkins Univ. Studies in
   Hist. and Polit. Science. v. 42)   *DLC, NN, CSmH, PU*
   *Biographical Sketch of Frederick Law Olmsted in " A Journey in
   the Seaboard Slave States With Remarks on Their Economy."*   Frederick Law Olmsted, Jr.   N. Y., 1904.   2 vols.   *DLC, NN, CSmH*

OLMSTED, GIDEON. *Captain Gideon Olmsted; Connecticut Privateersman in the Revolutionary War.* Louis F. Middlebrook. Salem, Mass., 1933. 172 p.   *DLC, NN, CSmH*

OLNEY, RICHARD. *Richard Olney and His Public Service.* Henry James. Boston, 1923. 335 p.   *DLC, NN, MWA, CSmH, PU*

OLNEY, STEPHEN. See BARTON, WILLIAM.

OMAR KHAYYAM. *Omar Khayyam, a Life.* Harold Lamb. N. Y., 1934. 316 p.   *DLC*

O'NEILL, EUGENE.

Eugene O'Neill. Barrett H. Clark. N. Y., 1926. 110 p.   *DLC, NN, PU*

Eugene O'Neill, the Man and His Plays. Barrett H. Clark. N. Y., 1929. rev. ed. London, 1933. 214 p.   *DLC, NN, PU*

Eugene O'Neill; a Critical Study . . . Sophus K. Winther. N. Y., 1934. 303 p.   *DLC, NN*

2:366–592

OP DEN GRAEFF, ABRAHAM and DIRCK. 2:521

ORAGE, ALFRED RICHARD. 2:236

ORCHARD, W. E. 2:487

O'REILLY, JOHN BOYLE. *The Life of John Boyle O'Reilly.* James J. Roche. N. Y., 1891. 790 p.   *DLC, NN, MWA, CSmH, PU*

ORIGEN. 2:371

ORLÉANS, ELISABETH CHARLOTTE. *The Rabelaisian Princess, Madame Royale of France.* Harold D. Eberlein. N. Y., 1931. 304 p.   *DLC, NN*

ORNSTEIN, LEO. 2:236

ORRUM, EILLEY. *Eilley Orrum, Queen of the Comstock.* Swift Paine. Indianapolis, 1929. 309 p.   *DLC, NN, MWA*

OSBORN, SARAH. *Memoirs of the Life of Mrs. Sarah Osborn.* Samuel Hopkins. Worcester, Mass., 1799. 380 p.   *DLC, NN, MWA, CSmH, RP:JCB*

OSBORNE, THOMAS MOTT.

There is No Truce; a Life of Thomas Mott Osborne. Rudolph W. Chamberlain. N. Y., 1935. 420 p.   *DLC, NN, PU*

Osborne of Sing Sing. Frank Tannenbaum. Chapel Hill, 1933. 343 p.   *DLC, NN*

OSGOOD, HERBERT LEVI. *Herbert Levi Osgood; an American Scholar.* Dixon R. Fox. N. Y., 1924. 167 p.   *DLC, NN, MWA, CSmH, PU*

OSLER, WILLIAM.

The Life of Sir William Osler. Harvey Cushing. Oxford, 1925. 2 vols.   *DLC, NN, CSmH, PU*

The Great Physician. A Short Life of Sir William Osler. Edith
G. Reid. N. Y., 1931. 299 p. *DLC, NN, PU*
OSWELL, WILLIAM COTTON. *William Cotton Oswell, Hunter and Explorer.* W. E. Oswell. N. Y., 1900. 2 vols. *DLC, NN, MWA*
OTEY, JAMES HERVEY. *Memoir of Rt. Rev. James Hervey Otey, the First Bishop of Tennessee.* William M. Green. N. Y., 1885. 359 p.
DLC, NN, MWA, CSmH
OTIS, HARRISON GRAY. *Life and Letters of Harrison Gray Otis.* Samuel E. Morison. Boston, 1913. 2 vols.
DLC, NN, CSmH, PU, MiD:B
OTIS, JAMES.
Life of James Otis. Francis Bowen. (L.A.B.)
DLC, NN, MWA, CSmH
James Otis, the Pre-Revolutionist. John C. Ridpath. Chicago,
1898. 112 p. *DLC, NN, PU, MiD:B*
James Otis. John C. Ridpath. Milwaukee, 1903. 184 p.
(Great Americans of History) *DLC, NN*
The Life of James Otis of Massachusetts. William Tudor.
Boston, 1823. 508 p. *DLC, NN, MWA, PU, MiU:C*
OTTERBEIN, PHILIP WILLIAM. *Life of Philip W. Otterbein. Founder of the Church of the United Brethren in Christ.* A. W. Drury.
Dayton, O., 1913. 384 p. *NN, PU*
OTWAY, THOMAS, AND LEE, NATHANIEL. *Otway and Lee; Biography From a Baroque Age.* Roswell G. Ham. New Haven, 1931. 250 p.
DLC, NN, CSmH
OUGHTRED, WILLIAM. *William Oughtred, a Great Seventeenth-Century Teacher of Mathematics.* Florian Cajori. Chicago, 1916. 100 p.
DLC, NN, CSmH, PU

OULD, MATTIE. 2:518
OVERTON, JOHN WILLIAMS. 2:425
OVID. 2:91
OWEN, JOSEPH. *Story of a Dedicated Life (Joseph Owen); With Sketch of the Life of H. J. Owen.* J. C. Moffat. Princeton, 1887.
DLC
OWEN, ROBERT. *Life of Robert Owen.* Frederic A. Packard. Phila.,
1866. 264 p. *DLC, NN, CSmH, PU*
2:331
OWEN, THOMAS JEFFERSON VANCE. . . . *Chicago's True Founder, Thomas J. V. Owen: a Pleading For Truth and Social Justice in Chicago History.* James R. Haydon. Lombard, Ill., 1934. 312 p.
(Privately Printed) *DLC, NN, CSmH*

OWENS, JOHN EDMOND. *Memoirs of the Professional and Social Life of John E. Owens.* Mrs. M. A. C. Owens. Balt., 1892. 292 p.
DLC, NN, MWA, CSmH

OZANAM, FREDERIC. *Frederic Ozanam, Professor at the Sorbonne. His Life and Works.* Kathleen O'Meara. N. Y., 1878. 345 p.
DLC, NN, PU

PADDOCK, BENJAMIN GREEN. *Memoir of Rev. Benjamin G. Paddock.* Zachariah Paddock. N. Y., 1875. 292 p. *NN, MWA, MiD:B*

PADEREWSKI, IGNACE J. 2:30–236–301

PAGE, HARLAN. *Memoir of Harlan Page.* William A. Hallock. N. Y., 1835. 230 p. *DLC, NN, MWA*

PAGE, THOMAS NELSON. *Thomas Nelson Page.* Roswell Page. N. Y., 1923. 210 p. *DLC, NN, MWA, CSmH, PU*
2:258

PAGE, WALTER HINES.

Training of an American. The Earlier Life and Letters of Walter Hines Page, 1855–1913. Burton J. Hendrick. Boston, 1928. 444 p. *DLC, NN, CSmH, PU*
Life and Letters of Walter Hines Page. Burton J. Hendrick. N. Y., 1925–26. 3 vols. *DLC, NN, CSmH, PU*
2:493

PAINE, ROBERT. *Life of Robert Paine, Bishop of M. E. Church, South.* R. H. Rivers. Nashville, 1884. 314 p. *DLC*

PAINE, ROBERT TREAT. *Two Men of Taunton, in the Course of Human Events, 1731–1829.* Ralph Davol. Taunton, Mass., 1912. 406 p.
DLC, NN

PAINE, ROBERT TROUP. *Memoir of Robert Troup Paine.* Martyn Paine and M. A. W. Paine. N. Y., 1852. 524 p.
DLC, NN, MWA, PU

PAINE, THOMAS.

Thomas Paine, Prophet and Martyr of Democracy. Mary A. Best. N. Y., 1927. 413 p. *DLC, NN, CSmH, PU, MiU:C*
The Life of Thomas Paine. James Cheetham. N. Y., 1809. 347 p. *DLC, NN, MWA, CSmH, MiU:C*
Life of Thomas Paine. Moncure D. Conway. N. Y., 1892. 2 vols. *DLC, NN, MWA, CSmH, PU, MiU:C*
Tom Paine—Liberty Bell. George Creel. N. Y., 1932. 173 p.
DLC, NN, MWA, PU
Thomas Paine, the Apostle of Religious and Political Liberty. John E. Remsburg. Boston, 1880. 134 p. *DLC, NN, CSmH*
Thomas Paine. Ellery Sedgwick. N. Y., 1899. 150 p. (Beacon Biographies) *DLC, NN*

Life of Thomas Paine. Gilbert Vail. N. Y., 1841. 192 p.
DLC, NN, MWA, CSmH, MiD:B, MiU:C

Life of Thomas Paine. William Van der Weyde. N. Y., 1925.
V. 1 of the Patriots Edition of " The Life and Works of Thomas
Paine ") *DLC, NN, CSmH*
> 2:89–150–334–562–660

PALESTRINA, GIOVANNI PIERLUIGI. 2:187

PALFREY, WILLIAM. *Life of William Palfrey.* John G. Palfrey.
(L.A.B.) *DLC, NN, MWA, CSmH*

PALMER, ALBERT GALLATIN. *A Memorial of Albert Gallatin Palmer,
Preacher, Pastor, Poet, and Scholar.* Edward T. Hiscox. Phila.,
1894. 348 p. *DLC, NN*

PALMER, ALICE FREEMAN. *Life of Alice Freeman Palmer.* G. H.
Palmer. Boston, 1908. 354 p. *DLC, NN, MWA, CSmH, PU*
> 2:6–506

PALMER, ALONZO BENJAMIN. *Memorial of Alonzo Benjamin Palmer
(1815–1887).* Henry S. Frieze. Cambridge, 1890. 196 p.
DLC, MWA, PU, MiD:B

PALMER, BENJAMIN MORGAN. *Life and Letters of Benjamin M.
Palmer.* T. C. Johnson. Richmond, 1906. 688 p.
DLC, NN, MWA, CSmH

PALMER, GEORGE HERBERT. *George Herbert Palmer.* Charles M.
Bakewell and Wm. E. Hocking. Cambridge, 1935. 80 p.
DLC, NN

PALMER, NATHANIEL BROWN. *Captain Nathaniel Brown Palmer, an
Old Time Sailor of the Sea.* John R. Spears. N. Y., 1922. 252 p.
DLC, NN, MWA

PALMER, WILLIAM J. *General William J. Palmer, Founder of Colorado
Springs, Builder of Denver and Rio Grande Railroad.* Jeannette
Turpin. Colorado Springs, 1924. 79 p. *DLC, NN*

PANNEBECKER, HENDRIK. *Hendrick Pannebecker, Surveyor of Lands
for the Penns, 1674–1754.* Samuel W. Pennypacker. Phila., 1894.
164 p. *DLC, NN, MWA*

PARACELSUS, THEOPHRASTUS. 2:348–394

PARÉ, AMBROISE. *Life and Times of Ambroise Paré (1510–1590) With
a New Translation of His " Apology " and an Account of His
Journeys in Divers Places.* Francis R. Packard. N. Y., 1921.
297 p. *DLC, NN, CSmH*

PARK, CARLTON. *Carlton Park, Builder.* Ethel M. Sandry. Brooklyn, 1931. 107 p. *DLC, NN*

PARK, EDWARDS AMASA. *Professor Park and His Pupils. A Biographical Sketch.* Boston, 1899. 168 p. *DLC, NN, MWA*

PARKER, CARLETON HUBBELL. *Life of Carleton H. Parker.* Cornelia S. Parker. Boston, 1919. 190 p. *DLC, NN, MWA*

PARKER, EDWIN WALLACE. *Life of Edwin Wallace Parker: Forty-One Years a Missionary in India.* J. H. Messmore. N. Y. and Chicago, 1903. 333 p. *DLC, NN*

PARKER, ELY SAMUEL. *The Life of Ely Samuel Parker.* A. C. Parker. Buffalo, 1919. 346 p. *CSmH*

PARKER, FRANCIS WAYLAND. *Francis Wayland Parker; an Interpretive Biography.* Ida C. Heffron. Los Angeles, 1934. 127 p. *DLC, NN*

PARKER, JOEL. *Memorial of Joel Parker.* Freehold, N. J., 1889. 130 p. *DLC, NN, CSmH, PU*

PARKER, LEONARD FLETCHER. *Leonard Fletcher Parker.* Jacob A. Swisher. Iowa City, 1927. 199 p. (Iowa Biographical Series) *DLC, NN, CSmH, PU, MiD:B*

PARKER, LINUS. *Linus Parker, the Editor Bishop: His Life and Writings.* C. B. Galloway. Nashville, 1886.

PARKER, NATHAN. *Memoir of the Rev. Nathan Parker.* Henry Ware, Jr. n.p., 1834. 92 p. *NN*

PARKER, PETER. 2:237

PARKER, THEODORE.

    Theodore Parker—Preacher and Reformer. John W. Chadwick. Boston, 1901. 422 p. *DLC, NN, MWA, CSmH*

    Theodore Parker. Henry S. Commager. Boston, 1936. 339 p. *DLC, NN, CSmH*

    Story of Theodore Parker. F. E. Cooke. Boston, 1889. 115 p. *DLC, NN, MWA*

    Theodore Parker. John Fiske. Boston, 1889.

    Theodore Parker: A Biography. Octavius B. Frothingham. Boston, 1874. 588 p. *NN, MWA, CSmH, PU*

    Life and Correspondence of Theodore Parker. John Weiss. N. Y., 1864. 2 vols. *NN, MWA, CSmH, PU*
    2:12–40–144–334

PARKMAN, FRANCIS.

    A Life of Francis Parkman. Charles H. Farnham. Boston, 1900. 394 p. *DLC, NN, MWA, CSmH, PU, MiD:B, MiU:C*

    Francis Parkman. A Sketch. O. B. Frothingham. Boston, 1894. (Mass. Hist. Soc. Proc.) *NN, MWA, CSmH*

    Francis Parkman. Henry D. Sedgwick. Boston, 1904. 345 p. (A.M.L.) *DLC, NN, CSmH, PU*

PARMENIUS, STEPHEN. *Memoir of Stephen Parmenius of Buda, With His Latin Poem Translated.* Abiel Holmes. (Mass. Hist. Soc. Coll. ser. I., vol. 9, 1804)   *DLC, NN, CSmH*

PARMLY, WHEELOCK HENDEE. *In Memoriam. Wheelock Hendee Parmly, D.D.* n.p., n.d.   176 p.   *NN, MWA*

PARRISH, JOSEPH. *A Memoir of the Life and Character of the Late Joseph Parrish, M.D.* George B. Wood. Phila., 1840.   72 p.
DLC, NN, MWA, PU, MiD:B

PARSON, RICHARD.   2:71

PARSONS, ALBERT. *Life of Albert Parsons.* Lucy E. Parsons. Chicago, 1889.   254 p.   *DLC, NN, MWA*

PARSONS, EMILY ELIZABETH. *Memoir of Emily E. Parsons.* Theophilus Parsons, ed. Boston, 1880.   159 p.
DLC, NN, MWA, CSmH

PARSONS, JOSEPH. *Cornet Joseph Parsons, One of the Founders of Springfield and Northampton, Mass.* H. M. Burt. N. Y., 1901.   187 p.   *DLC, NN*

PARSONS, LEVI. *Memoir of Rev. Levi Parsons, Late Missionary to Palestine.* Daniel O. Morton. Poultney, Vt., 1824.   431 p.
DLC, NN, MWA

PARSONS, SAMUEL. *Memories of Samuel Parsons, Landscape Architect of the Department of Public Parks, New York.* Mabel Parsons, ed. N. Y., 1926.   150 p.   *DLC, NN*

PARSONS, SAMUEL HOLDEN. *Life and Letters of Samuel H. Parsons, Maj.-Gen. in the Continental Army and Chief Judge of the Northwestern Territory, 1737–1789.* C. S. Hall. Binghamton, N. Y., 1905.   601 p.   *DLC, NN, MWA*

PARSONS, THEOPHILUS. *Memoir of Theophilus Parsons, Chief Justice of the Supreme Judicial Court of Massachusetts.* Theophilus Parsons. Boston, 1859.   476 p.
DLC, NN, MWA, CSmH, PU, MiD:B

PARSONS, USHER. *Memoir of Usher Parsons, M.D.* Charles W. Parsons. Providence, 1870.   72 p.   *DLC, NN, MWA, CSmH*

PARTON, SARA PAYSON. *Memoir of Fanny Fern in " Fanny Fern." A Memorial Volume.* James Parton. N. Y., 1877.   70 p.
DLC, NN

PASCHAL, AGNES. *Ninety-Four Years: Agnes Paschal.* George W. Paschal. Washington, 1871.   361 p.   *DLC, PU*

PASSAVANT, WILLIAM ALFRED. *Life and Letters of W. A. Passavant, D.D.* G. H. Gerberding. Greenville, Pa., 1906.   615 p.
DLC, NN

PASTEUR, LOUIS. *Pasteur.* Samuel J. Holmes. N. Y., 1924. 246 p.
DLC, NN, PU
2:5–79–176–670–675–678

PASTORIUS, FRANCIS DANIEL. *Life of Francis Daniel Pastorius, Founder of Germantown, Pa.* Marion D. Learned. Phila., 1908. 324 p. DLC, NN, PU

PATER, WALTER. *Walter Pater.* Ferris Greenslet. N. Y., 1903. 163 p.
DLC, NN, PU
2:91

PATERSON, ALEXANDER. *The Missionary of Kilmany, Being a Memoir of Alexander Paterson.* John Baillie. N. Y., 1853. 253 p. NN

PATERSON, JOHN. *The Life of John Paterson, Major-General in the Revolutionary Army.* Thomas Egleston. N. Y., 1894. 293 p.
DLC, NN, MWA, PU, MiD:B

PATERSON, WILLIAM. *William Paterson of New Jersey, 1745–1806.* Gertrude S. Wood. Fair Lawn, N. J., 1933. 217 p. DLC, NN

PATRICK, MARY MILLS. *An Educational Ambassador to the Near East; the Story of Mary Mills Patrick and an American College in the Orient.* Hester D. Jenkins. N. Y., 1925. 314 p. DLC, NN, PU

PATTEN, RUTH. *Memoirs of Mrs. Ruth Patten.* William Patten. Hartford, 1834. 148 p.
DLC, NN, MWA, CSmH, MiD:B, MiU:C

PATTERSON, ELIZABETH. 2:518

PATTERSON, JAMES. *Memoir of Rev. James Patterson . . .* Robert Adair. Phila., 1840. 324 p. DLC, NN

PATTERSON, JAMES KENNEDY. *A Biography of James Kennedy Patterson, President of the University of Kentucky from 1869 to 1910.* Mabel H. Pollitt. Louisville, 1925. 408 p. DLC, NN

PATTERSON, JOHN HENRY. *John H. Patterson: Pioneer in Industrial Welfare.* Samuel Crowther. N. Y., 1923. 364 p.
DLC, NN, CSmH

PATTERSON, ROBERT. *Concerning the Forefathers; Being a Memoir, With Personal Narrative Letters to Two Pioneers, Col. Robert Patterson and Col. John Johnson.* Charlotte R. Conover. N. Y., 1902. 432 p. DLC, NN, MWA

PATTON, WILLIAM. *Life and Times of Rev. William Patton and Annals of the Missouri Conference.* David R. M'Anally. St. Louis, 1858. 347 p. NN

PATTRI, JAMES. 2:46

PAUL, SAINT. *Life and Letters of Paul the Apostle.* Lyman Abbott. Boston, 1898. 332 p. DLC, NN
2:371–665

PAULDING, HIRAM. *Life of Hiram Paulding, Rear-Admiral, U. S. N.* Rebecca P. Meade. N. Y., 1910. 321 p.   *DLC, NN*

PAULDING, JAMES KIRKE.
James Kirke Paulding, Versatile American. Amos L. Herold. N. Y., 1926. 167 p. (Col. Univ. Studies in Eng.)
    DLC, NN, MWA, CSmH, PU
Literary Life of James K. Paulding. William I. Paulding. N. Y., 1867. 397 p.   *DLC, NN, MWA, CSmH, PU*

PAXSON, STEPHEN. *A Fruitful Life: Missionary Labors of Stephen Paxson.* Mrs. B. Paxson Drury. Phila., 1882. 217 p.
    NN, MiD:B

PAXTON, ELISHA FRANKLIN. *Memoir and Memorials: Elisha Franklin Paxton, Brigadier-General, C. S. A.* J. G. Paxton. N. Y., 1907. 114 p.   *DLC, NN, CSmH*

PAYNE, D. L. 2:358

PAYNE, HENRY CLAY. *Henry Clay Payne.* W. W. Wight. Milwaukee, 1907. 196 p. (Privately Printed)   *DLC, NN*

PAYNE, JOHN HOWARD.
John Howard Payne: A Biographical Sketch. Charles H. Brainard. Boston, 1885. 144 p.   *DLC, NN, CSmH, PU*
John Howard Payne; American Poet, Actor, Playwright, Consul and the Author of " Home, Sweet Home." Rosa P. Chiles. Washington, 1930. 89 p.   *DLC, NN, MWA, PU*
A Sketch of the Life of John Howard Payne. Theodore S. Fay. Boston, 1833. 27 p.   *DLC, CSmH*
The Early Life of John Howard Payne. W. T. Hanson. Boston, 1913. 226 p. (Privately Printed)
    DLC, NN, MWA, CSmH, PU
The Life and Writings of John Howard Payne, the Author of Home, Sweet Home . . . and Dramatic Works. Gabriel Harrison. Albany, N. Y., 1875. 410 p. *DLC, NN, MWA, CSmH, RP:JCB*
John Howard Payne: Dramatist, Poet, Actor, and Author of Home, Sweet Home; His Life and Writings. Gabriel Harrison. Phila., 1885. 404 p.   *DLC, NN, MWA, CSmH, PU*

PAYNE, ROGER. *Roger Payne and His Art.* William L. Andrews. N. Y., 1892. 35 p.   *NN, MWA*

PAYNTER, HENRY MARTYN. *Henry M. Paynter: A Memoir.* Alice M. Paynter. N. Y., 1895. 298 p.   *DLC*

PAYSON, EDWARD.
A Memoir of Rev. Edward Payson, D.D. Asa Cummings. N. Y., 1849. 486 p.   *DLC, NN, MWA, CSmH, MiD:B*

Mementos of Rev. Edward Payson, D.D.; Embracing a Sketch of His Life and Character, and Selections From His Works. E. L. Janes. N. Y., 1873. 351 p.   *DLC*

PAYTON, CORSE. *The Romance of a Western Boy; the Story of Corse Payton.* Gertrude N. Andrews. Brooklyn, N. Y., 1901. 121 p.
DLC, NN

PEABODY, ANDREW PRESTON. 2:519

PEABODY, EPHRAIM. 2:519

PEABODY, FRANCIS. *Memoir of Francis Peabody, Pres. of the Essex Institute.* Charles W. Upham. Salem, Mass., 1868. 80 p.
DLC, NN, MWA, CSmH, MiD:B

PEABODY, GEORGE.
A Brief Sketch of George Peabody. Jabez L. M. Curry. Cambridge, 1898. 161 p.   *DLC, NN, MWA, CSmH, MiD:B*
Life of George Peabody. Mrs. P. A. Hanaford. Boston, 1870. 308 p.   *DLC, NN, MWA, PU*
2:331

PEABODY, SELIM HOBART. *Selim Hobart Peabody; a Biography.* Katherine P. Girling. Urbana, Ill., 1923. 215 p.   *DLC, NN*

PEABODY, WILLIAM A. *Memoir of William A. Peabody.* Edwards A. Park. Boston, 1860. 106 p.   *MWA*

PEABODY, WILLIAM BOURN OLIVER. *Sermons by the Late William B. O. Peabody, With a Memoir.* O. W. B. Peabody, ed. Boston, 1849. 393 p.   *DLC, NN, MWA*

PEACOCK, THOMAS LOVE. *Life of Thomas Love Peacock.* Carl Van Doren. N. Y., 1911. 298 p.   *DLC, NN*

PEAKE, MARY S. *Memoir of Mary S. Peake.* (*The Colored Teacher at Fortress Monroe.*) L. C. Lockwood. Boston, 1863. 64 p.
NN

PEALE, CHARLES WILLSON. *Charles Willson Peale and His Public Services in the American Revolution.* Albert C. Peale. Washington, 1897. 31 p.   *DLC, NN, PU*

PEALE, REMBRANDT. 2:394

PEARSONS, DANIEL KIMBALL.
Daniel K. Pearsons; His Life and Works. Daniel K. Pearsons. Elgin, Ill., 1912. 405 p.   *DLC, NN, MWA*
Life of Dr. D. K. Pearsons. Edward F. Williams. N. Y. and Boston, 1911. 308 p.   *DLC*

PEARY, ROBERT EDWIN.
Peary, the Man Who Refused to Fail. Fitzhugh Green. N. Y., 1926. 404 p.   *DLC, NN*

Peary. William H. Hobbs. N. Y., 1936. 502 p.

DLC, NN, PU

2:388–396

PECK, EDMUND JAMES. *Life and Work of Rev. E. J. Peck Among the Eskimos.* Arthur Lewis. N. Y., 1904. 349 p. *NN*

PECK, JOHN MASON.

Forty Years of Pioneer Life. Memoir of Rev. J. M. Peck. Rufus Babcock, ed. Phila., 1864. 360 p. *CSmH, PU*

John Mason Peck and One Hundred Years of the Home Missions, 1817–1917. Austen K. DeBlois. N. Y., 1917. 134 p.

NN

Vanguard of the Caravans; a Life-Story of John Mason Peck. Coe S. Hayne. Phila., 1931. 157 p. *DLC, NN*

PEDDICORD, KELION FRANKLIN. *Kelion F. Peddicord, of Quirk's Scouts, Morgan's Kentucky Cavalry, C. S. A.: Biographical and Autobiographical.* Indiana W. P. Logan. N. Y., 1908. 170 p.

DLC, NN, CSmH

PEDDIE, JOHN. *John Peddie. Biographical Sketches Contributed by Friends.* Charles H. Banes, ed. Phila., n.d. 324 p. *MWA*

PEEBLES, JAMES MARTIN. *A Biography of James M. Peebles.* Edward Whipple. Battle Creek, Mich., 1901. 592 p. *DLC, NN*

PEET, JOSIAH. *Memoir . . . of Rev. Josiah Peet.* David Shepley. N. Y., 1844. 187 p. *NN, MWA*

PELHAM, JOHN. *The Life of the Gallant Pelham.* Philip Mercer. Macon, Ga., 1929. 180 p. *DLC, NN*

PEMBERTON, JAMES. 2:594

PENDLETON, GEORGE HUNT. *Life and Speeches of George H. Pendleton.* George Bloss. Cincinnati, 1868. *NN, MWA, MiD:B*

PENDLETON, WILLIAM NELSON. *Memoirs of William Nelson Pendleton, D.D.* Susan P. Lee. Phila., 1893. 490 p. *DLC, NN, CSmH*

PENN, WILLIAM.

William Penn as the Founder of Two Commonwealths. A. C. Buell. N. Y., 1904. 368 p. *DLC, NN, CSmH, MiD:B*

William Penn, 1644–1718. Robert J. Burdette. N. Y., 1882. 366 p. (Lives of American Worthies) *DLC, NN, PU, MiD:B*

Passages From the Life and Writings of William Penn. Thomas P. Cope. Phila., 1882. 512 p. *DLC, NN, CSmH*

History of William Penn. W. H. Dixon. N. Y., 1873. 337 p.

DLC, NN, MWA, CSmH, MiD:B, MiU:C

Life of William Penn. George E. Ellis. (L.A.B.)

DLC, NN, MWA, CSmH, MiD:B

The True William Penn. Sydney G. Fisher. Phila., 1900. 392 p.   *DLC, MWA, PU, MiU:C*

William Penn. G. Hodges. Boston, 1901. 140 p. (Riverside Biographies)   *DLC, NN*

William Penn. Rupert S. Holland. N. Y., 1915. 166 p.
             DLC, NN, PU

The Life of William Penn. Samuel M. Janney. Phila., 1852. 560 p.   *DLC, NN, MWA, CSmH, PU*

The Penns of Pennsylvania and England. Arthur Pound. N. Y., 1932. 349 p.   *DLC, NN, PU*

The Boy who Dared; the Story of Wm. Penn. Mary H. Wade. N. Y., 1929. 238 p.   *DLC*

The Life of William Penn. Mason L. Weems. Phila., 1819. 208 p.   *DLC, NN, MWA, CSmH, PU, MiD:B*
    2:55–594–675

PENNELL, JOSEPH. *Life and Letters of Joseph Pennell.* Elizabeth R. Pennell. Boston, 1929. 2 vols.   *DLC, NN, MWA, PU*

PENNELL, THEODORE LEIGHTON. 2:237

PENNINGTON, SAMUEL HAYES. *Samuel Hayes Pennington, M.D., LL.D., 1806–1900, 9th President of the New Jersey Hist. Society.* W. Nelson. Paterson, N. J., 1906. 9 p.   *DLC, NN, MWA*

PENNYPACKER, MRS. PERCY V. *Mrs. Percy V. Pennypacker.* Helen Knox. N. Y., 1916. 192 p.   *DLC, NN*

PENNYPACKER, SAMUEL WHITAKER. *Samuel W. Pennypacker.* Hampton L. Carson. Phila., 1917. 44 p.   *DLC, PU*

PENROSE, BOIES. *Power and Glory; the Life of Boies Penrose.* Walter Davenport. N. Y., 1931. 240 p.   *DLC, NN, MWA, PU*

PEPPER, WILLIAM. *William Pepper, M.D. (1843–1898) Provost of the University of Pennsylvania.* Francis N. Thorpe. Phila., 1904. 555 p.   *DLC, NN, PU*

PEPPERRELL, WILLIAM. *The Life of Sir William Pepperrell, Bart.* Usher Parsons. Boston, 1855. 352 p.
        DLC, NN, MWA, CSmH, MiD:B
    2:542

PEPYS, SAMUEL.
Soul of Samuel Pepys. Gamaliel Bradford. Boston, 1924. 261 p.   *DLC, NN, CSmH, PU*

Mr. Pepys Upon the State of Christ Hospital. Rudolf Kirk. Phila., 1935. 109 p.   *DLC, NN, CSmH, PU*

Mr. Pepys and Mr. Evelyn. Clara Marburg. Phila., 1935. 155 p.   *DLC, CSmH, PU*

Mr. Secretary Pepys; With Extracts From His Diary. James
G. Wilson. N. Y., 1867. 264 p. *DLC, NN*
2:7

PEPYS, MRS. SAMUEL. 2:93

PERCIVAL, JAMES GATES.
James Gates Percival. Henry E. Legler. Milwaukee, 1901.
61 p. (Mequon Club) *DLC, NN, CSmH*
The Life and Letters of James Gates Percival. Julius H. Ward.
Boston, 1866. 583 p. *DLC, NN, MWA, CSmH, MiD:B*

PERICLES. 2:286

PERINCHIEF, OCTAVIUS. *Octavius Perinchief: His Life of Trial and
Supreme Faith.* Charles Lanman. Washington, 1879. *DLC*

PERKINS, AUGUSTUS THORNDIKE. *Memoir of Augustus Thorndike
Perkins, A.M.* Wm. H. Whitmore. Cambridge, 1892. 14 p.
DLC, NN, MWA, MiD:B

PERKINS, EDWARD H. *Edward H. Perkins, a Brief Record of a Noble
Life . . .* Franklin Carter. New Haven, 1878. 56 p.
DLC, NN, MWA

PERKINS, GEORGE HAMILTON. *George H. Perkins, Commodore, U. S. N.*
Carroll S. Alden. Boston, 1914. 302 p. *DLC, NN*

PERKINS, JAMES HANDASYD. *The Memoir and Writings of James
Handasyd Perkins.* William H. Channing, ed. Boston, 1851. 2
vols. *DLC, NN, MWA, MiD:B*

PERKINS, THOMAS HANDASYD. *Memoir of Thomas H. Perkins.*
Thomas G. Cary. Boston, 1856. 304 p. *DLC, NN*

PERROT, NICHOLAS. *Nicholas Perrot: a Study in Wisconsin History.*
Gardner P. Stickney. 1895. 15 p. (Parkman Club Papers, No. 1)
DLC, NN, MWA
2:127

PERRY, ARTHUR LATHAM. *A Professor of Life. A Sketch of Arthur
Latham Perry, of Williams College.* Carroll Perry. Boston, 1923.
113 p. *DLC, NN, PU*

PERRY, MATTHEW CALBRAITH.
*The Great Commodore; the Exploits of Matthew Calbraith
Perry.* Edward M. Barrows. Indianapolis, N. Y., 1935. 397 p.
DLC, NN, CSmH
Matthew C. Perry; a Typical American Naval Officer. William
E. Griffis. Boston, 1887. 459 p. *DLC, NN, MWA, CSmH, PU*
2:78–396

PERRY, OLIVER HAZARD.
The Hero of Erie. James Barnes. N. Y., 1898. 167 p.
DLC, NN, MWA, CSmH

Oliver Hazard Perry. Charles J. Dutton. N. Y., 1935. 308 p.
DLC, NN

Commodore Hazard Perry and the War on the Lakes. Olin L. Lyman. N. Y., 1905. 246 p. *DLC, NN, CSmH, MiD:B*

The Life of Commodore Oliver Hazard Perry. Alex. S. Mackenzie. N. Y., 1840. 2 vols. *DLC, NN, MWA, CSmH, MiD:B*

Oliver Hazard Perry and the Battle of Lake Erie. James Cooke Mills. Detroit, 1913. 278 p. *DLC, NN, MWA, MiD:B*

Life of Commodore O. H. Perry. John M. Niles. Hartford, 1820. 376 p. *DLC, NN, MWA, CSmH, MiD:B*
2:396

PERRY, THOMAS SERGEANT. *Thomas Sergeant Perry; a Memoir.* John T. Morse. Boston, 1929. 181 p. *DLC, NN, MWA, PU*

PERSHING, JOHN JOSEPH.
Pershing, the Story of a Great Soldier. Harold McCracken. N. Y., 1931. 193 p. *DLC, NN*

Story of General Pershing. Everett T. Tomlinson. N. Y., 1919. 260 p. *DLC, NN, PU*
2:388

PETER THE GREAT.
History of Peter the Great, Emperor of Russia. Jacob Abbott. N. Y., 1875. 368 p. *DLC, NN, MWA*

Life of Peter the Great. J. Barrow. N. Y., 1903. 405 p. (Franklin Biography Series) *DLC, NN, MWA*

History of Peter the Great, Czar of Russia. Sarah H. Bradford. N. Y., 1858. 233 p. *DLC, NN*

Peter the Great. John L. Motley. London, 1887. N. Y., 1893. 70 p. *DLC, NN, PU*

Peter the Great, Emperor of Russia: Study of Historical Biography. Eugene Schuyler. N. Y., 1884. 2 vols. *DLC, NN, PU*

PETER, HUGH. *Hugh Peter, Preacher . . . Philanthropist.* Eleanor B. Peters. N. Y., 1902. 101 p. *CSmH*

PETER, SARAH. *Memoirs of the Life of Mrs. Sarah Peter.* Margaret R. King. Cincinnati, 1889. 2 vols. *DLC, NN*

PETERS, ANZONETTA REBECCA. *The Young Disciple; or, Memoir of Anzonetta R. Peters.* John A. Clark. Phila., 1836. 230 p.
NN, MWA, PU

PETERS, HUGH. *A History of the Rev. Hugh Peters.* Samuel Peters. N. Y., 1807. *RP:JCB*

PETIGRU, JAMES LOUIS.
   Life, Letters and Speeches of James Louis Petigru, the Union Man of South Carolina. James P. Carson. Washington, 1920. 497 p.   *DLC, CSmH, PU*
   James L. Petigru. A Biographical Sketch. W. J. Grayson. N. Y., 1866. 178 p.   *DLC, NN, MWA, CSmH, MiD:B* 2:225

PETIT, ADOLPH. *The Happy Ascetic, Adolph Petit of the Society of Jesus* . . . Joseph R. N. Maxwell. N. Y., 1936. 212 p.
                                                          DLC, NN

PETRIE, IRENE. *A Woman's Life for Kashmir. Irene Petrie; a Biography.* Mary L. G. Carus-Wilson. Chicago, 1901. 343 p.
                                                          DLC, NN

PETTIGREW, JAMES JOHNSTON. *Memorial of the Life of Brig.-Gen. J. J. Pettigrew.* William H. Trescot. Charleston, 1870. 65 p.
                                                      DLC, NN, CSmH

PEYSTER, JOHN WATTS. *John Watts de Peyster.* Frank Allaben. N. Y., 1908. 2 vols. (Allaben Biographical Series)
                                                  DLC, NN, CSmH, PU

PEYTON, JOHN HOWE. *Memoir of John Howe Peyton.* J. L. Peyton. Staunton, Va., 1894. 297 p. (Privately Printed)
                                              DLC, NN, MWA, CSmH, PU

PHELPS, ALMIRA HART LINCOLN. *Almira Hart Lincoln Phelps, Her Life and Work* . . . Emma L. Bolzau. Phila., 1936. 534 p.
                                              DLC, NN, CSmH, PU

PHELPS, ANSON GREENE. *A Memorial of Anson G. Phelps, Jr.* Henry B. Smith. N. Y., 1860. 188 p.   *DLC, NN*

PHELPS, AUSTIN. *Austin Phelps: a Memoir.* Elizabeth Stuart Phelps Ward. N. Y., 1891. 280 p.   *DLC, NN, MWA, MiD:B*

PHELPS, JOHN WOLCOTT. *Life and Public Services of Gen. John Wolcott Phelps.* Cecil H. C. Howard. Brattleboro, Vt., 1887. 58 p.
                                              DLC, NN, MWA, CSmH

PHELPS, MATTHEW. *Memoirs and Adventures of Captain Matthew Phelps.* Anthony Haswell. Bennington, Vt., 1802. 210 p.
                                          DLC, NN, MWA, CSmH, RP:JCB

PHELPS, WILLIAM LYON. 2:236

PHELPS, WILLIAM WALTER. *William Walter Phelps.* Hugh M. Herrick. N. Y., 1904. 462 p.   *DLC, NN*

PHILBRICK, JOHN DUDLEY. *A Memorial of the Life and Services of John D. Philbrick.* Larkin Dunton. Boston, 1888. 225 p.
                                          DLC, NN, MWA, PU, MiD:B

PHILIP. [INDIAN KING.]
King Philip. Jacob Abbott. N. Y., 1900. 410 p. DLC, NN
History of King Philip, Sovereign Chief of the Wampanoags.
J. S. C. Abbott. N. Y., 1857. 410 p. DLC, NN, MWA
PHILIP II. Philip II of Spain. David G. Loth. N. Y., 1932. 297 p.
DLC, NN
PHILIP, JOHN WOODWARD. Life and Adventures of " Jack " Philip,
Rear-Admiral, U. S. N. Edgar S. Maclay and Philip Barrett. N. Y.,
1903. 288 p. DLC, NN, MWA, CSmH, MiD:B
PHILIPS, KATHERINE. The Matchless Orinda. Philip W. Souers.
Cambridge, 1931. 326 p. (Harvard Studies in English)
DLC, NN, CSmH, PU
PHILLIPS, DAVID GRAHAM. David Graham Phillips and His Times.
Isaac F. Marcosson. N. Y., 1932. 308 p. DLC, NN, PU
PHILLIPS, EDWARD S. Life and Labors for Humanity of Rev. Edward
S. Phillips. W. Joyce. Pottsville, Pa., 1901. 144 p. DLC, NN
PHILLIPS, FREDERIC ILLSLEY. 2:519
PHILLIPS, SAMUEL. A Memoir of His Honor Samuel Phillips, LL.D.
John L. Taylor. Boston, 1856. 391 p.
DLC, NN, MWA, MiD:B
PHILLIPS, WENDELL.
Life and Times of Wendell Phillips. George L. Austin. Bos-
ton, 1888. 431 p. DLC, NN, MWA, CSmH, MiD:B
Wendell Phillips, the Agitator. Carlos Martyn. N. Y., 1890.
600 p. DLC, NN, MWA, CSmH
The Story of Wendell Phillips. Charles E. Russell. Chicago,
1914. 185 p. DLC, NN
Wendell Phillips, Orator and Agitator. Lorenzo Sears. N. Y.,
1909. 379 p. DLC, NN, CSmH, PU
2:150–330–624
PHILLIPPS, ADELAIDE. Adelaide Phillipps; a Record. Mrs. R. C.
Waterston. Boston, 1883. 170 p. DLC, NN
PHILO JUDAEUS. 2:371
PHIPS, WILLIAM. Life of Sir William Phips. Francis Bowen.
(L.A.B.) DLC, NN, MWA, CSmH
PHYSICK, PHILIP SYNG. A Memoir of the Life and Character of Philip
Syng Physick. Jacob Randolph. Phila., 1839. 114 p.
DLC, NN, MWA, PU
PIATT, DONN. Donn Piatt: His Work and His Ways. Charles G.
Miller. Cincinnati, 1893. 381 p. DLC, NN

PICKARD, HANNAH MAYNARD. *Memoir and Writings of Mrs. Hannah Maynard Pickard*. Edward Otheman. Boston, 1845. 311 p.
DLC, NN, MWA

PICKENS, ANDREW. 2:290

PICKERING, JOHN.
Life of John Pickering. Mary O. Pickering. Boston, 1887. 534 p. (Privately Printed) *DLC, NN, MWA, PU*
Memoir of Hon. John Pickering. William H. Prescott. Boston, 1849. (Mass. Hist. Soc. Coll. ser. 3, vol. 10)
DLC, NN, MWA, CSmH, MiD:B, MiU:C

PICKERING, TIMOTHY. *Life of Timothy Pickering*. Octavius Pickering. Boston, 1867–73. 4 vols.
DLC, NN, MWA, CSmH, PU, MiD:B, MiU:C

PICKETT, GEORGE EDWARD. *Soldier of the Civil War*. T. E. Pickett. Cleveland, 1900. 62 p. (Privately Printed) *DLC, CSmH*

PICKETT, JOSEPH WORTHY. *Memoirs of Joseph W. Pickett, Missionary*. William Salter. Burlington, Ia., 1880. 150 p. *NN, CSmH*

PIERCE, FRANKLIN.
The Life of Gen. Frank. Pierce, of New Hampshire, the Democratic Candidate for President of the United States. David V. G. Bartlett. Auburn, 1852. 300 p. *DLC, NN, MWA, MiD:B*
The Life of Franklin Pierce. Nathaniel Hawthorne. Boston, 1852. 144 p. (Included in a Shorter Form in " Sketches and Studies," 1883) *DLC, NN, MWA, CSmH, PU*
Franklin Pierce; Young Hickory of the Granite Hills. Roy F. Nichols. Phila., 1931. 615 p. *DLC, NN, CSmH, PU*

PIERCE, GEORGE FOSTER. *Life and Times of Bishop George F. Pierce*. G. G. Smith. Sparta, Ga., 1888. 688 p. *NN, MWA, CSmH*

PIERCE, JAMES MELVILLE. 2:497

PIERCE, JOHN. *Memoir of the Late Rev. John Pierce*. Abraham Hartwell. Lunenburg, n.d. 180 p. *NN, MWA*

PIERCE, JOHN DAVIS. *John D. Pierce, Founder of the Michigan School System: Study of Education in the Northwest*. C. O. Hoyt and R. C. Ford. Ypsilanti, Mich., 1905. 162 p.
DLC, NN, PU, MiD:B

PIERPONT, JOHN. *John Pierpont; Biographical Sketch*. Abbie A. Ford. Boston, 1909. 25 p. (Privately Printed) *DLC*

PIKE, ALBERT.
Albert Pike. F. W. Allsopp. Little Rock, Ark., 1928. 369 p.
DLC, NN, CSmH

Gen. Albert Pike's Poems. With Introductory Biographical Sketch. Lilian P. Roome. Little Rock, Ark., 1900. 21 p.
DLC, NN

PIKE, ROBERT. *The New Puritan; New England Two Hundred Years Ago. Some Account of the Life of Robert Pike.* James S. Pike. N. Y., 1879. 237 p. *DLC, NN, MWA*

PIKE, ZEBULON MONTGOMERY. *Life of Zebulon M. Pike.* Henry Whiting. (L.A.B.) *DLC, NN, MWA, CSmH*
2:262. See BROWN, JACOB.

PILCHER, ELIJAH HOMES. *Life and Labors of Elijah H. Pilcher of Michigan. Fifty-Nine Years a Minister of the M. E. Church.* James E. Pilcher. N. Y., 1892. 142 p. *DLC, NN, MiD:B*

PINCHOT, GIFFORD. 2:151

PINCKNEY, DARCY. *Darcy Pinckney.* Sue Pinckney. N. Y., 1907. 379 p. *DLC*

PINCKNEY, ELIZA. *Eliza Pinckney.* Harriet H. Ravenel. N. Y., 1896. 331 p. (Women of Colonial and Revolutionary Times)
DLC, NN, MWA, CSmH

PINCKNEY, THOMAS. *Life of General Thomas Pinckney.* Charles C. Pinckney. Boston, 1895. 237 p. *DLC, NN, MiU:C*

PINET, PIERRE FRANÇOIS. *Father Pierre François Pinet, S.J., and His Mission of the Guardian Angel of Chicago, 1696–1699.* F. R. Grover. Chicago, 1907. 28 p. (Chicago Hist. Soc. 1906)
DLC, NN, MWA, CSmH

PINKERTON, ALLAN and WILLIAM ALLAN. *The Pinkertons.* R. W. Rowan. N. Y., 1931. 350 p. *DLC, NN, MWA, PU*

PINKHAM, LYDIA ESTES. *Life and Times of Lydia E. Pinkham.* Robert C. Washburn. N. Y., 1931. 221 p. *DLC, NN, PU*

PINKHAM, SETH. *Through the Hawse-Hole; the True Story of a Nantucket Whaling Captain.* Florence B. Anderson. N. Y., 1932. 276 p. *DLC, NN*

PINKNEY, EDWARD COOTE. *Life and Works of Edward C. Pinkney.* T. O. Mabbott and F. L. Pleadwell. N. Y., 1926. 233 p.
DLC, NN, MWA, CSmH, PU
2:503

PINKNEY, WILLIAM.
Life of William Pinkney. William Pinkney. N. Y., 1853. 407 p. *DLC, NN, MWA, MiD:B*
Life of William Pinkney. Henry Wheaton. (L.A.B.)
DLC, NN, MWA, CSmH

Some Account of the Life, Writings and Speeches of William Pinkney. Henry Wheaton. N. Y., 1826. 616 p.

NN, MWA, PU, MiD:B, MiU:C

2:218

PITMAN, CHARLES. *The Life, Labors and Sermons of Rev. Charles Pitman . . . of the New Jersey Conference . . .* Caleb A. Malmsbury. Phila., 1887. 352 p. *DLC, NN*

PITT, WILLIAM. 2:330

PIUS IX.

A Popular Life of Pope Pius IX. R. Brennan. N. Y., 1887. 290 p.

A Life of Pope Pius IX. John R. G. Hassard. N. Y., 1878. 242 p. *DLC*

PIZARRO, FRANCISCO.

Pizarro and the Conquest of Peru. F. A. Ober. N. Y., 1906. 295 p. (Heroes of American History) *DLC, MiU:C*

Incredible Pizarro, Conqueror of Peru. Frank Shay. N. Y., 1932. 342 p. *DLC, NN, PU*

PLACIDE, HENRY. 2:367

PLANT, HENRY BRADLEY. *The Life of Henry Bradley Plant.* G. Hutchinson Smyth. N. Y., 1898. 344 p.

DLC, NN, MWA, CSmH, MiD:B

PLATO. 2:336

PLATT, JEANETTE HULME. *Life and Letters of Mrs. Jeanette H. Platt.* Cyrus Platt. Phila., 1882. 363 p. *DLC, NN, MWA*

PLATT, ORVILLE HITCHCOCK. *Old-Fashioned Senator, Orville H. Platt, of Connecticut: Story of a Life Unselfishly Devoted to the Public Service.* L. A. Coolidge. N. Y., 1910. 655 p. *DLC, NN*

PLATT, THOMAS. 2:14

PLENTY-COUPS. *American; the Life Story of a Great Indian, Plenty-Coups, Chief of the Crows.* Frank B. Linderman. N. Y., 1930. 313 p. *DLC, NN, PU*

PLINY. 2:91

PLUMB, PRESTON B. *The Life of Preston B. Plumb.* William E. Connelley. Chicago, 1913. 475 p. *DLC, NN, MWA, CSmH, PU*

PLUMER, WILLIAM. *Life of William Plumer.* William Plumer, Jr. Boston, 1857. 543 p. *DLC, NN, MWA, CSmH*

POCAHONTAS.

Princess Pocahontas. Mittie O. McDavid. N. Y., 1907. 125 p.

DLC, NN

Pocahontas and Her Companions. E. D. Neil. Albany, 1869. 32 p. *DLC, NN, MWA*

Princess Pocahontas. William L. Sheppard. Richmond, 1907. 17 p.   DLC, NN, CSmH

POE, EDGAR ALLAN.

Israfel: The Life and Times of Edgar Allan Poe. Hervey Allen. N. Y., 1926. 2 vols.   DLC, NN, MWA, CSmH, PU

Poe Cult . . . With a New Memoir. Eugene L. Didier. N. Y., 1909. 301 p.   DLC, NN, PU

Dark Glory. Dorothy Dow. N. Y., 1931. 287 p. (Fictionized Biography)   DLC, NN, MWA, PU

The Life of Edgar Allan Poe. W. F. Gill. N. Y., 1877. 347 p.
DLC, NN, MWA, CSmH, PU

Life and Letters of Edgar Allan Poe. James A. Harrison. N. Y., 1903. 2 vols.   DLC, NN, MWA, CSmH, PU

Edgar Allan Poe. J. A. Joyce. N. Y., 1901. 218 p.
DLC, NN, MWA

Edgar Allan Poe; a Study in Genius. Joseph W. Krutch. N. Y., 1926. 244 p.   DLC, NN, MWA, CSmH, PU

Edgar Allan Poe, the Man, the Master, the Martyr. Oliver Leigh. Chicago, 1906. 83 p.   DLC, NN, CSmH

Edgar Allan Poe. John A. Macy. N. Y., 1907. 112 p. (Beacon Biographies)   DLC

A Defense of Edgar Allan Poe. Life, Character and Dying Declarations of the Poet. John J. Moran. Washington, 1885. 87 p.
DLC

A Builder of the Beautiful; Some Unsuspected Aspects of Poe— Literary and Emotional Alike. Maxwell V. Morton. Boston, 1928. 64 p.   DLC

Edgar Allan Poe; the Man. Mary E. Phillips. Phila., 1926. 2 vols.   DLC, NN, MWA, CSmH, PU

Edgar Allan Poe; Memorial Volume. Sara S. Rice. Balt., 1877. 95 p.   DLC, NN, CSmH

Edgar A. Poe; a Psychopathic Study. John W. Robertson. N. Y., 1922. 331 p.   DLC, NN, MWA, PU

Edgar Allan Poe; How to Know Him. Charles A. Smith. Indianapolis, 1921. 350 p.   DLC, NN, MWA, PU

Edgar Allan Poe. Edmund C. Stedman. N. Y., 1881. 104 p.
DLC, NN, MWA, CSmH, PU

Memoir of Edgar Allan Poe. Richard H. Stoddard. N. Y., 1856. 170 p.   DLC, NN

The Home Life of Poe. Susan A. Weiss. N. Y., 1907. 229 p.
DLC, MWA

The Works of the Late Edgar Allan Poe: With Notices of His Life and Genius. N. P. Willis, J. R. Lowell, and R. W. Griswold. N. Y., 1850. 2 vols. N. Y., 1855. 3 vols.

DLC, NN, MWA, CSmH, PU

Edgar Allan Poe. George E. Woodberry. Boston, 1885. 354 p. (A.M.L.) *DLC, NN, MWA, CSmH, PU*

The Life of Edgar Allan Poe. George E. Woodberry. Boston, 1909. 2 vols. *DLC, NN, MWA, CSmH, PU*
2:503:660

POINDEXTER, GEORGE. *The Early Life of George Poindexter; a Story of the First Southwest.* Mack Swearingen. New Orleans, 1934. 194 p. *DLC, NN, MWA, CSmH, MiD:B*

POINSETT, JOEL ROBERTS.
. . . *The Diplomatic Career of Joel Roberts Poinsett.* Dorothy M. Parton. Washington, 1934. 162 p. *DLC, NN, CSmH*

Joel Roberts Poinsett; a Political Biography. Herbert E. Putnam. Washington, 1935. 240 p. *DLC, NN, CSmH*

Joel R. Poinsett, Versatile American. J. Fred Rippy. Durham, N. C., 1935. 257 p. *DLC, NN, CSmH, PU*

Life and Services of Joel R. Poinsett. Charles J. Stillé. Phila., 1888. 84 p. (Pamphlet) *DLC, NN, PU, MiD:B, MiU:C*

POLHEMUS, ABRAHAM. *Memorial of Rev. Abraham Polhemus, Late Minister of the North Reformed Dutch Church of Newark . . .* Abraham Polhemus. Newark, N. J., 1858. 201 p. *NN, MiD:B*

POLK, JAMES KNOX.
Life of James K. Polk. John S. Jenkins. Auburn, 1850. 395 p.
DLC, NN, MWA, CSmH, MiD:B

James K. Polk; a Political Biography. Eugene I. McCormac. Berkeley, Cal., 1922. 746 p. *DLC, NN, CSmH, PU*

POLK, LEONIDAS. *Leonidas Polk: Bishop and General.* William M. Polk. N. Y., 1893. 2 vols. New Ed. N Y., 1915.
DLC, NN, CSmH, PU
2:612

POLK, SARAH CHILDRESS. *Memorials of Sarah Childress Polk; Wife of the Eleventh President of the U. S.* Anson and Fanny Nelson. N. Y., 1892. 284 p. *DLC, NN, MWA*

POLLOK, ROBERT. *Life of Robert Pollok.* James Scott. N. Y., 1848. 364 p. *DLC, NN*

POLO, MARCO. 2:78:670

POMEROY, MARCUS MILLS. *Life of Mark M. Pomeroy.* Mary E. Tucker. N. Y., 1868. 230 p. *DLC, NN, MWA*

PONTE, LORENZO DA. *Lorenzo da Ponte; Poet and Adventurer.* Joseph L. Russo. N. Y., 1922. 166 p. (Col. Univ. Studies in Romance) *DLC, NN, CSmH*
2:71

PONTIAC. *The Life of Pontiac . . .* Edward S. Ellis. London, 1861, N. Y., 1910. 230 p. *DLC, NN, CSmH, MiU:C*

POPKIN, JOHN SNELLING. *A Memorial of the Rev. John Snelling Popkin, D.D.* Cornelius C. Felton, ed. Cambridge, 1852. 392 p. *DLC, NN, MWA*

PORTER, ALEXANDER. *Alexander Porter, Whig Planter of Old Louisiana.* Wendell H. Stephenson. Baton Rouge, La., 1934. 154 p. *DLC, NN, CSmH, PU*

PORTER, DAVID.
Memoir of Commodore David Porter. David D. Porter. Albany, 1875. 427 p. *DLC, NN, MWA, CSmH*
Commodore David Porter, 1780–1843. Archibald D. Turnbull. N. Y., 1929. 326 p. *DLC, NN, PU, MiD:B*
2:396.

PORTER, DAVID DIXON. *Admiral Porter.* James R. Soley. N. Y., 1903. 499 p. (G.C.) *DLC, NN, CSmH, PU*

PORTER, EBENEZER. *Memoir of . . . Ebenezer Porter . . . President of the Theological Seminary, Andover.* Lyman Matthews. Boston, 1837. 396 p. *DLC, NN, MWA, MiD:B*

PORTER, ELIPHALET. 2:681

PORTER, ELIZA CHAPPELL. *Eliza Chappell Porter; a Memoir.* Mary H. Porter. Chicago, 1892. 366 p. *NN*

PORTER, GENE STRATTON. *The Lady of the Limberlost; the Life and Letters of Gene Stratton-Porter.* Jeannette P. Meehan. Garden City, N. Y., 1928. 369 p. *DLC, NN*

PORTER, HORACE. *An American Soldier and Diplomat, Horace Porter.* Elsie P. Meade and Henry G. Pearson. N. Y., 1927. 390 p. *DLC, NN, MWA, CSmH, PU, MiD:B*

PORTER, NOAH. *Noah Porter.* George S. Merriam, ed. N. Y., 1893. 306 p. *DLC, NN, MWA, PU, MiD:B*

PORTER, WILLIAM SYDNEY. [O. HENRY]
Caliph of Bagdad; Being Arabian Night Flashes of the Life, Letters and Work of O. Henry. Robert H. Davis and Arthur B. Maurice. N. Y., 1931. 411 p. *DLC, NN, PU*
O. Henry; a Biography. Charles A. Smith. Garden City, N. Y., 1916. 258 p. *DLC, NN, MWA, CSmH, PU*

PORTER, WILLIAM TROTTER. *Life of William T. Porter.* Francis Brinley. N. Y., 1860. 273 p. *DLC, NN, MWA, CSmH*

POSEY, THOMAS. *Memoir of Thomas Posey.* James Hall. (L.A.B.) *DLC, NN, MWA, CSmH*

POST, TRUMAN MARCELLUS. *Truman Marcellus Post, D.D.: a Biography.* Truman A. Post. Boston, 1891. 507 p. *NN*

POTTER, ALONZO. *Memoirs of the Life and Services of Rt. Rev. Alonzo Potter.* M. A. de W. Howe. Phila., 1871. 427 p. *NN, PU*

POTTER, ANDREW JACKSON. *Andrew Jackson Potter, the Noted Parson of the Texan Frontier.* H. A. Graves. Nashville, 1881. 471 p. *DLC, NN, CSmH*

POTTER, HENRY CODMAN.
Henry Codman Potter, Seventh Bishop of New York. George Hodges. N. Y., 1915. 386 p. *DLC, NN, MiD:B*
Bishop Potter, the People's Friend. Harriette A. Keyser. N. Y., 1910. 196 p. *DLC, NN*
Henry Codman Potter, an American Metropolitan. James Sheerin. N. Y., 1933. 196 p. *DLC, NN*

POTTER, JENNIE O'NEILL. *The Story of Jennie O'Neill Potter.* Anna R. Diehl. N. Y., 1901. *NN*

POTTS, JAMES. *A Short Biographical Sketch of Major James Potts, 1752–1822.* Thomas M. Potts. n.p., 1877. 85 p. (Privately Printed) *DLC, MWA, CSmH*

POUNDS, JOHN. 2:406

POWELL, D. F. 2:358

POWELL, EDWARD L. 2:487

POWELL, JOAB. *Joab Powell: Homespun Missionary.* Marie L. Nichols. Portland, Ore., 1935. 116 p. *DLC, NN*

POWELL, LAZARUS WHITEHEAD. *Biographical Sketch of the Hon. Lazarus W. Powell . . . Governor of the State of Kentucky From 1851 to 1855.* Frankfort, Ky., 1868. 134 p. *DLC, NN, MiD:B*

POWELL, LEVEN. *A Biographical Sketch of Col. Leven Powell, Including His Correspondence During the Revolutionary War.* R. C. Powell, ed. Alexandria, Va., 1877. 104 p. *DLC, NN*

POWELL, WILLIAM DUMMER. *The Life of William Dummer Powell, First Judge of Detroit and Fifth Chief Justice at Upper Canada.* William R. Riddell. Lansing, Mich., 1924. 305 p. *DLC, NN, MWA, CSmH, PU, MiD:B*

POWER, JOHN J. *The Life of Very Rev. John J. Power, D.D.* John J. McGratty. Worcester, 1902. *MWA, MiD:B*

POWER, TYRONE. *Tyrone Power*. William Winter. N. Y., 1913. 192 p. *DLC, NN, MWA, CSmH*

POWERS, PETER. *Peter Powers, Pioneer; the Story of the First Settler in Hollis, New Hampshire*. Rudge Nichols and Caroline N. Poole. Concord, N. H., 1930. 130 p. *DLC, NN, MWA*

POWHATAN. 2:116

PRATT, DANIEL. *Hon. Daniel Pratt: a Biography*. Susan F. Tarrant. Richmond, 1904. 173 p. *DLC, NN, MWA*

PRATT, ENOCH. *Enoch Pratt; the Story of a Plain Man*. Richard H. Hart. Balt., 1935. 121 p. *DLC, NN, MWA, CSmH*

PRATT, RICHARD HENRY. *Pratt, the Red Man's Moses*. Elaine G. Eastman. Norman, Okla., 1935. 285 p. *DLC, NN, CSmH*

PRATT, SAMUEL. *Sketch of the Early Life of Samuel F. Pratt. With Some Account of the Early History of the Pratt Family*. William P. Letchworth. Buffalo, 1874. 211 p. *DLC, NN, MWA*

PRATT, WILLIAM. *Bill Pratt, the Saw-Buck Philosopher*. John S. Zelie and Carroll Perry. Williamstown, Mass., 1895. 156 p. *DLC, NN, MWA*

PRATT, ZADOCK. *Biography of Zadock Pratt of Prattsville, N. Y.* n.p., 1852. 506 p. *DLC, NN, MWA, CSmH, PU, MiD:B*

PREBLE, EDWARD. *Life of Edward Preble*. Lorenzo Sabine. (L.A.B.) *DLC, NN, MWA, CSmH*

PREBLE, HARRIET. *Memoir of the Life of Harriet Preble*. Richmond H. Lee. N. Y., 1856. 409 p. *DLC, MWA, PU*

PRENTICE, GEORGE DENNISON. *Prenticiana; . . . With a Biographical Sketch of George D. Prentice*. Gilderoy W. Griffin. Phila., 1860. 23 p. *DLC, NN, CSmH*
2:144–503

PRENTISS, ELIZABETH. *The Life and Letters of Elizabeth Prentiss*. George L. Prentiss. N. Y., 1882. 573 p. *DLC, NN, MWA, MiD:B*

PRENTISS, SEARGENT SMITH.
Memoir of S. S. Prentiss. G. L. Prentiss, ed. N. Y., 1855. 2 vols. *DLC, NN, CSmH, PU*
Life and Times of Seargent Smith Prentiss. Jos. D. Shields. Phila., 1884. 442 p. *DLC, NN, MWA, PU*

PRESCOTT, WILLIAM HICKLING.
Memoir of W. H. Prescott. C. H. Hart. Boston, 1868. 13 p. *DLC, NN, MWA*
William Hickling Prescott. Rollo Ogden. Boston, 1904. 239 p. (A.M.L.) *DLC, NN, CSmH, PU, MiD:B*

William H. Prescott. Harry T. Peck. London, 1905. 186 p. (E.M.L.)   *DLC, NN, CSmH*

Life of William Hickling Prescott. George Ticknor. Boston, 1864. 491 p.   *DLC, NN, MWA, CSmH, PU, MiD:B, MiU:C*

PRESTON, MARGARET JUNKIN. *The Life and Letters of Margaret Junkin Preston.* Elizabeth P. Allan. Boston, 1903. 378 p.
      DLC, NN, PU

   2:503

PRESTON, WILLIAM CAMPBELL. 2:431

PRETTY-SHIELD. *Red Mother.* Frank B. Linderman. N. Y., 1932. 256 p.   *DLC, NN, PU*

PRICE, PHILIP. *Memoir of Philip and Rachel Price.* Eli K. Price. Phila., 1852. 192 p.   *DLC, NN, MWA, PU*

PRICE, STERLING. 2:612

PRICE, THOMAS FREDERICK. *Father Price of Maryknoll; a Short Sketch of the Life of Rev. Thomas Frederick Price.* Patrick J. Byrne. Maryknoll, N. Y., 1923. 93 p.   *DLC, NN*

PRICHARD, JOHN LAMB. *Memoir of Rev. John L. Prichard, Late Pastor of the First Baptist Church, Wilmington, N. C.* James D. Hufham. Raleigh, 1867. 182 p.   *DLC, NN, CSmH*

PRIESTLEY, JOSEPH. *Priestley in America, 1794–1804.* Edgar F. Smith. Phila., 1930. 173 p.   *DLC, NN, MWA, PU*

   2:348–393

PRINCE, JOHN. 2:681

PRINCE, WILLIAM REED. *Memoir . . . of William Reed Prince.* Newell A. Prince. Portland, Me., 1846. 80 p.   *DLC, MWA*

PROCTER, BRYAN WALLER [BARRY CORNWALL]. *Barry Cornwall; a Biography of Bryan Waller Procter, With a Selected Collection of Hitherto Unpublished Letters.* Richard W. Armour. Boston, 1935. 370 p.   *DLC, NN, CSmH*

PROUD, ROBERT. *Notices of the Life and Character of Robert Proud.* Charles W. Thomson. Phila., 1826, 1864. 17 p. (Penn. Hist. Soc. Memoirs. Vol. 1)   *DLC, NN, MWA, CSmH, PU, MiU:C*

PROUDFIT, ALEXANDER. *Life of Alexander Proudfit.* John Forsyth. N. Y., 1846. 384 p.   *NN, PU*

PROVOOST, SAMUEL. *Life of Bishop Provoost of New York.* John N. Norton. N. Y., 1859. 183 p.   *DLC*

PRYNNE, WILLIAM. *William Prynne, a Study in Puritanism.* Ethyn W. Kirby. Cambridge, 1931. 228 p.   *DLC, NN, CSmH, PU*

PRYOR, THEODORICK BLAND. *The Life of Theodorick Bland Pryor, First Mathematical Fellow at Princeton College.* Thomas D. Suplee. San Francisco, 1879. 199 p.   *DLC, NN ·*

PULASKI, CASIMIR.
    Casimir Pulaski. Charles C. Jones, Jr. Savannah, 1873. 28 p.
                                            DLC, NN
    Life of Count Pulaski. Jared Sparks. (L.A.B.)
                               DLC, NN, MWA, CSmH

PULITZER, JOSEPH. *Joseph Pulitzer: His Life and Letters.* Don C.
Seitz. N. Y., 1924. 478 p.   *DLC, NN, MWA, PU*
2:672

PULLMAN, GEORGE MORTIMER. 2:623

PUMPELLY, RAPHAEL. 2:114

PURCELL, HENRY. 2:187

PUTNAM, GEORGE PALMER. *George Palmer Putnam.* George H. Putnam. N. Y., 1912. 476 p.   *DLC, NN, PU, MiD:B*

PUTNAM, ISRAEL.
    *Memoirs of the Life, Adventures and Military Exploits of Israel
Putnam.* Ithaca, N. Y., 1834. 119 p.
                    NN, MWA, CSmH, MiD:B, MiU:C
    Life of Israel Putnam. William Cutter. N. Y., 1847. 383 p.
                            DLC, NN, MWA, MiD:B
    Gen. Israel Putnam . . . a Biography. George C. Hill. Bos-
ton, 1858. 270 p.   *DLC, NN, CSmH, PU, MiD:B*
    Essay on the Life of . . . Maj.-Gen. Israel Putnam . . . David
Humphreys. Hartford, 1788. 187 p. *NN, MWA, CSmH, MiU:C*
    *Memoirs of the Life, Adventures and Military Exploits of Israel
Putnam.* David Humphreys. N. Y., 1815. 108 p.   *NN, CSmH*
    An Essay on the Life of . . . Maj.-General Israel Putnam. David
Humphreys. Boston, 1818. 276 p.
                    NN, MWA, CSmH, MiD:B, MiU:C
    *Life and Heroic Exploits of Israel Putnam, Major-General in
the Revolutionary War.* David C. Humphreys. Hartford, 1833.
190 p.   *NN, MWA, CSmH, PU*
    Israel Putnam, Pioneer, Ranger and Major-General, 1718–1790.
W. F. Livingston. N. Y., 1901. 442 p. (American Men of
Energy)   *DLC, NN, PU*
    Life of Israel Putnam. O. W. B. Peabody. (L.A.B.)
                          DLC, NN, MWA, CSmH, PU
    Gen. Israel Putnam and the Battle of Bunker Hill. Alfred P.
Putnam. Salem, Mass., 1901. 64 p.   *DLC, NN, MWA*
    Life of Israel Putnam, Major-General in the Continental Army.
Increase N. Tarbox. Boston, 1876. 389 p.
                          DLC, NN, MWA, MiD:B

The Life and Times of Israel Putnam, Maj.-Gen. in the Continental Army. Orville J. Victor. N. Y., 1876. 99 p. *DLC, NN* 2:358

PUTNAM, LOUISA DUNCAN. *Mary Louisa Duncan Putnam: William Clement Putnam.* Elizabeth D. Putnam. Davenport, Ia., 1907. 58 p. *DLC, MWA*

PUTNAM, RUFUS. *Memoirs of Rufus Putnam.* Rowena W. Buell, ed. Boston, 1903. 460 p. *DLC, NN, MWA, CSmH, RP:JCB*

PYLE, HOWARD. *Howard Pyle; a Chronicle.* Charles D. Abbott. N. Y., 1925. 249 p. *DLC, NN, CSmH, PU*

PYTHAGORAS. 2:336

QUANTRILL, WILLIAM CLARKE. *Quantrill and the Border Wars.* William E. Connelley. Cedar Rapids, Ia., 1910. 542 p.
DLC, NN, CSmH, PU

QUAYLE, WILLIAM ALFRED. 2:487

QUICK, HERBERT. 2:497

QUICK, THOMAS. *The Original Life and Adventures of Tom Quick, the Indian Slayer* ... James E. Quinlan. Monticello, 1851. Deposit, N. Y., 1894. 123 p. *DLC, NN, CSmH*

QUINCY, DOROTHY. *Dorothy Quincy, Wife of John Hancock, With Events of Her Time.* Ellen C. de Q. Woodberry. Washington, 1901. 259 p.

QUINCY, ELIZA SUSAN M. *Memoir of the Life of Eliza S. M. Quincy.* Eliza S. M. Quincy. Boston, 1861. 267 p. *DLC, NN, MWA*

QUINCY, JOHN. *John Quincy; Master of Mount Wollaston . . . Speaker of the Massachusetts House of Representatives.* Daniel M. Wilson. Boston, 1909. 84 p. *DLC, NN, MWA, PU*

QUINCY, JOSIAH.

Life of Josiah Quincy. Edmund Quincy. Boston, 1867. 560 p.
DLC, NN, MWA, CSmH, PU, MiU:C
Memoir of the Life of Josiah Quincy. Josiah Quincy, Jr. Boston, 1825. Rev. Ed. Boston, 1874. 431 p.
DLC, NN, MWA, PU, MiD:B
Memoir of Josiah Quincy. James Walker. Boston, 1867. 185 p. (Mass. Hist. Soc. Proc. Series I, vol. 9)
DLC, NN, MWA, CSmH, MiD:B

QUINN, JAMES. *Sketches of the Life and Labors of James Quinn.* John F. Wright. Cincinnati, 1851. 324 p.
DLC, NN, PU, MiD:B

QUITMAN, JOHN ANTHONY. *Life and Correspondence of John A. Quitman.* J. F. Claiborne. N. Y., 1860. 2 vols.
DLC, NN, CSmH, PU

RABELAIS, FRANÇOIS.
>*Book of Rabelais.* Herman Fetzer [Jake Falstaff]. N. Y., 1928. 246 p.   *DLC, NN*
>*Francis Rabelais; the Man and His Work.* Albert J. Nock and C. R. Wilson. N. Y. and London, 1929. 359 p.   *DLC, NN, PU*
>*François Rabelais; Man of the Renaissance; a Spiritual Biography.* Samuel Putnam. N. Y., 1929. 530 p.   *DLC, NN*

RACHEL, ELIZABETH FELIX. *Rachel. A Sketch of the Life of the Great Tragedienne.* Nina H. Kennard. Boston, 1886. 307 p.   *DLC, NN*

RADBURNE, JAMES. *El Jimmy (Radburne); Outlaw of Patagonia.* Herbert Childs. Phila., 1936. 399 p.   *DLC, NN*

RADCLIFFE, ANN. *Ann Radcliffe in Relation to Her Time.* Clara F. McIntyre. New Haven, 1920. 108 p. (Yale Studies in English, No. 62)   *DLC, NN, CSmH, PU*

RADFORD, WILLIAM. *Old Naval Days; Sketches From the Life of Rear-Admiral William Radford.* Sophie R. de Meissmer. N. Y., 1920. 389 p.   *DLC, NN, CSmH*

RADISSON, PIERRE ESPRIT. 2:127

RAFINESQUE, CONSTANTINE SAMUEL.
>*Life and Writings of Rafinesque.* R. E. Call. Louisville, 1895. 227 p. (Filson Club Pub. No. 10)   *DLC, NN, CSmH, MiD:B*
>*Rafinesque; a Sketch of His Life.* T. J. Fitzpatrick. Des Moines, 1911. 241 p.   *DLC, NN, CSmH*
>2:225

RAIKES, ROBERT. *The Rise and Progress of Sunday Schools. A Biography of Robert Raikes and William Fry.* J. C. Power. N. Y., 1864. 283 p.   *NN*

RAIN-IN-THE-FACE. 2:204

RALE, SEBASTIAN. *Life of Sebastian Rale.* Convers Francis. (L.A.B.)   *DLC, NN, MWA, CSmH*

RALEIGH, SIR WALTER.
>*Ralegh and His World.* Irvin W. Anthony. N. Y., 1934. 339 p.   *DLC, NN*
>*Sir Walter Raleigh; That Damned Upstart.* Donald B. Chidsey. N. Y., 1931. 315 p.   *DLC, NN*
>*Sir Walter Raleigh.* F. A. Ober. N. Y., 1909. 303 p. (Heroes of American History)   *DLC, NN*
>*Sir Walter Raleigh and His Colony in America . . .* Increase N. Tarbox. Boston, 1884. 329 p. (Prince Soc. Pub.)   *DLC, NN, MWA, CSmH, MiU:C*

Sir Walter Raleigh; Last of the Elizabethans. Edward J. Thompson. New Haven, 1935. 416 p. *DLC, NN, CSmH, PU*
Sir Walter Raleigh. Henry D. Thoreau. Boston, 1905. 106 p.
DLC, NN, MWA, CSmH
The Life and Times of Sir Walter Raleigh, Pioneer of Anglo-American Colonization. Charles K. True. Cincinnati, 1877. 271 p.
DLC

2:78

RALSTON, WILLIAM CHAPMAN.
Memorial of William C. Ralston. San Francisco, 1875. 43 p.
DLC, NN, CSmH, PU
The Man Who Built San Francisco. Julian Dana. N. Y., 1936. 397 p. *DLC, NN*
William Chapman Ralston, Courageous Builder. Cecil G. Tilton. Boston, 1935. 474 p. *DLC, NN, CSmH*
RAMSAY, MARTHA LAURENS. *Memoirs of the Life of Martha Laurens Ramsay.* David Ramsay. Charleston, 1811. 274 p.
DLC, NN, MWA, CSmH, MiD:B, MiU:C
RAMSAY, NATHANIEL. *A Sketch of the Life and Character of Nathaniel Ramsay.* W. F. Brand. Balt., 1887. 15 p. (Md. Hist. Soc. Fund-Publication No. 24. pp. 45–60) *DLC, NN, MWA, PU*
RAMSAY, SIR WILLIAM. 2:286
RAMUS, PETER. *Peter Ramus and the Educational Reformation of the Sixteenth Century.* Frank P. Graves. N. Y., 1912. 226 p.
DLC, NN, CSmH, PU
RANDALL, BENJAMIN. *The Life of Elder Benjamin Randall.* John Buzzell. Limerick, Me., 1827. 308 p. *DLC, NN, MWA, CSmH*
RANDOLPH, EDMUND. *Omitted Chapters of History, Disclosed in the Life and Papers of Edmund Randolph.* Moncure D. Conway. N. Y., 1888. 401 p. *DLC, NN, MWA, CSmH, PU, MiU:C*
RANDOLPH, EDWARD. *Edward Randolph.* Robert N. Toppan, ed. Boston, 1898–1909. 5 vols. (Prince Soc. Pub.)
DLC, NN, CSmH
RANDOLPH, JACOB. *Biographical Memoir of Jacob Randolph, M.D.* George W. Norris. Phila., 1848. 12 p. *DLC, NN, PU*
RANDOLPH, JOHN.
John Randolph. Henry Adams. Boston, 1882. 313 p. (A.S.) *DLC, NN, MWA, CSmH, PU, MiD:B*
Home Reminiscences of John Randolph of Roanoke. Powhatan Bouldin. Danville and Richmond, 1878. 320 p.
DLC, NN, MWA, CSmH

John Randolph of Roanoke, 1773–1833. William C. Bruce. N. Y., 1922. 2 vols. *DLC, NN, CSmH, PU*

John Randolph. R. H. Dabney. Milwaukee, 1903. 179 p. (Great Americans of History) *DLC, NN, CSmH, MiD:B*

The Life of John Randolph of Roanoke. H. A. Garland. N. Y., 1851. 2 vols. *DLC, NN, MWA, CSmH, PU, MiD:B, MiU:C*

Randolph of Roanoke; a Political Fantastic. Gerald W. Johnson. N. Y., 1929. 278 p. *DLC, NN, PU*

Biography of John Randolph. Lemuel Sawyer. N. Y., 1844. 132 p. *DLC, NN, MWA, CSmH, MiD:B*

John Randolph . . . and Other Sketches. Frederick Wm. Thomas. Phila., 1853. 375 p. *DLC, NN*
  2:35–89–511–654

RANKIN, JEANETTE. 2:395

RANTOUL, ROBERT. *Memoir . . . of Robert Rantoul, Jr.* Luther Hamilton. Boston, 1854. 864 p. *DLC, NN, MWA, CSmH*

RAPHAEL. *Raphael.* Moses F. Sweetser. Boston, 1877. 153 p. *DLC*
  2:248

RARY, ISAAC. *Memoir of Isaac Rary, M.D.* Thomas S. Kirkbride. Phila., 1881. 19 p.

RAUCH, CHRISTIAN DANIEL. *Life of Christian Daniel Rauch.* Ednah D. Cheney. Boston, 1893. 331 p. *DLC*

RAVENSCROFT, JOHN STARK. *The Life of Bishop Ravenscroft.* John N. Norton. N. Y., 1858. 152 p. *NN*
  2:295

RAWLE, WILLIAM. 2:110

RAWLINS, JOHN AARON. *The Life of John A. Rawlins.* James H. Wilson. N. Y., 1916. 514 p. *DLC, NN, CSmH*

RAWSON, EDWARD. *Memoir of Edward Rawson.* S. S. Rawson. Boston, 1849. 146 p. *DLC, NN, MWA*

RAYMOND, HENRY JARVIS. *Henry J. Raymond and the New York Press.* Augustus Maverick. Hartford, 1870. 501 p. *DLC, NN, MWA, CSmH, PU*

RAYMOND, JOHN HOWARD. *Life and Letters of John Howard Raymond.* Mrs. H. R. Lloyd, ed. N. Y., 1881. 744 p. *DLC, NN, PU*

RAYNER, ISIDOR. 2:218

READ, ELIZABETH T. *Memoir of Miss Elizabeth T. Read.* John S. C. Abbott. N. Y., 1847. 221 p. *MWA, MiD:B*

READ, GEORGE. *Life and Correspondence of George Read.* William T. Read. Phila., 1870. 575 p. *DLC, NN*

READ, MARY. 2:576

READ, NATHAN. *Nathan Read . . . a Contribution to the Early History of the Steamboat and Locomotive Engine.* David Read. N. Y., 1870. 201 p. *DLC, NN, MWA*

RECTOR, EDWARD. *Edward Rector; a Story of the Middle West.* George R. Grose. N. Y., 1928. 95 p. *DLC, NN*

RED CLOUD. 2:204

REDDINGTON, JOANNA WOODBERRY. *Memoir of Joanna Woodberry Reddington.* Samuel S. Mallery. Boston, 1837. 92 p. *MWA*

RED JACKET.

> *Red Jacket.* Buffalo, 1885. 117 p. *CSmH*
>
> *An Account of Sa-Go-Ye-Wat-Ha; or, Red Jacket and His People, 1750–1830.* J. Niles Hubbard. Albany, N. Y., 1836. 356 p. *DLC, NN, MWA, CSmH, MiU:C*
>
> *The Life and Times of Red Jacket, or Sa-Go-Ye-Wat-Ha; Being the Sequel to the History of the Six Nations.* William L. Stone. N. Y., 1841. 484 p. *DLC, NN, CSmH*
>
> *Life and Times of Sa-Go-Ye-Wat-Ha, or, Red Jacket.* W. L. Stone. Albany, 1866. 509 p. *NN, MWA, CSmH, RP:JCB*

REDPATH, JAMES. *The Life of James Redpath and the Development of the Modern Lyceum.* Charles F. Horner. N. Y., Newark, N. J., 1926. 301 p. *DLC, NN*

REED, ESTHER. *Life of Esther De Berdt, Afterwards Esther Reed . . .* W. D. Reed. Phila., 1853. 336 p. *DLC, NN, PU, MiD:B, MiU:C*

REED, JOHN.

> *John Reed; the Making of a Revolutionary.* Granville Hicks and John Stuart. N. Y., 1936. 445 p. *DLC, NN*
>
> *One of Us; the Story of John Reed; in Lithographs.* Lynd K. Ward and Granville Hicks. N. Y., 1935. 64 p. *DLC*

REED, JOSEPH.

> *Life of Joseph Reed.* Henry Reed. (L.A.B.) *DLC, NN, MWA, CSmH*
>
> *Life and Correspondence of Joseph Reed.* William B. Reed. Phila., 1847. 2 vols. *DLC, NN, MWA, CSmH, PU, MiD:B, MiU:C, RP:JCB*

REED, MARTHA. *Martha: a Memorial of an Only and Beloved Sister.* Andrew Reed. N. Y., 1835. 316 p. *DLC, NN*

REED, MARY. *Mary Reed, Missionary to the Lepers.* John Jackson.
N. Y., 1899. 127 p. *DLC, NN*

REED, THOMAS BRACKETT.
 Life of Thomas B. Reed. Samuel W. McCall. Boston, 1914.
303 p. *DLC, NN, MWA, CSmH, PU*
 Thomas B. Reed, Parliamentarian. William A. Robinson.
N. Y., 1930. 423 p. *DLC, NN, CSmH, PU*

REED, WALTER. *Walter Reed and Yellow Fever.* Howard A. Kelly.
N. Y., 1906. 293 p. *DLC, NN, PU*
 2:176–675

REHAN, ADA. *Ada Rehan: A Study.* William Winter. N. Y., 1893.
211 p. *DLC, NN, MWA, CSmH, PU*

REID, ELIZABETH MILLS. 2:425

REID, RICHARD. *Biography of Judge Richard Reid.* Elizabeth J.
Reid. Cincinnati, 1886. 584 p. *DLC, NN*

REID, WALLACE. *Wallace Reid; His Life Story as Related by His
Mother.* Bertha W. Reid. N. Y., 1923. 104 p. *DLC, NN*

REID, WHITELAW. *Life of Whitelaw Reid.* Royal Cortissoz. N. Y.,
1921. 2 vols. *DLC, NN, MWA, CSmH, PU*

REITZEL, ROBERT. *Robert Reitzel.* Adolf E. Zucker. Phila., 1917.
74 p. *DLC, NN, CSmH, PU*

REMBRANDT.
 Rembrandt. Moses F. Sweetser. Boston, 1878. 162 p.
DLC, NN
 *R.v.R.; Being the Last Years and Death of One Rembrandt
Harmenszoon van Rijn.* Hendrik W. Van Loon. N. Y., 1930.
570 p. (Biographical Fiction) *DLC, NN, PU*
 2:161

REMSEN, IRA. 2:286

RENAN, ERNEST. *Ernest Renan.* Lewis F. Mott. N. Y., 1921. 461 p.
DLC, NN, PU

REVERE, PAUL.
 Paul Revere and His Engraving. W. L. Andrews. N. Y., 1901.
170 p. *DLC, NN, MWA, CSmH*
 Sons of Liberty; a Story of the Life and Times of Paul Revere.
Walter A. Dyer. N. Y., 1920. 436 p. *DLC, MWA*
 *True Story of Paul Revere, His Mid-Night Ride, His Arrest and
Court-Martial, His Useful Public Services.* C. F. Gettemy. Bos-
ton, 1905. 294 p. *DLC, NN, MWA, PU, MiD:B*
 Life of Col. Paul Revere. Elbridge H. Goss. Boston, 1891.
2 vols. *DLC, MWA, CSmH, MiD:B, MiU:C*

Paul Revere, the Torch Bearer of the Revolution. Belle Moses. N. Y., 1916. 269 p. *DLC*

Paul Revere. Emerson G. Taylor. N. Y., 1930. 237 p.
DLC, NN, MWA, CSmH, PU

REYNOLDS, CATHERINE. *Memoir of Miss Catherine Reynolds, of Poughkeepsie, N. Y.: With Selections From Her Diary and Letters.* George Coles, ed. N. Y., 1844. 212 p. *NN*

REYNOLDS, CHARLEY. *Charley Reynolds, Soldier, Hunter, Scout and Guide.* John E. Remsburg. Kansas City, Mo., 1931. 88 p.
DLC, NN, CSmH

REYNOLDS, JOSHUA. *Sir Joshua Reynolds.* Moses F. Sweetser. Boston, 1878. 176 p. *DLC, NN, PU*
2–293

RHETT, ROBERT BARNWELL. *Robert Barnwell Rhett: Father of Secession.* Laura A. White. N. Y., 1931. 264 p.
DLC, NN, CSmH, PU

RHIND, JOHN MASSEY. 2:430

RHODES, JAMES FORD. *James Ford Rhodes, American Historian.* Mark A. de W. Howe. N. Y., 1929. 375 p. *DLC, NN, CSmH, PU*

RIBAULT, JOHN. *Life of John Ribault.* Jared Sparks. (L.A.B.)
DLC, NN, MWA, CSmH

RICE, AUSTIN. *Colonel Austin Rice.* Charles B. Rice. Boston, 1905. 65 p. *DLC, NN, MWA*

RICE, DAN. *The Life of Dan Rice.* Maria W. Brown. Long Branch, N. J., 1901. 501 p. *DLC, MWA*

RICE, JOHN HOLT. *A Memoir of the Rev. John H. Rice.* William Maxwell. Phila., 1835. 412 p. *NN, MWA, CSmH, PU*

RICE, LUTHER.
Luther Rice, Pioneer in Missions and Education. Edward B. Pollard. Phila., 1928. 125 p. *DLC, NN*
Memoir of Rev. Luther Rice, one of the First American Missionaries to the East. James B. Taylor. Balt., 1840. 344 p.
NN, MWA, CSmH

RICE, MARY S. *Reminiscences of Mrs. Mary S. Rice.* Mary H. Krout. Honolulu, T. H., 1908. 143 p. *MWA*

RICH, CHARLES COULSON. *Charles Coulson Rich; Pioneer Builder of the West.* John H. Evans. N. Y., 1936. 400 p.
DLC, NN, MWA, CSmH

RICH, THOMAS HILL. *Thomas Hill Rich, a Memorial.* Caroline W. Rich. Idlehaven, Me., 1896. 96 p. *DLC, NN, MWA*

RICHARD I. *History of King Richard the First of England.* Jacob Abbott. N. Y., 1857. 336 p. *DLC, NN, PU*

RICHARD II. *History of King Richard the Second of England.* Jacob Abbott. N. Y., 1886. 347 p. *DLC, NN, MWA*

RICHARDS, FRANKLIN DEWEY. *Life of Franklin D. Richards, President of the Council of the Twelve Apostles, Church of Jesus Christ of Latter Day Saints.* Franklin L. R. West. Salt Lake City, 1924. 275 p. *NN, CSmH*

RICHARDS, THEODORE WILLIAM. 2:286–388

RICHARDS, WILLIAM. *Memoirs of the Life . . . of Rev. William Richards.* John Evans. Chiswick, 1819. *RP:JCB*

RICHARDSON, HENRY HOBSON.
   The Architecture of Henry H. Richardson and His Times. Henry R. Hitchcock, Jr. N. Y., 1936. 310 p. *DLC, NN, MWA*
   Henry H. Richardson and His Works. Mariana G. Van Rensselaer. Boston, 1888. 152 p. *DLC, NN*

RICHARDSON, JOSEPH. 2:521

RICHARDSON, SAMUEL. 2:521

RICHARDSON, WILLIAM ADAMS. *A Sketch of the Life and Public Services of William Adams Richardson.* Frank W. Hackett. Washington, 1898. 145 p. *DLC, NN, MWA, PU*

RICHARDSON, WILLIAM MERCHANT. *Life of William M. Richardson, LL.D., Late Chief Justice of the Superior Court in New Hampshire.* Concord, 1830. 90 p. *MWA, CSmH*

RICHMOND, CORA L. V. *Life Work of Mrs. Cora L. V. Richmond.* Harrison D. Barrett. Chicago, 1895. 759 p. *DLC, NN*

RICHMOND, LEGH.
   Life of Legh Richmond. G. T. Bedell. Phila., 1829. 211 p. *DLC*
   A Memoir of the Rev. Legh Richmond. T. S. Grimshawe. N. Y., 1829. 262 p. *DLC, NN, MWA, CSmH*

RICHTER, JEAN PAUL. *Life of Jean Paul Richter . . . Preceded by His Autobiography.* Eliza B. Lee. Boston, 1864. 538 p. *DLC, NN, MWA, PU*

RIGDON, SIDNEY. *. . . Sidney Rigdon—Early Mormon . . .* Daryl Chase. Chicago, 1931. 236 p. *DLC, NN*

RIGHTER, CHESTER NEWELL. *The Bible in the Levant; or, the Life and Letters of the Rev. Chester N. Righter.* S. Irenaeus Prime. N. Y., 1859. 336 p. *DLC, NN*

RIIS, JACOB AUGUST. 2:340–507–672–675

RILEY, JAMES WHITCOMB.
 The Youth of James Whitcomb Riley. Marcus Dickey. Indianapolis, 1919. 425 p.   *DLC, NN, CSmH*
 The Maturity of James Whitcomb Riley. Marcus Dickey. Indianapolis, 1922. 427 p.   *DLC, NN, CSmH*
RIMBAUD, ARTHUR. 2:598
RIPLEY, ELEAZAR WHEELOCK. *Eleazar Wheelock Ripley of the War of 1812.* Nicholas Baylies. Des Moines, Ia., 1890. 192 p.
     DLC, NN

 See BROWN, JACOB.
RIPLEY, EZRA. 2:681
RIPLEY, GEORGE. *George Ripley.* O. B. Frothingham. Boston, 1882. 321 p. (A.M.L.)   *DLC, NN, MWA, CSmH, PU, MiD:B*
RIPLEY, SARAH ALDEN. 2:92
RISKE, CHARLOTTE. *Memoir of Charlotte Chambers.* Lewis H. Garrard. Phila., 1856. 135 p.   *DLC, NN, CSmH, MiD:B*
RISTORI, ADELAIDE. *Adelaide Ristori. A Biography.* Kate Field. N. Y., 1867. 69 p.   *NN*
RITCHIE, ALBERT CABELL. 2:218
RITCHIE, THOMAS. *Thomas Ritchie—A Study in Virginia Politics.* Charles H. Ambler. Richmond, 1913. 303 p.
     DLC, NN, CSmH, PU

RITSCHL, ALBRECHT. 2:371
RITTENHOUSE, DAVID.
 Memoirs of the Life of David Rittenhouse . . . With Various Notices of Many Distinguished Men. William A. Barton. Phila., 1813. 614 p.   *DLC, NN, MWA, PU, MiD:B*
 David Rittenhouse; His Life and Achievements. William E. and William B. Montague, comps. Norristown, Pa., 1924. 26 p.
     MWA, PU
 Life of David Rittenhouse. James Renwick. (L.A.B.)
     DLC, NN, MWA, CSmH, PU
 An Eulogium, Intended to Perpetuate the Memory of David Rittenhouse . . . Benjamin Rush. Phila., 1796. 46 p.
     DLC, NN, CSmH, PU, MiU:C
 2:521–707
RITTER, CARL. *The Life of Carl Ritter, Late Professor of Geography in the University of Berlin.* William L. Gage. N. Y., 1867. 242 p.
     DLC, NN, PU
RIXEY, PRESLEY MARION. *The Life Story of Presley Marion Rixey . . . Biography and Autobiography.* William C. Braisted and William H. Bell. Strasburg, Va., 1930. 518 p.   *DLC, NN*

RIZAL, JOSÉ.
   Lineage, Life and Labors of José Rizal, Poet, Patriot. Austin
   Craig, Manila, P. I., 1913. Yonkers-on-Hudson, 1914. 279 p.
                                                          DLC, NN
   *Hero of the Filipinos, the Story of José Rizal, Poet, Patriot, and
   Martyr.* Charles E. Russell. N. Y., 1923. 392 p.
                                                       DLC, NN, PU
ROACH, JOHN. 2:623
ROBERT-HOUDIN, JEAN. *A Master of Modern Magic; the Life and
   Adventures of Robert-Houdin.* Henry R. Evans. N. Y., 1932.
   58 p.   *DLC, NN*
ROBERTS, ABIGAIL. *Memoir of Mrs. Abigail Roberts; An Account of
   Her Birth, Early Education, Call to the Ministry.* Philetus Roberts.
   Irvington, N. J., 1858. 198 p.   *NN*
ROBERTS, BARTHOLOMEW. 2:71
ROBERTS, MARSHALL OWEN. 2:623
ROBERTSON, JAMES. *Gen. James Robertson.* T. E. Matthews. Nash-
   ville, 1934. 588 p.   *CSmH*
ROBERTSON, JAMES. *Life of James Robertson, Missionary Superin-
   tendent in the Northwest.* C. W. Gordon. N. Y., 1908. 403 p.
                                                          DLC, NN
ROBERTSON, WILLIAM JOSEPH. 2:258
ROBESON, PAUL. *Paul Robeson, Negro.* Eslanda C. Robeson. N. Y.,
   1930. 178 p.   *DLC, NN, PU*
   2:592
ROBESPIERRE, MAXIMILIEN. *Robespierre and the French Revolution.*
   Charles F. Warwick. Phila., 1909. 407 p.   *DLC, NN, PU*
ROBINSON, CHARLES. *The Life of Charles Robinson, the First State
   Governor of Kansas.* Frank W. Blackmar. Topeka, Kan., 1902.
   438 p.   *DLC, NN, MWA, CSmH, PU, MiD:B*
ROBINSON, EDWARD. *The Life, Writings and Character of Rev. E.
   Robinson.* R. D. Hitchcock and H. B. Smith. N. Y., 1863. 100 p.
                                                          DLC, NN
ROBINSON, EDWIN ARLINGTON.
   Edwin Arlington Robinson. Ben Ray Redman. N. Y., 1926.
   96 p.   *DLC, NN, MWA, CSmH, PU*
   Edwin Arlington Robinson. Mark Van Doren. N. Y., 1927.
   93 p.   *DLC, NN, MWA, PU*
ROBINSON, HENRIETTA. *Memoir of Henrietta Robinson.* David Wil-
   son. N. Y., 1855. 329 p.   *DLC, NN, MWA*
ROBINSON, HENRY MAURIS. 2:233

ROBINSON, JOHN.
Pastor of the Pilgrims: a Biography of John Robinson. Walter
H. Burgess. N. Y., 1930. 426 p.   *DLC, NN, MWA*
John Robinson, the Pilgrims' Pastor. Ozora S. Davis. Boston,
1903. 366 p.   *DLC, NN, MWA*
    2:141

ROBINSON, MONCURE. *Professional Biography of Moncure Robinson,
Civil Engineer.* Richard B. Osborne. Phila., 1889. 47 p.   *PU*

ROBINSON, RICHARD ALEXANDER. *Richard A. Robinson, a Memoir.*
Temple Bodley. Louisville, 1903. 172 p.   *NN, PU*

ROBINSON, THERESE. *The Life and Works of Mrs. Therese Robinson.*
Irma E. Voigt. Chicago, 1914. 148 p.   *DLC, NN, PU*

ROBINSON, WILLIAM. *Memoir of the Rev. William Robinson, Formerly
Pastor of the Congregational Church in Southington, Conn.* Edward Robinson. N. Y., 1859. 214 p. (Privately Printed)
    DLC, NN, MWA

ROBUSTI, JACOPO. [TINTORETTO.] *Life and Genius of Jacopo Robusti, Called Tintoretto.* Frank P. Stearns. N. Y., 1894. 327 p.
    NN

ROCKEFELLER, JOHN DAVISON.
Rockefeller; Giant, Dwarf, Symbol. William H. Allen. N. Y.,
1930. 619 p.   *DLC, NN*
*A Study of John D. Rockefeller, the Wealthiest Man in the
World.* Marcus M. Brown. Cleveland, 1905. 150 p.   *DLC*
God's Gold; the Story of Rockefeller and His Times. John T.
Flynn. N. Y., 1932. 520 p.   *DLC, NN, PU*
John D. Rockefeller and His Career. Silas Hubbard. N. Y.,
1904. 192 p.   *DLC, NN*
John D.; a Portrait in Oils. John K. Winkler. N. Y., 1929.
256 p.   *DLC, NN*
    2:325

ROCKNE, KNUTE.
Rockne. Warren Brown. Chicago, 1931. 234 p.
    DLC, NN, MWA
Goals, the Life of Knute Rockne. Huber W. Hurt. N. Y.,
1931. 271 p.   *DLC, NN*
*Salesman From the Sidelines; Being the Business Career of
Knute K. Rockne.* McCready Huston. N. Y., 1932. 235 p.
    DLC, NN
Rockne of Notre Dame. Delos W. Lovelace. N. Y., 1931.
235 p.   *DLC, NN*

Knute Rockne; Man Builder. Harry A. Stuhldreher. Phila., 1931. 335 p. *DLC, NN, PU*

ROCKWELL, PORTER. *Holy Murder; the Story of Porter Rockwell.* Charles Kelly and Hoffman Birney. N. Y., 1934. 313 p.
DLC, NN, MWA, CSmH

RODGERS, JAMES. *James Rodgers of New London, Conn.* James Rogers. Boston, 1902. 514 p.

RODGERS, JAMES. *My Husband, Jimmie Rodgers.* Carrie C. Rodgers. San Antonio, 1935. 264 p. *DLC, NN*

RODGERS, JOHN. *Commodore John Rodgers, Captain, Commodore and Senior Officer of the American Navy, 1773–1838; A Biography.* Charles O. Paullin. Cleveland, 1910. 434 p.
DLC, NN, MWA, CSmH, PU

RODGERS, JOHN. *Memoirs of the Rev. John Rodgers . . .* Samuel Miller. N. Y., 1913. 432 p. *DLC, NN, MWA, CSmH*

RODGERS, JOHN KEARNY. *Biographical Sketch of J. Kearny Rodgers, M.D.* Edward Delafield. N. Y., 1852. 28 p.
DLC, NN, MWA, PU

ROE, EDWARD PAYSON. *E. P. Roe: Reminiscences of His Life.* Mary A. Roe. N. Y., 1899. 235 p. *DLC, NN*

ROE, FRANCIS ASBURY. *Francis Asbury Roe.* Marcus Benjamin. Washington, 1903. 43 p. (Memorial Papers of Soc. of Colonial Wars in D. C., no. 4) *DLC, NN, CSmH, MiD:B*

ROEDING, GEORGE CHRISTIAN. *George Christian Roeding, 1868–1928. The Story of California's Leading Nursery Man and Fruit Grower.* Henry W. Kruckeberg. Los Angeles, 1930. 109 p. *NN*

ROGERS, B. P. 2:40

ROGERS, BRUCE. *Bruce Rogers. With a List of Books Printed Under Mr. Rogers's Supervision.* Frederic Warde. Cambridge, 1925. 74 p. *DLC, NN, CSmH*

ROGERS, EARL. *Take the Witness; Life of Earl Rogers.* Alfred Cohn and Joe Chisholm. N. Y., 1934. 315 p. *DLC, NN, MWA*

ROGERS, FAIRMAN. *F. R.: A Memoir.* H. H. Furness. Phila., 1903. 20 p. (Privately Printed) *DLC, NN, MWA, CSmH, PU*

ROGERS, HENRY HUTTLESTONE. 2:331

ROGERS, ROBERT. *Life of Robert Rogers.* Allan Nevins. Chicago, 1914. 173 p. (in *Ponteach or The Savages of America*)
DLC, NN, CSmH, PU, MiU:C

2:542

ROGERS, WILL.
Our Will Rogers. Jack Lait. N. Y., 1935. 117 p.
DLC, NN

An Appreciation of Will Rogers. David R. Milsten. San Antonio, 1935. 258 p. *DLC, NN*

Will Rogers, Ambassador of Good Will, Prince of Wit and Wisdom. Patrick J. O'Brien. Phila., 1935. 288 p. *DLC, NN*

2:366

ROGERS, WILLIAM. *Reminiscences of William Rogers.* R. H. Hadden, comp. N. Y., 1888. 228 p. *DLC, NN, PU*

ROGERS, WILLIAM BARTON.

William Barton Rogers, Founder of the Massachusetts Institute of Technology. James P. Munroe. Boston, 1904. 52 p. *NN*

Life and Letters of William Barton Rogers. Mrs. William B. Rogers. Boston, 1896. 2 vols. *DLC, NN*

ROLAND, MANON PHLIPON.

History of Madame Roland. J. S. C. Abbott. N. Y., 1850. 304 p. *DLC, NN, MWA*

Manon Phlipon Roland; Early Years. Evangeline W. Blashfield. N. Y., 1922. 383 p. *DLC, NN*

Madame Roland. Mathilde Blind. Boston, 1886. 318 p. *DLC, NN*

A Daughter of the Seine; the Life of Madame Roland. Jeanette Eaton. N. Y., 1929. 324 p. *DLC, NN*

Madame Roland: Biographical Study. Ida M. Tarbell. N. Y., 1896. 328 p. *DLC, NN, CSmH*

Madame Roland; a Biographical Study. Gerald Tate. N. Y., 1917. 106 p. *NN*

Lady Who Loved Herself; the Life of Madame Roland. Catharine Young. N. Y., 1930. 318 p. *DLC, NN*

2:138

ROLLIER, AUGUST E. 2:175

ROLLINS, EDWARD HENRY. *Life of Edward H. Rollins.* James O. Lyford. Boston, 1906. 547 p. *DLC, CSmH*

ROLLINS, JAMES SIDNEY. *James Sidney Rollins. Memoir.* William B. Smith. N. Y., 1891. 317 p.

ROLPH, JAMES. *The Life of James Rolph, Jr.* David W. Taylor. San Francisco, 1934. 126 p. *DLC, NN, CSmH*

ROMAN NOSE. 2:204

ROMANET, LOUIS. *Kabluk of the Eskimo.* Lowell J. Thomas. Boston, 1932. 275 p. *DLC, NN*

RONALDS, SIR FRANCIS. 2:25

ROOSEVELT, FRANKLIN D.

Franklin D. Roosevelt the Man. Erich Brandeis. N. Y., 1936. 55 p. *NN*

Our President, Franklin Delano Roosevelt, a Biography . . .
Joseph Lasky. N. Y., 1933. 58 p.   *DLC, NN*
    Franklin D. Roosevelt; a Career in Progressive Democracy.
Ernest K. Lindley. Indianapolis, 1931. 379 p.
                                    DLC, NN, MWA, PU
    This Man Roosevelt. Earle Looker. N. Y., 1932. 233 p.
                                             DLC, NN
    Franklin Delano Roosevelt, the Minute Man of '33. Belle
Moses. N. Y., 1933. 201 p.   *DLC, NN*
    From Boyhood to President With Franklin Delano Roosevelt.
Samuel Nisenson and F. Vitelli. Cleveland, 1934. 123 p.
                                             DLC, NN
    This Democratic Roosevelt; the Life Story of " F. R."; an
Authentic Biography. Leland M. Ross and A. W. Grobin. N. Y.,
1932. 312 p.   *DLC*
ROOSEVELT, QUENTIN. *Quentin Roosevelt. A Sketch With Letters.*
Kermit Roosevelt. N. Y., 1921. 282 p.   *DLC, NN, PU*
    2:425
ROOSEVELT, SARA DELANO. *Gracious Lady; the Life of Sara Delano*
Roosevelt. Rita H. Kleeman. N. Y., 1935. 333 p.   *DLC, NN*
ROOSEVELT, THEODORE.
    Theodore Roosevelt, Twenty-Sixth President of the United
States. C. E. Banks and L. Armstrong. Chicago, 1902. 413 p.
                                          DLC, NN, CSmH
    Roosevelt and the Republic. John W. Bennett. N. Y., 1908.
424 p.   *DLC, NN*
    Theodore Roosevelt and His Time Shown in His Own Letters.
Joseph B. Bishop. N. Y., 1920. 2 vols. *DLC, NN, MWA, CSmH*
    Theodore Roosevelt, the American. Edward H. Cotton. Bos-
ton, 1926. 192 p.   *DLC, NN, MWA*
    Many-Sided Roosevelt: Anecdotal Biography. G. W. Douglas.
N. Y., 1907. 272 p.   *DLC, NN, CSmH*
    Theodore Roosevelt, His Life and Work . . . Frederick E.
Drinker and J. H. Mowbray. Phila., 1919. 471 p.   *DLC, NN*
    Roosevelt: His Mind in Action. Lewis D. Einstein. Boston,
1930. 259 p.   *DLC, NN, PU*
    From the Ranch to the White House; Life of Theodore Roose-
velt . . . Edward S. Ellis. Chicago, 1927. 373 p.   *DLC, NN*
    Adventures of Theodore Roosevelt. Edwin Emerson. N. Y.,
1928. 336 p.   *DLC, NN*

Roosevelt, the Happy Warrior. Bradley Gilman. Boston, 1921. 376 p. *DLC, NN, CSmH, PU*

Roosevelt, the Prophet of Unity. Hermann Hagedorn. N. Y., 1924. 142 p. *DLC, NN, PU*

Roosevelt in the Bad Lands. Hermann Hagedorn. Boston. 491 p. *DLC, NN, MWA, CSmH, PU*

Life of Theodore Roosevelt. Murat Halstead. Akron, Ohio, 1902. 391 p. *DLC*

The Life and Sayings of Theodore Roosevelt. Thomas Handford. Chicago, 1903. 315 p. *DLC, NN*

Theodore Roosevelt. The Pride of the Rough Riders. Thomas W. Handford. Chicago, 1899. 256 p. *DLC, NN*

Theodore Roosevelt. Norman Hapgood. N. Y., 1905. 14 p. *DLC*

Great Heart; the Life Story of Theodore Roosevelt. Daniel M. Henderson. N. Y., 1919. 224 p. *DLC, NN*

Theodore Roosevelt: the Man as I Knew Him. Ferdinand C. Iglehart. N. Y., 1919. 442 p. *DLC, NN*

The Man Roosevelt: a Portrait Sketch. F. E. Leupp. N. Y., 1904. 341 p. (Historic Lives Series) *DLC, NN*

Life of Theodore Roosevelt. William D. Lewis. Phila., 1919. 480 p. *DLC, NN, MWA, PU*

Theodore Roosevelt. Walter F. McCaleb. N. Y., 1931. 383 p. *DLC, NN, MWA, PU*

The Story of Theodore Roosevelt. Joseph W. McSpadden. N. Y. and Newark, N. J., 1923. 186 p. *DLC, NN*

Theodore Roosevelt, Patriot and Statesman. R. C. V. Meyers. Phila. and Chicago, 1902. 526 p. *DLC, CSmH, MiD:B*

Theodore Roosevelt, the Boy and the Man. James Morgan. N. Y., 1907. 324 p. *DLC, NN, MWA, CSmH*

The Life Story of Theodore Roosevelt. Charles Morris. Phila., 1909. 424 p. *DLC, NN*

The Marvelous Career of Theodore Roosevelt. Charles Morris. Phila., 1910. 390 p. *DLC, NN, CSmH*

Theodore Roosevelt. Edmund L. Pearson. N. Y., 1920. 159 p. *DLC, NN, PU*

Life of Theodore Roosevelt. F. M. Perry. N. Y., 1903. 126 p. (Famous Americans Series) *DLC, NN*

Theodore Roosevelt. Henry F. Pringle. N. Y., 1931. 627 p. *DLC, NN, CSmH, PU*

Theodore Roosevelt, the Citizen. Jacob Riis. N. Y., 1904. 471 p. *DLC, NN, CSmH, PU, MiD:B*

My Brother, Theodore Roosevelt. Corinne Roosevelt Robinson. N. Y., 1921. 365 p. *DLC, NN, MWA, CSmH, PU*

Theodore Roosevelt, an Intimate Biography. William Thayer. Boston, 1919. 474 p. *DLC, NN, MWA, CSmH, PU*

The Life and Meaning of Theodore Roosevelt. Eugene Thwing. N. Y., 1919. 367 p. *DLC, NN*

Theodore Roosevelt: The Logic of His Career. Charles G. Washburn. Boston, 1916. 245 p. *DLC, NN, MWA, CSmH, PU*

The Heart of Roosevelt; an Intimate Life-Story of Theodore Roosevelt. Wayne Whipple. Phila., 1923. 256 p. *DLC, MWA*

Roosevelt in the Rough. John Willis. N. Y., 1931. 246 p. *DLC, NN, MWA*

Roosevelt; the Story of a Friendship. Owen Wister. N. Y., 1930. 372 p. *DLC, NN, PU*

    2:6–14–47–77–94–388–525–660

ROOSEVELT, THEODORE, JR. 2:546

ROOT, ELIHU. 2:388

ROOT, JOHN WELLBORN. *John Wellborn Root: Study of His Life and Work.* Harriet Monroe. Boston, 1896. 291 p. *DLC, NN*

ROPES, JOHN CODMAN. *John Codman Ropes, a Memoir.* Joseph May. Cambridge, 1900. 28 p. (Also in Proc. of Mass. Hist. Soc. 1900) *DLC, NN, MWA, CSmH, PU*

ROSECRANS, WILLIAM STARKE. 2:634

ROSS, BETSY. *Betsy Ross, Quaker Rebel.* Edwin S. Parry. Phila., 1930. 252 p. *DLC, NN, MWA, PU, MiU:C*

ROSS, JAMES. *Life and Times of Senator James Ross.* James I. Brownson. Washington, Pa., 1910. 52 p. *DLC, PU*

ROSS, REUBEN. *Life and Times of Elder Reuben Ross.* James Ross. Phila., 1882. 426 p. *DLC, NN, MiD:B*

ROSS, ROBERT. *Martyr of Today: Life of Robert Ross.* James H. Ross. Boston, 1894. 180 p. *DLC*

ROSS, ROLAND. 2:176

ROSS, WILLIAM P. *The Life and Times of Hon. William P. Ross.* Fort Smith, Ark., 1893. 272 p.

ROSSETTI. *The Rossettis: Dante Gabriel and Christina.* Elizabeth L. Cary. N. Y., 1900. 310 p. *DLC, NN*

ROSSINI, GIOACHINO ANTONIO. 2:187

ROTHSCHILD, MEYER ANSELM. 2:331

ROUSSEAU, JEAN JACQUES. *Jean-Jacques Rousseau.* Matthew Josephson. N. Y., 1931. 546 p. *DLC, NN, PU*
2:144–334

ROUX, PIERRE PAUL EMIL. 2:176

ROWAN, STEPHEN CLEGG. *Sketch of the Life and Services of Vice-
Admiral Stephen C. Rowan, U. S. N.* S. C. Ayres. Cincinnati,
1910. 17 p. *DLC, NN, CSmH*

ROWSON, SUSANNA HASWELL.
Memoir of Mrs. Susanna Haswell Rowson. Elias Nason. Al-
bany, N. Y., 1870. 212 p. *DLC, NN, MWA, CSmH, MiU:C*
*Susanna Haswell Rowson, the Author of Charlotte Temple; a
Bibliographical Study.* Robert W. G. Vail. Worcester, Mass.,
1933. 116 p. *DLC, NN, MWA, CSmH*

ROYALL, ANNE. *Life and Times of Anne Royall.* Sarah H. Porter.
Cedar Rapids, 1909. 298 p. *DLC, NN, PU*
2:703

ROYDEN, AGNES MAUDE. 2:487

RUBENS, PETER PAUL. *The Life of Rubens.* George H. Calvert.
Boston, 1876. 219 p. *DLC, NN, MWA*
2:161–248

RUBRUQUIS, WILLIAM. 2:680

RUFFIN, EDMUND.
Edmund Ruffin, Southerner; a Study in Secession. Avery O.
Craven. N. Y., 1932. 283 p. *DLC, NN, CSmH, PU*
Edmund Ruffin. Henry Ellis. (Branch Hist. Papers, III.
June, 1910) *NN*

RUMPFF, ELIZA ASTOR. *Memoir of Mrs. Eliza Astor Rumpff, and of
the Duchess De Broglie.* Robert Baird. N. Y., 1839. 159 p.
DLC, NN, MWA, MiD:B

RUMSEY, JAMES. *James Rumsey, Pioneer in Steam Navigation.* Ella
M. Turner. Scottdale, Pa., 1930. 245 p.
DLC, NN, MWA, CSmH

RUSH, BENJAMIN.
Benjamin Rush and His Services to American Education. Harry
G. Good. Berne, Indiana, 1918. 283 p. *DLC, NN, PU*
Benjamin Rush, Physician and Citizen. Nathan G. Goodman.
Phila., 1934. 421 p. *DLC, NN, CSmH, PU*
An Eulogium Upon Benjamin Rush, M.D. . . . David Ramsay.
Phila., 1813. 139 p. (In Medical Biographies and Other Papers)
DLC, NN, PU

RUSK, JEREMIAH McCLAN. *" Uncle Jerry." Life of General Jeremiah M. Rusk, Stage Driver, Farmer, Soldier, Legislator, Governor, Cabinet Officer.* Henry Casson. Madison, Wis., 1895. 490 p.
DLC, NN

RUSKIN, JOHN. 2:246

RUSSELL, CHARLES HANDY.
Memoir of Charles H. Russell, 1796–1884. Charles Howland Russell. N. Y., 1903. 109 p. *DLC, NN*

RUSSELL, CHARLES HOWLAND. *Charles Howland Russell, 1851–1921.* Charles H. Russell. N. Y., 1935. 134 p. *DLC, NN*

RUSSELL, MARY BAPTIST. *Life of Mother Mary Baptist Russell, Sister of Mercy.* Matthew Russell. N. Y., 1901. 187 p.
DLC, CSmH

RUTH, GEORGE HERMAN. 2:425

RUTLEDGE, JOHN. 2:230–290–666

RYAN, ABRAM JOSEPH. 2:503

RYAN, JOHN DENNIS. 2:233

RYAN, STEPHEN VINCENT. *Memorial of the Life and Labors of Rt. Rev. Stephen V. Ryan, Second Bishop of Buffalo, N. Y.* Patrick Cronin. Buffalo, 1896. *MiD:B*

RYDER, ALBERT PINKHAM. 2:161

RYDER, RUSSELL. *Russell Ryder.* D. B. Conklin. N. Y., 1902. 333 p.
DLC, NN

RYDER, WILLIAM HENRY. *Biography of William Henry Ryder.* J. W. Hanson. Boston, 1891. 303 p. *DLC, NN*

SABINE, WALLACE CLEMENT. *Wallace Clement Sabine; a Study in Achievement.* William D. Orcutt. Norwood, Mass., 1933. 376 p. (Privately Printed) *DLC, NN*

SABSOVITCH, HIRSCH LOEB. *Adventures in Idealism; a Personal Record of the Life of Professor Sabsovich.* Katharine Sabsovich. N. Y., 1922. 208 p. (Privately Printed) *DLC, NN, PU*

SACHS, HANS. 2:406

SAFFORD, DANIEL. *A Memoir of Daniel Safford.* Mrs. A. E. Safford. Boston, 1861. 384 p. *NN, MWA, CSmH*

SAILER, RANDOLPH. *A Memoir of Randolph Sailer.* Henry Bower. Phila., 1871. 144 p. *DLC, NN, PU*

SAINT-GAUDENS, AUGUSTUS. 2:340–430

SAINT-JUST, LOUIS ANTOINE.
Saint-Just, Apostle of Terror. Geoffrey Bruun. Boston, 1932. 168 p. *DLC, NN*

Saint-Just, Colleague of Robespierre. Eugene N. Curtis. N. Y., 1935. 402 p.   *DLC, NN, PU*

SAINTE-BEUVE, CHARLES AUGUSTUS.

    Charles-Augustus Sainte-Beuve. George M. Harper. Phila., 1909. 388 p.   *DLC, NN, PU*

    Sainte-Beuve. Lewis F. Mott. N. Y., 1925. 521 p.
        DLC, NN, PU

SAINTE-MARTHE, CHARLES DE. *Charles De Sainte-Marthe.* Caroline Ruutz-Rees. N. Y., 1910. 664 p. (Col. Univ. Studies in Romance)   *DLC, NN, PU*

SALADIN. *Saladin, Prince of Chivalry.* Charles J. Rosebault. N. Y., 1930. 305 p.   *DLC, NN*

SALMON, JOSHUA S. *Memorials of the Honorable Joshua S. Salmon of Boonton, New Jersey.* Andrew M. Sherman. Morristown, N. J., 1904. 171 p.   *NN*

SALOMON, HAYM.

    Haym Salomon. Madison C. Peters. N. Y., 1911, 1915. 47 p.
        DLC, NN, PU

    Haym Salomon and the Revolution. Charles E. Russell. N. Y., 1930. 317 p.   *DLC, NN, CSmH, PU*

SALTER, WILLIAM. *Rev. William Salter, 1821–1910, Minister of the Congregational Church and Society of Burlington, Iowa, 1846–1910.* James L. Hill. Des Moines, 1911. 644 p.   *DLC, NN, MiD:B*

SALTUS, EDGAR. *Edgar Saltus, the Man.* Marie Saltus. Chicago, 1925. 324 p.   *DLC, NN, MWA, CSmH, PU*

SAMPSON, AUGUSTA F. *Memorial of Augusta F. Sampson.* Henry J. Van Dyke. Brooklyn, 1862. 16 p.   *DLC*

SAMPSON, DEBORAH. *The Female Review. Life of Deborah Sampson, the Female Soldier in the War of the Revolution.* Herman Mann. Boston, 1866. 267 p.   *DLC, NN, MWA, CSmH, MiU:C* 2:703

SAMPSON, FRANCIS SMITH. *A Memorial of the Christian Life and Character of Francis S. Sampson.* Robert L. Dabney. Richmond, 1855. 122 p.   *NN*

SAMS, ISAAC. *Sketch of the Life and Professional Services of Isaac Sams.* H. S. Doggett. Cincinnati, 1880. 83 p.   *DLC, MiD:B*

SANBORN, KATE. *Kate Sanborn; July 11, 1839–July 9, 1917.* Edwin W. Sanborn. Boston, 1918. 76 p.   *DLC, NN, MWA*

SAND, GEORGE. [AMANTINE, BARONESS DUDEVANT.]

    George Sand; the Search For Love. Marie H. J. Howe. N. Y., 1927. 351 p.   *DLC, NN, PU*

Seven Strings of the Lyre; the Romantic Life of George Sand, 1804–1876. Elizabeth W. Schermerhorn. N. Y., 1927. 327 p.
DLC, NN

2:90
SANDBURG, CARL. 2:236–366
SANDERS, ALVIN HOWARD. 2:497
SANDERS, JAMES HARDY. 2:497
SANDOZ, JULES. *Old Jules.* Mari Sandoz. Boston, 1935. 424 p.
DLC, NN, CSmH
SANFORD, DAVID. *Memoir of Rev. David Sanford, Pastor of the Village Church in Medway, Mass.* William M. Cornell. Middleboro, 1878. 90 p. *NN, MWA*
SANFORD, JOSEPH. *Memoir of the Rev. Joseph Sanford.* Robert Baird. Phila., 1836. 268 p. *DLC, NN, MWA, CSmH*
SANFORD, MARIA. *Maria Sanford.* Helen Whitney. Minneapolis, 1922. 322 p. *DLC, NN*
SANKEY, IRA DAVID. See MOODY, DWIGHT L.
SANTA ANNA, ANTONIO LOPEZ.
Santa Anna. Wilfrid H. Calcott. Norman, Okla., 1936. 361 p.
DLC, NN, PU
Santa Anna; the Napoleon of the West. Frank C. Hanighen. N. Y., 1934. 326 p. *DLC, NN, PU*
El Presidente; a Sketch of the Life of General Santa Anna. Clarence R. Wharton. Austin, 1924. 197 p.
DLC, NN, CSmH, PU
SARGENT, JOHN SINGER. *John S. Sargent; His Life and Work.* William H. Downes. Boston, 1925, London, 1926. 313 p.
DLC, NN, CSmH, PU

2:123–388–429
SARLE, AMARANCY PAINE. *Saint Indefatigable. A Sketch of the Life of Amarancy Paine Sarle.* W. F. Davis. Boston, 1883. 97 p.
DLC, NN
SATTERLEE, CHURCHILL. *Fisher of Men: Churchill Satterlee, Priest and Missionary.* Hamilton Schuyler. N. Y., 1905. 202 p.
DLC, NN
SATTERLEE, HENRY YATES. *Master Builder: the Life of Henry Yates Satterlee, Bishop of Washington.* Charles H. Brent. N. Y., 1916. 477 p. *DLC, NN, MiD:B*
SAUGRAIN, ANTOINE FRANÇOIS. *The First Scientist of the Mississippi Valley. A Memoir of the Life and Work of Doctor Antoine François Saugrain.* William V. Byars. St. Louis, 1905. 18 p. *NN*

SAVERY, WILLIAM.
A Journal of the Life, Travels and Religious Labors of W. Savery
. . . William Savery. London, 1844, Phila., 1873. 485 p.
DLC, NN, CSmH
Life of William Savery of Philadelphia, 1750–1804. Francis R.
Taylor. N. Y., 1925. 474 p.
DLC, NN, MWA, CSmH, PU, MiD:B
SAVONAROLA, GIROLAMO.
Savonarola, His Life and Times. William R. Clark. Chicago,
1890. 352 p. DLC, NN, PU
Girolamo Savonarola, a Prophet of Righteousness. William H.
Crawford. Cincinnati, 1907. 260 p. DLC, NN
Jerome Savonarola. A Sketch. J. L. O'Neil. Boston, 1898.
232 p. DLC, NN, PU
Was Savonarola Really Excommunicated? An Inquiry. J. L.
O'Neil. Boston, 1900. 202 p. DLC, NN
Savonarola; a Study in Conscience. Ralph Roeder. N. Y.,
1930. 307 p. DLC, NN
2:330–573
SAWYER, CAROLINE MEHITABLE AND THOMAS JEFFERSON. Life of
Thomas J. and Caroline M. Sawyer. R. Eddy. Boston, 1900.
458 p. DLC, NN
SAY, THOMAS.
A Short Compilation of the Extraordinary Life and Writings of
Thomas Say . . . Benjamin Say. Phila., 1796. 151 p.
DLC, NN, MWA, CSmH, MiU:C
Thomas Say: Early American Naturalist. Harry B. Weiss and
Grace M. Liegler. Springfield, Ill., 1931. 260 p.
DLC, NN, MWA, PU
SCAMMELL, ALEXANDER. 2:149
SCANDERBEG, GEORGE. George Castriot, Surnamed Scanderbeg, King
of Albania. Clement C. Moore. N. Y., 1850. 267 p.
DLC, NN, MWA
SCATTERGOOD, THOMAS. Memoirs of Thomas Scattergood, Late of
Philadelphia, a Minister of the Gospel of Christ. William and T.
Evans. London, 1845. 464 p. NN
SCHAFF, PHILIP. The Life of Philip Schaff. David S. Schaff. N. Y.,
1897. 526 p. DLC, NN, PU
SCHAMYL. Life of Schamyl; and Narrative of Circassian War of In-
dependence Against Russia. J. Milton Mackie. Cleveland, 1856.
300 p. DLC, NN, MWA

SCHAUDINN, FRITZ. 2:175

SCHAUMBURG, EMILIE. 2:518

SCHENCK, ROBERT CUMMING. 2:128

SCHIFF, JACOB HENRY. *Jacob H. Schiff: His Life and Letters.* Cyrus
Adler. N. Y., 1928. 2 vols. *DLC, NN, PU*

SCHILLER, FRIEDRICH. *Life and Works of Friedrich Schiller.* Calvin
Thomas. N. Y., 1901. 481 p. *DLC, NN, PU*
See GOETHE, JOHANN W.

SCHLATTER, FRANCIS. *Biography of Francis Schlatter, the Healer, With
His Life, Works and Wanderings.* Harry B. Magill. Denver,
1896. 206 p. *NN*

SCHLATTER, MICHAEL. *The Life of Rev. Michael Schlatter, With a
Full Account of His Travels and Labors Among the Germans in
Pennsylvania, New Jersey, Maryland, and Virginia (1716–1790).*
H. Harbaugh. Phila., 1857. 375 p. *DLC, NN, PU*

SCHLIERMACHER, FRIEDRICH ERNST DANIEL. 2:98–371

SCHMAUK, THEODORE EMANUEL. *Theodore Emanuel Schmauk, D.D.,
LL.D., a Biographical Sketch, With Liberal Quotations From His
Letters and Other Writings.* George W. Sandt. Phila., 1921. 291 p.
DLC, NN

SCHMUCKER, SAMUEL SIMON. *Life and Times of Rev. S. S. Schmucker.*
P. Anstadt. York, Pa., 1896. 392 p. *PU*

SCHNEIDER, JAMES M. AND EDWARD M. *Memoir of James M. Schneider
and Edward M. Schneider.* Increase N. Tarbox. Boston, 1867.
357 p. *DLC, MWA*

SCHOONMAKER, JAMES M. *Col. J. M. Schoonmaker and the Pittsburgh
and Lake Erie Railroad; a Study of Personality and Ideals.* Harrington Emerson. N. Y., 1913. 152 p. *DLC, NN, CSmH*

SCHOPENHAUER, ARTHUR. *Schopenhauer, Pessimist and Pagan.* V.
J. McGill. N. Y., 1931. 312 p. *DLC, NN*
2:332

SCHUBERT, FRANZ. *Franz Schubert; the Man and His Circle.* Walter
N. Flower. N. Y., 1928. 369 p. *DLC, NN, PU*
2:187

SCHUETZE, WILLIAM HENRY. *William Henry Schuetze.* William Mc-
Adoo. Wash., 1903. 164 p. *CSmH*

SCHUMANN, ROBERT. 2:187

SCHUMANN-HEINK, ERNESTINE. *Schumann-Heink, the Last of the
Titans.* Mary Lawton. N. Y., 1928. 390 p. *DLC, NN, PU*

SCHURZ, CARL.
The Americanization of Carl Schurz. Chester V. Easum. Chicago, 1929. 374 p. *DLC, NN, CSmH, PU*

Carl Schurz, Reformer. Claude M. Fuess. N. Y., 1932. 421 p.
DLC, NN, CSmH, PU

Carl Schurz, Militant Liberal. Joseph Schafer. Madison, Wis., 1930. 270 p. (Wisconsin Biography Series)
DLC, NN, MWA, CSmH, MiD:B
2:340–672

SCHUYLER, CATHERINE. *Catherine Schuyler.* M. G. Humphreys. N. Y., 1897. 251 p. (Women of Colonial and Revolutionary Times)
DLC, NN

SCHUYLER, ELIZABETH. *Elizabeth Schuyler.* Mary E. Springer. N. Y., 1903. 256 p.
DLC, NN

SCHUYLER, GEORGINA AND LOUISA. 2:519

SCHUYLER, LOUIS SANDFORD. *A Memorial of Louis Sandford Schuyler, Priest.* N. Y., 1879. 153 p.
DLC, NN, MWA

SCHUYLER, PHILIP.
The Life and Times of Philip Schuyler. Benson J. Lossing. N. Y., 1860. 504 p.
NN, MWA, CSmH

The Life and Times of Philip Schuyler. Benson J. Lossing. N. Y., 1873. 2 vols.
DLC, NN, MiD:B, MiU:C

Colonial New York; Philip Schuyler and His Family. G. W. Schuyler. N. Y., 1885. 2 vols.
DLC, NN, CSmH

Life of General Philip Schuyler, 1733–1804. Bayard Tuckerman. N. Y., 1903. 277 p.
DLC, NN, CSmH, PU

SCHWANN, THEODORE. 2:678

SCHWEITZER, ALBERT. *Albert Schweitzer, the Man and His Work.* John D. Regester. N. Y., 1931. 145 p.
DLC, NN
2:675

SCOFIELD, CYRUS INGERSON. *Life Story of C. I. Scofield.* C. G. Trumbull. N. Y., 1920. 138 p.
CSmH

SCOTT, GEORGE ROBERT WHITE. *In Memoriam. Rev. George Robert White Scott . . .* Mary D. Scott. Boston, 1905. 239 p.
DLC, NN, MWA, PU

SCOTT, JAMES. [DUKE of MONMOUTH] *James Crofts, the Beauty Man and His Love.* Fred Erick. Boston, 1926. 235 p.
DLC, NN

SCOTT, JOHN. *Colonel John Scott of Long Island, 1634–1696.* Wilbur C. Abbott. New Haven, 1918. 93 p. DLC, NN, CSmH, MiD:B
2:7

SCOTT, JOSIAH. *A Memoir of the Life and Character of Josiah Scott.* Robert C. Colmery. Columbus, O., 1881. 190 p. NN, MWA

SCOTT, ORANGE. *Life of Rev. Orange Scott.* Lucius C. Mattack. N. Y., 1851. 307 p. *DLC, NN*

SCOTT, ROBERT. 2:507

SCOTT,.THOMAS A. *Captain Thomas A. Scott, Master Diver.* Francis H. Smith. Boston, 1908. 76 p. (True American Types Series)
DLC, NN, MWA, PU

SCOTT, WINFIELD.
Illustrated Life of General Winfield Scott, Commander-in-Chief of the Army of Mexico. N. Y., 1847. 144 p. *DLC, NN*
The Giant of Three Wars; a Life of General Winfield Scott. James Barnes. N. Y., 1903. 241 p. *DLC, NN*
The Lives of Winfield Scott and Andrew Jackson. J. T. Headley. N. Y., 1852. 341 p. *DLC, NN, MWA, PU, MiD:B*
The Life of Winfield Scott. J. T. Headley. San Francisco, 1861. 202 p. *NN, MWA*
Life and Services of General Winfield Scott. E. D. Mansfield. N. Y., 1852. 538 p. *DLC, NN, MWA, CSmH, PU, MiD:B*
Life, Military and Civil Services of Gen. Winfield Scott. Orville J. Victor. N. Y., 1861. 118 p. (Beadle's Dime Biographical Library) *NN, MWA, CSmH*
General Scott. Marcus J. Wright. N. Y., 1894. 349 p. (G.C.) *DLC, NN, CSmH, PU, MiD:B*
2:590

SCOVEL, SYLVESTER. *Memoir of Sylvester Scovel, D.D., Late President of Hanover College, Ia., and Formerly Domestic Missionary and Missionary Agent in the West.* James Wood. New Albany, 1851. 213 p. *DLC, NN, CSmH*

SCRIPPS, EDWARD WYLLIS.
E. W. Scripps. Negley D. Cochran. N. Y., 1933. 315 p.
DLC, NN, PU
Lusty Scripps; the Life of E. W. Scripps (1854–1926). Gilson Gardner. N. Y., 1932. 274 p. *DLC, NN, MWA*

SCUDDER, DAVID COIT. *Life and Letters of David Coit Scudder, Missionary in Southern India.* Horace E. Scudder. N. Y., 1864. 402 p.
NN, MWA, PU

SCUDDER, JANE. 2:430

SCUDDER, JOHN. *Memoir of the Rev. John Scudder, M.D., Thirty-Six Years Missionary in India.·* Jared B. Waterbury. N. Y., 1870. 307 p. *NN*
2:237

SCULL, GUY HAMILTON. *Guy Hamilton Scull, Soldier, Writer, Explorer and War Correspondent.* Henry Jay Case, comp. N. Y., 1922. 267 p. *DLC, NN*

SEABURY, SAMUEL. [1729–1796]
Life and Correspondence of Rev. S. Seabury, First Bishop of Connecticut and of the Episcopal Church in the United States. E. E. Beardsley. Boston, 1881. 498 p. *DLC, NN, PU*
The Life of the Rt. Rev. Samuel Seabury, D.D., Bishop of Connecticut. John N. Norton. N. Y., 1857. 107 p. *NN, MWA*
Memoir of Bishop Seabury: (First American Bishop). W. J. Seabury. N. Y., 1908. 453 p. *DLC, NN*

SEABURY, SAMUEL. *Samuel Seabury; a Challenge.* Walter Chambers. N. Y., 1932. 389 p. *DLC, NN, CSmH, PU*

SEABURY, WARREN BARTLETT. *The Vision of a Short Life.* A Memorial of Warren Bartlett Seabury, One of the Founders of the Yale Mission College in China. J. B. Seabury. Cambridge, 1909. 192 p. *DLC*

SEARS, BARNAS. *Barnas Sears, a Christian Educator.* Alvah Hovey. N. Y., 1902. 184 p. *DLC, PU*

SEATON, WILLIAM WINSTON. *William Winston Seaton of the National Intelligence. A Biographical Sketch.* Josephine Seaton. Boston, 1871. 385 p. *DLC, MWA, CSmH, PU*

SEDGWICK, CATHERINE MARIA. *Life and Letters of Catherine Maria Sedgwick.* Mary E. Dewey, ed. N. Y., 1871. 446 p.
DLC, NN, MWA, CSmH, PU, MiD:B
2:43

SEDGWICK, JOHN. *John Sedgwick, Major-General.* Emily S. Welch. n.p., 1899. 24 p. (Privately Printed) *DLC, NN, MWA, PU*

SEDGWICK, WILLIAM THOMPSON. *A Pioneer of Public Health, William Thompson Sedgwick.* Edwin O. Jordan. New Haven, 1924. 193 p. *DLC, NN*

SEE, THOMAS JEFFERSON JACKSON. *Brief Biography . . . of T. J. J. See.* William L. Webb. Lynn, Mass., 1913. 298 p.
DLC, NN, MWA, CSmH, PU

SEELY, CATHERINE. *Memoirs of Catherine Seely and Deborah S. Roberts, Late of Darien, Connecticut.* N. Y., 1844. 252 p. *NN*

SEELYE, LAURENUS CLARK. *Laurenus Clark Seelye, First President of Smith College.* Harriet C. Rhees. Boston, 1929. 342 p.
DLC, NN, MWA, CSmH, PU

SEMMELWEIS, IGNAZ PHILIPP. 2:175

SEMMES, RAPHAEL. *Raphael Semmes.* Colyer Meriwether. Phila., 1913. 367 p. (A.C.B.) *DLC, NN, MiD:B*

SENECA. 2:332

SENNETT, MACK. *Father Goose, the Story of Mack Sennett.* Gene Fowler. N. Y., 1934. 407 p. *DLC, NN*

SERGEANT, JOHN. 2:110

SEROFF, VICTOR ILYITCH. *To Whom it May Concern; the Story of Victor Ilyitch Seroff.* Morris Werner. N. Y., 1931. 277 p. *DLC, NN*

SERRA, JUNÍPERO.
 Junipero Serra; the Man and His Work. Abigail H. Fitch. Chicago, 1914. 364 p. *DLC, NN, CSmH, PU*
 Historical Account of the Life and Apostolic Labors of the Venerable Fr. Junípero Serra. Francisco Palou. Pasadena, 1913. 338 p. *DLC, NN, CSmH*
 Junípero Serra; Pioneer Colonist of California. Agnes Repplier. N. Y., 1933. 312 p. *DLC, NN, MWA, CSmH, PU*
 2:680

SETON, ELIZABETH.
 Elizabeth Seton, Foundress of the American Sisters of Charity. Agnes Sadlier. N. Y., 1905. 289 p. *DLC*
 Memoir, Letters and Journal of Elizabeth Seton. (Sister of Charity). R. Seton. N. Y., 1869. 2 vols. *NN*
 Life of Mrs. Eliza A. Seton, Foundress . . . of the Sisters . . . of Charity . . . in the United States. Charles I. White. N. Y., 1851. 581 p. *DLC, NN, CSmH*
 Life of Eliza A. Seton. Chas. I. White. Balt., 1879. 504 p. *DLC, NN*

SETTLE, ELKANAH. *Elkanah Settle: His Life and Works.* Frank C. Brown. Chicago, 1910. 170 p. *DLC, NN, CSmH, PU*

SEVERANCE, CAROLINE M. *The Mother of Clubs: Caroline M. Seymour Severance: an Estimate and an Appreciation.* Caroline M. S. Severance. Los Angeles, 1906. 191 p. *DLC, NN, CSmH*

SEVIER, JOHN.
 John Sevier; Pioneer of the Old Southwest. Carl S. Driver. Chapel Hill, 1932. 240 p. *DLC, NN, MWA, CSmH, PU*
 John Sevier as a Commonwealth Builder. James R. Gilmore. (Edmund Kirke.) N. Y., 1887. 321 p. *DLC, NN, MWA, CSmH*
 Life of Gen. John Sevier. Francis M. Turner. N. Y., 1910 226 p. *DLC, NN*

SÉVIGNÉ, MME DE. 2.93

SEWALL, JOTHAM. *Memoir of Rev. Jotham Sewall, of Chesterville, Maine.* Jotham Sewall. Boston, 1853. 408 p.

DLC, MWA, MiD:B

SEWALL, SAMUEL. *Samuel Sewall and the World He Lived in.* N. H. Chamberlain. Boston, 1897. 319 p.

DLC, NN, MWA, CSmH, PU, MiD:B

SEWALL, SAMUEL EDMUND. *Samuel E. Sewall: a Memoir.* Nina M. Tiffany. Boston, 1898. 175 p. *DLC, NN, MWA, CSmH*

SEWARD, ANNA. *The Singing Swan; an Account of Anna Seward and Her Acquaintance with Dr. Johnson, Boswell, and Others of Their Time.* Margaret E. Ashmun. New Haven, 1931. 298 p.

DLC, NN, CSmH, PU

SEWARD, WILLIAM HENRY.
The Life of William H. Seward. George E. Baker, ed. N. Y., 1855. 410 p. *DLC, NN, MWA, CSmH, MiD:B*
Life of William Henry Seward. Frederic Bancroft. N. Y., 1900. 2 vols. *DLC, NN, MWA, CSmH, PU*
William H. Seward. Edward E. Hale, Jr. Phila., 1910. 388 p. (A.C.B.) *DLC, NN*
William Henry Seward. Thornton K. Lothrop. Boston, 1899. 423 p. (A.S.) *DLC, NN, MWA, CSmH, PU, MiD:B*
Seward at Washington as Senator and Secretary of State; A Memoir of His Life With Selections From His Letters. Frederick W. Seward. N. Y., 1891. 2 vols. *DLC, NN, MWA, CSmH, PU*
2:40–96–107–329–349–590

SEYBERT, JOHN. *The Life and Labors of John Seybert, First Bishop of the Evangelical Association.* Samuel P. Spreng. Cleveland, 1888. 439 p. *NN*

SEYMOUR, HORATIO.
The Life and Public Services of Horatio Seymour . . . [and] a . . . Life of Francis P. Blair, Jr. James D. McCabe, Jr. N. Y., 1868. 503 p. *DLC, NN, MWA, MiD:B*
A Sketch of the Life of Horatio Seymour, 1810–1886. Alexander J. Wall. N. Y., 1929. 111 p.

DLC, NN, MWA, CSmH, PU, MiD:B, MiU:C
Seymour and Blair: Their Lives and Services. David G. Croly. N. Y., 1868. 275 p. *DLC, NN, CSmH*
2:128–590

SHACKLETON, ERNEST. 2:675

SHADWELL, THOMAS. *Thomas Shadwell, His Life and Comedies.* Alfred S. Borgman. N. Y., 1928. 269 p. *DLC, NN, CSmH*

SHAFTER, OSCAR LOVELL. *Life, Diary and Letters of Oscar Lovell Shafter, Associate Justice, Supreme Court of California, Jan. 1, 1864, to Dec. 31, 1868.* Flora H. Loughead, ed. San Francisco, 1915. 323 p.   *DLC, NN, CSmH*

SHAFTESBURY, EARL of. [ANTHONY ASHLEY COOPER.] ... *The First Earl of Shaftesbury.* Louise F. Brown. N. Y., 1933. 350 p.
     DLC, NN, CSmH, PU

SHAKESPEARE, WILLIAM.
     Life of William Shakespeare. Joseph Q. Adams. Boston, 1923. 560 p.   *DLC, NN, CSmH, PU*
     Shakespeare. Raymond M. Alden. N. Y., 1922. 377 p. (Master Spirits of Literature)   *DLC, NN, CSmH, PU*
     Shakespeare, Actor-Poet; as Seen by His Associates, Explained by Himself, and Remembered by the Succeeding Generation. Clara L. Comtesse de Chambrun. N. Y., 1927. 356 p. *DLC, NN, PU*
     Life, Art and Character of Shakespeare. H. N. Hudson. N. Y., 1883. 2 vols.   *DLC, NN, PU*
     Shakespeare and Voltaire. Thomas R. Lounsbury. N. Y., 1902. 463 p.   *DLC, NN, CSmH, PU*
     William Shakespeare; Poet. H. W. Mabie. N. Y., 1900. 421 p.
     Life of William Shakespeare. W. J. Rolfe. Boston, 1902. 531 p.   *DLC, NN, PU*
     Memoirs of the Life of William Shakespeare. Richard G. White. Boston, 1865. 425 p.   *DLC, NN, CSmH, PU*
     2:82–144

SHARP, MARTHA THOMPSON. *Memoir of Martha Thompson Sharp.* James I. Helm. Phila., 1849. 198 p.   *DLC, NN*

SHARSWOOD, GEORGE.
     Sketch of George Sharswood, Chief Justice of the Supreme Court of Penna. G. W. Biddle. Phila., 1883. 53 p.   *DLC, NN, MWA*
     Memoir of George Sharswood. Charles H. Hart. Phila., 1884. 10 p.   *NN, MWA, CSmH, MiD:B*

SHAW, ANNA HOWARD. 2:506

SHAW, GEORGE BERNARD.
     George Bernard Shaw: His Life and Works. Archibald Henderson. Cincinnati, 1911. 528 p.   *DLC, NN, CSmH, PU*
     Bernard Shaw; Playboy and Prophet. Archibald Henderson. N. Y., 1932. 871 p.   *DLC, NN*
     George Bernard Shaw; a Critical Study. Joseph McCabe. N. Y., 1914. 261 p.   *DLC, NN, CSmH, PU*
     2:301

SHAW, HENRY WHEELER. See BILLINGS, JOSH.

SHAW, JOHN. *Poems By . . . Doctor John Shaw . . . [with] a Biographical Sketch of the Author.* J. E. Hall. Boston, 1810. 252 p.
NN, MWA, CSmH

SHAW, LEMUEL. *Lemuel Shaw, Chief Justice of the Supreme Judicial Court of Massachusetts, 1830–1860.* Frederic H. Chase. Boston, 1918. 330 p.
DLC, NN, MWA, CSmH

SHAW, ROBERT GOULD. *Sketch of the Life and Death of Col. Robert G. Shaw.* Robert T. Teamoh. Boston, 1904. 49 p. *DLC, NN*

SHAW, SAMUEL. *The Journals of Major Samuel Shaw, the First American Consul at Canton. With a Memoir of the Author.* Josiah Quincy. Boston, 1847. 360 p.
DLC, NN, MWA, CSmH, MiD:B, MiU:C

SHAW, WILLIAM SMITH. *Memorials of William Smith Shaw.* Joseph B. Felt. Boston, 1852. 346 p.
DLC, NN, MWA

SHEA, JOHN GILMARY. *John Gilmary Shea, Father of American Catholic History, 1824–1892.* Peter Guilday. N. Y., 1926. 171 p.
DLC, NN

SHEDD, WILLIAM AMBROSE. *The Measure of a Man; the Life of William Ambrose Shedd, Missionary to Persia.* Mary L. Shedd. N. Y., 1922. 280 p.
DLC, NN

SHEEHAN, JOHN. *A True Narrative of the Life of . . . John Sheehan Who Was Executed in Boston, on Thursday, No. 22, 1787, for Burglary.* Boston, 1787.

SHELBY, JOSEPH ORVILLE. 2:314

SHELDON, WILLIAM. *Life and Labors of William Sheldon.* Lucy Sheldon. Mendota, Ill., 1902. 304 p.
DLC

SHELLEY, PERCY BYSSHE.

The Magic Plant; the Growth of Shelley's Thought. Carl Grabo. Chapel Hill, 1936. 450 p. *DLC, NN, PU*

Shelley; His Life and Work. Walter E. Peck. Boston, 1927. 2 vols. *DLC, NN, CSmH, PU*

Percy Bysshe Shelley as a Philosopher and Reformer. Charles Sotheran. N. Y., 1876. 51 p. *DLC, NN, CSmH*

Anecdote Biography of Percy B. Shelley. R. H. Stoddard. N. Y., 1877. 290 p. *DLC, NN, MWA*

Mad Shelley. James R. Ullman. Princeton, 1930. 120 p.
DLC, NN, CSmH, PU

2:701

SHEPARD, CYRUS. *Missionary Teacher; a Memoir of Cyrus Shepard.* Zachariah A. Mudge. N. Y., 1848. 221 p.

SHEPARD, FRED DOUGLAS.   2:237

SHEPARD, THOMAS.

The Life of Thomas Shepard. John A. Albro. Boston, 1847.
324 p. (Lives of the Chief Fathers of New England, vol. IV)
DLC, NN, MWA, CSmH, MiU:C
Thomas Shepard, Pilgrim Father and Founder of Harvard.
Alexander Whyte. Edinburgh, 1909. 252 p.
2:405–464

SHERIDAN, PHILIP HENRY.

The Gallant Trooper. General Philip H. Sheridan. James P.
Boyd. Phila., 1888. 224 p.   CSmH
Life of Gen. Philip H. Sheridan: Its Romance and its Reality.
F. A. Burr and R. J. Hinton. Providence, 1888. 445 p.
DLC, NN, MWA, CSmH, MiD:B
General Sheridan. H. E. Davies. N. Y., 1895. 332 p. (G.C.)
DLC, NN, CSmH
Illustrious Life, Campaigns, and Public Services of Maj.-Gen. P.
H. Sheridan. C. Denison. Phila., 1865. 197 p.   DLC, CSmH
The Life of Philip Henry Sheridan, the Dashing, Brave and
Successful Soldier. Joseph Faulkner. N. Y., 1888. 149 p.
DLC, NN, CSmH
Fighting Phil; the Life and Military Career of Philip Henry
Sheridan, General of the Army of the United States. Phineas C.
Headley. Boston, N. Y., 1889. 380 p.   DLC, NN, CSmH
Sheridan; a Military Narrative. Joseph Hergesheimer. Bos-
ton, 1931. 381 p.   DLC, NN, MWA
The Life of Gen. P. H. Sheridan, the Hero of the Shenandoah.
Julian K. Larke. N. Y., 1864. 108 p.   DLC, CSmH
General Philip H. Sheridan, a Story of His Life and Military
Services. William H. Van Orden. N. Y., 1896. 214 p.
DLC, MWA, CSmH
2:104–624–634

SHERMAN, ELLEN EWING. See EWING, ELLEN.

SHERMAN, JOHN.

John Sherman . . . Life and Public Services. S. A. Bronson.
Columbus, O., 1880. 272 p.   DLC, NN, MWA, MiD:B
John Sherman. Theodore E. Burton. Boston, 1906. 449 p.
(A.S.)   DLC, NN, MWA, CSmH, PU, MiD:B
John Sherman. G. U. Harn. Columbus, O., 1908. 30 p.
DLC, MWA

John Sherman; His Life and Public Services. Winfield S. Kerr. Boston, 1908. 2 vols. *DLC, NN, MWA, CSmH, PU*
  The Life and Public Services of John Sherman. Benjamin P. Poore. Cincinnati, 1880. 43 p.
  DLC, NN, MWA, CSmH, MiD:B
SHERMAN, ROGER. *Life of Roger Sherman.* L. H. Boutell. Chicago, 1896. 361 p. *DLC, NN, MWA*
  2:406
SHERMAN, STUART PRATT. *The Life and Letters of Stuart P. Sherman.* Jacob Zeitlin and Homer Woodbridge. N. Y., 1929. 2 vols.
  DLC, NN, PU

SHERMAN, WILLIAM TECUMSEH.
  Sherman and His Campaigns. A Military Biography. S. M. Bowman and R. B. Irvin. N. Y., 1865. 512 p.
  DLC, NN, MWA, CSmH, PU
  The Life of William T. Sherman. James P. Boyd. Phila., 1891. 608 p. *DLC*
  Memorial Life of Gen. William T. Sherman. Edward Chase. Chicago, 1891. 558 p. *CSmH*
  The Life of Gen. W. T. Sherman. T. R. Dawley. N. Y., 1864. 108 p. *DLC*
  Life of . . . Gen. Wm. T. Sherman. Thomas C. Fletcher. Balt., 1891. 479 p. *CSmH*
  General Sherman. M. F. Force. N. Y., 1899. 353 p. (G.C.)
  DLC, NN, CSmH
  Life and Military Career of Gen. W. T. Sherman. P. C. Headley. N. Y., 1865. 368 p. *DLC, NN, MWA, CSmH*
  Life of William T. Sherman. Willis F. Johnson. Phila., 1891. 607 p. *DLC, NN, MWA, CSmH, MiD:B*
  Sherman, Fighting Prophet. Lloyd Lewis. N. Y., 1932. 690 p.
  DLC, NN, PU
  Life and Deeds of General Sherman. Henry D. Northrop. Cleveland, 1891. 568 p. *DLC, NN, CSmH*
  William T. Sherman. Edward Robins. Phila., 1905. 352 p. (A.C.B.) *DLC, NN, CSmH*
  Life of Gen. W. T. Sherman. W. H. Van Orden. N. Y., 1895. 201 p. *DLC, CSmH, MiD:B*
  2:96–104–624
SHERWOOD, ADIEL. *Memoir of Adiel Sherwood, D.D.* Julia L. Sherwood. Phila., 1884. 416 p. *DLC*

SHIELDS, JAMES. *Life of Major General James Shields.* Wm. H. Condon. Chicago, 1900. 387 p. *DLC, NN*

SHIPMAN, ANDREW JACKSON. *A Memorial of Andrew J. Shipman; His Life and Writings.* Conde B. Pallen, ed. N. Y., 1916. 362 p. *DLC, NN*

SHIPP, SCOTT. *Personal Memoir of the Life and Services of Scott Shipp.* Jennings C. Wise. Lexington, Va., 1915. 56 p. *DLC, NN*

SHIPPEN, EDWARD. *Memoir of Edward Shippen, Chief Justice of Pennsylvania.* Lawrence Lewis, Jr. Phila., 1883. 24 p. *PU*

SHIRLAW, WALTER. 2:52

SHIRLEY, WILLIAM. *William Shirley.* G. A. Wood. N. Y., 1920. 435 p. (Columbia Univ. Studies. XCII)
DLC, NN, MWA, CSmH, PU

SHOLES, CHRISTOPHER. 2:343

SHOUP, PAUL. 2:233

SHORT, CHARLES. *Memoir of the Life of Charles Short.* C. Lancaster Short. Newcastle, Me., 1892. 39 p.
DLC, NN, MWA, PU, MiD:B

SHORT, THOMAS. *Thomas Short, First Printer of Conn.* W. D. Love. Hartford, 1901. 48 p. *DLC, NN, MWA, CSmH*

SHOVEL, CLOUDSLEY. 2:406

SHUCK, HENRIETTA HALL.
Pioneering For Jesus; the Story of Henrietta Hall Shuck. Thomas S. Dunaway. Nashville, 1930. 160 p. *DLC, NN*
Memoir of Henrietta Shuck, First Female Missionary to China. J. Jeter. Boston, 1846. 251 p. *DLC, NN, CSmH*

SIBERT, WILLIAM LUTHER. *William L. Sibert, the Army Engineer, Major General, Retired; Builder Gatun Locks and Dam, Panama Canal ...* Edward B. Clark. Phila., 1930. 206 p. *DLC, NN*

SIBLEY, HENRY HASTINGS. *The Ancestry, Life and Times of Hon. Henry Hastings Sibley, LL.D.* Nathaniel West. St. Paul, Minn., 1889. 596 p. *DLC, NN, MWA, MiD:B*

SIDDONS, SARAH. *Mrs. Siddons.* Nina H. Kennard. Boston, 1887. 354 p. *DLC, NN, PU*

SIDNEY, ALGERNON. *Life of Algernon Sidney; With Sketches of Some of His Contemporaries and Extracts From His Correspondence and Political Writings.* George Van Santvoord. N. Y., 1851. 334 p.
DLC, NN, MWA

SIDNEY, SIR PHILIP. *Immortal Sidney.* Emma M. Denkinger. N. Y., 1931. 317 p. *DLC, NN, CSmH*

SIGOURNEY, LYDIA HOWARD. *Mrs. Sigourney, the Sweet Singer of Hartford.* Gordon S. Haight. New Haven, 1930. 201 p.
DLC, NN, MWA, CSmH, PU

SILL, EDWARD ROWLAND. *Edward Rowland Sill: His Life and Work.* William B. Parker. Boston, 1915. 307 p.
DLC, NN, CSmH, PU

See GILDER, RICHARD W.

SILLIMAN, BENJAMIN. *Life of Benjamin Silliman.* G. P. Fisher. N. Y., 1866. 2 vols. *DLC, NN, CSmH, PU, MiD:B*

SIMMS, FLORENCE. *Florence Simms; a Biography.* Richard Roberts. N. Y., 1926. 292 p. *DLC, NN*

SIMMS, WILLIAM GILMORE. *William Gilmore Simms.* William P. Trent. Boston, 1892. 351 p. (A.M.L.)
DLC, NN, MWA, CSmH, PU, MiD:B
2:503

SIMPSON, SIR JAMES Y. 2:675

SIMPSON, JEROME. *The Story of Jerry Simpson.* Annie L. Diggs. Wichita, Kan., 1908. 274 p. *DLC, NN*

SIMPSON, MATTHEW.
Life of Bishop Matthew Simpson of the M. E. Church. George R. Crooks. N. Y., 1890. 512 p. *DLC, NN, MWA, PU*
Peerless Orator, the Rev. Matthew Simpson, Bishop of the M. E. Church. Ezra M. Wood. Pittsburgh, 1909. 206 p. *DLC*

SIMPSON, THOMAS. *Thomas Simpson and His Times.* Frances M. Clarke. N. Y., 1929. 215 p. *DLC, NN, PU*

SIMS, WILLIAM SOWDEN. 2:396

SINCLAIR, UPTON. *Upton Sinclair, a Study in Social Protest.* Floyd Dell. N. Y., 1927. 194 p. *DLC, NN, PU*
2:366

SITTING BULL.
Sitting Bull and the Indian War of 1890–91. Willis F. Johnson. Phila., 1891. 544 p. *DLC, NN, MWA, CSmH*
Sitting Bull, Champion of the Sioux, a Biography. Stanley Vestal. Boston, 1932. 350 p. *DLC, NN, PU*
2:204

SKEELE, AMOS. *A Sketch of the Life of Amos Skeele, S.T.D., in " The Salt of the Earth and Other Sermons."* Francis L. Palmer. Milwaukee, 1921. 48 p. *DLC, MWA*

SKILES, WILLIAM WEST. *William West Skiles; a Sketch of Missionary Life at Valle Crucis in Western North Carolina.* Susan F. Cooper. N. Y., 1890. 141 p. *DLC, NN, MWA*

SKINNER, JOHN STUART. *Biographical Sketch of John Stuart Skinner.* Benjamin P. Poore. N. Y., 1854. 34 p. *DLC, NN* 2:497

SLAFTER, JOHN. *Memorial of John Slafter.* Boston, 1869. 155 p. (Privately Printed) *DLC, NN, MWA*

SLATER, SAMUEL. *Memoirs of Samuel Slater, The Father of American Manufactures, With a History of the Rise and Progress of Cotton Manufacture in England and America.* George S. White. Phila., 1836. 448 p. *DLC, NN, MWA, CSmH, PU*

SLATTERY, CHARLES LEWIS. *Charles Lewis Slattery.* Howard C. Robbins. N. Y., 1931. 341 p. *DLC, NN, PU*

SLESSOR, MARY. *Mary Slessor of Calibar; Pioneer Missionary.* William P. Livingstone. N. Y., 1916. 347 p. *DLC, NN* 2:506

SLIDELL, JOHN.
John Slidell. Louis M. Sears. Durham, N. C., 1925. 252 p. *DLC, NN, MWA, CSmH, PU*
John Slidell and the Confederates in Paris (1862–65). Beckles Willson. N. Y., 1932. 296 p. *DLC, NN, MWA, CSmH, PU*

SLOANE, JAMES RENWICK WILSON. *Life and Works of J. R. W. Sloane . . . Professor of Theology in the Reformed Presbyterian Seminary at Allegheny City, Penn., 1868–1886.* William M. Sloane. N. Y., 1888. 440 p. *DLC, PU*

SLOAT, JOHN DRAKE. *Life of the Late Rear-Admiral John Drake Sloat, U. S. N.* Edwin A. Sherman. Oakland, Cal., 1902. 258 p. *DLC, NN, CSmH*

SLOCUM, FRANCES.
Biography of Frances Slocum, the Lost Sister of Wyoming. John F. Meginness. Williamsport, Pa., 1891. 238 p. *DLC, NN, MWA*
Frances Slocum, the Lost Sister of Wyoming. Martha B. Phelps. N. Y., 1905. 167 p. *DLC, NN, MWA*
The Lost Sister of Wyoming. An Authentic Narrative. John Todd. Northampton, 1842. 160 p. *DLC, CSmH*

SLOCUM, HENRY WARNER. *Life of Major-General Henry W. Slocum.* C. E. Slocum. Toledo, O., 1913. 391 p. *DLC, NN, CSmH*

SLUYTER, RICHARD. *A Memoir of the Rev. Richard Sluyter, Late Pastor of the Reformed Protestant Dutch Church of Claverack, N. Y.* R. O. Currie. N. Y., 1846. 132 p. *DLC, NN*

SMEDLEY, FRANKLIN. *Franklin Smedley.* Caroline W. Smedley. n.p., n.d. 10 p. (Papers of Frankford Hist. Soc., Phila., Pa.)

SMET, PIERRE JEAN. *Life, Letters and Travels of Father Pierre Jean de Smet, S.J., 1801–1873.* H. M. Chittenden and A. T. Richardson. N. Y., 1905. 4 vols. *DLC, NN, CSmH*

SMILEY BROTHERS. 2:6

SMITH, ALBERT. *Mont Blanc Sideshow; the Life and Times of Albert Smith.* James M. Thorington. Phila., 1934. 255 p. *DLC, NN*

SMITH, ALFRED EMANUEL.
The Life of Al Smith. (Told in Forty-Eight Pictures.) Jerry Costello. N. Y., 1928. 52 p. *DLC, NN*

Alfred E. Smith. Henry Moskowitz. N. Y., 1924. 312 p. *DLC, NN, PU*

Up From the City Streets, Alfred E. Smith, a Biographical Study in Contemporary Politics. Norman Hapgood and Henry Moskowitz. N. Y., 1927. 349 p. *DLC, NN*

Alfred E. Smith: A Critical Study. Henry F. Pringle. N. Y., 1927. 402 p. *DLC, NN, PU*
2:151

SMITH, AMANDA. *Life, Travels, Labors and Helpers of Mrs. Amanda Smith, the Famous Negro Missionary Evangelist.* Marshall W. Taylor. Cincinnati, 1886. 63 p.

SMITH, BYRON CALDWELL.
The Love-Life of Byron Caldwell Smith. N. Y., 1930. 24 p. *DLC, NN*

A Young Scholar's Letters; Being a Memoir of Byron Caldwell Smith. D. O. Kellogg, ed. N. Y., 1897. 370 p. *DLC, NN*

SMITH, CHARLES EASTWISK. *Memoir of Charles E. Smith, President of the Phila. and Reading R. R. and Iron Master, 1820–1900.* E. Alexander Scott. Buffalo, 1902. 83 p. *PU*

SMITH, DABNEY HOWARD. *Life, Army Record, and Public Services of D. Howard Smith.* Sydney K. Smith. Louisville, 1890. 211 p. *DLC, NN, CSmH*

SMITH, EDMUND KIRBY. *General Kirby-Smith.* Arthur H. Noll. Sewanee, Tenn., 1907. 293 p. *DLC*

SMITH, ELIHU HUBBARD. *A Lesser Hartford Wit, Dr. Elihu Hubbard Smith, 1771–1798.* Marcia E. Bailey. Orono, Me., 1928. 150 p. (Univ. of Me. Studies, Second Series, No. 11) *DLC, NN, MWA, CSmH, PU*

SMITH, ELIZABETH. *Fragments, in Prose and Verse, by Miss Elizabeth Smith. With Some Account of Her Life and Character.* H. M. Bowdler. Burlington, N. J., 1811. 261 p. *DLC, NN, MWA, MiU:C*

SMITH, GEORGE ARCHIBALD. *A Memorial of the Rev. George Archibald Smith, A.M.* Philip Slaughter. N. Y., 1889. 74 p.

MWA, CSmH

SMITH, GEORGE RAPPEEN. *Life of George R. Smith, Founder of Sedalia, Mo.* Samuel B. Harding. Sedalia, Mo., 1904. 398 p. (Privately Printed) *NN, CSmH, PU, MiD:B*

SMITH, GERRIT. *Gerrit Smith; a Biography.* O. B. Frothingham. N. Y., 1878. 381 p. *DLC, NN, MWA, CSmH, PU, MiD:B*

SMITH, HENRY. *Life and Times of Henry Smith, the First American Governor of Texas.* J. H. Brown. Dallas, 1887. 395 p.

DLC, NN, CSmH, PU

SMITH, HENRY BOYNTON.
Henry Boynton Smith. Lewis F. Stearns. Boston, 1892. 368 p.

DLC, MWA

Henry Boynton Smith, His Life and Work. H. B. Smith. N. Y., 1881. 482 p. *NN, PU*

SMITH, HENRY DICKINSON. *Henry Dickinson Smith: A Biography.* Henry D. Porter. N. Y., 1908. 175 p. *DLC*

SMITH, HEZEKIAH. *Chaplain Smith and the Baptists: Life, Journals, etc. of Hezekiah Smith, 1737–1805.* Reuben A. Guild. Phila., 1885. 429 p. *NN, MWA, MiD:B*

SMITH, JEDEDIAH. 2:41

SMITH, JEFFERSON RANDOLPH. *Reign of Soapy Smith: Monarch of Misrule, in the Last Days of the Old West and the Klondike Gold Rush.* Wm. R. Collier and Edwin V. Westrate. N. Y., 1935. 299 p. *DLC, NN*

SMITH, JEREMIAH. *Life of the Hon. Jeremiah Smith, LL.D.* John H. Morison. Boston, 1845. 516 p. *DLC, NN, MWA*

SMITH, JOHN.
The Life and Adventures of Captain John Smith. Phila., 1813. 90 p. *MWA*

The Life and Adventures of Captain John Smith. W. C. Armstrong. N. Y., 1868. 264 p. *DLC, NN, PU*

John Smith—Also Pocahontas. John G. Fletcher. N. Y., 1928. 308 p. *DLC, NN, PU*

Adventures of Captain John Smith. Francis L. Hawks. N. Y., 1842. 201 p. *DLC, NN, CSmH, PU, MiD:B, MiU:C*

Captain John Smith, Founder of Virginia. George C. Hill. Boston, 1858. 286 p. *DLC, NN, PU, MiD:B*

Life of Captain John Smith. George S. Hillard. (L.A.B.)

DLC, NN, MWA, CSmH, PU, MiD:B

Captain John Smith. Tudor Jenks. N. Y., 1904. 259 p.
DLC, NN, CSmH

Captain John Smith, 1579–1631. Rossiter Johnson. N. Y., 1915. 194 p. (True Stories of Great Americans)
DLC, NN, MWA

Captain John Smith and His Critics. Charles Poindexter. Richmond, 1893. 74 p. *DLC, NN, CSmH*

The Exciting Adventures of Captain John Smith. Vernon Quinn. N. Y., 1928. 315 p. *DLC, NN*

Adventures of Captain John Smith. E. P. Roberts. N. Y., 1902. 307 p. *DLC*

Life of Captain John Smith, the Founder of Virginia. William G. Simms. N. Y., 1846. 379 p.
DLC, NN, CSmH, PU, MiD:B, MiU:C

Life of Captain John Smith, Planter of Virginia. Charles K. True. N. Y., 1882. 267 p. *MWA*

Captain John Smith (1579–1631), Sometime Governor of Virginia and Admiral of New England: Study of His Life and Writings. Charles D. Warner. N. Y., 1881. 307 p. (Lives of American Worthies) *DLC, NN, MWA, CSmH, PU, MiD:B, MIU:C*

True Story of Captain John Smith. Katherine P. Woods. N. Y., 1901. 382 p. *DLC, NN, MWA*

SMITH, JOSEPH.

Joseph Smith and His Mormon Empire. Harry M. Beardsley. Boston, 1931. 421 p. *DLC, NN, CSmH*

The Life of Joseph Smith, the Prophet. George Q. Cannon. Salt Lake City, 1888. 512 p. *NN, MWA*

Joseph Smith, an American Prophet. John H. Evans. N. Y., 1933. 447 p. *DLC, NN, CSmH, PU*

Prophet of Palmyra: Mormonism Reviewed and Examined in the Life and Character of Its Founder Joseph Smith. T. Gregg. N. Y., 1890. 552 p. *DLC, NN*

Biographical Sketches of Joseph Smith, the Prophet, and His Progenitors for Many Generations. Lucy Smith. Liverpool, 1853. 371 p. *DLC, NN, MWA*

SMITH, JUNIUS. *Junius Smith; a Biography of the Founder of the Atlantic Liner.* Edgar LeRoy Pond. N. Y., 1927. 292 p.
DLC, NN, MiD:B

SMITH, LOWELL. *Lowell and Abigail, a Realistic Idyll.* Mary D. Frear. New Haven, 1934. 324 p. (Privately Printed)
DLC, NN, CSmH, PU, MiD:B

SMITH, MATTHEW HALE. *Review of the Life and Writings of M. Hale Smith.* L. C. Browne. Boston, 1847. 360 p. *DLC*

SMITH, MARTHA HAZELTINE. *Memoir of . . . Martha Hazeltine Smith.* Sarah Sleeper. Boston, 1843. 294 p. *MWA*

SMITH, NATHAN. *Life and Letters of Nathan Smith.* Emily A. Smith. New Haven, 1914. 185 p. *DLC, NN, MWA*

SMITH, RICHARD PENN. *The Life and Writings of Richard Penn Smith, With a Reprint of His Play, " The Deformed," 1830.* Bruce W. McCullough. Menasha, Wis., 1917. 100 p.
DLC, NN, CSmH, PU

SMITH, ROSWELL. *A Memory of Roswell Smith.* George W. Cable. N. Y., 1892. 69 p. (Privately Printed) *NN, MWA, CSmH*

SMITH, SAMUEL. 2:218

SMITH, SARAH LANMAN. *Memoir of Mrs. Sarah Lanman Smith, Late of the Mission in Syria.* Edward W. Hooker. Boston, 1839. 407 p.
DLC, NN, MWA

SMITH, SEBA. *Two American Pioneers, Seba Smith and Elizabeth Oakes Smith.* Mary A. Wyman. N. Y., 1927. 251 p. (Col. Univ. Studies in English) *DLC, NN, MWA, PU*

SMITH, SOPHIA. *Sophia Smith and . . . Smith College.* Elizabeth D. Hanscom. Northampton, 1925. 120 p. *CSmH*

SMITH, STEPHEN R. *Memoirs of Rev. Stephen R. Smith.* Thomas J. Sawyer. Boston, 1852. 423 p. *DLC*

SMITH, THEOBALD. 2:176

SMITH, THOMAS. *Life and Times of Thomas Smith, 1745–1809.* Burton A. Konkle. Phila., 1904. 303 p. *DLC, NN, MWA, PU*

SMITH, THOMAS KILBY. *Life and Letters of Thomas Kilby Smith, Brevet Maj.-Gen. U. S. Volunteers, 1820–1887.* Walter G. Smith. N. Y., 1897. 487 p. *DLC, NN, CSmH, PU*

SMITH, WILLIAM. *Memoirs of Gov. William Smith of Virginia.* J. W. Bell. N. Y., 1891. 461 p. *DLC, NN, CSmH*

SMITH, WILLIAM. *Colonel William Smith and Lady. The Romance of Washington's Aide and Young Abigail Adams.* Katherine M. Roof. Boston, 1929. 347 p. *DLC, NN, MWA*

SMITH, WILLIAM.
The Life and Correspondence of the Reverend William Smith. H. W. Smith. Phila., 1879–80. 2 vols.
DLC, NN, PU, MiD:B, MiU:C
A Memoir of the Rev. William Smith, Provost of the College, Academy and Charitable School of Philadelphia. Charles J. Stillé. Phila., 1869. 63 p. *DLC, PU, MiD:B*

SMITH, WILLIAM AUSTIN. *William Austin Smith.* Charles L. Slattery. N. Y., 1925. 244 p. *DLC, NN*

SMITH, WILLIAM FARRAR. *Life and Services of William Farrar Smith . . . in the Civil War.* James H. Wilson. Wilmington, Del., 1904. 130 p. *DLC, NN, PU*

SMITH, WILLIAM RUSSELL. *William Russell Smith of Alabama, His Life and Works; Including the Entire Text of " The Uses of Solitude."* Anne Easby-Smith. Phila., 1931. 298 p. *DLC, NN, CSmH*

SMITH, WILLIAM AND LUCY. *Story of William and Lucy Smith.* G. S. Merriam, ed. Boston, 1889. 666 p. *DLC, NN, MWA, CSmH*

SMITH, WORTHINGTON. *Select Sermons of Rev. Worthington Smith. With a Memoir of His Life.* Joseph Torrey. Andover, 1861. 115 p. *DLC*

SMITHSON, JAMES.

James Smithson. S. P. Langley. Washington, 1904. 25 p. *DLC, NN*

James Smithson and His Bequest. William J. Rhees. Washington, 1880. 68 p. *DLC, NN, PU, MiD:B*

SMYTH, ALBERT HENRY. *Biographical Notice of Albert Henry Smyth.* Jos. G. Rosengarten. Phila., 1907. 10 p. (Reprinted from Proceedings of the American Philosophical Soc. V. 46. 1907) *NN, PU*

SMYTH, FREDERICK. *Sketches of the Life and Public Services of Frederick Smyth of New Hampshire.* Benjamin P. Poore, comp. Manchester, N. H., 1885. 459 p. *DLC, NN, MWA, MiD:B*

SNOW, LORENZO. *Biography and Family Record of Lorenzo Snow.* Eliza R. Snow Smith. Salt Lake City, 1884. 581 p. *DLC, NN, MWA, CSmH*

SOCRATES. 2:332–665

SOMERVILLE, MARY. 2:337

SOTO, FERDINAND DE.

De Soto and the Conquistadores. Theodore Maynard. N. Y., 1930. 297 p. *DLC, NN, PU*

Ferdinand de Soto and the Invasion of Florida. Frederick A. Ober. N. Y., 1906. 290 p. *DLC, NN, CSmH*

Life, Travels and Adventures of Ferdinand de Soto. Lambert A. Wilmer. Phila., 1858. 532 p. *DLC, NN, CSmH, PU*

SOULE, ALFRED B. *Major Soule. A Memorial of Alfred B. Soule, Late Major of the Twenty-Third Regiment, Maine Volunteers.* Chislon. Salem, 1866. 199 p. *DLC, CSmH*

SOULE, HENRY BIRDSALL. *Memoir of Rev. H. B. Soule.* Caroline A.
Soule. N. Y., 1852. 396 p. *NN, MWA*

SOULE, JOSHUA. *Life of Joshua Soule.* Horace M. Du Bose. Nashville, 1911. 285 p. *DLC, NN*

SOUTHEY, ROBERT. *The Early Life of Robert Southey, 1774–1803.*
William Haller. N. Y., 1917. 353 p. (Col. Univ. Studies in
Eng.) *DLC, NN, CSmH, PU*

SOUTHWELL, ROBERT. *An Appreciation of Robert Southwell.* Sister
Rose Anita Morton. Phila., 1929. 103 p. *DLC, NN, CSmH, PU*

SPAETH, ADOLPH. *Adolph Spaeth, D.D.* Harriet R. Spaeth, ed.
Phila., 1916. 439 p. *DLC, PU*

SPALDING, FRANKLIN SPENCER. *Franklin Spencer Spalding, Man and
Bishop.* John H. Melish. N. Y., 1917. 297 p.
DLC, NN, MiD:B

SPALDING, HENRY HARMON. *Henry Harmon Spalding.* Clifford M.
Drury. Caldwell, Idaho, 1936. 438 p. *DLC, NN, MWA, MiD:B*

SPALDING, LYMAN. *Dr. Lyman Spalding.* James A. Spalding. Boston, 1916. 380 p. *DLC, NN, PU*

SPALDING, MARTIN JOHN. *The Life of the Most. Rev. M. J. Spalding,
D.D., Archbishop of Baltimore.* John L. Spalding. N. Y., 1873.
468 p. *DLC, NN*

SPALLANZANI, LAZARO. 2:176

SPARKS, JARED.

The Life and Writings of Jared Sparks. Herbert B. Adams.
Boston, 1893. 2 vols. *DLC, NN, MWA, CSmH, PU, MiD:B*
Memoir of Jared Sparks. George E. Ellis. Cambridge, 1869.
102 p. (Reprinted from Mass. Hist. Soc. Proc. May, 1868)
DLC, NN, MWA, CSmH, PU
Memoir of Jared Sparks. Brantz Mayer. Balt., 1867. 36 p.
DLC, NN, MWA, CSmH

SPARROW, WILLIAM. *Life and Correspondence of Rev. William Sparrow . . . of the Episcopal Theological Seminary of Virginia.* Cornelius Walker. Phila., 1876. 433 p. *DLC, CSmH, PU*

SPEED, JAMES. *James Speed: A Personality.* James Speed. Louisville, 1914. 136 p. *DLC, NN, PU*

SPEICHER, EUGENE. *Eugene Speicher.* Frank J. Mather. N. Y.,
1931. 54 p. *DLC, NN*

SPENCER, A. P. 2:175

SPENCER, CORNELIA PHILLIPS. *Old Days in Chapel Hill, Being the
Life and Letters of Cornelia Phillips Spencer.* Hope S. Chamberlain. Chapel Hill, 1926. 325 p. *DLC, NN, MWA, CSmH*

SPENCER, HERBERT. 2:332

SPENCER, ICHABOD SMITH. *Rev. Ichabod S. Spencer, Sermons, With a Sketch of His Life.* J. M. Sherwood. 1855. 2 vols. *DLC, MWA*

SPENCER, LEVI. *Memoir of Rev. Levi Spencer . . . Pastor of the Congregational Church at Canton, Bloomington and Peoria, Illinois.* J. Blanchard. Cincinnati, 1856. 193 p. *MWA*

SPENCER, THOMAS. *Memoirs of Rev. Thomas Spencer.* Thomas Raffles. Hartford, 1815. 360 p. *DLC, NN, MWA, CSmH*

SPENER, PHILIP JACOB. *Philip J. Spener and His Work; Augustus H. Francke and His Work.* Marie E. Richard. Phila., 1897. 154 p. *DLC*

SPINOZA, BENEDICTUS. *Blesséd Spinoza.* Lewis Browne. N. Y., 1932. 334 p. *DLC, NN*
    2:332

SPOFFORD, HARRIET PRESCOTT. *Harriet Prescott Spofford, a Romantic Survival.* Elizabeth K. Halbeisen. Phila., 1935. 273 p. *DLC, NN, CSmH, PU*

SPOHR, LUDWIG. 2:187

SPOTTED TAIL. 2:204

SPOTSWOOD, ALEXANDER. *Alexander Spotswood, Governor of Colonial Virginia, 1710–1722.* Leonidas Dodson. Phila., 1932. 323 p. *DLC, NN, CSmH, PU*

SPRAGUE, CHARLES EZRA. *Charles Ezra Sprague.* Helen S. Mann. N. Y., 1931. 67 p. *DLC, NN, MWA*

SPRAGUE, WILLIAM. *The Last of the War Governors. A Biographical Appreciation of Colonel William Sprague, Governor of Rhode Island, 1860–1863.* Henry W. Shoemaker. Altoona, Pa., 1916. 103 p. *DLC, NN*

SPRECHER, SAMUEL. *Portraiture of the Life of Samuel Sprecher, D.D., Pastor, President of Wittenberg College and Seminary, and Author.* P. G. Bell. Phila., 1907. 146 p. *DLC*

SPURGEON, CHARLES HADDON.
    Life of Charles H. Spurgeon. Russell H. Conwell. Phila., 1892. 616 p. *NN*
    The Shadow of the Broad Brim; the Life Story of Charles Haddon Spurgeon, Heir of the Puritans. Richard E. Day. Phila., 1934. 236 p. *DLC, NN, PU*
    Charles Haddon Spurgeon. James J. Ellis. N. Y., 1890. 219 p. *DLC, NN*
    Charles Haddon Spurgeon, the Puritan Preacher in the Nineteenth Century. George C. Lorimer. Boston, 1892. 230 p. *NN*

Life and Labors of Charles H. Spurgeon. G. C. Needham, comp. Boston, 1882. 638 p. NN

Life and Work of Rev. Charles H. Spurgeon. Henry D. Northrop. Cincinnati, 1890. 512 p.

C. H. Spurgeon. His Life and Ministry. Jesse Page. n.p. 160 p. NN

Life of Charles H. Spurgeon, Pastor of the Metropolitan Tabernacle. Godfrey H. Pike. N. Y., 1892. 397 p. DLC

From the Usher's Desk to the Tabernacle Pulpit; the Life and Labors of Charles Haddon Spurgeon. Robert Shindler. N. Y., 1892. 316 p. DLC, NN
2:98

STABLER, EDWARD. *A Memoir of the Life of Edward Stabler ... With a Collection of His Letters.* William Stabler. Phila., 1846. 312 p. NN, MWA

STAËL-HOLSTEIN, ANNE LOUISE. *Madame de Staël.* Bella Duffy. Boston, 1887. 239 p. DLC, NN, PU

STALIN, JOSEF. *Stalin.* Isaac D. Levine. N. Y., 1931. 421 p. DLC, NN, PU
2:276

STANDISH, MILES.
Miles Standish, Captain of the Pilgrims. John S. C. Abbott. N. Y., 1872. 372 p. DLC, NN, MiD:B

Captain Myles Standish. Tudor Jenks. N. Y., 1905. 250 p. DLC, PU

The Exploits of Myles Standish. Henry Johnson. N. Y., 1897. 278 p. DLC, NN
2:141

STANFORD, JANE. *Mrs. Leland Stanford; an Intimate Biography.* Bertha Berner. Stanford U., Calif., 1935. 231 p. DLC, NN, CSmH

STANFORD, JOHN. *Memoir of the Rev. John Stanford, D.D.* Charles G. Sommers. N. Y., 1835. 417 p. DLC, NN, MWA, CSmH

STANFORD, LELAND. *Leland Stanford, War Governor of California, Railroad Builder and Founder of Stanford University.* George T. Clark. Stanford U., Calif., 1931. 491 p. DLC, NN, CSmH

STANFORD, LELAND, JR. *In Memoriam. Leland Stanford, Jr.* H. C. Nash. n.p., n.d. 249 p. CSmH

STANLEY, HENRY MORTON.
Life of Henry M. Stanley. A. M. Godbey. Chicago, 1902. 612 p. (Biographies of Famous Men)

Henry M. Stanley: His Life, Works, and Explorations. H. W.
Little. Phila., 1890. 456 p.   *DLC*
    2:190–262

STANSBURY, ELIJAH. *The Life and Times of Hon. Elijah Stansbury,
an "Old Defender" and Ex-Mayor of Baltimore.* Archibald
Hawkins. Balt., 1874. 298 p.   *DLC, NN, MiD:B*
STANTON, EDWIN McMASTERS.
    In Memoriam, Edwin McMasters Stanton; His Life and Work.
Joseph B. Doyle. Steubenville, O., 1911. 405 p.
                     DLC, NN, CSmH
    *Edwin McMasters Stanton, the Autocrat of Rebellion, Emanci-
pation, and Reconstruction.* Frank A. Flower. Akron, O., 1905.
445 p.   *DLC, NN, MWA, CSmH, PU, MiD:B*
    Life and Public Services of Edwin M. Stanton. George C.
Gorham. Boston, 1899. 2 vols.   *DLC, NN, CSmH, PU*
    2:96–624

STANTON, ELIZABETH CADY. *Elizabeth Cady Stanton.* Theodore
Stanton and Harriot S. Blatch, ed. N. Y., 1922. 2 vols.
                     DLC, NN, PU
    2:9

STANTON, WILLIAM A. *A Memoir of William A. Stanton, S.J.* Wil-
liam T. Kane, S.J. St. Louis, 1918. 262 p.   *DLC*
STARK, JOHN.
    Life of John Stark. Edward Everett. (L.A.B.)
                     DLC, NN, MWA, CSmH, PU
    *Memoir . . . of Gen. John Stark; With Notices of Several Other
Officers of the Revolution.* Caleb Stark. Concord, 1860. 495 p.
            DLC, NN, MWA, CSmH, MiD:B, MiU:C
STARR, THOMAS. *Life and Character of Thomas Starr.* Enoch Hun-
tington. Middletown, 1797.
STATELER, L. B. *Life of Rev. L. B. Stateler; or, Sixty-Five Years on
the Frontier.* Edwin J. Stanley. Nashville, 1907. 356 p.
                     NN, CSmH
STAUGHTON, WILLIAM. *Memoir of the Rev. William Staughton, D.D.*
S. W. Lynd. Boston, 1834. 312 p.   *DLC, NN*
ST. CLAIR, ARTHUR. *The St. Clair Papers: Life and Public Services of
Arthur St. Clair, Soldier of the Revolutionary War.* William H.
Smith. Cincinnati, 1882. 2 vols.
         DLC, NN, MWA, CSmH, PU, MiU:C
STEARNS, GEORGE LUTHER. *Life and Public Services of George Luther
Stearns.* F. P. Stearns. Phila., 1907. 401 p.
                     DLC, NN, CSmH, PU

STEARNS, GEORGE MUNROE. *The Parson's Devil, the Life Story of George M. Stearns, One of the Ablest, Wittiest and Best Loved American Lawyers.* Clifton Johnson. N. Y., 1927. 296 p.
DLC, NN, MWA

STEARNS, MARY EMMELINE. *Mary E. Stearns.* Millicent Todd. Cambridge, 1909. 362 p. *DLC, NN, CSmH, PU*

STEARNS, SAMUEL HORATIO. *The Life and Character of Rev. Samuel H. Stearns.* W. A. Stearns. Boston, 1839. 252 p.

STEBBINS, HORATIO. *Horatio Stebbins, His Ministry and His Personality.* Charles A. Murdock. Boston, 1921. 269 p. *DLC, NN*

STEDMAN, EDMUND CLARENCE. *Life and Letters of Edmund Clarence Stedman.* Laura Stedman and G. M. Gould. N. Y., 1910. 2 vols.
DLC, NN, CSmH, PU

STEELE, JOEL DORMAN. *Joel Dorman Steele, Teacher and Author.* Anna C. Palmer. N. Y., 1900. 215 p. *DLC, PU*

STEELE, RICHARD. *Sir Richard Steele.* Willard Connely. N. Y., 1934. 462 p. *DLC, NN, CSmH, PU*

STEELE, ROBERT WILBUR. *Robert Wilbur Steele, Defender of Liberty.* Walter L. Wilder. Denver, 1913. 327 p. *DLC, NN, CSmH*

STEENDAM, JACOB. *Jacob Steendam, Nochvaster: a Memoir of the First Poet in New Netherlands.* W. L. Andrews. N. Y., 1908. 62 p. *DLC, NN, CSmH*

STEICHEN, EDWARD. *Steichen, the Photographer.* Carl Sandburg. N. Y., 1929. 70 p. (Ltd. Autographed Ed.) *DLC, NN*

STEIN, CHARLOTTE VON. *Charlotte Von Steinn; a Memoir.* George H. Calvert. Boston, 1877. 280 p. *DLC, NN*

STEINER, EDWARD ALFRED. 2:672

STEINMETZ, CHARLES PROTEUS.
Charles Proteus Steinmetz; a Biography. John W. Hammond. N. Y., 1924. 489 p. *DLC, NN, PU*
Loki: the Life of Charles Proteus Steinmetz. Jonathan N. Leonard. N. Y., 1929. 291 p. *DLC, NN, MWA, PU*
2:150

STELL, ANDREW TAYLOR. *Dr. A. T. Stell, Founder of Osteopathy.* M. A. Lane. Chicago, 1918. 217 p. *DLC*

STELLER, GEORGE WILHELM. *George Wilhelm Steller, the Pioneer of Alaskan Natural History.* Leonhard H. Stejneger. Cambridge, 1936. 623 p. *DLC, NN, MWA, CSmH, PU*

STEPHENS, ALEXANDER HAMILTON.
Alexander H. Stephens, in Public and Private; With Letters and Speeches, Before, During and Since the War. Henry Cleveland. Phila., 1866. 833 p. *DLC, NN, MWA, CSmH*

Life of Alexander H. Stephens. Richard M. Johnston and William H. Browne. Phila., 1878. 619 p. *DLC, NN, MWA, PU*
   Alexander H. Stephens. L. B. Pendleton. Phila., 1908. 406 p. (A.C.B.) *DLC, NN, MWA, CSmH, PU*
   Little Alec; a Life of Alexander H. Stephens. Eudora R. Richardson. Indianapolis, 1932. 359 p. *DLC, NN, CSmH, PU*
   2:88–128–654

STEPHENS, LINTON. *Biographical Sketch of Linton Stephens, Late Associate Justice of the Supreme Court of Georgia, Containing a Selection of His Letters, Speeches, State Papers, etc.* James D. Waddell, ed. Atlanta, 1877. 434 p. *DLC, NN, CSmH*

STEPHENSON, GEORGE. 2:5

STERLING, JOHN WILLIAM. *John William Sterling, Class of 1864, Yale College, a Biographical Sketch.* John A. Graver. New Haven, 1929. 113 p. *DLC, NN, PU*

STERNBERG, GEORGE MILLER. *George Miller Sternberg; a Biography.* Martha L. Sternberg. Chicago, 1920. 331 p. *DLC, NN, PU*

STERNE, LAURENCE. *Life and Times of Laurence Sterne.* Wilbur L. Cross. N. Y., 1909. 2nd ed. rev. New Haven, 1925. 2 vols. 3rd ed. 2 vols. in 1. New Haven, 1929. 670 p.
   DLC, NN, CSmH, PU

STERNE, SIMON. *Life and Public Services of Simon Sterne.* John Foord. N. Y., 1903. 348 p. *DLC, NN, CSmH, PU, MiD:B*

STEUER, MAX. *Max Steuer; Magician of the Law.* Richard O. Boyer. N. Y., 1932. 223 p. *DLC, NN, MWA*
   2:236

STEVENS, BENJAMIN. *Memoir of Benjamin Franklin Stevens.* G. Manville Fenn. London, 1903. 310 p.
   DLC, NN, MWA, CSmH, PU, MiD:B, MiU:C

STEVENS, GEORGE BARKER. *Prof. George Barker Stevens, D.D., LL.D.* Williston Walker. New Haven, 1907. 29 p. *DLC, NN, MWA*

STEVENS, ISAAC INGALLS. *The Life of Isaac Ingalls Stevens.* Hazard Stevens. Boston, 1900. 2 vols. *DLC, NN, CSmH, PU*

STEVENS, JOHN. *John Stevens; an American Record.* Archibald D. Turnbull. N. Y., 1928. 545 p. *DLC, NN, MWA, PU, MiD:B*
   2:343

STEVENS, ROBERT LIVINGSTON. 2:343

STEVENS, THADDEUS.
   Thaddeus Stevens: Commoner. E. B. Callender. Boston, 1882. 210 p. *DLC, NN, MWA, MiD:B*

Thaddeus Stevens. Samuel W. McCall. Boston, 1899. 369 p.
(A.S.) *DLC, NN, MWA, CSmH, PU, MiD:B*
Life of Thaddeus Stevens. James A. Woodburn. Indianapolis,
1913. 620 p. *DLC, NN, MWA, CSmH, PU*
Thaddeus Stevens. Thomas F. Woodley. Harrisburg, 1934.
664 p. *DLC, NN, CSmH, PU*

STEVENSON, ADLAI EWING. See BRYAN, WILLIAM JENNINGS.
STEVENSON, ROBERT LOUIS.
The True Stevenson. George S. Hellman. Boston, 1925. 253 p.
DLC, NN
An Intimate Portrait of R. L. Stevenson. Lloyd Osborne. N. Y.,
1924. 155 p. *DLC, NN, PU*
STEVENSON, MRS. ROBERT LOUIS. *Life of Mrs. R. L. Stevenson.* Nel-
lie Sanchez. N. Y., 1920. 337 p. *DLC, CSmH, PU, MiD:B*
STEWART, ALEXANDER TURNEY. 2:331–623
STEWART, BISHOP. *Life of Bishop Stewart, of Quebec.* John N. Nor-
ton. N. Y., 1859.
STEWART, JAMES. *Stewart of Lovedale: Life of James Stewart, D.D.,
M.D.* James Wells. N. Y., 1909. 419 p. *NN*
STEWART, VIRGIL A. *History of Virgil A. Stewart and His Adventures
in Capturing and Exposing the Great " Western Land Pirate " and
His Gang . . .* H. R. Howard, comp. N. Y., 1836. 273 p.
DLC, NN, MWA, CSmH, PU
STIEGEL, " BARON " WILLIAM. 2:225
STIEGLITZ, ALFRED. *America and Alfred Stieglitz; a Collective Por-
trait.* Waldo Frank. N. Y., 1935. 339 p. *DLC, NN*
2:236
STIER, RUDOLPH. *The Life of Rudolph Stier (From German Sources).*
John P. Lacroix. N. Y., 1874. 332 p. *DLC, NN, MWA, PU*
STILES, EZRA.
The Life of Ezra Stiles, D.D., LL.D. Abiel Holmes. Boston,
1798. 402 p. *DLC, NN, MWA, CSmH, PU, MiD:B, RP:JCB*
Life of Ezra Stiles. James L. Kingsley. (L.A.B.)
DLC, NN, MWA, CSmH
STILLMAN, JAMES.
Portrait of a Banker; James Stillman, 1850–1918. Anna R.
Burr. N. Y., 1927. 370 p. *DLC, NN*
The First Billion; the Stillmans and the National City Bank.
John K. Winkler. N. Y., 1934. 277 p. *DLC, NN*
STILWELL, SAMUEL. *The Life of Samuel Stilwell.* Samuel S. Doughty.
N. Y., 1877. 51 p. *DLC, NN*

STIRLING, EARL OF. See ALEXANDER, WILLIAM.

STOCKTON, ROBERT FIELD. *A Sketch of the Life of Com. Robert F. Stockton; With an Appendix.* Samuel J. Bayard. N. Y., 1856. 210 p. *DLC, NN, CSmH, PU, MiD:B*

STODDARD, CHARLES. *Memorials of Charles Stoddard.* Mary S. Johnson. Boston, 1876. 525 p. *DLC, NN, MWA*

STODDARD, DAVID TAPPAN. *Memoir of the Rev. David Tappan Stoddard, Missionary to the Nestorians.* Joseph P. Thompson. Boston, 1858. 422 p. *DLC, NN, MWA*

STODDARD, JOHN LAWSON. *John L. Stoddard; Traveler, Lecturer, Literateur.* Daniel C. Taylor. N. Y., 1935. 325 p. *DLC, NN*

STODDART, CLELAND. *Cleland.* William W. Stoddart. Boston, 1935. 357 p. *DLC, NN*

STOKES, WILLIAM. 2:678

STONE, ALVAN. *Memoir of Alvan Stone of Goshen, Mass.* David Wright. Boston, 1837. 256 p. *DLC, NN, MiD:B*

STONE, BARTON WARREN. *Barton Warren Stone, Pathfinder of Christian Union; a Story of His Life and Times.* Charles C. Ware. St. Louis, 1932. 357 p. *DLC, NN*

STONE, JAMES KENT. *Fidelis of the Cross, James Kent Stone.* Walter G. and Helen G. Smith. N. Y., 1926. 467 p. *DLC, NN*

STONE, LUCY. *Lucy Stone, Pioneer of Women's Rights.* Alice S. Blackwell. Boston, 1930. 313 p. *DLC, NN, MWA, PU*

STONER, NICHOLAS. *Trappers of New York: or, a Biography of Nicholas Stoner and Nathaniel Foster . . .* Jeptha R. Simms. Albany, 1850. 280 p. *DLC, NN, MWA, CSmH*

STOREY, MOORFIELD. *Portrait of an Independent; Moorfield Storey, 1845–1929.* M. A. De Wolfe Howe. Boston, 1932. 384 p. *DLC, NN, MWA, CSmH*

STORROW, JAMES JACKSON. *Son of New England; James Jackson Storrow.* Henry G. Rearson. Boston, 1932. 292 p. *DLC, NN, MWA*

STORRS, EMERY ALEXANDER. *Life of Emery A. Storrs.* I. E. Adams. Boston, 1886. 800 p. *DLC, MWA, CSmH*

STORY, JOSEPH. *Life and Letters of Joseph Story.* Wm. W. Story, ed. Boston, 1851. 2 vols. *DLC, NN, MWA, CSmH, PU, MiU:C*

STORY, WILLIAM WETMORE. *William Wetmore Story and His Friends.* Henry James. Boston, 1903. 2 vols. *DLC, NN, CSmH, PU*

STOVER, ANN, FANNIE and MARIA. 2:703

STOW, BARON.
    The Model Pastor. A Memoir of the Life and Correspondence of Rev. Baron Stow, D.D. John C. Stockbridge. Boston, 1871. 376 p. *DLC, NN, MWA, CSmH*

Memoir of Rev. Baron Stow. J. C. Stockbridge, comp. Boston, 1894. 392 p. *DLC*

STOWE, HARRIET BEECHER.
Harriet Beecher Stowe. Martha F. Crow. N. Y., 1913. 310 p.
DLC, NN, CSmH
Life and Letters of Harriet Beecher Stowe. Annie Fields, ed. Boston, 1897. 406 p. *DLC, NN, MWA, CSmH, PU, MiD:B*
Life-Work of the Author of " Uncle Tom's Cabin." Florine T. McCray. N. Y., 1889. 440 p. *DLC, NN, CSmH*
Life of Harriet Beecher Stowe. Charles E. Stowe. Boston, 1889. 530 p. *CSmH*
Harriet Beecher Stowe: The Story of Her Life. Charles E. and Lyman B. Stowe. Boston, 1911. 313 p.
DLC, NN, CSmH, PU, MiD:B
2:9–40–92–581

STRAIGHT, WILLARD. *Willard Straight.* Herbert D. Croly. N. Y., 1924. 569 p. *DLC, NN, PU*
2:425

STRANDBERG, OVE. 2:175

STRANG, JAMES JESSE.
A Moses of the Mormons. H. E. Legler. Milwaukee, 1897. 2 vols. (Parkman Club Papers Nos. 15, 16)
DLC, NN, MWA, CSmH
A Moses of the Mormons (James J. Strang). Henry E. Legler. Lansing, Mich., 1903. (Michigan Pioneer and Hist. Soc., Vol. 32)
DLC, NN, CSmH
Crown of Glory; the Life of James J. Strang, Moses of the Mormons. Oscar W. Riegel. New Haven, 1935. 281 p.
DLC, CSmH, MiD:B

STRATTON, CHARLES SHERWOOD. *Sketch of the Life, Personal Appearance, Character and Manners of Charles S. Stratton, the Man in Miniature, Known as General Tom Thumb . . .* N. Y., 1847, 1849, 1860. 24 p. *DLC, NN, MWA, CSmH*

STRAUS, NATHAN. 2:672

STRAUSS, RICHARD. *Richard Strauss; the Man and His Works.* Henry T. Finck. Boston, 1917. 328 p. *DLC, NN, PU*

STREETER, GEORGE WELLINGTON. *Captain Streeter, Pioneer.* E. G. Ballard. Chicago, 1914. 295 p. *CSmH*

STREETER, MILTON WHIPPLE. *Life of Milton W. Streeter, Who Murdered His Wife at Southbridge, Mass.* H. F. Tingley. Pawtucket, R. I., 1850. 96 p. *DLC, NN*

STRINDBERG, AUGUST.
>*August Strindberg, the Bedeviled Viking.* Vivian J. McGill. N. Y., 1930. 459 p.   *DLC, NN, PU*
>*Strindberg, and His Plays.* Vance Thompson. N. Y., 1921. 32 p.   *DLC*

STRINGFIELD, THOMAS. *Life of Scout Two Braids (Thomas String-field).* Carl F. and J. R. Wheeler. San Antonio, 1909. 50 p.
      DLC, NN

STRONG, RICHARD MARVIN. *Memoir of Richard M. Strong, a Member of the Albany Bar.* Albany, 1863. 66 p. *DLC, NN, CSmH, PU*

STUART, ALEXANDER HUGH HOLMES. *Alexander Hugh H. Stuart, 1807–1891; a Biography.* Alexander F. Robertson. Richmond, 1925. 484 p.   *DLC, NN, CSmH, PU*

STUART, CHARLES EDWARD. *Bonnie Prince Charlie (Charles Edward Stuart).* Donald B. Chidsey. N. Y., 1928. 330 p. *DLC, NN*

STUART, ELBRIDGE AMOS. 2:233

STUART, GEORGE RUTLEDGE. *George R. Stuart, Life and Work.* William W. Pinson. Nashville, 1927. 276 p.   *DLC, NN*

STUART, GILBERT. *Life and Works of Gilbert Stuart.* George C. Mason. N. Y., 1879. 286 p.
      DLC, NN, MWA, CSmH, PU, MiD:B, RP:JCB
>2:123–394–429

STUART, JAMES EWELL BROWN.
>*Life and Campaigns of Maj.-Gen. J. E. B. Stuart.* H. B. Mc-Clellan. Boston, 1885. 468 p.   *DLC, NN, CSmH*
>*J. E. B. Stuart, Commander of the Cavalry Corps, Army of Northern Va., C. S. A.* Theodore S. Garnett. N. Y., 1907. 67 p.
      DLC, NN, CSmH
>
>*Jeb Stuart.* John W. Thomason. N. Y., 1930. 512 p.
      DLC, NN, PU
>
>2:88–612

STUART, MARY. *Scottish Queen (Mary Stuart).* Herbert S. Gorman. N. Y., 1932. 605 p.   *DLC, NN*
>2:337

STUYVESANT, PETER.
>*Peter Stuyvesant, the Last Dutch Governor of New Amsterdam.* John S. C. Abbott. N. Y., 1873. 362 p.   *DLC, NN, MiD:B*
>*Peter Stuyvesant, Director-General for the West India Co., in New Netherland.* Bayard Tuckerman. N. Y., 1893. 193 p.
>(Makers of America)   *DLC, NN, MWA, MiD:B, MiU:C*

Life and Times of Pieter Stuyvesant. Hendrik W. Van Loon. N. Y., 1928. 336 p. *DLC, NN, CSmH, PU* 2:660

SUCRE, ANTONIO JOSÉ DE. *Antonio José de Sucre (Gran Mariscal de Ayacucho) Hero and Martyr of American Independence; a Sketch of His Life.* Guillermo A. Sherwell. Washington, 1924. 236 p. *DLC, NN, MWA, PU*

SULEYMAN, SULTAN. *Grand Turke; Suleyman the Magnificent; Sultan of the Ottomans.* Fairfax D. Downey. N. Y., 1929. 333 p. *DLC, NN*

SULLIVAN, ALGERNON SYDNEY.
Algernon Sydney Sullivan. Anne M. Holmes. N. Y., 1929. 359 p. *DLC, NN*
A Memoir of Algernon Sydney Sullivan Together With Memorial Tributes. G. H. Sullivan. N. Y., 1890. 143 p. *NN*

SULLIVAN, JAMES. *Life of James Sullivan: With Selections From His Writings.* Thomas C. Amory. Boston, 1859. 2 vols. *DLC, NN, MWA, MiU:C*

SULLIVAN, JOHN.
Military Services and Public Life of Maj.-Gen. John Sullivan. T. C. Amory. Boston and Albany, 1868. 320 p. *DLC, NN, MWA, CSmH, MiD:B*
Life of John Sullivan. O. W. B. Peabody. (L.A.B.) *DLC, NN, MWA, CSmH*
A New Hampshire Lawyer in General Washington's Army. A Biographical Sketch of the Hon. John Sullivan, LL.D. Oscar E. Rising. Geneva, N. Y., 1915. 120 p. *DLC, NN, MWA*

SULLIVAN, JOHN LAWRENCE. *John L. Sullivan; an Intimate Narrative.* Roy F. Dibble. Boston, 1925. 209 p. *DLC, NN, PU*

SULLIVAN, MARY MILDRED. *Mary Mildred Sullivan; A Biography.* Anne M. Holmes. Concord, N. H., 1924. 196 p. *DLC, NN, MWA*

SULLY, THOMAS. *Life and Works of Thomas Sully (1783–1872).* Edward Biddle and Mantle Fielding. Phila., 1921. 411 p. *DLC, NN, MWA, PU*

SUMMERFIELD, JOHN.
Memoirs of the Life and Ministry of the Rev. John Summerfield, A.M. John Holland. N. Y., 1830. 360 p. *DLC, NN, MWA, CSmH, MiD:B*
Rev. John Summerfield. A New Life. William M. Willett. Phila., 1857. 256 p. *DLC, NN, PU*

SUMNER, CHARLES.
The Life of Charles Sumner. Jeremiah and J. D. Chaplin. Boston and Dover, N. H., 1874. 504 p.   *DLC, NN*
Charles Sumner. Anna L. Dawes. N. Y., 1892. 330 p. (Makers of America Series)   *DLC, NN, CSmH*
Life of Charles Sumner, Scholar in Politics. A. H. Grimké. N. Y., 1892. 415 p. (American Reformer Series)
DLC, NN, MWA
Life of Charles Sumner. D. A. Harsha. N. Y., 1856. 329 p.
DLC, NN, MWA, CSmH, MiD:B
Charles Sumner. G. H. Haynes. Phila., 469 p. (A.C.B.)
DLC, NN, PU, MiD:B
Charles Sumner. John F. Kirk. Phila., 1892. 6 p.   *DLC*
Life and Public Services of Charles Sumner. Charles E. Lester. N. Y., 1874. 596 p.   *DLC, NN, MWA, CSmH, MiD:B*
Life and Times of Charles Sumner. Elias Nason. Boston, 1874. 356 p.   *DLC, NN, MWA, CSmH, PU, MiD:B*
Memoir and Letters of Charles Sumner. Edward L. Pierce. Boston, 1878–94. 4 vols.   *DLC, NN, MWA, CSmH, PU, MiD:B*
Life of Charles Sumner. W. G. Shotwell. N. Y., 1910. 733 p.
DLC, NN, CSmH
Charles Sumner. Moorfield Storey. Boston, 1900. 466 p. (A.S.)   *DLC, NN, MWA, CSmH, PU, MiD:B*
2:96–107–144–624
SUMNER, JOHN SAXTON. 2:546
SUMNER, WILLIAM GRAHAM. *William Graham Sumner.* Harris E. Starr. N. Y., 1925. 557 p.   *DLC, NN*
SUMTER, THOMAS. *Thomas Sumter.* Anne K. Gregorie. Columbia, S. C., 1931. 313 p.   *DLC, NN, CSmH, MiU:C*
SUN YAT-SEN.
Sun Yat Sen, Liberator of China. Henry B. Restarick. New Haven, 1931. 167 p.   *DLC, NN*
Sun-Yat-Sen; His Life and Its Meaning. Albie M. Sharman. N. Y., 1935. 418 p.   *NN, PU*
2:276
SUNDAY, WILLIAM ASHLEY.
Billy Sunday, the Man and the Method. Frederick F. Betts. Boston, 1916. 69 p.   *DLC, NN*
Real Billy Sunday, the Life and Work of Rev. William Ashley Sunday, the Baseball Evangelist. Elijah P. Brown. N. Y., 1914. 285 p.   *DLC, NN, MWA*

Billy Sunday, the Man and His Message. William T. Ellis. Phila., 1936. 519 p.   *DLC, NN, MWA, MiD:B*
Spectacular Career of Rev. Billy Sunday, Famous Baseball Evangelist. Theodore T. Frankenberg. Columbus, O., 1913. 231 p.
     DLC, NN, MiD:B
     2:190

Surcouf, Robert. 2:488

Sutter, John Augustus.
     Sutter of California. Julian Dana. N. Y., 1934. 423 p.
     DLC, NN, MWA, CSmH
     Life and Times of Gen. John A. Sutter. T. J. Schoonover. Sacramento, 1895. 136 p.   *DLC, NN, CSmH, MiD:B*
     2:41–46–225

Swain, Robert. *Memoir of Robert Swain.* J. H. Morrison. Boston, 1847. 259 p.   *DLC*

Swedenborg, Emanuel.
     Life of Emanuel Swedenborg, With Some Account of His Writings. Benjamin F. Barrett. N. Y., 1841. 160 p.   *DLC, NN*
     Life of Emanuel Swedenborg. Nathaniel Hobart. Boston, 1845. 230 p.   *DLC, NN, MWA*
     Life of Emanuel Swedenborg. Together With a Brief Synopsis of His Writings, Both Philosophical and Theological. William White. Phila., 1881. 266 p.   *DLC, NN, MWA, PU*
     The Life and Mission of Emanuel Swedenborg. Benjamin Worcester. Boston, 1901. 473 p.   *DLC, NN*
     2:232

Sweet, John Edson. *John Edson Sweet. A Story of Achievement in Engineering and Influence Upon Men.* Albert W. Smith. N. Y., 1925. 220 p. (American Soc. of Mechanical Engineers)
     DLC, NN, CSmH, PU

Swenson, S. M. *Hyphenated; or, The Life Story of S. M. Swenson.* August Anderson. Austin, 1916. 290 p.   *DLC, NN*

Swett, John. *John Swett; the Biography of an Educational Pioneer.* William G. Carr. Santa Ana, Calif., 1933. 173 p.
     DLC, NN, CSmH

Swift, Gustavus Franklin. *Yankee of the Yards; the Biography of Gustavus F. Swift.* Louis F. Swift and Arthur Van Vlissingen. N. Y., 1928. 218 p.   *DLC, NN, CSmH, PU*

Swift, Jonathan. *Swift.* Carl Van Doren. N. Y., 1930. 279 p.
     DLC, NN, PU

SWIFT, LUCIUS B. *Lucius B. Swift.* Wm. D. Foulke. Indianapolis, 1930. 153 p. *CSmH*

SWINBURNE, ALGERNON.
Swinburne. Samuel C. Chew. Boston, 1929. 335 p.
DLC, NN, PU
Swinburne. George E. Woodberry. N. Y., 1905. 317 p.
DLC, NN, PU

SWING, DAVID. *David Swing, Poet-Preacher.* Joseph F. Newton. Chicago, 1909. 273 p. *DLC, NN*

SYDENHAM, THOMAS. *Thomas Sydenham, Clinician.* David Riesman. N. Y., 1926. 52 p. *DLC, NN, PU*

SYDENSTRICKER, ANDREW. *Fighting Angel.* Pearl Buck. N. Y., 1936. 302 p. *DLC, NN*

SYDENSTRICKER, CAROLINE. *The Exile.* Pearl Buck. N. Y., 1936. 315 p. *DLC, NN*

SYMMES, JOHN CLEVES. 2:225

SYMONDS, JOHN ADDINGTON. *John Addington Symonds.* Van Wyck Brooks. N. Y., 1914. 234 p. *DLC, NN*

SYMONDS, WILLIAM LAW. *The Life and Writings of William Law Symonds.* William Winter, comp. 1908. 668 p. (Privately Printed) *DLC, NN, MWA*

TABB, JOHN BANNISTER.
John Banister Tabb, the Priest-Poet. Mary P. Finn. Washington, 1915. 153 p. *DLC, NN*
Father Tabb: a Study of His Life and Works. Francis A. Litz. Balt., 1923. 303 p. *DLC, PU*
Father Tabb; His Life and Work. Jennie M. Tabb. Boston, 1921. 174 p. *DLC, NN, PU*

TABOR, HORACE A. W. AND ELIZABETH McC.
The Tabors; a Footnote to Western History. Lewis C. Gandy. N. Y., 1934. 291 p. *DLC, NN, MWA, PU*
Silver Dollar; the Story of the Tabors. David Karsner. N. Y., 1932. 354 p. *DLC, NN, MWA*

TAFT, ALPHONSO. *Life of Alphonso Taft.* Lewis A. Leonard. N. Y., 1920. 307 p. *DLC, NN, MWA*

TAFT, STEPHEN HARRIS. *An Empire Builder of the Middle West; Biography of Stephen H. Taft . . .* Fred H. Taft. Los Angeles, 1929. 259 p. *DLC, NN, CSmH*

TAFT, WILLIAM HOWARD.
William Howard Taft, a Character Study. Edward H. Cotton. Boston, 1932. 83 p. *DLC, NN*

William Howard Taft, the Man of the Hour. Oscar K. Davis. Phila., 1908. 406 p.   *DLC, NN, MWA, PU*

William Howard Taft. Herbert S. Duffy. N. Y., 1930. 345 p.   *DLC, NN*

William Howard Taft, American. Robert L. Dunn. Boston, 1908. 263 p.   *DLC, NN*

President and Chief-Justice; the Life and Public Services of William Howard Taft. Francis McHale. Phila., 1931. 321 p.   *DLC, NN, MWA*

TALBOT, SILAS. *The Life of Silas Talbot, a Commodore in the Navy of the U. S.* Henry T. Tuckerman. N. Y., 1850. 137 p.   *DLC, NN, CSmH*

TALLEYRAND, CHARLES-MAURICE.

Talleyrand; the Training of a Statesman, 1754–1838. Anna B. Dodd. N. Y., 1927. 531 p.   *DLC, NN, PU*

Talleyrand; a Biographical Study. Joseph McCabe. N. Y., 1907. 373 p.   *DLC, NN*

Life of Prince Talleyrand, With Extracts From His Speeches and Writings. Charles K. McHarg. N. Y., 1857. 382 p. *DLC, NN* 2:95

TALMADGE. *The Talmadge Sisters, Norma, Constance, Natalie; an Intimate Story of the World's Most Famous Screen Family.* Margaret L. Talmadge. Phila., 1924. 245 p.   *DLC, NN, PU*

TALMAGE, THOMAS DE WITT.

Life and Sermons of T. De Witt Talmage. C. F. Adams, Jr. Chicago, 1903. 429 p.   *DLC, NN*

Authorized and Authentic Life and Works of T. De Witt Talmage. C. E. Banks and G. C. Cook. Chicago, 1902. 479 p.   *DLC*

T. De Witt Talmage; His Life and Work. Biographical Edition. Louis A. Banks, ed. Phila., 1902. 500 p.   *DLC, NN, MWA*

Life and Death of T. De Witt Talmage, D.D. J. Lobb. N. Y., 1902. 222 p.   *DLC*

Life and Teachings of T. De Witt Talmage. T. De Witt Talmage. Phila., 1902. 511 p.   *DLC*

TAMAHAY. 2:204

TAMERLANE. *Tamerlane, the Earth Shaker.* Harold Lamb. N. Y., 1928. 340 p.   *DLC, NN*

TAMMANY. *The Life, Exploits and Precepts of Tammany, the Famous Indian Chief . . .* Samuel L. Mitchill. N. Y., 1795. 36 p.   *DLC, NN, MWA, CSmH*

TAMMEN, HARRY HEYE.   See BONFILS, F. G.

TANEY, ROGER BROOKE.

    Roger B. Taney: Jacksonian Jurist.   Charles W. Smith.   Chapel Hill, 1936.   242 p.   *DLC, NN, PU*

    Life of Roger Brooke Taney.   Bernard C. Steiner.   Balt., 1922. 553 p.   *DLC, NN, CSmH*

    Roger B. Taney.   Carl B. Swisher.   N. Y., 1935.   608 p.

           DLC, NN, CSmH, PU

    Memoir of Roger Brooke Taney, Chief Justice of the Supreme Court of the U. S.   Samuel Tyler.   Balt., 1872.   659 p.

        DLC, NN, MWA, CSmH, PU, MiD:B, MiU:C

    2:218–634–666

TAPPAN, ARTHUR.   *Life of Arthur Tappan...L. Tappan.*   N. Y., 1870. 432 p.   *DLC, NN, MWA, CSmH*

TAPPAN, HENRY PHILIP.   *Henry Philip Tappan, Philosopher and University President.*   Charles M. Perry.   Ann Arbor, 1933.   475 p.

           DLC, NN, PU, MiD:B

TAPPAN, SARAH.   *Memoir of Mrs. Sarah Tappan.*   Lewis Tappan. N. Y., 1834.   156 p.   *DLC, NN*

TARKINGTON, BOOTH.   *Booth Tarkington.*   Robert C. Holliday.   N. Y., 1918.   218 p.   *DLC, NN, CSmH, PU*

    2:366

TATTNALL, JOSIAH.   *The Life and Services of Commodore Josiah Tattnall.*   Charles C. Jones, Jr.   Savannah, 1878.   255 p.   *DLC, NN*

TAYLOR, BAYARD.

    Bayard Taylor, Laureate of the Gilded Age.   Richmond C. Beatty.   Norman, Okla., 1936.   379 p.   *DLC, NN, CSmH, PU*

    Life, Travels and Literary Career of Bayard Taylor.   Russell H. Conwell.   Boston, 1881.   357 p.   *DLC, NN, MWA, PU*

    Bayard Taylor.   Henry W. Longfellow.   Cambridge, 1879.

           DLC, CSmH

    Bayard Taylor.   Albert H. Smyth.   Boston, 1896.   320 p. (A.M.L.)   *DLC, NN, MWA, CSmH, PU, MiD:B*

    Life and Letters of Bayard Taylor.   Marie H. Taylor and Horace E. Scudder.   Boston, 1884.   2 vols.

        DLC, NN, MWA, CSmH, PU

TAYLOR, BENJAMIN.   *Memoir of Elder Benjamin Taylor, a Minister of the Christian Connexion and Pastor of the Bethel Church in Providence, R. I.*   Edward Edmunds.   Boston, 1850.   144 p.

        DLC, NN, MWA

TAYLOR, CHARLES FREDERICK.   2:521

TAYLOR, CHARLES HENRY. *Charles H. Taylor, Builder of the Boston Globe.* James Morgan. Boston, 1923. 213 p. *DLC, NN, MWA*

TAYLOR, EDWARD THOMPSON.

Father Taylor. Robert Collyer. Boston, 1906. 58 p.
DLC, NN

Father Taylor, the Sailor Preacher. Incidents and Anecdotes of Rev. Edward T. Taylor. Gilbert Haven and Thomas Russell. Boston, 1872. 445 p. *DLC, NN, MWA, CSmH, MiD:B*

Life of Father Taylor, the Sailor Preacher. E. T. Taylor. Boston, 1904. 472 p. *DLC, NN*

TAYLOR, FANNIE. 2:518

TAYLOR, FREDERICK WINSLOW. *Frederick W. Taylor, Father of Scientific Management.* Frank B. Copley. N. Y., 1923. 2 vols.
DLC, NN, PU

TAYLOR, GEORGE BOARDMAN. *Life and Letters of Rev. George Boardman Taylor.* George Braxton Taylor. Lynchburg, Va., 1908. 413 p. *DLC*

TAYLOR, JAMES BRAINERD.

Memoir of James Brainerd Taylor. John H. and Benjamin H. Rice. N. Y., 1833. 441 p. *DLC, NN, MWA, MiD:B*

Life and Times of James B. Taylor. George B. Taylor. Phila., 1872. 359 p. *DLC, NN, CSmH*

TAYLOR, JAMES MONROE. *Life and Letters of James Monroe Taylor; the Biography of an Education.* Eliz. H. Haight. N. Y., 1919. 391 p. *DLC, NN, CSmH, PU*

TAYLOR, JANE. *Memoirs of Jane Taylor.* Isaac Taylor. Lowell, Mass., 1829. 96 p. *DLC, NN, MWA, CSmH*

TAYLOR, JOHN. *Life of John Taylor.* Brigham H. Roberts. Salt Lake City, 1892 468 p. *CSmH*

TAYLOR, JOHN.

John Taylor, Prophet of Secession. Wm. E. Dodd. Richmond, 1908. (Branch Hist. Papers, II) *DLC, NN*

Life of John Taylor; the Story of a Brilliant Leader in the Early Virginia State Rights School. Henry H. Simms. Richmond, 1932. 234 p. *DLC, NN, PU*

TAYLOR, OLIVER ALDEN. *Memoirs of Oliver A. Taylor.* T. A. Taylor. Boston, 1853. 396 p. *DLC, MWA*

TAYLOR, ROBERT LOVE AND ALFRED ALEXANDER.

Bob and Alf Taylor; Their Lives and Lectures; the Story of Senator Robert Love Taylor and Governor Alfred Alexander Taylor. Paul D. Augsburg. Morristown, Tenn., 1925. 334 p. *DLC, NN*

Life and Career of Senator Robert Love Taylor (Our Bob). James P., Alf A. and Hugh L. Taylor. Nashville, 1913. 370 p.

DLC, NN

TAYLOR, SARAH LOUISA. *Memoir of Mrs. Sarah Louisa Taylor.* Lot Jones. N. Y., 1838. 324 p. *DLC, NN, MWA*

TAYLOR, WILLIAM. *William Taylor of California.* Wm. Taylor. London, 1897. 411 p. *CSmH*

TAYLOR, WILLIAM. *The Soul Digger; or, Life and Times of William Taylor.* John H. Paul. Upland, Ind., 1928. 318 p. *DLC, NN*

TAYLOR, ZACHARY.

The Life of General Taylor, the Hero of Okee Chobee, Palo Alto, Resaca de la Palma, Monterey, and Buena Vista. Phila., 1847. 214 p. *DLC, NN*

A Life of Gen. Zachary Taylor. J. R. Fry. Phila., 1848. 332 p.

DLC, NN, MWA, CSmH, MiU:C

Life of Gen. Zachary Taylor. Henry Montgomery. Auburn, N. Y., 1847. 360 p. *DLC, NN, MWA, CSmH, PU, MiD:B*

Life of Gen. Zachary Taylor, the Whig Candidate for the Presidency. Benjamin P. Poore. Boston, 1848. 16 p. *DLC, MWA*

Life of Major General Zachary Taylor. C. Frank Powell. N. Y., 1847. 121 p. *DLC, NN, MWA, PU*

TAZEWELL, LITTLETON WALLER. *Discourse on the Life and Character of the Hon. Littleton Waller Tazewell.* Hugh B. Grigsby. Norfolk, Va., 1860. 123 p. *DLC, NN, MWA, CSmH, PU*

TECUMSEH.

Life of Tecumseh and of His Brother the Prophet. Benjamin Drake. Cincinnati, 1841. 235 p. *DLC, NN, MWA, CSmH*

Tecumseh and the Shawnee Prophet. Edward Eggleston and Lillie E. Seelye. N. Y., 1878. 327 p. *DLC, NN, MWA*

Life of Tecumseh, the Shawnee Chief, Including Biographical Notices of Black-Hoof, Cornstalk, Little Turtle, Tarhe (The Crane), Captain Logan, Keokuk. Edward S. Ellis. N. Y., 1861. 98 p.

NN, PU

TEFFT, THOMAS ALEXANDER. *The Architect and Monetarian, a Memoir of T. A. Tefft.* Edwin M. Stone. Providence, 1869. 64 p.

DLC, NN, MWA, MiD:B

TE-HO-RA-GWA-NE-GEN. *Life of Te-ho-ra-gwa-ne-gen, Alias Thomas Williams, a Chief of the Caughnawaga Tribe of Indians in Canada.* Eleazer Williams. Albany, 1859. 91 p.

DLC, NN, MWA, CSmH, MiU:C, RP:JCB

TEKAKWITHA, KATERI. *Life and Times of Kateri Tekakwitha, the Lily of the Mohawks.* Ellen H. Walworth. Buffalo, 1891. 314 p.
DLC, NN, CSmH

TEMPLE, DANIEL. *Life and Letters of Rev. Daniel Temple . . . a Missionary . . . in Western Asia.* Daniel H. Temple. Boston, 1855. 492 p.
DLC, NN, MWA

TEMPLE, SHIRLEY. *Shirley Temple.* Jerome Beatty. Akron, O., 1935. 107 p.
DLC, NN

TEMPLE, WILLIAM. *Sir William Temple; a Seventeenth Century " Libertin."* Clara Marburg. New Haven, 1932. 128 p.
DLC, NN, CSmH, PU

TENNYSON, ALFRED LORD.
Tennyson; His Home, His Friends and His Work. Elizabeth L. Cary. N. Y., 1898. 312 p.
DLC, NN
Life and Times of Tennyson From 1809 to 1850. Thomas R. Lounsbury. New Haven, 1915. 661 p. *DLC, NN, CSmH, PU*

TERESA, SAINT. *The Little Flower of Carmel.* Michael Williams. N. Y., 1925. 103 p.
DLC, NN

TERRY, DAVID SMITH. *The Life of David S. Terry. An Authentic, Impartial and Vivid History of His Eventful Life and Tragic Death.* Alexander E. Wagstaff, ed. San Francisco, 1892. 526 p.
NN, CSmH

THACKERAY, WILLIAM MAKEPEACE.
The Spiritual Drama in the Life of Thackeray. Nathaniel W. Stephenson. N. Y., 1913. 192 p.
DLC, NN
Anecdote Biographies of Thackeray and Dickens. Richard H. Stoddard. N. Y., 1874. 305 p.
DLC, NN, CSmH

THAYER, NATHANIEL. 2:681

THEOBALD, LEWIS. *Lewis Theobald; His Contribution to English Scholarship; With Some Unpublished Letters.* Richard F. Jones. N. Y., 1919. 363 p.
DLC, NN, CSmH, PU

THEODORE, SAINT. 2:371

THERESA, SAINT. *Saint Theresa of Avila.* Mrs. Bradley Gilman. Boston, 1889. 203 p.
DLC, NN, PU

THIERS, ADOLPHE. *Monsieur Thiers.* John M. S. Allison. N. Y., 1932. 294 p.
DLC, NN

THIRLWALL, CONNOP. *Connop Thirlwall; Historian and Theologian.* John C. Thirwall. N. Y., 1936. 271 p.
NN

THOBURN, ISABELLA. *Life of Isabella Thoburn.* James M. Thoburn. N. Y., 1903. 373 p.
DLC

THOBURN, JAMES MILLS. *Thoburn—Called of God.* W. F. Oldham. N. Y., Cincinnati, 1918. 188 p. *DLC, NN*

THOLUCK, FRIEDRICH AUGUST GOTTREU. *Sketch of the Life and Character of Prof. Tholuck.* Edwards A. Park. Edinburgh, 1840. 32 p. *DLC, NN*
2:519

THOM, JOHN CULBERTSON. *Memoir of the Rev. John C. Thom.* R. F. Sample. Phila., 1868. 284 p. *CSmH*

THOMAS À BECKET. *The Development of the Legend of Thomas Becket . . .* Paul A. Brown. Phila., 1930. 302 p. (Privately Printed) *DLC, NN, CSmH, PU*

THOMAS, GEORGE H.
General Thomas. Henry Coppée. N. Y., 1893. 332 p. (G.C.) *DLC, NN, MWA, CSmH*
Memoir of Maj.-Gen. G. H. Thomas. Richard W. Johnson. Phila., 1881. 322 p. *DLC, NN, CSmH*
Gen. George H. Thomas. Don Piatt and H. V. Boynton. Cincinnati, 1891. 658 p. *DLC, NN, MWA, CSmH*
Life of Major-General George H. Thomas. T. B. Van Horne. N. Y., 1882. 502 p. *DLC, NN, CSmH, PU*
2:96–104

THOMAS, ISAIAH.
Memoir of Isaiah Thomas. Samuel M. Burnside. Cambridge, 1836. 13 p. (Trans. . . . of Amer. Antiq. Soc., Vol. 2)
DLC, NN, MWA, CSmH, PU, MiU:C
From 'Prentice to Patron; the Life Story of Isaiah Thomas. Annie R. Marble. N. Y., 1935. 326 p.
DLC, NN, MWA, CSmH, MiU:C
Memoir of Isaiah Thomas. Benjamin F. Thomas. Boston, 1874. 73 p. *DLC, NN, MWA, PU*

THOMAS, JOHN. 2:149

THOMAS, JOHN WILSON. *John W. Thomas. A Memorial.* Nashville, 1906. 179 p. *DLC, NN*

THOMAS, JOSHUA. *The Parson of the Islands; a Biography of . . . Rev. Joshua Thomas.* Adam Wallace. Phila., 1861. 412 p. *DLC, MiD:B*

THOMAS, RICHARD HENRY. *Richard H. Thomas, M.D. Life and Letters.* Anna B. Thomas. Chicago, 1905. 438 p. *NN*

THOMAS, THEODORE.
American Orchestra and Theodore Thomas. Charles E. Russell. N. Y., 1927. 344 p. *DLC, NN*

Memoirs of Theodore Thomas. Rose Thomas. N. Y., 1911.
569 p.   *DLC, NN*
   2:340

THOMASON, THOMAS TRUEBODY. *Life of . . . T. T. Thomason.* John
Sargent. N. Y., 1833. 356 p.   *DLC, NN, MWA, PU*

THOMPSON, BENJAMIN. [COUNT RUMFORD]
   Memoir of Sir Benjamin Thompson, Count Rumford. George
E. Ellis. Cambridge, 1871. 680 p.   *DLC, NN, MWA, CSmH, PU*
   Life of Benjamin Thompson, Count Rumford. James Renwick.
(L.A.B.)   *DLC, NN, MWA, CSmH*
   Count Rumford of Massachusetts. James A. Thompson. N. Y.,
1935. 275 p.   *DLC, NN, MWA*

THOMPSON, DANIEL PIERCE. *The Novelist of Vermont: A Biographical
and Critical Study of Daniel Pierce Thompson.* John E. Flitcroft.
Cambridge, 1929. 329 p.   *DLC, NN, MWA, CSmH, PU*

THOMPSON, JOHN REUBEN. 2:503

THOMPSON, W. 2:52

THOMPSON, WILLIAM BOYCE. *The Magnate: William Boyce Thompson and His Time (1869–1930).* Hermann Hagedorn. N. Y.,
1935. 343 p.   *DLC, NN, MWA*

THOMPSON, WILLIAM HALE. *Hizzoner, Big Bill Thompson; an Idyll
of Chicago.* John Bright. N. Y., 1930. 302 p.
           DLC, NN, MWA, PU

THOMSEN, MORITZ. 2:233

THOMSON, CHARLES. *Life of Charles Thomson, Secretary of the Continental Congress and Translator of the Bible from the Greek.*
L. R. Harley. Phila., 1900. 244 p.
         DLC, NN, CSmH, PU, MiD:B

THOMSON, EDWARD. *Life of Edward Thomson, D.D., Late a Bishop
of the M. E. Church.* Edward Thomson. N. Y., 1885. 336 p.
                DLC

THOMSON, JAMES
   James Thomson: Biographical and Bibliographical Sketch.
Adolph Growoll. N. Y., 1893. 14 p.
   Life and Poetry of James Thomson (B.V.). James E. Meeker.
New Haven, 1917. 148 p.   *DLC, NN, PU*

THOMSON, JOSEPH. *Joseph Thomson, African Explorer.* James B.
Thomson. N. Y., 1898. 358 p.   *DLC*

THOMSON, JOSEPH JOHN. 2:348

THOREAU, HENRY.
   Henry Thoreau, the Cosmic Yankee. J. B. Atkinson. N. Y.,
1927. 158 p.   *DLC, NN, CSmH, PU*

Thoreau, The Poet-Naturalist. William E. Channing. Boston, 1873. 396 p. *DLC, NN, CSmH, PU*

Thoreau: His Life and Aims. A Study. Alexander H. Japp. (H. A. Page.) Boston, 1877. 234 p. *DLC, NN*

Thoreau: His Home, Friends and Books. Annie R. Marble. N. Y., 1902. 343 p. *DLC*

David Henry Thoreau. Joseph Palmer. Chapel Hill, 1929. 3 p. (Reprinted from Boston *Advertiser*, July 15, 1862) *PU*

Henry David Thoreau. H. S. Salt. N. Y., 1896. 208 p. (Great Writers Series) *DLC, NN*

Henry D. Thoreau. F. B. Sanborn. Boston, 1882. 324 p. (A.M.L.) *DLC, NN, MWA, CSmH, PU*

The Life of Henry David Thoreau. F. B. Sanborn. Boston, 1917. 541 p. *DLC, NN, CSmH, PU*

Henry David Thoreau, a Critical Study. Mark Van Doren. Boston, 1916. 138 p. *DLC, NN, MWA*
2:332

THORNTON, MATTHEW. *Matthew Thornton of New Hampshire, a Patriot of the American Revolution.* Charles T. Adams. Phila., 1903. 61 p. *DLC, NN, MWA, MiD:B*

THORNWELL, JAMES HENLEY. *The Life and Letters of James Henley Thornwell, D.D., LL.D., Ex-President of the South Carolina College . . .* Benjamin M. Palmer. Richmond, 1875. 614 p.
DLC, NN, CSmH

THROOP, ENOS THOMPSON. 2:349

THURAT, FRANÇOIS. 2:488

THURMAN, ALLEN GRANBERRY. 2:128

THURMAN, JOHN. See CLEVELAND, GROVER.

THURSTON, JOHN LAWRENCE. *A Life With a Purpose: Memorial of John L. Thurston, First Missionary of the Yale Mission.* Henry B. Wright. N. Y., 1908. 317 p. *DLC, MWA, PU*

THURSTON, ROBERT HENRY. *Robert H. Thurston.* William F. Durand. N. Y., 1929. 301 p. (American Soc. of Mechanical Engineers) *DLC, NN*

THWAITES, REUBEN GOLD. *Reuben Gold Thwaites; a Memorial Address.* Frederick J. Turner. Madison, 1914. 94 p.
DLC, NN, MWA, CSmH, MiD:B, MiU:C

TIBBETTS, THEODORE. *A Memorial of Rev. Theodore Tibbetts.* E. C. Towne. Boston, 1863. 27 p.

TICHENOR, ISAAC TAYLOR. *Isaac Taylor Tichenor, the Home Mission Statesman.* J. S. Dill. Nashville, 1908. 168 p. *DLC, NN*

TICKNOR, FRANCIS ORRAY. 2:503
TICKNOR, GEORGE.
    Memoir of George Ticknor. Charles H. Hart. Phila., 1871.
24 p.   *DLC, NN, MWA, CSmH, MiD:B*
    Life, Letters and Journals of George Ticknor. G. S. Hillard and
Anna Ticknor, eds. Boston, 1876. 2 vols.
                DLC, NN, MWA, CSmH, PU, MiD:B
TIERNEY, RICHARD HENRY. *Richard H. Tierney, Priest of the Society
of Jesus.* Francis X. Talbot. N. Y., 1930. 200 p.   *DLC*
TIFFANY, CHARLES LOUIS. 2:623
TIFFIN, EDWARD. *Life of Edward Tiffin, First Governor of Ohio.* W.
E. Gilmore. Chillicothe, O., 1897. 149 p. *DLC, MWA, MiD:B*
TILDEN, SAMUEL JONES.
    The Life of Samuel J. Tilden. John Bigelow. N. Y., 1895. 2
vols.   *DLC, NN, MWA, CSmH, PU*
    The Life of Samuel J. Tilden. Theodore P. Cook. N. Y., 1876.
434 p.   *NN*
    Life of Samuel J. Tilden of New York. John Esten Cooke.
N. Y., 1876.
    *Life and Public Services of Samuel J. Tilden . . . to Which is
Added a Sketch of the Life of T. A. Hendricks.* Theodore P. Cook.
N. Y., 1876. 434 p.   *DLC, NN, MiD:B*
    *Life of Hon. Samuel J. Tilden, With a Sketch of the Life of Hon.
Thomas A. Hendricks.* William M. Cornell. Boston, 1876. 336 p.
                      DLC, NN, MWA
    *Lives and Public Services of Samuel J. Tilden and Thomas A.
Hendricks.* C. Edwards Lester. N. Y., 1876. 192 p. *DLC, NN*
      2:107–590
TILESTON, THOMAS. *Thomas Tileston, 1793–1864.* Mary W. F.
Tileston. N. Y., 1925. 2 vols.   *DLC, NN*
TILGHMAN, BENJAMIN CHEW. 2:343
TILGHMAN, TENCH. *Memoir of Lieut. Col. Tench Tilghman, Secre-
tary and Aid to Washington.* Oswald Tilghman. Albany, 1876.
176 p.   *DLC, NN, MWA, CSmH, MiU:C*
TILGHMAN, WILLIAM. *Life of . . . William Tilghman, Late Chief
Justice of the State of Pennsylvania.* John Golder. Phila., 1829.
148 p.   *DLC, NN, CSmH, MiD:B*
    2:110
TILLETT, JOHN. *The Iron Duke of the Methodist Itinerancy; an Ac-
count of the Life and Labors of Rev. John Tillett of North Carolina.*
A. W. Plyler. Nashville, 1925. 216 p.   *DLC, NN*

TIMON, JOHN. *The Life and Times of the Rt. Rev. John Timon, D.D., . . . First Roman Catholic Bishop of Buffalo.* Charles G. Deuther. Buffalo, 1870. 338 p. *DLC, NN, MWA*

TIMROD, HENRY.
Henry Timrod, Laureate of the Confederacy. Henry T. Thompson. Columbia, S. C., 1928. 147 p. *DLC, NN, CSmH, PU*
Henry Timrod: Man and Poet, a Critical Study. George A. Wauchope. Columbia, S. C., 1915. 30 p. *DLC, NN*
2:503

TITIAN. *Titian.* Moses F. Sweetser. Boston, 1877. 160 p.
DLC, NN
2:161

TODD, CHARLES STEWART. *Memoir of Col. Charles S. Todd.* Gilderroy W. Griffin. Phila., 1873. 174 p.
DLC, NN, CSmH, MiD:B

TODD, JOHN *John Todd; the Story of His Life Told Mainly by Himself.* John E. Todd. N. Y., 1876. 529 p.
DLC, NN, MWA, PU, MiD:B

TOGO, HEIHECHIRO. *Togo and the Rise of Japanese Sea Power.* Edwin A. Falk. N. Y., 1936. 508 p. *DLC, NN, PU*

TOLSTOY, LEV N.
Life of Count Lyoi N. Tolstoi. Nathan H. Dole. N. Y., 1911. 467 p. *DLC, NN*
Tolstoy the Man. E. A. Steiner. N. Y., 1904. 310 p.
DLC, NN, PU
Lev. N. Tolstoy; an Analysis of His Life and Works. Leo Wiener. Boston, 1905. 105 p. *DLC, NN, PU*

TOMPKINS, DANIEL AUGUSTUS. *Daniel A. Tompkins, Builder of the New South; Being the Story of His Life Work.* George T. Winston. N. Y., 1920. 403 p. *DLC, NN, PU*

TOMPKINS, DANIEL D. 2:349

TOMPSON, BENJAMIN.
Works of Benjamin Tompson, With a Biographical Introduction. Howard J. Hall. Boston, 1924. 164 p. *DLC, NN, MWA, MiU:C*
Benjamin Tompson, a Graduate of Harvard College, . . . Samuel A. Green. Boston, 1895. 25 p. *NN*

TONSTENSON, LENNART. *Lennart Tonstenson, Grand Master of the Swedish Artillery.* J. W. De Peyster. Poughkeepsie, N. Y., 1855. 308 p. *DLC*

TONTI, HENRI. *The Man With the Iron Hand.* John C. Parrish. Boston, 1913. 288 p. *DLC, CSmH*

TONTY, HENRI DE. *Henry de Tonty.* Henry E. Legler. Milwaukee, 1896. 57 p. *DLC, NN, MWA*

TOOKE, JOHN HORNE. *John Horne Tooke.* Minnie C. Yarborough. N. Y., 1926. 252 p. (Col. Univ. Studies in Eng.)
DLC, NN, CSmH, PU

TOOMBS, ROBERT.
Life of Robert Toombs. Ulrich B. Phillips. N. Y., 1913. 281 p.
DLC, NN, MWA, CSmH, PU
Life of Robert Toombs. Pleasant A. Stovall. N. Y., 1892. 396 p. *DLC, NN, MWA, CSmH*
2:88–654

TORREY, CHARLES TURNER. *Memoir of Rev. Charles T. Torrey Who Died in the Penitentiary of Maryland Where He Was Confined for Showing Mercy to the Poor.* J. C. Lovejoy. Boston, 1847. 364 p.
DLC, NN, MWA, PU

TORREY, JASON. *Memoir of Major Jason Torrey of Bethany, Wayne County, Pa.* David Torrey. Scranton, Pa., 1885. 131 p.
DLC, NN, MWA, CSmH, MiD:B

TOUR, CHARLES. 2:127

TOURGÉE, ALBION WINEGAR. *Albion W. Tourgée.* Roy F. Dibble. N. Y., 1921. 160 p. *DLC, NN, CSmH, PU*

TOUSSAINT, PIERRE. *Memoir of Pierre Toussaint.* Hannah F. Lee. Boston, 1854. 124 p. *DLC, NN, MWA, CSmH*

TOUSSAINT L'OUVERTURE.
Life of Toussaint L'Ouverture, Warrior and Statesman. R. C. O. Benjamin. Los Angeles, Cal., 1888. 109 p. *DLC, NN, PU*
The Black Napoleon, the Story of Toussaint Louverture. Percy Waxman. N. Y., 1931. 298 p. *DLC, NN, PU*

TOWNSEND, ROBERT. See HALE, NATHAN.

TRADER, ELLA KING. *The Florence Nightingale of the Southern Army* ... Jacob F. Richard, comp. N. Y., 1914. 101 p. *DLC, NN*

TRAIL, ARIANA McELFRECH. *Ariana McElfrech Trail. A Memorial.* Florence Trail. Boston, 1929. 102 p. *DLC, NN, MWA*

TRAIN, GEORGE FRANCIS. *The People's Candidate for President, 1872, George Francis Train.* John W. Nichols. N. Y., 1872. 94 p.
DLC, NN

TRAUBEL, HORACE. *Horace Traubel, His Life and Work.* David Karsner. N. Y., 1919. 160 p. *DLC, NN, MWA, CSmH*

TRELAWNY, EDWARD JOHN. 2:598

TREVISAN, BERNARD. 2:348

TROBRIAND, COMTE REGIS. *Life and Memoirs of Comte Regis de Trobriand, Major General, U. S. A.* Marie C. De T. Post. N. Y., 1910. 539 p. *DLC, NN, CSmH*

TROLLOPE, ANTHONY. 2:91–109

TROTSKY, LEON. *Leon Trotsky; the Portrait of a Youth.* Max F. Eastman. N. Y., 1925. 181 p. *DLC, NN, PU*

TROUIN, DUGUAY. 2:488

TROUP, GEORGE MICHAEL. *Life of George Michael Troup.* Edward J. Harden. Savannah, 1859. 536 p. *DLC, NN, MWA, CSmH*

TRUDEAU, EDWARD LIVINGSTON. *Beloved Physician: Edward Livingston Trudeau.* Stephen Chalmers. Boston, 1916. 73 p.
DLC, NN, MWA, PU
2:507

TRUETT, GEORGE W. 2:487

TRUMBULL, HENRY CLAY. *Life Story of Henry C. Trumbull, Missionary, Army Chaplain, Editor and Author.* Philip E. Howard. Phila., 1905. 525 p. *DLC, NN, PU*

TRUMBULL, JOHN.
John Trumbull, Connecticut Wit. Alexander Cowie. Chapel Hill, 1936. 230 p. *DLC, NN, CSmH, PU, MiD:B*
John Trumbull, a Brief Sketch of His Life. John F. Weir. N. Y., 1901. 79 p. *DLC, NN, PU*
2:394

TRUMBULL, JONATHAN.
Life of Jonathan Trumbull, Governor of Connecticut. Isaac W. Stuart. Boston, 1859. 700 p.
DLC, NN, MWA, CSmH, MiD:B, MiU:C
Jonathan Trumbull, Governor of Connecticut, 1769–1784. Jonathan Trumbull. Boston, 1919. 362 p. *DLC, NN*

TRUMBULL, LYMAN. *Life of Lyman Trumbull.* Horace White. Boston, 1913. 458 p. *DLC, NN, CSmH, PU*

TRYON, DWIGHT WILLIAM. *The Life and Art of Dwight William Tryon.* Henry C. White. Boston, 1930. 226 p. *DLC, NN*
2:123

TRYON, WILLIAM. *Governor William Tryon and His Administration in the Province of North Carolina, 1765–1771.* Marshall D. Haywood. Raleigh, 1903. 223 p. *DLC, NN, CSmH, PU*

TUBMAN, HARRIET. *Scenes in the Life of Harriet Tubman.* Sarah H. Bradford. Auburn, N. Y., 1869. 132 p. *DLC, NN, MWA, CSmH*

TUCK, AMOS. *Amos Tuck.* Charles R. Corning. Exeter, N. H., 1902. 99 p. *DLC, NN, MWA*

TUCKER, JOHN IRELAND. *Doctor Tucker; Priest-Musician.* Christopher W. Knauff. N. Y., 1897. 351 p.   *DLC, NN, MWA*

TUCKER, JOHN RANDOLPH. *Life of Rear-Admiral John Randolph Tucker . . . and Biographical Sketch of the Author.* James H. Rochelle. Washington, 1903. 112 p.   *DLC, NN*

TUCKER, LUTHER. 2:497

TUCKER, SAMUEL. *Life of Samuel Tucker.* John H. Sheppard. Boston, 1868. 384 p.   *DLC, NN, MWA, CSmH, MiU:C*

TUKE, JAMES HACK. *James Hack Tuke.* E. Fry, comp. N. Y., 1899. 354 p.

TURGENEV, IVAN. *Turgenev, the Man—His Art—and His Age.* Avraham Yarmolinsky. N. Y., 1926. 386 p.   *DLC, NN, PU*

TURNER, ASA. *Asa Turner . . . and His Times.* George F. Magoun. Boston, 1889. 345 p.   *DLC, MWA*

TURNER, HENRY MCNEAL. *Life and Times of Henry M. Turner.* M. M. Ponton. Atlanta, 1917. 173 p.   *DLC, NN*

TURNER, JONATHAN BALDWIN. *The Life of Jonathan Baldwin Turner.* Mary T. Carriel. Jacksonville, Ill., 1911. 298 p.   *DLC, NN*

TURNER, JOSEPH. *Turner.* Moses F. Sweetser. Boston, 1878. 164 p.   *DLC, NN*

TUTTLE, CHARLES WESLEY. *Memoir of Charles W. Tuttle.* John W. Dean. Boston, 1888. 21 p. (Privately Printed)
    DLC, NN, MWA, CSmH, PU, MiD:B, MiU:C

TUTTLE, JAMES HARVEY. *Rev. James Harvey Tuttle: A Memoir.* Marion D. Shutter. Boston, 1905. 294 p.   *DLC, NN, MWA*

TUTTLE, LUCIUS. *Lucius Tuttle; an Appreciation.* Hayes Robbins. Boston, 1915. 61 p.   *DLC, NN, MWA*

TUTTLE, WILLIAM. *Life of William Tuttle.* Joseph F. Tuttle, comp. N. Y., 1852. 304 p.   *DLC, MWA*

TWAIN, MARK. See CLEMENS, SAMUEL LANGHORNE.

TWEED, WILLIAM MARCY. *" Boss " Tweed.* Denis T. Lynch. N. Y., 1927. 433 p.   *DLC, NN, MWA, CSmH*

TWO STRIKE. 2:204

TYLERS. *The Letters and Times of the Tylers.* Lyon G. Tyler. Richmond, 1884–1896. 3 vols. *DLC, NN, MWA, CSmH, PU, MiU:C*

TYLER, BENNETT. *Memoir of Rev. Bennett Tyler in His " Lectures on Theology."* Nahum Gale. Boston, 1859. 149 p. *DLC, MWA*

TYLER, JAMES BRAINERD. *A Memorial of the Rev. James Brainerd Tyler . . . of . . . Groton, Conn.* J. H. DeForest, ed. N. Y., 1872. 210 p.   *NN, MWA*

TYLER, JOHN.
> *Life of John Tyler.* N. Y., 1844. 256 p.
> *History of the Life, Administration and Times of John Tyler.* John R. Irelan. Chicago, 1888. 493 p.   *DLC, NN, MWA*
> 2:258

TYLER, MOSES COIT. *The Life of Moses Coit Tyler.* Howard M. Jones. Ann Arbor, Mich., 1933. 354 p.   *DLC, NN, CSmH*

TYNDALE, HECTOR. *A Memoir of Hector Tyndale, Brigadier-General and Brevet Major-General, U. S. Volunteers . . .* John McLaughlin. Phila., 1882. 118 p.   *DLC, NN, CSmH, PU*

TYNDALE, WILLIAM. *William Tyndale.* James J. Ellis. N. Y., 1890. 105 p.   *DLC*

TYNDALL, JOHN. 2:335

TYNG, STEPHEN HIGGINSON. *Record of the Life and Works of Stephen Higginson Tyng.* Charles R. Tyng. N. Y., 1890. 682 p.   *DLC*

TYSON, ELISHA. *Life of Elisha Tyson, the Philanthropist.* J. S. Tyson. Balt., 1825. 142 p.   *DLC, NN, MWA, CSmH, PU*

TYSON, THORNTON KELLY. *Thornton Kelly Tyson, Pioneer Home Missionary.* Brady A. Loving. Kansas City, Mo., 1915. 151 p.
> *DLC, NN*

UNDERHILL, JOHN.
> *Captain John Underhill; Gentleman, Soldier of Fortune.* L. E. De Forest and Anne Lawrence. N. Y., 1934. 104 p.
> *DLC, NN, MWA, CSmH, MiU:C*
> *John Underhill, Captain of New England and New Netherland.* Henry C. Shelley. N. Y., 1932. 473 p.   *DLC, NN, CSmH*

UNDERWOOD, OSCAR WILDER. 2:395

UNIAC, EDWARD H. *Edward H. Uniac: His Life, Struggle, and Fall.* John W. Berry. Boston, 1871. 217 p.   *DLC, MWA*

UNTERMYER, SAMUEL. 2:546

UPHAM, CHARLES WENTWORTH. *Memoir of Charles Wentworth Upham.* George E. Ellis. Cambridge, 1877. 43 p.
> *DLC, NN, MWA, MiU:C*

UPTON, EMORY. *The Life and Letters of Emory Upton, Colonel of the Fourth Regiment of Artillery.* Peter S. Michie. N. Y., 1885. 511 p.
> *DLC, NN, CSmH*

URQUHART, THOMAS. 2:71

USSELINX, WILLEM. *Willem Usselinx, Founder of the Dutch and Swedish West India Companies.* J. F. Jameson. N. Y., 1887. 234 p. (Amer. Hist. Assoc. Papers, V. 2, No. 3)
> *DLC, NN, MWA, CSmH, PU, MiU:C*

VAIL, THEODORE NEWTON. *In One Man's Life; Being Chapters From the Personal and Business Career of Theodore N. Vail.* Albert B. Paine. N. Y., 1921. 359 p. *DLC, NN, PU*

VALENTINO, RUDOLPH.
Rudolph Valentino, His Romantic Life and Death. Ben-Allah Newman. Hollywood, Calif., 1926. 132 p. *DLC, NN*
Valentino As I Knew Him. S. George Ullman. N. Y., 1926. 218 p. *DLC, NN*

VALLANDIGHAM, CLEMENT LAIRD. *A Life of Clement L. Vallandigham.* J. L. Vallandigham. Balt., 1872. 573 p. *NN, MWA*

VALTON, JOHN. *Life of Rev. John Valton.* Joseph Sutcliffe. N. Y., 1837. 163 p.

VANAMEE, PARKER. *Vanamee.* Mary C. Vanamee. N. Y., 1930. 307 p. *DLC, NN, PU*

VAN BUREN, MARTIN.
The American Talleyrand; the Career and Contemporaries of Martin Van Buren, Eighth President. Holmes Alexander. N. Y., 1935. 430 p. *DLC, NN, MWA, PU*
Martin Van Buren, To the End of His Public Career. George Bancroft. N. Y., 1889. 239 p.
DLC, NN, MWA, CSmH, PU, MiD:B, MiU:C
Martin Van Buren: Lawyer, Statesman and Man. William A. Butler. N. Y., 1862. 47 p. *DLC, NN, MWA*
The Life of Martin Van Buren, Heir-Apparent to the " Government " and the Appointed Successor of General Andrew Jackson. David Crockett. Phila., 1835. 209 p.
DLC, NN, MWA, CSmH, PU, MiD:B
Sketches of the Life of Martin Van Buren. Moses Dawson. Cincinnati, 1840. 216 p.
Biography of Martin Van Buren, Vice-President of the United States. William Emmons. Washington, 1835. 196 p.
DLC, NN, MWA, MiU:C
The Life and Political Opinions of Martin Van Buren, Vice-President of the United States. William M. Holland. Hartford, 1835. 364 p. *DLC, NN, MWA, MiD:B, MiU:C*
History of the Life, Administration and Times of Martin Van Buren . . . Seven Years Seminole War and Period of Great Financial Convulsions. John R. Irelan. Chicago, 1887. 624 p. *DLC, NN*
An Epoch and a Man: Martin Van Buren and His Times. Denis T. Lynch. N. Y., 1929. 566 p.
DLC, NN, MWA, CSmH, PU

The Life and Times of Martin Van Buren. William L. Mackenzie. Boston, 1846. 308 p.

        DLC, NN, MWA, CSmH, PU, MiD:B

Life of Martin Van Buren. Thomas M'Elhiney. Pittsburgh, 1853. 126 p.   *DLC*

    Martin Van Buren. Edward M. Shepard. Boston, 1888. 404 p. (A.S.)   *DLC, NN, MWA, CSmH, PU, MiD:B*

    2:349–501

VAN CAMPEN, MOSES. *Sketches of the Border Adventures in The Life and Times of Major Moses Van Campen.* John N. Hubbard. Bath, N. Y., 1841. 310 p.   *DLC, NN, MWA, CSmH*

VANCE, ZEBULON BAIRD. *Life of Zebulon B. Vance.* Clement Dowd. Charlotte, N. C., 1897. 493 p.

        DLC, NN, MWA, CSmH, PU, MiD:B

VAN COTT, MAGGIE NEWTON. *Life and Labors of Mrs. Maggie Newton Van Cott, the First Lady Licensed to Preach in the M. E. Church in the United States.* John O. Foster. Cincinnati, 1872. 339 p.   *DLC, MWA*

VANCOUVER, GEORGE. 2:387

VAN DEN BROEK. *Story of Father Van den Broek, O.P.: Study of Holland and the Story of the Early Settlement of Wisconsin.* Sr. Mary Alphonso. Chicago, 1907. 94 p.   *DLC*

VANDERBILTS. *The Vanderbilts and the Story of Their Fortune.* W. A. Croffut. N. Y., 1886. 310 p.   *DLC, NN, PU*

VANDERBILT, CORNELIUS. *Commodore Vanderbilt; an Epic of American Achievement.* Arthur D. H. Smith. N. Y., 1927. 339 p.

        DLC, NN, PU

    2:451–511–623

VANDERBILT, GERTRUDE. 2:425

VAN DYCK, ANTHONY. *Van Dyck.* Moses F. Sweetser. Boston, 1878. 157 p.   *DLC, NN*

    2:248

VAN DYKE, HENRY. *Henry Van Dyke; a Biography.* Tertius Van Dyke. N. Y., 1935. 444 p.   *DLC, NN*

    2:388

VAN DYKE, HENRY JACKSON. *Henry Jackson Van Dyke: a Memorial.* H. J. Van Dyke. 1892. 168 p.

VANE, HENRY.

    Life of Young Sir Henry Vane. Jas. K. Hosmer. Boston, 1889. 581 p.   *DLC, NN, MWA, CSmH, MiD:B, MiU:C*

Life of Sir Henry Vane, the Younger. W. W. Ireland. N. Y., 1906. 513 p.   *DLC, NN, CSmH, PU, MiD:B, MiU:C*
Sir Henry Vane, Jr., Governor of Massachusetts and Friend of Roger Williams and Rhode Island. Henry M. King. Providence, 1909. 207 p.   *DLC, NN, MWA, PU*
Life of Sir Henry Vane. Charles W. Upham. (L.A.B.)
    DLC, NN, MWA, CSmH, PU

VAN HORNE, WILLIAM. *The Life and Work of Sir William Van Horne.* Walter Vaughan. N. Y., 1920. 388 p.   *DLC, NN*

VAN LENNEP, MARY E. *Memoir of Mrs. Mary E. Van Lennep . . . Missionary to Turkey.* Hartford, 1848. 382 p.
    DLC, NN, MWA, MiD:B

VAN LOON, HENDRIK WILLEM. 2:236–366

VAN RENSSELAER, HENRY. *Life and Letters of Henry Van Rensselaer, S.J.* E. P. Spillane. N. Y., 1908. 293 p.   *DLC, NN*

VAN SCHAACK, HENRY. *Memoirs of the Life of Henry Van Schaack, Embracing Selections From His Correspondence During the American Revolution.* Henry C. Van Schaack. Chicago, 1892. 233 p.
    NN, CSmH, MiD:B

VAN SCHAACK, PETER. *Life of Peter Van Schaack.* Henry C. Van Schaick. N. Y., 1842. 490 p.   *DLC, MWA, CSmH, PU, MiU:C*

VAN WAGNER, W. M. *The Life and Labors of Rev. W. M. Van Wagner.* S. H. Tyng, Jr. N. Y., 1867.

VARAGINE, JACOBUS DE. *Materials For a Life of Jacopo de Varagine.* Ernest C. Richardson. N. Y., 1935.   *DLC, NN, CSmH, PU*

VARDAMAN, JAMES KIMBLE. *Biographical Sketches of James Kimble Vardaman.* Archibald S. Coody. Jackson, Miss., 1922. 232 p.
    DLC, NN

VASSAR, JOHN. *Uncle John Vassar; or, the Fight of Faith.* T. E. Vassar. N. Y., n.d. 217 p. (Privately Printed)
    DLC, NN, MWA, PU

VAUGHAN, FRANCES. *The True Story of Frances, the Falconer's Daughter, Wife of William Dungan, Gentleman, of London . . .* Eliz. N. White. Providence, 1932. 176 p.   *DLC, NN*

VAUGHAN, WILLIAM. *Memoirs of Rev. William Vaughan, D.D.* Thomas M. Vaughan. Louisville, 1878. 336 p.   *NN*

VEBLEN, THORSTEIN. *Thorstein Veblen and His America.* Joseph Dorfman. N. Y., 1934. 556 p.   *DLC, NN, PU*

VEDDER, ELIHU. 2:429

VEGA, LOPE DE. *Lope de Vega, Monster of Nature.* Angel Flores. N. Y., 1930. 214 p.   *DLC, NN, PU*

VEGO, FRANCESCO. *Vego, a Forgotten Builder of the American Republic.* Bruno Roselle. Boston, 1933. 280 p. **DLC**

VELASQUEZ. 2:161

VENIZELOS, ELEUTHERIOS. *Venizelos.* Herbert A. Gibbons. Boston, 1920. 384 p. (Modern Statesmen Series) **DLC, NN, PU**
2:30

VERENDYRE, PIERRE GAULTIER. 2:127

VERNHAM, ADA. *Ada Vernham, Actress.* Richard Marsh. Boston, 1900. 272 p. **DLC**

VERY, JONES. 2:87

VESALIUS, ANDREAS.
Andreas Vesalius, Reformer of Anatomy. James M. Ball. St. Louis, 1910. 149 p. **DLC, NN, CSmH**
Vesalius, Reformer and Martyr of Science: a Historical Sketch. Charles Born. Cincinnati, 1907. 227 p. **DLC**

VESPUCIUS, AMERICUS.
Life of Americus Vespucius, His Voyages and Discovery of the New World. Charles E. Lester and Andrew Foster. N. Y., 1845. 431 p. **DLC, NN, MWA, CSmH, PU, MiU:C**
Amerigo Vespucci. F. A. Ober. N. Y., 1907. 297 p. (Heroes of American History) **DLC, NN**

VIANNEY, JOHN BAPTIST. *Priestly Virtue and Zeal; a Study of the Life of St. John Baptist Vianney, the Curé d'Ars and Patron of Priests, Applied to the Sacerdotal Life of Today.* Joseph L. J. Kirlin. N. Y., Cincinnati, 1928. 179 p. **DLC, NN**

VICTORIA, QUEEN. *Queen Victoria, Her Glorious Life and Illustrious Reign.* Thomas W. Handford. Indianapolis, 1901. 496 p. **DLC**
2:1

VIGO, FRANCIS. 2:225

VILLA, FRANCISCO.
Viva Villa! A Recovery of the Real Pancho Villa, Peon, Bandit, Soldier, Patriot. Edgcumb Pinchon. N. Y., 1933. 383 p.
DLC, NN
Here Comes Pancho Villa; the Anecdotal History of a Genial Killer. Louis Stevens. N. Y., 1930. 309 p. **DLC, NN**

VILLENEUVE-BARGEMENT. *Villeneuve-Bargement, Precursor of Modern Social Catholicism.* Mary I. Ring. Milwaukee, 1935. 265 p.
DLC, NN

VINCENT DE PAUL, SAINT. 2:680

VINCENT, JOHN HEYL. *John Heyl Vincent; a Biographical Sketch.* Leon H. Vincent. N. Y., 1925. 319 p. **DLC, NN, PU**

VINCI, LEONARDO.
　　Mind of Leonardo da Vinci. Edward McCurdy. N. Y., 1928.
360 p. 　　　　　　　　　　　　　　　　　*DLC, NN, PU*
　　Leonardo da Vinci. Moses F. Sweetser. Boston, 1879. 145 p.
　　　　　　　　　　　　　　　　　　　　　　DLC, NN
　　2:161–248
VIRGIL. 2:82
VIVIAN, CHARLES ALGERNON S. *A Biographical Sketch of the Life of Charles Algernon Sidney Vivian, Founder of the Order of Elks, Together With Anecdotes and Reminiscences of His Works and Travels.* Imogen H. Vivian. San Francisco, 1904. 103 p. 　*DLC, NN*
VOLTA, ALESSANDRO. 2:25
VOLTAIRE, [FRANÇOIS M. AROUET]
　　The Young Voltaire. Cleveland B. Chase. N. Y., 1926. 253 p.
　　　　　　　　　　　　　　　　　　　　　DLC, NN, PU
　　Life of Voltaire. James Parton. Boston, 1881. 2 vols.
　　　　　　　　　　　　　　　　　　　　　DLC, NN, PU
　　Voltaire, Genius of Mockery. Victor Thaddeus. N. Y., 1928.
291 p. 　　　　　　　　　　　　　　　　　　*DLC, NN*
　　2:5–86–332
VON HUMBOLDT, ALEXANDER. *Life, Travels and Books of A. Von Humboldt.* Richard H. Stoddard. N. Y., 1859. 482 p.
　　　　　　　　　　　　　　　　　　　　　　DLC, NN
VONNOK, BESSIE POTTER. 2:430
VON STEUBEN, FRIEDRICH WILHELM.
　　The Army of the American Revolution and Its Organizer . . .
　　Rudolf Cronau. N. Y., 1923. 150 p. *DLC, NN, CSmH, MiD:B*
　　Frederick William Von Steuben and the American Revolution.
　　Joseph B. Doyle. Steubenville, Ohio, 1913. 399 p.
　　　　　　　　　　　　　　　　DLC, NN, MWA, CSmH, PU
　　The Life of Frederick William Von Steuben, Major General in the Revoutionary Army. Frederick Kapp. N. Y., 1859. 735 p.
　　　　　　　　　　　DLC, NN, MWA, CSmH, PU, MiD:B
VOORHEES, DANIEL WOLSEY. *The Tall Sycamore of the Wabash.*
　　Leonard S. Kenworthy. Boston, 1936. 155 p. 　*DLC, NN, PU*
WADE, BENJAMIN FRANKLIN. *Life of Benjamin F. Wade.* A. G.
　　Riddle. Cleveland, 1886. 310 p. *DLC, NN, MWA, CSmH, PU*
WADE, JONATHAN. *The Wades. Jonathan Wade, D.D., Deborah B. Wade: A Memorial.* Walter N. Wyeth. Phila., 1891. 196 p.
　　　　　　　　　　　　　　　　　　　　　　　NN

WADHAMS, EDGAR PHILIP. *Reminiscences of Edgar P. Wadhams, First Bishop of Ogdensburg.* Clarence A. Walworth. N. Y., 1893. 197 p.
DLC, NN

WADSWORTH, JAMES SAMUEL. *James S. Wadsworth of Geneseo.* Henry G. Pearson. N. Y., 1913. 321 p.
DLC, NN, CSmH, PU, MiD:B

WADSWORTH, JAMES WOLCOTT, JR. *James W. Wadsworth, Jr.; a Biographical Sketch.* Henry F. Holthusen. N. Y., 1926. 243 p.
DLC, NN, MWA

WAGNE-JAUREGG. 2:175

WAGNER, RICHARD.
Richard Wagner. Nathan H. Dole. N. Y., 1904. 32 p.
DLC, NN

Wagner and His Works. H. T. Finck. N. Y., 1893. 2 vols.
DLC, NN, CSmH

2:187

WAGNER, ROBERT FERDINAND. 2:546

WAINRIGHT, JONATHAN MAYHEW. *Life of Bishop J. M. Wainright.* J. N. Norton. N. Y., 1858. 184 p.
NN, MWA

WALKER, FRANCIS AMASA. *Life of Francis Amasa Walker.* James P. Munroe. N. Y., 1923. 449 p.
DLC, NN, CSmH, PU

WALKER, GEORGE WASHINGTON. *Brief Recollections of the Late Rev. George W. Walker.* Maxwell P. Gaddis. Cincinnati, 1857. 538 p.
DLC, NN

WALKER, HORATIO. 2:123

WALKER, JAMES. *Jimmie Walker, the Story of a Personality.* Louis J. Gribetz. N. Y., 1932. 353 p.
DLC, NN
2:546

WALKER, ROBERT JOHN. *Robert J. Walker, Imperialist.* William E. Dodd. Lynchburg, Va., 1915. 23 p. (Randolph-Macon Woman's College Bulletin. V. 1, No. 2)
DLC, NN, CSmH, PU

WALKER, WILLIAM. *Filibusters and Financiers; the Story of William Walker and His Associates.* W. O. Scroggs. N. Y., 1916. 408 p.
DLC, NN, CSmH, PU

2:172

WALL, RACHEL. *Life, Last Words and Dying Confession of Rachel Wall . . .* Boston, 1789.

WALLACE, CALEB. 8:225

WALLACE, HENRY. 2:497

WALLACE, WILLIAM HENRY L. *Life and Letters of Gen. W. H. L. Wallace.* Isabel Wallace. Chicago, 1909. 231 p.
DLC, NN, CSmH

WALLACE, WILLIAM ALEXANDER ANDERSON. *The Adventures of Big-Foot Wallace, the Texas Ranger and Hunter.* John C. Duval. 1870. 309 p. DLC, NN, MWA, CSmH

WALLACK, JAMES WILLIAM. *A Sketch of the Life of James W. Wallack, Sr.* Thomas H. Morrell, comp. N. Y., 1865. 61 p.
DLC, NN, CSmH, PU

WALPOLE, HORACE. *Horace Walpole and Madame du Deffand: an Eighteenth Century Friendship.* Anna De Koven. N. Y., 1929. 198 p. DLC, NN, CSmH, PU
2:86–87

WALSH, THOMAS. *The Life and Death of Thomas Walsh . . .* James Morgan. Phila., 1792. 356 p. NN, MWA, RP:JCB

WALSH, WILLIAM FRANCIS. *A Shepherd of the Far North; the Story of William Francis Walsh (1900–1930).* Robert Glody. San Francisco, 1934. 237 p. DLC, NN

WALTER, ISAAC N. *Memoir of Elder Isaac N. Walter.* Arthur L. McKinney. Cincinnati, 1859. 464 p. NN

WALTHER, CARL FERDINAND WILHELM.
The Story of C. F. W. Walther. William G. Polack. St. Louis, 1935. 138 p. DLC, NN
Doctor Carl Ferdinand Wilhelm Walther . . . Diedrich H. Steffens. Phila., 1917. 401 p. DLC, NN

WALTON, OCTAVIA. 2:518

WALTON, WILLIAM CLAIBORNE. *Memoir of William C. Walton . . . of the Second Presbyterian Church in Alexandria, Va. . . . and . . . in Hartford, Conn.* Joshua N. Danforth. Hartford, 1837. 319 p.
NN, MWA

WALWORTH, CLARENCE AUGUSTUS. *Life Sketches of Father Walworth, With Notes and Letters.* Ellen H. Walworth. Albany, 1907. 370 p. DLC

WANAMAKER, JOHN.
John Wanamaker; a Study. Joseph H. Appel. Camden, N. J., 1927. 103 p. DLC, NN
Business Biography of John Wanamaker, Founder and Builder, America's Merchant Pioneer From 1861 to 1922; With Glimpses of Rodman Wanamaker and Thomas B. Wanamaker. Joseph H. Appel. N. Y., 1930. 469 p. DLC, NN, MWA, CSmH, PU
Romantic Rise of a Great American (John Wanamaker). Russell H. Conwell. N. Y., 1924. 225 p. DLC, NN, PU
John Wanamaker. Herbert A. Gibbons. N. Y., 1926. 2 vols.
DLC, NN, PU

WARD, ARTEMAS. *Life of Artemas Ward, the First Commander-in-Chief of American Revolution.* Charles Martyn. N. Y., 1921. 334 p. (Privately Printed)

DLC, NN, MWA, CSmH, PU, MiD:B, MiU:C

WARD, ARTEMUS. See BROWNE, CHARLES F.

WARD, DURBIN. *Life of . . . Durbin Ward of Ohio.* Eliz. P. Ward, comp. Columbus, O., 1888. 601 p. *DLC, NN, MiD:B*

WARD, FREDERICK TOWNSEND. *A Yankee Adventurer; the Story of Frederick T. Ward and the Taiping Rebellion.* Holger Cahill. N. Y., 1930. 296 p. *DLC, NN, PU*

WARD, GILES F. *A Memorial of Giles F. Ward, Jr.* W. T. Budington. N. Y., 1866. 99 p. *DLC, MWA, CSmH*

WARD, JOHN QUINCY ADAMS. 2:430

WARD, JOSEPH. *Joseph Ward of Dakota.* George H. Durand. Boston, 1913. 252 p. *DLC, NN*

WARD, LESTER FRANK. *Lester F. Ward; a Personal Sketch.* Emily P. Cape. N. Y., 1922. 208 p. *DLC, NN, PU*

WARD, NATHANIEL.
    A Memoir of the Rev. Nathaniel Ward, A.M., Author of the "Simple Cobbler of Agawam in America." John W. Dean. Albany, 1868. 213 p. *NN, MWA, CSmH, MiD:B*
    Sketch of the Rev. Nathaniel Ward, of Ipswich. Stephen H. Phillips. Salem, 1864. (Essex Inst. Hist. Coll., Vol. VI)

NN, CSmH

    2:464

WARD, SALLIE. 2:518

WARD, SAMUEL.
    Life of Samuel Ward. William Gammell. (L.A.B.)

DLC, NN, MWA, CSmH

    Life and Services of Gov. Samuel Ward . . . John Ward. Providence, 1877. *RP:JCB*

WARE, HARRIET. *A Memoir of Harriet Ware, First Superintendent of the Children's Home in Providence.* Francis Wayland. Providence, 1850. 151 p. *NN, MWA*

WARE, HENRY. *Memoir of the Life of Henry Ware, Jr.* John Ware. Boston, 1846. 484 p. *DLC, NN, MWA, MiD:B*
    2:581

WARE, MARY LOVELL. *Memoir of Mary L. Ware, Wife of Henry Ware, Jr.* Edward B. Hall. Boston, 1857. 434 p.

DLC, NN, MWA, PU, MiD:B

    2:43

WARNER, CHARLES DUDLEY. *Charles Dudley Warner.* Annie A. Fields. N. Y., 1904. 209 p. (Contemporary Men of Letters Series) *DLC, NN, MWA, PU*

WARNER, SUSAN.

Susan Warner. Anna B. Warner. N. Y., 1904. 509 p. *DLC, NN*

Letters and Memories of Susan and Anna Bartlett Warner. Olivia E. P. Stokes. N. Y., 1925. 229 p. *DLC, NN*

WARREN, GOUVERNEUR KEMBLE. *Gouverneur Kemble Warren; the Life and Letters of an American Soldier, 1830–1882.* Emerson G. Taylor. Boston, 1932. 256 p. *DLC, NN, PU*

WARREN, JOHN. *The Life of John Warren, M.D.* Edward Warren. Boston, 1874. 568 p. *DLC, MWA, PU*

WARREN, JOHN COLLINS. *The Life of John Collins Warren, M.D. Compiled Chiefly From His Autobiography and Journals.* Edward Warren, comp. Boston, 1860. 2 vols.

DLC, NN, MWA, RP:JCB

WARREN, JONATHAN MASON. *Memoir of Jonathan Mason Warren, M.D.* Howard P. Arnold. Boston, 1886. 329 p. *DLC, NN*

WARREN, JOSEPH.

Life of Joseph Warren. Alexander H. Everett. (L.A.B.)

DLC, NN, MWA, CSmH, PU

Life and Times of Joseph Warren. Richard Frothingham. Boston, 1865. 558 p. *DLC, NN, MWA, CSmH, MiD:B, MiU:C*

WARREN, JOSIAH. *Josiah Warren, the First American Anarchist: a Sociological Study.* William Bailie. Boston, 1906. 134 p.

DLC, NN, MWA, PU

WARREN, MERCY. *Mercy Warren.* Alice Brown. N. Y., 1896. 317 p. (Women of Colonial and Revolutionary Times)

DLC, NN, MWA, CSmH, PU, MiD:B

WASHBURN, CHARLES GRENFILL. *The Life of Charles G. Washburn.* George H. Haynes. Boston, 1931. 302 p. *DLC, NN, MWA*

WASHBURN, ICHABOD. *Autobiography and Memoir of Ichabod Washburn.* H. T. Cheever, ed. Boston, 1879. 222 p. *MWA, MiD:B*

WASHBURN, ISRAEL. *Israel, Elihu, and Cadwallader Washburn.* Gaillard Hunt. N. Y., 1925. 397 p. *DLC, NN*

WASHBURNE, ELIHU BENJAMIN. 2:128

WASHINGTON, BOOKER TALIAFERO.

From Slave to College President: Being the Life Story of Booker T. Washington. Godfrey H. Pike. London, 1902. 111 p.

DLC, NN

Life and Times of Booker T. Washington. Benjamin F. Riley.
N. Y., 1916. 301 p. *DLC, NN*
Booker T. Washington, Builder of Civilization. Emmet J. Scott
and Lyman B. Stowe. N. Y., 1916. 331 p. *DLC, NN, CSmH*
*A Joshua in the Camp, the Life of Booker T. Washington of
Tuskegee, Alabama.* H. Rufus White. Tawson, Ind., 1895. 15 p.
DLC, MWA

2:6–190–205–325–336–493
WASHINGTON, BUSHROD. 2:110
WASHINGTON, GEORGE.

*The Life of General Washington, Present President of the United
States. Also of the Brave Montgomery.* Phila., 1794. 32 p.
George Washington; or, Life in America One Hundred Years Ago.
John S. C. Abbott. N. Y., 1875. 360 p.
DLC, NN, CSmH, MiD:B
George Washington and the West. Charles H. Ambler. Chapel
Hill, 1936. 270 p. *DLC, NN, CSmH, PU*
Life of George Washington. S. G. Arnold. N. Y., 1840. 228 p.
DLC, NN, CSmH, PU, MiU:C
*Early Sketches of George Washington. Reprinted With Bio-
graphical and Bibliographical Notes.* William S. Baker. Phila.,
1894. 150 p. *DLC, NN, MWA, CSmH*
Washington After the Revolution; 1784–1799. William S.
Baker. Phila., 1897. 366 p. *NN, MWA, CSmH*
The Life of George Washington, Commander-in-Chief . . .
Aaron Bancroft. Boston, 1826. 2 vols.
DLC, NN, MWA, CSmH, PU, MiD:B, RP:JCB
*The Father of His Country; How the Boy Washington Grew in
Stature and Spirit and Became a Great Soldier and President.* Wil-
liam E. Barton. Indianapolis, 1928. 301 p. *DLC, NN*
*A Short Sketch of General Washington's Life and Character.
Annexed to Charles Henry Wharton's " Poetical Epistle to His Ex-
cellency George Washington, etc."* John Bell. Annapolis, 1779.
NN, CSmH
*The True Story of George Washington, Called the Father of His
Country.* Elbridge S. Brooks. Boston, 1895. 204 p.
DLC, NN, CSmH
*The Soul of George Washington; an Overlooked Side of His
Character.* Joseph Buffington. Phila., 1936. 173 p. *DLC, NN*
Washington. Alonzo M. Bullock. Watertown, Wis., 1904. 95 p.
(Headlights of American History Series) *MWA, CSmH*

Washington, the Soldier. H. B. Carrington. Boston, 1898. 431 p.   *DLC, NN, MWA, CSmH, PU, MiU:C*

Life of General Washington, Late President of the United States. Jonathan Clark. Albany, 1813. 143 p.   *DLC, CSmH*

Biographical Memoirs of the Illustrious Gen. George Washington . . . also, A Sketch of His Private Life. Thomas Condie. Phila., 1800. 243 p.   *DLC, NN, MWA, CSmH, RP:JCB*

The Unknown Washington; Biographic Origins of the Republic. John Corbin. N. Y., 1930. 454 p.

         DLC, NN, CSmH, PU, MiU:C

Recollections and Private Memoirs of Washington. George W. P. Custis. Washington, 1860. 644 p.

         DLC, NN, MWA, CSmH, PU, MiD:B

The Life of George Washington. Edward Everett. N. Y., 1860. 348 p.   *DLC, NN, MWA, CSmH, PU, MiD:B*

George Washington Himself. A Common-Sense Biography Written From His Manuscripts. John C. Fitzpatrick. Indianapolis, 1933. 544 p.   *DLC, NN, MWA, CSmH, PU*

The True George Washington. Paul L. Ford. Phila., 1897. 319 p.   *DLC, NN, MWA, CSmH, PU, MiD:B*

George Washington. Worthington C. Ford. N. Y., 1900. 2 vols.   *DLC, NN, MWA, CSmH, PU, MiU:C*

George Washington. Worthington C. Ford. Boston, 1911. 169 p. (Beacon Biographies)   *DLC, NN, MWA, CSmH, PU*

Pictorial Life of George Washington. John Frost. Phila., 1847. 588 p.   *DLC, CSmH, PU*

Washington, Commander-in-Chief. Thomas G. Frothingham. Boston, 1930. 404 p.   *DLC, NN, MWA, CSmH, PU*

Life of George Washington. Francis Glass. N. Y., 1835. 245 p. (Written in Latin Prose)   *DLC, NN, MWA, CSmH, PU*

Washington and the Generals of the American Revolution. Rufus W. Griswold. Phila., 1848. 2 vols.   *DLC, NN, CSmH*

George Washington, 1732–1799. John Habberton. N. Y., 1884. 345 p. (Lives of American Worthies)

         DLC, MWA, CSmH, PU

The Life of George Washington, Studied Anew. Edward E. Hale. N. Y., 1888. 392 p.   *DLC, NN, MWA, CSmH*

Washington's Life and Military Career. M. H. Hancock. Chicago, 1902. 563 p.   *NN, CSmH, PU*

George Washington. Norman Hapgood. N. Y., 1901. 419 p.

         DLC, NN, CSmH

George Washington, Patriot, Soldier, Statesman. J. A. Harrison. N. Y., 1906. 481 p.   *DLC, NN, CSmH, PU*

George Washington, Country Gentleman. Paul L. Haworth. Indianapolis, 1925. 336 p.   *DLC, NN, MWA, CSmH, MiU:C*

Washington and His Generals. Joel T. Headley. N. Y., 1847. 2 vols.   *DLC, NN, MWA, CSmH, PU*

Life of George Washington. Joel T. Headley. N. Y., 1856. 477 p.   *NN, CSmH*

The Illustrated Life of Washington . . . Joel T. Headley. N. Y., 1859. 516 p.   *DLC, NN, CSmH*

George Washington, Patron of Learning. Leonard C. Helderman. N. Y., 1932. 187 p.   *DLC, NN, CSmH*

Life of Washington. Leonard Henley. N. Y., n.d. 207 p.   *PU*

Washington, the Man of Action. Frederick T. Hill. N. Y., 1914. 329 p.   *DLC, NN, MWA, CSmH*

George Washington; the Soul of a Nation. Mabel D. Holmes. Phila., 1932. 385 p.   *DLC, NN, MWA*

George Washington. Rupert Hughes. N. Y., 1926–1930. 3 vols.   *DLC, NN, PU*

Life of George Washington. Washington Irving. N. Y., 1855–1859. 5 vols.   *DLC, NN, MWA, CSmH, PU, MiD:B, RP:JCB*

General Washington. Bradley T. Johnson. N. Y., 1894. 338 p. (G.C.)   *DLC, NN, CSmH, PU, MiD:B*

George Washington, Day By Day. Elizabeth B. Johnston. Washington, 1894. 207 p.   *DLC, NN, CSmH*

George Washington, the Christian. William J. Johnstone. N. Y., 1919. 299 p.   *DLC, NN*

Memoirs of Washington. Caroline M. S. Kirkland. N. Y., 1857. 516 p.   *DLC, NN, MWA, CSmH, PU, MiD:B*

Everybody's Washington. Alden A. Knipe. N. Y., 1931. 282 p.   *DLC, NN, CSmH, PU*

George Washington. Shelby M. Little. N. Y., 1929. 481 p.   *DLC, NN, CSmH, PU, MiD:B*

Typical American, George Washington. C. E. Locke. N. Y., 1902. 28 p. (Hero Series)   *DLC, CSmH*

George Washington. Henry C. Lodge. Boston, 1889. 2 vols. (A.S.)   *DLC, NN, MWA, CSmH, PU, MiD:B*

Life of Washington; a Biography, Personal, Military, and Political. Benson J. Lossing. N. Y., 1860. 3 vols.   *DLC, NN, MWA, CSmH*

Greatest of Men, Washington . . . Alfred W. McCann. N. Y., 1927. 271 p. *DLC, NN*

Washington, a Virginia Cavalier. William H. Mace. N. Y., 1916. 180 p. *DLC, NN, CSmH*

Washington and Lincoln. Robert W. McLaughlin. N. Y., 1912. 278 p. *DLC, NN, MWA, CSmH*

Life of George Washington. John Marshall. Phila., 1804–07. 5 vols. rev. ed. 2 vols. Phila., 1832.
DLC, NN, MWA, CSmH, PU, MiD:B, MiU:C, RP:JCB

The American Patriot and Hero. A Brief Memoir of the Illustrious Conduct and Character of His Excellency General Washington . . . John Maxwell. Lancaster, 1785. 64 p. *DLC*

Family Life of George Washington. Charles Moore. Boston, 1926. 250 p. *DLC, NN, MWA, CSmH*

True and Authentic History of His Excellency George Washington. Jedidiah Morse. Phila., 1790. 21 p. *DLC, NN, CSmH*

The Master of Mount Vernon. Belle Moses. N. Y., 1932. 255 p. *DLC, NN*

The Ancestry and Earlier Life of George Washington. Edward D. Neill. Phila., 1892. 37 p. *DLC, NN, MWA, CSmH*

The Life of George Washington. John N. Norton. N. Y., 1860. 400 p. *DLC, NN, MWA, CSmH*

George Washington. Eugene Parsons. Milwaukee, 1903. 180 p. (Great Americans of History) *DLC, NN, CSmH, PU*

A Life of Washington. James K. Paulding. N. Y., 1835. 2 vols. (Harpers Family Library . . . 1836)
DLC, NN, MWA, CSmH, MiD:B

George Washington, In Love and Otherwise. Eugene Prussing. Chicago, 1925. 183 p. *DLC, NN, CSmH, MiU:C*

The Life of George Washington . . . David Ramsay. N. Y., 1807. Boston, 1811. Balt., 1825. 376 p.
DLC, NN, MWA, CSmH, PU, MiD:B, MiU:C, RP:JCB

Washington in Domestic Life, From Original Letters and Manuscripts. Richard Rush. Phila., 1857. 85 p.
DLC, NN, MWA, CSmH, PU, MiD:B, MiU:C

Washington. Joseph D. Sawyer. N. Y., 1927. 2 vols.
DLC, NN, MWA, PU

Life and Times of George Washington. Samuel M. Schmucker. Phila., 1859. 432 p. *CSmH, PU, MiD:B*

WASHINGTON

Life and Times of George Washington, Containing a Particular Account of National Principles and Events, and of Illustrious Men of the Revolution. John F. Schroeder. N. Y., 1857. 2 vols.

DLC, NN, MWA, CSmH, PU, MiD:B

Life and Times of George Washington. Schroeder-Lossing. Albany, 1903. 4 vols. DLC, NN, MWA, CSmH

George Washington. Horace E. Scudder. Boston, 1889. 248 p.

DLC, NN, MWA, CSmH, PU, MiD:B, MiU:C

George Washington. Louis M. Sears. N. Y., 1932. 560 p.

DLC, NN, CSmH, PU

The Lives of George Washington and Thomas Jefferson: With a Parallel. Stephen Simpson. Phila., 1833. 390 p.

DLC, NN, CSmH, MiD:B

The Life and Writings of George Washington. Jared Sparks. Boston, 1834–37; Boston, 1837. 12 vols.

DLC, NN, MWA, CSmH

The Life of George Washington. Jared Sparks. Vol. 1 of the *Life and Writings.* Boston, 1839. 562 p.

DLC, NN, MWA, CSmH, PU

George Washington. William O. Stoddard. N. Y., 1886. 307 p.

DLC, NN, MWA, CSmH

An Eulogy on General George Washington. Joseph Story. Salem, 1800. 24 p. DLC, NN, CSmH

From Farmhouse to White House: Life of George Washington. W. M. Thayer. Chicago, 1890. 503 p. DLC, NN, CSmH

George Washington. William R. Thayer. Boston, 1922. 274 p.

DLC, NN, CSmH, PU

George Washington. Thora Thorsmark. Chicago, 1931. 293 p.

DLC, NN, CSmH

Life of Washington. Virginia F. Townsend. N. Y., 1887. 267 p.

DLC, MWA, CSmH

Life of George Washington. James Trumbull. N. Y., 1829. 166 p. MWA, CSmH

The Character and Portraits of George Washington. H. T. Tuckerman. N. Y., 1859. 104 p. DLC, NN, MWA, CSmH

Washington, an Exemplification of the Principles of Free Masonry. Stephen H. Tyng. N. Y., 1852. 31 p.

DLC, NN, MWA, CSmH, MiD:B

The Life of Gen. Washington, First President of the United States. Charles W. Upham. Boston, 1840. 2 vols.

DLC, NN, MWA, CSmH, MiD:B

George Washington, Son of His Country. Paul Van Dyke. N. Y., 1931. 310 p. *DLC, NN, MWA, CSmH, PU*

A History of the Life and Death, Virtues and Exploits of General George Washington. Mason L. Weems. Georgetown, Phila., 1800. 84 p. *DLC, NN, MWA, CSmH, PU, MiU:C, RP:JCB*

A Life of George Washington, With Curious Anecdotes, Equally Honorable to Himself and Exemplary to His Young Countrymen ... Mason L. Weems. Phila., 1806. 228 p.
DLC, NN, MWA, CSmH, PU, MiD:B, MiU:C, RP:JCB

Life of George Washington, Embracing Anecdotes Illustrious of His Character. Horatio H. Weld. Phila., 1845. 222 p.
DLC, NN, PU, MiD:B

George Washington. Woodrow Wilson. N. Y., 1896. 333 p.
DLC, NN, MWA, CSmH, PU, MiD:B

Seven Ages of Washington. Owen Wister. N. Y., 1907. 263 p.
DLC, NN, MWA, CSmH, PU

George Washington: The Image and the Man. W. E. Woodward. N. Y., 1926. 460 p. *DLC, NN, PU*
2:77–144–264–329–386–435–505–562–654–662

WASHINGTON, MARTHA. *Martha Washington.* Anne H. Wharton. N. Y., 1897. 306 p. (Women of Colonial and Revolutionary Times) *DLC, CSmH, PU*
2:147–453

WASHINGTON, MARY.

Memoirs of the Mother and Wife of Washington. Margaret C. Conkling. Auburn, N. Y., 1850. 179 p.
DLC, NN, MWA, CSmH, PU, MiD:B

Mary and Martha; the Mother and the Wife of George Washington. Benson J. Lossing. N. Y., 1886. 348 p.
DLC, NN, MWA, CSmH

The Mother of Washington and Her Times. Mrs. Roger A. Pryor. N. Y., 1903. 367 p. *DLC, NN, MWA, CSmH*

The Mother of Washington. Nancy B. Turner and Sidney Gunn. N. Y., 1930. 284 p. *DLC, NN, PU*
2:147–337

WATERS, ABIGAIL. *Memoirs of the Life of Mrs. Abigail Waters.* Boston, 1817. *RP:JCB*

WATERS, WILBURN. *The Life and Adventures of Wilburn Waters, the Famous Hunter and Trapper of White Mountain Top.* Charles B. Coale. Richmond, 1878. 265 p. *DLC, NN, CSmH*

WATIE, STAND. *Life of General Stand Watie, the Only Indian Brigadier General of the Confederate Army and the Last General to Surrender.* Mabel W. Anderson. Pryor, Okla., 1915. 58 p.
DLC, NN, CSmH, MiD:B

WATKINS, W. H. *Life and Labors of W. H. Watkins.* T. L. Millen, ed. Nashville, 1886.

WATSON, ELKANAH. 2:542

WATSON, ELLEN. *Record of Ellen Watson.* Anna Buckland, ed. N. Y., 1884. 279 p. DLC, NN, PU

WATSON, RICHARD. *Life of Rev. Richard Watson.* Stephen B. Wickems. N. Y., 1856. 312 p. DLC

WATSON, THOMAS EDWARD.
The Life of Thomas E. Watson. William W. Brewton. Atlanta, 1926. 408 p. DLC, NN
The Life and Speeches of Thomas E. Watson. Thomas E. Watson. Nashville, 1908. 367 p.

WATT, JAMES. *James Watt.* Andrew Carnegie. N. Y., 1905. 241 p.
DLC, NN, PU

WATTS, ISAAC. *Memoirs of the Lives, Characters and Writings of Those Two Eminently Pious and Useful Ministers of Jesus Christ, Dr. Isaac Watts and Dr. Philip Doddridge.* Jeremy Belknap. Boston, 1793. 301 p. DLC, NN, MWA, CSmH, RP:JCB

WAYLAND, FRANCIS.
Francis Wayland. James O. Murray. Boston, 1891. 293 p. (American Religious Leaders) DLC, MWA, PU
A Memoir of the Life and Labors of Francis Wayland, Late President of Brown University. Francis and H. L. Wayland. N. Y., 1867. 2 vols. DLC, NN, MWA, PU

WAYNE, ANTHONY.
Life of Anthony Wayne. John Armstrong. (L.A.B.)
DLC, NN, PU
Hero of Stony Point; Anthony Wayne. James Barnes. N. Y., 1916. 209 p. DLC, PU
Mad Anthony Wayne. Thomas A. Boyd. N. Y., 1929. 351 p.
DLC, NN, PU
Anthony Wayne, Third General-in-Chief of the United States Army. John W. DePeyster. 1886. 34 p. DLC, NN, MiD:B
Mad Anthony, the Story of Anthony Wayne. Rupert S. Holland. N. Y., 1931. 259 p. DLC, NN
Life and Services of Gen. Anthony Wayne. H. N. Moore. Phila., 1845. 210 p. DLC, NN, CSmH, MiD:B

Anthony Wayne. Samuel W. Pennypacker. Phila., 1908. 45 p.
DLC, MWA, PU

A Gentleman Rebel; the Exploits of Anthony Wayne. John H. Preston. N. Y., 1930. 370 p. *DLC, NN, PU*

Anthony Wayne. Sometimes Called "Mad Anthony." John R. Spears. N. Y., 1903. 249 p. *DLC, NN, MWA, MiD:B*

Maj.-Gen. Anthony Wayne and the Penna. Line in the Continental Army. C. J. Stillé. Phila., 1893. 441 p.
DLC, NN, PU, MiD:B

The Life and Services of Anthony Wayne. Orville J. Victor. N. Y., 1861. 95 p. *NN, CSmH, MiD:B*
2:135

WEAVER, JAMES BAIRD. *James Baird Weaver.* Fred E. Haynes. Iowa City, 1919. 494 p. (Iowa State Hist. Soc.)
DLC, NN, CSmH, PU, MiD:B

WEAVER, JONATHAN. *Biography of Jonathan Weaver.* Henry A. Thompson. Dayton, O., 1901. 477 p. *DLC*

WEBB, SAMUEL BLATCHLEY. *Reminiscences of Gen'l. Samuel B. Webb, of the Revolutionary Army.* James W. Webb. N. Y., 1882. 402 p.
DLC, NN, CSmH, MiD:B

WEBER, JOSEPH, and FIELDS, LOUIS. *Weber and Fields; Their Tribulations, Triumphs and Their Associates.* Felix Isman. N. Y., 1924. 345 p. *DLC, NN, PU*

WEBER, KARL VON. 2:187

WEBSTER, DANIEL.
Godlike Daniel. Samuel H. Adams. N. Y., 1930. 426 p.
DLC, NN, MWA

American Statesman; or, Illustrations of the Life and Character of Daniel Webster. Joseph Banvard. 1853. 334 p.
DLC, MWA

Memoir of Daniel Webster. Charles H. Bell. Cambridge, 1881. 20 p. *DLC, MWA, MiD:B*

Daniel Webster. Allan L. Benson. N. Y., 1929. 402 p.
DLC, NN, PU, MiD:B

The Life, Eulogy, and Great Orations of Daniel Webster. L. G. Clark. N. Y., 1853. 72 p. *DLC, NN*

Life of Daniel Webster. George T. Curtis. N. Y., 1870. 2 vols. *DLC, NN, MWA, CSmH, PU, MiD:B*

The Last Years of Daniel Webster, a Monograph. George T. Curtis. N. Y., 1878. 55 p. *DLC, NN, MWA*

The True Daniel Webster. Sydney G. Fisher. Phila., 1911.
516 p.   *DLC, NN, PU*
Daniel Webster. Claude M. Fuess. Boston, 1930. 2 vols.
                              DLC, NN, MWA, CSmH, PU
Daniel Webster. Norman Hapgood. Boston, 1899. 119 p.
(Beacon Biographies)   *DLC, NN*
Reminiscences and Anecdotes of Daniel Webster. Peter Harvey.
Boston, 1877. 480 p.   *DLC, NN, MWA, CSmH, PU*
Daniel Webster. M. M. Jackson. Madison, Wis., 1885. 17 p.
                                                  DLC
Real Daniel Webster. Elijah R. Kennedy. N. Y., 1924. 271 p.
                                              DLC, NN
A Memoir of the Life of Daniel Webster. Samuel L. Knapp.
Boston, 1831. 234 p.   *DLC, NN, MWA, MiD:B*
Private Life of Daniel Webster. Charles Lanman. N. Y.,
1852. 205 p.   *DLC, NN, MWA, CSmH, MiD:B*
Daniel Webster. Henry C. Lodge. Boston, 1883. 372 p.
(A.S.)   *DLC, NN, MWA, CSmH, PU, MiD:B*
Life and Memorials of Daniel Webster. S. P. Lyman, Phila.,
1853. 2 vols. 1855–58. 3 vols.   *DLC, NN, CSmH, MiD:B*
Daniel Webster. Samuel W. McCall. Boston, 1902. 124 p.
                                              DLC, NN
Daniel Webster. John B. McMaster. N. Y., 1902. 343 p.
                                      DLC, NN, CSmH, PU
Daniel Webster and His Contemporaries. C. W. March. N. Y.,
1850. 295 p.   *DLC, NN, MWA, CSmH, MiD:B*
Daniel Webster. Frederic A. Ogg. Phila., 1914. 433 p.
(A.C.B.)   *DLC, NN, PU*
Daniel Webster. Eliz. A. Reed. Milwaukee, 1903. 180 p.
(Great Americans of History)   *DLC, NN*
Life, Speeches and Memorials of Daniel Webster. Samuel M.
Schmucker. Boston, 1859. 548 p.   *NN, MWA, CSmH, MiD:B*
Daniel Webster, His Life and Character. Benjamin F. Tefft.
Phila., 1854. 498 p.   *DLC, NN, CSmH*
Life . . . of Daniel Webster. Fletcher Webster. Boston, 1856.
2 vols.   *DLC*
Daniel Webster, the Expounder of the Constitution. Everett P.
Wheeler. N. Y., 1905. 188 p.   *DLC, NN, MWA*
    2:77–85–107–329–431–511–590
WEBSTER, GEORGE SMEDLEY. *George Smedley Webster.* Caroline W.
Smedley. n.p., n.d. 14 p. (Papers of Hist. Soc. of Frankford,
Phila., Pa.)

WEBSTER, NOAH.
Notes of the Life of Noah Webster. Emily E. F. Ford, comp.
N. Y., 1912. 2 vols. (Privately Printed)
DLC, NN, MWA, CSmH, PU
Noah Webster. H. E. Scudder. Boston, 1882. 302 p.
(A.M.L.) *DLC, NN, MWA, CSmH, PU, MiD:B*
Noah Webster. Ervin Shoemaker. N. Y., 1936. 347 p.
DLC, NN
Noah Webster; Schoolmaster to America. Harry R. Warfel.
N. Y., 1936. 460 p. *DLC, NN, CSmH, PU*
2:681
WEBSTER, REBECCA GAIR. *Biography of Mrs. Rebecca Gair Webster.*
T. D. P. Stone. Boston, 1848. 420 p. *DLC, MWA*
WEED, THURLOW. *Memoir of Thurlow Weed.* T. W. Barnes. Boston, 1884. (Vol. II of *Life of Thurlow Weed, Including His Autobiography and a Memoir*) *DLC, NN, MWA, CSmH, PU*
WEEKS, JOHN WINGATE. *Life of John W. Weeks.* Charles G. Washburn. Boston, 1928. 349 p. *DLC, NN, MWA, PU*
WEEMS, MASON LOCKE.
Parson Weems of the Cherry-Tree. Harold Kellock. N. Y., 1928. 212 p. *DLC, NN, MWA, PU*
Parson Weems; a Biographical and Critical Study. Lawrence C. Wroth. Balt., 1911. 104 p. *DLC, NN, MWA, MiU:C*
WEISER, CONRAD. *Life of Conrad Weiser, the German Pioneer, Patriot, and Patron of Two Races.* Clement Weiser. Reading, Pa., 1876. 449 p. *DLC, NN, MWA, PU*
WELD, FRANCIS MINOT. *Diaries and Letters of Francis Minot Weld, M.D. With a Sketch of His Life.* Sarah S. W. Blake. Boston, 1925. 245 p. *DLC, NN, MWA*
WELLINGTON, DUKE OF [ARTHUR WELLESLEY]. *Life of the . . . Duke of Wellington.* Francis L. Clarke and William Dunlap. N. Y., 1814. 423 p. *NN, MWA*
WELLONS, WILLIAM BROCK. *Life and Labors of Rev. William Brock Wellons, D.D.* J. W. Wellons and R. H. Holland. Raleigh, 1881. 448 p. *MWA*
WELLS, WILLIAM. 2:424
WELLS, WILLIAM CHARLES. *A Brief Study of . . . William Charles Wells, M.D.* Elisha Bartlett. Louisville, 1849. 32 p.
DLC, NN, PU, MiU:C
WENCKEBACH, CAROLA. *Carola Wenckebach, Pioneer.* Margarethe Muller. Boston, 1908. 289 p. *DLC, NN, MWA, PU*

WENDELL, BARRETT. *Barrett Wendell and His Letters*. Mark A. De
W. Howe. Boston, 1924. 250 p. *DLC, NN, MWA, CSmH, PU*
WENDELL, EVERT JANSEN. 2:425
WENTWORTH, JOHN. *John Wentworth, Governor of New Hampshire,*
1767–1775. Lawrence S. Mayo. Cambridge, 1921. 208 p.
DLC, NN, CSmH, PU, MiD:B
2:7
WESLEY, CHARLES. *Charles Wesley, Evangelist and Poet.* F. Luke
Wiseman. N. Y., 1932. 231 p. *DLC, NN, CSmH*
WESLEY, JOHN.
Life of John Wesley. B. W. Bond. Nashville, 1885. 210 p.
The Life of Rev. John Wesley, A.M. George Bourne. Balt.,
1807. 348 p. *MWA*
Rediscovery of John Wesley. George C. Cell. N. Y., 1935.
420 p. *DLC, NN, CSmH*
John Wesley; a Portrait. Abram Lipsky. N. Y., 1928. 305 p.
DLC, NN, PU
John Wesley. John D. Wade. N. Y., 1920. 301 p.
DLC, NN
Life of John Wesley. Caleb T. Winchester. N. Y., 1906. 301 p.
DLC, NN, PU
2:205–334
WESLEY, SUSANNA.
Susanna Wesley. Eliza Clarke. Boston, 1886. 301 p.
NN, MWA, PU
The Mother of the Wesleys. A Biography. John Kirk. Cin-
cinnati, 1865. 398 p. *NN*
WEST, BENJAMIN. *Benjamin West: His Life and Work.* H. E. Jack-
son. Phila., 1900. 115 p. *DLC, NN*
2:394–429
WEST, SIMEON HENRY. *Life and Times of S. H. West.* Simeon H.
West. Bloomington, Ill., 1908. 298 p. *DLC*
WESTCOTT, EDGAR NOYES. *An Account of the Life of Edgar Noyes*
Westcott in " The Teller, A Story." Forbes Heermans. N. Y.,
1901. 113 p. *DLC, NN, CSmH*
WESTINGHOUSE, GEORGE.
George Westinghouse, His Life and Achievements. Frank Crane.
N. Y., 1925. 34 p. *DLC, NN, PU*
George Westinghouse, His Life and Achievement. Francis E.
Leupp. Boston, 1918. 304 p. *DLC, NN*
Life of George Westinghouse. Henry G. Prout. N. Y., 1922.
375 p. *DLC, NN, PU*

WESTLEY, HELEN. 2:236

WETHERILL, CHARLES MAYER. *Charles M. Wetherill, 1825–1871.* Edgar F. Smith. Phila., 1929. 83 p. (Reprinted from the Jour. of Chem. Education) *NN, MWA*

WETZEL, LEWIS.

Life and Adventures of Lewis Wetzel, the Virginia Ranger. Cecil B. Hartley. Phila., 1860. 320 p. *DLC, NN, MiD:B*

Life and Adventures of Lewis Wetzel, Virginia Ranger and Scout. R. C. V. Meyers. N. Y., 1883. 414 p. *DLC, NN, MWA*

WHARTON, EDITH. *Edith Wharton.* Robert M. Lovett. N. Y., 1925. 91 p. (Modern American Writers) *DLC, NN, MWA, CSmH, PU*

WHEATON, ELIZA BAYLIES. *Life of Eliza Baylies Wheaton: Chapter in the History of the Higher Education of Women.* Harriet E. Paine, ed. Cambridge, 1907. 286 p. *DLC*

WHEATON, ROBERT. *Memoir of Robert Wheaton, With Selections From His Writings.* Boston, 1854. 124 p. *DLC, MWA, PU*

WHEATSTONE, SIR CHARLES. 2:25

WHEELER, JOSEPH.

Joseph Wheeler, the Man, the Statesman, the Soldier. T. C. De Leon. Atlanta, 1898. 142 p. *DLC, CSmH*

Gen. Joseph Wheeler. J. W. DuBose. N. Y., 1912. 476 p. *DLC, NN, CSmH, PU*

WHEELER, MARY COLMAN. *Mary C. Wheeler, Leader in Art and Education.* Blanche E. Williams. Boston, 1934. 244 p. *DLC, NN, MWA*

WHEELER, WAYNE BIDWELL. *Wayne Wheeler, Dry Boss; an Uncensored Biography of Wayne B. Wheeler.* Justin Steuart. N. Y., 1928. 304 p. *DLC, NN*

WHEELOCK, ELEAZAR. *Memoirs of the Rev. Eleazar Wheelock, D.D., Founder and President of Dartmouth College.* David McClure and Elijah Parish. Newburyport, 1811. 336 p. *DLC, NN, MWA, CSmH, MiD:B, MiU:C*

WHEELWRIGHT, JOHN.

Memoir of John Wheelwright. Charles H. Bell. Boston, 1876. 78 p. (Prince Soc. Publications) *DLC, NN, MWA, CSmH, PU, MiD:B, MiU:C*

John Wheelwright, 1592–1679. John Heard, Jr. Boston, 1930. 137 p. *DLC, NN, MWA, CSmH, MiD:B*

WHISTLER, GEORGE WASHINGTON. *A Sketch of the Life of George W. Whistler, Civil Engineer.* G. L. Vose. Boston and N. Y., 1887. 45 p. *DLC, NN, MWA*

WHISTLER, JAMES ABBOTT MCNEILL. *Life of James McNeill Whistler.*
Elizabeth R. and Joseph Pennell. Phila., 1908. 2 vols.
DLC, NN, CSmH, PU
2:84–114–123–429

WHITAKER, FESS. *History of Corporal Fess Whitaker.* Fess Whitaker. Louisville, 1918. 152 p. DLC, NN

WHITALL, JOHN MICKLE. *John M. Whitall; the Story of His Life.*
Hannah W. Smith. Phila., 1879. 338 p. DLC, NN

WHITE, CATHERINE PAYNE. *Frontier Mother, Catherine Payne White.*
Owen P. White. N. Y., 1929. 101 p. DLC, NN

WHITE, EDWARD. 2:395

WHITE, HENRY. *Henry White; Thirty Years of American Diplomacy.*
Allan Nevins. N. Y., 1930. 518 p. DLC, NN, CSmH, PU

WHITE, HUGH AUGUSTUS. *Sketches of . . . Capt. Hugh A. White.*
W. S. White. Columbia, 1864. 124 p. CSmH

WHITE, HUGH LAWSON. *Memoir of Hugh Lawson White.* Nancy N.
Scott. Phila., 1856. 455 p. DLC, NN, CSmH

WHITE, JAMES WILLIAM. *J. William White, M.D. A Biography.*
Agnes Repplier. Boston, 1919. 283 p.
DLC, NN, MWA, CSmH, PU

WHITE, JENNY C. *Memoir and Letters of Jenny C. White.* Rhoda E.
White. Boston, 1868. 363 p. DLC

WHITE, JOHN. *Memorials of Elder John White . . .* Allyn S. Kellogg. Hartford, 1860. 321 p. DLC, NN, CSmH

WHITE, JOHN. *John White, the Patriarch, of Dorchester (Dorset) and
the Founder of Massachusetts, 1575–1648.* Frances Rose-Troup.
N. Y., 1930. 483 p. DLC, NN, MiU:C
2:464

WHITE, JOSEPH. See CHURCHMAN, JOHN.

WHITE, JOSIAH. *Memoir of Josiah White.* Richard Richardson.
Phila., 1873. 133 p. DLC, NN, MWA, PU

WHITE, M. MORRIS. *M. Morris White, 1830–1913.* Mary C. Johnson. n.p., 1917. 134 p. (Privately Printed) NN

WHITE, PETER. *Hon. Peter White, a Biographical Sketch of the Lake
Superior Iron Country.* Ralph D. Williams. Cleveland, 1905.
205 p. DLC, NN, MWA, CSmH, PU, MiD:B, MiU:C

WHITE, WILLIAM.
The Life of Rt. Rev. William White, Bishop of Pennsylvania.
John N. Norton. N. Y., 1856. 103 p. DLC, NN, CSmH
Life and Times of Bishop White. Julius H. Ward. N. Y., 1892.
199 p. (Makers of America) DLC, NN

Memoir of the Life . . . of William White, D.D., Bishop of the Protestant Episcopal Church in . . . Pennsylvania. Bird Wilson. Phila., 1839. 430 p.　　　*DLC, NN, MWA, CSmH, PU*

WHITE, WILLIAM ALANSON. 2:592

WHITE, WILLIAM ALLEN. 2:592

WHITE BEAVER. 2:358

WHITE BULL. *Warpath; the True Story of the Fighting Sioux Told in a Biography of Chief White Bull.* Stanley Vestal. Boston, 1934. 291 p.　　　*DLC, NN, CSmH*

WHITEFIELD, GEORGE.

George Whitefield: a Biography With Special Reference to His Labors in America. Joseph Belcher, comp. N. Y., 1857. 514 p.
　　　DLC, NN, MWA, CSmH, MiD:B

Memoirs of Rev. George Whitefield . . . With an Extensive Collection of His Sermons and Other Writings. John Gillies. Middletown, Conn., 1798. 245 p.
　　　DLC, NN, MWA, CSmH, MiD:B, MiU:C

Life of Rev. George Whitefield. Daniel Newell. N. Y., 1846. 218 p.　　　*PU*

George Whitefield, Prophet-Preacher. Edward S. Ninde. N. Y., 1924. 222 p.　　　*DLC, NN*

WHITING, ALBERT BENNET. *Golden Memories of an Earnest Life. A Biography of A. B. Whiting: Together With Selections From His Poetical Compositions and Prose Writings.* Rachel A. Whiting. Boston, 1872. 293 p.　　　*DLC, NN*

WHITMAN, BERNARD. *Memoir of the Rev. Bernard Whitman.* Jason Whitman. Boston, 1837. 215 p.　　　*DLC, MWA*

WHITMAN, MARCUS.

Marcus Whitman, Pathfinder and Patriot. Myron Eells. Seattle, 1909. 349 p.　　　*DLC, NN, PU*

Marcus Whitman and the Early Days of Oregon. W. A. Mowry. N. Y. and Boston, 1901. 341 p.　　　*DLC, NN, CSmH*
2:41

WHITMAN, HELEN. *Poe's Helen.* Caroline Ticknor. N. Y., 1916. 292 p.　　　*DLC, NN, CSmH*

WHITMAN, WALT.

Whitman and Burroughs, Comrades. Clara Barrus. Boston, 1931. 392 p.　　　*DLC, NN, PU*

Walt Whitman. Richard M. Bucke. Phila., 1883. 236 p.
　　　DLC, NN, CSmH

Whitman: A Study. John Burroughs. Boston, 1902. 268 p.
　　　DLC, NN, MWA, CSmH, PU

Walt Whitman. George R. Carpenter. N. Y., 1909. 125 p. (E.M.L.) *DLC, NN, PU*

Walt Whitman, the Man. Thomas Donaldson. N. Y., 1896. 278 p. *DLC, NN, CSmH, PU*

Walt Whitman (The Camden Sage) as Religious and Moral Teacher, a Study. William N. Guthrie. Cincinnati, 1897. 105 p. (Pamphlet) *DLC, NN*

Whitman; an Interpretation in Narrative. Emory Holloway. N. Y., 1926. 330 p. *DLC, NN, CSmH, PU*

Whitman, the Poet-Liberator of Women. Mabel M. Irwin. N. Y., 1905. 77 p. *DLC, NN, MiD:B*

Walt Whitman, the Poet of Wider Selfhood. Mila T. Maynard. Chicago, 1903. 145 p. *DLC, NN*

Walt Whitman: A Brief Biography With Reminiscences. Harrison S. Morris. Cambridge, 1929. 122 p. *DLC, NN, PU*

Walt Whitman, His Life and Work. Bliss Perry. Boston, 1906. rev. ed. 1908. 334 p. (A.M.L.) *DLC, NN, MWA, CSmH, PU*

Walt Whitman. Isaac H. Platt. Boston, 1904. 147 p. (Beacon Biographies) *DLC, NN, CSmH, PU*

Magnificent Idler; the Story of Walt Whitman. Cameron Rogers. N. Y., 1926. 312 p. *DLC, NN, PU*

Walt Whitman, the Prophet-Poet. Ronald D. Sawyer. Boston, 1913. 76 p. *DLC, NN, MWA, PU*

With Walt Whitman in Camden. Horace Traubel. Vol. 1, Boston, 1906. Vol. 2, N. Y., 1908. Vol. 3, N. Y., 1914. 3 vols. *DLC, NN, CSmH,* (1906, 474 p.) *PU*

2:47–87

WHITNEY, ELI. 2:343–707

WHITNEY, JOSIAH DWIGHT. *Life and Letters of Josiah Dwight Whitney.* Edwin T. Brewster. Boston, 1909. 411 p. *DLC, NN, MWA, PU, MiD:B*

WHITTEMORE, THOMAS. *Memoir of Thomas Whittemore, D.D.* J. G. Adams. Boston, 1878. 388 p. *DLC*

WHITTIER, JOHN GREENLEAF.

John Greenleaf Whittier. Richard E. Burton. Boston, 1901. 134 p. (Beacon Biographies) *DLC, NN, MWA*

John Greenleaf Whittier. G. R. Carpenter. Boston, 1903. 311 p. (A.M.L.) *DLC, NN, MWA, CSmH, PU*

Whittier: Prophet, Seer and Man. B. O. Flower. Boston, 1896. 160 p. *DLC, NN, MWA, CSmH, PU*

John Greenleaf Whittier. Thomas W. Higginson. N. Y., 1902.
196 p. (E.M.L.) *DLC, NN, MWA, CSmH, PU*
John Greenleaf Whittier: His Life, Genius and Writings. W. S.
Kennedy. Boston, 1882. rev. ed. N. Y., 1892. 311 p.
DLC, NN, MWA, CSmH
John G. Whittier, the Poet of Freedom. W. S. Kennedy. N. Y.,
1892. 330 p. (American Reformer Series) *NN, CSmH*
Quaker Militant, John Greenleaf Whittier. Albert Mordell.
Boston, 1933. 354 p. *DLC, NN, CSmH, PU*
Life and Letters of John Greenleaf Whittier. S. F. Pickard.
Boston, 1894. 2 vols. *DLC, NN, MWA, CSmH, PU*
John Greenleaf Whittier. A Biography. F. H. Underwood.
Boston, 1884. 413 p. *DLC, NN, CSmH, PU*
2:6–40

WHITTINGHAM, WILLIAM R. *Life of William R. Whittingham.* W. F.
Brand. N. Y., 1886. 2 vols. *DLC, PU*

WICKES, LAMBERT. *Lambert Wickes, Sea Raider and Diplomat; the
Story of a Naval Captain of the Revolution.* William B. Clark.
New Haven, 1932. 466 p. *DLC, NN, CSmH*

WICKLIFF, JOHN. *The Life of Rev. John Wickliff.* Daniel Curry.
N. Y., 1846. 326 p. *DLC*

WIGGIN, KATE DOUGLAS. *Kate Douglas Wiggin as Her Sister Knew
Her.* Nora A. Smith. Boston, 1925. 382 p. *DLC, NN, CSmH*

WIGGLESWORTH, MICHAEL. *Memoir of the Rev. Michael Wigglesworth,
Author of the "Day of Doom."* John W. Dean. Albany, 1871.
160 p. *DLC, NN, MWA, CSmH, MiU:C*

WIGHT, ORLANDO WILLIAMS. *Memorial of O. W. Wight, M.D.* Jarvis
S. Wight. Cambridge, 1890. 266 p. *DLC, NN, PU*

WILBUR, CURTIS DWIGHT. 2:546

WILDE, RICHARD HENRY. *Life, Literary Labors and Neglected Grave
of Richard Henry Wilde.* C. C. Jones. Augusta, Ga., 1885. 21 p.
DLC, NN, MWA, CSmH
2:503

WILDER, JOHN THOMAS. *General John T. Wilder, Commander of the
Lightning Brigade . . .* Samuel C. Williams. Bloomington, Ill.,
1936. 105 p. *DLC, NN*

WILDER, MARSHALL PINCKNEY. *Memoir of Marshall P. Wilder.* John
H. Sheppard. Boston, 1867. 54 p. *DLC, NN, MWA, MiD:B*

WILEY, ALLEN. *Life and Times of Rev. Allen Wiley, A.M.* F. C.
Holliday. Cincinnati, 1853. 391 p. *DLC, NN, MiD:B*

WILEY, ISAAC WILLIAM. *Isaac W. Wiley, Late Bishop of the M. E. Church; a Monograph.* Richard S. Rusty. Cincinnati, 1906. 233 p.
NN

WILHELM, WILLIAM HERMAN. *William Herman Wilhelm.* Ethan A. Weaver. Wilmington, 1904. (Mem. Papers of the Soc. of Col. Wars in D. C., no. 3)
DLC, NN, MiD:B

WILKES, CHARLES. 2:262

WILKINSON, JAMES.
The Finished Scoundrel. General James Wilkinson, Sometime Commander-in-Chief of the Army of the United States. Royal O. Shreve. Indianapolis, 1933. 319 p.
DLC, NN

Wilkinson, Soldier and Pioneer. James Wilkinson. New Orleans, 1935. 238 p.
DLC, NN, CSmH, PU

WILKINSON, JEMIMA. *Memoir of Jemima Wilkinson, a Preacheress of the Eighteenth Century.* David Hudson. Bath, N. Y., 1844. 288 p.
DLC, NN, MWA, CSmH, MiU:C

WILLARD, EMMA.
Emma Willard and Her Pupils; or, Fifty Years of Troy Female Seminary, 1822–1872. M. J. M. Fairbanks, ed. N. Y., 1898. 895 p.
DLC, NN, PU

The Life of Emma Willard. John Lord. N. Y., 1873. 351 p.
DLC, NN, MWA, PU

Emma Willard, Daughter of Democracy. Alma Lutz. Boston, 1929. 291 p.
DLC, NN, MWA, CSmH, PU

WILLARD, FRANCES ELIZABETH.
The Beautiful Life of Frances E. Willard. Anna A. Gordon. Chicago, 1898. 416 p.
DLC, NN, MWA, CSmH

Life of Frances E. Willard. Anna A. Gordon. Evanston, Ill., 1912. 337 p.
DLC, PU

Frances Willard: Her Life and Work. Ray Strachey. N. Y., 1913. 310 p.
DLC, NN
2:9–92–180–325–506

WILLARD, SAMUEL.
Memoir of S. Willard. William W. Wherldon. Boston, 1865. 272 p.

Life of Rev. Samuel Willard . . . of Deerfield, Mass. Samuel Willard. Boston, 1892. 188 p.
NN, MWA

WILLARD, SIMON. *Willard Memorial; or, Life and Times of Major Simon Willard; With Notices of Three Generations of His Descendants.* Joseph Willard. Boston, 1858.
DLC, NN, MWA, RP:JCB

WILLIAM THE CONQUEROR.
 History of William the Conqueror. Jacob Abbott. N. Y.,
1878. 291 p.   *DLC, NN, PU*
 William the Conqueror. Phillips Russell. N. Y., 1933. 344 p.
          DLC, NN
WILLIAM OF ORANGE. *William the Silent, Prince of Orange, the Modern
Man of the Sixteenth Century* . . . Ruth Putnam. N. Y., 1895.
2 vols.   *DLC, NN, CSmH, PU*
WILLIAMS, CHARLES D.   2:487
WILLIAMS, DAVID ROGERSON. *Life and Legacy of David Rogerson
Williams.* Harvey T. Cook. N. Y., 1916. 338 p.   *DLC, NN*
WILLIAMS, ELEAZER. *Eleazer Williams: His Forerunners, Himself.*
W. W. Wight. Milwaukee, 1896. 263 p. (Parkman Club Papers,
No. 7)   *DLC, NN, MWA, MiD:B*
WILLIAMS, EPHRAIM.   2:542
WILLIAMS, SIR GEORGE.   2:675
WILLIAMS, JAMES LEON. *The Life and Work of James Leon Williams*
 . . . George W. Clapp. N. Y., 1925. 299 p.   *DLC, NN*
WILLIAMS, JOHN. *A Biographical Memoir of the Rev. John Williams,
First Minister of Deerfield, Massachusetts.* Stephen W. Williams.
Greenfield, Mass., 1837. 127 p.

          DLC, NN, MWA, CSmH, MiU:C
WILLIAMS, JOHN SHARP. *An Old-Fashioned Senator. A Story-Biog-
raphy of John Sharp Williams.* Harris Dickson. N. Y., 1925.
204 p.   *DLC, NN, PU*
WILLIAMS, RICHARD. *A Memoir of Richard Williams, Surgeon, Cate-
chist to the Patagonian Missionary Society in Tierra del Fuego.*
James Hamilton. N. Y., 1854. 255 p.   *DLC, NN, MWA*
WILLIAMS, ROGER.
 *Roger Williams; A Study of His Life, Times and Character of
a Political Pioneer.* Edmund J. Carpenter. N. Y., 1909. 253 p.
(Grafton Hist. Series)   *DLC, NN, MWA, CSmH, PU, MiD:B*
 Roger Williams, Prophet and Pioneer. Emily Easton. Boston,
1930. 399 p.   *DLC, NN, CSmH, PU*
 Roger Williams and the Baptists. E. C. Eddy. Boston, 1861.
          NN, MWA
 Life of Roger Williams. Romeo Elton. London and Provi-
dence, 1853. 173 p.   *DLC, NN, MWA, MiD:B*
 Roger Williams, New England Firebrand. James E. Ernst.
N. Y., 1932. 538 p.   *DLC, NN, MWA, CSmH, PU*

Life of Roger Williams. William Gammell. Boston, 1845.
221 p. *DLC, NN, MWA, CSmH*

Life of Roger Williams. William Gammell. Boston, 1854.
221 p. (L.A.B.) *DLC, NN, MWA*

Roger Williams. May E. Hall. Boston, 1917. 212 p.
DLC, NN, MWA

Spirit of Roger Williams. Lorenzo D. Johnson. Boston, 1839.
94 p. *DLC, NN, MWA, MiD:B*

Memoir of Roger Williams, the Founder of the State of Rhode Island. James D. Knowles. Boston, 1834. 437 p.
DLC, NN, MWA, PU, MiD:B, MiU:C, RP:JCB

Foot-Prints of Roger Williams; a Biography. Zachariah A. Mudge. N. Y., 1871. 285 p. *DLC, NN, MWA, CSmH*

Roger Williams, the Pioneer of Religious Liberty. Oscar S. Straus. N. Y., 1894. 257 p.
DLC, NN, MWA, CSmH, PU, MiD:B, RP:JCB

Roger Williams. Arthur B. Strickland. Boston, 1919. 152 p.
DLC, NN, CSmH

2:141

WILLIAMS, SAMUEL WELLS. *The Life and Letters of Samuel Wells Williams, LL.D.* Frederick W. Williams. N. Y., 1889. 490 p.
DLC, NN, MWA, PU

WILLIAMS, TALCOTT. *Talcott Williams, Gentleman of the Fourth Estate.* Elizabeth Dunbar. Brooklyn, 1936. 400 p. *DLC, NN, PU*

WILLIAMS, THOMAS. *Life and Speeches of Thomas Williams, Orator, Statesman and Jurist, 1806–1872.* Burton A. Konkle. Phila., 1905. 2 vols. *DLC, NN*

WILLIAMS, THOMAS. See TE-HO-RA-GWA-NE-GEN.

WILLIAMS, WILLIAM. *Old Bill Williams, Mountain Man.* Alpheus H. Favour. Chapel Hill, 1936. 229 p. *DLC, MWA, PU*

WILLIAMS, WILLIAM. *Oneida County Printer; William Williams, Printer, Publisher, Editor.* John C. Williams. N. Y., 1906. 211 p.
DLC, NN, MWA, CSmH, MiD:B

WILLIAMSON, HUGH.

A Biographical Memoir of Hugh Williamson. David Hosack. N. Y., 1820. 78 p. [Also in N. Y., Hist. Soc. Col. 1st Ser. Vol. V. p. 3] *DLC, NN, MWA, CSmH, MiD:B, MiU:C*

Life and Public Services of Hugh Williamson. John W. Neal. Durham, N. C., 1919. (Hist. Papers. Trinity College Hist. Soc. Series XIII. pp. 62–111) *NN, CSmH, PU*

WILLIAMSON, ISAIAH V. *The Life of Isaiah V. Williamson.* John Wanamaker. Phila., 1928. 170 p. *DLC, NN*

WILLIAMSON, JOHN. *John Williamson of Hard Scrabble.* M. A. Mc-
Coid. Chicago, 1902. 341 p. *DLC*

WILLIAMSON, JOHN POAGE. *John P. Williamson; a Brother to the
Sioux.* Winifred W. Barton. N. Y., 1919. 269 p. *DLC, NN*

WILLING, THOMAS. *Willing Letters and Papers; Edited With a Biographical Essay of Thomas Willing of Philadelphia (1731–1821).*
Thomas W. Balch. Phila., 1922. 227 p.

DLC, NN, MWA, MiD:B

WILLINGHAM, ROBERT JOSIAH. *Life of Robert Josiah Willingham.*
Elizabeth W. Willingham. Nashville, 1917. 282 p. *DLC, NN*

WILLIS, NATHANIEL PARKER. *Nathaniel Parker Willis.* Henry A.
Beers. Boston, 1885. 365 p. (A.M.L.)

DLC, NN, MWA, CSmH, PU, MiD:B

WILMARTH, BUTLER. *Memoir of Butler Wilmarth, M.D.* Wm. H.
Fish. Boston, 1854. 256 p. *DLC*

WILMER, RICHARD HOOKER. *Richard H. Wilmer, Second Bishop of
Alabama.* Walter C. Whitaker. Phila., 1907. 315 p. *DLC, NN*

WILMOT, DAVID. *David Wilmot, Free Soiler.* Charles B. Going. N. Y.,
1924. 787 p. *DLC, NN, CSmH, PU*

WILSON, ALEXANDER.

Sketch of the Life of Alexander Wilson. George Ord. N. Y.,
1828–29. 121 p. (in Wilson's *American Ornithology*)

DLC, NN, CSmH, PU

Life of Alexander Wilson. W. B. O. Peabody. (L.A.B.)

DLC, NN, MWA, PU

Alexander Wilson, Poet-Naturalist. James S. Wilson. N. Y.,
1906. 179 p. *DLC, NN*

WILSON, ALPHEUS WATERS. *Alpheus W. Wilson, a Prince in Israel.*
Carlton D. Harris. Louisville, 1917. 209 p. *DLC, NN*

WILSON, BIRD. *A Memorial of the Rev. Bird Wilson, D.D., LL.D.*
W. White Bronson. Phila., 1864. 212 p. *DLC, NN, MWA, PU*

WILSON, DANIEL. *Life, Last Words and Dying Confession of Daniel
Wilson, Who Was Executed at Providence, R. I., April 24, 1774.*
Boston, 1774.

WILSON, DANIEL.

Life and Correspondence of Rev. Daniel Wilson. Josiah Bate-
man. N. Y., 1860. 2 vols. *NN*

Life of Bishop Wilson of Calcutta. John N. Norton. N. Y.,
1863. 334 p. *DLC*

WILSON, ELIZABETH. *A Faithful Narrative of Elizabeth Wilson, Who
Was Executed at Chester, Jan. 3rd, 1786, Charged With the Murder
of Her Twin Infants.* Carlisle, 1786. *DLC*

WILSON, ERNEST HENRY. *Ernest H. Wilson, Plant Hunter.* Edward I. Farrington. Boston, 1931. 197 p.   *DLC, NN, MWA, PU*

WILSON, HENRY.
   Life and Public Services of Henry Wilson. Elias Nason. Boston, 1872. 419 p. (Famous American Series)   *NN, MiD:B*
   The Life and Public Speeches of Henry Wilson, Late Vice-President of the United States. Elias Nason and Thomas Russell. Boston, 1876. 452 p.   *DLC, NN, MWA*

WILSON, HENRY. *Henry Wilson, One of God's Best.* Madile Wilson and Albert B. Simpson. N. Y., 1908. 197 p.

WILSON, JAMES. *James Wilson (1742–1798) Signer of the Declaration of Independence.* Lucien H. Alexander, ed. Boston, 1907. 19 p.   *DLC, MWA, CSmH, MiD:B*

WILSON, JAMES. *Tama Jim.* Earley V. Wilcox. Boston, 1930. 196 p.
     DLC, NN

WILSON, JAMES. *Memoir of the Life of James Wilson . . . of Woodville.* James Hamilton. N. Y., 1859. 395 p.   *NN, PU*

WILSON, JOHN. 2:405–428

WILSON, SAMUEL THOMAS. *A Light of the Church in Kentucky; or, The Life, Labors and Character of the Very Rev. Samuel Thomas Wilson . . . Pioneer Educator and the First Provincial of a Religious Order in the U. S.* Victor F. O'Daniel. Washington, 1932. 333 p.
     DLC, NN, CSmH

WILSON, WOODROW.
   Woodrow Wilson; a Character Study. Robert E. Annin. N. Y., 1924. 404 p.   *DLC, NN, PU*
   Woodrow Wilson: Life and Letters. Ray S. Baker. N. Y., 1927–35. 6 vols.   *DLC, NN, CSmH, PU*
   Life of Woodrow Wilson. Josephus Daniels. Phila., 1924. 371 p.   *DLC, NN*
   Woodrow Wilson and His Work. William E. Dodd. N. Y., 1920. 369 p.   *DLC, NN, CSmH, PU*
   Woodrow Wilson: The Man and His Work. Henry J. Ford. N. Y., 1916. 322 p.   *DLC, CSmH, PU*
   Woodrow Wilson: the Story of His Life. William B. Hale. N. Y., 1912. 233 p.   *DLC, NN, CSmH*
   Woodrow Wilson. His Career, His Statesmanship, and His Public Policies. Hester E. Hosford. N. Y., 1912. 234 p.
     DLC, NN, PU
   Woodrow Wilson, the Dreamer and the Dream. Lucian L. Knight. Atlanta, 1924. 135 p.   *DLC, NN, MWA, PU*

True Story of Woodrow Wilson. David Lawrence. N. Y., 1924. 368 p. *DLC, NN, PU*

Woodrow Wilson; the Caricature, the Myth and the Man. Edith G. Reid. N. Y., 1934. 242 p. *DLC, NN*

Wilson the Unknown; an Explanation of an Enigma of History. Wells Wells. N. Y., 1931. 358 p. *DLC, NN*

Woodrow Wilson, the Man, His Times and His Task. William A. White. Boston, 1924. 527 p. *DLC, NN, CSmH, PU*

Woodrow Wilson, the Man Who Lives On. John K. Winkler. N. Y., 1933. 310 p. *DLC, NN*

2:77–94–116–205–325–388–395–493–670

WILSON, WILLIAM BAUCHOP. *W. B. Wilson and the Department of Labor.* Roger W. Babson. N. Y., 1919. 276 p. *DLC, NN*

WIMAR, CARL. *Carl Wimar: Biography.* W. R. Hodges. Galveston, Tex., 1908. 37 p. *DLC, NN, CSmH, PU*

WI-NE-MA. *Wi-Ne-Ma (the Woman Chief). Her People.* Alfred B. Meacham. Hartford, 1876. 168 p. *DLC, NN, MWA, PU*

WING, HENRY EBENESER. *A Reporter for Lincoln; Story of Henry E. Wing, Soldier and Newspaperman.* Ida M. Tarbell. N. Y., 1927. 78 p. *DLC, NN, MWA*

WING, JOSEPH ELWYN. 2:497

WINGATE, PAINE. *Life and Letters of Paine Wingate . . .* Charles E. L. Wingate. Medford, Mass., 1930. 2 vols. (Privately Printed) *DLC, NN, MWA, CSmH, PU*

WINKWORTH, SUSANNA. *Memorials of Two Sisters, Susanna and Caroline Winkworth.* Margaret J. Shain, ed. N. Y., 1908. 341 p. *DLC, NN*

WINSLOW, CHARLES LATHROP. *Memoir of Charles Lathrop Winslow, 1821–1832.* E. C. Hutchings. N. Y., 1837. 107 p. *NN, MWA*

WINSLOW, EDWARD. 2:141

WINSLOW, FRANCIS. *Francis Winslow; His Forebears and Life.* Arthur Winslow. Norwood, Mass., 1935. 352 p. (Privately Printed) *DLC, NN, MWA*

WINSLOW, HARRIET WADSWORTH LATHROP. *Memoir of Mrs. Harriet L. Winslow, . . . of the American Mission in Ceylon.* Miron Winslow. N. Y., 1840. 478 p. *DLC, NN, MWA*

WINSLOW, JOHN ANCRUM. *Life of John A. Winslow, Rear-Admiral, U. S. N.* J. M. Ellicott. N. Y., 1902. 281 p. *DLC, NN, CSmH*

WINSLOW, MARY. *Life in Jesus: a Memoir of Mrs. Mary Winslow.* Octavius Winslow. N. Y., 1860. 426 p. *DLC, NN*

WINSOR, JUSTIN. *Justin Winsor; a Memoir.* Horace E. Scudder. Cambridge, 1899. 32 p. *MWA, MiU:C*

WINTHROP, JOHN.
John Winthrop and the Great Colony; or, Sketches of the Settlement of Boston. Charles K. True. N. Y., 1875. 207 p. *DLC*
John Winthrop, First Governor of Massachusetts. Joseph H. Twichell. N. Y., 1891. 245 p. (Makers of America)
NN, MWA, CSmH
Life and Letters of John Winthrop. Robert C. Winthrop, ed. Boston, 1864–67. 2 vols.
DLC, NN, MWA, CSmH, PU, MiD:B, MiU:C
2:141–464

WINTHROP, JOHN. *A Sketch of the Life of John Winthrop the Younger, Founder of Ipswich, Massachusetts, in 1633.* Thomas F. Waters. 1899. 78 p. (Pub. of the Ipswich Hist. Soc.)
DLC, NN, CSmH, PU, MiD:B, MiU:C

WINTHROP, MARGARET. *Margaret Winthrop.* Alice M. Earle. N. Y., 1895. 341 p. (Women of Colonial and Revolutionary Times)
DLC, NN, MWA, CSmH

WINTHROP, ROBERT CHARLES. *Memoir of Robert Charles Winthrop.* Robert C. Winthrop, Jr. Boston, 1897. 358 p.
DLC, NN, MWA, CSmH, PU

WINTHROP, THEODORE. *Biographical Sketch of Theodore Winthrop.* George W. Curtis. Boston, 1861. 15 p. [in *Cecil Dreeme*]
DLC, NN, CSmH, PU

WIRT, WILLIAM. *Memoirs of the Life of William Wirt.* John P. Kennedy. Phila., 1849. 2 vols.
DLC, NN, MWA, CSmH, PU, MiD:B
2:218

WISE, HENRY AUGUSTUS.
A Biographical Sketch of Henry A. Wise, With a History of the Political Campaign in Virginia in 1855. James P. Hambleton. Richmond, 1856. 509 p. *DLC, NN, CSmH*
Life of Henry A. Wise. Barton H. Wise. N. Y., 1899. 434 p.
DLC, NN, CSmH, PU

WISE, ISAAC MAYER. *Isaac M. Wise, the Founder of American Judaism.* M. B. May. N. Y., 1916. 415 p. *DLC, NN*

WISHARD, LUTHER DELORAINE. *Luther D. Wishard, Projector of World Movements.* Charles K. Ober. N. Y., 1927. 199 p. *DLC, NN*

WISTAR, CASPAR.
Tribute to the Memory of the Late Caspar Wistar, M.D. David Hosack. N. Y., 1818. 17 p. *DLC, PU*

An Eulogium in Commemoration of Doctor Caspar Wistar. William Tilghman. Phila., 1818. 47 p. (in Medical Biographies and Other Papers) *DLC, PU*

WITHERSPOON, JOHN. *President Witherspoon . . .* Varnum L. Collins. Princeton, N. J., 1925. 2 vols. *DLC, NN, CSmH, PU*

WITHERSPOON, JOHN. *John Witherspoon.* D. W. Woods, Jr. N. Y., 1906. 295 p. *DLC, NN, MWA*

WITHINGTON, HIRAM. *Memoirs of Rev. Hiram Withington.* J. H. Allen. Boston, 1849. 190 p. *DLC, NN, MWA*

WITT, DANIEL. *The Life of Rev. Daniel Witt, D.D. of Prince Edward County, Va.* Jeremiah B. Jeter. Richmond, 1875. 276 p.

DLC, CSmH

WOEHLER, FRIEDRICH. 2:348

WOLCOTT, ROGER. *Roger Wolcott.* William Lawrence. Boston, 1902. 238 p. *DLC, NN, MWA, PU, MiD:B*

WOOD, FERNANDO.

A Model Mayor. Early Life, Congressional Career, and Triumphal Municipal Administration of Hon. Fernando Wood. A Citizen of New York. N. Y., 1855. 126 p.

DLC, NN, MWA, MiD:B

A Biography of Fernando Wood. A History of the Forgeries, Perjuries, and Other Crimes of Our "Model" Mayor. Abijah Ingraham. N. Y., 1856. 32 p. *DLC, NN, MWA*

Biography of Hon. Fernando Wood. Donald MacLeod. N. Y., 1856. 335 p. *DLC, NN, MWA, PU, MiD:B*

WOOD, LEONARD.

That Human Being, Leonard Wood. Hermann Hagedorn. N. Y., 1920. 126 p. *DLC, NN, PU*

Leonard Wood; a Biography. Hermann Hagedorn. N. Y., 1931. 2 vols. *DLC, NN, PU*

Leonard Wood, Administrator, Soldier and Citizen. W. H. Hobbs. N. Y., 1920. 272 p. *DLC, NN, PU, MiD:B*

Life of Leonard Wood. J. G. Holme. N. Y., 1920. 228 p.

DLC, NN, MWA, PU

Leonard Wood, Prophet of Preparedness. Isaac D. Marcosson. N. Y., 1917. 92 p. *DLC, NN, PU*

Career of Leonard Wood. Joseph H. Sears. N. Y., 1919. 272 p.

DLC, NN, PU

Leonard Wood: Conservator of Americanism. Eric F. Wood. N. Y., 1920. 351 p. *DLC, NN, PU*

WOOD, SAMUEL N. *Memorial of Samuel N. Wood.* Margaret L.
Wood. Kansas City, 1892. 251 p. *DLC, NN*

WOOD, T. W. 2:52

WOODBRIDGE, JOHN. *Memoir of Rev. John Woodbridge.* Sereno D.
Clark. Boston, 1877. 473 p. *DLC, NN*

WOODBRIDGE, MARY A. *Life and Labors of Mrs. Mary A. Woodbridge*
. . . Aaron M. Hills. Ravenna, O., 1895. 401 p. *DLC, NN*

WOODBRIDGE, WILLIAM. *The Life of William Woodbridge.* Charles
Lanman. Washington, 1867. 236 p. *DLC, NN, MWA, MiD:B*

WOODFILL, SAMUEL. *Woodfill of the Regulars; a True Story of Adventure From the Arctic to the Argonne.* Lowell Thomas. Garden
City, N. Y., 1929. 325 p. *DLC, NN*

WOODHOUSE, JAMES. *James Woodhouse, a Pioneer in Chemistry, 1770–
1809.* Edgar F. Smith. Phila., 1918. 299 p.
DLC, NN, MWA, PU

2:406

WOODHULL, VICTORIA. *Terrible Siren, Victoria Woodhull (1838–
1927).* Emanie L. Sachs. N. Y., 1928. 423 p.
DLC, NN, MWA

WOODRUFF, WILFORD. *Wilford Woodruff, Fourth President of the
Church of Jesus Christ of Latter-Day Saints, History of His Life
and Labors, as Recorded in His Daily Journals* . . . Matthias F.
Cowley. Salt Lake City, 1909. 702 p. *DLC, NN*

WOODS, LEONARD. *The Life and Character of Leonard Woods.* Edwards A. Park. Andover, 1880. 52 p. *DLC, NN, MWA*

WOODS, ROBERT ARCHEY. *Robert A. Woods, Champion of Democracy.*
Eleanor H. Woods. Boston, 1929. 376 p. *DLC, NN, MWA*

WOODWARD, ELLEN M. *Memoir of Ellen M. Woodward.* George D.
Miles. Phila., 1850. 199 p. *DLC*

WOODWARD, HENRY. *Dr. Henry Woodward, the First English Settler
in South Carolina and Some of His Descendants.* Joseph W. Barnwell. Charleston, 1908. 13 p. *NN*

WOODWARD, JOHN BLACKBURNE. *John B. Woodward; a Biographical
Memoir.* Elijah R. Kennedy. N. Y., 1897. 222 p.
DLC, NN, CSmH, MiD:B

WOOL, JOHN ELLIS. See WORTH, WILLIAM J.

WOOLLEY, EDWARD MOTT. *Memoir of Rev. Edward Mott Woolley.*
Fidelia W. Gillett and B. G. Grosh. Boston, 1855. 360 p.
DLC, MWA, MiD:B

WOOLSEY, MELANCTHON LLOYD. *Melancthon Lloyd Woolsey (1758–
1819). A Memoir.* M. Lloyd Woolsey. Champlain, N. Y., 1929.
33 p. *CSmH*

WOOLSON, CONSTANCE FENIMORE. *Constance Fenimore Woolson, Literary Pioneer.* John D. Kern. Phila., 1934. 198 p.

DLC, NN, CSmH, PU

WORCESTER, NOAH. *Memoirs of the Rev. Noah Worcester, D.D.* Henry Ware, Jr. Boston, 1844. 155 p. *DLC, NN, MWA*
2:406

WORCESTER, SAMUEL AUSTIN. *Cherokee Messenger (Samuel Austin Worcester).* Althea Bass. Norman, Okla., 1936. 348 p.

DLC, NN, MWA, CSmH

WORCESTER, SAMUEL. *Life and Labors of Rev. Samuel Worcester.* Samuel M. Worcester. Boston, 1852. 2 vols. *DLC, NN*

WORCESTER, THOMAS. *A Biographical Sketch of Thomas Worcester, D.D. . . . of the Boston Society of the New Jerusalem.* Sampson Reed. Boston, 1880. 140 p. *DLC, NN, MWA*

WORDSWORTH, WILLIAM.
William Wordsworth; His Life, Works and Influence. George M. Harper. N. Y., 1916. 2 vols. *DLC, NN, CSmH, PU*
Rediscovery of Wordsworth. Cornelius H. Patton. Boston, 1935. 258 p. *DLC, NN, PU*

WORTH, WILLIAM JENKINS. *Life of General Worth; To Which is Added a Sketch of the Life of Brigadier-General Wool.* N. Y., 1856. 256 p. *DLC, NN, MWA*

WOTTON, HENRY. *Life and Letters of Sir Henry Wotton.* Logan P. Smith. Oxford, 1907. 2 vols. *DLC, NN, CSmH, PU*

WRIGHT, CALEB. *Caleb Wright.* J. Habberton. Boston, 1901. 461 p.
DLC, NN

WRIGHT, CHAUNCEY.
Chauncey Wright. Philosophical Discussions. With a Biographical Sketch. Charles E. Norton. N. Y., 1877. 434 p.
DLC, NN
Letters of Chauncey Wright; With Account of His Life. James B. Thayer. Cambridge, 1878. 392 p. *DLC, NN, MWA*

WRIGHT, EDWARD. *Incidents in the Life of Edward Wright.* Edward Leach. Phila., 1871. 344 p. *NN*

WRIGHT, FRANCES. *Frances Wright.* William R. Waterman. N. Y., 1924. 267 p. *DLC, NN, CSmH*
2:150

WRIGHT, HENRY BURT. *Life of Henry B. Wright.* George Stewart. N. Y., 1925. 250 p. *DLC, NN*

WRIGHT, ORVILLE AND WILBUR. *Wright Brothers, Fathers of Flight.* John R. McMahon. Boston, 1930. 308 p. *DLC, NN, PU*
2:301–388

WRIGHT, SILAS.

A Life of Silas Wright, 1795–1847, United States Senator From New York, 1833–44, Governor of the State of New York, 1844–46. William E. Chancellor. N. Y., 1913. 128 p.   DLC, NN

The Life and Times of Silas Wright. R. H. Gillet. Albany, 1874. 2 vols.   DLC, NN, CSmH, PU

Life and Times of Silas Wright. Jabez D. Hammond. N. Y., 1848. 749 p.   NN, MWA, CSmH

The Life of Silas Wright, Late Governor of the State of New York. John S. Jenkins. Auburn, N. Y., 1847. 378 p.
     DLC, NN, MWA, CSmH, PU

2:349

WYANT, ALEXANDER HELWIG. 2:123

WYCHERLEY, WILLIAM. Brawny Wycherley; First Master in English Modern Comedy. Willard Connely. N. Y., 1930. 352 p.
     DLC, NN, CSmH, PU

WYLIE, ELINOR. Elinor Wylie; the Portrait of an Unknown Lady. Nancy Hoyt. N. Y., Indianapolis, 1935. 203 p. DLC, NN, PU

WYLLYS, JOHN P. See HALE, NATHAN.

WYMAN, JEFFRIES. Memoir of Jeffries Wyman, 1814–1874. A. S. Packard. Wash., 1878. 126 p.   PU

XENOPHON. Xenophon, Soldier of Fortune. Leo V. Jacks. N. Y., 1930. 230 p.   DLC, NN, PU

XERXES. History of Xerxes the Great. Jacob Abbott. N. Y., 1878. 302 p.   DLC, NN

YAMAGATA, AROMITO. 2:276

YANCEY, WILLIAM LOWNDES. The Life and Times of William Lowndes Yancey. John W. Du Bose. Birmingham, Ala., 1892. 752 p.
     DLC, NN, CSmH, PU

YATES, JOSEPH CHRISTOPHER. 2:349

YATES, RICHARD. The Life and Public Services of Richard Yates, the War Governor of Illinois. Logan U. Reavis. St. Louis, 1881. 37 p.
     DLC, NN

YEAMAN, WILLIAM POPE. Life and Writings of Rev. William Pope Yeaman. Joseph C. Maple. Columbia, Mo., 1906. 388 p. DLC

YORK, ALVIN.

Sergeant York and His People. Samuel K. Cowan. N. Y., 1922. 292 p.   DLC, NN

Sergeant York; Last of the Long Hunters. Tom Skeyhill. Phila., 1924. 240 p.   DLC, MWA

YORK, SARA EMILY. *Memoir of Mrs. Sara Emily York . . . Missionary to Greece.* Rebecca B. Medberry. Boston, 1853.   *MWA*

YOUMANS, EDWARD LIVINGSTON. *Edward Livingston Youmans, Interpreter of Science to the People.* John Fiske. N. Y., 1894. 597 p.
DLC, NN, MWA, CSmH, PU

YOUNG, BRIGHAM.

The Life of Brigham Young. Edward H. Anderson. Salt Lake City, 1893. 173 p.   *NN*

Brigham Young and His Mormon Empire. Frank J. Cannon and George L. Knapp. N. Y., 1913. 398 p.
DLC, NN, MWA, PU

Life Story of Brigham Young. Susa Gates and Leah E. Widstoe. N. Y., 1930. 338 p.   DLC, NN, MWA, CSmH

Life of Brigham Young. Edward W. Tullidge. N. Y., 1876. 168 p.   DLC, NN, CSmH

Brigham Young. M. R. Werner. N. Y., 1925. 478 p.
DLC, NN, MWA, CSmH, PU

Pictures and Biographies of Brigham Young and His Wives. Brigham Young. Salt Lake City, 1896. 40 p.
NN, MWA, CSmH

2:46–180

YOUNG, EDWARD. *The Life and Letters of Edward Young.* Henry C. Shelley. N. Y., 1914. 289 p.   DLC, NN, PU

YOUNG, ELLA FLAGG. *Ella F. Young and a Half-Century of the Chicago Public Schools.* John T. McManis. Chicago, 1916. 238 p.
DLC, NN

YOUNG, JOHN. 2:349

YOUNG, OWEN D. *Owen D. Young.* Ida M. Tarbell. N. Y., 1932. 353 p.   DLC, NN, MWA, PU

YOUNG, VIRGINIA CUSTIS. *A Gallant Life; Memories of Virginia Custis Young.* Edith Wathen. N. Y., 1934. 162 p.   DLC, NN

YOUNGER, ROBERT AND COLE. *Life of Bob and Cole Younger With Quantrell; Daring and Startling Episodes in the Lives of These Notorious Bandits.* Clarence E. Ray. Chicago, 1916. 189 p.
DLC, NN

ZAMORANO, DON AUGUSTIN V. *Don Augustin V. Zamorano; Statesman, Soldier, Craftsman, and California's First Printer.* George L. Harding. Los Angeles, 1934. 308 p.   DLC, NN, CSmH

ZAPATA, EMILIANO. *The Crimson Jester, Zapata of Mexico.* Harry H. Dunn. N. Y., 1933. 304 p.   DLC, NN

ZEISBERGER, DAVID. *Life and Times of David Zeisberger.* Edmund A. De Schweinitz. Phila., 1870. 747 p.

DLC, NN, MiD:B, MiU:C

ZELLE, MARGARETHA G. *Mata Hari; Courtesan and Spy.* Thomas Coulson. N. Y. and London, 1930. 312 p. *DLC, NN, PU*

2:576

ZENGER, JOHN PETER. *John Peter Zenger, His Press, His Trial . . .* Livingston Rutherford. N. Y., 1904. 275 p.

DLC, NN, MWA, CSmH, PU, MiU:C

2:660

ZEPPELIN, FERDINAND. *Ferdinand, Graf von Zeppelin.* Margaret Goldsmith. N. Y., 1931. 278 p. *DLC, NN, PU*

ZIEGFELD, FLORENZ. *Ziegfeld, the Great Glorifier.* Eddie Cantor and David Freedman. N. Y., 1934. 166 p. *DLC, NN*

ZOLA, EMILE. *Zola and His Time.* Matthew Josephson. N. Y., 1928. 558 p. *DLC, NN*

ZOROASTER. 2:665

ZUKOR, ADOLPH. *House That Shadows Built.* William H. Irwin. N. Y., 1928. 293 p. *DLC, NN*

ZWINGLI, ULRICH. *Life of Ulrich Zwingli, the Swiss Patriot and Reformer.* Samuel Simpson. N. Y., 1902. 297 p. *DLC, NN*

NOTE

Subjects are itemized under the titles of
Collective Biographies except in those cases
where the individuals exceed twenty in number.

PART II

COLLECTIVE BIOGRAPHIES

Listed by Authors

1. ABBOTT, JOHN S. C. *Kings and Queens; or, Life in the Palace.* N. Y., 1848. 312 p.

    Josephine and Maria Louisa, Louis Philippe, Ferdinand of Austria, Nicholas, Isabella II, Leopold, Victoria and Louis Napoleon. *DLC, NN, MWA, PU*

2. ABBOTT, JOHN S. C. *Lives of the Presidents . . . from Washington to the Present Time.* Boston, 1867. 480 p.

    DLC, NN, MWA, CSmH, MiD:B

3. ABBOTT, JOHN S. C., AND CONWELL, RUSSELL H. *Lives of the Presidents . . . from Washington to the Present Time.* Portland, Me., 1882. 640 p. *DLC, NN, MWA, CSmH, MiD:B*

4. ABBOTT, JOHN S. C., AND CONWELL, RUSSELL H. *Lives of the Presidents.* Chicago, 1902. 3 vols. *DLC, NN*

5. ABBOTT, LAWRENCE FRASER. *Twelve Great Modernists.* N. Y., 1927. 301 p.

    St. Francis, Erasmus, Herodotus, Voltaire, Thomas Jefferson, John Marshall, François Millet, George Stephenson, Beethoven, Emerson, Darwin, Pasteur. *DLC, NN*

6. ABBOTT, LYMAN. *Silhouettes of My Contemporaries.* N. Y., 1921. 361 p.

    P. T. Barnum, Edwin Booth, the Smiley Brothers, John B. Gough, Alice Freeman Palmer, John Fiske, Edward Everett Hale, John G. Whittier, General Samuel Chapman Armstrong, General William Booth, Daniel Bliss, Dwight Lyman Moody, Henry Ward Beecher, Phillips Brooks, Booker T. Washington, Rutherford B. Hayes, Abraham Lincoln, Theodore Roosevelt, Jacob Abbott. *DLC, NN, PU*

7. ABBOTT, WILBUR C. *Conflicts with Oblivion.* New Haven, 1924. 404 p.

    Pepys, Benjamin Disraeli, Sir William Monson, Colonel Thomas Blood, Oliver Cromwell, Sir John Wentworth, Venerable Bede, Colonel John Scott. *DLC, NN, CSmH, PU*

8. ABBOTT, WILBUR C. *Adventures in Reputation.* Cambridge, 1935. 264 p.
Thomas B. Macaulay, Lord Chesterfield, Queen Victoria, Oliver Cromwell, David Hume, James Bloxham.
DLC, NN, CSmH, PU

9. ADAMS, ELMER C., AND FOSTER, WARREN D. *Heroines of Modern Progress.* N. Y., 1913. 324 p.
Elizabeth Fry, Mary Lyon, Elizabeth Cady Stanton, Harriet Beecher Stowe, Florence Nightingale, Clara Barton, Julia Ward Howe, Frances E. Willard, J. Ellen Foster, Jane Addams.
DLC, NN, CSmH

10. ADAMS, H. G. *Cyclopedia of Female Biography.* N. Y., 1869. 788 p. *DLC, CSmH*

11. ADAMS, OSCAR FAY. *Dictionary of American Authors.* Boston, 1897. 444 p. Boston, 1905. 587 p.
DLC, NN, MWA, CSmH

12. ADDISON, DANIEL DULANEY. *Clergy in American Life and Letters.* N. Y., 1900. 400 p.
Timothy Dwight, William Ellery Channing, Theodore Parker, Horace Bushnell, Henry Ward Beecher, Phillips Brooks.
DLC, NN, CSmH, PU

13. AIKENS, ANDREW J., AND PROCTOR, L. A., eds. *Men of Progress.* Milwaukee, 1897. 640 p. *DLC, NN*

14. ALEXANDER, DE A. S. *Four Famous New Yorkers.* N. Y., 1923. 488 p.
Grover Cleveland, Thomas Platt, David Hill, Theodore Roosevelt. *DLC, NN*

15. ALLEN, DEVERE, ed. *Adventurous Americans.* N. Y., 1932. 346 p. *DLC, NN*

16. ALLEN, WILLIAM, ed. *American Biographical and Historical Dictionary.* Cambridge, 1809. 632 p.
DLC, NN, MWA, CSmH, MiD:B, MiU:C, RP:JCB

17. ALLISON, JOHN, ed. *Notable Men of Tennessee.* Atlanta, 1905. 2 vols. *DLC, NN*

18. *American Biography.* N. Y., 1876. 2 vols. *DLC, NN, PU*

19. *American Blue Book of Biography; Men of 1912.* Chicago, 1913. 656 p. *DLC, NN, CSmH, PU*

20. *American History and Biography.* N. Y., 1838. 258 p.
DLC, NN

21. *American Military Biography.* Cincinnati, 1825. 184 p.
DLC, NN, CSmH, MiD:B

22. *American Political and Military Biography.* n.p., 1825.   424 p.
    DLC, NN, PU, MiD:B, MiU:C
23. *American Portrait Gallery.*   N. Y., 1877.
    Presidents, Statesmen, Military and Naval Heroes, Clergymen,
    Authors, Poets, etc.   *DLC, NN, CSmH, PU*
24. *America's Greatest Men and Women.*   St. Louis, n.d.   256 p.
    NN
25. APPLEYARD, ROLLO.   *Pioneers of Electrical Communication.*   N.
    Y., 1930.   347 p.
    Maxwell, Ampere, Volta, Wheatstone, Hertz, Oersted, Ohm,
    Heaviside, Chappe, Ronalds.   *DLC, NN*
26. ARMOR, WILLIAM CRAWFORD.   *Lives of the Governors of Penn-*
    sylvania.   Phila., 1872.   528 p.   *DLC, NN, CSmH, PU*
27. ASHE, SAMUEL A'COURT, ed.   *Biographical History of North*
    Carolina.   Greensboro, N. C., 1905–17.   8 vols.
    DLC, NN, CSmH
28. ATKINSON, GEORGE W., AND GIBBENS, A. F.   *Prominent Men of*
    West Virginia.   Wheeling, W. Va., 1890.   1022 p.   *NN*
29. ATKINSON, WILLIAM BIDDLE, ed.   *The Physicians and Surgeons*
    of the United States.   Phila., 1878.   788 p.
    DLC, NN, MWA, CSmH, PU
30. BAGGER, EUGENE S.   *Eminent Europeans: Studies in Continental*
    Reality.   N. Y., 1922.   302 p.
    Queen Marie of Roumania, King Ferdinand of Roumania,
    Eleutherios Venizelos, Thomas G. Masaryk, John Bratiano, Jr.,
    Count Michael Karolyi, Ignace Jan Paderewski, Edward Benes,
    Admiral Horthy.   *DLC, NN, PU*
31. BAILEY, ISAAC.   *American Naval Biography.*   1815.   *DLC*
32. BAKER, JAMES H.   *Lives of the Governors of Minnesota.*   St.
    Paul, Minn., 1908.   480 p.   *DLC, NN, MWA, CSmH*
33. BALCH, MARSTON, ed.   *Modern Short Biographies.*   N. Y., 1935.
    383 p.
    Young Weston, Florence Nightingale, James Boswell, Leonardo
    da Vinci, H. M. King George III, The Wife of Abraham Lin-
    coln, The Sorrows of the Young Werther, Leuwenhoek, Aunt
    Mary Emerson, George Bellows, Hindenburg, Talleyrand, Ham-
    merstein, Margaret Baxter, Miss Ormerod, Helen Keller, Wil-
    liam Congreve, Dorothy Osbourne.   *DLC, NN, PU*
34. BALDWIN, CHARLES N.   *Universal Biographical Dictionary.*   N. Y.,
    1825.   444 p.   *DLC, NN, MWA, CSmH, MiD:B*

35. BALDWIN, JOSEPH GLOVER. *Party Leaders.* N. Y., 1855. 369 p.
Thomas Jefferson, Alexander Hamilton, Andrew Jackson, Henry
Clay, John Randolph of Roanoke.
DLC, NN, CSmH, PU, MiD:B

36. BARDEEN, CHARLES W. *Dictionary of Educational Biography.*
Syracuse, N. Y., 1901. 287 p. *DLC, NN*

37. BARNARD, HENRY, ed. *Educational Biography.* N. Y., 1859.
524 p. *DLC, NN, CSmH, PU*

38. BARNES, WILLIAM HORATIO. *The American Government.* N. Y.,
1873–74. 3 vols. *DLC, NN*

39. BARRETT, WALTER. *Old Merchants of New York.* N. Y., 1863–
66. 4 vols. *DLC, NN, CSmH, MiU:C*

40. BARTLETT, DAVID W. *Modern Agitators: or, Pen Portraits of
Living American Reformers.* N. Y., 1855. 396 p.
B. P. Rogers, Theodore Parker, Frederick Douglass, Ichabod
Codding, Harriet Beecher Stowe, Elihu Burritt, William Lloyd
Garrison, John B. Gough, Charles G. Finney, Joshua R. Gid-
dings, William Cullen Bryant, Lyman Beecher, Henry Ward
Beecher, E. H. Chapin, John G. Whittier, Horace Bushnell,
William H. Seward, James Russell Lowell, Horace Greeley,
Thurlow Weed Brown. *DLC, NN, MWA*

41. BASHFORD, HERBERT. *Stories of Western Pioneers.* San Fran-
cisco, 1928. 192 p.
Lewis and Clark, Jedediah Smith, Dr. John McLoughlin, Kit
Carson, John Charles Frémont, Ezra Meeker, Joaquin Miller,
Captain John A. Sutter, Dr. Marcus Whitman, Bret Harte,
Thomas Starr King, John Swett, Mark Twain, John Muir, The
Pioneer Mother. *DLC, NN*

42. BAY, W. V: N. *Reminiscences of the Bench and Bar of Missouri.*
St. Louis, 1878. 611 p. *DLC, NN, MWA, CSmH*

43. BEACH, SETH C. *Daughters of the Puritans.* Boston, 1905.
286 p.
Catherine M. Sedgwick, Mary L. Ware, Lydia M. Child, Dorothea L. Dix, Margaret Fuller Ossoli. *DLC*

44. BEARD, ANNIE E. *Our Foreign Born Citizens.* N. Y., 1922.
288 p. *DLC, NN, PU*

45. BEARD, RICHARD. *Early Ministers of the Cumberland Presbyterian Church.* Nashville, 1867. 319 p. *DLC, NN*

46. BECHDOLT, FREDERICK R. *Giants of the Old West.* N. Y., 1930.
245 p.
John Colter, Ashley and His Young Men, Stephen Fuller

Austin, William Becknell, James Pattri, Brigham Young, John Augustus Sutter, Alexander Majors, Charles Goodnight.

DLC, NN, MWA, PU

47. BEERS, HENRY A. *Four Americans.* New Haven, 1919. 90 p. Roosevelt, Hawthorne, Emerson, Whitman.

DLC, NN, CSmH, PU

48. BELKNAP, JEREMY. *American Biography.* Boston, 1794–98. 2 vols. 1857. 3 vols.

DLC, NN, MWA, CSmH, PU, MiD:B, MiU:C, RP:JCB

49. BELL, CHARLES H. *The Bench and Bar of New Hampshire.* Boston, 1894. 795 p. *DLC, NN, MWA*

50. BENESCH, ADOLPH B. *Men of Ohio in Nineteen Hundred.* Cleveland, 1901. 273 p. *NN*

51. BENGTSON, B. E. *Pen Pictures of Pioneers.* Holdrege, Neb., 1926. 2 vols. *DLC, NN*

52. BENJAMIN, S. G. W. *Our American Artists.* Boston, 1886. 193 p.

W. H. Beard, A. F. Bellows, R. S. Gifford, W. M. Chase, S. R. Gifford, W. Shirlaw, J. J. Enneking, T. W. Wood, S. Colman, W. Thompson, G. L. Brown, D. Neal. *DLC*

53. BENNETT, DeROBIGNE MORTIMER. *The World's Sages, Thinkers and Reformers.* N. Y., 1876. 1075 p. *DLC, NN*

54. BENTON, GUY PORTER, ed. *Memorials of Vermonters.* N. Y., 1917. 337 p. *DLC, NN*

55. BEST, MARY AGNES. *Rebel Saints.* N. Y., 1925. 333 p. George Fox, Margaret Fell, Thomas Lurting, Mary Fisher, Katherine Evans, Sarah Chevers, William Penn, Edward Burrough, Mary Dyer, Elizabeth Haddon. *DLC, NN, PU*

56. *Biographia Americana.* N. Y., 1825. 356 p. *DLC, NN, MiU:C*

57. *Biographical Cyclopedia and Portrait Gallery* [of Ohio]. Cincinnati, 1883–87. 4 vols. *DLC, NN*

58. *Biographical Cyclopedia of Representative Men of Rhode Island.* Providence, 1881. 589 p. *DLC, NN*

59. *Biographical Directory of the State of New York, 1900.* N. Y., 1900. 567 p. *DLC, NN, CSmH*

60. *Biographical Encyclopaedia of Illinois of the Nineteenth Century.* Philadelphia, 1875. 529 p. *DLC, NN*

61. *Biographical Encyclopaedia of Ohio of the 19th Century.* Cincinnati, 1876. 672 p. *DLC, NN*

62. *Biographical Encyclopaedia of Texas.* N. Y., 1880. 300 p. *NN*

63. *Biographical History of Central Kansas.* N. Y., 1902. 1633 p.
    DLC, NN
64. *Biographical History of Eminent and Selfmade Men of the State of Indiana.* Cincinnati, 1880. 2 vols. *DLC, NN*
65. *Biographical History of Northern Michigan; Containing Biographies of Prominent Citizens.* Indianapolis, 1905. 855 p.
    NN
66. Biographical Publishing Company. *Men of West Virginia.* Chicago, 1903. 2 vols. *NN*
67. *Biographical Review of the Leading Citizens of Columbia County, New York.* Boston, 1894. 603 p.
68. *Biographical Sketches of Members of the Indiana State Government, State and Judicial Officials, and Members of the 51st Legislative Assembly, 1879.* Indianapolis, 1879. 167 p. *NN*
69. *Biographical Souvenir of Georgia and Florida.* Chicago, 1889. 880 p. *NN*
70. *Biography of the American Military and Naval Heroes, of the Revolutionary and Late Wars.* N. Y., 1826. 2 vols. *NN*
71. BISHOP, MORRIS. *A Gallery of Eccentrics; or A Set of Twelve Originals & Extravagants from Elagabalus, the Waggish Emperor, to Mr. Professor Parson, the Tippling Philologer, Designed to Serve, by Example, for the Correction of Manners & for the Edification of the Ingenious.* N. Y., 1928. 244 p.
    Elagabalus, Brusquet, Jan Baptista van Helmont, Sir Thomas Urquhart, Sir Jeffrey Hudson, François Timolean de Choisy, Duke Mazrin, Captain Bartholomew Roberts, Bampflyde-Moore Carew, Edward Wortley Montagu, jun., Lorenzo da Ponte, Richard Parson. *DLC, NN, CSmH, PU*
72. BLAKE, JOHN LAURIS. *A Biographical Dictionary: Comprising a Summary Account of the Lives of the Most Distinguished Persons of All Ages, Nations and Professions; Including More Than Two Thousand Articles of American Biography.* Philadelphia, 1856. 1366 p. *DLC, NN, MWA, MiD:B*
73. BLANCHARD, CHARLES, comp. *The Progressive Men of the Commonwealth of Pennsylvania.* Logansport, Ind., 1900. 2 vols.
    DLC, NN
74. BLUMENFELD, RALPH DAVID. *R. D. B's Procession.* N. Y., 1935. 285 p.
    Thumbnail Sketches of some Fifty Famous Personages, among whom are: H. G. Wells, Mark Twain, P. T. Barnum, Sarah Bernhardt, Ellen Terry, Lloyd George, Buffalo Bill, Lawrence of Arabia, and eight Presidents of the U. S. *DLC, NN*

75. BOLTON, CHARLES KNOWLES. *The Founders; Portraits of Persons Who Came to the Colonies in North America before the Year 1701.* Boston, 1919–26. 3 vols.

DLC, NN, MWA, CSmH

76. BOLTON, SARAH K. *Famous American Authors.* N. Y., 1887. 325 p. *DLC, NN, MWA*

77. BOLTON, SARAH K. *Famous American Statesmen.* N. Y., 1888, 1925.

George Washington, Benjamin Franklin, Thomas Jefferson, John Adams, Alexander Hamilton, John Marshall, James Madison, Andrew Jackson, Daniel Webster, Henry Clay, Abraham Lincoln, John Hay, Theodore Roosevelt, Woodrow Wilson.

DLC, NN

78. BOLTON, SARAH K. *Famous Voyagers and Explorers.* N. Y., 1893. 509 p.

Christopher Columbus, Marco Polo, Ferdinand Magellan, Sir Walter Raleigh, Sir John Franklin, Dr. Kane, C. F. Hall and others, David Livingstone, Matthew Calbraith Perry, General A. W. Greely and other Arctic explorers.

79. BOLTON, SARAH K. *Famous Men of Science.* N. Y., 1899. 333 p.

Nikolaus Copernicus, Galileo Galilei, Sir Isaac Newton, Carl Linnaeus, Sir William Herschel, Baron Cuvier, Alexander Humboldt, Sir Humphrey Davy, John James Audubon, Michael Faraday, Sir Charles Lyell, Louis Agassiz, Charles Robert Darwin, Louis Pasteur, John Henry Fabre, Lord Kelvin, Thomas Henry Huxley. *DLC, MWA*

80. BOLTON, SARAH K. *Lives of Poor Boys Who Became Famous.* N. Y., 1913. 367 p. *DLC, NN*

81. BOYLE, ESMERELDA. *Biographical Sketches of Distinguished Marylanders.* Baltimore, 1877. 374 p. *DLC, NN, MWA*

82. BOYNTON, HENRY WALCOTT. *The World's Leading Poets.* N. Y., 1912. 346 p.

Homer, Virgil, Dante, Shakespeare, Milton, Goethe.

83. BRADFORD, ALDEN. *Biographical Notices of Distinguished Men of New England.* Boston, 1842. 464 p.

Statesmen, Patriots, Physicians, Lawyers, Clergymen, Mechanics. *DLC, NN, MWA*

84. BRADFORD, GAMALIEL. *American Portraits.* Boston, 1920–22. 248 p.

Mark Twain, Henry Adams, Sidney Lanier, James McNeill

Whistler, James G. Blaine, Grover Cleveland, Henry James, Joseph Jefferson. *DLC, NN, CSmH, PU*

85. BRADFORD, GAMALIEL. *As God Made Them: Portraits of Some Nineteenth-Century Americans.* Boston, 1929. 294 p.
Daniel Webster, Henry Clay, John Caldwell Calhoun, Horace Greeley, Edwin Booth, Francis James Child, Asa Gray.
DLC, NN, MWA, CSmH, PU

86. BRADFORD, GAMALIEL. *Bare Souls.* N. Y., 1924. 340 p.
Voltaire, Thomas Gray, Horace Walpole, William Cowper, Charles Lamb, John Keats, Gustave Flaubert, Edward Fitzgerald. *DLC, NN, CSmH, PU*

87. BRADFORD, GAMALIEL. *Biography and the Human Heart.* Boston, 1932. 283 p.
Henry Wadsworth Longfellow, Walt Whitman, Charlotte Cushman, William Morris Hunt, An American Pepys: John Beauchamp Jones, Jones Very, Letters of Horace Walpole, Biography by Mirror. *DLC, NN, CSmH, PU*

88. BRADFORD, GAMALIEL. *Confederate Portraits.* Boston, 1914. 291 p.
Joseph E. Johnston, J. E. B. Stuart, James Longstreet, P. G. T. Beauregard, Judah P. Benjamin, Alexander H. Stephens, Robert Toombs, Raphael Semmes. *DLC, NN, CSmH, PU*

89. BRADFORD, GAMALIEL. *Damaged Souls.* Boston, 1923. 284 p.
Benedict Arnold, Thomas Paine, Aaron Burr, John Randolph of Roanoke, John Brown, Phineas Taylor Barnum, Benjamin F. Butler. *DLC, NN, MWA, CSmH, PU*

90. BRADFORD, GAMALIEL. *Daughters of Eve.* Boston, 1930. 303 p.
Eve in the Apple-Orchard, Ninon de Lenclos, Madame de Maintenon, Madame de Guyon, Mlle de Lespinasse, Catherine the Great, George Sand, Sarah Bernhardt.

91. BRADFORD, GAMALIEL. *Naturalist of Souls.* Boston, 1917. 292 p. N. Y., 1926. 368 p.
1917 ed. Psychography, The Poetry of Donne, A Pessimist Poet (Giacomo Leopardi), Anthony Trollope, An Odd Sort of Popular Book (Anatomy of Melancholy) Alexander Dumas, The Novel Two Thousand Years Ago, A Great English Portrait Painter (Edward Hyde, Earl of Clarendon), Letters of a Roman Gentleman (Pliny), Ovid Among the Goths, Portrait of a Saint (Francis of Sales).
1926 ed. Psychography, Walter Pater, The Poetry of Donne, A Pessimist Poet, Anthony Trollope, An Odd Sort of Popu-

lar Book, Alexander Dumas, A French Lamb (Jules Le-
maître), A Great English Portrait Painter, A Gentleman of
Athens (Xenophon), Letters of a Roman Gentleman, Ovid
Among the Goths, and the Portrait of a Saint.

DLC, NN, PU

92. BRADFORD, GAMALIEL. *Portraits of American Women.* Boston,
1917–19. 276 p.
Abigail Adams, Sarah Alden Ripley, Mary Lyon, Harriet
Beecher Stowe, Margaret Fuller Ossoli, Louisa May Alcott,
Frances Elizabeth Willard, Emily Dickinson.

DLC, NN, CSmH, PU

93. BRADFORD, GAMALIEL. *Portraits of Women.* Boston, 1916.
201 p.
Lady Mary Wortley Montagu, Lady Holland, Miss Austen,
Madame D'Arblay, Mrs. Pepys, Madame de Sévigné, Madame
du Deffand, Madame de Choiseul, and Eugénie de Guérin.

DLC, NN, PU

94. BRADFORD, GAMALIEL. *The Quick and the Dead.* N. Y., 1931.
282 p.
Theodore Roosevelt, Woodrow Wilson, Thomas Edison, Henry
Ford, Nikolai Lenin, Benito Mussolini, Calvin Coolidge.

DLC, NN, MWA, PU

95. BRADFORD, GAMALIEL. *Saints and Sinners.* Boston, 1932. 261 p..
Caesar Borgia, Saint Francis of Assisi, Casanova, Thomas à
Kempis, Talleyrand, Fénelon, Byron. *DLC, NN, PU*

96. BRADFORD, GAMALIEL. *Union Portraits.* Boston, 1916. 330 p.
George B. McClellan, Joseph Hooker, George G. Meade, George
Henry Thomas, William Tecumseh Sherman, Edwin M. Stan-
ton, William H. Seward, Charles Sumner, Samuel Bowles.

DLC, NN, CSmH, PU

97. BRADFORD, GAMALIEL. *Wives.* N. Y., 1925. 298 p.
Confessions of a Biographer, Mrs. Abraham Lincoln, Mrs.
Benedict Arnold, Theodosia Burr, Mrs. James Madison, Mrs.
Jefferson Davis, Mrs. Benjamin F. Butler, Mrs. James Gil-
lespie Blaine. *DLC, NN, CSmH, PU*

98. BRASTOW, LEWIS O. *Representative Modern Preachers.* N. Y.,
1904. 423 p.
Friedrich Daniel Ernst Schleiermacher, Frederick William Rob-
ertson, Henry Ward Beecher, Horace Bushnell, Phillips Brooks,
John Henry Newman, James Bowling Mozley, Thomas Guthrie,
Charles Haddon Spurgeon. *DLC, PU*

99. BRAYMAN, JAMES O. *Daring Deeds of American Heroes.* N. Y., 1859. 499 p.   *DLC, NN, MWA, CSmH*

100. BRENDON, JOHN A. *Great Navigators and Discoverers.* N. Y., 1930. 281 p.   *DLC, NN, PU*

101. BRENNAN, J. FLETCHER, ed. *Biographical Cyclopaedia and Portrait Gallery of Distinguished Men . . . of Ohio.* Cincinnati, 1879. 504 p.   *DLC, NN*

102. *Brief Biographies: A Biographical Dictionary of Who's Who in Maine.* Lewiston, Me., 1926.   *DLC, NN*

103. BROCKETT, LINUS PIERPONT. *Men of our Day; or Biographical Sketches of Patriots, Orators, Statesmen, Generals, Reformers, Financiers, and Merchants.* Phila., 1872. 696 p.
     DLC, NN, CSmH, PU, MiD:B

104. BROCKETT, LINUS PIERPONT. *Our Great Captains.* N. Y., 1865. 292 p.
Grant, Sherman, Thomas, Sheridan, Farragut.
     DLC, NN, MWA, CSmH

105. BROOKS, ELBRIDGE S. *The Century Book of Famous Americans.* N. Y., 1896. 251 p.   *DLC, NN, CSmH*

106. BROOKS, ELBRIDGE S. *Historic Americans.* N. Y., 1899. 384 p.
     DLC, NN, CSmH

106a. BROOKS, ELIZABETH. *Prominent Women of Texas.* Akron, O., 1896. 206 p.   *CSmH*

107. BROOKS, NOAH. *Statesmen.* N. Y., 1895. 347 p.
Henry Clay, Daniel Webster, John C. Calhoun, Thomas H. Benton, William H. Seward, Salmon P. Chase, Abraham Lincoln, Charles Sumner, Samuel J. Tilden, James G. Blaine, James A. Garfield, Grover Cleveland.
     DLC, NN, MWA, CSmH, MiD:B

108. BROOKS, ULYSSES R. *South Carolina Bench and Bar.* Columbia, S. C., 1908. 381 p.   *DLC, NN, CSmH*

109. BROWN, CHARLES REYNOLDS. *They Were Giants.* N. Y., 1934. 279 p.
Benjamin Franklin, Horace Bushnell, Anthony Trollope, Peter Cooper, Edward Everett Hale, Silas Weir Mitchell, Phillips Brooks, David Starr Jordan, Washington Gladden, Abraham Lincoln.   *DLC, NN*

110. BROWN, DAVID PAUL. *The Forum; or, Forty Years Full Practice at the Philadelphia Bar.* Phila., 1856. 2 vols.
Thomas M'Kean, Bushrod Washington, William Tilghman, Hugh Henry Brackenridge, John Bannister Gibson, William

Lewis, Jared Ingersoll, William Bradford, William Rawle, Alexander J. Dallas, Sampson Levy, Henry Baldwin, Robert C. Grier, Jeremiah S. Black, Ellis Lewis, John Sergeant, and the Sitting Judges of the Supreme Court, Philadelphia County Court, and the Court of Common Pleas.

DLC, NN, MWA, CSmH, PU

111. BROWN, JOHN HOWARD. *American Naval Heroes.* Boston, 1899. 607 p. *NN, MiU:C*

112. BROWN, JOHN HOWARD. *Cyclopaedia of American Biographies.* Boston, 1897–1903. 7 vols. *DLC, NN*

113. BROWN, JOHN HOWARD, ed. *Biographical Dictionary of America.* 1906. 10 vols. *DLC, NN, PU*

114. BROWN, ROLLO W. *Lonely Americans.* N. Y., 1929. 319 p. Charles W. Eliot, James McNeill Whistler, Edward MacDowell, George Bellows, Charles Eliot Norton, Raphael Pumpelly, Emily Dickinson, Abraham Lincoln. *DLC, NN, MWA*

115. BRUCE, J. E., comp. *Short Biographical Sketches of Eminent Negro Men and Women in Europe and the U. S.* Yonkers, 1910. *CSmH*

116. BRUCE, PHILIP ALEXANDER. *The Virginia Plutarch.* Chapel Hill, 1929. 2 vols. *DLC, NN, MWA, CSmH*

117. BUCHHOLZ, HEINRICH EWOLD. *Governors of Maryland from the Revolution to the Year 1908.* Balt., 1908. 300 p. *DLC, NN, MWA*

118. *Builders of the Nation.* N. Y., 1892. 2 vols. *DLC, NN, PU*

119. BUNGAY, GEORGE W. *Off-Hand Takings; or, Crayon Sketches of the Noticeable Men of Our Age.* N. Y., 1854. 408 p. *DLC, NN, MWA, PU, MiD:B*

120. BURTON, GEORGE WARD. *Men of Achievement in the Great Southwest.* Los Angeles, 1904. 149 p. *DLC, NN, CSmH*

121. BUSCH, NIVEN, JR. *Twenty-one Americans.* N. Y., 1930. 332 p. *DLC, NN*

122. BYRNE, THOMAS. *Professional Criminals of America.* 1895. *DLC*

123. CAFFIN, CHARLES H. *American Masters of Sculpture.* N. Y., 1902. 195 p. *NN* George Inness, John La Farge, James A. McNeill Whistler, John Singer Sargent, Winslow Homer, Edwin A. Abbey, George Fuller, Homer D. Martin, George de Forest Brush, Alexander H. Wyant, Dwight W. Tryon, Horatio Walker, Gilbert Stuart. *DLC, NN, PU*

124. CALDWELL, JOSHUA W. *Sketches of the Bench and Bar of Tennessee.* Knoxville, 1898. 399 p.   *DLC, NN, MWA*

124a. *California Masonry.* Los Angeles, 1936. 3 vols.

125. CAMPBELL, J. H. *Georgia Baptists.* Macon, 1874. 502 p. *NN*

126. CAMPBELL, JOHN A., ed. *Biographical History of Prominent Men of the Great West.* Chicago, 1902. 688 p.   *DLC, NN*

127. CAMPBELL, THOMAS J. *Pioneer Laymen of North America.* N. Y., 1915. 2 vols.

> I. Jacques Cartier, Pedro Menendez, Samuel Champlain, Charles de la Tour, Maisonneuve, Charles Le Moyne, Pierre Esprit Radisson; II. Le Moyne de Longueuil, Nicolas Perrot, Le Moyne d'Iberville, Frontenac, La Salle, Le Moyne de Bienville, Pierre Gaultier de Verendyre, John McLoughlin.   *DLC, NN*

128. CARROLL, HOWARD. *Twelve Americans: Their Lives and Times.* N. Y., 1883. 473 p.

> Horatio Seymour, Charles Francis Adams, Peter Cooper, Hannibal Hamlin, John Gilbert, Robert C. Schenck, Frederick Douglass, William Allen, Allen G. Thurman, Joseph Jefferson, Elihu B. Washburne, Alexander H. Stephens.
>   *DLC, NN, MWA, PU, MiU:C*

129. CARSON, HAMPTON L. *History of the Supreme Court of the U. S.* Phila., 1904. 2 vols.   *DLC, NN, MWA, CSmH*

130. CARTER, NATHAN F. *Native Ministry of New Hampshire.* Concord, N. H., 1906. 1017 p.   *DLC, NN, MWA, CSmH*

131. CATTELL, JAMES M. *American Men of Science. A Biographical Directory.* N. Y., 1906–1933. 1278 p.
    DLC, NN, MWA, CSmH, PU

131a. CATTELL, JAMES M. *Leaders in Education.* N. Y., 1932. 1037 p.   *CSmH*

132. *Century Biographical Encyclopedia.* N. Y., 1922.
    DLC, NN, MiD:B

133. CHADWICK, EARL L. *Conservative Advocate: Biographies of Connecticut's Successful Men.* Hartford, 1909. 122 p.
    DLC, NN

134. CHAMBERLAIN, J. S., ed. *Makers of Millions; or, The Marvelous Success of America's Self-Made Men.* Chicago, 1899. 598 p.
    NN

134a. CHAMPLIN, J. D. *Cyclopedia of Painters.* N. Y., 1886–87. 4 vols.   *CSmH*

135. CHAPPELL, ABSALOM HARRIS. *Miscellanies of Georgia.* Atlanta, 1874. 3 parts.

1: The Oconee War; Alexander McGillivray, General Elijah Clark, Col. Benjamin Hawkins. 2: Middle Georgia; Middle Georgia and the Negro, Middle Georgia and the Land Lottery System, The Pine Mountain, King's Gap and King's Trails, The Pine Barren Speculation in 1794–1795, The Yazoo Fraud. 3: General James Jackson, General Anthony Wayne.

NN, CSmH

136. CHASE, HENRY, ed. *Representative Men of Maine.* Portland, Me., 1893. 250 p. *DLC, NN*

137. CHEEVER, GEORGE B. *Poets of America.* Hartford, 1847. 405 p. *DLC, NN, MWA*

138. CHILD, LYDIA M. *The Ladies Family Library.* Boston, 1832. 248 p. Boston, 1833. 288 p.
1. Lady Russell and Madame Guyon; 2. Madame de Staël and Madame Roland; 3. Biographies of Good Wives.

DLC, NN, MWA, CSmH

139. CHILDE, CROMWELL, comp. *Pocket History of the Commanders of the American Army.* N. Y., 1899. 95 p. *DLC*

140. CLARK, BARRETT H., ed. *Great Short Biographies of the World.* N. Y., 1928. 1407 p. *DLC, NN, MWA, PU*

141. CLARK, MARY. *Biographical Sketches of the Fathers of New England.* Concord, N. H., 1836. 180 p.
John Robinson, John Carver, Edward Winslow, William Brewster, William Bradford, Robert Cushman, Miles Standish, John Winthrop, Roger Williams. *DLC, NN, MWA*

142. CLARK, RUFUS WHEELWRIGHT. *Heroes of Albany.* Albany, 1867. 870 p. *DLC, NN, MWA, CSmH*

143. CLARK, W. J., JR. *Great American Sculptors.* Phila., 1877. 144 p. *DLC, NN, MWA*

144. CLARKE, JAMES FREEMAN. *Memorial and Biographical Sketches.* Boston, 1878. 434 p.
John Albion Andrew, James Freeman, Charles Sumner, Theodore Parker, Samuel Gridley Howe, William Ellery Channing, Walter Channing, Ezra Stiles Gannett, Samuel Joseph May, Susan Dimock, George Keats, Robert J. Breckenridge, George Denison Prentice, Junius Brutus Booth, Washington, Shakespeare, Jean Jacques Rousseau, William Hull.

DLC, NN, MWA, PU

145. CLARKE, RICHARD HENRY. *Lives of the Deceased Bishops of the Catholic Church in the U. S.* N. Y., 1872–88. 3 vols.

DLC, NN, CSmH, MiD:B

146. CLEMENS, WILL M. *Famous Funny Fellows.* N. Y., 1882. 214 p. *DLC, NN, PU*

147. CLEMENT, J., ed. *Noble Deeds of American Women.* Auburn, N. Y., 1854. 480 p.
Mother of Washington, Wife of Washington, Wife of John Adams, Ann H. Hudson. *NN, CSmH, PU, MiD:B*

148. CLEVELAND NEWS and CLEVELAND LEADER. *Men of Ohio.* n.p., n.d. 193 p. *NN*

149. COFFIN, CHARLES, comp. *Lives and Services.* N. Y., 1845. 222 p.
Major General John Thomas, Colonel Thomas Knowlton, Colonel Alexander Scammell, Major-General Henry Dearborn. *DLC, NN, MWA, MiU:C*

150. COLEMAN, MCALISTER. *Pioneers of Freedom.* N. Y., 1929. 222 p.
Thomas Paine, Thomas Jefferson, Frances Wright, Wendell Phillips, John P. Altgeld, Henry George, Samuel Gompers, Eugene Debs, John Mitchell, Charles Steinmetz. *DLC, NN, PU*

151. COLLINS, FREDERICK LEWIS. *Our American Kings.* N. Y., 1924. 257 p.
Calling on Governors, The " Wet " Smiths, The " Dry " Pinchots, Percy Baxter, Vic Donahey, Jake and Mrs. Jake, and Jack; The Blaines of Boscobel, Ephraim Morgan, Nestos from Norway, Working Hard With Ritchie, Pat and His Hat, Richardson of California, Hart of Washington, The Big Man in the Little White House, A. J., a Lonely Soul; Cross Country, Some Conclusions. *DLC, NN, MWA, PU*

152. COLLINS, JOSEPH. *The Doctor Looks at Biography.* N. Y., 1925. 344 p. *DLC, NN, PU*

153. *Contemporary American Biography.* N. Y., 1892. 1 vol. *DLC, NN, MiD:B*

154. COOPER, JAMES FENIMORE. *Lives of Distinguished Naval Officers.* Phila., 1846. 2 vols. *DLC, NN, CSmH*

155. CORNELL, WILLIAM MASON. *Lives of Clergymen, Physicians, and Eminent Business Men of the 19th Century.* Boston, 1881. 1 vol. *NN, MWA*

156. CORNELL, WILLIAM MASON. *Recollections of " Ye Olden Time."* Boston, 1878. 436 p. *DLC, NN*

157. COURNOS, JOHN. *A Modern Plutarch.* Indianapolis, 1928. 428 p. *DLC, NN, PU*

158. **Coursey, Oscar William.** *Who's Who in South Dakota*. Mitchell, S. D., 1916–25. 3 vols. *DLC, NN*

159. **Cowley, Matthias F.** *Prophets and Patriarchs of the Church of Jesus Christ of Latter-Day Saints.* Chattanooga, 1902. 505 p. *NN*

160. **Coxe, J. R.** *Female Biography.* 2 vols.

161. **Craven, Thomas.** *Men of Art.* N. Y., 1931. 524 p.
Giotto, Leonardo Da Vinci, Michelangelo, Titian, Rubens, Rembrandt, El Greco, Velasquez, Goya, Hogarth, Blake, Turner, Ryder, Delacroix, Cézanne. *DLC, NN, PU*

162. **Crawford, Mary Caroline.** *Famous Families of Massachusetts.* Boston, 1930. 2 vols. *DLC, NN, MWA*

163. **Creegan, C. C., and Goodnow, J. A. B.** *Great Missionaries of the Church.* N. Y., 1895. 404 p. *NN*

164. **Creel, George.** *Sons of the Eagle.* Indianapolis, 1927. 321 p. *DLC, NN, MWA*

165. **Crockett, Walter Hill, ed.** *Vermonters: Book of Biographies.* Brattleboro, 1931. 254 p. *DLC, NN, MWA, PU*

166. **Crosby, Nathan.** *Annual Obituary Notices of Eminent Persons in the U. S.* Boston, 1858–59. 2 vols. *DLC, NN, MWA, CSmH, PU*

167. **Cullum, G. W.** *Campaigns of War of 1812–15.* N. Y., 1879. 412 p. *DLC, NN, CSmH*

168. **Cutler, Julia P.** *Founders of Ohio.* Cincinnati, 1888. 28 p. *DLC, NN, CSmH*

169. **Cutter, William Richard, ed.** *Memorial Encyclopaedia of the State of Massachusetts.* N. Y., 1917. 3 vols. *NN*

170. **Daniell, Lewis E.** *Personnel of the Texas State Government.* Austin, 1887. 317 p. *DLC, NN, CSmH*

171. **Daniell, Lewis E.** *Types of Successful Men of Texas.* Austin, 1890. 631 p. *DLC, NN, CSmH*

172. **Davis, Richard Harding.** *Real Soldiers of Fortune.* N. Y., 1906. 233 p.
Major-General Henry Ronald Douglas MacIver, Baron James Harden-Hickey, Winston Spencer Churchill, Captain Philo Norton McGiffin, General William Walker, the King of the Filibusters, Major Burnham, Chief of Scouts. *DLC, NN, CSmH*

173. **Davis, William T.** *Bench and Bar of the Commonwealth of Massachusetts.* Boston, 1895. 2 vols. *DLC, MWA*

174. **De Goesbriand, Louis.** *Catholic Memoirs of Vermont and New Hampshire.* Burlington, Vt., 1886. 166 p. *DLC, NN, MWA*

175. DE KRUIF, PAUL H. *Men Against Death.* N. Y., 1932. 363 p.
Semmelweis, Banting, Minot, Spencer, Evans, McCoy, Schaudinn, Bordet, Wagne-Jauregg, Finsen, Rollier, Strandberg.

DLC, NN

176. DE KRUIF, PAUL H. *Microbe Hunters.* N. Y., 1926. 363 p.
Leeuwenhoek, Spallanzani, Pasteur, Koch, Roux, Behring, Metchnikoff, Theobald Smith, David Bruce, Roland Ross, Batista Grassi, Walter Reed, Paul Ehrlich. *DLC, NN, PU*

177. DELAPLAINE, JOSEPH. *Delaplaine's Repository of Distinguished American Characters.* Philadelphia, 1815. 106 p.

DLC, NN, MWA, CSmH, MiU:C

178. DENVER PRESS CLUB. *Who's Who in the Rockies.* Denver, 1923. 168 p. *DLC, NN*

179. DERBY, G., comp. *National Cyclopedia of American Biography.* N. Y., 1893. 752 p. *NN*

180. DIBBLE, ROY F. *Strenuous Americans.* N. Y., 1923. 370 p.
Jesse James, Admiral Dewey, Brigham Young, Frances E. Willard, James J. Hill, P. T. Barnum, Mark Twain.

DLC, NN

181. DICKINSON, ASA DON, ed. *Stories of Achievement.* N. Y., 1916. 6 vols.
Inspiration and Suggestion, Warriors and Statesmen, Orators and Reformers, Authors and Journalists, Scientists, Inventors and Explorers, Men of Affairs. *DLC, NN*

182. *Distinguished Men of Philadelphia and of Pennsylvania.* Phila., 1913. 102 p. *DLC, NN*

183. *Distinguished Successful Americans of Our Day.* Chicago, 1911. 590 p. *DLC, NN, CSmH, PU*

184. DIX, JOHN R. *Pulpit Portraits.* Boston, 1854. 256 p.

DLC, MWA

185. DIXON, SAMUEL HOUSTON. *The Men Who Made Texas Free.* Houston, 1924. 345 p. *DLC, NN*

186. DODD, WILLIAM E. *Statesmen of the Old South.* N. Y., 1911. 242 p.
Thomas Jefferson, John C. Calhoun, Jefferson Davis.

DLC, NN, CSmH, PU

187. DOLE, NATHAN H. *Famous Composers.* N. Y., 1902. 2 vols.
Vol. 1. Da Palestrina, Purcell, Bach, Händel, Gluck, Haydn, Mozart, Beethoven, Rossini, von Weber. Vol. 2. Schubert, Spohr, Meyerbeer, Mendelssohn, Schumann, Chopin, Glinka, Berlioz, Liszt, Wagner. *DLC, NN, CSmH*

188. Donovan, George Francis. *The Pre-Revolutionary Irish in Massachusetts.* St. Louis, 1931. 159 p. *DLC, NN, CSmH*

189. Downes, W. H. *Twelve Great Artists.* Boston, 1900. 172 p. *DLC, NN, MWA*

190. Downie, Ralph Ernest. *Orphans All.* Seattle, 1936. 258 p. Andrew Jackson, Andrew Johnson, Rutherford B. Hayes, James A. Garfield, Herbert Hoover, Charles Curtis, Stonewall Jackson, Lloyd George, Cardinal Hayes, Eamon de Valera, Henry M. Stanley, " Billy " Sunday, James E. West, Toyohiko Kagawa, Booker T. Washington. *DLC, NN*

191. Doyle, Richard Davis. *The Pre-Revolutionary Irish in New York.* St. Louis, 1932. 278 p. [Ms. St. Louis Univ. Library.] *DLC*

192. Drake, Francis S., ed. *Dictionary of American Biography.* Boston, 1872. 1019 p. *DLC, NN, MWA, CSmH, PU, MiU:C*

193. Drake, Samuel Adams. *Our World's Great Benefactors.* Chicago, 1888. 702 p. *NN, MiD:B*

194. Drake, Samuel G. *Biography and History of the Indians of North America.* Boston, 1837. 588 p. *DLC, NN, MWA, CSmH, PU, MiU:C*

195. Dudley, Dean, ed. *Officers of Our Union Army and Navy.* Boston, 1862. 148 p. *DLC, NN, CSmH, MiD:B*

196. Durant, William J. *Story of Philosophy.* N. Y., 1926. 577 p. *DLC, NN, PU*

197. Duyckinck, Evert Augustus. *Lives and Portraits of the Presidents of the United States from Washington to Johnson.* N. Y., 1865. 208 p. *DLC, NN, CSmH*

198. Duyckinck, Evert Augustus. *Lives and Portraits of the Presidents of the United States from Washington to Arthur.* N. Y., 1881. 271 p. *NN, CSmH, MiD:B, MiU:C*

199. Duyckinck, Evert Augustus, and Duyckinck, G. L. *Cyclopaedia of American Literature.* N. Y., 1855. 2 vols. *DLC, NN, MWA, CSmH, PU*

200. Dwight, Nathaniel. *The Lives of the Signers of the Declaration of Independence.* N. Y., 1840. 373 p. *DLC, NN, MWA, PU*

201. Dye, Charity. *Some Torch Bearers in Indiana.* Indianapolis, 1917. 327 p. *DLC, NN*

202. Dyer, Oliver. *Great Senators of the United States.* N. Y., 1889. 316 p. *DLC, NN, MWA, CSmH, MiD:B*

203. Earle, Helen L. *Biographical Sketches of American Artists.* Lansing, Mich., 1924.   *DLC, NN, CSmH*

204. Eastman, (Ohiyesa) Charles Alexander. *Indian Heroes and Great Chieftains.* Boston, 1918. 241 p.
Red Cloud, Spotted Tail, Little Crow, Tamahay, Gall, Crazy Horse, Sitting Bull, Rain-in-the-Face, Two Strike, American Horse, Dull Knife, Roman Nose, Chief Joseph, Little Wolf, Hole-in-the-Day.   *DLC*

205. Eddy, Sherwood, and Page, Kirby. *Makers of Freedom.* N. Y., 1926. 311 p.
William Lloyd Garrison, Booker T. Washington, Francis of Assisi, Martin Luther, John Wesley, J. Keir Hardie, Susan B. Anthony, Woodrow Wilson.   *DLC, NN*

206. Edwards, Bela B. *Biography of Self Taught Men.* Boston, 1832. 2 vols.   *DLC, NN, MWA, PU*

207. Eggleston, Edward, and Others. *Famous American Indians.* N. Y., 1878–80. 5 vols.   *DLC, NN, MWA*

208. Eliot, Charles W. *Four American Leaders.* Boston, 1906. 126 p.
Franklin, Washington, Channing, Emerson.
                    DLC, NN, MWA, CSmH

209. Eliot, John. *A Biographical Dictionary.* Boston, 1809. 511 p.
                    DLC, NN, MWA, PU, RP:JCB

210. Eliot, Samuel Atkins. *Biographical History of Massachusetts.* Boston, 1909. 2 vols.   *DLC, NN, MWA*

211. Ellet, Elizabeth F. *Pioneer Women of the West.* N. Y., 1852. 434 p.   *DLC, NN, MWA, CSmH, MiD:B*

212. Ellet, Elizabeth F. *Women of the American Revolution.* N. Y., 1848–1850. 3 vols.   *DLC, NN, MWA, CSmH, PU, MiD:B*

213. Ellis, James A., ed. *Memorial Encyclopaedia of the State of New Hampshire.* N. Y., 1919. 332 p.   *DLC, NN*

214. Ellis, James A., ed. *Memorial Encyclopaedia of the State of Pennsylvania.* N. Y., 1919. 208 p.   *DLC, NN*

215. *Encyclopaedia of Connecticut Biography.* Boston, 1917. 4 vols.
                    DLC, NN

216. *Encyclopaedia of Contemporary Biography of New York.* N. Y., 1878–90. 6 vols.   *DLC, NN*

217. *Encyclopaedia of Contemporary Biography of West Virginia.* N. Y., 1894. 293 p.   *DLC, NN*

218. Essary, Jesse Frederick. *Maryland in National Politics, from Charles Carroll to Albert C. Ritchie.* Baltimore, 1932. 352 p.

Charles Carroll of Carrollton, John Hanson, James McHenry, Luther Martin, Samuel Chase, General Samuel Smith, William Pinkney, William Wirt, Roger B. Taney, Reverdy Johnson, Henry Winter Davis, Montgomery Blair, Arthur P. Gorman, Isidor Rayner, Albert C. Ritchie, Conclusion. *DLC, NN, PU*

218a. *Evangelical Biography* . . . Phila., 1798. *RP:JCB*

219. EVANS, F. W. *Compendium . . . of the United Society of Believers in Christ's Second Appearing.* N. Y., 1867. 192 p.
DLC, NN, CSmH

220. EVANS, MADISON. *Biographical Sketches of the Pioneer Preachers of Indiana.* Phila., 1862. 422 p. *DLC, NN*

221. EVANS, THOMAS H., ed. *Men of Affairs of the Empire State.* N. Y., 1895. *NN*

222. EVENING NEWS ASSOCIATION, THE. *Men of Progress.* Detroit, 1900. 528 p. *NN*

223. EVEREST, CHAS. W. *Poets of Connecticut.* Hartford, 1843. 468 p. *DLC, NN, MWA, CSmH*

224. FARIS, JOHN THOMSON. *Makers of Our History.* Boston, N. Y., 1917. 387 p. *DLC, NN*

225. FARIS, JOHN THOMSON. *The Romance of Forgotten Men.* N. Y., 1928. 313 p.
" Baron " Henry W. Stiegel, John Bartram, Three Bradfords, Caleb Wallace, Christopher Ludwick, Francis Vigo, Harm Jan Huidekoper, Joshua Humphreys, John Cleves Symmes, Constantine Samuel Rafinesque, Elihu Burritt, John Augustus Sutter, James L. Petrigu, Sheldon Jackson.
DLC, NN, MWA, PU

226. FIELD, CLAUDE H. A. F. *Heroes of Missionary Enterprise.* Phila., 1907. 334 p. *DLC, NN*

227. FINGER, CHARLES JOSEPH. *Romantic Rascals.* N. Y., 1927. 251 p. *DLC, NN*

227a. FISKE, JOHN. *Essays Historical and Literary.* N. Y., 1902. 2 vols. *DLC, NN, CSmH*

228. FITCH, CHARLES ELLIOTT, ed. *Encyclopaedia of Biography of New York.* N. Y., 1916–25. 8 vols.
DLC, NN, MWA, CSmH

229. FITZHUGH, HARRIET LLOYD, AND FITZHUGH, PERCY K. *Concise Biographical Dictionary.* N. Y., 1935. 777 p. *DLC, NN*

230. FLANDERS, HENRY. *Lives and Times of the Chief Justices of the Supreme Court.* Phila., 1855–58. 2 vols.
John Jay, John Rutledge, William Cushing, Oliver Ellsworth, John Marshall. *DLC, NN, MWA, CSmH, PU*

231. FORBES, ABNER, AND GREENE, J. W. *Rich Men of Massachusetts.* Boston, 1852. 224 p. *DLC, NN, MWA*

232. FORBES, BERTIE CHARLES. *Men Who Are Making America.* N. Y., 1926. 442 p. *DLC, NN*

233. FORBES, BERTIE CHARLES. *Men Who Are Making the West.* N. Y., 1923. 343 p.
Herbert Fleishhacker, John B. Miller, Elbridge Amos Stuart, Edward L. Doheny, Kenneth R. Kingsbury, Wigginton Ellis Creed, Charles L. Anceney, Robert Dollar, Amadeo P. Giannini, John D. Ryan, Paul Shoup, Henry M. Robinson, Moritz Thomsen, Harry W. Child. *DLC, NN, MWA, CSmH*

234. FORBES, BERTIE CHARLES, AND FOSTER, D. D. *Automotive Giants of America.* N. Y., 1926. 295 p. *DLC, NN*

235. FRANCIS, SAMUEL WARD. *Distinguished Living New York Physicians.* N. Y., 1867. 228 p. *DLC, NN, CSmH*

236. FRANK, WALDO DAVID. *Time Exposures.* N. Y., 1926. 187 p.
Otto H. Kahn, William Lyon Phelps, Georgia O'Keeffe, Ignace Paderewski, Max Steuer, Carl Sandburg, Helen Westley, Thomas Beer, Ernest Bloch, Charles Chaplin, Dr. Abraham Arden Brill, Hendrik Willem Van Loon, Horace B. Liveright, John Dewey, Sinclair Lewis, Leo Ornstein, A. R. Orage, Theodore Dreiser, Katherine Cornell, Alfred Stieglitz.
DLC, NN, PU

237. FRANKLIN, JAMES HENRY. *Ministers of Mercy.* N. Y., 1919. 239 p.
Theodore Leighton Pennell, Christine Iverson Bennett, Fred Douglas Shepard, James Curtis Hepburn, Joseph Plumb Cochran, Catherine L. Mabie, Peter Parker, John Kenneth Mackenzie, The Neves of Kashmir, John Scudder. *DLC, NN*

238. FRENCH, BENJAMIN FRANKLIN. *Biographia Americana.* N. Y., 1825. 356 p. *NN, MiD:B, MiU:C*

239. FRENCH, BENJAMIN FRANKLIN. *Memoirs of Eminent Female Writers.* Phila., 1827. 183 p. *DLC, NN*

240. FROST, JOHN. *American Generals, From the Founding of the Republic to the Present Time.* Hartford, 1849. 916 p.
DLC, NN

241. FROST, JOHN. *Heroes of the Revolution.* N. Y., 1844. 240 p.
DLC, NN

242. FROST, JOHN. *Lives of American Merchants.* N. Y., 1844. 240 p.
DLC, NN, MiD:B

243. FROST, JOHN. *Lives of the Heroes of the American Revolution.* Boston, 1847. 370 p.   *DLC, NN, CSmH, PU, MiD:B*

244. FROST, JOHN. *Pictorial Book of the Commodores.* Phila., 1845. 440 p.   *DLC, NN, CSmH*

245. FROST, JOHN. *Presidents of the U. S. from Washington to Cleveland.* Boston, 1889. 547 p.   *DLC, NN, CSmH*

246. FROTHINGHAM, PAUL REVERE. *All These.* Cambridge, 1927. 314 p.
Introduction, by M. A. De W. Howe; Memoirs, by R. Grant; John Cotton; John Fiske; John Ruskin; The Historian as Preacher; Maeterlinck; By Way of Contrast; Edward Everett Hale; William Everett; George Hodges; Cromwell; Charles W. Eliot.   *DLC, NN, CSmH*

247. GALLAHER, JAMES E., ed. *Representative Deaf Persons of the U. S. of America.* Chicago, 1898. 222 p.   *DLC, NN*

248. GARESCHÉ, EDWARD F. *Great Christian Artists.* Milwaukee, 1924. 209 p.
Leonardo Da Vinci, Raphael Santi, Michelangelo, Fra Angelico, Bartolomé Murillo, Peter Paul Rubens, and Anthony Van Dyck.   *DLC*

249. GATES, MERRILL E., ed. *Men of Mark in America.* Washington, D. C., 1905–06. 2 vols.   *DLC, NN*

250. GIDDINGS, EDWARD. *American Christian Rulers; or, Religion and Men of Government.* N. Y., 1890. 590 p. *DLC, NN, MWA*

251. GILMER, GEORGE R. *Sketches of Some of the First Settlers of Upper Georgia, of the Cherokees, and the Author.* Americus, Ga., 1855. 458 p.   *DLC, MWA, CSmH*

252. GLAZIER, WILLARD. *Heroes of Three Wars.* Phila., 1880. 446 p.
War of the Revolution, War with Mexico, War for the Union.   *DLC, NN, MWA, MiD:B*

253. GODWIN, PARKE, ed. *Cyclopedia of Biography.* N. Y., 1851, 1878. 1153 p.   *DLC, NN, MWA, MiD:B*

254. GODWIN, PARKE. *Handbook of Universal Biography.* N. Y., 1852. 821 p.   *DLC, NN*

255. GOODRICH, CHARLES A. *Lives of the Signers of the Declaration of Independence.* N. Y., 1829. 460 p.
    DLC, NN, MWA, CSmH, PU

256. GOODRICH, SAMUEL G. *Lives of Celebrated American Indians.* Boston, 1843. 315 p.   *DLC, NN, MWA, CSmH*

257. GOODRICH, SAMUEL G. *Popular Biography.* N. Y., 1854. 526 p.   *DLC, NN*

258. GORDON, ARMISTEAD CHURCHILL. *Virginian Portraits.* Staunton, Va., 1924. 137 p.
John Tyler, William Green, William Joseph Robertson, William Gordon M'Cabe, Thomas Nelson Page. *NN*

259. GORRIE, PETER DOUGLAS. *Lives of Eminent Methodist Ministers.* Auburn, N. Y., 1852. 408 p. *DLC, NN*

260. *Governors of Massachusetts, 1629–1885.* Boston, 1885. *NN*

261. *Great American Book of Biography.* Phila., 1896. 735 p.
Bk. 1. The Great Founders of the Republic; Bk. 2. The Noble Builders of Our Union; Bk. 3. The Great Generals of the Civil War; Bk. 4. The Heroes of the American Navy; Bk. 5. Our Great Presidents and Statesmen; Bk. 6. Our Giants of Inventive Achievement; Bk. 7. Our Successful Men of Business; Bk. 8. Our Great Pulpit Orators and Reformers; Bk. 9. Our Noted Literary Men and Women; Bk. 10. The Political Leaders of the Present Day. *DLC*

262. GREELY, ADOLPHUS WASHINGTON. *Explorers and Travelers.* N. Y., 1902. 373 p.
Louis Joliet; Peter Le Moyne, Sieur d'Iberville; Jonathan Carver; Captain Robert Gray; Captain Meriwether Lewis and Lieut. William Clark; Zebulon Montgomery Pike; Charles Wilkes; John Charles Frémont; Elisha Kent Kane; Isaac Israel Hayes; Charles Francis Hall; George Washington De Long; Paul Belloni Du Chaillu; Stanley Africanus.
DLC, NN, MWA, MiD:B

263. GRIFFITH, FRANK CARLOS. *Maine's Hall of Fame.* South Poland, Me., 1905. 12 p. *DLC, NN*

264. GRIGGS, EDWARD H. *American Statesmen; An Interpretation of Our History and Heritage.* Croton-on-Hudson, N. Y., 1927. 364 p.
Washington, Franklin, Jefferson, Hamilton, Lee, Lincoln.
DLC, NN, MWA, PU

265. GRISWOLD, R. W. *Biographical Annual.* N. Y., 1841. 307 p.
NN, MWA, CSmH

266. GRISWOLD, RUFUS W. *Female Poets of America.* Phila., 1849. 400 p. *DLC, NN, MWA, CSmH*

267. GRISWOLD, RUFUS W. *The Poets and Poetry of America.* Phila., 1842. 666 p. *DLC, NN, MWA, CSmH, PU*

268. GRISWOLD, RUFUS W. *Poets and Poetry of England in the 19th Century.* N. Y., 1845. 504 p. *DLC, NN, MWA, PU*

269. GRISWOLD, RUFUS W. *The Sacred Poets of England and America.* N. Y., 1849. 552 p. *DLC, NN, MWA*

270. GRISWOLD, RUFUS W. *The Prose Writers of America.* Phila., 1847. 552 p. *DLC, NN, CSmH, MiU:C*

271. GRISWOLD, RUFUS W. *Washington and the Generals of the American Revolution.* Phila., 1848. 2 vols. *DLC, NN, CSmH, MiD:B*

272. GROSS, S. D. *Lives of Eminent American Physicians and Surgeons of the 19th Century.* Phila., 1861. 836 p. *DLC, NN*

272a. HADLEY, MILTON. *True Stories of Our Famous Men and Women.* Phila., 1900. 256 p. *CSmH*

273. HALE, EDWARD EVERETT. *Lights of Two Centuries.* N. Y., 1887. 603 p. *DLC, NN*

274. HALE, W. T. *Great Southerners.* Nashville, 1901. 252 p. *DLC, NN*

275. HALL, HENRY. *America's Successful Men of Affairs.* N. Y., 1895. 2 vols. *DLC, NN, MiD:B*

276. HALL, JOSEF WASHINGTON. *Eminent Asians.* N. Y., 1929. 510 p.
Sun Yat-sen, Yamagata, Ito, Mustapha Kemal, Josef Stalin, Mahatma Gandhi. *DLC, NN*

277. HALL, T. W. *Heroes of Our Revolution.* N. Y., 1900. 317 p. *DLC*

278. HAMERSLY, LEWIS R. *Biographical Sketches of Distinguished Officers of the Army and Navy.* N. Y., 1905. 383 p. *DLC, NN, MWA, CSmH*

279. HAMERSLY, LEWIS R. *First Citizens of the Republic.* N. Y., 1906. 239 p. *DLC, NN*

280. HAMM, MARGHERITA A. *Builders of the Republic.* N. Y., 1902. 410 p. *DLC, NN, MiD:B*

281. HAMM, MARGHERITA A. *Famous Families of New York.* N. Y., 1902. 2 vols. *DLC, NN, MWA*

281a. HANAFORD, PHEBE. *Daughters of America.* Augusta, Me., 1882. 750 p. *CSmH*

282. HARDIE, JAMES. *The New Universal Biographical Dictionary and American Remembrancer of Departed Merit.* N. Y., 1801–1802. 4 vols. *DLC, NN, MWA, CSmH, MiD:B*

283. HARLOW, REX F. *Oklahoma Leaders.* Oklahoma City, 1928. 530 p. *DLC, NN*

284. HARLOW, REX F. *Successful Oklahomans.* Oklahoma City, 1927. 239 p. *DLC, NN*

285. HARRISON, MITCHELL C., comp. *New York's Prominent and Progressive Men.* N. Y., 1900–02. 3 vols.   *DLC, NN*

286. HARROW, BENJAMIN. *Eminent Chemists of Our Time.* N. Y., 1920. 248 p.

Perkin and Coal-Tar Dyes, Mendeleeff and the Periodic Law, Ramsay and the Gases of the Atmosphere, Richards and Atomic Weights; van't Hoff and Physical Chemistry, Arrhenius and the Theory of Electrolytic Dissociation, Moissan and the Electric Furnace, Madame Curie and Radium, Victor Meyer and the Rise of Organic Chemistry, Remsen and the Rise of Chemistry in America, Fischer and the Chemistry of Foods.

DLC, NN

287. HARSHA, DAVID A. *The Most Eminent Orators and Statesmen of Ancient and Modern Times.* Phila., 1854. 520 p.

DLC, NN, PU

288. HARSHBERGER, JOHN W. *The Botanists of Philadelphia and Their Work.* Phila., 1899. 457 p.   *DLC, NN, PU*

289. HART, JOHN S. *Female Prose Writers of America.* Phila., 1852. 432 p.   *DLC, NN, CSmH*

290. HARTLEY, CECIL B. *Heroes and Patriots of the South.* Phila., 1860. 320 p.

General Francis Marion, General William Moultrie, General Andrew Pickens, Governor John Rutledge.   *DLC, NN, MWA*

291. HATHAWAY, ESSE VIRGINIA. *The Book of American Presidents.* N. Y., 1931. 367 p.   *DLC*

292. HAWKS, FRANCIS L., ed. *Appleton's Cyclopedia of Biography.* N. Y., 1856. 1058 p.   *DLC, NN, CSmH, PU*

293. HAWKS, FRANCIS L. *Lives and Anecdotes of Illustrious Men.* N. Y., 1850. 1 vol.

Oliver Cromwell, Hernando Cortez, Sir Joshua Reynolds, Dr. Adam Clarke, Sir Humphrey Davy, Lindley Murray, Baron Cuvier, Reverend George Crabbe.   *NN*

294. HAY, CHARLES AUGUSTUS. *Memoirs of Rev. Jacob Goering, Rev. George Lochman, and Rev. Benjamin Kurtz.* Phila., 1888. 211 p.   *DLC, NN*

295. HAYWOOD, MARSHALL DE L. *Lives of the Bishops of North Carolina.* Raleigh, N. C., 1910. 270 p.

John Stark, John S. Ravenscroft, Levi Lilliman Ives, Thomas Atkinson, Theodore Benedict Arnold.   *DLC, NN, MWA*

296. HEADLEY, JOEL TYLER. *The Chaplains and Clergy of the Revolution.* N. Y., 1864. 402 p.   *DLC, NN, MWA, CSmH*

297. HEADLEY, JOEL TYLER. *Napoleon and His Marshals.* N. Y., 1847. 2 vols.   *DLC, NN, MWA, PU*

298. HEADLEY, PHINEAS C. *Public Men of Today.* Hartford, 1883. 799 p.   *DLC, NN*

299. HEATHCOTE, CHARLES WM. *The Signers of the Declaration of Independence.* West Chester, Pa., 1932. 76 p.   *DLC, NN*

300. HEMPHILL, JAMES C., ed. *Men of Mark in South Carolina.* Washington, 1907–09. 4 vols.   *DLC, NN*

301. HENDERSON, ARCHIBALD. *Contemporary Immortals.* N. Y., 1930. 208 p.

     Albert Einstein, Mahatma Gandhi, Thomas Edison, Benito Mussolini, George Bernard Shaw, Guglielmo Marconi, Jane Addams, Orville Wright, Ignace Jan Paderswski, Marie Curie, Henry Ford, Rudyard Kipling.   *DLC, NN, PU*

302. HERRING, JAMES, AND LONGACRE, JAMES B. *National Portrait Gallery of Distinguished Americans.* N. Y., 1834–39. 4 vols.   *DLC, NN, MWA, CSmH, PU, MiD:B*

303. HERRINGSHAW, THOMAS W. *American Blue Book of Biography; Prominent Americans of 1914.* Chicago, 1915. 1016 p.   *DLC, NN, CSmH, PU*

304. HERRINGSHAW, THOMAS W. *Herringshaw's Encyclopaedia of American Biography of the 19th Century.* Chicago, 1898. 1046 p.   *DLC, NN, MWA, CSmH, MiD:B*

305. HERRINGSHAW, THOMAS W. *Herringshaw's National Library of American Biography.* Chicago, 1914. 5 vols.   *DLC, NN, CSmH*

306. HIGGINSON, THOMAS WENTWORTH. *English Statesmen.* N. Y., 1875. 363 p.   *DLC, NN, CSmH*

307. HILLS, FREDERICK SIMON, comp. *Men of Vermont State.* Albany, 1925.   *NN*

308. HILLS, FREDERICK SIMON, ed. *New York State Men.* Albany, 1906. 366 p.   *DLC, NN*

309. HINCHMAN, WALTER S., AND GUMMERE, FRANCIS B. *Lives of Great English Writers.* Boston, 1908. 569 p. *DLC, NN, PU*

310. HISSRICH, RICHARD. *Biographies of All the Candidates for the Offices of President and Vice-President of the U. S. from 1789 to 1884.* Wheeling, 1884. 123 p.   *DLC*

311. *History of the Bench and Bar of New York.* N. Y., 1897. 2 vols.   *DLC, NN*

312. HOLE, CHARLES. *A Brief Biographical Dictionary.* N. Y., 1866. 453 p.   *DLC, NN, MWA, CSmH, PU*

313. HOLLAND, MARY A. GARDNER, comp. *Our Army Nurses.* Boston, 1895. 548 p.   *DLC, NN, MWA, CSmH*

314. HOLLISTER, W. R., AND NORMAN H. *Five Famous Missourians.* Kansas City, Mo., 1900. 386 p.
S. L. Clemens, R. P. Bland, C. Clark, J. M. Greenwood, and J. O. Shelby.   *DLC, NN*

315. HOLLOWAY, LAURA C. *Famous American Fortunes and the Men Who Have Made Them.* Phila., 1883. 784 p.
    DLC, NN, PU

316. HOLLOWAY, LAURA C. *Ladies of the White House . . . from Washington to Hayes.* Phila., 1880. 598 p.
    DLC, NN, MWA, CSmH

317. HOLMES, PRESCOTT. *Lives of the Presidents.* Phila., 1898. 282 p.
    DLC, NN

318. HORNE, CHARLES FRANCIS, ed. *Great Men and Famous Women.* N. Y., 1894. 4 vols.   *DLC, NN, PU*

319. HOTCHKIN, SAMUEL FITCH. *Early Clergy of Pennsylvania and Delaware.* Phila., 1890. 280 p.   *DLC, NN, PU*

320. HOUGH, FRANKLIN BENJAMIN. *American Biographical Notes.* Albany, 1875. 442 p.   *DLC, NN, MWA, CSmH, MiU:C*

321. HOUGHTON, WALTER R., ed. *Kings of Fortune; or, Triumphs of Self-Made Men.* N. Y., 1885. 621 p.   *NN, MiD:B*

322. HOWARD, WILLIAM A. *The Nebraska Legislature and National and State Officers of Nebraska.* Lincoln, Neb., 1895. 300 p.
    NN

323. HOWE, HENRY. *Adventures and Achievements of Americans.* N. Y., 1859. 732 p.   *DLC, NN*

324. HOWE, HENRY. *Memoirs and Lives of American and European Mechanics.* N. Y., 1847. 482 p.   *DLC, NN, PU*

325. HOWE, M. A. DE WOLFE. *Causes and Their Champions.* Boston, 1926. 331 p.
Clara Barton, Phillips Brooks, Frances E. Willard, the Rockefellers, Samuel Gompers, Susan B. Anthony, Booker T. Washington, Woodrow Wilson.   *DLC, NN, PU*

326. HOWE, M. A. DE WOLFE. *Classic Shades; Five Leaders of Learning and Their Colleges.* Boston, 1928. 199 p.
Timothy Dwight of Yale, Mary Lyon and Mount Holyoke, Mark Hopkins and Williams, Princeton and James McCosh, The Harvard Figure of Charles William Eliot.
    DLC, NN, MWA, PU

327. HOWES, DURWARD, ed. *American Women; the Official Who's Who Among the Women of the Nation, 1935–36.* Los Angeles, 1935. 665 p. *DLC, NN, CSmH*

328. HOWES, DURWARD, ed. *America's Young Men; the Official Who's Who Among the Young Men of the Nation, 1934.* Los Angeles, 1934. 678 p. *DLC, NN, CSmH*

329. HUBBARD, ELBERT. *Little Journeys to the Homes of American Statesmen.* N. Y., 1898. 436 p.
George Washington, Benjamin Franklin, Alexander Hamilton, Samuel Adams, John Hancock, John Quincy Adams, Thomas Jefferson, Daniel Webster, Henry Clay, John Jay, William H. Seward, Abraham Lincoln. *DLC, NN, MWA, CSmH*

330. HUBBARD, ELBERT. *Little Journeys to the Homes of Eminent Orators.* East Aurora, N. Y., 1903. 2 vols.
Bk. 1. Pericles, Mark Antony, Savonarola, Martin Luther, Edmund Burke, William Pitt. Bk. 2. Jean Paul Marat, Robert Ingersoll, Patrick Henry, Starr King, Henry Ward Beecher, Wendell Phillips. *DLC, NN, MWA, PU*

331. HUBBARD, ELBERT. *Little Journeys to the Homes of Great Business Men.* East Aurora, N. Y., 1909. 2 vols.
Bk. 1. Robert Owen, James Oliver, Stephen Girard, Mayer A. Rothschild, Philip Armour, John J. Astor. Bk. 2. Peter Cooper, Andrew Carnegie, George Peabody, A. T. Stewart, H. H. Rogers, James J. Hill. *DLC, NN, MWA, PU*

332. HUBBARD, ELBERT. *Little Journeys to the Homes of Great Philosophers.* East Aurora, N. Y., 1904. 2 vols.
Bk. 1. Socrates, Seneca, Aristotle, Marcus Aurelius, Spinoza, Swedenborg. Bk. 2. Immanuel Kant, Auguste Comte, Voltaire, Herbert Spencer, Schopenhauer, Henry D. Thoreau.
DLC, NN, PU

333. HUBBARD, ELBERT. *Little Journeys to the Homes of Great Lovers.* East Aurora, N. Y., 1906. 2 vols.
Josiah and Sarah Wedgwood, William Godwin and Mary Wollstonecraft, Dante and Beatrice, John Stuart Mill and Harriet Taylor, Charles Parnell and Kitty O'Shea, Petrarch and Laura, Dante Gabriel Rossetti and Elizabeth Eleanor Siddal, Balzac and Madame Hanska, Fénelon and Madame Guyon, Ferdinand Lassalle and Helene von Donniges, Lord Nelson and Lady Hamilton, Robert Louis Stevenson and Fanny Osbourne.
DLC, NN, PU

334. HUBBARD, ELBERT. *Little Journeys to the Homes of Great Reformers.* East Aurora, N. Y., 1907. 2 vols.
Bk. 1. John Wesley, Henry George, Garibaldi, Richard Cobden, Thomas Paine, John Knox. Bk. 2. John Bright Bradlaugh, Theodore Parker, Oliver Cromwell, Anne Hutchinson, Jean Rousseau. *DLC, NN, MWA, PU*

335. HUBBARD, ELBERT. *Little Journeys to the Homes of Great Scientists.* East Aurora, N. Y., 1905. 2 vols.
Bk. 1. Copernicus, Galileo, Sir Isaac Newton, Humboldt, Sir William Herschel, Charles Darwin. Bk. 2. Ernst Haeckel, Carl von Linnaeus, Thomas H. Huxley, John Tyndall, Alfred R. Wallace, John Fiske. *DLC, NN, PU*

336. HUBBARD, ELBERT. *Little Journeys to the Homes of Great Teachers.* East Aurora, N. Y., 1908. 2 vols.
Bk. 1. Moses, Confucius, Pythagoras, Plato, King Alfred, Friedrich Froebel. Bk. 2. Booker T. Washington, Thomas Arnold, Erasmus, Hypatia, St. Benedict, Mary Baker Eddy.
DLC, NN, PU

337. HUMPHREY, GRACE. *Story of the Marys.* Phila., 1923. 203 p.
Mary Stuart, Mary Chilton, Mary Washington, Marie Antoinette, Mary Ann Evans, Mary Liverman, Mary Lamb, Mary Somerville, Mary Lynne, Mary the Virgin. *DLC, PU*

338. HUNT, FREEMAN. *Lives of American Merchants.* N. Y., 1858.
2 vols. *DLC, NN, MWA, CSmH, PU, MiU:C*

339. HUNT, WILLIAM. *American Biographical Panorama.* Albany, 1849. 480 p. *DLC, NN, MiD:B*

339a. HUNTER, HENRY. *Sacred Biography* . . . Boston, 1794. 3 vols. *RP:JCB*

340. HUSBAND, JOSEPH. *Americans by Adoption.* Boston, 1920. 153 p.
Stephen Girard, John Ericsson, Louis Agassiz, Carl Schurz, Theodore Thomas, Andrew Carnegie, James J. Hill, Augustus Saint-Gaudens, Jacob A. Riis. *DLC, NN, PU*

341. HUTTON, LAURENCE, AND WATERS, C. E. *Artists of the 19th Century and Their Works.* Boston, 1879, 1907. 2 vols.
DLC, NN, PU

341a. HYLANDER, CLARENCE JOHN. *American Inventors.* N. Y., 1934. 216 p. *DLC*

342. HYLANDER, CLARENCE JOHN. *American Scientists.* N. Y., 1935. 186 p. *DLC, PU*

343. ILES, GEORGE. *Leading American Inventors.* N. Y., 1912. 447 p.
John and Robert Livingston Stevens, Robert Fulton, Eli Whitney, Thomas Blanchard, Samuel Finley Breese Morse, Charles Goodyear, John Ericsson, Cyrus Hall McCormick, Christopher Latham Sholes, Elias Harvey, Benjamin Chew Tilghman, Ottmar Mergenthaler. *DLC, NN, MWA, PU*

344. *Illinois Blue Book of Biography.* Chicago, 1916. 229 p.
DLC, NN, PU

345. *Illustrated Album of Biography of Southwestern Minnesota and Northwestern Iowa.* Chicago, 1889. 1080 p. *DLC, NN*

346. IRELAN, JOHN R. *The Republic; or, A History of the U. S. of America in the Administrations from the Monarchic Colonial Days to the Present Time.* Chicago, 1886–88. 15 vols.
DLC, NN, MWA, CSmH, PU, MiD:B

347. IVINS, LESTER SYLVAN, AND WINSHIP, A. E. *Fifty Famous Farmers.* N. Y., 1924. 407 p. *DLC, NN*

348. JAFFE, BERNARD. *Crucibles; the Lives and Achievements of the Great Chemists.* N. Y., 1930. 377 p.
Bernard Trevisan, Theophrastus Paracelsus, John Joachim Becher, Joseph Priestley, Henry Cavendish, Antoine Laurent Lavoisier, John Dalton, John Jacob Berzelius, Amadeo Avogadro, Friedrich Woehler, Dmitri I. Mendeleeff, Svante Arrhenius, Marie Skladowska Curie, Joseph John Thomson, Henry G. J. Moseley, Irving Langmuir. *DLC, NN, PU*

349. JENKINS, JOHN STILWELL. *Lives of the Governors of the State of New York.* N. Y., 1851. 826 p.
George Clinton, John Jay, Morgan Lewis, Daniel D. Tomkins, De Witt Clinton, Joseph C. Yates, Martin Van Buren, Enos T. Throop, William L. Marcy, William H. Seward, William C. Bouck, Silas Wright, John Young, Hamilton Fish.
DLC, NN, MWA, CSmH, PU

350. JENKINS, JOHN STILWELL. *Lives of Patriots and Heroes of the American Revolution.* Auburn, 1847. 293 p. *DLC*

351. JENSSON, J. C. *American Lutheran Biographies.* Milwaukee, 1890. 901 p. *DLC, NN*

352. JOHNSON, ALLEN, AND MALONE, DUMAS, eds. *Dictionary of American Biography.* N. Y., 1928–36. 20 vols.
DLC, NN, CSmH, MiU:C

353. JOHNSON, ROSSITER, ed. *Twentieth Century Biographical Dictionary of Noted Americans.* Boston, 1904. 10 vols.
DLC, NN

354. JOHNSTON, CHARLES HAVEN LADD. *Famous American Athletes of Today*. Boston, 1928. 445 p. DLC, NN

355. JOHNSTON, CHARLES HAVEN LADD. *Famous American Athletes of Today*. Boston, 1930. 328 p. (Second Series)
DLC, NN

356. JOHNSTON, CHARLES HAVEN LADD. *Famous Frontiersmen and Heroes of the Border*. Boston, 1925. 359 p. DLC, NN

357. JOHNSTON, CHARLES HAVEN LADD. *Famous Generals of the Great War*. Boston, 1919. 310 p. DLC, NN

358. JOHNSTON, CHARLES HAVEN LADD. *Famous Scouts of the Frontier*. Boston, 1911. 340 p.
General Israel Putnam, Daniel Boone, Simon Kenton, Captain Samuel Brady, The Two Athletic Poes and Major Sam Mc-Culloch, Lewis and Clark, Colonel Davy Crockett, General Sam Houston, Kit Carson, General William S. Harvey, Wild Bill Hickok, Captain D. L. Payne, White Beaver, Dr. D. F. Powell, William F. Cody. DLC, NN

359. JONES, A. D. *The American Portrait Gallery of the Principal Actors in American History*. N. Y., 1855. 768 p.
DLC, NN, MWA, PU

360. JONES, A. D. *Illustrated American Biography*. N. Y., 1853. 1 vol. DLC, NN, CSmH, MiD:B

361. JONES, CHARLES C., JR. *Biographical Sketches of the Delegates from Georgia to the Continental Congress*. Boston, 1891. 211 p. DLC, NN, CSmH

362. JONES, EDGAR DE WITT. *American Preachers of Today*. Indianapolis, 1933. 317 p. DLC, NN

363. JONES, M. *Biographies of Great Men*. N. Y., 1866. 128 p.
DLC, NN

364. JORDAN, JOHN W. *Encyclopedia of Pennsylvania Biography*. 1914–30. 20 vols. DLC, NN, PU

365. JUDSON, L. CARROLL. *Biography of the Signers of the Declaration of Independence*. Phila., 1839. 354 p.
DLC, NN, CSmH, PU

366. KARSNER, DAVID. *Sixteen Authors to One*. N. Y., 1928. 290 p.
Theodore Dreiser, James Branch Cabell, Sherwood Anderson, Sinclair Lewis, Booth Tarkington, Eugene O'Neill, Edgar Lee Masters, Carl Sandburg, Christopher Morley, Clarence Darrow, Hendrik Willem Van Loon, Will Durant, Ben Hecht, Konrad Bercovici, Upton Sinclair, Will Rogers. DLC, NN

367. KEESE, WILLIAM LINN. *A Group of Comedians.* N. Y., 1901. 91 p.
Henry Placide, William Rufus Blake, John Brougham, George Holland, Charles Fisher. *DLC, NN, MWA, CSmH, PU*

368. KELLY, HOWARD A., AND BURRAGE, WALTER L. *American Medical Biographies.* Baltimore, 1920. 1320 p.
DLC, NN, MWA, PU

369. KENNEDY, JAMES H. *Bench and Bar of Cleveland.* Cleveland, 1889. 358 p. *NN*

370. KERNODLE, PETER JEFFERSON. *Lives of Christian Ministers.* Richmond, 1909. 408 p. *DLC*

371. KERSHNER, FREDERICK D. *Pioneers of Christian Thought.* Indianapolis, 1930. 373 p.
Philo, Paul of Tarsus, Marcion, Origen, Athanasius, Theodore, Augustine, Anselm, Abelard, Aquinas, Erasmus, Luther, Calvin, Arminius, Schleiermacher, Ritschl. *DLC, NN*

372. KILBOURN, DWIGHT C. *Bench and Bar of Litchfield County, Conn.* Litchfield, Conn., 1909. 344 p. *DLC, NN*

373. KING, MOSES. *Notable New Yorkers.* N. Y., 1899. 616 p.
DLC, NN, MWA, CSmH

374. KINGSTON, JOHN. *The New American Biographic Dictionary.* Baltimore, 1810. 303 p. *DLC, NN, MWA*

375. KNAPP, SAMUEL L. *Biographical Sketches of Eminent Lawyers, Statesmen, and Men of Letters.* Boston, 1839. 360 p.
DLC, NN, MWA, MiD:B, MiU:C

376. KNAPP, SAMUEL L. *Female Biography . . . Distinguished Women in Different Nations and Ages.* Phila., 1846. 501 p.
DLC, NN, MWA

377. KNAPP, SAMUEL L. *Sketches of Public Characters.* N. Y., 1830. 260 p. *DLC, NN, CSmH, MiU:C*

378. KNIGHT, LUCIAN LAMAR, AND CAWSTON, A. H., eds. *Encyclopaedia of Georgia Biography.* Atlanta, 1931. *DLC, NN*

379. KNIGHT, LUCIAN LAMAR. *Georgia's Bi-Centennial Memoirs and Memories.* Atlanta, 1931–33. 4 vols. *DLC, NN*

380. LABREE, BENJAMIN, ed. *Notable Men of Kentucky.* Louisville, 1902. 228 p. *NN*

381. *Lamb's Biographical Dictionary of the United States.* Boston, 1900–03. 7 vols. *DLC, NN, CSmH*

382. LAND, JOHN E. *Indiana's Representative Men in 1881.* Indianapolis, 1881. 128 p. *NN*

383. Langford, Laura (Carter) Holloway. *Famous American Fortunes*. Phila., 1885. 784 p.   *DLC, NN, CSmH*

384. Lanman, Charles. *Biographical Annals of the Civil Government of the United States*. Washington, 1876. 676 p.
          DLC, NN, MWA, CSmH, PU, MiD:B, MiU:C

385. Lanman, Charles. *Leading Men of Japan*. Boston, 1883. 421 p.   *DLC, NN*

386. Larned, Josephus Nelson. *A Study of Greatness in Men*. Boston, 1911. 303 p.
     Napoleon I, Oliver Cromwell, George Washington, Abraham Lincoln.   *DLC, NN, PU*

387. Laut, Agnes C. *Vikings of the Pacific*. N. Y., 1905. 349 p.
     Bering, Outlaw Hunters of Russia, Benjowsky, Cook, Vancouver, Gray.   *DLC, NN, CSmH*

388. Law, Frederick H. *Modern Great Americans*. N. Y., 1926. 286 p.
     Alexander Graham Bell, Luther Burbank, John Burroughs, Andrew Carnegie, Alexis Carrel, Samuel Langhorne Clemens, Thomas A. Edison, George W. Goethals, William C. Gorgas, Albert A. Michelson, Robert A. Millikan, Robert E. Peary, John J. Pershing, Theodore W. Richards, Theodore Roosevelt, Elihu Root, John S. Sargent, Henry Van Dyke, Woodrow Wilson, Wilbur and Orville Wright.   *DLC, NN*

389. Lee, Anna Maria. *Memoirs of Eminent Female Writers*. Phila., 1827. 183 p.   *DLC, NN, MWA*

390. Lee, Cuthbert. *Contemporary American Portrait Painters*. N. Y., 1929. 108 p.   *DLC, NN, PU*

391. Lee, Cuthbert. *Early American Portrait Painters*. New Haven, 1929. 350 p.   *DLC, NN, MWA, CSmH*

392. Leiter, Mrs. Mary Theresa. *Biographical Sketches of the Generals of the Continental Army of the Revolution*. Cambridge, 1889. 167 p.   *DLC, NN, CSmH, PU*

393. Leonard, Jonathan Norton. *Crusaders of Chemistry*. N. Y., 1930. 307 p.
     Roger Bacon, Nicholas Flamel, Paracelsus, Robert Boyle, Joseph Priestley, Henry Cavendish, Antoine Laurent Lavoisier.
          DLC, NN, PU

394. Lester, Charles E. *The Artists of America*. N. Y., 1846. 257 p.
     Washington Allston, Henry Inman, Benjamin West, Gilbert Charles Stuart, John Trumbull, James De Veaux, Rembrandt Peale, Thomas Crawford.   *DLC, NN, PU*

395. Leupp, Francis E. *National Miniatures.* N. Y., 1918. 302 p.
President Wilson, William J. Bryan, Chief Justice White, Oscar
W. Underwood, Jeanette Rankin, Emma Goldman, William J.
Burns, Jane Addams. *DLC, NN*

396. Lewis, Charles Lee. *Famous American Naval Officers.* Bos-
ton, 1924. 374 p.
Paul Jones, Stephen Decatur, Isaac Hull, David Porter, Oliver
Hazard Perry, Thomas Macdonough, Matthew Calbraith Perry,
David Glasgow Farragut, Alfred Thayer Mahan, Robert Edwin
Peary, George Dewey, William Sowden Sims. *DLC, NN*

397. Lewis, Charles Lee. *Famous Old-World Sea Fighters.* Boston, 1929. 362 p. *DLC, NN*

398. Lewis, William Draper, ed. *Great American Lawyers.* Phila.,
1907. 8 vols. *DLC, NN, PU*

399. Lincoln, Charles Z. *The Bench and Bar of Cattaraugus
County, N. Y.* 1893. 416 p. *DLC, NN*

400. Lincoln, Robert W. *Lives of the Presidents of the United
States.* N. Y., 1836. 508 p. *DLC, NN, MWA, MiD:B*

401. Linder, Usher F. *Reminiscences of the Early Bench and Bar
of Illinois.* Chicago, 1879. 406 p. *CSmH*

402. Link, Samuel Albert. *Pioneers of Southern Literature.* Nashville and Dallas, 1899–1900. 2 vols. *DLC, NN, CSmH*

403. Lippmann, Walter. *Men of Destiny.* N. Y., 1927. 244 p.
DLC, NN, PU

404. *Literary Doctors of Medicine.* 1926. 306 p. (Privately
Printed) *DLC*

405. *Lives of the Chief Fathers of New England.* Boston, 1846–49.
5 vols.
John Cotton, John Wilson, John Norton, John Eliot, Thomas
Shepard, Increase Mather. *DLC, NN*

406. *Lives of Distinguished Shoemakers.* Portland, Me., 1849. 340 p.
Saint Crispin, James Lackington, Timothy Bennett, Roger
Sherman, William Carey, Robert Bloomfield, Simon Antoine,
Hans Sachs, William Gifford, Thomas Holcroft, Thomas Hardy,
Cloudsley Shovel, George Fox, James Woodhouse, Jacob Beh-
men, Noah Worcester, John Pounds. *NN*

407. *Lives of Eminent Individuals, Celebrated in American History.*
Boston, 1839. 380 p. *DLC, NN*

408. Livingston, John. *Portraits of Eminent Americans.* N. Y.,
1853–54. 4 vols. *DLC, NN, MWA, PU, MiD:B*

409. LOCKWOOD, FRANCIS CUMMINS. *Arizona Characters.* Los Angeles, 1928. 230 p.   *DLC, NN, MWA*

410. LONGFELLOW, HENRY W. *Poets and Poetry of Europe.* Phila., 1871. 916 p.   *DLC, NN, MWA, CSmH, PU*

411. LOSSING, BENSON J. *Biographical Sketches of the Signers of the Declaration of Independence.* Phila., 1848. 384 p.
    DLC, NN, MWA, MiU:C

412. LOSSING, BENSON J. *Eminent Americans.* N. Y., 1857. 416 p.
    DLC, NN, MWA, PU, MiD:B

413. LOSSING, BENSON J. *Our Countrymen.* N. Y., 1855. Var. Vol.
    DLC, NN, MWA, CSmH

414. LOUISIANA HISTORICAL AND BIOGRAPHICAL ASSOCIATION. *"Louisianians and Their State."* New Orleans, 1919. 144 p.
    DLC, NN

415. LOYLESS, THOMAS W. *Georgia's Public Men.* Atlanta, 1902. 307 p.   *NN*

416. LYNCH, JAMES D. *Bench and Bar of Mississippi.* N. Y., 1881. 539 p.   *DLC, MWA*

417. LYNCH, JAMES D. *The Bench and Bar of Texas.* St. Louis, 1885. 610 p.   *DLC, NN, MWA, CSmH*

418. McAFEE, JOHN J. *Kentucky Politicians.* Louisville, 1886. 259 p.
    DLC, NN

419. McALPIN, FRANK. *Our Album of Authors.* Phila., 1885. 416 p.
    MWA

420. McCABE, JAMES DABNEY, JR. *Great Fortunes and How They Were Made.* Phila., 1870. 633 p.   *DLC, PU*

421. McCABE, JOSEPH. *Empresses of Constantinople.* Boston, n.d. 341 p.   *DLC, NN, PU*

422. McCABE, JOSEPH. *Empresses of Rome.* N. Y., 1911. 357 p.
    DLC, NN, PU

423. MacCRACKEN, H. M. *Lives of Church Leaders.* N. Y., 1900.
    DLC

424. McDONALD, JOHN. *Biographical Sketches.* Cincinnati, 1838. 267 p.
Gen. Nathaniel Massie, Gen. Duncan McArthur, Capt. Wm. Wells, and Gen. Simon Kenton.   *DLC, NN, MWA*

425. McGOVERN, JOHN TERENCE. *Diogenes Discovers Us.* N. Y., 1933. 304 p.
Gilmour C. Dobie, Evert Jansen Wendell, Lord Burghley, George Herman Ruth, Elizabeth Mills Reid, Frank A. Hinkey, Sir Thomas Lipton, Lady Astor, Edward Kimball Hall, Dever-

eux Milburn, Willard Dickerman Straight, Quentin Roosevelt, John Williams Overton, Hobart Baker, Gertrude Vanderbilt Whitney, Gustavus Town Kirby. *DLC, NN*

426. McKAY, FREDERIC E., AND WINGATE, CHARLES. *Famous American Actors of Today.* N. Y., 1896. 399 p.

DLC, NN, MWA, PU

427. McKENNEY, THOS. L., AND HALL, JAMES. *History of the Indian Tribes of North America.* Phila., 1838–44. 3 vols.

DLC, NN, MWA, CSmH, PU

428. MACLURE, ALEXANDER WILSON. *Lives of the Chief Fathers of New England.* Boston, 1846. 305 p.

John Wilson, John Norton, John Davenport. *DLC, NN*

429. McSPADDEN, JOSEPH WALKER. *Famous Painters of America.* N. Y., 1907. 361 p.

Benjamin West, John Singleton Copley, Gilbert Stuart, George Inness, Elihu Vedder, Winslow Homer, John La Farge, James A. McNeill Whistler, John Singer Sargent, Edwin Austin Abbey, William Merritt Chase. *DLC, NN*

430. McSPADDEN, JOSEPH WALKER. *Famous Sculptors of America.* N. Y., 1924. 377 p.

John Quincy Adams Ward, Augustus St. Gaudens, Frederick MacMonnies, Daniel Chester French, Paul Wayland Bartlett, George Grey Barnard, Gutzon Borglum, John Massey Rhind, James Earle Fraser, Hermon Atkins MacNeil, Harriet Hosmer, Anna Vaughn Hyatt, Janet Scudder, Bessie Potter Vonnok.

DLC, NN

431. MAGOON, ELIAS LYMAN. *Living Orators in America.* N. Y., 1849. 462 p.

Daniel Webster, Edward Everett, Henry Clay, John C. Calhoun, George McDuffie, Lewis Cass, Thomas H. Benton, William C. Preston, Thomas Corwin. *DLC, NN, MWA, MiD:B*

432. MAGOON, ELIAS LYMAN. *Orators of the American Revolution.* N. Y., 1848. 456 p. *DLC, NN, MWA, CSmH, MiU:C*

433. *Makers of America.* Washington, 1915–22. 4 vols.

DLC, NN, CSmH

434. MALLETT, DANIEL T. *Index of Artists.* N. Y., 1935. 493 p.

DLC, NN, MWA

435. MANSHIP, ANDREW. *National Jewels. Washington, Lincoln and the Fathers of the Revolution.* Phila., 1865. 123 p.

DLC, NN, CSmH

436. MARBLE, ANNIE RUSSELL. *The Nobel Prize Winners in Literature, 1901–1931.* N. Y., 1932. 312 p. *DLC, NN, MWA, PU*

437. MATHER, COTTON. *Magnalia Christi Americana: or, The Ecclesiastical History of New England.* London, 1702. Hartford, 1820, 1853. *DLC, NN, MWA, CSmH, PU*

438. MATTHEWS, BRANDER, AND HUTTON, LAURENCE. *Actors and Actresses of Great Britain and the U. S. from the Days of David Garrick to the Present Time.* N. Y., 1886. 5 vols.
DLC, NN, MWA, CSmH, PU

439. MAURY, SARAH MYTTON. *The Statesmen of American in 1846.* Phila., 1847. 261 p. *DLC, NN, MWA, CSmH, PU*

440. MAY, CAROLINE, ed. *American Female Poets.* Phila., 1848. 532 p. *DLC, NN, MWA, PU*

441. MEANY, EDMOND STEPHEN. *Governors of Washington.* Seattle, 1915. 114 p. *DLC, NN, CSmH*

442. *Memorial and Biographical Record; the Black Hills Region.* Chicago, 1898. 399 p. *DLC, NN*

443. *Memorial Record of the Northern Peninsula of Michigan.* Chicago, 1895. 642 p. *NN*

443a. *Men and Women of America.* N. Y., 1910. 1592 p.

444. *Men of America.* John W. Leonard. N. Y., 1908. 2188 p.

445. *Men of Progress in the State of Connecticut.* Boston, 1898. 480 p. *DLC, NN*

446. *Men of Progress in the Commonwealth of Massachusetts.* Boston, 1896. 1027 p. *DLC, NN*

447. *Men of the Time; or, Sketches of Living Notables.* N. Y., 1852. 564 p. *DLC, NN, CSmH, PU*

448. MICHIGAN HISTORICAL COMMISSION; *Michigan Biographies.* Lansing, 1924. 2 vols. *DLC, NN, MWA, CSmH, PU*

449. MILLER, PEYTON F. *A Group of Great Lawyers of Columbia County, New York.* 1904. 264 p. *DLC, NN, MWA*

450. MILLER, STEPHEN F. *The Bench and Bar of Georgia.* Phila., 1858. 2 vols. *DLC, NN, MWA, CSmH, PU*

451. MINNIGERODE, MEADE. *Certain Rich Men.* N. Y., 1927. 210 p. Stephen Girard, John Jacob Astor, Jay Cooke, Daniel Drew, Cornelius Vanderbilt, Jay Gould, Jim Fisk. *DLC, NN, PU*

452. MINNIGERODE, MEADE. *Lives and Times; Four Informal American Biographies.* N. Y., 1925. 215 p. Stephen Jumel, William Eaton, Theodosia Burr, Edmund C. Genêt. *DLC, NN, PU*

453. MINNIGERODE, MEADE. *Some American Ladies.* N. Y., 1926. 287 p.
Martha Washington, Abigail Adams, Dolly Madison, Elizabeth Monroe and Louisa Adams, Rachel Jackson, Peggy Eaton.
DLC, NN, PU

454. MOORE, FRANK, ed. *Heroes and Martyrs: Notable Men of the Time.* N. Y., 1862. 253 p. *DLC, NN, CSmH*

455. MOORE, FRANK. *The Patriot Preachers of the American Revolution.* N. Y., 1862. 368 p. *DLC, NN*

456. MOORE, FRANK. *The Portrait Gallery of the War, Civil, Military, and Naval.* N. Y., 1864. 353 p. *DLC, NN, MWA*

457. MOORE, FRANK. *Women of the War: Their Heroism and Self-Sacrifice.* Hartford, 1866. 596 p.
DLC, NN, MWA, CSmH, PU

458. MOORE, JACOB BAILEY. *Memoirs of American Governors.* Washington, 1846. 439 p. (Plymouth and Massachusetts Bay)
DLC, NN, MWA

459. MOORE, JOHN WEEKS. *Historical, Biographical, and Miscellaneous Gatherings Relative to Printers, Printing, Publishing, and Editing.* Concord, 1886. 604 p.
DLC, NN, MWA, CSmH, PU, MiU:C

460. MOORE, MATTHEW H. *Pioneers of Methodism in North Carolina and Virginia.* Nashville, 1884. 314 p. *DLC, NN*

461. MORAIS, HENRY SAMUEL. *Eminent Israelites of the Nineteenth Century.* Phila., 1880. 371 p. *DLC, NN*

462. MORAN, THOMAS F. *American Presidents; Their Individualities and Their Contributions to American Progress.* N. Y., 1928. 318 p. *DLC, NN*

463. MORGAN, JAMES. *Our Presidents.* N. Y., 1924. 325 p. N. Y., 1935. 398 p. *DLC, NN, MWA, PU*

464. MORISON, SAMUEL E. *Builders of the Bay Colony.* Boston, 1930. 365 p.
John White, Governor Winthrop, Thomas Shepard, John Hull, Henry Dunster, Nathaniel Ward, Robert Child, John Eliot, Mistress Anne Bradstreet.
DLC, NN, MWA, CSmH, PU, MiU:C

465. MORRIS, CHARLES. *The Blue Book of Biography.* Phila., 1911. 697 p. *DLC, NN*

466. MORRIS, CHARLES. *The Handy Dictionary of Biography.* Phila., 1901. 607 p. *DLC, NN, MWA*

467. MORRIS, CHARLES. *Heroes of Discovery in America.* Phila., 1906. 344 p. *DLC, CSmH*

468. MORRIS, CHARLES. *Heroes of the Army in America.* Phila., 1919. 354 p. *DLC, NN, CSmH*

469. MORRIS, CHARLES. *Heroes of the Navy in America.* Phila., 1907. 320 p. *DLC, NN*

470. MORRIS, CHARLES. *Heroes of Progress in America.* Phila., 1919. 372 p. *DLC, NN*

471. MORRIS, CHARLES. *Makers of New York.* Phila., 1895. 348 p. *DLC, NN*

472. MOSES, GEORGE HIGGINS, comp. *New Hampshire Men.* Concord, N. H., 1893. 408 p. *DLC, NN*

473. MOSES, JOHN, ed. *Biographical Dictionary and Portrait Gallery of the Representative Men of the U. S.* Chicago, 1896. 2 vols. *DLC, NN*

474. MOSES, MONTROSE J. *Famous Actor Families in America.* N. Y., 1906. 341 p.
Today and Yesterday, The Booths, The Jeffersons, The Sotherns, The Boucicaults, The Hacketts, The Drews and the Barrymores, The Wallacks, The Davenports, The Hollands, The Powers. *DLC, NN, CSmH, PU*

475. MOLTON, AUGUSTUS FREEDOM, ed. *Memorials of Maine.* N. Y., 1916. 415 p. *DLC, NN*

476. MOWRY, W. A. AND A. M. *American Heroes and Heroism.* N. Y., 1903. 223 p. *DLC*

477. MOWRY, W. A. AND A. M. *American Inventions and Inventors.* N. Y., 1900. 298 p. *DLC, NN*

478. MOWRY, W. A. AND A. M. *American Pioneers.* N. Y., 1905. 363 p. *DLC*

479. MUNRO, WILFRED HAROLD. *Memorial Encyclopedia of the State of Rhode Island.* N. Y., 1916. 428 p. *DLC, NN*

480. MURRAY, JOHN O'KANE. *Catholic Pioneers of America.* N. Y., 1882. 433 p. *DLC*

481. MURRAY, JOHN O'KANE. *Lives of the Catholic Heroes and Heroines of America.* N. Y., 1880. 878 p. *DLC, NN*

482. MYERS, JAY ARTHUR. *Fighters of Fate.* Balt., 1927. 318 p. *DLC, NN*

483. NASH, ELIZABETH TODD. *Fifty Puritan Ancestors, 1628–1660.* New Haven, 1902. 182 p. *DLC, NN, MWA*

484. *National Encyclopedia of American Biography.* N. Y., 1893–1936. 25 vols. *DLC, NN, CSmH*

485. *National Cyclopaedia of the Colored Race.* Montgomery, Ala., 1919.   *DLC, NN*

486. *National Portrait Gallery of Distinguished Americans.* N. Y., 1852. 2 vols.   *DLC, NN, CSmH*

487. NEWTON, JOSEPH FORT. *Some Living Masters of the Pulpit.* N. Y., 1923. 261 p.
George A. Gordon, John A. Hutton, Dean Inge of St. Paul's, Charles E. Jefferson, W. E. Orchard, Charles D. Williams, A. Maude Royden, Samuel McChord Crothers, T. Reaveley Glover, S. Parkes Cadman, Reginald J. Campbell, William A. Quayle, George W. Truett, Edward L. Powell, Frank W. Gunsaulus: In Memoriam.   *DLC, NN*

488. NORMAN, CHARLES B. *Corsairs of France.* N. Y., 1929. 314 p.
Jean Bart, Leville of Dunkirk, Jacques Cassard of Nantes, Duguay Trouin and Robert Surcouf of St. Malo, and François Thurat of Boulogne.   *DLC, NN, CSmH*

489. NORTHEN, WILLIAM J. *Men of Mark in Georgia.* Atlanta, 1907–12. 6 vols.   *DLC, NN*

490. NORTON, FREDERICK CALVIN. *Governors of Connecticut.* Hartford, 1905. 385 p.   *DLC, NN, MWA*

491. *Notable Men of Illinois and Their State.* Chicago, 1912. 429 p.
    DLC, NN

492. *Notables of the Southwest.* Los Angeles, 1912.   *DLC*

493. ODUM, HOWARD WASHINGTON, ed. *Southern Pioneers in Social Interpretation.* Chapel Hill, 1925. 221 p.
A Southern Promise, by H. W. Odum; Woodrow Wilson, by G. W. Johnson; Walter Hines Page, by R. D. W. Connor; Charles Brantley Aycock, by E. A. Alderman; Seaman A. Knapp, by J. Davis; Augustus Baldwin Longstreet, by J. D. Wade; Joel Chandler Harris, by Julia C. Harris; Booker T. Washington, by M. N. Work; Madeline McDowell Breckenridge, by S. P. Breckenridge; Edward Kidder Graham, by R. D. W. Connor.   *DLC, NN, CSmH, PU*

494. *Officers of the Army and Navy (Regular) Who Served in the Civil War.* Phila., 1894. 177 p.   *DLC, NN, CSmH*

495. *Officers of the Army and Navy (Volunteer) Who Served in the Civil War.* Phila., 1894. 177 p.   *DLC, NN, CSmH*

496. OGDEN, MARY DEPUE, ed. *Memorial Cyclopedia of New Jersey.* Newark, N. J., 1915.   *DLC, NN, MWA*

497. OGILVIE, WILLIAM EDWARD. *Pioneer Agricultural Journalists.* Chicago, 1927. 128 p.

John Stuart Skinner, Judge Jesse Buel, Luther Tucker, Orange Judd, Norman J. Colman, William Dempster Hoard, Wilmer Atkinson, James Harvey Sanders, Alvin Howard Sanders, William Ransdell Goodwin, Joseph E. Wing, Herbert Quick, Henry Wallace, James Melville Pierce, Herbert W. Collingwood.

DLC, NN, MiU:C

498. OMAHA DAILY BEE. *" Nebraskans," 1854–1904.* Omaha, Neb., 1904. 305 p. *DLC, NN*

499. *One Thousand American Men of Mark of Today.* Chicago, 1916. 446 p. *DLC, NN*

500. O'NEALL, J. B. *Biographical Sketches of the Bench and Bar of South Carolina.* Charleston, 1859. 2 vols.
Chief Justices, Law Judges, Chancellors, Recorders, Attorney Generals, U. S. District Attorneys, Solicitors, and Members of the Bar. *DLC, NN, MWA, PU*

501. ORTH, S. P. *Five American Politicians.* Cleveland, 1906. 447 p.
Aaron Burr, DeWitt Clinton, Martin Van Buren, Henry Clay, Stephen A. Douglas. *DLC, NN, PU*

502. *Our Famous Women.* Hartford, 1884. 715 p.
NN, MWA, CSmH, PU

503. PAINTER, F. V. N. *Poets of the South.* N. Y., 1903. 230 p.
Francis Scott Key, Richard Henry Wilde, George D. Prentice, William Gilmore Simms, Edward Coate Pinkney, Philip Pendleton Cooke, Theodore O'Hara, Francis Orrery Ticknor, John R. Thompson, Margaret J. Preston, Edgar Allan Poe, Paul Hamilton Hayne, Henry Timrod, Sidney Lanier, Abram J. Ryan. *DLC,. NN, PU*

504. PARKER, JOHN R. *Musical Biography.* Boston, 1825. 250 p.
NN, MWA, PU

505. PARKER, THEODORE. *Historic Americans.* Boston, 1866–71. 312 p.
Franklin, Washington, John Adams, Thomas Jefferson.
DLC, NN, MWA, CSmH, PU, MiD:B

506. PARKMAN, MARY R. *Heroines of Service.* N. Y., 1917. 322 p.
Mary Lyon, Alice Freeman Palmer, Clara Barton, Frances E. Willard, Julia Ward Howe, Anna Howard Shaw, Mary Antin, Alice C. Fletcher, Mary Slessor, Marie Sklodowska, Jane Addams. *DLC, NN*

507. PARKMAN, MARY R. *Heroes of Today.* N. Y., 1917. 326 p.
John Muir, John Burroughs, Wilfred Grenfell, Captain Robert Scott, Jacob Riis, Edward L. Trudeau, George Washington

Goethals, Bishop Rowe, Samuel Pierpont Langley, Rupert Brooke, Herbert C. Hoover. *DLC, NN*

508. PARTON, JAMES. *Captains of Industry.* Boston, 1855. 114 p.
DLC, NN, MWA

509. PARTON, JAMES. *Daughters of Genius.* Phila., 1886.
NN, CSmH

510. PARTON, JAMES, ed. *Eminent Women of the Age.* Hartford, 1869. 628 p. *NN, CSmH, PU*

511. PARTON, JAMES. *Famous Americans of Recent Times.* Boston, 1867. 473 p.
Henry Clay, Daniel Webster, John C. Calhoun, John Randolph, Stephen Girard and his College, James Gordon Bennett and the *New York Herald,* Charles Goodyear, Henry Ward Beecher and His Church, Commodore Vanderbilt, Theodosia Burr, John Jacob Astor. *DLC, NN, PU*

512. PARTON, JAMES. *Illustrious Men and Their Achievements.* N. Y., n.d. 841 p. *NN, MWA*

513. PARTON, JAMES. *People's Book of Biography.* Hartford, 1868. 624 p. *DLC, NN, MWA, PU*

514. PARTON, JAMES, ed. *Sketches of Men of Progress.* Hartford, 1870–71. 668 p. *DLC, NN, PU*

515. PARTON, JAMES, ed. *Some Noted Princes, Authors, and Statesmen of Our Time.* N. Y., 1885. 354 p.
DLC, NN, MWA, PU

516. PATTEN, JAMES ALEXANDER. *Lives of the Clergy of New York and Brooklyn.* N. Y., 1874. 635 p. *DLC, NN, MWA*

517. PAYNTER, LAWRENCE W. *Medical History of Washington County (Indiana).* Salem, Indiana, 1931. 47 p. *NN*

518. PEABODY, FRANCIS GREENWOOD. *Reminiscences of Present-Day Saints.* Boston, 1927. 307 p.
Ephraim Peabody, Andrew Preston Peabody, James Freeman Clarke, Friedrich August Gottreu Tholuck, Edward Everett Hale, Charles Carroll Everett, Alfred Tredway White, Phillips Brooks, Samuel Chapman Armstrong, Henry Drummond, Carl Hilty, Louisa and Georgina Schuyler, Frederic Illsley Phillips, Charles William Eliot. *DLC, NN, MWA, PU*

519. PEACOCK, VIRGINIA T. *Famous American Belles of the Nineteenth Century.* Phila., 1901. 297 p.
Marcia Burns, Theodosia Burr, Elizabeth Patterson, The Caton Sisters, Margaret O'Neill, Cora Livingston, Emily Marshall, Octavia Walton, Fanny Taylor, Jessie Benton, Sallie Ward,

Harriet Lane, Adele Cutts, Emilie Schaumburg, Kate Chase, Mattie Ould, Jennie Jerome, Nellie Hazeltine, Mary Victoria Leiter, New York as a Social Center. *DLC, NN, MWA, PU*

520. PEELE, WILLIAM JOSEPH. *Lives of Distinguished North Carolinians.* Raleigh, 1898. 605 p.   *NN*

521. PENNYPACKER, SAMUEL W. *Historical and Biographical Sketches.* Phila., 1883. 416 p.

David Rittenhouse, Christopher Dock, Abraham and Dirck Op Den Graeff, William Moore of Moore Hall, Samuel Richardson, Captain Joseph Richardson, Samuel John Atlee, James Abram Garfield, Henry Armett Brown, Charles Frederick Taylor.   *DLC, NN, MWA, PU*

522. PERINE, GEORGE CORBIN. *The Poets and Verse-Writers of Maryland.* Cincinnati, 1898. 318 p.   *DLC, NN*

523. PERRY, BENJAMIN F. *Biographical Sketches of Eminent American Statesmen.* Phila., 1887. 612 p. *DLC, NN, MWA, PU*

524. PERRY, CHARLES E., ed. *Founders and Leaders of Connecticut.* Boston, 1934. 319 p.   *DLC, NN, CSmH*

525. PERRY, F. M., AND ELISON, H. W. *Four Great American Presidents.* N. Y., 1904. 362 p.

Garfield, McKinley, Cleveland, Roosevelt. *DLC, NN, CSmH*

526. PERRY, WILLIAM STEVENS. *Episcopate in America.* N. Y., 1895. 378 p.   *DLC, NN*

527. PETERS, WILLIAM A. *Lives of Our Presidents.* N. Y., 1884. 415 p.   *DLC, NN, CSmH*

528. PETERSON, CHARLES JACOBS. *Military Heroes of the American Revolution.* Phila., 1848. 487 p.   *NN, MWA*

529. PETERSON, CHARLES JACOBS. *Military Heroes of the War of 1812.* Phila., 1858. 208 p.   *DLC, NN, MWA, CSmH*

530. PETERSON, CHARLES JACOBS. *Military Heroes of the War With Mexico.* Phila., 1858. 282 p.   *DLC, NN, CSmH*

531. PHELPS, ALONZO, ed. *Contemporary Biography of California's Representative Men.* San Francisco, 1881. 441 p.

Bancroft, H. H., California's Biography; Davidson, G., The Application of Irrigation to California; Fitzgerald, O. P., The Education of California; Le Conte, J., The Geology of California.   *NN, CSmH*

532. PHILLIPS, LAWRENCE BARNETT. *Dictionary of Biographical Reference.* N. Y., 1871. 1020 p.

DLC, NN, MWA, CSmH, PU, MiU:C

533. PILCHER, JAMES EVELYN. *The Surgeon Generals of the Army of the U. S. of America.* Carlisle, Pa., 1905. 114 p.
DLC, NN

534. PITTSBURGH LEADER. *The Book of Prominent Pennsylvanians.* Pittsburgh, Pa., 1913. 258 p. *DLC, NN*

535. *Poets of the West; a Selection of Favorite American Poems, with Memoirs of Their Authors.* London, 1859. 127 p. *NN*

536. POND, J. B. *Eccentricities of Genius.* N. Y., 1900. 564 p.
DLC, NN, MWA, PU

537. POPE, CHARLES HENRY. *Pioneers of Massachusetts.* Boston, 1900. 549 p. *DLC, NN, MWA*

538. POPE, CHARLES HENRY. *Pioneers of Maine and New Hampshire, 1623 to 1660.* Boston, 1908. 252 p. *DLC, NN, MWA*

539. *Portrait and Biographical Record of Arizona.* Chicago, 1901. 1034 p. *DLC, NN*

540. *Portrait and Biographical Record of Colorado.* Chicago, 1909. 1492 p. *DLC*

540a. *Portrait Biographical Album of Lake County, Ill.* Chicago, 1891. 782 p.

541. *Portrait, Genealogical and Biographical Record of the State of Utah.* Chicago, 1902. 499 p. *DLC, NN*

542. POUND, ARTHUR. *Native Stock; the Rise of the American Spirit Seen in Six Lives.* N. Y., 1931. 267 p.
The William Pepperrells, John Bradstreet, Ephraim Williams, Robert Rogers, James Clinton, Elkanah Watson.
DLC, NN, MWA

543. POWELL, THOMAS. *The Living Authors of America.* N. Y., 1850. 366 p. *DLC, NN, MWA, CSmH, PU*

544. POTTER, CHARLES F. *Story of Religion as Told in the Lives of Its Leaders.* N. Y., 1929. 627 p. *DLC, NN, PU*

545. *Presidents of the U. S., 1789–1894.* N. Y., 1894. 526 p.
DLC, NN

546. PRINGLE, HENRY F. *Big Frogs.* N. Y., 1928. 276 p.
Herbert Hoover, Jimmy Walker, Rev. S. Parkes Cadman, Kenesaw M. Landis, Ivy L. Lee, Bernarr McFadden, Samuel Untermyer, Frank Hedley, William H. Anderson, Will H. Hays, Robert F. Wagner, Curtis D. Wilbur, Theodore Roosevelt, Jr., John S. Sumner. *DLC, NN, MWA*

547. PROCTOR, LUCIEN BROCK. *Bench and Bar of New York.* N. Y., 1870. 779 p. *DLC, NN, MWA*

548. *Progressive Men of Northern Ohio.* Cleveland, 1906. 264 p.
DLC, NN

549. *Progressive Men of Western Colorado.* Chicago, 1905. 876 p.
DLC, NN

550. *Progressive Men of the State of Wyoming.* Chicago, 1903. 965 p.
DLC, NN

551. *Prominent Families of New York.* N. Y., 1897. 641 p.
DLC, NN

552. *Public Characters; or, Contemporary Biography.* Baltimore,
1803. 496 p. *DLC, NN, CSmH*

553. RAMEY, W. SANFORD. *Kings of the Battle-Field.* Phila., 1885.
525 p. *DLC, NN, CSmH*

554. RAND, EDWARD K. *Founders of the Middle Ages.* Cambridge,
1928. 365 p.
St. Ambrose the Mystic, St. Jerome the Humanist, Boethius
the First of the Scholastics. *DLC, NN, CSmH, PU*

555. RAYMOND, IDA. *Southland Writers; Female Writers of the South.*
Phila., 1870. 2 vols. *NN*

556. RAYMOND, WILLIAM. *Biographical Sketches of Distinguished
Men of Columbia County* [*N. Y.*]. Albany, 1851. 104 p.
DLC, NN, MWA

557. REDMOND, GEORGE F. *Financial Giants of America.* Boston,
1922. 2 vols. *DLC, NN, PU*

558. REED, GEORGE IRVING, ed. *Encyclopedia of Biography of Indiana.* Chicago, 1895–99. 2 vols. *DLC, NN*

559. REED, PARKER M. *Bench and Bar of Wisconsin.* Milwaukee,
1882. 542 p. *DLC, NN, MWA*

560. REES, JAMES. *Dramatic Authors of America.* Phila., 1845. 144 p.
DLC, NN, MWA, CSmH, PU

561. REID, WHITELAW. *Ohio in the War; her Statesmen, Generals
and Soldiers.* Columbus, 1893. 2 vols.
DLC, NN, MWA, CSmH

562. REMSBURG, JOHN E. *Six Historic Americans.* N. Y., 1906.
182 p.
Washington, Paine, Jefferson, Franklin, Lincoln, Grant.
DLC, NN, CSmH

563. REMSBURG, JOHN E. *The Fathers of Our Republic.* Boston,
1887. 45 p.
Paine, Jefferson, Washington, Franklin. *DLC*

564. RENO, CONRAD. *Memoirs of the Judiciary and Bar of New
England for the Nineteenth Century.* Boston, 1900. 2 vols.
DLC

565. *Representative Men of Colorado in the Nineteenth Century.* N. Y., 1902. 272 p.   *DLC, NN*

566. *Representative New Mexicans.* Denver, 1912. 1 vol.   *DLC, NN*

567. *Republicans of Illinois.* Chicago, 1905. 379 p.   *DLC, NN*

568. *Republicans of New York.* N. Y., 1906. 444 p.   *DLC, NN*

569. REUSS, FRANCIS X. *Biographical Cyclopaedia of the Catholic Hierarchy of the U. S., 1784–1898.* Milwaukee, 1898. 129 p.   *NN*

570. RICH, ELIHU, ed. *Appleton's Cyclopaedia of Biography.* N. Y., 1856. 1058 p.   *DLC, NN, CSmH*

571. RILEY, BENJAMIN FRANKLIN. *Makers and Romance of Alabama History.* Birmingham, 1914. 618 p.   *DLC, NN, CSmH*

572. ROBINSON, VICTOR. *Pathfinders in Medicine.* N. Y., 1913. 810 p.   *DLC, NN, PU*

573. ROEDER, RALPH. *Men of the Renaissance. Four Lawgivers.* N. Y., 1933. 540 p.
Savonarola, Machiavelli, Castiglione, Aretino.   *DLC, NN, CSmH, PU*

574. ROGERS, AUGUSTUS C. *Sketches of Representative Men, North and South.* N. Y., 1873. 510 p.   *DLC, NN*

575. ROGERS, AUGUSTUS C., ed. *United States Diplomatic and Consular Service.* N. Y., 1876. 540 p.   *DLC, NN, PU*

576. ROGERS, CAMERON. *Gallant Ladies.* N. Y., 1928. 363 p.
Mata Hari, Mary Read and Anne Bonny, Calamity Jane, Adrienne Lecouvreur, Lola Montez.   *DLC, NN*

577. ROGERS, THOMAS J. *A New American Biographical Dictionary.* Easton, Pa., 1813. 424 p.   *DLC, CSmH*

578. ROGERS, THOMAS J., comp. *A New American Biographical Dictionary.* Easton, Pa., 1824. 504 p. (3d ed.)   *DLC, NN, PU, MiD:B*

579. ROGERS, THOMAS J. *Lives of the Departed Heroes, Sages and Statesmen of America.* N. Y., 1834. 400 p.   *DLC, NN*

580. ROSELAND, JENS CHRISTIAN. *American Lutheran Biographies.* Milwaukee, 1905. 901 p.   *DLC, NN*

581. ROURKE, CONSTANCE MAYFIELD. *Trumpets of Jubilee.* N. Y., 1927. 445 p.
Lyman Beecher, Henry Ward Beecher, Harriet Beecher Stowe, Horace Greeley, and Phineas T. Barnum.   *DLC, NN, MWA, PU*

582. Row, Augustus. *Masonic Biography and Dictionary.* Phila., 1868. 365 p. *DLC*

583. Sabine, Lorenzo. *American Loyalists.* Boston, 1847. 733 p. *DLC, NN, PU, MiU:C*

584. Sabine, Lorenzo. *Biographical Sketches of the Loyalists of the American Revolution.* Boston, 1864. 2 vols. *DLC, NN, MWA, CSmH, PU, MiU:C*

585. Sanderson, John, et al. *Biography of the Signers of the Declaration of Independence.* Phila., 1828. 5 vols. *DLC, NN, MWA, CSmH, PU, RP:JCB*

586. Savage, Charles C. *Illustrated Biography.* Buffalo, 1856. 600 p.
Statesmen, Philosophers, Heroes, Artists, Reformers, Philanthropists, Mechanics, Navigators, Authors, Poets, Divines, Soldiers, Savants. *DLC, NN*

587. Savage, John. *Our Living Representative Men.* Phila., 1860. 503 p. *DLC, NN, CSmH, PU*

588. Scott, William J. *Biographic Etchings of Ministers and Laymen of the Georgia Conferences.* Atlanta, 1895. 317 p. *DLC, NN*

589. Seawell, Molly Elliot. *Twelve Naval Captains.* N. Y., 1897. 233 p. *DLC, NN, CSmH*

590. Seitz, Don Carlos. *The " Also Rans "; Great Men Who Missed Making the Presidential Goal.* N. Y., 1928. 356 p.
Aaron Burr, William H. Crawford, John C. Calhoun, Henry Clay, Lewis Cass, Daniel Webster, Winfield Scott, John C. Frémont, Stephen A. Douglas, William H. Seward, George B. McClellan, Horatio Seymour, Horace Greeley, Samuel J. Tilden, Winfield S. Hancock, James G. Blaine, Benjamin F. Butler, W. J. Bryan. *DLC, NN, PU*

591. Seitz, Don Carlos. *Uncommon Americans.* Indianapolis, 1925. 328 p. *DLC, NN, PU*

592. Sergeant, Elizabeth Shepley. *Fire Under the Andes.* N. Y., 1927. 331 p.
Introduction, Amy Lowell, Robert Edmond Jones, William Alanson White, Eugene O'Neill, Elinor Wylie, Charles Townsend Copeland, Pauline Lord, William Allen White, Paul Robeson, Alice Hamilton, H. L. Mencken, Willa Cather, Robert Frost, Oliver Wendell Holmes. *DLC, NN, PU*

593. Seymour, Charles C. B. *Self-Made Men.* N. Y., 1858. 588 p. *NN, MWA*

594. SHARPLESS, ISAAC. *Political Leaders of Provincial Pennsylvania.*
N. Y., 1919. 248 p.
Introduction, William Penn, Thomas Lloyd, David Lloyd,
James Logan, John Kinsey, Isaac Norris, James Pemberton,
John Dickinson. *DLC, NN, PU*

595. SHEA, JOHN DAWSON G. *The American Nation Illustrated in
the Lives of Her Fallen, Brave, and Living Heroes.* N. Y.,
1862. *NN, CSmH, MiD:B*

596. SHEA, JOHN DAWSON G. *The Fallen Brave.* N. Y., 1861. 224 p.
DLC, NN, CSmH, PU

597. SHEA, JOHN DAWSON G. *Our Faith and Its Defenders.* 1892.
NN

598. SHEAHAN, HENRY BESTON. *The Book of Gallant Vagabonds.*
N. Y., 1925. 231 p.
John Ledyard, Giovanni Belzoni, Edward John Trelawny,
Thomas Morton of Merry-Mount, James Bruce, Arthur Rim-
baud. *DLC, NN, PU*

599. SHERMAN, DAVID. *Sketches of New England Divines.* N. Y.,
1860. 443 p. *DLC, NN*

600. SHOEMAKER, FLOYD CALVIN. *Missouri's Hall of Fame.* Columbia, Mo., 1918. 269 p. *DLC, NN*

601. SIMMONS, RALPH B., comp. *Utah's Distinguished Personalities.*
Salt Lake City, 1933. *DLC, NN*

602. SIMMONS, WILLIAM J. *Men of Mark; Eminent, Progressive and
Rising.* Cleveland, 1887. 1141 p. *DLC, NN, CSmH*

603. SIMPSON, HENRY, ed. *The Lives of Eminent Philadelphians, Now
Deceased.* Phila., 1859. 993 p. *DLC, NN, PU*

604. SISSON, CHARLES JASPER, ed. *Thomas Lodge and Other Eliza-
bethans.* Cambridge, 1933. 526 p.
Thomas Lodge and His Family, Barnabe Barnes, Lodowick
Bryskett and His Family, John Lyly, Sir George Buc.
DLC, NN, CSmH, PU

605. *Sketches of Men of Mark.* N. Y., 1871. 847 p. *DLC, NN*

606. *Sketches of Successful New Hampshire Men.* Manchester, 1882.
315 p. *DLC, NN*

607. *Sketches of Washingtonians.* Seattle, 1906. 320 p. *DLC, NN*

608. SMEETON, GEORGE, ed. *The Unique; or, Biography of Many
Distinguished Characters.* Boston, 1829. 253 p. *DLC, NN*

609. SMITH, CHARD P. *Annals of the Poets.* N. Y., 1935. 523 p.
DLC, NN, CSmH

610. SMITH, HELEN AINSLIE. *One Hundred Famous Americans.* N. Y., 1902. 574 p. *DLC, NN*

610a. SMITH, WILLIAM HENRY. *History of the Cabinet of the United States.* Balt., 1925. 537 p. *CSmH*

611. SMITH, WILLIAM HENRY. *Speakers of the House of Representatives of the U. S.* Balt., 1928. 261 p. *DLC, NN, CSmH*

612. SNOW, WILLIAM PARKER. *Southern Generals; Their Lives and Campaigns.* N. Y., 1866. 500 p.
Robert Edward Lee, Thomas J. Jackson, P. G. T. Beauregard, Jos. E. Johnston, Samuel Cooper, James Longstreet, Braxton Bragg, R. S. Ewell, J. E. B. Stuart, A. P. Hill, John B. Hood, A. S. Johnston, Leonidas Polk, Sterling Price, E. Kirby Smith, John H. Morgan, Wm. J. Hardee, Wade Hampton.
DLC, NN, MWA

613. SNOW, WILLIAM PARKER. *Lee and His Generals.* N. Y., 1867. 500 p. *DLC, NN, CSmH*

614. SOUTHERN BIOGRAPHICAL ASSOCIATION. *Men of the South.* New Orleans, 1922. 792 p. *DLC*

615. SPARKS, JARED, ed. *Library of American Biography.* N. Y., 1864. 25 vols. *DLC, NN, MWA, CSmH, MiD:B, MiU:C*

616. SPEER, WILLIAM S., AND BROWN, J. H., eds. *Encyclopedia of the New West.* Marshall, Texas, 1881. 1014 p.
DLC, NN, CSmH

617. SPEER, WILLIAM S. *Sketches of Prominent Tennesseans.* Nashville, 1888. 579 p. *DLC, NN*

618. SPENCER, RICHARD HENRY, ed. *Genealogical and Memorial Encyclopedia of the State of Maryland.* N. Y., 1919. 2 vols.
DLC, NN, MWA

619. SPENCER, WILBUR DANIEL. *Maine Immortals.* Augusta, Me., 1932. 316 p. *DLC, NN*

620. SPRAGUE, WILLIAM B. *Annals of the American Pulpit.* N. Y., 1857–69. 9 vols. *DLC, NN, MWA, CSmH, PU, MiD:B*

621. SPRAGUE, WILLIAM B. *Annals of the American Episcopal Pulpit.* N. Y., 1859. 822 p. *DLC, NN*

622. STILES, EDWARD HOLCOMB. *Recollections and Sketches of Notable Lawyers and Public Men of Early Iowa.* Des Moines, 1916. 988 p. *DLC, NN*

623. STODDARD, WILLIAM OSBORN. *Men of Business.* N. Y., 1893. 317 p.
John Jacob Astor, Cornelius Vanderbilt, Charles Louis Tiffany, John Roach, Levi Parsons Morton, Edwin Denison Morgan,

Cyrus West Field, Chauncey Mitchell Depew, Alexander Turner, Philip Danforth Armour, Horace Brigham Claflin, Marshall Owen Roberts, George Mortimer Pullman, Peter Cooper, Marshall Field, Leland Stanford.

DLC, NN, CSmH, MiD:B

624. STOWE, HARRIET BEECHER. *Men of Our Times.* Hartford, 1868. 575 p.

Lincoln, Grant, Garrison, Sumner, Chase, Wilson, Greeley, Farragut, Andrew, Colfax, Stanton, Douglas, Buckingham, Sherman, Sheridan, Howard, Phillips, Beecher.

DLC, NN, MWA, CSmH, PU, MiD:B

625. STRANG, LEWIS C. *Celebrated Comedians of Light Opera and Musical Comedy in America.* Boston, 1900. 293 p.

DLC, NN

626. STRANG, LEWIS C. *Famous Actors of Today in America.* Boston, 1900. 2 vols. *DLC, NN*

627. STRANG, LEWIS C. *Famous Actors of the Day in America.* Boston, 1902. 343 p. *DLC, NN*

628. STRANG, LEWIS C. *Famous Actresses of the Day in America.* Boston, 1901. 2 vols. *DLC*

629. STRANG, LEWIS C. *Famous Actresses of the Day in America.* Boston, 1899. 360 p. *DLC, NN*

630. SUCCESSFUL AMERICANS. *Sketches and Portraits of Representative Men and Women.* N. Y., 1900–07. *NN, CSmH*

631. SULLIVAN, WILLIAM. *Public Men of the Revolution.* Phila., 1847. 463 p. *DLC, NN, CSmH, MiU:C*

632. SUMMERS, THOMAS OSMOND, ed. *Biographical Sketches of Eminent Itinerant Ministers of the Methodist Episcopal Church South.* Nashville, 1858.

633. SWAIN, DAVID L. *Lives of Distinguished Carolinians.* Raleigh, 1898. *DLC*

633a. SWISS-AMERICAN HISTORICAL SOCIETY. *Prominent Americans of Swiss Origin.* N. Y., 1932. 1 vol. *CSmH*

634. TAGGART, JOSEPH. *Biographical Sketches of Eminent American Patriots.* Kansas City, Mo., 1907. 299 p.

Charles Carroll, Roger Brooke Taney, W. Starke Rosecrans, J. Barry, Philip H. Sheridan. *DLC, NN*

635. TAYLOR, JAMES B. *Lives of Virginia Baptist Ministers.* Richmond, 1838. N. Y., 1860. *NN, MWA, CSmH*

636. TEMPLE, OLIVER PENY. *Notable Men of Tennessee, from 1833 to 1875.* N. Y., 1912. 467 p. *DLC, NN*

637. THACHER, JAMES. *American Medical Biography.* Boston, 1828. 2 vols. *DLC, NN, MWA, CSmH, PU*

638. THATCHER, B. B. *Biography of North American Indians Who Have Been Distinguished as Orators, Warriors, Statesmen.* N. Y., 1832. 2 vols. *DLC, NN, MWA, CSmH*

639. THAYER, WILLIAM MAKEPEACE. *Onward to Fame and Fortune; or, Climbing Life's Ladder.* N. Y., 1897. 446 p. *DLC, NN*

640. THAYER, WILLIAM ROSCOE. *Throne Makers.* Boston, 1899. 329 p. *DLC, NN, PU*

641. THOMAS, E. A. *Comprehensive Dictionary of Biography.* Boston, 1876. 590 p. *NN, MWA, PU*

642. THOMAS, ISAIAH. *The History of Printing in America and a Biography of Printers.* Worcester, Mass., 1810. 2 vols. *DLC, NN, MWA, CSmH, PU, MiU:C*

643. THOMAS, JOSEPH. *Universal Pronouncing Dictionary of Biography and Mythology.* Phila., 1870. 2 vols. *DLC, NN, MWA, CSmH, PU*

644. THOMAS, R. *The Glory of America.* N. Y., 1834. 574 p. *CSmH, MiD:B*

645. THWING, CHARLES FRANKLIN. *Friends of Men.* N. Y., 1933. 479 p. *DLC, NN, MWA, PU*

646. THWING, CHARLES FRANKLIN. *Guides, Philosophers and Friends.* N. Y., 1927. 476 p. *DLC, NN, MWA, PU*

647. TOMLINSON, EVERETT T. *Book of Pioneers.* N. Y., 1926. 251 p. *DLC, NN*

648. TOOMEY, DANIEL O. *Massachusetts of Today.* Boston, 1892. 619 p. *DLC, NN*

649. TOWLE, GEORGE MAKEPEACE. *Heroes and Martyrs of Invention.* Boston, 1890. 202 p. *DLC, NN*

650. TOWNSEND, JOHN WILSON. *Kentuckians in History and Literature.* N. Y., 1907. 189 p. *DLC, NN, CSmH*

651. TOWNSEND, VIRGINIA F. *Our Presidents; or, The Lives of the Twenty-Three Presidents of the U. S.* 1889. 378 p. *DLC, NN, CSmH*

652. TRACY, HENRY C. *American Naturalists.* N. Y., 1930. 282 p. *DLC, NN, PU*

653. TRENT, W. P., ed. *Biographies of Leading Americans.* N. Y., n.d. 4 vols. *NN, CSmH*

654. TRENT, W. P. *Southern Statesmen of the Old Régime.* N. Y., 1897. 293 p. *CSmH, PU*

Washington, Jefferson, Randolph, Calhoun, Stephens, Toombs, Jefferson Davis. *DLC, NN*

655. TRISSAL, FRANCIS MARION. *Public Men of Indiana; a Political History from 1860 to 1890.* Hammond, Ind., 1922. 226 p.
DLC, NN

656. TUCKERMAN, HENRY THEODORE. *Biographical Essays; or, Studies of Character.* Boston, 1857. 475 p.
DLC, NN, MWA, PU, MiD:B

657. TUCKERMAN, HENRY THEODORE. *Book of the Artists. American Artist Life.* N. Y., 1867. 639 p.
DLC, NN, MWA, CSmH

658. TYLER, LYON GARDINER, ed. *Encyclopedia of Virginia Biography.* N. Y., 1915. 5 vols. *DLC, NN, MWA, CSmH*

659. TYLER, MOSES COIT. *Three Men of Letters.* N. Y., 1895. 200 p. George Berkeley, Timothy Dwight, Joel Barlow.
DLC, NN, MWA, CSmH, PU

659a. ULLERY, JACOB. *Men of Vermont.* Brattleboro, 1894. 3 pts.
CSmH

660. ULMANN, ALBERT. *New Yorkers.* N. Y., 1928. 267 p. Peter Minuit, Peter Stuyvesant, Thomas Dongan, John Peter Zenger, Thomas Paine, Alexander Hamilton, Robert Fulton, De Witt Clinton, Washington Irving, Samuel F. B. Morse, Peter Cooper, Edgar Allan Poe, Theodore Roosevelt.
DLC, NN

661. UNDERWOOD, FRANCIS HENRY. *Builders of American Literature.* Boston, 1893. 302 p. *DLC*

662. *Unique, The; or Biography of Many Distinguished Characters.* Boston, 1829. 234 p. De Witt Clinton, George Washington, George Canning, Jacob Hays, La Fayette, Benjamin Franklin, John Adams, John Quincy Adams, Washington Irving, Patrick Henry, James Monroe, Thomas Jefferson, James Madison, Andrew Jackson.
DLC, NN, MWA, CSmH

663. *United States Biographical Dictionary and Portrait Gallery.* Chicago and N. Y., 1877. 698 p. *NN*

664. *Universal Biography.* N. Y., 1810. 2 vol. *DLC, NN*

665. VAN BUSKIRK, WILLIAM R. *Saviors of Mankind.* N. Y., 1929. 537 p. Lao-Tze, Confucius, Gautama, Zoroaster, Aakhnatan, Moses, Isaiah of Babylon, Socrates, Jesus of Nazareth, Saul of Tarsus, Mahomet. *DLC, NN, PU*

666. VAN SANTVOORD, G. *Sketches of the Chief Justices of the Supreme Court of the United States.* Albany, 1854. 740 p.
Jay, Rutledge, Ellsworth, Marshall, Taney.
DLC, NN, CSmH, PU

667. VENABLE, EMERSON, ed. *Poets of Ohio.* Cincinnati, 1909. 356 p.
DLC, NN, MWA

668. VICTOR, ORVILLE JAMES. *Men of Time.* N. Y., 1862–63. 3 vols.
Generals Halleck, Pope, Siegel, Corcoran, Prentiss, Kearney, Hatch, Augur, Butler, Banks, Burnside, Baker, Stevens, Wilcox, Weber, Hooker, Rosecrans, Grant, McClernand, Mitchell.
DLC, NN, CSmH

669. WALE, J. S. *The Officers of Our Society for Fifty Years.* Washington, 1936. 46 p. (Reprinted from Proc. of Entomological Society of Wash., D. C. Vol. 38. No. 6. June, 1936)
DLC, NN

670. WADE, MARY H. *Adventurers All.* N. Y., 1927. 267 p.
Charles Lindbergh, Marco Polo, Louis Pasteur, Elizabeth Fry, St. Francis of Assisi, Mary Alessor of Calabar, Woodrow Wilson.
DLC, NN

671. WADE, MARY H. *Real Americans.* Boston, 1922. 277 p. *DLC*

672. WADE, MARY H. *Pilgrims of To-Day.* Boston, 1916. 253 p.
John Muir, Jacob Riis, Mary Antin, Edward A. Steiner, Carl Schurz, Nathan Straus, Joseph Pulitzer.
DLC, NN

673. WALDRON, D. G., ed. *Biographical Sketches of Delegates to Convention to Frame a Constitution for California.* San Francisco, 1878. 176 p.
DLC, NN, CSmH

674. WALDRON, WILLIAM WATSON. *Washington Irving and Contemporaries.* N. Y., n.d. 247 p.
DLC, NN

675. WALLACE, ARCHER. *Heroes of Peace.* N. Y., 1929. 133 p.
Charles A. Lindbergh, Sir Ernest Shackleton, Albert Schweitzer, William Penn, Sir James Young Simpson, Benjamin Franklin, George Washington Goethals, Louis Pasteur, Alexander Graham Bell, George Washington Carver, Sir George Williams, William H. P. Anderson, Jacob Riis, George Muller, Dr. Walter Reed, George Reed.
DLC, NN

676. WALLACE, ARCHER. *Men Who Played the Game.* N. Y., 1891. 127 p.
DLC, NN

677. WALSH, JAMES J. *Catholic Churchmen in Science.* Phila., 1906. 221 p.
DLC, NN, PU

678. WALSH, JAMES J. *Makers of Modern Medicine.* N. Y., 1907. 362 p.
Morgagni, Auenbrugger, Jenner, Galvani, Laennec, Graves, Stokes, Corrigan, Muller, Schwann, Claude Bernard, Pasteur, O'Dwyer. *DLC, NN, PU*

679. WALSH, JAMES J. *Our American Cardinals.* N. Y., 1926. 352 p.
Cardinals McCloskey, Gibbons, Farley, O'Connell, Dougherty, Mundelein, Hayes. *DLC, NN*

680. WALSH, JAMES JOSEPH, comp. *These Splendid Priests.* N. Y., 1926. 248 p.
St. Benedict, Friar William de Rubruquis, Friar Odoric, St. Ignatius Loyola, St. Francis Xavier, Father James Marquette, St. Vincent de Paul, Father Isaac Jogues, Father Jerome Lobo, Friar Junípero Serra, Father John MacEnery. *DLC, NN*

681. WARE, WM., ed. *American Unitarian Biography.* 1850. 2 vols.
Noah Webster, John Prince, Ezra Ripley, James Freeman, Eliphalet Porter, Aaron Bancroft, Joseph Mottey, John Allyn, Henry Ware, Thaddeus M. Harris, John T. Kirkland, Nathaniel Thayer, Abiel Abbot. *DLC, NN, MWA, PU*

682. WATERLOO, STANLEY, AND HANSON, J. W., eds. *Famous American Men and Women.* Chicago, 1896. 519 p. *DLC, NN*

683. WATSON, IRVING A., ed. and comp. *Physicians and Surgeons of America.* Concord, N. H., 1896. 843 p. *DLC, NN, PU*

684. WAUCHOPE, GEORGE ARMSTRONG. *Writers of South Carolina.* Columbia, S. C., 1910. 420 p. *DLC, NN, PU*

685. WEAVER, GEORGE SUMNER. *Lives and Graves of Our Presidents.* Chicago, 1884, 1897. 554 p. *DLC, NN, MWA*

686. WHITMAN, C. M. *American Orators and Oratory.* N. Y., 1884. 1120 p. *DLC, NN*

687. WILDMAN, EDWIN. *The Founders of America in the Days of the Revolution.* Boston, 1924. 326 p. *DLC, NN*

688. WILLIAMS, STEPHEN WEST. *American Medical Biography, or, Memoirs of Eminent Physicians.* Greenfield, Mass., 1845. 664 p. *DLC, NN, MWA, CSmH, PU*

689. WILLIAMSON, LELAND, ed. *Prominent and Progressive Pennsylvanians of the Nineteenth Century.* Phila., 1898. 3 vols. *DLC, NN, PU*

690. WILLIS, WILLIAM. *A History of the Law, the Courts, and the Lawyers of Maine.* Portland, 1863. 712 p. *DLC, NN, MWA*

691. WILMER, JAMES JONES. *The American Nepos.* Baltimore, 1805. 408 p. *DLC, NN, CSmH*

692. WILSON, FRED T. *Pen Pictures of the Presidents.* Nashville, 1932. 554 p. *DLC, NN*

693. WILSON, JAMES GRANT. *Biographical Sketches of Illinois Officers Engaged in the War Against the Rebellion of 1861.* Chicago, 1862. 120 p. *DLC, NN, MWA, CSmH, PU*

694. WILSON, JAMES GRANT. *Presidents of the United States, 1789–1914.* N. Y., 1914. 4 vols. *DLC, NN, CSmH*

695. WILSON, JAMES GRANT. *Sketches of Illustrious Soldiers.* N. Y., 1880. 484 p. *DLC, NN, MWA, CSmH*

696. WILSON, JAMES GRANT, AND FISKE, JOHN, eds. *Appleton's Cyclopedia of American Biography.* N. Y., 1886–89. 6 vols. *DLC, NN, MWA, CSmH, PU*

697. WILSON, JOHN L. *The Dead of the Synod of Georgia.* Atlanta, 1869. 377 p. *DLC*

698. WILSON, THOMAS. *Biography of the Principal American Military and Naval Heroes.* N. Y., 1817. 2 vols. *DLC, NN, MWA, CSmH, MiU:C*

699. WINCHESTER, PAUL. *Men of Maryland Since the Civil War.* Balt., 1923. 1 vol. *DLC, NN*

700. WINGATE, C. E. L., AND McKAY, F. E., eds. *Famous American Actors of Today.* N. Y., 1896. 2 vols. *DLC, NN, PU*

701. WINWAR, FRANCES. *The Romantic Rebels.* Boston, 1935. 507 p.
Byron, Shelley, Keats. *DLC, NN*

702. WOOD, NORMAN B. *Lives of Famous Indian Chiefs.* Aurora, Ill., 1906. 771 p. *DLC, NN, CSmH*

702a. WOOLLEN, WILLIAM W. *Biographical and Historical Sketches of Early Indiana.* Indianapolis, 1883. 568 p. *CSmH*

703. WRIGHT, RICHARDSON L. *Forgotten Ladies.* Phila., 1928. 307 p.
The Savage Maid, Ann, Fanny, and Maria Stover, Sophy Hopkey, Deborah Sampson, Maria Monk, Anne Royal, Sarah Josepha Hale, Margaret and Catherine Fox, Belle Boyd. *DLC, NN, MWA*

704. WRIGHT, R. W. *The Poets and Poetry of Connecticut.* (Papers of the New Haven Colony Hist. Soc. Vol. II) *NN, MWA, CSmH*

705. WYATT, THOMAS. *Memoirs of the Generals, Commodores, and Other Commanders of Distinction in the American Army and*

Navy During the Wars of the Revolution and 1812. Phila.,
1848. 315 p.   *DLC, NN, MWA, CSmH, MiD:B, RP:JCB*

706. WYL, W. *Mormon Portraits.* Salt Lake City, 1886. 320 p.
   DLC, CSmH

707. WYNNE, JAMES. *Lives of Eminent Literary and Scientific Men
of America.* N. Y., 1850. 356 p.
Benjamin Franklin, Jonathan Edwards, Robert Fulton, John
Marshall, David Rittenhouse, Eli Whitney.   *DLC, NN*